Survey of
Financial Princip...

MELICHER

Texas A&M University
LARRY WOLKEN

Wiley Custom Learning Solutions

D1467404

Copyright © 2014 by John Wiley & Sons, Inc.

All rights reserved.

Cover Image © GTS Production /Shutterstock

No part of this publication may be reproduced, stored in a retrieval system or transmitted in any form or by any means, electronic, mechanical, photocopying, recording, scanning or otherwise, except as permitted under Sections 107 or 108 of the 1976 United States Copyright Act, without either the prior written permission of the Publisher, or authorization through payment of the appropriate per-copy fee to the Copyright Clearance Center, Inc., 222 Rosewood Drive, Danvers, MA 01923, website www.copyright.com. Requests to the Publisher for permission should be addressed to the Permissions Department, John Wiley & Sons, Inc., 111 River Street, Hoboken, NJ 07030-5774, (201)748-6011, fax (201)748-6008, website http://www.wiley.com/go/permissions.

To order books or for customer service, please call 1(800)-CALL-WILEY (225-5945).

Printed in the United States of America.

ISBN 978-1-118-93502-6
Printed and bound by SCI.

Brief Contents

INTRODUCTION TO FINANCE

Markets, Investments, and Financial Management

FIFTEENTH EDITION

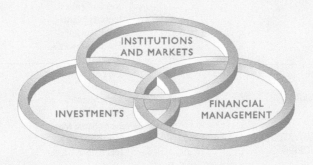

Ronald W. Melicher

Professor of Finance
University of Colorado at Boulder

Edgar A. Norton

Professor of Finance
Illinois State University

WILEY

*To my parents, William and Lorraine, and
to my wife, Sharon, and our children,
Michelle, Sean, and Thor*

Ronald W. Melicher

*To my best friend and wife, Becky,
and our gifts from God, Matthew and Amy*

Edgar A. Norton

VICE PRESIDENT & EXECUTIVE PUBLISHER	George Hoffman
EXECUTIVE EDITOR	Joel Hollenbeck
CONTENT EDITOR	Jennifer Manias
ASSISTANT EDITOR	Courtney Luzzi
SENIOR EDITORIAL ASSISTANT	Erica Horowitz
DIRECTOR OF MARKETING	Amy Scholz
ASSISTANT MARKETING MANAGER	Puja Katariwala
MARKETING ASSISTANT	Mia Brady
EDITORIAL OPERATIONS MANAGER	Yana Mermel
PRODUCT DESIGNER	Allison Morris
SENIOR MEDIA SPECIALIST	Elena Santa Maria
SENIOR PRODUCTION AND MANUFACTURING MANAGER	Janis Soo
ASSOCIATE PRODUCTION MANAGER	Joel Balbin

This book was set in 10/12 Minion by Aptara Corp. and printed and bound by RRD/JC. The cover was printed by RRD/JC.

This book is printed on acid free paper. ∞

Founded in 1807, John Wiley & Sons, Inc. has been a valued source of knowledge and understanding for more than 200 years, helping people around the world meet their needs and fulfill their aspirations. Our company is built on a foundation of principles that include responsibility to the communities we serve and where we live and work. In 2008, we launched a Corporate Citizenship Initiative, a global effort to address the environmental, social, economic, and ethical challenges we face in our business. Among the issues we are addressing are carbon impact, paper specifications and procurement, ethical conduct within our business and among our vendors, and community and charitable support. For more information, please visit our website: www.wiley.com/go/citizenship.

Copyright © 2014, 2008, 2005 John Wiley & Sons, Inc. All rights reserved. No part of this publication may be reproduced, stored in a retrieval system or transmitted in any form or by any means, electronic, mechanical, photocopying, recording, scanning, or otherwise, except as permitted under Sections 107 or 108 of the 1976 United States Copyright Act, without either the prior written permission of the Publisher, or authorization through payment of the appropriate per-copy fee to the Copyright Clearance Center, Inc., 222 Rosewood Drive, Danvers, MA 01923, (978)750-8400, fax (978)750-4470 or on the web at www.copyright.com. Requests to the Publisher for permission should be addressed to the Permissions Department, John Wiley & Sons, Inc., 111 River Street, Hoboken, NJ 07030-5774, (201)748-6011, fax (201)748-6008, or online at http://www.wiley.com/go/permissions.

Evaluation copies are provided to qualified academics and professionals for review purposes only, for use in their courses during the next academic year. These copies are licensed and may not be sold or transferred to a third party. Upon completion of the review period, please return the evaluation copy to Wiley. Return instructions and a free of charge return shipping label are available at www.wiley.com/go/returnlabel. Outside of the United States, please contact your local representative.

Library of Congress Cataloging-in-Publication Data

Melicher, Ronald W.

[Finance]

Introduction to finance : markets, investments, and financial management / Ronald W. Melicher, Professor of Finance University of Colorado at Boulder, Edgar A. Norton, Professor of Finance, Illinois State University—15th ed.

p. cm.

Revised edition of the authors' Finance.

Includes index.

ISBN 978-1-118-49267-3 (pbk.)

1. Finance. 2. Finance—United States. I. Norton, Edgar, 1957- II. Title.

HG173.M398 2014

332—dc23

2013033077

Printed in the United States of America

• PREFACE •

The fifteenth edition of *Introduction to Finance: Markets, Investments, and Financial Management* builds upon the successes of its earlier editions while maintaining a fresh and up-to-date coverage of the field of finance.

Our text is designed to present a more balanced first course in finance, one that offers students perspectives on financial markets, investing, and financial management. We use a successful pedagogy that reviews markets and institutions, then the world of investments, and finally the concepts and applications of business financial management.

A movement has been growing to offer a more balanced first course in finance. Previous editions were developed for such an "overview" first course, and this new edition continues in that vein. Eighteen chapters cover the three major financial areas involving the financial system, investments, and business finance. For the student who does not plan to take additional courses in finance, this book provides a valuable overview of the discipline's major concepts. For the student who wants to take additional courses in finance, the overview presented provides a solid foundation upon which future courses can build.

Introduction to Finance is meant to be used in a course whose purpose is to survey the foundations of the finance discipline. As such, it is designed to meet the needs of students in various programs. Specifically, *Introduction to Finance* can be used in any of the following four ways:

1. As the first course in finance at a college or university where the department wants to expose students to a broad foundational survey of the discipline.

2. As the first and only course in finance for nonfinance business students.

3. As an appropriate text to use at a school that seeks to provide liberal arts majors with a business minor or business concentration. The writing level is appropriate to provide students with a good foundation in the basics of our discipline.

4. As a "lower division" service course whose goal is to attract freshmen and sophomores to business and to attract them to become finance majors.

The philosophy behind the book is threefold. First, we believe that a basic understanding of the complex world of finance should begin with a survey course that covers an introduction to financial markets, investments, and financial management or business finance. Students can gain an integrated perspective of the interrelationships among these three areas. They will appreciate how businesses and individuals are affected by markets and institutions, as well as how markets and institutions can be used to meet the goals of individuals or firms. Given the events in the financial markets and the economy in recent years, this integrated perspective adds value to student learning and understanding of the field.

Second, we wrote the book as an introductory survey of finance with a readable and user-friendly focus in mind. We seek to convey basic knowledge, concepts, and terms that will serve the nonfinance major into the future and that will form a foundation upon which the finance major can build. Some finer points, discussions of theory, and complicated topics are reserved for "Learning Extensions" in selected chapters. We aim to make students using our text financially literate and cognizant of the richness of finance. The book provides a good foundation for students to build upon in later courses in financial management, investments, or financial markets.

Third, we focus on the practice of finance in the settings of markets, investments, and financial management. We focus on the descriptive in each of these fields. We don't want students to be unable to see the forest of finance because the trees of quantitative methods obscure their view or scare them away. When we do introduce equations and mathematical concepts that are applicable to finance, we will show step-by-step solutions.

By learning about markets (including gaining knowledge about institutions), investments, and management as the three major strands of finance, students will finish their course with a greater understanding of how these three fields interrelate. Financial markets will be seen as the arena to which businesses and financial institutions go to raise funds and as the mechanism through which individuals can invest their savings to meet their future goals. The topic of investments is important in facilitating the savings-investment process. Understanding the trade-off of risk and return, as well as the valuation of bonds and stocks, is essential to investors and businesses raising financial capital. Understanding how securities markets work is equally important. Financial management uses information it obtains from securities and other financial markets to efficiently and profitably manage assets and to raise needed funds in a cost-efficient manner.

A broad exposure to the discipline of finance will meet the needs of nonmajors who should know the basics of finance so they can read the *The Wall Street Journal*, visit business-related Internet sites, and analyze other business information sources intelligently. It will help the nonfinance major work as a member of a cross-functional work team, a team that will include finance professionals. In addition, this overview of finance will start the finance major off on the right foot. Rather than receiving a compartmentalized idea of finance—often viewed through the corporate finance lens that many texts use—the finance major will receive a practical introduction to the different disciplines of finance and will better appreciate their relationships to one another.

Part 1 of the book contains six chapters on the financial system, with primary emphasis on financial markets and the tools and skills necessary to better understand how such markets work. We begin with an overview of the three main subfields of finance, identify the "six principles of finance," and discuss career opportunities. The principles of finance are the following:

1. Money has a time value.
2. Higher returns are expected for taking on more risk.
3. Diversifying one's investments can reduce risk.
4. Financial markets are efficient in pricing securities.
5. The objectives of managers and stockholders may differ.
6. Reputation matters.

We discuss finance and the role and functions of the financial system to a nation's economy. The role of banks, other financial intermediaries, and the Federal Reserve are reviewed, as are their functions in the financial system. Part 1 introduces the international role of finance and how modern economies are affected by exchange rates, trade, and the flow of global funds.

Following this introduction to the financial system, Part 2 focuses on investments. We review the role of savings in an economy and the ways in which funds flow to and from different sectors. Interest rates are introduced, and the discussion centers on making the student aware of the different influences on interest rate levels and why the rates change over time. Because interest rates measure the cost of moving money across time, this section reviews basic time-value-of-money concepts with many worked-out examples, including the keystrokes that students can use with financial calculators.

Next, after reviewing the characteristics of bonds and stocks, students will learn to apply time-value-of-money concepts to find the prices of these securities. Continuing our overview of investments, we discuss investment banking basics and the operations of securities markets, as well as the fundamentals of investment risks and returns to conclude Part 2. Advanced classes may want to review the financial derivatives basics, which are explained in a learning extension to Chapter 11's discussion of securities and markets.

The raising of funds by businesses in the institutional and market environments is covered in Parts 1 and 2. Next, in Part 3, the final six chapters of the text introduce students to financial management. The discussion begins with the different ways in which to organize a business and the financial implications of each organizational form. We introduce accounting concepts, such as the balance sheet, income statement, and statement of cash flows with simple examples. We discuss financial ratios, which assist in the process of analyzing a firm's strengths and weaknesses. We review their use as a means to help managers plan ahead for future asset and financing needs. Strategies for managing a firm's current assets and current liabilities are examined, as are the funding sources firms use to tap the financial markets for short-term financing. Finally, we introduce students to capital budgeting basics and capital structure concepts.

New and Improved

The content of *Introduction to Finance* has been updated to incorporate many of the economic and financial events of the past few years. The financial crisis of 2007–2009, the subsequent recession and recovery—along with the behavior of the Federal Reserve and securities markets—provide a means to highlight causes, effects, and the integration of finance into our everyday lives, as well as the implications for markets, investments, and business finance. A *financial crisis* margin icon is placed next to relevant text material.

We continue our innovation from previous editions by featuring a real firm (Walgreens, the retail drugstore chain) in many of the chapters on investments and financial management as a means of presenting and analyzing data.

In addition to these broad improvements, all chapters have been updated and revised to reflect recent events and data. Specific notable changes in this fifteenth edition include the following:

Chapter 1, The Financial Environment, provides an overview of the financial system and environment. Economic and financial developments during the first part of the twenty-first century are identified, including the financial crisis and the 2007–2009 Great Recession.

Chapter 2, Money and the Monetary System, has been updated and the relationship between money supply and economic activity is discussed in light of the recent financial crisis and the associated credit crunch.

Chapter 3, Banks and Other Financial Institutions, features new material relating to how the financial crisis impacted on financial institutions. Falling housing prices, mortgage loan defaults, and declining values on mortgage-backed securities resulted in many financial institutions not having adequate equity capital to continue to operate and, thus, had to merge or be "bailed out."

Chapter 4, Federal Reserve System, describes the current structure and operations of the Fed including the Fed's response to the recent financial crisis and the Great Recession that followed. We also discuss the Fed's use of a new non-traditional monetary policy that became known as quantitative easing.

Chapter 5, Policy Makers and the Money Supply, describes how the U.S. government responded to the perfect financial storm involving the financial crisis and the subsequent Great Recession.

Chapter 6, International Finance and Trade, updates information on the European Union (EU) membership and the eurozone countries that have adopted the euro as their single currency.

Chapter 7, Savings and Investment Process, discusses how the increased use of debt by consumers to finance their spending contributed to the recent financial crisis and the Great Recession. Because home ownership has been an important component in the savings-investment process of individuals, we have incorporated materials on real estate mortgages and the mortgage markets into this chapter.

Chapter 8, Interest Rates, discusses the factors that explain differences in interest rates at a point in time as well as over time. In this chapter, we also cover the Fed's easy money policy, including the impact of quantitative easing on interest rates resulting in historical lows.

Chapter 9, Time Value of Money, conveys the importance of compounding (earning interest on interest) in building wealth over time. Examples are used to illustrate how to perform calculations with formulas, with interest factor tables, step-by-step financial calculator keystrokes, and Excel spreadsheets. We discuss the implications of the current low interest rate environment.

Chapter 10, Bond and Stocks: Characteristics and Valuations, has its bond valuation section rewritten to use the annual percentage rate (APR) approach as opposed to the effective interest rate (EAR) approach. The chapter contains updated data and improved discussions of bonds and stocks. We have revised the discussion of the risks facing investors in a low interest rate environment sustained by the Fed since the Great Recession. Spreadsheet examples show how to apply time value concepts to calculate bond prices and stock prices.

Chapter 11, Securities and Markets, incorporates changes in securities trading, including the New York Stock Exchange and IntercontinentalExchange (NYSE–ICE) merger as well as an overview of the Facebook initial public offering (IPO) and some of its problems.

Chapter 12, Financial Returns and Risk Concepts, is one of the more mathematical chapters; it shows how to do calculations with step-by-step calculator keystrokes and spreadsheet functions.

Chapter 13, Business Organization and Financial Data, features data from Walgreens' financial statements. We maintain that a firm's goal is to maximize shareholder wealth, and we discuss "sustainability" in light of this goal. In response to the financial crisis, we review problems with using stock options as an incentive mechanism for managers and the balance sheet implications of the government bailout for some U.S. auto companies.

Chapter 14, Financial Analysis and Long-Term Financial Planning, uses updated data from Walgreens and the retail drugstore industry in a practical example of financial ratio analysis using industry averages.

Chapter 15, Managing Working Capital, expands the discussion of managing cash in a difficult business environment with low interest rates. We discuss a new reason why firms hold large amounts of cash, with the tax cost of repatriating the funds back to the home country.

Chapter 16, Short-Term Business Financing, was revised to improve pedagogy and to update the material. It contains information on real firms' working capital financing strategies and on the implications of the financial crisis on a firm's ability to obtain short-term financing. We include a section on the American Energy and Infrastructure Jobs Act of 2012 (JOBS Act of 2012), a tool to help small firms obtain financing, including the use of "crowdfunding."

Chapter 17, Capital Budgeting Analysis, relates the cash flow estimation process for a project to the firm's statement of cash flows from Chapter 13 and reviews standard capital budgeting analysis tools such as net present value (NPV), internal rate of return (IRR), profitability index (PI), and modified internal rate of return (MIRR).

Chapter 18, Capital Structure and the Cost of Capital, contains updated discussions of trends in the use of debt by corporations and the use of debt financing in the low interest rate environment that has existed since the Great Recession.

LEARNING AND TEACHING AIDS

The fifteenth edition of *Introduction to Finance* offers the following aids for students and instructors:

CHAPTER OPENERS: Each chapter begins with the following:

- Chapter Learning Objectives, which students can use to review the chapter's main points and which instructors can use as a basis for in-class lecture or discussion;
- Where We Have Been statements that remind students of what was covered in the previous chapters;
- Where We Are Going, which are previews of chapters to come;
- How This Chapter Applies To Me that explain how the content of the chapter, no matter how technical or business specific, has applications to the individual student.

APPLYING FINANCE TO: These boxes show how the topic of each chapter relates to the finance fields of institutions and markets, investments, and financial management.

INTERNET MARGIN NOTES: We direct the student to relevant Web sites at different points in each chapter.

MARGIN DEFINITIONS: Margin definitions of key terms are provided to assist students in learning the language of finance.

CONCEPT CHECKS: These features appear in the margins near the end of every section to quiz students on what they have learned and how well they have learned it. Concept Checks reinforce the topical material and help students determine what they need to review.

MARGIN ICONS: These are placed in the margin to indicate discussions of finance principles, implications of the recent financial crisis, financial or business ethical issues, and global or international discussions.

SPREADSHEET ILLUSTRATIONS: We show how to use spreadsheets to solve problems and to teach students about the power of spreadsheet functions and analysis.

BOXED FEATURES: Throughout the book, boxes are used to focus on current topics or applications of interest. They are designed to illustrate concepts and practices in the dynamic field of finance.

- Small Business Practice boxes highlight aspects of the chapter topics relating directly to small businesses and entrepreneurship.
- Career Opportunities in Finance boxes provide information about various careers in finance and appear in many chapters.
- Personal Financial Planning boxes provide insight into how the chapter's content can be applied to an individual's finances.

LEARNING EXTENSIONS: Chapter appendixes, called Learning Extensions, are included in many chapters. Learning Extensions provide additional in-depth coverage of topics related to their respective chapters, and many challenge students to use their mathematical skills.

END-OF-CHAPTER MATERIALS: Each chapter provides the following:

- Discussion Questions that review chapter material
- Exercises for students to solve and exercise their mathematical skills
- Problems that are more difficult and that should be solved by using spreadsheets

COMPANION WEB SITE: The text's Web site at www.wiley.com/college/melicher contains a myriad of resources and links to aid learning and teaching.

INSTRUCTOR'S MANUAL AND TEST BANK: The Instructor's Manual is available to adopters of this text. It features detailed chapter outlines, lecture tips, and answers to end-of-chapter questions and problems. The manual includes an extensive test bank of true/false and multiple choice questions with answers, revised and expanded for this edition by Kevin Cochrane of College of the Desert.

COMPUTERIZED TEST BANK: This program is for use on a PC running Windows. The Computerized Test Bank contains content from the test bank provided within a Test Generating Program that allows instructors to customize their exams.

POWERPOINT PRESENTATIONS: Created by the authors, a PowerPoint presentation is provided for each chapter of the text. Slides include outline notes on the chapter, additional presentation topics, and figures and tables from the text.

STUDENT PRACTICE QUIZZES: A set of quizzes, revised by Leslie Mathis of University of Memphis, allows students to practice their knowledge and understanding of each chapter. These multiple-choice quizzes are auto-graded to provide students with instant feedback on their work.

SPREADSHEET SOFTWARE: A set of Excel-compatible templates, developed by Robert Ritchey of Texas Tech University, are available on the text's Web site. Students can use the templates to help solve some of the end-of-chapter problems and challenge problems.

ACKNOWLEDGMENTS

We would like to thank the Wiley Publishing team of Executive Editor Joel Hollenbeck, Assistant Editor Courtney Luzzi, and Senior Editorial Assistant Erica Horowitz for their role in preparing and publishing the fifteenth edition of *Introduction to Finance*.

In addition, we are especially grateful to the reviewers for their comments and constructive criticisms of this and previous editions:

Saul W. Adelman, *Miami University, Ohio*

Linda K. Brown, *St. Ambrose University*

Lisa Johnson, *Centura College*

Barbara L. Purvis, *Centura College*

Tim Alzheimer, *Montana State University*

Allan Blair, *Palm Beach Atlantic College*

Stewart Bonem, *Cincinnati State Technical and Community College*

Joseph M. Byers, *Community College of Allegheny County, South Campus*

Robert L. Chapman, *Orlando College*

William Chittenden, *Texas State University*

Will Crittendon, *Bronx Community College*

David R. Durst, *University of Akron*

Sharon H. Garrison, *Florida Atlantic University*

Asim Ghosh, *Saint Joseph's University*

Lester Hadsell, *University of Albany*

Irene M. Hammerbacher, *Iona College*

Kim Hansen, *Mid-State Technical College*

Jeff Hines, *Davenport College*

Jeff Jewell, *Lipscomb University*

Ed Krohn, *Miami Dade Community College*

P. John Limberopoulos, *University of Colorado Boulder*

Leslie Mathis, *University of Memphis*

John K. Mullen, *Clarkson University*

Michael Murray, *Winona State University*

Napoleon Overton, *University of Memphis*

Michael Owen, *Montana State University*

Marco Pagani, *San Jose State University*

Alan Questell, *Richmond Community College*

Ernest Scarbrough, *Arizona State University*

Raymond Shovlain, *St. Ambrose University*

Amir Tavakkol, *Kansas State University*

Jim Washam, *Arkansas State University*

Howard Whitney, *Franklin University*

David Zalewski, *Providence College*

Likewise, we appreciate the comments from students and teachers, who have used previous editions, and the assistance from the dozens of reviewers, who have commented about the early editions. Special recognition goes to Carl Dauten, who coauthored the first four editions, and Merle Welshans, who was a coauthor on the first nine editions of the book. Finally, and perhaps most importantly, we wish to thank our families for their understanding and support during the writing of the fifteenth edition.

Ronald W. Melicher, *Boulder, Colorado*
Edgar A. Norton, *Normal, Illinois*

FEATURES OF THIS BOOK

Chapter Openers

- **Chapter Learning Objectives** that students can use to review the chapter's main points and instructors can use as a basis for in-class lecture or discussion.
- **Where We Have Been** briefly summarizes material from previous chapters.
- **Where We Are Going** briefly previews coverage in future chapters.
- **How This Chapter Applies to Me** briefly outlines personally relevant issues.

Concept Checks appear in the margins near the end of every section to quiz students on what they have just learned and how well they have learned it. Concept checks reinforce the topical material and help students determine what they need to review.

Boxed Features throughout the book are used to focus on current topics or applications of interest. They are designed to illustrate concepts and practices in the dynamic field of finance.

- **Small Business Practice** boxes highlight aspects of the chapter topics relating directly to small businesses and entrepreneurship.
- **Personal Financial Planning** boxes incorporate relevant information on how the chapter's content can be applied to an individual's finances.
- **Career Opportunities in Finance** boxes appear in several chapters and provide information about various careers in finance.
- **Applying Finance To** boxes show how the chapter relates to the finance fields of institutions and markets, investments, and financial management.

Spreadsheet Illustrations explain how to use spreadsheets to solve problems while showing students the powers of spreadsheet function and analysis.

Learning Extensions are chapter appendices, which provide additional in-depth coverage of topics related to their respective chapters. Many challenge students to use their mathematical skills.

End-of-Chapter Materials provide discussion questions, exercises, and special challenge problems that present students with more difficult questions that should be solved using Excel spreadsheets.

Icons:

Concept Check	Internet Activity	Ethics	Global	Finance	Financial Crisis
CONCEPT CHECK	INTERNET ACTIVITY	ETHICAL ISSUES	GLOBAL DISCUSSION	FINANCE PRINCIPLE	FINANCIAL CRISIS

· AUTHOR BIOS ·

Ron Melicher is a professor of finance and previously served three different terms as chair of the Finance Division, Leeds School of Business, University of Colorado Boulder. He is a past president of the Financial Management Association. Ron earned undergraduate, M.B.A., and doctoral degrees from Washington University in St. Louis, Missouri. While at the University of Colorado, he has received several distinguished teaching awards and was designated a university-wide President's Teaching Scholar. Ron teaches corporate finance and financial strategy and valuation in the M.B.A. and Executive M.B.A. programs, in addition to entrepreneurial finance and investment banking to undergraduate students. His research has been published in major finance journals, including the *Journal of Finance, Journal of Financial and Quantitative Analysis*, and *Financial Management*. He is also the coauthor of *Entrepreneurial Finance*, fourth edition (South-Western/Cengage Learning).

Edgar A. Norton is professor of finance in the College of Business at Illinois State University. He holds a double major in computer science and economics from Rensselaer Polytechnic Institute and received his M.S. and Ph.D. from the University of Illinois at Urbana–Champaign. A Chartered Financial Analyst (CFA), he regularly receives certificates of achievement in the field of investments. He has consulted with COUNTRY Financial, Maersk, and the CFA Institute; does pro bono financial planning; and is a past president of the Midwest Finance Association. His research has appeared in numerous journals, such as *Financial Review, Journal of Business Venturing*, and *Journal of Business Ethics*. He has coauthored four textbooks, including *Introduction to Finance*.

• BRIEF CONTENTS •

• CONTENTS •

INTRODUCTION TO FINANCE

Markets, Investments, and Financial Management

PART I

INSTITUTIONS AND MARKETS

INTRODUCTION

Ask someone what he or she thinks "finance" is about. You'll probably get a variety of responses: "It deals with money." "It is what my bank does." "The New York Stock Exchange has something to do with it." "It's how businesses and people get the money they need—you know, borrowing and stuff like that." And they'd all be correct!

Finance is a broad field. It involves national and international systems of banking and financing business. It also deals with the process you go through to get a car loan and what a business does when planning for its future needs.

It is important to understand that while the U.S. financial system is complex, it generally operates efficiently. However, on occasion, imbalances can result in economic, real estate, and stock market "bubbles," which when bursts cause havoc on the workings of the financial system. The decade of the 2000s began with the bursting of the "tech" or technology bubble and the "dot.com" bubble. Then in mid-2006, the real estate bubble in the form of excessive housing prices burst. This was followed by the peaking of stock prices in 2007 followed by a steep decline that continued into early 2009. Economic activity began slowing in 2007 and progressed into an economic recession beginning in mid-2008, which was accompanied by double-digit unemployment rates. The result was the 2007–2008 financial crisis and the 2008–2009 Great Recession that produced the most financial distress on the U.S. financial system since the Great Depression years of the 1930s.

Within the general field of finance, there are three areas of study: financial institutions and markets, investments, and financial management. These areas are illustrated in the accompanying diagram. Financial institutions collect funds from savers and lend them to or invest them in businesses or people that need cash. Examples of financial institutions are commercial banks, investment banks, insurance companies, and mutual funds. Financial institutions operate as part of the financial system. The financial system is the environment of finance. It includes the laws and regulations that affect financial transactions. The financial system encompasses the Federal Reserve System, which controls the supply of money in the U.S. economy. It also consists of the mechanisms that have been constructed to facilitate the flow of money and financial securities among countries. Financial markets represent ways for bringing together those that have money to invest with those that need funds. Financial markets, which include markets for mortgages, securities, and currencies, are necessary for a financial system to operate efficiently. Part 1 of this book examines the financial system and the role of financial institutions and financial markets in it.

Securities markets play important roles in helping businesses and governments raise new funds. Securities markets also facilitate the transfer of securities between investors. A securities market can be a central location for the trading of financial claims, such as the New York Stock Exchange. It may also take the form of a communications network, as with the over-the-counter market, which is another means by which stocks and bonds can be traded. When people invest funds, lend or borrow money, or buy or sell shares of a company's stock, they are participating in the financial markets. Part 2 of this book examines the role of securities markets and the process of investing in bonds and stocks.

The third area of the field of finance is financial management. Financial management studies how a business should manage its assets, liabilities, and equity to produce a good or service. Whether or

2

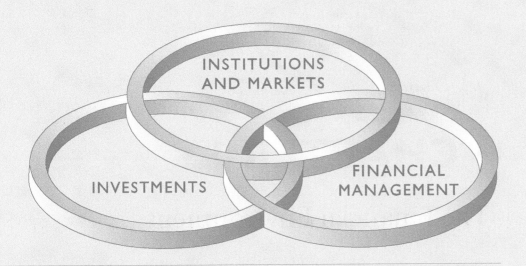

not a firm offers a new product or expands production, or how it invests excess cash, are examples of decisions that financial managers are involved with. Financial managers are constantly working with financial institutions and watching financial market trends as they make investment and financing decisions. Part 3 discusses how financial concepts can help managers better manage their firms.

There are few clear distinctions or separations between the three areas of finance. The diagram intentionally shows institutions and markets, investments, and financial management overlapping one another. Financial institutions operate in the environment of the financial markets and work to meet the financial needs of individuals and businesses. Financial managers do analyses and make decisions based on information they obtain from the financial markets. They also work with financial institutions when they need to raise funds and when they have excess funds to invest. Participants investing in the financial markets use information from financial institutions and firms to evaluate different investments in securities such as stocks, bonds, and certificates of deposit. A person working in one field must be knowledgeable about all three. Thus, this book is designed to provide you with a survey of all three areas of finance.

Part 1, Institutions and Markets, presents an overview of the financial system and its important components of policy makers, a monetary system, financial institutions, and financial markets. Financial institutions operate within the financial system to facilitate the work of the financial markets. For example, you can put your savings in a bank and earn interest. But your money doesn't just sit in the bank: The bank takes your deposit and the money from other depositors and lends it to Kathy, who needs a short-term loan for her business; to Ron for a college loan; and to Roger and Maria, who borrow the money to help buy a house. Banks bring together savers and those who need money, such as Kathy, Ron, Roger, and Maria. The interest rate the depositors earn and the interest rate that borrowers pay are determined by national and even international economic forces. Just what the bank does with depositors' money and how it reviews loan applications is determined to some extent by bank regulators and financial market participants, such as the Federal Reserve Board. Decisions by the president and Congress relating to fiscal policies and regulatory laws may also directly influence financial institutions and markets and alter the financial system.

Chapter 2 presents an overview of the role of money in the operation of the U.S. monetary and financial systems, including discussion of how funds are transferred among individuals, firms, and countries. Depository institutions, such as banks and savings and loans, as well as other financial institutions, involved in the financial intermediation process are the topic of Chapter 3. The Federal Reserve System, the U.S. central bank that controls the money supply, is discussed in Chapter 4. Chapter 5 places the previous chapters in perspective, discussing the role of the Federal Reserve and the banking system in helping meet national economic goals for the United States, such as economic growth, low inflation, and stable exchange rates. Part 1 concludes with an explanation of international trade and the topic of international finance in Chapter 6.

• CHAPTER 1 •

The Financial Environment

Chapter Learning Objectives... AFTER STUDYING THIS CHAPTER, YOU SHOULD BE ABLE TO DO THE FOLLOWING:

- Define *finance* and explain why finance should be studied.
- Identify several major career opportunities in finance.
- Identify and describe the six principles of finance.
- Identify characteristics and components of an effective financial system.
- Describe the financial functions performed in an effective financial system.
- Briefly describe the four types of financial markets.

Where We Have Been... As we progress through this book, we start each chapter with a brief review of previously covered materials. This will provide you with a reference base for understanding the transition from topic to topic. After completing the text, you will be at the beginning of what we hope is a successful business career.

Where We Are Going... The financial environment within which we live and work is composed of a financial system, institutions, and markets. Part 1 of this text focuses on developing an understanding of the financial institutions and markets that operate to make the financial system work efficiently. Chapter 2 describes the U.S. monetary system, including how it is intertwined with the capital formation process and how it has evolved. Current types of money are described, and we discuss why it is important to control the growth of the money supply. In following chapters, we turn our attention to understanding how financial institutions, policy makers, and international developments influence how the financial system functions.

How This Chapter Applies to Me... While it is impossible to predict what life has in store for each of us in terms of health, family, and career, everyone can be a productive member of society. Nearly all of us will take part in making social, political, and economic decisions. A basic understanding of the financial environment that encompasses economic and financial systems will help you in making informed economic choices.

Let us begin with the following quote by George Santayana, a U.S. philosopher and poet:

Those who cannot remember the past are condemned to repeat it.[1]

While this quotation refers to the need to know something about history so individuals can avoid repeating bad social, political, and economic decisions, it is equally important to the field of finance. All individuals have the responsibility to be able to make informed public choices involving the financial environment. By understanding the financial environment and studying the financial system, institutions and markets, investments, and financial management, individuals will be able to make informed economic and financial choices that will lead to better financial health and success. After studying the materials in this book, you will be better informed in making choices that affect the economy and the financial system, as well as be better prepared for a business career, possibly one in the field of finance.

---

1. George Santayana, *Reason in Common Sense, The Life of Reason,* Vol. 1 (Charles Scribner's Sons, 1905), p. 284.

HOW HAS THE FINANCIAL ENVIRONMENT CHANGED?

The first twelve years of the twenty-first century have been a difficult time in the United States and worldwide. Whereas the 1990s decade was a period of economic growth and prosperity, the early part of the twenty-first century has been characterized by economic and financial markets volatility along with many individuals "treading water" in trying to maintain the standards of living they had achieved.

A price bubble for technology stocks, including so-called dot.com start-ups, burst in the United States in 2000. An economic downturn followed and was exacerbated by the September 11, 2001 terrorist attack. Economic recovery occurred over several years until the housing price bubble burst in 2006 and housing values declined. Securities tied to housing prices declined causing concerns that "over-borrowed" financial institutions might fail because they held insufficient equity capital resources to cover the decline in values of the home mortgages and housing-related debt securities they held. This led to the 2007–2008 financial crisis. A major economic recession (sometimes called the Great Recession) began in early 2008 and continued through mid-2009 and turned out to be the deepest and longest recession since the Great Depression of the 1930s. Unemployment rates exceeded 10 percent in 2009 and remained above the 7 percent level as of the end of 2012.

The health of economies, financial institutions, and markets are linked throughout the world. European and other major foreign financial institutions were caught in the 2007–2008 financial crisis and most foreign economies suffered economic downturns near the end of the 2000s decade. Even China, which had been growing its economy at a double-digit rate during the decade of the 2000s, had a slowing economic activity during the past couple of years. This has worldwide implications since many developed and developing economies are tied to demand for natural resources and other products by Chinese firms.

We believe the analysis and understanding of past developments in economic activity and financial markets is useful to governments, businesses, and individuals in planning their futures. By learning from the past, we may be able to avoid, or mediate, similar pitfalls in the future.

WHAT IS FINANCE?

Finance is the study of how individuals, institutions, governments, and businesses acquire, spend, and manage money and other financial assets. Understanding finance is important to all students regardless of the discipline or area of study because nearly all business and economic decisions have financial implications. The decision to spend or consume (for new clothes or dinner at a fancy restaurant) rather than save or invest (for spending or consuming more in the future) is an everyday decision that we face.

The *financial environment* encompasses the financial system, institutions or intermediaries (we will use these terms interchangeably throughout this text), financial markets, business firms, individuals, and global interactions that contribute to an efficiently operating economy. Figure 1.1 depicts the three areas of finance within the financial environment: institutions and markets, investments, and financial management. Though we identify three distinct finance areas, these areas do not operate in isolation but rather interact or intersect with each other. Our focus in this book is to provide the reader with exposure to all three areas, as well as to show how they are integrated. Of course, students pursuing a major or area of emphasis in finance will take multiple courses in one or more of these areas.

Financial institutions are organizations or intermediaries that help the financial system operate efficiently and transfer funds from savers and investors to individuals, businesses, and governments that seek to spend or invest the funds in physical assets (inventories, buildings, and equipment). *Financial markets* are physical locations or electronic forums that facilitate the flow of funds among investors, businesses, and governments. *Investments* involve the sale or marketing of securities, the analysis of securities, and the management of investment risk through portfolio diversification. *Financial management* involves financial planning, asset management, and fund-raising decisions to enhance the value of businesses.

Finance has its origins in economics and accounting. Economists use a supply and demand framework to explain how the prices and quantities of goods and services are determined in a free-market economic system. Accountants provide the record-keeping mechanism for showing

finance
study of how individuals, institutions, governments, and businesses acquire, spend, and manage money and other financial assets

financial environment
financial system, institutions or intermediaries, financial markets, business firms, individuals, and global interactions that contribute to an efficiently operating economy

financial institutions
organizations or intermediaries that help the financial system operate efficiently and transfer funds from savers and investors to individuals, businesses, and governments that seek to spend or invest the funds in physical assets

financial markets
physical locations or electronic forums that facilitate the flow of funds among investors, businesses, and governments

investments
involve the sale or marketing of securities, the analysis of securities, and the management of investment risk through portfolio diversification

financial management
involves financial planning, asset management, and fund-raising decisions to enhance the value of businesses

FIGURE 1.1
Graphic Illustration of the Financial Environment

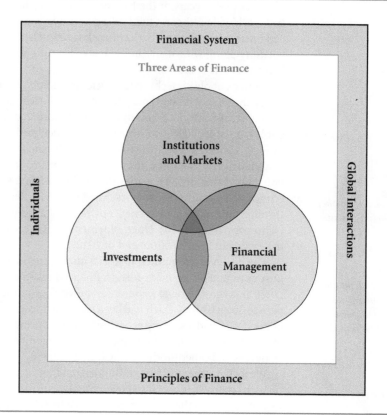

ownership of the financial instruments used in the flow of financial funds between savers and borrowers. Accountants record revenues, expenses, and profitability of organizations that produce and exchange goods and services.

Efficient methods of production and specialization of labor can exist if there is an effective means of paying for raw materials and final products. Businesses can obtain the money needed to buy capital goods such as machinery and equipment only if a mechanism has been established for making savings available for investment. Similarly, federal and other governmental units, such as state and local governments and tax districts, can carry out their wide range of activities if efficient means exist for raising money, for making payments, and for borrowing.

Financial institutions, financial markets, and investment and financial management are crucial elements of the financial environment and well-developed financial systems. Financial institutions are intermediaries, such as banks, insurance companies, and investment companies that engage in financial activities to aid the flow of funds from savers to borrowers or investors.

Financial markets provide the mechanism for allocating financial resources or funds from savers to borrowers. Individuals make decisions as investors and financial managers. Investors include savers and lenders as well as equity investors.

While we are focusing on financial managers in this book, we recognize that individuals must be continuously involved in managing their personal finances. Investment management involves making decisions relating to issuing and investing in stocks and bonds. Financial management in business involves making decisions relating to the efficient use of financial resources in the production and sale of goods and services. The goal of the financial manager in a profit-seeking organization is to maximize the owners' wealth. This is accomplished through effective financial planning and analysis, asset management, and the acquisition of financial capital. Financial managers in not-for-profit organizations aim to provide a desired level of services at acceptable costs and perform the same financial management functions as their for-profit counterparts.

entrepreneurial finance
study of how growth-driven, performance-focused, early-stage firms raise financial capital and manage their operations and assets

personal finance
study of how individuals prepare for financial emergencies, protect against premature death and the loss of property, and accumulate wealth over time

CONCEPT CHECK

What are the three areas of finance?

What two finance themes are carried throughout this book?

INTERNET ACTIVITY

Go to the Small Business Administration Web site, http://www.sba.gov, and explore what is involved in deciding whether to start a new business.

TWO THEMES

As we progress through this book, we offer two themes within the financial institutions and markets, investments, and financial management topic areas. In each chapter, we provide boxed materials relating to small business practice and personal financial planning. Successful businesses typically progress through a series of life cycle stages from the idea stage to exiting the business. More specifically, the successful business typically moves through five stages: development stage, startup stage, survival stage, rapid growth stage, and maturity stage. Individuals who choose to become small business owners do so for a number of different reasons. Some small business owners focus on salary replacement opportunities where they seek income levels comparable to what they could have earned by working for much larger firms. Other individuals pursue lifestyle small business opportunities where they get paid for doing things they like to do. Entrepreneurs seek to own and run businesses that stress high growth rates in sales, profits, and cash flows.

Entrepreneurial finance is the study of how growth-driven, performance-focused, early-stage (from development through early rapid growth) firms raise financial capital and manage their operations and assets. Our small business practice boxes focus on operational and financial issues faced by early-stage firms. *Personal finance* is the study of how individuals prepare for financial emergencies, protect against premature death and the loss of property, and accumulate wealth over time. Our personal financial planning boxes focus on planning decisions made by individuals in regards to saving and investing their financial resources.

WHY STUDY FINANCE?

There are several reasons to study finance. Knowledge of the basics of finance covered in this text should help you make informed: economic decisions, personal and business investment decisions, and career decisions.

1. ***To make informed economic decisions.***

    As we will see, the operation of the financial system and the performance of the economy are influenced by policy makers. Individuals elect many of these policy makers in the United States, such as the president and members of Congress. Since these elected officials have the power to alter the financial system by creating laws and since their decisions can influence economic activity, individuals must be informed when making political and economic choices. Do you want a balanced budget, lower taxes, free international trade, low inflation, and full employment? Whatever your financial and economic goals may be, you need to be an informed participant if you wish to make a difference. Every individual should attain a basic understanding of finance as it applies to the financial system. Part 1 of this book focuses on understanding the roles of financial institutions and markets and how the financial system works.

SMALL BUSINESS PRACTICE
Importance of Small Firms in the U.S. Economy

As the U.S. economy moved from the industrial age to the information age, dramatic changes occurred in the importance of small businesses. As large firms with five hundred or more employees continued to downsize and restructure throughout the 1990s and into the twenty-first century, small firms provided the impetus for economic growth.

During the mid-1970s through the 1980s period, firms with fewer than five hundred employees provided over half of total employment and nearly two-thirds of the net new jobs in the United States. Small firms provided most of the net new jobs during the 1990s. And, while the decade of the 2000s involved a housing price collapse, a major financial crisis, and economic recession, small firms continued to be the primary supplier of new jobs.

Why have small firms been so successful in creating new jobs? A U.S. Small Business Administration (SBA) white paper suggests two reasons. First, small firms provide a crucial role in technological change and productivity growth. Market economies change rapidly, and small firms can adjust quickly. Second, small firms provide the mechanism and incentive for millions of individuals to pursue the opportunity for economic success.

Others may argue that entrepreneurial spirit and activity account for the importance of small firms in the U.S. economy. Whatever the reasons, the ongoing growth of small businesses continues to be an important stimulus to the economy in the early years of the twenty-first century.

For current statistics, visit the SBA Office of Advocacy Web site at http://www.sba.gov/advo.

2. ***To make informed personal and business investment decisions.***
An understanding of finance should help you better understand how the institution, government unit, or business that you work for finances its operations. At a personal level, the understanding of investments will enable you to better manage your financial resources and provide the basis for making sound decisions for accumulating wealth over time. Thus, in addition to understanding finance basics relating to the financial system and the economy, you need to develop an understanding of the factors that influence interest rates and security prices. Part 2 of this book focuses on understanding the characteristics of stocks and bonds and how they are valued, securities markets, and how to make risk-versus-return investment decisions.

3. ***To make informed career decisions based on a basic understanding of business finance.***
Even if your business interest is in a nonfinance career or professional activity, you will likely need to interact with finance professionals within and outside your firm or organization. Doing so will require a basic knowledge of the concepts, tools, and applications of financial management. Part 3 of this book focuses on providing you with an understanding of how finance is applied within a firm by focusing on decision making by financial managers.

Of course, you may be interested in pursuing a career in finance or at least want to know what people who work in finance do. Throughout this text, you will find discussions of career opportunities in finance as well as a boxed feature entitled Career Opportunities in Finance.

CONCEPT CHECK

Give three reasons for studying finance.

INTERNET ACTIVITY

Go to The Wall Street Journal *Web site section at http://www.careerjournal. com, and find information relating to job hunting.*

CAREERS IN FINANCE

Career opportunities in finance are available in financial management, depository financial institutions, contractual savings and real property organizations, and securities markets and investment firms. While you may aspire to own your own business or to be a chief executive officer (CEO) or chief financial officer (CFO) in a major corporation, most of us must begin our careers in an entry-level position. Following are four ways to get started in a finance career.

1. ***Financial management***
Larger businesses or corporations divide their finance activities into treasury and control functions, whereas smaller firms often combine these functions. The treasurer is responsible for managing the firm's cash, acquiring and managing the firm's assets, and selling stocks and bonds to raise the financial capital necessary to conduct business. The controller is responsible for cost accounting, financial accounting, and tax record-keeping activities. Entry-level career opportunities include the following:

   - *Cash management analyst* involves monitoring and managing the firm's day-to-day cash inflows and outflows
   - *Capital expenditures analyst* involves estimating cash flows and evaluating asset investment opportunities
   - *Credit analyst* involves evaluating credit applications and collecting amounts owed by credit customers
   - *Financial analyst* involves evaluating financial performance and preparing financial plans
   - *Cost analyst* involves comparing actual operations against budgeted operations
   - *Tax analyst* involves preparing financial statements for tax purposes

2. ***Depository financial institutions***
Banks and other depository institutions offer the opportunity to start a finance career in consumer or commercial lending. Banks hold and manage trust funds for individuals and other organizations. Entry-level career opportunities include the following:

   - *Loan analyst* involves evaluating consumer and/or commercial loan applications
   - *Bank teller* involves assisting customers with their day-to-day checking and banking transactions
   - *Investments research analyst* involves conducting research on investment opportunities for a bank trust department

3. *Contractual savings and real property organizations*

Insurance companies, pension funds, and real estate firms provide opportunities for starting a career in finance. These institutions need various employees willing to blend marketing or selling efforts with financial expertise. Entry-level career opportunities include the following:

- *Insurance agent (broker)* involves selling insurance to individuals and businesses and participating in the processing of claims
- *Research analyst* involves analyzing the investment potential of real property and securities for pension fund holdings
- *Real estate agent (broker)* involves marketing and selling or leasing residential or commercial property
- *Mortgage analyst* involves analyzing real estate loan applications and assisting in the arranging of mortgage financing

4. *Securities markets and investment firms*

Securities firms and various investment-related businesses provide opportunities to start a finance career in the investments area. Opportunities include buying and selling seasoned securities, analyzing securities for investment potential, marketing new securities issues, and helping individuals plan and manage their personal financial resources. Entry-level career opportunities include the following:

- *Stockbroker (account executive)* involves assisting clients in purchasing stocks and bonds and building investment wealth
- *Security analyst* involves analyzing and making recommendations on the investment potential of specific securities
- *Investment banking analyst* involves conducting financial analysis and valuation of new securities being issued
- *Financial planner assistant* involves analyzing individual client insurance needs and investment plans to meet retirement goals

While we have focused on entry-level careers in profit-motivated businesses and financial organizations, careers in finance are available in government or not-for-profit organizations. Finance opportunities at the federal or state government levels include managing cash funds, making asset expenditure decisions, and issuing debt securities to raise funds. Hospitals and other not-for-profit organizations also need expert financial managers to manage assets, control costs, and obtain funds. Government units and not-for-profit organizations hire financial and other analysts to perform these tasks.

All of these entry-level finance job opportunities can be found in the international setting. For example, many businesses engaged in producing and marketing products and services in foreign markets often offer employees opportunities for international job assignments. Large U.S. banks offer international job experiences through their foreign banking operations. Furthermore, since worldwide securities markets exist, securities analysts and financial planners often must analyze and visit foreign-based firms.

CAREER OPPORTUNITIES IN FINANCE
You Are Likely to Have More than One Business Career

Students are advised to prepare for several business careers during their working lifetimes. Corporate America continues to restructure and reinvent itself. At the same time, new industries associated with the information age are developing, and old industries are dropping by the wayside. These developments mean you will have more opportunities for multiple business careers.

Graduates of Harvard University are periodically surveyed concerning their work experiences and careers. Responses to one survey of individuals twenty-five years after graduation found that over half had

worked for four or more employers, and one-fourth had been fired or, in kinder terms, "involuntarily terminated". Over half of the men and women respondents had had at least two substantially different careers, and in many instances significant retraining was required.

Remember as you read this book that even if you do not plan on a career in finance, learning about finance might become important to you in your working lifetime. No matter where your business career takes you, you will always need to know and understand your personal finances.

CONCEPT CHECK

What are the major areas for possible careers in finance?

FINANCE PRINCIPLE

Several detailed Career Opportunities in Finance boxes are presented in selected chapters. We hope these materials provide a better understanding of some of the many career opportunities that exist in the finance field. We are sure new finance job opportunities will occur as the field continues to develop and change. It is time to begin learning about finance.

SIX PRINCIPLES OF FINANCE

Finance is founded on six important principles. The first five relate to the economic behavior of individuals, and the sixth one focuses on ethical behavior. Knowing about these principles will help us understand how managers, investors, and others incorporate time and risk into their decisions, as well as why the desire to earn excess returns leads to information-efficient financial markets in which prices reflect available information. Unfortunately, sometimes greed associated with the desire to earn excess returns causes individuals to risk losing their reputations by engaging in questionable ethical behavior and unethical behavior in the form of fraud or other illegal activities. The bottom line is "Reputation matters." The following are the six principles that serve as the foundation of finance:

1. Money has a time value.
2. Higher returns are expected for taking on more risk.
3. Diversification of investments can reduce risk.
4. Financial markets are efficient in pricing securities.
5. Manager and stockholder objectives may differ.
6. Reputation matters.

TIME VALUE OF MONEY

Let's look at these principles one by one. Money in hand today is worth more than the promise of receiving the same amount in the future. The time value of money exists because a sum of money today could be invested and grow over time. For example, assume you have $1,000 and that it could earn $60 (6 percent) interest over the next year. Thus, $1,000 today would be worth $1,060 at the end of one year (i.e., $1,000 plus $60). As a result, a dollar today is worth more than a dollar received a year from now. The time value of money principle helps us understand the economic behavior of individuals and the economic decisions of the institutions and businesses they run. This finance principle pillar is apparent in many of our day-to-day activities, and knowledge of it will help us understand the implications of time-varying money decisions. We explore the details of the time value of money in Chapter 9, but this first principle of finance will be apparent throughout this book.

RISK VERSUS RETURN

A trade-off exists between risk and expected return in all types of investments, both assets and securities. Risk is the uncertainty about the outcome or payoff of an investment in the future. For example, you might invest $1,000 in a business venture today. After one year, the firm might be bankrupt, and you would lose your total investment. On the other hand, after one year your investment might be worth $2,400. This variability in possible outcomes is your risk. Instead, you might invest your $1,000 in a U.S. government security, where after one year the value may be $950 or $1,100. Rational investors would consider the business venture investment to be riskier and would choose this investment only if they feel the expected return is high enough to justify the greater risk. Investors make these trade-off decisions every day.

Business managers make similar trade-off decisions when they choose between different projects in which they could invest. Understanding the risk/return trade-off principle helps us understand how individuals make economic decisions. While we specifically explore the trade-off between risk and expected return in greater detail in Part 2, this second principle of finance is involved in many financial decisions throughout this text.

DIVERSIFICATION OF RISK

While higher returns are expected for taking on more risk, all investment risk is not the same. Some risk can be removed or diversified by investing in several different assets or securities. Let's return to the example involving a $1,000 investment in a business venture where after one year the investment we could provide a return of either zero dollars or $2,400. Let's assume an opportunity exists to invest $1,000 in a second unrelated business venture in which the outcomes would be zero dollars or $2,400. Let's further assume we will put half of our $1,000 investment funds in each investment opportunity such that the individual outcomes for each $500 investment would be zero dollars or $1,200.

Though both investments could lose everything (i.e., return zero dollars) or return $1,200 each (a total of $2,400), one investment could go broke and the other return $1,200. So, four outcomes are possible:

POSSIBLE OUTCOMES	COMBINED INVESTMENT	POSSIBLE RETURNS		COMBINED RETURN
Outcome 1:	$500 + $500	$0 + $0	=	$0
Outcome 2:	$500 + $500	$0 + $1,200	=	$1,200
Outcome 3:	$500 + $500	$1,200 + $0	=	$1,200
Outcome 4:	$500 + $500	$1,200 + $1,200	=	$2,400

If each outcome has an equal one-fourth (25 percent) chance of occurring, most of us would prefer this diversified investment. Though our combined investment of $1,000 ($500 in each investment) at the extremes could return zero dollars or $2,400, it is also true that we have a 50 percent chance of getting $1,200 back for our $1,000 investment. As a result, most of us would prefer investing in the combined or diversified investment rather than in either of the two investments separately. We will explore the benefits of investment diversification in Part 2 of this text.

FINANCIAL MARKETS ARE EFFICIENT

A fourth finance-related aspect of economic behavior is that individuals seek to find undervalued and overvalued investment opportunities involving real and financial assets. It is human nature, economically speaking, to search for investment opportunities that will provide returns higher than those expected for undertaking a specified risk level. This attempt by many to earn excess returns or to beat the market leads to financial markets being information efficient. However, at the same time, consistently earning returns higher than those expected in a risk/return trade-off framework becomes almost impossible. Rather than looking at this third pillar of finance as a negative consequence of human economic behavior, we prefer to couch it positively in that it leads to information-efficient financial markets.

A financial market is said to be information efficient if the prices of securities reflect all information available to the public. When new information becomes available, prices change to reflect that information. For example, let's assume a firm's stock is currently trading at $20 per share. If the market is efficient, potential buyers and sellers of the stock know that $20 per share is a fair price. Trades should be at $20, or near to it, if the demand (potential buyers) and supply (potential sellers) are in reasonable balance. Let's assume the firm announces the production of a new product that is expected to increase sales and profits. Investors might react by bidding up the price to, say, $25 per share to reflect this new information. Assuming this new information is assessed properly, the new fair price becomes $25 per share. This informational efficiency of financial markets exists because a large number of professionals are continually searching for mispriced securities. As soon as new information is discovered, it becomes immediately reflected in the price of the associated security. Information-efficient financial markets play an important role in the marketing and transferring of financial assets between investors by providing liquidity and fair prices. The importance of information efficient financial markets is examined throughout this text and specifically in Chapter 12.

MANAGEMENT VERSUS OWNER OBJECTIVES

A fifth principle of finance is related to management objectives differing from owner objectives. Owners or equity investors want to maximize the returns on their investments but often hire professional managers to run their firms. However, managers may seek to emphasize the size of firm sales or assets, have company jets or helicopters available for their travel, and receive company-paid country club memberships. Owner returns may suffer as a result of manager objectives. To bring manager objectives in line with owner objectives, the company must tie manager compensation to measures of performance beneficial to owners. Managers are often given a portion of the ownership positions in privately held firms and are provided stock options and bonuses tied to stock price performance in publicly traded firms.

The possible conflict between managers and owners is sometimes called the *principal-agent problem*. We will explore this problem in greater detail and describe how owners provide incentives to managers to manage in the best interests of equity investors or owners in Chapter 13.

REPUTATION MATTERS

ETHICAL ISSUES

ethical behavior
how an individual or organization treats others legally, fairly, and honestly

The sixth principle of finance is "Reputation matters." An individual's reputation reflects his or her ethical standards or behavior. **Ethical behavior** is how an individual or organization treats others legally, fairly, and honestly. The ethical behavior of organizations reflects the ethical behaviors of their directors, officers, and managers. For institutions or businesses to be successful, they must have the trust and confidence of their customers, employees, and owners, as well as the community and society within which they operate. Firms have an ethical responsibility to provide safe products and services, to have safe working conditions for employees, and to not pollute or destroy the environment. Laws and regulations exist to ensure minimum levels of protection and the difference between unethical and ethical behavior. Examples of high ethical behavior include when firms establish product safety and working-condition standards well above the legal or regulatory standards.

Unfortunately, and possibly due in part to the greed for excess returns (such as higher salaries, bonuses, more valuable stock options, personal perquisites), directors, officers, managers, and other individuals sometimes are guilty of unethical behavior for engaging in fraudulent or other illegal activities. Reputations are destroyed, criminal activities are prosecuted, and involved individuals may receive jail sentences. The unethical behavior of directors, officers, and managers may lead to a loss of reputation and destruction of the institutions and businesses for which they work.

Many examples of fraudulent and illegal unethical behavior have been cited in the financial press over the past few decades, and most seem to be tied to greed for personal gain. In such cases, confidential information was used for personal benefit, illegal payments were made to gain business, accounting fraud was committed, business assets were converted to personal use, and so forth. In the early 1980s, a number of savings and loan association managers were found to have engaged in fraudulent and unethical practices, and some managers were prosecuted and sent to prison, and their institutions were dissolved or merged with other institutions.

In the late 1980s and early 1990s, fraudulent activities and unethical behavior by investment banking firms resulted in several high-profile financial wheeler-dealers going to prison. This resulted in the collapse of Drexel, Burnham, Lambert and the near collapse of Salomon Brothers. By the early part of the twenty-first century, such major firms as Enron, its auditor Arthur Andersen, and WorldCom ceased to exist because of fraudulent and unethical behavior on the part of their managers and officers. In addition, key officials of Tyco and Adelphia were charged with illegal actions and fraud. In 2009, Bernie Madoff was convicted and sent to prison for operating a Ponzi scheme that resulted in investors losing billions of dollars. Returns in a Ponzi scheme are fictitious and unearned. Early investors receive their returns from the contributions of subsequent investors. Ultimately, such a scheme collapses when new investors cannot be found and when existing investors want to sell their investments.

While the financial press chooses to highlight examples of unethical behavior, most individuals exhibit sound ethical behavior in their personal and business dealings and practices. In fact, the sixth principle of finance depends on most individuals practicing high-quality ethical behavior and believing that reputation matters. To be successful, an organization or business must have the trust and confidence of its various constituencies, including customers, employees, owners, and the community. High-quality ethical behavior involves treating others fairly and honestly and goes beyond meeting legal and regulatory requirements. High reputation value reflects high-quality ethical behavior, so employing high ethical standards is the right thing to do. Many organizations and businesses have developed and follow their own code of ethics. The importance of practicing sound ethical behavior is discussed throughout this text.

CONCEPT CHECK

What are the six principles of finance?

OVERVIEW OF THE FINANCIAL SYSTEM

financial system
a complex mix of financial intermediaries, markets, instruments, policy makers, and regulations that interact to expedite the flow of financial capital from savings into investments

The **financial system** is a complex mix of financial intermediaries, markets, instruments, policy makers, and regulations that interact to expedite the flow of financial capital from savings into investment. We present a brief overview of the financial system in Chapter 1 and then follow with more detailed coverage in the remaining chapters of Part 1.

CHARACTERISTICS AND REQUIREMENTS

Figure 1.2 provides a graphic review of the U.S. financial system. First, an effective financial system must have several sets of *policy makers* who pass laws and make decisions relating to fiscal and monetary policies. These policy makers include the president, Congress, the U.S. Treasury, and the Federal Reserve Board. Since the United States operates within a global economy, political and economic actions of foreign policy makers influence, although indirectly, the U.S. financial system and its operations. Major economic goals are identified and policy maker actions designed to achieve those goals are discussed in Chapter 5.

Second, an effective financial system needs an efficient monetary system, which is composed of a central bank and a banking system able to create and transfer a stable medium of exchange called money. In the United States, the dollar is the medium of exchange, the central bank is the Federal Reserve System, and the banking system is commonly referred to as the commercial banking system. Characteristics of money and the monetary system are discussed in Chapter 2, and the Federal Reserve System is covered in Chapter 4.

Third, an effective financial system must have *financial institutions* or intermediaries that support capital formation either by channeling savings into investment in physical assets or by fostering

INTERNET ACTIVITY

Go to the BusinessWeek *Web site, http://www.businessweek. com, and identify a major business development relating to the financial environment*

FIGURE 1.2
Graphic View of the U.S. Financial System

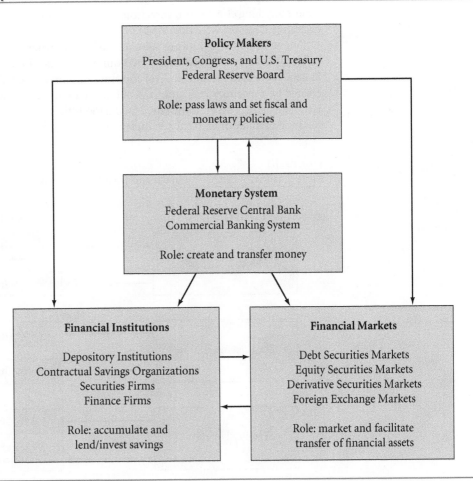

direct financial investments by individuals in financial institutions and businesses. The process of accumulating and then lending and investing savings is referred to as the savings-investment process. Four types of financial intermediaries are listed in Figure 1.2. Depository institutions, contractual savings organizations, securities firms, and finance firms are discussed in Chapter 3.

Fourth, an effective financial system requires financial assets or instruments necessary for the savings-investment process to work efficiently. We cover the types of financial asset instruments and securities used in the United States throughout the text and cover how the savings-invest-ment process works in Chapter 7.

Fifth, an effective financial system must also have *financial markets* that facilitate the transfer of financial assets among individuals, institutions, businesses, and governments. Figure 1.2 iden-tifies three types of financial markets: debt securities markets, equity securities markets, and derivative securities markets. We briefly discuss these markets later in this chapter and then provide more detailed coverage of the various securities markets throughout the text.

CONCEPT CHECK

What five requirements are necessary for a financial system to be effective?

FINANCIAL SYSTEM COMPONENTS AND FINANCIAL FUNCTIONS

We can express the roles of the monetary system, financial institutions, and financial markets as financial functions necessary in an effective financial system. Figure 1.3 indicates that the mone-tary system is responsible for creating and transferring money. Financial institutions efficiently accumulate savings and then lend or invest these savings. Financial institutions play important roles in the savings-investment process through financial intermediation activities and in facili-tating direct investments by individuals. Financial markets, along with certain securities firms, are responsible for marketing and transferring financial assets or claims.

Creating Money

Since money is something accepted as payment for goods, services, and debts, its value lies in its purchasing power. Money is the most generalized claim to wealth since it can be exchanged for almost anything else. Most transactions in today's economy involve money, and most would not take place if money were unavailable.

One of the most significant functions of the monetary system within the financial system is creating money, which serves as a medium of exchange. In the United States, the Federal Reserve System is primarily responsible for the amount of money created although most of the money is created by depository institutions. A sufficient amount of money is essential if economic activity is to take place at an efficient rate. Having too little money constrains economic growth. Having too much money often results in increases in the prices of goods and services.

FIGURE 1.3

Three Financial System Components and Their Financial Functions

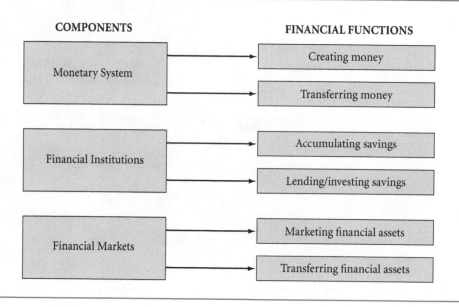

PERSONAL FINANCIAL PLANNING
People Are the Financial System

The main participant in the financial system is not the large institution or corporation. Instead, it's you and others like you. Households, families, and individuals provide up to 80 percent of the savings flows in the U.S. economy in any year. Three main sources of savings exist: personal savings, business savings (that is, retained earnings), and government surpluses. Personal savings far outweigh the other two sources combined as a source of savings flows in the United States.

You can look at this is another way: Where do financial institutions get the funds they invest and loan? Banks get their funds mainly from individuals' checking and savings accounts and from certificates of deposit (CDs). Pension funds obtain their cash from the savings of working people. Insurance firms accumulate funds to invest from policyholders' payments of premiums for their life, health, car, and home insurance. Mutual funds obtain investable cash by selling their shares to investors like you who want to accumulate savings and returns on savings to fund a future goal such as retirement, a new car, a house down payment, or children's college expenses.

Transferring Money

Individuals and businesses hold money for purchases or payments they expect to make in the future. One way to hold money is in checkable deposits at depository institutions. When money is held in this form, payments can be made easily by check. The check is an order to the depository institution to transfer money to the party who received the check. This is a great convenience since checks can be written for the exact amount of payments, can be safely sent in the mail, and can provide a record of payment. Institutions can also transfer funds between accounts electronically, making payments without paper checks. Funds transfers can be made by telephone, at automated teller machines (ATMs) connected to a bank's computer, and via the Internet.

Accumulating Savings

A function performed by financial institutions is the accumulation or gathering of individual savings. Most individuals, businesses, and organizations do not want to take the risks involved in having cash on hand. Even if relatively small, cash amounts are put into a depository institution for safekeeping. When all the deposits are accumulated in one place, they can be used for loans and investments in amounts much larger than any individual depositor could supply. Depository institutions regularly conduct advertising campaigns and other promotional activities to attract deposits.

Lending and Investing Savings

Another basic function of financial institutions is lending and investing. The money that has been put into these intermediaries may be lent to businesses, farmers, consumers, institutions, and governmental units. It may be lent for varying periods and for different purposes, such as to buy equipment or to pay current bills. Some financial institutions make loans of almost all types. Others specialize in one or two types of lending. Other financial institutions invest all or part of their accumulated savings in the stock of a business or in debt obligations of businesses or other institutions.

Marketing Financial Assets

New financial instruments and securities are created and sold in the primary securities market. For example, a business may want to sell shares of ownership, called stock, to the general public. It can do so directly, but the process of finding individuals interested in investing funds in that business is likely to be difficult, costly, and time consuming. One particular financial intermediary, an investment banking firm, can handle the sale of shares of ownership. The function of the investment banking firm is one of merchandising. Brokerage firms market existing, or seasoned, instruments and securities.

Transferring Financial Assets

Several types of financial institutions facilitate or assist the processes of lending and selling securities. Brokerage firms market and facilitate the transferring of existing or seasoned instruments

CONCEPT CHECK
What are the financial functions that take place in the financial system?

money markets
where debt securities with maturities of one year or less are issued and traded

capital markets
where debt instruments or securities with maturities longer than one year and corporate stocks or equity securities are issued and traded

primary markets
where the initial offering or origination of debt and equity securities takes place

secondary markets
physical locations or electronic forums where debt (bonds and mortgages) and equity securities are traded

CONCEPT CHECK
How do money markets and capital markets differ?

How do primary markets differ from secondary markets?

debt securities
obligations to repay borrowed funds

debt markets
where money market securities, bonds (corporate, financial institution, and government), and mortgages are originated and traded

and securities. If shares of stock are to be sold to the general public, it is desirable to have a ready market in which such stocks can be resold when the investor desires. Organized stock exchanges and the over-the-counter market provide active secondary markets for existing securities. The ability to buy and sell securities quickly and at fair market values is important in an efficient financial system.

FINANCIAL MARKETS CHARACTERISTICS

Financial markets facilitate the raising of financial capital by government entities and business firms. Government entities can issue or sell debt securities to finance the building of roads and bridges or to provide added services to people. Business firms can issue debt securities, and corporations can sell equity securities or stocks to raise funds to invest in and grow their businesses. Financial markets facilitate the transferring of previously issued debt and equity securities from existing to new investors.

MONEY AND CAPITAL MARKETS

Money markets are where debt securities with maturities of one year or less are issued and traded. These markets are generally characterized by high liquidity whereby *money market securities* can be easily sold or traded with little loss of value. These short-lived securities generally have low returns and low risk. In Chapter 2, we will discuss money market securities.

Capital markets are where debt instruments or securities with maturities longer than one year and corporate stocks or equity securities are issued and traded. *Capital market securities* are generally issued to finance the purchase of homes by individuals, buildings and equipment by businesses, and the providing of infrastructure (roads, bridges, buildings, etc.) by governments. Business firms and governments issue long-term debt securities, called bonds, to finance their assets and operations. Mortgages are issued to finance homes and buildings. Corporations also issue stocks to meet their financing needs. In Part 2, we will cover capital market securities.

PRIMARY AND SECONDARY MARKETS

Primary and secondary markets exist for debt (bonds and mortgages) and equity securities. The initial offering or origination of debt and equity securities takes place in *primary markets*. Proceeds from the sale of new securities after issuing costs go to the issuing business or government issuer. The primary market is the only "market" where the security issuer directly benefits (receives funds) from the sale of its securities. Mortgage loans provide financing for the purchase of homes and other real property.

Secondary markets are physical locations or electronic forums where debt (bonds and mortgages) and equity securities are traded. Secondary markets for securities facilitate the transfer of previously issued securities from existing investors to new investors. Security transactions or transfers typically take place on organized security exchanges or in the electronic over-the-counter market. Individuals and other investors can actively buy and sell existing securities in the secondary market. While these secondary market investors may make gains or losses on their securities investments, the issuer of the securities neither benefits nor loses from these activities. The secondary market for securities is typically divided into short-term (money) and long-term (capital) market categories. We discuss primary and secondary securities markets in detail in Chapter 11. In addition, an active secondary market for real estate mortgages exists. We will discuss the basics of secondary markets for mortgages in Chapter 7.

MAJOR TYPES OF FINANCIAL MARKETS

Four main types of financial markets exist: debt securities markets, equity securities markets, derivative securities markets, and foreign exchange markets. *Debt securities* are obligations to repay borrowed funds. *Debt securities markets* are markets where money market securities, bonds (corporate, financial institution, and government), and mortgages are originated and

bond markets
where debt securities with longer-term maturities are originated and traded

mortgage markets
where loans to purchase real estate (buildings and houses) are originated and traded

common stocks
ownership shares in corporations

equity securities markets
where ownership rights in corporations are initially sold and traded

derivative securities markets
where financial contracts or instruments that derive their values from underlying debt and equity securities are originated and traded

foreign exchange markets
electronic markets in which banks and institutional traders buy and sell various currencies on behalf of businesses and other clients

CONCEPT CHECK

How do bond securities and common stocks differ?

What are the four major types of financial markets, and how do they differ?

traded. **Bond markets** are where debt securities with longer-term maturities are originated and traded. Government entities (federal, state, and local), financial institutions, and business firms can issue bonds. While bonds and bond markets are discussed throughout this text, we will focus on them in Chapter 10. **Mortgage markets** are where loans to purchase real estate (buildings and houses) are originated and traded. Mortgage markets are discussed in Chapter 7.

Common stocks are ownership shares in corporations. **Equity securities markets** are markets where ownership rights in corporations are initially sold and traded. Corporations can raise funds either through a *private placement*, which involves issuing new securities directly to specific investors, or through a *public offering*, which involves selling new securities to the general public. Financial institutions can also raise equity capital by selling stocks in their firms. Equity securities and markets are discussed in detail in Chapter 11.

In addition to money and capital markets, **derivative securities markets** are markets where financial contracts or instruments that derive their values from underlying debt and equity securities are originated and traded. A familiar form of *derivative security* is the opportunity to buy or sell a corporation's equity securities for a specified price and within a certain amount of time. Derivative securities may be used to speculate on the future price direction of the underlying financial assets or to reduce price risk associated with holding the underlying financial assets. Organized exchanges handle standardized derivative security contracts, and negotiated contracts are handled in electronic markets often involving commercial banks or other financial institutions. We discuss derivative securities in the Learning Extension to Chapter 11.

Foreign exchange markets (FOREX markets) are electronic markets in which banks and institutional traders buy and sell various currencies on behalf of businesses and other clients. In the global economy, consumers may want to purchase goods produced or services provided in other countries. Likewise, an investor residing in one country may wish to hold securities issued in another country. For example, a U.S. consumer may wish to purchase a product in a foreign country. If the product is priced in the foreign country's currency, it may be necessary to exchange U.S. dollars for the foreign currency to complete the transaction. Businesses that sell their products in foreign countries usually receive payment in the foreign currencies. However, because the relative values of currencies may change, firms often use the currency exchange markets to reduce the risk of holding too much of certain currencies. We discuss currency exchange rates and foreign exchange markets in Chapter 6.

THE PLAN OF STUDY

The subject matter of this book includes the entire scope of the financial environment from the perspective of the financial system and the three areas of finance: institutions and markets, investments, and financial management. You will learn about the markets in which funds are traded and the institutions that participate in and assist these flows of funds. You will learn about the investment area of finance, including the characteristics of issued debt and equity securities, securities markets, and investment risk-return concepts. You will study the financial management principles and concepts that guide financial managers to make sound financial planning, asset acquisition, and financing decisions. International finance applications are integrated throughout the text.

Part 1 focuses on the financial institutions, markets, and other participants that make the U.S. financial system operate effectively domestically and globally. Chapter 2 introduces the role of money within the overall financial system and its monetary system component. Chapter 3 focuses on the financial intermediation roles of depository and other financial institutions, as well as how they operate within the financial system. Chapter 4 discusses the Federal Reserve System. Chapter 5 discusses economic objectives, the role and actions of policy makers, and how money and credit are provided to meet the needs of the economy. We conclude Part 1 with Chapter 6 on international finance and trade because of its importance in understanding market economies worldwide.

Part 2 is concerned with the investments area of finance. Chapter 7 discusses the savings and investment process and its major role in the U.S. market economy. This is followed by Chapter 8,

INTERNET ACTIVITY

The Monster.com Web site, http://www.monster.com, provides information on available finance jobs. Click on "Jobs". In the "Keywords or company name box, type "Finance" or "Economics" and list some of the entry-level finance positions.

CONCEPT CHECK

What do the three parts of this book cover?

which describes the structure of interest rates. Time value of money concepts are covered in Chapter 9, and Chapter 10 covers the characteristics and valuations of bonds and stocks. Chapter 11 discusses the characteristics and workings of the securities markets. Part 2 concludes with Chapter 12, which describes financial return and risk concepts for a single asset or security, and for portfolios of securities.

Part 3 focuses on the financial management of businesses. We begin Chapter 13 with an introduction and overview of the types of business organizations and follow with a review of basic financial statements and financial data important to the financial manager. Chapter 14 discusses the need for, and the way in which to conduct, financial analysis of past performance and concludes with a section on long-term financial planning. Chapter 15 covers the management of working capital, while Chapter 16 focuses on sources of short-term business financing. We then turn our attention in Chapter 17 to the process and methods for conducting capital budgeting analysis. We conclude Part 3 with Chapter 18, which provides a discussion of capital structure and cost of capital concepts.

As we illustrated in Figure 1.1, the three areas of finance are dependent and continue to interact or overlap. For example, financial institutions provide an important financial intermediation role by getting individual savings into the hands of businesses so financial managers can use and invest those funds. Financial managers rely on the investments area of finance when carrying out their financial management activities. Corporations often need to raise funds in the primary securities markets, and secondary securities markets, in turn, provide investors with the liquidity to buy and sell previously issued securities. Our approach in this book is to survey all three areas of finance.

APPLYING FINANCE TO

INSTITUTIONS AND MARKETS	INVESTMENTS	FINANCIAL MANAGEMENT
Financial institutions and financial markets are necessary components of an efficient financial system. Institutions perform an important financial intermediation role by gathering the savings of individuals and then lending the pooled savings to businesses that want to make investments.	Securities markets are important components of an efficient financial system. The primary securities market facilitates raising funds by issuing new debt and equity securities. The secondary market for securities facilitates the transfer of ownership of existing securities among investors.	Business firms continually interact with financial institutions as they carry out their day-to-day operations. Businesses often seek to raise additional funds to finance investment in inventories, equipment, and buildings needed to support sales growth. Bank loans and mortgage loans are important financing sources, along with the proceeds from the issuance of new debt and equity securities.

SUMMARY

Finance is the study of how businesses and others acquire, spend, and manage money and other financial resources. More specifically, finance is composed of three areas: financial institutions and markets, investments, and financial management. However, these three areas intersect and overlap. A survey approach to the study of finance covers all three areas.

An effective financial system requires policy makers, a monetary system, and financial institutions and financial markets to facilitate the flow of financial capital from savings into investments. Policy makers pass laws and set fiscal and monetary policies designed to manage the economy. A monetary system creates and transfers money. Financial institutions accumulate and lend/invest individual savings. Financial markets facilitate the transfer of securities and other financial assets. Four types of financial markets exist: debt securities markets, equity securities markets, derivative securities markets, and foreign exchange markets. These activities operate together to create a smooth and efficient financial system.

KEY TERMS

bond markets	ethical behavior	investments
capital markets	finance	money markets
common stocks	financial environment	mortgage markets
debt securities	financial institutions	personal finance
debt securities markets	financial management	primary markets
derivative securities markets	financial markets	secondary markets
entrepreneurial finance	financial system	
equity securities markets	foreign exchange markets	

DISCUSSION QUESTIONS

1. Briefly describe how the financial environment has changed during the past few years.

2. What is finance?

3. What is meant by the term financial environment?

4. What are the three areas of finance?

5. Briefly describe the terms *entrepreneurial finance* and *personal finance.*

6. Identify and briefly describe several reasons for studying finance.

7. Indicate some of the career opportunities in finance available to business graduates.

8. What are the six principles of finance?

9. Describe what is meant by *ethical behavior.*

10. What are the basic requirements of an effective financial system?

11. Identify and briefly describe the financial functions in the financial system.

12. Briefly describe the differences between money and capital markets.

13. What are the differences between primary and secondary markets?

14. How do debt securities and common stocks differ?

15. Identify the four types of major financial markets.

EXERCISES

1. Match the following dates with the associated events:

Year		Event
a.	2000	(1) great recession
b.	2001	(2) U.S. terrorist attack
c.	2006	(3) financial crisis
d.	2007–08	(4) technology stock bubble
e.	2008–09	(5) housing price bubble

2. The U.S. financial system is composed of (1) policy makers, (2) a monetary system, (3) financial institutions, and (4) financial markets. Indicate which of these components is associated with each of the following roles:

a. accumulate and lend/invest savings

b. create and transfer money

c. pass laws and set fiscal and monetary policies

d. market and facilitate transfer of financial assets

3. Financial markets may be categorized as (1) debt securities markets, (2) equity securities markets, (3) derivative securities markets, and (4) foreign exchange markets. Indicate in which of these markets the following securities trade:

a. mortgages

b. bonds

c. common stocks

d. currencies

4. In business, ethical dilemmas or situations occur frequently. Laws and regulations exist to define unethical behavior. However, the practicing of high-quality ethical behavior often goes beyond meeting laws and regulations. Indicate how you would respond to the following situations.

a. Your boss has told you that tomorrow the Federal Drug Administration (FDA) will announce its approval of your firm's marketing of a new breakthrough drug. As a result of this information, you are considering purchasing shares of stock in your firm this afternoon. What would you do?

b. In the past, your firm has complied with regulatory standards relating to product safety. However, you have heard through the company grapevine that some of your firm's products have failed resulting in injuries to customers. You are considering quitting your job due to personal moral concerns. What would you do?

5. Obtain several recent issues of the *The Wall Street Journal* or *Bloomberg Businessweek.* Identify, read, and be prepared to discuss at least one article relating to one of the six principles of finance.

6. Obtain several recent issues of the *The Wall Street Journal* or *Bloomberg Businessweek.* Identify, read, and be prepared to discuss at least one article relating to one of the four types of financial markets identified in this chapter.

7. Obtain several recent issues of the *The Wall Street Journal* or *Bloomberg Businessweek.* Identify, read, and be prepared to discuss at least one article relating specifically to recent changes in the financial environment.

8. Go to the U.S. Small Business Administration (SBA) Web site, http://www.sba.gov, and search for sources of information on starting a new business. Identify and prepare a written summary of the *startup basics* described on the SBA site.

• CHAPTER 2 •

Money and the Monetary System

Chapter Learning Objectives . . .

AFTER STUDYING THIS CHAPTER, YOU SHOULD BE ABLE TO DO THE FOLLOWING:

- Briefly discuss the developments that led to the recent financial crisis.
- Describe the three ways in which money is transferred from savers to businesses.
- Identify the major components of the monetary system.
- Describe the functions of money.
- Give a brief review of the development of money in the United States.
- Describe types of major money market securities.
- Briefly explain the M1 and M2 definitions of the money supply.
- Explain possible relationships between money supply and economic activity.
- Comment on developments in the international monetary system.

Where We Have Been . . .

In Chapter 1, we provided a general overview of the financial environment including the three areas of finance: institutions and markets, investments, and financial management. We hope we provided you with a convincing argument as to why you should study finance and have provided an understanding of the career opportunities available in finance. We described six principles of finance. You should know what is required for a financial system to be effective and know the available types of financial markets to aid the transfer of financial assets.

Where We Are Going . . .

As we progress through Part 1, we build on our understanding of the U.S. financial system. Chapter 3 focuses on understanding the importance of depository and other institutions in the financial system. We discuss how your savings are pooled with the savings of other individuals in financial institutions and then are made available to businesses, governments, and other individuals who may want to invest in inventories, invest in highways, or purchase homes. The remaining chapters in Part 1 focus on the Federal Reserve System, the role of policy makers, and how international developments influence the financial system.

How This Chapter Applies to Me . . .

Each of us needs money. While you may feel you need more or less money than your friend, money is necessary for each of us to conduct day-to-day activities. You may have to buy gas for your car or pay for public transportation to school or work. Your may need money for lunch or supplies. You may even want to borrow money to purchase a house someday. After reading this chapter, you should have a clearer understanding of the functions and types of money available to you.

John Kenneth Galbraith, a U.S. economist, said the following about money:

> *Money is a singular thing. It ranks with love as man's greatest source of joy. And with death as his greatest source of anxiety. Over all history it has oppressed nearly all people in one of two ways: either it has been abundant and very unreliable, or reliable and very scarce.*[1]

---

1. John Kenneth Galbraith. *The Age of Uncertainty*. Houghton Mifflin, 1977. Print.

Why should any singular thing be so important? Money is what makes the financial system work. Money is a measure of wealth. Money can be used to purchase goods and services. Money is acceptable to repay debts. Creating and transferring money are integral parts of the capital formation process. However, too much money in an economy is associated with unsustainable economic growth and rapidly rising prices. On the other hand, too little money in an economy is associated with poor economic performance and sometimes recession. Of course, the relationships between supply and economic activity and money supply and rising prices are impacted by a number of other factors as we will see later in this chapter and in other chapters.

THE 2007–2008 FINANCIAL CRISIS

FINANCIAL CRISIS

A number of negative economic and financial trends and events came together to contribute to the financial crisis of 2007–2008 and the Great Recession of 2008–2009. A rapid decline in housing prices caused a credit crunch, which in turn, contributed to high unemployment and a major decline in economic activity. These developments occurred at a time when individuals, financial institutions, and business firms were heavily in debt. The result was a so-called "perfect financial storm" accompanied by a fear that the financial system might collapse.

Though some disagreement continues as to the specific causes of the financial crisis, most economists and others trace the beginning of the crisis to the bursting of the U.S. housing bubble in mid-2006. Prior to mid-2006, housing prices were continually rising every year with some areas of the United States experiencing annual double-digit housing price increases. The first part of the twenty-first century was a time when U.S. federal government policies encouraged home ownership. Lenders were willing to lend to financially risky borrowers seeking mortgage loans to make home purchases, and individual borrowers were willing to take on excessive amounts of mortgage debt, all in the belief that housing prices would continue to rise. Once housing prices declined, many homeowners had the equity in their homes wiped out and many mortgage loans became "underwater" which occurs when mortgage debt on the homes exceeded the value of the homes. This rapid decline in housing values was accompanied by a major loss of jobs in home construction and related industries.

Many home mortgage loans were combined into pools of loans and then mortgage-backed securities were issued with the mortgage loan pools as backing or collateral. Since large amounts of mortgage-backed securities were held by banks and other financial institutions, as home prices collapsed, it became clear these mortgage-backed securities had been previously overvalued. They declined sharply in value. A credit crunch occurred when banks and other financial institutions found they had inadequate equity capital to cover their large mortgage loan and other debt commitments. As a result, financial institutions were forced to layoff many employees. Businesses found it difficult to borrow from banks and other financial institutions because of the credit crunch causing higher levels of unemployment.

During 2008, the federal government helped some financial institutions to merge, bailed out a number of institutions and businesses, and allowed other financial institutions to fail. The financial crisis and the associated credit crunch were accompanied by the 2008–2009 economic downturn which began in early 2008 and ended in mid-2009 with economic activity declining more than 10 percent and the unemployment rate exceeding 10 percent. The 2008–2009 economic downturn is referred to as the Great Recession since it involved the largest economic downturn since the Great Depression of the 1930s.

CONCEPT CHECK

What were some of major developments that led to the financial crisis?

We will discuss more details relating to the financial crisis and the Great Recession at various points throughout the first section of this textbook. We begin this chapter with a discussion of money and the monetary system. Many economists and others believe a link exists between the supply or availability of money and economic activity. The argument is that monetary policy makers can stimulate economic activity through increased monetary liquidity by making more money available at lower borrowing costs to businesses, investors, and others. It is presumed the investment of these low-cost funds will result in more economic growth. However, opinion differs as to how direct the relationship is between the availability of money and economic activity. We will provide further discussion later in the chapter.

PROCESS OF MOVING SAVINGS INTO INVESTMENTS

Financial institutions and markets move or transfer money from individuals and institutions with excess money to business firms and others who have needs for more money. We usually look at individuals in total or in the aggregate as an economic unit. Financial institutions, business firms, and governments (federal, state, and local) are viewed as economic units. A *surplus economic unit* generates more money than it spends, and thus, it has excess money to save or invest. A *deficit economic unit* spends more money than it brings in and must balance its money receipts with money expenditures by obtaining money from surplus units.

surplus economic unit
generates more money than it spends, and thus, it has excess money to save or invest

Individuals taken as a group have generally been a surplus economic unit in the past. Even though some individuals are saving, others are borrowing to cover the purchase of goods and services. Individuals desiring to purchase homes also borrow by taking out mortgage loans. Some business firms are savers when their revenues exceed their costs of operation and reinvestment back in the businesses. Other businesses choose to borrow or sell stock to finance their operations and grow their businesses with the intent of providing higher returns to their investors. Private sector financial institutions have responsibilities to provide returns to their investor-owners and sometimes borrow heavily to grow their institutions and hopefully provide higher returns. Sometimes, government entities (federal, state, and local) have tax revenues that exceed expenditures and thus are surplus economic units. However, when government entities spend more than they receive from tax revenues, they must borrow the money shortfall and, thus, are deficit economic units.

deficit economic unit
spends more money than it brings in and must balance its money receipts with money expenditures by obtaining money from surplus units

For the U.S. financial system to operate depends on each of the three overall economic units (individuals, business firms, and government entities) to achieve a reasonable balance between their aggregate revenues and expenditures. When expenditures exceed revenues for extended periods of time, deficit economic units must build up large amounts of debt. A major factor in the severity of the 2007–2008 financial crisis and the 2008–2009 Great Recession was the massive amounts of debt taken on by individuals, business firms, financial institutions, and government entities during the decade leading up to the crisis. In an effort to survive the financial crisis and recover from the Great Recession, government entities, through increased expenditures in the form of stimulus programs, have increased their deficits and, in the case of the U.S. government, dramatically increased the size of the national debt.

savings-investment process
involves the direct or indirect transfer of individual savings to business firms in exchange for their debt or stock securities

Our primary focus is on the *savings-investment process* that involves the direct or indirect transfer of individual savings to business firms in exchange for their debt and stock securities. Figure 2.1 shows three ways whereby money is transferred from savers to a business firm. As illustrated in the top part, savers can directly purchase the securities (stocks or debt instruments) of a business firm by exchanging money for the firm's securities. No financial institution is used in this type of savings-investment transaction since it involves only a saver and the business firm.

The use of indirect transfers is the more common way by which money is transferred from savers to investors. The middle part of Figure 2.1 shows how the transfer process usually takes place when savers purchase new securities issued by a business. In Chapter 1, we mentioned this indirect transfer involves use of the primary securities market. In this process, financial institutions operate to bring savers and security issuers together. Savers provide money to purchase the business firm's securities. However, rather than a direct transfer taking place, financial institutions, such as investment banks, may facilitate the savings-investment process by first purchasing the securities being issued by a corporation and then reselling the securities to savers. No additional securities are created in this type of indirect transfer.

The bottom part of Figure 2.1 illustrates the typical capital formation process involving a financial institution. Savers deposit or invest money with a financial institution such as a bank, insurance company, or mutual fund. The financial institution issues its own securities to the saver. For example, a saver may give money in the form of currency to a bank in exchange for the bank's savings or time-deposit obligation. The bank, in turn, may lend money to a business firm in exchange for that firm's "I owe you" (IOU) in the form of a loan. As money passes from savers through a financial institution to a business firm, a debt instrument or security is created by the financial institution and by the business firm. In Chapter 3, we will discuss this process of financial intermediation further.

FIGURE 2.1

Savings-Investment Process: From Individual Savers to a Business Firm

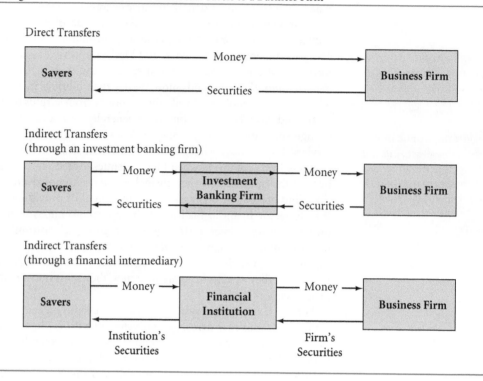

The savings-investment process could, however, focus on the flow of money from savers to government entities that are operating at deficits caused by expenditures greater than tax revenues. The U.S. government and state and local governments can sell their debt securities directly to savers who might be individuals, business firms, or financial institutions. Indirect transfers could take place with the aid of financial institutions to facilitate the movement of government entity debt securities to savers. A financial institution may operate as a conduit in the primary securities market. Alternatively, the financial institution may purchase the government entity's debt securities and, in turn, issue its own debt securities to individuals and other savers.

The savings-investment process could focus on moving the savings of individuals and other savers to those individuals, businesses, institutions, and governments that want to finance real estate investments. Many individuals want to own their own homes and can do so only by taking on mortgage debt or home loans. Other organizations may wish to invest in real property in the form of offices, manufacturing facilities, or other buildings. To do this often requires the need to finance a part of the purchase price with a mortgage loan on the real property being purchased. While our focus in this text is primarily on the savings-investment process involving the raising of money or financial capital by business firms, we will discuss the process for financing deficits by government entities in Chapter 5, and in Chapter 7, we will address the financing of residential and commercial property.

CONCEPT CHECK

What are surplus economic units and deficit economic units?

How does the savings-investment process take place when financial institutions are involved?

Which economic units, in addition to business firms, might need money from savers to invest?

OVERVIEW OF THE MONETARY SYSTEM

The monetary system is responsible for carrying out the financial functions of creating and transferring money. Money is needed to conduct day-to-day activities, facilitate the capital investment process, and support economic growth. Businesses need money to invest in inventories, equipment, and buildings. Governments need money to construct roads, buildings, parks, and other infrastructure for the people. Individuals need money to purchase goods, services, and homes.

Figure 2.2 indicates the major participants in the U.S. monetary system. A central bank is needed to define and regulate the amount of the money supply in the financial system. A central bank facilitates the transferring of money by processing and clearing checks, a form of money

FIGURE 2.2
The U.S. Monetary System

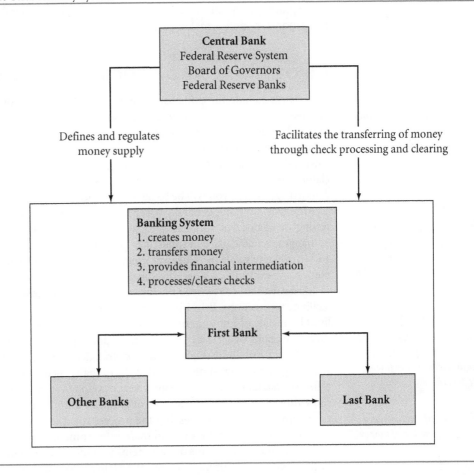

called deposit money. The central bank in the United States is called the Federal Reserve System (or Fed for short). In Chapter 4, we will discuss the characteristics and operation of the Fed, and in Chapter 5, we will cover its policy-making activities.

An efficient banking system is needed. Not all types of financial institutions are the same. For example, even though insurance companies and investment companies can provide a financial intermediation function between savers and investors, only depository institutions as a group can create money. Depository institutions include commercial banks, savings and loan associations (S&Ls), savings banks, and credit unions. For purposes of presentation, we commonly refer to all depository institutions as banks, and they are part of the banking system. In Chapter 3, we will discuss the characteristics of depository and other major financial institutions.

The banking system, as depicted in Figure 2.2, is composed of all the banks in the system. For illustration purposes, there is a first bank and a last bank. The banking system creates money (technically deposit money) and, along with the Fed, clears checks and transfers money within the overall financial system. Checks can be cleared either through other banks in the banking system or with the aid of the Fed. In Chapters 3 and 4, we will examine the check clearing process.

While an individual bank, such as First Bank, cannot create money, the banking system can. Let's assume that First Bank receives $1,000 from the ABC business firm and sets up a checking account (demand deposit) for the firm. The $1,000 received by First Bank is called "reserves" and represents money held by First Bank so that it can pay off checks written by ABC against its checking account balance. However, rather than holding the full $1,000 in reserves, First Bank will hold a fraction (e.g., 20 percent, or $200) in reserves and will lend the remaining $800 to the XYZ firm. As long as XYZ places the $800 loan proceeds in its checking account at a bank (e.g., Last Bank) somewhere in the banking system, the initial $1,000 demand deposit established for ABC has increased to $1,800 (the $1,000 for ABC plus the $800 for XYZ). As long as deposit

CONCEPT CHECK

Who are the major participants in the U.S. monetary system?

money keeps coming back into the banking system, more deposit money is created. In practice, the Fed specifies the percentage of reserves that banks must hold against demand deposits. We will explore the deposit money creation process in greater detail in Chapter 5 when we discuss the Fed's monetary policy-making activities.

IMPORTANCE AND FUNCTIONS OF MONEY

real assets
include the direct ownership of land, buildings or homes, equipment, inventories, durable goods, and precious metals

financial assets
money, debt instruments, equity securities, and other financial contracts that are backed by real assets and the earning abilities of issuers

money
anything generally accepted as a means of paying for goods, services, and paying off debts

medium of exchange
the basic function of money

barter
exchange of goods or services without using money

store of value
money held for some period of time before it is spent

liquidity
the ease with which an asset can be exchanged for money or other assets

Real assets include the direct ownership of land, buildings or homes, equipment, inventories, durable goods, and precious metals. **Financial assets** are money, debt instruments, equity securities, and other financial contracts that are backed by real assets and the earning abilities of issuers. A loan to you to purchase an automobile usually provides for the lender to hold the auto title (ownership) until the loan is repaid. Long-term debt issued by a corporation may represent a claim against specific assets, such as buildings and equipment, or the general assets of the issuer. A mortgage loan to you will be backed by the house against which the loan is being made.

Money is anything generally accepted as a means of paying for goods and services and for paying off debts. For something to serve successfully as money, it must be easily divisible so exchanges can take place in small or large quantities, relatively inexpensive to store and transfer, and reasonably stable in value over time. Money must perform three basic functions: serving as a medium of exchange, a store of value, and a standard of value.

Money was first developed to serve as a **medium of exchange**, the basic function of money, to facilitate transactions. Primitive economies consisted largely of self-sufficient units or groups that lived by means of hunting, fishing, and simple agriculture. People had little need or occasion to exchange goods or services. As economies developed, however, the process of exchange became important. Some individuals specialized, to a degree at least, in herding sheep, raising grain, or shaping gold as metalsmiths. To aid in the exchanging of goods or services without using money, called **barter**, tables of relative values were developed from experience. For example, a table might show the number of furs, measures of grain, or amount of cloth agreed to equal one cow. This arrangement eased exchanges, but the process still had many serious drawbacks. For example, if a person had a cow and wanted to trade it for some nuts and furs, he or she would need to find someone who had an excess of these items to trade. The need for a simpler means of exchange led to the development of money, with its relatively low storage and transfer costs, to be used as a medium of exchange.

Money may be held for some period of time as a **store of value**. That is, money may be spent immediately after it is received or after it has been held for some time. While money is being held, it is a liquid asset and provides its owner with flexibility, but the owner pays for this flexibility by giving up the potential return that could be earned through investment or the satisfaction that could be gained from spending it for goods and services. Money can perform its function as a store of value only if its purchasing power is relatively stable over time. Under this condition, the spending decision is separated from the income decision. Once income is received, the holder of the income can spend it or save it. If the decision is to save, then that money can be made available through the savings-investment process to those who may want to invest now.

Any asset other than money can serve as a store of value as long as that asset can be converted into money quickly and without significant loss of value. We refer to this quality as **liquidity**,

SMALL BUSINESS PRACTICE
Starting Your Small Business

Today, with modern telecommunication facilities and the Internet, many small businesses can be located wherever their owners want to live and work. At the same time, certain cities and geographical areas in the United States may be more conducive to helping small businesses succeed.

The Dun & Bradstreet Company (D&B) provides a wealth of information relating to the starting of a new business. D&B provides

information on how to establish, manage, and grow your small business. When considering whether to establish or start a business, you must ask this: "Are you really ready to start?" You must plan your business, as well as understand legal and tax issues.

which is the ease with which an asset can be exchanged for money or other assets. Money is perfectly liquid since it is a generally accepted medium of exchange. Other assets, such as savings deposits held at depository institutions, approach the liquidity of money. The existence of such liquid assets reduces the need for holding money as a store of value.

Money serves as a *standard of value*, which means that prices and contracts for deferred payments are expressed in terms of the monetary unit. For example, in the United States, prices and debts are usually expressed in terms of dollars without stating whether the purchase will be cash or credit. If money is to perform its function as a standard of value, the value of the monetary unit must be relatively stable over time. For example, if one dollar can be used to purchase two ballpoint pens today but only one tomorrow, such money would be ineffective as a store of value or a standard of value.

Though money is the fundamental measure of wealth, an individual's net worth usually consists of more than just money. *Individual net worth* is the sum of an individual's money, real assets, and financial assets or claims against others less the individual's debt obligations. Real assets include the automobile you own, your house (if you have one) and its contents, clothes, and jewelry or precious stones. You may own shares of stock in a mutual fund. While these are financial assets, they remain part of your net worth. However, you may have borrowed from a bank to purchase your automobile, and you probably have a mortgage loan on the house you purchased. These financial claims are held by others against some of your real property. You must subtract debt obligations or financial claims against you or your real property to determine your individual net worth. Probably more than eight million millionaires are in the world with about one-third of them being in the United States. If you wish to join this group someday, you will have to accumulate a net worth in excess of $1 million. Good luck!

DEVELOPMENT OF MONEY IN THE UNITED STATES

The two basic components of money supply in the United States are physical money (coin and currency) and deposit money. A review of the development of money in the United States will help us understand the characteristics of money today, as well as how well U.S. money performs the three functions of money listed.

PHYSICAL MONEY (COIN AND PAPER CURRENCY)

The first function of successful money is that it serves as a medium of exchange. Physical money is the coin and paper currency used to purchase goods and services and to settle debts. We will first examine how U.S. coins have changed in terms of their precious metal (gold and silver) content over time. Then, we will examine how U.S. paper currency has changed in terms of its physical characteristics and its "backing" with precious metals.

U.S. Coins

While barter was undoubtedly important in early American history, the government moved swiftly toward a monetary system based on precious metals that would serve as an efficient medium of exchange. During much of the seventeenth and eighteenth centuries, the American colonies relied primarily on the Spanish dollar to conduct business transactions.[2] In 1785, the word *dollar* was adopted by the U.S. Congress as the standard monetary unit or standard of value. The first monetary act in the United States, passed in 1792, provided for a *bimetallic standard*, usually based on silver and gold. The dollar was defined in both grains of pure silver and grains of pure gold. All silver and gold coins were to be *full-bodied money* because their metal content was worth the same as their face values. For example, one silver dollar was to contain one dollar's worth of silver, a ten-dollar gold coin was to contain ten dollars' worth of gold, and so on.

standard of value
prices and contracts for deferred payments are expressed in terms of the monetary unit

individual net worth
sum of an individual's money, real assets, and financial assets or claims against others less the individual's debt obligations

CONCEPT CHECK

How do real assets and financial assets differ?

What is money?

What are the three functions performed by money?

bimetallic standard
monetary standard based on two metals, usually silver and gold

full-bodied money
coins that contain the same value in metal as their face value

---

2. The Spanish dollar often was cut into eight pieces or "bits" to make change. Sometimes, the U.S. quarter-dollar is referred to as "two bits." This term originated from the cutting the Spanish dollar into "pieces of eight."

A law enacted in 1837 modified the weight for the silver dollar to 412.5 grains of silver with .900 fineness. Copper of .100 fineness was used to make the coins last longer. The result was that each dollar contained .77344 ounce of pure silver. Since the value of the silver content was to be $1, silver was valued at $1.29 per ounce ($1/.77344).

Figure 2.3 shows examples of full-bodied and token U.S. coins. The top portion shows the front side (obverse) of the peace-type dollar and the Franklin half-dollar. The peace-type dollar was produced from 1921 to 1935. The Franklin half-dollar, produced from 1948 to 1963, contained .36169 ounce of pure silver. Since silver prices had been gradually rising, the Franklin half-dollar was full-bodied money at a silver price of $1.38 ($.50/.36169). Depending on the prevailing market price of silver, a silver coin, such as the half-dollar, could be less than, greater than, or exactly full-bodied.

For full-bodied money, its store of value was reflected in the value of its precious metal content, and as long as the price of precious metals moved in unison with the prices of goods and services, this money's store of value reflected the store of purchasing power.

token coins
coins with face values higher than the value of their metal content

Rapidly rising silver prices in the 1960s, however, made silver coins worth more as melted bullion than their face values. As a result, the U.S. government debased its full-bodied money by replacing silver content with copper and nickel. Coins with face values higher than the value of their metal content are called ***token coins***. The bottom portion of Figure 2.3 shows two copper-nickel-clad (token) U.S. coins. The Eisenhower dollar was minted from 1971 to 1978. Kennedy

FIGURE 2.3

Examples of Full-Bodied and Token (Copper-Nickel-Clad) U.S. Coins

Two Full-Bodied Coins
[Face value and silver metal content were equal when coin was issued]

Peace Type Dollar
(issued 1921–35)
[contains .77344
ounces of silver]

Franklin Half Dollar
(issued 1948–63)
[contains .36169
ounces of silver]

Two Token Coins
[Face value much greater than metal (no silver) content]

Eisenhower Dollar
(issued 1971–78)
[contains only
copper and nickel]

Kennedy Half Dollar
(issued 1971–present)
[contains only
copper and nickel]

half-dollars were full-bodied coins in 1964, were changed to silver-clad (reduced silver content) coins from 1965 to 1970, and have been copper-nickel–clad coins since 1971.

The production of gold coins began in 1795 with $5 and $10 coins. The issuance of full-bodied gold dollars was authorized in 1849, and production continued through 1889. For several decades, the value of a U.S. dollar was expressed in terms of silver and of gold. All gold coin production was stopped in 1933, and in 1934, U.S. citizens were prohibited from holding monetary gold in the United States. In 1961, this restriction was extended to gold held abroad by U.S. citizens. In 1975, all restrictions on holding gold in money form were removed.

Paper Currency

INTERNET ACTIVITY

Go to the U.S. Treasury Web site, http://www.treas.gov. Go to Services, and click on "Coins and Currency". Click on "Bureau of Engraving and Printing" in the second paragraph of text. Find recent information on redesigned currency.

representative full-bodied money
paper money that is backed by an amount of precious metal equal in value to the face amount of the paper money

fiat money
legal tender proclaimed to be money by law

The evolution and use of paper currency in the United States have been characterized by an erratic history. While some paper money was issued by individual colonies, the first effort of a government to issue paper money occurred when the Continental Congress authorized the issuance of notes called Continentals to finance the Revolutionary War. While these notes were denominated in dollars, they had no backing in silver or gold. Rather, they were backed only by possible future tax revenues to be gathered when the colonies became independent. As you might guess, the Continentals became worthless. This led to a long period of distrust of paper money. After a brief experience with two national banks, American banking went through a period of no federal regulation and nonuniformity in operating laws. State-chartered banks issued their own paper currency almost at will and, in many cases, with no or little backing of their notes with gold or silver deposits.[3]

Paper money may be representative full-bodied money or fiat money. ***Representative full-bodied money*** is paper money that is backed by an amount of precious metal equal in value to the face amount of the paper money. The U.S. government has issued two types of representative full-bodied money. From 1865 to 1928, gold certificates were issued, and since they could be redeemed for gold with a value equal to the paper currency's face amount, they were considered "as good as gold." However, because most gold certificates were issued in large denominations, they were not intended to be used in general circulation but rather to settle institutional gold accounts. The issuance of silver certificates was authorized beginning in 1878. A switch to "small-size" silver certificates occurred in 1929, and they continued to be issued and used through 1963.

Figure 2.4 shows examples of full-bodied and fiat U.S. paper currency. The top portion shows a silver certificate. These certificates could be exchanged for silver dollars or silver bullion when presented to the U.S. Treasury. Like full-bodied silver coins, these silver certificates became worth more in terms of the bullion value of silver relative to their face values as silver prices began climbing in the 1960s. As a result, the U.S. government halted the redemption of silver certificates in silver dollars, and in 1968, redemption in silver bullion was stopped.

Today, almost all paper money in circulation is in the form of Federal Reserve Notes, which were authorized under the Federal Reserve Act of 1913. The bottom portion of Figure 2.4 shows a Federal Reserve Note. These notes, which are not backed by gold or silver, are called ***fiat money***, being legal tender proclaimed to be money by law, because the government decreed the notes to be legal tender for the purposes of making payments and discharging public and private debts. Of course, the copper-nickel–clad, or token, coins of today are fiat money because their metal content values are less than their face values.

The reliance on the use of fiat money can be problematic. First, fiat money generally becomes worthless if the issuing government fails. As an example, Confederate currency was issued during the U.S. Civil War. However, when the Confederacy lost the war, this fiat money became worthless. Second, since there is no required backing in gold or silver, issuing more fiat money is relatively easy. Issuing too much money can, in turn, lead to rising prices and a lack of confidence in the government. An effective monetary system with a strong central bank and prudent policy makers are needed when a financial system relies on fiat money to carry out its transactions.

Several major changes in Federal Reserve Notes have taken place over time. In 1929, the size of the notes was reduced about 30 percent from large notes (7.42 inches by 3.13 inches) to smaller

---

3. By 1865, about one-third of the circulating paper currency was counterfeit. As a result, the U.S. Treasury established the U.S. Secret Service to control counterfeiting activities.

FIGURE 2.4

Examples of Representative Full-Bodied and Fiat U.S. Paper Currency

Representative Full-Bodied Paper Currency
[Face value and silver metal "backing" were equal when the bill was issued]

Silver Certificate (small size issued 1929–63)
[exchangeable for silver dollars or silver bullion equal to face amount]

Fiat Paper Currency
[No "backing" with silver (or other precious metal) deposits]

Federal Reserve Note (small size issued 1929–present)
[U.S. government states on each note: "This note is legal tender for all debts, public and private"]

ETHICAL ISSUES

notes (6.14 inches by 2.61 inches). This change made production less expensive and made it easier to handle and less costly to store and transfer paper money. Figure 2.5 shows the old and current design of the $20 Federal Reserve Note. The "small portrait" $20 note is shown in the top portion of the figure.

When it comes to money, how individuals behave ranges from exhibiting high ethical standards down to deceit, fraud, and counterfeiting. How you acquire and deal with money affects your reputation. Individuals who work hard, follow the law, and treat other individuals they are involved with in money transactions fairly and honestly are able to find success, accumulate wealth, and build high-quality reputations. However, probably almost from the origins of money creation, there have been individuals driven by greed who have engaged in counterfeiting activities to illegally get money rather than work for it. Most of us have trouble understanding such extreme unethical behavior, which typically results in getting caught, serving prison time, and destroying reputations of those involved.

Unfortunately, attempts to counterfeit U.S. currencies represent a big illegal business for some individuals and organizations. Furthermore, the ability to counterfeit currency has been aided in recent years by the introduction of high-quality color copiers. To thwart counterfeiting efforts, the U.S. Treasury Department's Bureau of Engraving and Printing has developed new currency designs in recent years. A new series of notes that made use of microprinting and an embedded security

FIGURE 2.5
Old and Current Designs of the $20 U.S. Federal Reserve Note

Old Design $20 Bill
[Relatively easy to copy and counterfeit]

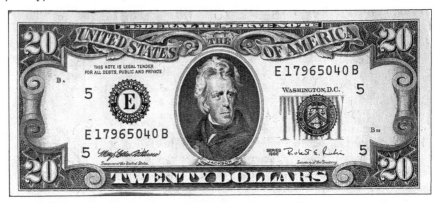

Old Design $20 Federal Reserve Note (small size issued 1929–97)

Current Design $20 Bill
[More difficult to copy and counterfeit]

Current Design $20 Federal Reserve Note (issued beginning in 2003)

strip was introduced in 1990 to improve security and to make counterfeiting more difficult. A more complete design change began with the $100 "large-portrait" bill in 1996. Large-portrait $50 bills were introduced in 1997, and in 1998, $20 bills were placed in circulation. New $5 and $10 bills were introduced in 2000 so only the $1 bill continues to use the small-portrait format.

In 2003, more currency design changes were implemented. The bottom portion of Figure 2.5 shows the most recent "large-portrait" $20 bill, which still features Andrew Jackson. In the 1998 version, the larger portrait was for the first time placed off-center to allow the inclusion of a watermark that is visible from both sides when held up against a light. The bill contains a vertically embedded security thread, which glows red when exposed to ultraviolet light, at the far left of the portrait. Color-shifting ink, fine-line printing, and microprinting were added. In the 2003 version, U.S. currency began taking on added colors. Peach and light blue hues were added to the previous green-and-black bills. Other changes included removing the circle around Andrew Jackson's head and adding a faded bald eagle to the left of the portrait and the words "Twenty USA" and "USA Twenty" to the right of the portrait.

These anti-counterfeiting efforts, while very costly, are essential to maintaining the public's trust and confidence in fiat money. Of course, even though the appearance of U.S. paper money may be changing, the government honors all previously issued U.S. paper currency at full face value. No requirement or time limit exists for exchanging old notes for new ones. Old notes continue to remain in circulation until depository institutions return them to the Fed to be retired.

CONCEPT CHECK

What is meant by full-bodied money?

What is meant by fiat money?

PERSONAL FINANCIAL PLANNING
Local Currency: Another Form of Savings and Spending Power

The monetary system has evolved from barter of goods and services to today's credit money. Money is a means to facilitate exchange. Rather than carpenter Jim trading a chair for new shirts sewn by seamstress Jane, Jim and Jane use Federal Reserve Notes to buy chairs and shirts from each other.

Some areas of the United States have two monetary systems. About 30 cities and towns print their own versions of money used for transactions within a locality. One reason communities do so is to keep money in the community. For example, local currency circulates in the following locations: Ithaca, New York; Madison, Wisconsin; Takoma Park, Maryland; Detroit, Michigan; Austin, Texas; and Waldo County, Maine. Such currency is legal, but it must be printed in a size smaller than the U.S. $1 bill and issued in denominations of at least $1.

Ithaca's local currency is denominated in Ithaca Hours; each Hour is worth about $10, the area's average hourly wage. Denom-

inations range from one-eighth of an Hour up to two Hours. Since it started in 1991, Hours have been earned and spent by 1,500 people and are accepted by 300 businesses. Most stores accept them only as partial payment for goods; they require the balance to be paid in U.S. currency. An advisory board oversees the supply of Hours.

The idea of local currency in the United States has had a long history. You may have experience with traveler's checks; they are a form of private currency. One purchases traveler's checks with cash; the checks can then be used as currency because they represent this cash. The recognizable name and good credit of the issuer (e.g., American Express or Thomas Cook), rather than that of the individual making the payment, guarantees the value of the checks. Since lost or stolen traveler's checks can be reported, payment stopped, and new checks issued in their place, they provide users with a safety level unavailable with cash.

DEPOSIT MONEY

The use of physical money (coin and currency) to complete transactions can be costly and inefficient if large amounts and/or long distances are involved. As a result of these constraints on the use of physical money, along with confidence in the banking system, a special type of credit money called *deposit money* has grown readily in importance in the U.S. monetary system. **Credit money** is money backed by the creditworthiness of the issuer.[4] Deposit money is backed by the creditworthiness of the depository institution that issued the deposit.

credit money
money backed by the creditworthiness of the issuer

Deposit money takes the form of demand deposits held at commercial banks or other checkable deposits held at S&Ls, savings banks, and credit unions. A demand deposit gets its name from the fact that the owner of a deposit account "demands" that all or a portion of the amount in his or her demand deposit account be transferred to another individual or organization. Checks or drafts have traditionally been used to transfer demand deposit or other checkable deposit amounts. Let's return to our example where the ABC business firm deposits $1,000 at First Bank to set up a $1,000 demand deposit account in ABC's name. ABC then writes a $1,000 check against its deposit account and sends the check to an equipment manufacturer as payment for purchase of equipment. The equipment manufacturer deposits the check in its own demand deposit account in a bank, e.g., Last Bank. The check must be processed and cleared through the banking system, with or without the assistance of the Fed. That is, it must be returned to First Bank, which will pay the check amount to Last Bank and deduct $1,000 from the business firm's demand deposit account at First Bank. To aid and speed the clearing process, copies of checks can be sent electronically rather than having to wait for actual paper checks to be delivered.

automatic transfer service (ATS) accounts
used to make direct deposits to, and payments from, checkable deposit accounts

The use of electronic ways to transfer funds held in demand and other checkable deposit accounts continues to increase and replace the use of more costly and time-consuming paper checks. **Automatic transfer service (ATS) accounts** are used to make direct deposits to, and payments from, checkable deposit accounts. Employers often have their employees' wages deposited directly in their employees' checking accounts rather than issuing payroll checks. Electronic funds transfers for payment of utility bills, mortgage loans, credit card balances, and so forth, are increasingly common.

---

4. Fiat money is a form of credit money. However, while the government declares fiat money to be legal tender, other forms of credit money such as deposit money do not have governmental support or backing.

debit cards
provide for the immediate direct transfer of deposit amounts

CONCEPT CHECK
Why is deposit money said to be credit money?

money market securities
debt instruments or securities with maturities of one year or less

Treasury bill
short-term debt obligation issued by the U.S. federal government to meet its short-term borrowing needs when imbalances exist between tax revenues and government expenditures

negotiable certificate of deposit (negotiable CD)
short-term debt instrument issued by depository institutions to individual or institutional depositors

commercial paper
short-term unsecured promissory note issued by a high credit-quality corporation

Debit cards provide for the immediate direct transfer of deposit amounts. For example, when a debit card is used to purchase merchandise at a retailer's point-of-sale (POS) cash register or from its Internet sites, the card holder's bank transfers the designated amount from the purchaser's demand account to the retailer's account. Debit cards are used to make cash withdrawals from automated teller machines (ATMs). When cash is dispersed, the user's demand deposit account's balance is immediately reduced by the amount of cash withdrawn.

MONEY MARKET SECURITIES

As noted in Chapter 1, *money markets* are the markets where debt securities with maturities of one year or less are originated (primary markets) or traded (secondary markets). **Money market securities** are debt instruments or securities with maturities of one year or less. In general, money markets securities have low default risk and high liquidity. That is, issuers are expected to meet their debt obligations when due and short maturities and secondary markets for many of these securities allow them to be sold with little loss of value.

Figure 2.6 identifies and provides characteristics of major money market securities. A **Treasury bill** is a short-term debt obligation issued by the U.S. federal government to meet its short-term borrowing needs when imbalances exist between tax revenues and government expenditures. Treasury bills are generally issued with maturities between three months (technically 91 days) and one year. Investors buy Treasury bills for safety and liquidity reasons. First, the federal government will probably never default on its debt obligations. Second, an active secondary money market for Treasury bills exists, so investors can sell them at any time before maturity if cash needs arise.

A **negotiable certificate of deposit (negotiable CD)** is a short-term debt instrument issued by depository institutions to individual or institutional depositors. Negotiable certificates of deposit are issued by commercial banks in denominations of $100,000 or more with typical maturities ranging from one month to one year. Negotiable CDs are money market securities with an active secondary market that allows short-term investors to easily match their cash or liquidity needs when they arise. It is important, of course, to recognize that negotiable CDs differ from smaller-denomination CD time deposits offered by depository institutions to individual depositors. Small-deposit CDs are nonnegotiable and must be redeemed with the issuer, and thus, no secondary securities market exists for them. In fact, owners of nonnegotiable CDs redeemed before maturity usually are charged an interest deduction penalty.

Businesses often find it necessary to borrow short-term to meet temporary imbalances between when cash is received from sales and when bills must be paid. **Commercial paper** is a short-term unsecured promissory note issued by a high credit-quality corporation. Maturities on commercial

FIGURE 2.6
Major Money Market Securities

TYPE	TYPICAL MATURITIES	ISSUERS	INVESTORS	SECONDARY MARKET
Treasury bills	91 days to 1 year	U.S. government	Individuals, business firms, and institutions	High activity
Commercial paper	1 day to 9 months	Business firms and institutions	Business firms and institutions	Moderate activity
Negotiable certificates of deposit (Negotiable CDs)	Up to 1 year	Depository institutions	Business firms	Low activity
Banker's acceptances	Up to six months	Banks	Business firms	High activity
Repurchase agreements	Up to 1 year	Business firms and institutions	Business firms and institutions	No market
Federal funds	1 day to 1 week	Depository institutions	Depository institutions	No market

paper are generally one to three months in length. However, since an active secondary money market for commercial paper exists, purchasers can sell their commercial paper holdings at any time to meet their cash needs.

banker's acceptance
promise of future payment issued by a firm and guaranteed by a bank

A **banker's acceptance** is a promise of future payment issued by a firm and guaranteed by a bank. Banker's acceptances are used to finance international trade and typically have maturities from one to six months. For example, a U.S. exporter that is sending goods to an importer in a foreign country may not know the credit quality of the importer. To facilitate the transaction, a bank may be asked to guarantee payment of the "draft" or bill for the goods, which will be due at a future date. The accepted draft is sent to the exporter. The importer pays the amount of the draft, plus a fee for the guarantee, to the bank when due.

The bank, in turn, pays the exporter or whoever is holding the draft at the time of maturity. Exporters often sell their banker's acceptances at a discount to obtain cash prior to the due date. There is an active secondary market for banker's acceptances with other business firms often buying banker's acceptances as a source of low default risk, high liquidity short-term investments. In Chapter 6, we will discuss the process of conducting international in greater detail.

repurchase agreement
short-term debt security sold by a business firm or financial institution to another business or institution where the seller agrees to repurchase the security at a specified price and date

A **repurchase agreement** is a short-term debt security sold by a business firm or financial institution to another business or institution where the seller agrees to repurchase the security at a specified price and date. Repurchase agreements may be as short as one day or involve several months. Most repurchase agreements utilize Treasury bills but may include commercial paper or negotiable certificates of deposit.

Brokers and dealers, through an electronic network, facilitate the bringing together of organizations with excess funds with those in need of funds. Since cash receipts relative to cash expenditures can change almost daily for business firms, a firm might be a seller of a repurchase agreement at one time and a buyer of a repurchase agreement at another time. No secondary market exists for repurchase agreements.

federal funds
short-term loans, usually with maturities of one day to one week made between depository institutions

Federal funds are short-term loans, usually with maturities of one day to one week made between depository institutions. For example, a commercial bank with excess funds may make a short-term loan to another depository institution with a shortage of funds. The interest rate on federal funds is determined by supply and demand for short-term loans by banks. The Federal Reserve, as we will see in Chapters 4 and 5, can influence the federal funds rate as it carries out monetary policy.

Federal funds brokers bring together banks who want to purchase federal funds with those who want to sell funds. Transactions typically start at $5 million with the interbank loan volume being in the billions of dollars. No secondary market exists for federal funds due to their short maturities. A one day or overnight loan is highly liquid. Although there is some credit risk concerning the ability of the borrowing depository institution to repay the loan, short maturities mitigate such risk.

CONCEPT CHECK

What are the major types of money market securities?

MEASURES OF THE U.S. MONEY SUPPLY

Now that we have a basic understanding how money developed in the United States, we must examine how we measure the money supply or "stock" today. Since we want to "count" the money supply in the financial system as of a point in time, this can be viewed as the amount of money stock on a particular date. We will start with a narrow definition of the money supply, referred to as M1, and then consider M2, which is a broader definition.

M1 MONEY SUPPLY

M1 money supply
consists of currency, travelers' checks, demand deposits, and other checkable deposits at depository institutions

As noted, the basic function of money is that it must be acceptable as a medium of exchange. The M1 definition of the money supply includes only types of money that meet this basic function. More specifically, the **M1 money supply** consists of currency, traveler's checks, demand deposits, and other checkable deposits at depository institutions. For December, 2012, the Fed reports the not seasonally adjusted M1 and its four components as follows:

M1 COMPONENT	$BILLIONS	PERCENTAGE
Currency	1092.4	43.7
Traveler's checks	3.8	.2
Demand deposits	951.7	38.1
Other checkable deposits	449.9	18.0
Total M1	**2,497.8**	**100.0**

All four components are types of credit money. Currency is U.S. physical money in the form of coins and paper currency. The coins are token money, and the paper currency is fiat money in the form of Federal Reserve Notes. However, U.S. currency (coins and paper money) is accepted for making payments and retiring debts and, thus, serves as an important medium of exchange. Currency comprises nearly 44 percent of the M1 money supply. Traveler's checks, offered by banks and other organizations, promise to pay on demand the face amounts of the checks with their acceptance based on the creditworthiness of the issuer. Since traveler's checks are a widely accepted medium of exchange, they qualify as a component of the M1 money supply. Even so, their relative importance is small, as they represent substantially less than 1 percent of the M1 total.

Demand deposits (checking accounts) at commercial banks, and other checkable deposits at S&Ls, savings banks, and credit unions, also are considered to be credit money, since these deposits are backed solely by the creditworthiness of the issuing institutions when checks are presented for collection. Demand deposits at commercial banks account for 38 percent of the money supply. Other checkable deposits represent 18 percent of M1, include ATS accounts and negotiable order of withdrawal (NOW) accounts at depository institutions, credit union share draft accounts, and demand deposits at S&Ls, credit unions, and savings banks.

Taken together, demand deposit and other checkable deposit accounts comprise a little less than half of the M1 money supply. This high percentage shows the importance of the banking system and its money creating function within the monetary system and in terms of the broader U.S. financial system.

Before moving to a broader definition of the money supply, we should point out some of the adjustments or exclusions that take place when estimating the M1 money supply or stock. M1 measures transaction balances. These sums of money can be spent without first converting them to some other asset and are held for anticipated or unanticipated purchases or payments in the immediate future. Essentially, only those amounts that represent the purchasing power of units in the U.S. economy other than the federal government are counted. Specifically excluded from M1 is currency in the vaults of depository institutions or held by the Fed and the U.S. Treasury. Demand deposits owed to depository institutions, the federal government, and foreign banks and governments are excluded. An adjustment is made to avoid double-counting checks being processed. The vault cash and deposits belonging to depository institutions do not represent purchasing power and, therefore, are not money. However, they serve as reserves, an important element of our financial system that will be discussed in the next several chapters.

INTERNET ACTIVITY

Go to the Federal Reserve Bank of San Francisco's Web site, http://www.frbsf.org. Go to the Consumer tab and click on "Consumer Information & Assistance". Find information relating to consumer rights and the use of credit and debit cards.

M2 money supply
M1 plus highly liquid financial assets, including savings accounts, small time deposits, and retail money market mutual funds (MMMFs)

M2 MONEY SUPPLY

The Fed's second definition of the money stock, M2, is a broader measure than M1 because it emphasizes money as a store of value in addition to its function as a medium of exchange. In general terms, the *M2 money supply* includes M1 plus highly liquid financial assets, including savings accounts, small time deposits, and retail money market mutual funds (MMMFs). Most of the financial assets added to M2 provide their owners with a higher rate of return than would M1 components. More specifically, M2 adds the following to M1: savings deposits (including money market deposit accounts), small-denomination time deposits (under $100,000) less individual retirement account (IRA) and Keogh account balances at depository institutions, plus balances in retail MMMFs less IRA and Keogh balances at money market mutual funds.

As of December 2012, the Fed reported M2 at $10,475.6 billion which is over four times the size of M1. Some of the owners of the assets included in M2 hold them as long-term savings instruments. Other individuals and firms hold these M2 specific assets even though they plan to spend the funds within a few days because the assets are liquid. M1, thus, understates purchasing power by the amount of these M2 balances held for transaction purposes.

The components of M2 illustrate the difficulties the Fed has faced in drawing the boundaries of these definitions. For example, MMDAs provide check-writing privileges and can therefore be used for transaction purposes. Some analysts argue on this basis that money market deposit account (MMDA) balances should be a part of M1. The Fed has included MMDA balances in M2, but not in M1, because MMDAs are different from traditional money components and because MMDAs seem to be used more as savings instruments than as transaction balances. On the other hand, it can be argued that small time deposits should be excluded from M2 because they are not, in practice, liquid. Small time deposit holders, who wish to cash them in before maturity, are penalized by having to forfeit some of the interest they have earned. However, small

money market mutual funds (MMMFs)
issue shares to customers and invest the proceeds in highly liquid, short maturity, interest-bearing debt instruments called money market investments

time deposits are included because they are considered to be close substitutes for some of the other savings instruments included in M2. Savings deposits, including MMDAs, at depository institutions are greater than the M1 total.

Money market mutual funds (MMMFs) issue shares to customers and invest the proceeds in highly liquid, short-maturity, interest-bearing debt instruments called *money market investments.* MMMFs get their name from the type of investments they make. The nature of their investments, coupled with payment of interest daily, keeps MMMF shares valued at $1. Many MMMFs allow shareholders to write checks against their accounts. When checks are cleared and presented to the MMMF for payment, the number of shares owned by the shareholder is reduced accordingly. This process, of course, is similar to writing checks against checkable deposits held at depository institutions. However, rather than including retail MMMF balances in M1, the Fed decided that consumers use the accounts more as a store of purchasing power and less as a medium of exchange.

EXCLUSIONS FROM THE MONEY SUPPLY

credit cards
provide predetermined credit limits to consumers at the time the cards are issued

The Fed excludes certain stores of value and borrowings from its money supply definitions. For example, stock and bond mutual funds held by individuals represent stores of value, and some permit limited check writing against these accounts. However, because the value of shares in these funds often fluctuates and individuals may hold these security investments for a long time, the Fed does not consider these to be part of the money supply.

Credit cards provide predetermined credit limits to consumers at the time the cards are issued. No checkable or other deposits are established at the time of issue. Thus, neither credit card limits nor outstanding balances are part of the money supply. Rather, credit cards allow their holders to borrow up to a predetermined limit. However, the use of credit cards can affect the rate of turnover of the money supply and may contribute to money supply expansion. If credit card borrowing stimulates the demand for goods and services, a given money supply can support a higher level of economic activity. We will explore the relationship between money supply and economic activity in the next section. When you use your credit card to purchase a product for, say, $50 at a retailer, the bank that issued the credit card lends you $50 and increases the retailer's demand deposit account by $50. As your credit card balance increases as you purchase goods and services on credit, the checkable deposit accounts of those who sold the goods and services also increase. Of course, users of credit cards must pay off their debts.

CONCEPT CHECK

What is the definition of the M1 money supply?

How do the M1 and M2 money supply definitions differ?

How does the use of credit cards affect the money supply?

MONEY SUPPLY AND ECONOMIC ACTIVITY

Many economists believe that money supply matters when they manage economic activity. They have observed that economic activity, money supply, and the price levels of goods and services generally move together over time. However, economists disagree as to how these relationships are to be explained.

gross domestic product (GDP)
a measure of the output of goods and services in the economy

The output of goods and services in the economy is referred to as the **gross domestic product (GDP)**. Since we typically measure output in current dollars, we are measuring "nominal" GDP. Some economists called *monetarists* believe the amount of money in circulation determines the GDP level or economic activity. If we divide GDP by the money supply (MS), we get the number of times the money supply turns over to produce GDP. Economists refer to the turnover of money as the velocity of money. More specifically, the **velocity of money** (VM) measures the rate of circulation of the money supply. For example, if the annual GDP is $15 million and the money supply is $5 million, the VM is three times (i.e., $15 million/$5 million). In alternative form, we can say that:

velocity of money
measures the rate of circulation of the money supply

$$MS \times VM = GDP \tag{2.1}$$

We have this example:

$$\$5 \text{ million} \times 3 = \$15 \text{ million}$$

Economists express nominal GDP as being equal to real output (RO) times the price level (PL) of goods and services, or this equation:

$$RO \times PL = GDP \qquad (2.2)$$

For example, if the RO in the economy is 150,000 products and the average price is $100, the GDP is $15 million (e.g., 150,000 × $100). Putting these two equations together, we have this equation:

$$MS \times VM = RO \times PL \qquad (2.3)$$

An increase in the money supply and/or velocity causes nominal GDP to increase. For nominal GDP to increase, RO and/or PL must increase. For example, let's assume the money supply increases by 10 percent or $500,000 to $5.5 million while the velocity stays at three times. Nominal GDP will increase to this level:

$$\$5.5 \text{ million} \times 3 = \$16.5 \text{ million}$$

Since GDP equals RO × PL, some change in RO or PL (or a combination of the two) needs to take place. One possibility is for RO to increase by 15,000 products or units to 165,000 with no change in prices. GDP then would be the following:

$$165,000 \text{ units} \times \$100 = \$16.5 \text{ million}$$

Monetarists believe that when the money supply exceeds the amount of money demanded, the public will spend more rapidly, causing real economic activity or prices to rise. A too-rapid rate of growth in the money supply will result in rising prices or inflation because excess money will be used to bid up the prices of existing goods. ***Inflation*** is a rise or increase in the prices of goods and services that is not offset by increases in their quality. Because of the difficulty in measuring changes in quality, a more operational definition of inflation is a continuing rise in prices. For example, instead of the $1.5 million increase in GDP from $15 million to $16.5 million being due to a 10 percent increase in the money supply, the increase might have been due solely to inflation. Let's assume that the quantity of products sold remains at the original 150,000-unit level but that the average price increases by 10 percent to $110. GDP would be calculated as the following:

$$150,000 \text{ units} \times \$110 = \$16.5 \text{ million}$$

Of course, almost unlimited combinations of ROs and PLs could occur, including reducing one of the variables that could produce the same new GDP.

Other economists, called *Keynesians* in honor of John Maynard Keynes, believe that a change in the money supply has a less direct relationship with GDP. They argue that a change in money supply first causes a change in interest rate levels, which in turn, alters the demand for goods and services. For example, an increase in the money supply might cause interest rates to fall (at least initially) because more money is being supplied than is being demanded. Lower interest rates, in turn, will lead to an increase in consumption and/or investment spending, causing the GDP to grow.[5] In contrast, a decrease in the money supply will likely cause interest rates to rise. As a result, the GDP will grow more slowly or even decline depending on how the higher interest rates affect consumption and spending decisions.

As you might guess, it is impossible to say that one group of economists (monetarists or Keynesians) is right and the other is wrong. The ability to identify relationships among GDP, money supply, and price levels has been complicated by the fact that the VM has increased and the various measures of the have grown at different rates. M1 velocity has increased as credit card

INTERNET ACTIVITY

Go to the Federal Reserve Bank of St. Louis Web site, http:// www.stlouisfed.org, access the Federal Reserve Economic Database (FRED) and find information on the current money supply. Determine the current size of M1 and its four components, along with the size of M2.

inflation
a rise or increase in prices of goods and services that is not offset by increases in their quality

INTERNET ACTIVITY

Go to the Federal Reserve Bank of St. Louis Web site, http:// www.stlouisfed.org, and click on the Research & Data tab. Click on FRED Economic Data. Find the current size of the M1 money supply and the annual gross domestic product (GDP), and then calculate the velocity of money.

---

5. If the increase in money supply leads to price level increases (inflation), nominal interest rates that include inflation expectations might actually increase. We will cover the determinants of market interest rates in Chapter 8.

usage has replaced the more traditional use of currency and deposit money when purchasing goods and services. The velocity of M1 money has increased as the public has made more use of MMMFs and other liquid accounts that serve as stores of value relative to their usage of traditional deposit money in demand and other checkable accounts.

Recent developments have made it difficult to interpret the near-term impact of changes in the money supply. Decreasing regulation and increasing competition among financial institutions have led to changes in the types of deposit money that individuals use for medium of exchange purposes. Likewise, changes are ongoing in how individuals use "near-cash" accounts for store of value purposes. Thus, recent changes in growth rates for different definitions of the money supply reflect in part changes in how individuals pay bills and store purchasing power. This is one reason why the Fed simultaneously keeps track of more than one measure of the money supply.

Some economists believe a "psychological" factor impacts the relationship between money supply and economic activity. The action of increasing the money supply does not automatically result in higher GDP. Businesses and individual may choose not to borrow low-cost funds due to perceived uncertainty about future economic conditions. Some view the practice of increasing the money supply and liquidity akin to "trying to push on a string" in terms of increased economic activity. If businesses and individuals choose not to increase their investments and expenditures, the link between money supply and GDP may be difficult to observe.

As a result of the economic downturn in 2001 and the September 11, 2001, terrorist attacks, the Federal Reserve moved to maintain financial liquidity through continued increases in M1 and M2 and by lowering federal funds rates to historically low levels. Continued monetary easing occurred during the latter-half of the decade of the 2000s in response to the 2007–2008 financial crisis and the 2008–2009 Great Recession. We will explore how the Fed administers monetary policy in our dynamic and complex financial system in Chapters 4 and 5.

CONCEPT CHECK

What is meant by the equation "money supply times velocity of money equals real output times price level" (MS × VM = RO × PL)?

INTERNATIONAL MONETARY SYSTEM

The international monetary system was historically tied to the gold standard. An international gold standard was used to conduct most international trade during the latter part of the 1800s and the early part of the 1900s. However, a breakdown in the gold standard occurred during World War I, and less formal exchange systems continued during the worldwide depression of the 1930s and during World War II.

In 1944, many of the world's economic powers met at Bretton Woods, New Hampshire. They agreed to an international monetary system tied to the U.S. dollar or gold via fixed or pegged exchange rates. One ounce of gold was set equal to $35. Each participating country had its currency pegged to gold or the U.S. dollar. This system of fixed exchange rates became known as the Bretton Woods System and was maintained through 1971.

By early 1973, major currencies were allowed to float against each other, resulting in a flexible or floating exchange rate system. While free market forces have been allowed to operate today, central monetary authorities attempt to intervene in exchange markets when they believe that exchange rates between two currencies are harming world trade and the global economy. This makes the current international monetary system a managed floating exchange rate system.

GLOBAL DISCUSSION

currency exchange rate
the value of one currency
relative to another

Virtually all international transactions now involve the exchange of currencies or checkable deposits denominated in various currencies. Exchanges occur for goods and services, for financial claims, or for other currencies. A **currency exchange rate** reflects the value of one currency relative to another. The relationship between currencies depends on the supply and demand for each currency relative to the other. The supply of a currency in international markets depends largely on the imports of the issuing country, that is, how much of its currency the country spends in world markets. Demand for a currency depends on the amount of exports that currency will buy from the issuing country. Demand depends on the confidence of market participants in the restraint and stability of the monetary authority issuing the currency. If demand for a particular currency falls relative to its supply, then the exchange rate will fall and the international purchasing power of that nation's money supply will drop. Domestic inflation, political instability, or an excess of imports over exports can cause one currency to decline relative to another currency. If a currency is widely accepted, the demand for it may be increased by the desire of people worldwide to hold it as an international medium of exchange. Such is the case of the U.S. dollar, which is

euro
a single currency that has replaced the individual currencies of some of the member countries of the European Union

CONCEPT CHECK

What is meant by the currency exchange rate between two countries?

widely held internationally because of its general acceptance and ability to hold its value. In Chapter 6, we will discuss international finance is discussed in detail.

A major international development occurred on January 1, 1999, when twelve European Union (EU) countries gave up their individual currencies and adopted a unified currency called the *euro.* For example, the French gave up the franc, the Germans the mark, the Italians the lira, and the Spanish the peseta. All members of the European Union do not currently use the euro either because they have chosen to keep their own national currencies or do not qualify for adoption due to fiscal deficit and other constraints. The creation of the Euro was accompanied by the formation of the European Central Bank (ECB), which replaces the central banks of each of the participating countries.

Although our focus is on the U.S. monetary system, we operate in a global economy. Thus, we must interact with other monetary systems, and a change in either the EU or Japanese monetary systems will affect the U.S. monetary system. For example, when the ECB increases interest rates in the EU, the value of the U.S. dollar weakens relative to the euro. This increases the cost of products imported into the United States unless the Federal Reserve takes countering actions.

APPLYING FINANCE TO...

INSTITUTIONS AND MARKETS

The monetary system is composed of a central bank, the Federal Reserve System, and a banking system. For the monetary and financial systems to work, money must be accepted as the medium of exchange by each of us. Commercial banks in the aggregate help create and transfer money and, thus, help the monetary system operate efficiently. Other financial institutions help in the savings-investment process when individual savings are pooled and lent or invested in business firms.

Occasionally, the savings of some individuals are directed to other individuals who want to purchase homes using mortgage loans. Individual, institutional, and business savings may be directed to help government entities to finance deficits caused by tax revenues being exceeded by expenditures.

INVESTMENTS

Money is the fundamental store of wealth. While we often think of money in terms of coin and currency, the money supply (MS) includes demand deposits and other checkable deposits. Some definitions of the money supply include savings accounts, time deposits, and money market mutual funds. An individual's net worth consists of real assets such as automobiles and houses, mutual fund shares held, and holdings of the various types of money less any debts.

Money markets are where debt securities with maturities of one year or less are originated and sometimes traded. Major money market securities include Treasury bills, commercial paper, negotiable certificates of deposit, banker's acceptances, repurchase agreements, and federal funds.

FINANCIAL MANAGEMENT

Business firms rely on financial institutions to help them raise funds from the savings of individuals. Businesses need money to conduct their day-to-day operations and need an efficient monetary system for collecting funds from customers and for paying their own bills in a timely fashion. Some businesses make use of money market securities for short-term investment purposes when they have surplus funds. Other businesses borrow in the money markets to help finance their short-term debt needs. Some business firms issue, while others invest in, commercial paper and repurchase agreements. Other business firms may hold their money market investments in Treasury bills or negotiable certificates of deposit. While money market securities are originated in primary markets, some trade actively in secondary markets.

SUMMARY

A working knowledge of the U.S. monetary system is essential to understanding the broader U.S. financial system and how businesses and financial institutions operate within the financial system. The monetary system is responsible for creating and transferring money and is intertwined with the savings-investment process. Major participants in the monetary system in the United States include a central bank called the Federal Reserve and a banking system composed of depository institutions. Money must provide several functions for a monetary system to succeed. Money must serve as a medium of exchange, as a store of value, and as a standard of value.

Prior to the development of money, barter was used to exchange goods and services. The American colonies moved quickly to money based on precious metals (gold and silver) to conduct transactions. Early U.S. coins were full-bodied money in that the value of their precious metal content was equal to their face value. Today, U.S. coins are token coins in that they are no longer backed by precious metals but instead by the creditworthiness of the U.S. government. For some time, the government issued gold certificate notes and silver certificate notes that were considered representative full-bodied money because they could be exchanged for precious metals worth the same as the face value of the notes. Today, U.S. paper currency is fiat money, which gets its name from the government decreeing that the notes are legal tender for paying public and private debts. Deposit money is demand deposit and other checkable deposit balances held at depository institutions and backed by the creditworthiness of the issuing institutions.

An efficient financial system sometimes needs more than just "money" to operate efficiently. Over time several important money market securities have evolved in the United States. Included are Treasury bills, negotiable certificates of deposit, commercial paper, banker's acceptances, repurchase agreements, and federal funds.

As the U.S. monetary system became more complex, definitions of the money supply (MS) changed as forms of payment increased to meet the needs of the economy. Today, the money supply is measured primarily in terms of M1 and M2. M1 focuses on currency and deposit money that serve primarily as mediums of exchange. M2 adds types of money that are viewed more as stores of value, such as money market mutual funds (MMMFs).

Economists believe a link exists between money supply and economic activity. Monetarists contend the money supply and gross domestic product (GDP) have a direct link via the velocity of money (VM). Keynesians believe the link is less direct because changes in money supply first affect interest rates, which, in turn, influence GDP through changes in consumption and investment. Evidence does not indicate that one group is right and the other wrong. By recognizing both views, we develop a better understanding of the importance of the role of monetary policy in achieving real economic growth.

Historically, the international monetary system was tied to the gold standard. In 1944, the exchange rates between the currencies of most industrialized countries were fixed relative to the U.S. dollar or gold. By the early 1970s, exchange rates between major currencies were allowed to float against one another. While we are focusing on characteristics of the U.S. monetary system, we must recognize that our monetary system does not and cannot operate in isolation from the monetary systems in other countries.

KEY TERMS

automatic transfer service (ATS) accounts

banker's acceptance

barter

bimetallic standard

commercial paper

credit cards

credit money

currency exchange rate

debit cards

deficit economic unit

euro

federal funds

fiat money

financial assets

full-bodied money

gross domestic product (GDP)

individual net worth

inflation

liquidity

medium of exchange

M1 money supply

M2 money supply

money

money market mutual funds (MMMFs)

money market securities

negotiable certificate of deposit (negotiable CD)

real assets

representative full-bodied money

repurchase agreement

savings-investment process

standard of value

store of value

surplus economic unit

token coins

Treasury bill

velocity of money

DISCUSSION QUESTIONS

1. Briefly discuss the developments that led to the 2007–2008 financial crisis.

2. How do surplus economic units and deficit economic units differ?

3. Describe the three basic ways whereby money is transferred from savers to business firms.

4. Identify economic units in addition to business firms who might need funds from savers.

5. Identify the major participants in the U.S. monetary system.

6. Indicate how real assets and financial assets differ.

7. Define money and indicate the basic functions of money.

8. Describe how an individual's net worth is determined.

9. Briefly describe the development of money, from barter to the use of precious metals.

10. What is the difference between full-bodied money and token coins?

11. Describe how representative full-bodied money and fiat money differ.

12. What is deposit money, and how is it "backed"?

13. What are automatic transfer service (ATS) accounts?

14. What are debit cards, and how are they used?

15. Define money market securities and briefly describe the major types of these securities.

16. Describe the M1 definition of the money supply and indicate the relative significance of the M1 components.

17. How does M2 differ from M1? What are money market mutual funds?

18. Briefly describe the monetarists' view of the relationship between money supply and economic activity.

19. How do Keynesians view the relationship between money supply and economic activity?

20. Briefly describe the development of the international monetary system.

EXERCISES

1. Match the following money market securities with their issuers.

Securities	Issuers
a. Treasury bills	1. depository institutions
b. negotiable CDs	2. U.S. government
c. commercial paper	3. banks
d. banker's acceptances	4. business firms and institutions

2. Match the following money market securities with the level of secondary market activity.

a. Treasury bills	1. no activity
b. commercial paper	2. low activity
c. federal funds	3. moderate activity
d. negotiable CDs	4. high activity

3. Go to the Web site of the Federal Reserve Bank of St. Louis at http://www.stlouisfed.org. Go to "Research and Data" and click on "FRED Economic Data" to access the Federal Reserve Economic Database (FRED). Compare the present size of M1 and M2 money stock measures with the data presented in the Measures of the U.S. Money Supply section of this chapter. Find the current sizes of these M1 components: currency, traveler's checks, demand deposits, and other checkable deposits. Express each component as a percentage of M1 and compare your percentages with those presented in the chapter.

4. Find several recent issues of *Bloomberg Businessweek*. Identify articles relating to developments in the U.S. monetary system. Search for possible developments occurring in foreign monetary systems.

5. We are faced with ethics decisions involving money almost every day. For example, we all probably have seen money in the form of coin or currency lying on the ground or floor somewhere. We may have at some time discovered a lost wallet. Should it matter if the amount of money is small or large? Should it matter if no one else is around and/or there is no evidence of who lost the money? Sometimes, we hear the finders-keepers argument being used to rationalize an individual's decision. How would you react to the following scenarios?

a. You are walking down a street and find a dollar bill lying on the ground. No one else is close by. You consider picking up the dollar, acknowledging your good luck, and putting it in your pocket. What would you do?

b. While you are shopping in a grocery store, you see a wallet lying on the floor. You don't know who dropped the wallet. You consider holding on to the wallet until you get home and then search for the owner's identification so you might contact the owner with information you have the wallet. Alternatively, you could just give the wallet to the store manager. What would you do?

PROBLEMS

1. Determine the size of the M1 money supply using the following information:

Currency plus Traveler's checks	$25 million
Negotiable CDs	$10 million
Demand deposits	$13 million
Other checkable deposits	$12 million

2. Determine the size of the M1 money supply using the following information:

Currency	$700 billion
Money market mutual funds	$2,000 billion
Demand deposits	$300 billion
Other checkable deposits	$300 billion
Traveler's checks	$10 billion

3. Determine the size of the demand deposits component of the M1 money supply using the following information:

Currency	$350 million
Traveler's checks	$10 million
Other checkable deposits	$200 million
Small time deposits	$100 million
M1 money supply	$800 million

4. Following are components of the M1 money supply at the end of last year. What will be the size of the M1 money supply at the end of next year if currency grows by 10 percent, demand deposits grow by 5 percent, other checkable deposits grow by 8 percent, and the amount of traveler's checks stays the same?

Currency	$700 billion
Demand deposits	$300 billion
Other checkable deposits	$300 billion
Traveler's checks	$10 billion

5. The following information is available to you: traveler's checks = $1 million; coin and paper currency = $30 million; repurchase agreements and Eurodollars = $15 million; demand deposits = $25 million; retail money market mutual funds = $60 million; savings accounts at depository institutions = $40 million; checkable deposits at depository institutions = $35 million; large-denomination time deposits = $50 million; institutional money market mutual funds = $65 million; and small-denomination time deposits = $45 million. Using Fed definitions, determine the dollar sizes of the following:

a. M1 money supply

b. M2 money supply

6. A country's gross domestic product (GDP) is $20 billion, and its money supply (MS) is $5 billion. Answer the following questions:

a. What is the country's velocity of money (VM)?

b. If the money supply stays at the same level next year while the VM "turns over" 4.5 times, what will the GDP level be?

c. Assume that the VM will turn over 4 times next year. If the country wants a GDP of $22 billion at the end of next year, what will have to be the size of the money supply? What percentage increase in the money supply will be necessary to achieve the target GDP?

7. Assume that the real output (RO) for a country is expected to be 2.4 million products. Answer the following questions:

a. If the price level (PL) is $250 per product, what will be the amount of the gross domestic product (GDP)?

b. Now assume that the GDP is projected to be $8 million next year. What will the PL of the products need to be to reach the GDP target?

c. Now assume that the RO of 2.4 million products is composed of equal amounts of two types of products. The first product sells for $100 each, and the second product sells for $500 each. What will be the size of the GDP?

8. Assume that a country estimates its M1 money supply at $20 million. A broader measure of the money supply, M2, is $50 million. The country's gross domestic product is $100 million. Production or real output for the country is 500,000 units or products.

   a. Determine the velocity of money based on the M1 money supply.

   b. Determine the velocity of money based on the M2 money supply.

   c. Determine the average price for the real output.

9. Using the data in Problem 7 along with the monetarists' view of the relationship between money supply and the gross domestic product (GDP), answer the following:

   a. If the M1 money supply increases by 10 percent and the M1 velocity of money does not change, what is the expected value of the GDP for next year?

   b. Based on the information from (a), if real output does not change next year, what is the expected average price for the products? What percentage change, if any, would take place in the price level?

   c. If the M2 money supply decreases by 10 percent and the M2 velocity of money does not change, what is the expected value of GDP next year?

   d. Based on information from (c), if the price level does not change next year, what will the expected real output in units or products be?

10. The following information was gathered for the XYZ economy: velocity of money = 3.8 times; average price level = $85; and real output = 10,000 units. Answer the following questions:

   a. What is the nominal gross domestic product (GDP) for the XYZ economy?

   b. What is the size of the money supply for the XYZ economy?

   c. If real output increases by 10 percent next year, but the price level and velocity of money do not change, what money supply amount will be needed to support this real growth in economic activity?

   d. What will be the money supply needed to support economic activity next year if real output increases to 12,000 units, the average price increases to $90, and velocity increases to four times?

11. The One Product economy, which produces and sells only personal computers (PCs), expects that it can sell 500 more, or 12,500 PCs, next year. Nominal gross domestic product (GDP) was $20 million this year, and the money supply was $7 million. The central bank for the One Product economy plans to increase the money supply by 10 percent next year. Answer the following questions:

   a. What was the average selling price for the personal computers this year?

   b. What is the expected average selling price next year for PCs if the velocity of money remains at this year's turnover rate? What percentage change in price level is expected to occur?

   c. If the objective is to keep the price level the same next year (i.e., no inflation), what percentage increase in the money supply should the central bank plan for?

   d. How would your answer in (c) change if the velocity of money is expected to be three times next year? What is it now?

12. **Challenge Problem** The following problem requires a basic knowledge about probabilities and the calculation of expected values. The problem is more easily solved using Excel spreadsheet software.

Scenario	A	B	C	D	E	Metric
Probability	.10	.20	.40	.20	.10	Percent
Velocity of money	1.75	2.5	3.0	3.5	4.25	Turnover
Real output	375	450	500	550	625	Units in thousands
Price level	75	90	100	110	125	Dollars

   a. Calculate the dollar amount of the money supply under each scenario or outcome.

   b. Calculate the expected value of the money supply, taking into consideration each scenario and its probability of occurrence.

   c. Scenario C is the most likely scenario given that its probability of occurrence is 40 percent. Show how the amount of the money supply would change holding real output at 500,000 units and the price level at $100 for each of the velocity of money turnover rates (you have previously calculated the money supply under Scenario C for a turnover of 3.0 times).

   d. Repeat the Scenario C exercise in (c) but hold the velocity of money at 3.0 times and price level at $100 and allow real output to change.

   e. Repeat the Scenario C exercise in (c) but hold the velocity of money at 3.0 times and real output at 500,000 units and allow price level to change.

INSTITUTIONS
AND MARKETS

INVESTMENTS

FINANCIAL
MANAGEMENT

• CHAPTER 3 •

Banks and Other Financial Institutions

Chapter Learning Objectives . . . AFTER STUDYING THIS CHAPTER, YOU SHOULD BE ABLE TO DO THE FOLLOWING:

- Describe how financial institutions were impacted by the financial crisis.
- Identify the major financial institutions and their roles in the financial system.
- Describe the differences between commercial banking and investment banking.
- Identify the functions of banks and of the banking system
- Discuss general regulation of the banking system and how depositors' funds are protected.
- Describe the structure of banks in terms of bank charters, branch banking, and bank holding companies.
- Briefly describe the bank balance sheet and the major account categories that it contains.
- Discuss bank management in terms of bank liquidity and bank solvency.
- Briefly explain why and how bank capital is managed.
- Describe the characteristics of several foreign banking systems.

Where We Have Been . . . *In Chapter 2, we presented an overview of the U.S. monetary system. We discussed how the monetary system is intertwined with the savings-investment process, and we identified the major participants in the monetary system. Money has three functions, which are a medium of exchange, a store of value, and a standard of value. An understanding of how money developed in the United States over time, as well as knowing current definitions of the U.S. money supply, will be useful as we move through Part 1. Having an understanding of the relationship between the money supply and the economy will help us understand how the actions of policy makers influence economic activity and the financial system.*

Where We Are Going . . . *As we move through Part 1, we continue to build on our understanding of the U.S. financial system. Chapter 4 focuses on the Federal Reserve System. We will describe the structure of the Fed and discuss the Fed's functions. The Fed directs monetary policy by setting reserve requirements and interest rates on loans to depository institutions and through buying and selling U.S. government securities. We will discuss the Fed's supervisory and regulatory responsibilities. The last two chapters in Part 1 focus on the role of the policy makers (those responsible for carrying out fiscal policy, monetary policy, and debt management) and on how international developments influence the financial system.*

How This Chapter Applies to Me . . . *You probably have a checking account at a depository institution. You may have a savings account or own some shares in a mutual fund. You may have an automobile loan or a home mortgage. Each of these activities requires an interaction with a financial institution. After reading this chapter you should have a better understanding of what depository and other financial institutions do in carrying out the savings-investment process and how banks operate and are managed.*

Webster's New English Dictionary defines *bank* as the following:

> *an establishment for the deposit, custody, and issue of money, for making loans and discounts, and for making easier the exchange of funds by checks, notes, etc.*

Webster also defines *bank* as:

> *the funds of a gambling establishment; the fund or pool by the banker or dealer in some gambling games*

Most of us associate the first definition with our perception of banks and banking in the United States. However, there have been examples throughout history and recently where the second definition seems to fit. For example, isolated fraudulent behavior on the part of some commercial bank and savings and loan association (S&L) officers has resulted in criminal indictments and in prison sentences. Overall, of course, banks and other financial institutions have performed well in getting savings to investors and contributing to an efficient financial system.

FINANCIAL INSTITUTION DISTRESS DURING THE FINANCIAL CRISIS

FINANCIAL CRISIS

mortgage
loan backed by real property in the form of buildings and houses

mortgage-backed security
debt security created by pooling together a group of mortgage loans whose periodic payments belong to the holders of the security

Homeowners typically finance a portion of the purchase of their houses with mortgage loans. A *mortgage* is a loan backed by real property in the form of buildings and houses. Banks and other mortgage lenders engaged during the decade of the 2000s in "pooling" together loans they originated into securities. Other financial intermediaries "repackaged" mortgage loans into mortgaged-backed securities. A *mortgage-backed security* is a debt security created by pooling together a group of mortgage loans whose periodic payments belong to the holders of the security. The value of these mortgage-backed securities depended on the value of the homes against which the underlying mortgages were issued.

As previously noted, housing prices peaked in 2006, and after, home values declined sharply. These falling house prices, in turn, caused the value of mortgage loans, and associated mortgage-backed securities, on those houses to drop. In many instances, the value of houses declined to levels below the amounts of the underlying mortgages wiping out all equity the homeowners had in the houses. When mortgage loans exceed the value of the underlying houses, the mortgage loans are said to be "underwater." Furthermore, many homeowners lost their jobs during the 2008–2009 Great Recession. These developments resulted in many home foreclosures. Banks and other holders of these mortgages and mortgage-backed securities found that the value of their asset holdings declined so much that many of the institutions had inadequate capital to meet their liabilities causing them to be on the verge of bankruptcy.

In March 2008, Bear Stearns, a major financial institution, was on the verge of failing due to the collapse of the values of mortgage-backed securities and had to be acquired by the JPMorgan Chase & Co. with the help of the Federal Reserve and the U.S. Treasury. By September 2008, the financial crisis was at its peak. Lehman Brothers, a major investment bank, was allowed to fail, and Merrill Lynch was sold to Bank of America.

Shortly after the Lehman bankruptcy and the Merrill sale, American International Group (AIG), the largest insurance firm in the United States, was "bailed out" by the Federal Reserve with the U.S. government receiving an ownership interest in AIG. Like Merrill, the Federal National Mortgage Association (FNMA or Fannie Mae), and the Federal Home Loan Mortgage Corporation (FHLMC or Freddie Mac), AIG was considered "too big to fail" due to its potential impact on the global financial markets.

CONCEPT CHECK

What is a mortgage loan?

What are mortgage-backed securities?

What role did banks play in the financial crisis?

In late September 2008, Washington Mutual, the largest savings and loan in the United States, failed with most of its assets being purchased by JPMorgan Chase & Co. Wachovia Bank, then the fourth largest commercial bank in the United States, was also on the brink of bankruptcy before finally agreeing to be purchased by Wells Fargo Bank. Citigroup and the Bank of America, the first and second largest U.S. banks, respectively, were suffering financial difficulties.

TYPES AND ROLES OF FINANCIAL INSTITUTIONS

The current system of financial institutions or intermediaries in the United States, like the monetary system, evolved to meet the needs of the country's citizens and to facilitate the savings-investment process. Individuals may save and grow their savings with the assistance of financial institutions. While individuals can invest directly in the securities of business firms and government units, most individuals invest indirectly through financial institutions that do the lending and investing for them. *Financial intermediation* is the process by which individual savings are accumulated in depository institutions and, in turn, lent or invested.

Figure 3.1 shows the major types of financial institutions grouped into four categories: depository institutions, contractual savings organizations, securities firms, and finance companies. *Depository institutions* accept deposits or savings from individuals and then lend these pooled savings to businesses, governments, and individuals. Depository institutions include commercial banks, S&Ls, savings banks, and credit unions. *Contractual savings organizations* collect premiums on insurance policies and employee/employer contributions from pension fund participants and provide retirement benefits and insurance against major financial losses. Insurance companies and pension funds are the two important forms of contractual savings organizations.

Securities firms accept and invest individual savings and also facilitate the sale and transfer of securities between investors. In addition to pooling individual savings and investments, securities firms receive funds from other financial intermediaries. Investment companies (mutual funds), investment banking firms, and brokerage firms are the primary types of securities firms that we will cover. *Finance firms* provide loans directly to consumers and businesses as well as help borrowers obtain mortgage loans on real property. Our emphasis will be on finance companies and mortgage banking firms when discussing finance firms.

Few of today's financial intermediaries existed during the American colonial period. Only commercial banks and insurance companies (life and property) can be traced back prior to 1800. During the early 1800s, savings banks and S&Ls began developing. Investment banking firms (and organized securities exchanges) can be traced back to the first half of the 1800s. No new major financial intermediaries evolved during the last half of the nineteenth century. Credit unions, pension funds, mutual funds, and finance companies began during the early part of the 1900s. Thus, throughout much of the 1900s and into the twenty-first century, emphasis has been on redefining and restructuring existing financial intermediaries rather than introducing new ones.

FIGURE 3.1
Types of Financial Institutions

FINANCIAL INSTITUTIONS CATEGORIES	PRIMARY SOURCES OF FUNDS
DEPOSITORY INSTITUTIONS	
Commercial banks	Individual savings
Savings and loan associations	Individual savings
Savings banks	Individual savings
Credit unions	Individual savings
CONTRACTUAL SAVINGS ORGANIZATIONS	
Insurance companies	Premiums paid on policies
Pension funds	Employee/employer contributions
SECURITIES FIRMS	
Investment companies (mutual funds)	Individual savings (investments)
Investment banking firms	Other financial institutions
Brokerage firms	Other financial institutions
FINANCE FIRMS	
Finance companies	Other financial institutions
Mortgage banking firms	Other financial institutions

financial intermediation process by which individual savings are accumulated in depository institutions and, in turn, lent or invested

depository institutions accept deposits from individuals and then lend these pooled savings to businesses, governments, and individuals

contractual savings organizations collect premiums on insurance policies and employee/employer contributions from participants and provide retirement benefits and insurance against major financial losses

securities firms accept and invest individual savings and also facilitate the sale and transfer of securities between investors

finance firms provide loans directly to consumers and businesses as well as help borrowers obtain mortgage loans on real property

CONCEPT CHECK
What is meant by financial intermediation?

What are the four major categories of financial institutions?

commercial banks
depository institutions that accept deposits, issue check-writing accounts, and make loans to businesses and individuals

thrift institutions
noncommercial bank depository institutions referred to as savings and loan associations, savings banks, and credit unions that accumulate individual savings and lend primarily to other individuals

savings banks
accept the savings of individuals and lend pooled savings to individuals primarily in the form of mortgage loans

savings and loan associations (S&Ls)
accept individual savings and lend pooled savings to individuals, primarily in the form of mortgage loans, and to businesses

credit unions
cooperative nonprofit organizations that exist primarily to provide member depositors with consumer credit

CONCEPT CHECK

What are the four types of depository institutions?

insurance companies
provide financial protection to individuals and businesses for life, property, liability, and health uncertainties

pension funds
receive contributions from employees and/or their employers and invest the proceeds on behalf of the employees

DEPOSITORY INSTITUTIONS

When we refer to banks and the banking system in the United States, we primarily think in terms of commercial banking. **Commercial banks** are depository institutions that accept deposits, issue check-writing accounts, and make loans to businesses and individuals. Depository institutions also include three thrift institutions in addition to commercial banks. **Thrift institutions** are noncommercial bank depository institutions referred to as S&Ls, savings banks, and credit unions that accumulate individual savings and lend primarily to other individuals. S&Ls engage in some lending to businesses but focus primarily on loans to individuals. Savings banks and credit unions focus on providing consumer and home mortgage loans to individuals seeking to purchase items such as automobiles and houses.

Savings banks made their appearance in 1812, emphasizing individual thrift savings and safety of principal. **Savings banks** accept the savings of individuals and lend pooled savings to individuals primarily in the form of mortgage loans. Often, the trustees of these banks were prominent local citizens, serving without pay, who regarded their service as an important civic duty. Today, savings banks operate almost entirely in New England, New York, and New Jersey, with most of their assets continuing to be invested in mortgage loans.

In 1831, savings and loan associations, known also as savings and loans or S&Ls, came on the scene. The basic mission of these institutions, which were first known as building societies and then as building and loan associations, was to provide home mortgage financing. In distinguishing between savings banks and savings and loans, it might be said that originally the savings banks' emphasis was on thrift and the safety of savings while the emphasis of the S&Ls was on home financing. Today, **savings and loan associations** accept individual savings and lend pooled savings to individuals, primarily in the form of mortgage loans, and to businesses. In contrast with the limited geographic expansion of savings banking, savings and loan activity spread throughout the United States.

Credit unions came on the American scene later than the other thrift institutions. **Credit unions** are cooperative nonprofit organizations that exist primarily to provide member depositors with consumer credit, including the financing of automobiles and the purchase of homes. Credit unions are made up of individuals who possess common bonds of association, such as occupation, residence, or church affiliation. These institutions derive their funds almost entirely from their members' savings. The first official credit union was formed in the United States in 1909, but it was not until the 1920s that credit unions became important as a special form of depository institution.

Figure 3.2 illustrates the role of financial institutions in directing savings to *business firms* that want to make investments to maintain and grow their firms. Individuals make deposits in commercial banks that in turn make loans to and purchase debt securities of business firms. Since thrift institutions focus primarily on gathering the savings of individuals and in turn lending those funds to individuals, they are not depicted on Figure 3.2.

CONTRACTUAL SAVINGS ORGANIZATIONS

Contractual savings organizations in the form of insurance companies and pension funds play important roles by collecting premiums and contributions and using these pooled funds to purchase the debt and equity securities of business firms, as is depicted in Figure 3.2. Of course, contractual savings organizations actively purchase the debt securities issued by governmental units. **Insurance companies** provide financial protection to individuals and businesses for life, property, liability, and health uncertainties. Policyholders pay premiums to insurance companies that invest these funds until the insured claims must be paid. Life insurance provides economic security for dependents in the event of premature death of the insured individual. Health insurance provides protection against possible catastrophic medical expenses in the event the insured individual becomes ill or is in an accident. Property insurance protects a policyholder against possible financial loss from fire, theft, and other insured perils. Liability insurance protects a policyholder against possible financial loss from a claim of negligence charged by another individual.

Pension funds receive contributions from employees and/or their employers and invest the proceeds on behalf of the employees. The purpose of a pension plan is to provide income during an individual's retirement years. Pension funds are private pension plans or government-sponsored plans. Many business organizations provide private pension plans for their employees. A private pension plan may be insured or noninsured. A contractual plan with a life insurance

FIGURE 3.2
Role of Financial Institutions in Directing Savings to Business Firms

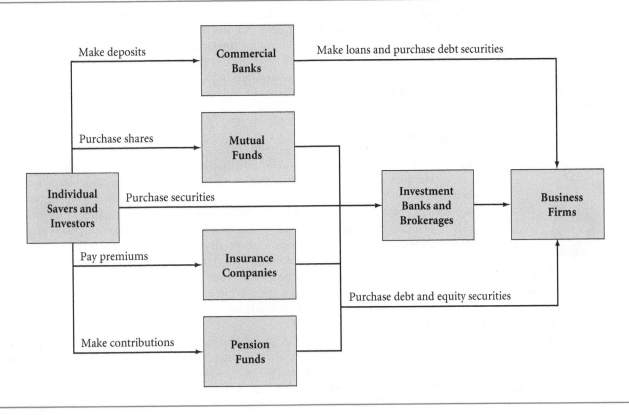

CONCEPT CHECK

What are the two basic types of contractual savings organizations?

company is an insured plan. An uninsured plan uses a trustee, often a commercial bank or trust company, to manage, invest, and distribute benefits as established in the trust arrangement. Government-sponsored plans may involve the federal government or state and local governments. Social Security is the largest federal pension plan. The Social Security plan is funded by currently working individuals paying Social Security taxes. Social Security is designed to provide only minimum retirement benefits, so most individuals will need to accumulate additional funds before retirement. The federal government provides pension plans for its employees, known as civil servants, as well as for military employees. State and local government pension plans typically are established to cover teachers, police and fire employees, and other civil servants.

SECURITIES FIRMS

Securities firms perform several financial functions. Some securities firms are active in the savings-investment process, while others are concentrating primarily on marketing new securities and facilitating the transfer of existing securities between investors. **Investment companies** sell shares in their firms to individuals and others and invest the pooled proceeds in corporate and government securities. An investment company may be a closed-end fund or an open-end fund. A closed-end fund issues a fixed number of its shares to investors and invests the pooled funds in securities. Shares in a closed-end fund are bought and sold in secondary securities markets once they have been initially issued.

Open-end funds, typically called **mutual funds**, can issue an unlimited number of their shares to their investors and use the pooled proceeds to purchase corporate and government securities. However, unlike with closed-end funds, investors purchase new shares or redeem old shares directly with their mutual fund rather than buying and selling the shares in a secondary securities market. Figure 3.2, which focuses on getting funds to business firms, depicts the important role that mutual funds play by selling shares to individual investors and then using the proceeds to purchase debt and equity securities issued by business firms. Mutual funds grow by investing the funds of their existing investors in securities that will pay or distribute cash and will appreciate in value. Successful mutual funds attract more investor funds and, in turn, invest in more securities.

investment companies
sell shares in their firms to individuals and others and invest the pooled proceeds in corporate and government securities

mutual funds
open-end investment companies that can issue an unlimited number of their shares to their investors and use the pooled proceeds to purchase corporate and government securities

investment banking firms

sell or market new securities issued by businesses to individual and institutional investors

brokerage firms

assist individuals who want to purchase new or existing securities issues or who want to sell previously purchased securities

Investment banking firms, referred to as investment banks, sell or market new securities issued by businesses to individual and institutional investors. *Brokerage firms* assist individuals who want to purchase new or existing securities issues or who want to sell previously purchased securities. Investment banking and brokerage activities are often combined in the same firms. However, in contrast with mutual funds, investment banking firms and brokerage firms do not gather the savings of individuals but rather market or sell securities issued by corporations directly to individuals, as depicted in Figure 3.2. Investment banking and brokerage firms obtain financial capital to carry out their activities from their own resources or from other financial institutions.

FINANCE FIRMS

Finance firms, while an important type of financial institution, are not included in Figure 3.2 because they focus largely on providing loans to individuals for meeting credit needs and purchasing durable goods and homes. *Finance companies* provide loans directly to consumers and businesses or aid individuals in obtaining financing. Sales and consumer finance companies lend to individuals. *Sales finance companies* finance installment loan purchases of automobiles and other durable goods such as washers, dryers, and refrigerators. *Consumer finance companies* provide small loans to individuals and households. *Commercial finance companies* provide loans to businesses unable to obtain financing from commercial banks. However, commercial finance companies are not included in Figure 3.2 because they do not accumulate the savings of individuals but rather get funds for making loans to businesses from other financial institutions.

Mortgage banking firms, or mortgage companies, help individuals obtain mortgage loans by bringing together borrowers and institutional investors. A *mortgage loan* is a loan on real property, such as a house, whereby the borrower pledges the property as collateral to guarantee the loan will be repaid. The primary mortgage market, where home and other real property loans are "originated," is important to the success of the financial system. Traditionally, once a mortgage loan was originated, it was held by the lender until maturity or until the loan was prepaid. However, as individual mortgage loans become more standardized, secondary mortgage markets have appeared, in which existing real property mortgages are bought and sold.

CONCEPT CHECK

What are some basic types of securities firms?

finance companies

provide loans directly to consumers and businesses or aid individuals in obtaining financing

mortgage banking firms

help individuals obtain mortgage loans by bringing together borrowers and institutional investors

OVERVIEW OF THE BANKING SYSTEM

We turn our attention to the development of a basic understanding of the current U.S. banking system. First we describe the traditional differences between commercial banking and investment banking and their combination to provide universal banking. Then we cover the functions of banks and the banking system.

COMMERCIAL, INVESTMENT, AND UNIVERSAL BANKING

When we refer to banks and the banking system in the United States, we primarily think in terms of commercial banking. As previously noted, a *commercial bank* accepts deposits, issues check-writing accounts to facilitate purchases and paying bills, and makes loans to individuals and businesses. This definition of a bank is consistent with the Webster's dictionary definition cited at the

CONCEPT CHECK

What are two basic types of finance firms?

SMALL BUSINESS PRACTICE
Types of Credit Used by Small Businesses

At various times, the Fed conducts national surveys of small business finances. These are nationally representative surveys of small businesses designed to gather data on bank and nonbank participants in the supplying of credit to small businesses.

Data are gathered on six types of loans: credit lines used, mortgage loans, equipment loans, vehicle loans, capital leases, and other loans. Data on trade credit and credit card debt are not gathered. Bank credit lines used is the single most important source of the six types of credit used by small businesses. Lines of credit are bank loans against which small businesses can "draw down" or borrow against.

FIGURE 3.3

Commercial Banking and Investment Banking Intermediation Activities

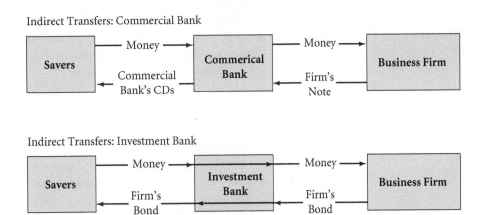

CONCEPT CHECK

What are the major financial institutions involved in directing savings of individuals to business firms?

---

investment bank

helps businesses sell their new debt and equity securities to raise financial capital

beginning of the chapter. In contrast, an ***investment bank*** helps businesses sell their new debt and equity securities to raise financial capital.

Figure 3.3 depicts these two types of indirect transfers to and from savers to a business firm. You should be able to recall a similarity between this figure and Figure 2.1 in Chapter 2, which included direct transfers between individuals and business firms whereby no financial institution performs an intermediary role by bringing individual investors together with business firms desiring to sell securities. Direct investments are relatively rare occurrences. The top portion of Figure 3.3 shows the traditional role of the commercial bank as a financial institution that accepts the deposits of savers in exchange for the bank's securities, e.g., certificates of deposit (CDs). The bank then lends money to the business firm in exchange for the firm's promise (e.g., a note) to repay the loan. The bottom portion of Figure 3.3 shows that the investment bank markets the business firm's securities (e.g., a bond) to savers. This can be done either by first purchasing the securities from the firm and then reselling the securities (a practice called "underwriting," as we will see in Chapter 11) or by marketing the securities on behalf of the issuing firm to savers.

Glass-Steagall Act of 1933

provided for separation of commercial banking and investment banking activities in the United States

In the midst of the Great Depression, Congress passed the *Banking Act of 1933*. This legislation, commonly known as the ***Glass-Steagall Act of 1933*** in recognition of the individuals responsible for introducing and supporting the act, provided for the separation of commercial banking and investment banking in the United States. Many banks failed during the late 1920s and early 1930s, and efforts were undertaken to assess why banks failed. Some politicians, regulators, and others thought many of the bank failures had been caused, in part, by investment banking activities involving underwriting and the holding of equity securities. The result was passage of the Glass-Steagall Act.

Gramm-Leach-Bliley Act of 1999

repealed the separation of commercial banking and investment banking provided for in the Glass-Steagall Act of 1933

After more than six decades, the Glass-Steagall Act was repealed with the passage of the ***Gramm-Leach-Bliley Act of 1999***. When Glass-Steagall was enacted, many officials and individuals believed that government regulation was the answer to avoiding banking excesses and mismanagement. An underlying belief was that competition and free markets represent the best way to manage banking risks and create stability in the financial system. Commercial banks were no longer prohibited from engaging in investment banking and insurance underwriting. Likewise, insurance companies and investment banking firms could engage in commercial banking. Universal banking was permitted in the United States, as in various other countries. A ***universal bank*** is a bank that engages in commercial banking and investment banking. Germany also has universal banking, and the United Kingdom does not legally separate commercial banking from investment banking.

universal bank

bank that engages in commercial banking and investment banking

However, as a result of the 2007–2008 financial crisis and the 2008–2009 Great Recession, government officials and others promoted the need to move toward more re-regulation of financial institutions to help restore financial stability in the United States. The result was the passage in 2010 of the Dodd-Frank Wall Street Reform and Consumer Protection Act, which we will discuss later in this chapter.

FUNCTIONS OF BANKS AND THE BANKING SYSTEM

banking system
commercial banks, S&Ls,
savings banks, and credit
unions

Depository institutions accept deposits, make loans, and issue checkable deposit accounts. Like commercial banks, S&Ls, savings banks, and credit unions perform these activities. The U.S. **banking system** includes commercial banks, S&Ls, savings banks, and credit unions. Today, all depository institutions are commonly referred to as banks. Banks and the banking system perform five functions: accepting deposits, granting loans, issuing checkable deposit accounts, clearing checks, and creating deposit money. To the extent that commercial banks perform investment banking operations (i.e., are universal banks), they perform a sixth function: raising financial capital for businesses.

In accepting deposits, banks provide a safe place for the public to keep money for future use. Individuals and businesses seldom wish to spend their money as it becomes available; without depository facilities such funds may lie idle. The banking system puts the accumulated deposits to use through loans to persons and businesses that have an immediate use for them. This, of course, is the financial intermediation activity of depository institutions in the savings-investment process.

Banks play an important role in the payments process or mechanism in place in the U.S. financial system by creating deposit money. Through check writing against demand and other checkable deposits, it is easier for individuals and businesses to make purchases and to pay bills or debts. Of course, it is not enough to permit check writing; an efficient mechanism must exist for processing the checks so they can be presented to the bank that authorized the check for payment.

Let's take a brief look at how checks are "cleared" or processed in the United States. Let's assume you owe $100 for the purchase of a product on credit from the ABC firm. You write a $100 check against your checkable deposit account, held at First Bank, payable to ABC and mail the check to ABC. An ABC employee opens the envelope containing your check and deposits the check in ABC's deposit account held at Last Bank.

A check can clear in three ways through the U.S. banking system:

1. Bank to bank
2. Through a bank clearinghouse
3. Through a Federal Reserve Bank

Figure 3.4 shows these three ways of processing or collecting a check. Last Bank could present your check directly to First Bank for payment. First Bank pays the check and deducts the amount of the check from your checkable deposit account. Since First Bank authorized or issued the deposit money, confidence in its creditworthiness is important in making the clearing process work.

However, since direct check presentation is costly and time consuming, most banks use bank clearinghouses. This is particularly useful when the two banks are in different cities. In our example, the bank clearinghouse would receive the check from Last Bank, credit the bank's account at the clearinghouse, and subtract the amount of your check from First Bank's account at the clearinghouse. At the end of each day, all of a bank's transactions handled through the clearinghouse are "netted out," with the result being an increase or decrease in the bank's account with the clearinghouse. Of course, when presented with your check, First Bank will reduce your checkable deposit account accordingly.

Sometimes banks work closely with and hold deposit accounts at other banks, known as correspondent banks, in distant cities. For example, Last Bank may hold a deposit account at one of its correspondent banks called Middle Bank, which is in the same city as First Bank. In this case, when Last Bank receives your check from ABC, it is deposited in Last Bank's account at Middle Bank. Middle Bank, in turn, either presents your check directly to First Bank or uses the bank clearinghouse in its and in First Bank's city.

Most depository institutions with large checkable deposit accounts are required to hold accounts with the Federal Reserve. Actually, the funds are held with the Federal Reserve Bank responsible for its city or area as we will see in the next chapter. If Last Bank wants to use the Federal Reserve for check clearing purposes, it will first deposit your check with its Federal Reserve Bank, where Last Bank's account will be increased. The Fed Bank will reduce First Bank's account held at the Federal Reserve even if it is held at a different Federal Reserve Bank. The check then is returned to First Bank so that your checkable account balance can be reduced by the $100.

When paper checks were physically transferred and cleared through the financial system, the process was an expensive, time-consuming enterprise. Today, with the use of electronic check

FIGURE 3.4
How Checks Are Processed or Cleared Through the Banking System

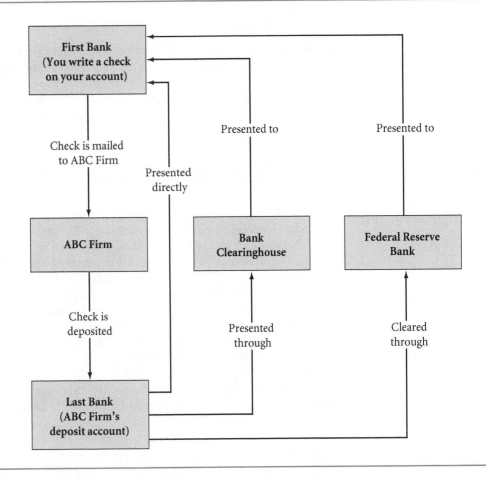

clearing mechanisms, the clearing process is much more efficient. In Chapter 4, we will examine the Fed's check-clearing process in greater detail.

The banking system has the unique ability to create deposit money and, thus, expand the money supply (MS). The ability to create more deposit money is almost limitless as long as the deposit money keeps coming back into the banking system, unless banks are required to hold a portion of their checkable deposits in the form of reserves. We examine deposit, reserves, and other accounts later in this chapter. Chapter 4 will cover how the Fed can regulate the money supply by setting reserve requirements that banks must hold against their checkable deposits. Chapter 5 will explore how reserve requirements and other Fed tools can be used to set monetary policy.

CONCEPT CHECK

How did a commercial bank used to differ from an investment bank?

What are the functions performed by banks and the banking system?

HISTORICAL DEVELOPMENT OF THE U.S. BANKING SYSTEM

Before we examine the current structure of the banking industry, we will review a little U.S. banking history. We know you are about to ask, "Why should I learn anything about the history of banking?" First, a basic understanding of how the banking system evolved should help us better understand how and why the system operates the way it does today. Second, to paraphrase the quotation at the beginning of Chapter 1, "Those who don't study history are doomed to repeat its mistakes."

BEFORE THE CIVIL WAR

Until the Civil War, banking in the United States developed under confusing and difficult circumstances. The population lived for the most part on farms. Families were self-sufficient, and transportation and communications were poor. The friction between those who supported a strong central government and those who did not existed in the early years of U.S. history, as it does today. The country had little experience in money and financial management, and much controversy raged over the power to charter and regulate banks.

Early Chartered Banks

During the colonial period, small unincorporated banks were established to ease the shortage of financial capital for businesses. Their operations consisted largely of issuing their own paper money. Outside of the larger towns, deposit banking was of minor significance. It was not until 1782 that the first incorporated bank, the Bank of North America, was created. Robert Morris established it in Philadelphia to assist in financing prior Revolutionary War expenditures. This bank set a good example for successful banking: Its notes served as a circulating medium of exchange, it lent liberally to the U.S. government, and it redeemed its own notes in metallic coins upon demand. Two years later, the Bank of Massachusetts and the Bank of New York were established. Until 1790, these three incorporated banks were the only such banks.

First Bank of the United States

Alexander Hamilton was the first secretary of the Treasury of the United States. For several years he had harbored the idea of a federally chartered bank that would support the growing economy and would give financial assistance to the government during its crises. His recommendations were submitted to the House of Representatives of the United States in 1790, and in 1791, a twenty-year charter was issued to the First Bank of the United States. This bank served the nation by issuing notes, transferring funds from region to region, and curbing the excessive note issues of state banks by presenting such notes periodically to the issuing banks for redemption. However, strong opposition existed to the renewal of its charter, and in 1811, it ceased operations. The antagonism of state banking interests was an important cause of the demise of the First Bank.

Following the expiration of the charter of the First Bank, the number of state banks increased rapidly, as did the volume of their note issues. Abuses of banking privileges were extensive. The capital of many banks was largely fictitious, and a flood of irredeemable notes was issued to the public.

Second Bank of the United States

The Second Bank of the United States was chartered primarily to restore order to the chaotic banking situation that had developed after the First Bank of the United States ceased operations in 1811. Like the First Bank, it received a twenty-year federal charter. The Second Bank began operations in 1816 and ably served individuals, businesses, and the government. It accepted deposits, made loans, and issued notes. Furthermore, it restrained the note issuing practices of state banks by periodically presenting their notes for redemption. The Second Bank served as the fiscal agent for the government. It received all deposits of government funds and reported regularly on all government receipts and expenditures.

In 1833, President Andrew Jackson and many of his associates began such a vigorous campaign against the Second Bank that it became apparent its charter would not be renewed in 1836 when it expired. Jackson claimed the bank was being run to benefit private interests and was operated in such a way as to weaken government policies. Like the First Bank, it became a victim of political pressure. Not until 1863 was another bank in the United States to receive a federal charter.

State Banks from 1836 to the Civil War

When the Second Bank's charter expired, the excesses that had plagued the period between 1811 and 1816 began again. This period is characterized as one of "wildcat" banking.[1] Although many state banks operated on a conservative and sound basis, the majority engaged in risky banking practices through excessive note issues, lack of adequate bank capital, and insufficient reserves against their notes and deposits.

Because the notes of even well-established banks were often of inferior quality, it was easy for skillful counterfeiters to increase the denomination of notes. Because of the poor communications that existed between various sections of the country, a banker often had trouble being certain

---

1. This nickname was used to refer to banks located in wilderness areas that were more accessible to wildcats than people. This made it difficult for anyone to redeem these banks' notes.

whether notes presented for payment were real. Skillfully prepared counterfeit notes frequently circulated with greater freedom than did the legitimate notes of weak and little-known banks.

In spite of the many abuses of state banks during this period, New York, Massachusetts, and Louisiana originated sound banking legislation, much of which provided the basis for the 1863 establishment of the National Banking System.

ENTRY OF THRIFT INSTITUTIONS

The chaotic banking conditions of the early 1800s left individuals with few safe institutions in which they could place their savings. The lack of safe depository institutions, in turn, inhibited the effective development of home financing. The rapidly growing population depended to a large extent on individual financial arrangements to meet its need for housing. The accumulated savings of most individual home buyers, then as now, were inadequate to buy a house. In response to this problem, two new forms of depository institutions, known as *thrift institutions*, came into being: savings banks and savings and loan associations. Credit unions developed later.

CONCEPT CHECK

Why was the First Bank of the United States authorized, and what did it do?

What are the three types of depository institutions in addition to commercial banks?

REGULATION OF THE BANKING SYSTEM

The purpose of this section is to provide a brief review of major legislation that has shaped the development of the U.S. banking system. We separate our discussion into general banking legislation, the savings and loan crisis, and legislation enacted to protect depositors' funds.

GENERAL BANKING LEGISLATION

A variety of laws have been passed in the United States to regulate the banking system. Early laws focused on establishing a system of federally chartered banks followed by a system of central banks. More recent legislation has focused on deregulating banking activities and improving the effectiveness of monetary policy.

National Banking Act of 1864

The *National Banking Act of 1864* allowed banks to receive federal charters. This legislation provided the basis for the present national banking laws. As in the cases of the First and Second Banks of the United States, the reasons for federal interest in the banking system were to provide for a sound banking system and to curb the excesses of the state banks. An important additional purpose of the National Banking Act of 1864 was to provide financing for the Civil War. Secretary of the Treasury Salmon P. Chase and others believed that government bonds could be sold to the nationally chartered banks, which could issue their own notes based in part on the government bonds they had purchased.

Through the National Banking Act of 1864, various steps were taken to promote safe banking practices. Among other things, minimum capital requirements were established for banks with federal charters, loans were regulated with respect to safety and liquidity, a system of supervision and examination was instituted, and minimum reserve requirements against notes and deposits were established. In general, while these reform measures were constructive, they were viewed by some as too restrictive. For example, loans against real estate were not allowed. Much of the criticism of the national banking system, in fact, was caused by the inflexibility of its rules.

INTERNET ACTIVITY

Go to the Citibank Web site, http://www.citibank.com. Find information on the savings alternatives and interest rates currently being paid.

Federal Reserve Act of 1913

The *Federal Reserve Act of 1913* brought to the American economy a system of central banks. The Federal Reserve System was designed to eliminate many of the weaknesses that had persisted under the National Banking Act of 1864 and to increase the effectiveness of commercial banking in general. It included strong central domination of banking practices and many services for commercial banks. We describe the structure and functions of the Federal Reserve System in Chapter 4, and in Chapter 5, we will discuss implementation and management of monetary policy.

Banking Act of 1933

As previously noted, this legislation, commonly referred to as the Glass-Steagall Act of 1933, was passed during the Great Depression. This act provided for the separation of commercial banking activities and investment banking activities in the United States. Some politicians, regulators, and others thought that many bank failures during the late 1920s and early 1930s were caused by high risk investment banking activities involving securities underwriting and the holding of equity securities. As a result, the Glass-Steagall Act was passed.

Depository Institutions Deregulation and Monetary Control Act of 1980

In 1980, President Jimmy Carter signed into law the *Depository Institutions Deregulation and Monetary Control Act*, which for ease of reference is often just called the *Monetary Control Act*. This act represents a major step toward deregulating banking in the United States and improving the effectiveness of monetary policy. The two main provisions of the act are deregulation and monetary control.

Depository Institutions Deregulation

The Depository Institutions Deregulation part of the Monetary Control Act was designed to reduce or eliminate interest rate limitations imposed on the banking system, increase the various sources of funds, and expand the uses of the funds of S&Ls. One significant change affected the Fed's Regulation Q, which established interest rate ceilings on time and savings deposits. By early 1986, most provisions of Regulation Q had been phased out. Furthermore, state-imposed interest rate ceilings were substantially modified, and state restrictions on deposit interest rates for insured institutions were eliminated.

To enable depository institutions to compete for funds that were flowing in large amounts to money market mutual funds (MMMFs), negotiable orders of withdrawal (NOW) accounts were authorized. While NOW accounts carried interest rates more competitive with MMMF accounts, they still fell under Regulation Q restrictions. Credit unions were permitted to issue draft accounts that for all intents and purposes were the same as NOW accounts. Federal deposit insurance, which we discuss in greater detail later, was increased from $40,000 to $100,000 for each account. This large increase in deposit protection, although politically popular at the time, is now described as an undue expansion of protection. The U.S. Treasury has stated this increase undermined market discipline and enabled depository institutions to make high-risk loans for which the taxpayers in the long run have become liable. To enhance competition among depository institutions, Title IV of the Monetary Control Act amended the Home Owners' Loan Act of 1933 (HOLA). Federally chartered S&Ls were permitted to invest up to one-fifth of their assets in corporate debt securities, commercial paper, and consumer loans. Prior residential mortgage loan restrictions relating to geographical areas and first mortgage lending requirements were removed. Greater authority was permitted for granting real estate development and construction loans by federally chartered S&Ls. In addition, federal savings banks were allowed to make a small number of commercial loans and accept some checkable deposits.

PERSONAL FINANCIAL PLANNING
Saving with a Credit Union

Banks' fondness for charging fees can make banking expensive for individuals who do not shop around for the bank that best and most inexpensively meets their needs. For individuals, the best place to bank may not be a bank but rather a credit union. Credit union members, who have some kind of common affiliation, such as an employer or religious organization membership, run these. Credit unions are tax-exempt depository institutions. Although they do not pay any taxes, any interest or dividends received by their members is taxable.

While commercial banks and credit unions accept the savings deposits of individuals, their lending objectives differ. Commercial banks provide loans to businesses and individuals, whereas credit unions emphasize consumer loans.

Credit unions often pay slightly higher interest rates than their commercial bank counterparts on interest-bearing checking accounts, savings accounts, and certificates of deposit (CDs). At the same time, credit union members often receive lower credit card and new car loan interest rates than what they would have to pay at a commercial bank. However, interest rates on home equity loans tend to be about the same at credit unions and commercial banks. Of course, to compare and take advantage of possible differences in savings and borrowing rates between a commercial bank and a credit union, you must first become a member of a credit union.

Monetary Control

The Monetary Control Act was designed to extend the Fed's control to thrift institutions and to commercial banks that are not members of the system. This was accomplished by extending reserve requirements and general controls to these institutions. Because the Fed had more stringent regulations than many state regulatory agencies, many commercial banks had given up their membership in the system to become state-chartered nonmember banks. The Monetary Control Act, therefore, has had the effect of halting the declining system membership by transferring much regulatory control from the state to the federal level.

In the past, reserve requirements imposed by the Fed applied only to member banks. The requirements were based on a complicated formula involving size, location, and type of charter. These differential reserve requirements have been eliminated. Even foreign banks and offices operating in this country have been included in these simplified reserve requirements. Along with the broadening of control by the Fed, there has been a broadening of privileges to those institutions brought under its control. All depository institutions may borrow from the Fed on the same basis, and the fee schedule for services rendered by the Fed applies to all regulated depository institutions.

Garn-St. Germain Depository Institutions Act of 1982

There had been high hopes that the Monetary Control Act would have a quick and beneficial effect on the banking system as well as on the effectiveness of monetary control by the Fed. However, this was not the case. In late 1980 and 1981, interest rates dramatically increased. S&Ls and savings banks were faced with heavy increases in their cost of funds as depositors shifted from low-interest passbook savings to the higher-yielding NOW accounts and savings certificates. Furthermore, since the interest rates on NOW accounts were restricted by Regulation Q, MMMFs had a clear competitive advantage in attracting funds. Rapidly increasing federal deficits and troubles in the automobile and housing industries added to the demand for legislation to address these problems. The *Garn-St. Germain Act of 1982* resulted.

Although the Garn-St. Germain Act had many provisions, its principal focus was to assist the savings and loan industry, which had deteriorated to dangerous levels. Depository institutions in general were authorized, among other things, to issue a new money market deposit account with no regulated interest-rate ceiling. S&Ls were authorized to make nonresidential real estate loans, commercial loans, and variable-rate mortgages.

Gramm-Leach-Bliley Act of 1999

As previously noted, after more than 60 years, the Glass-Steagall Act was repealed and replaced by the Gramm-Leach-Bliley Act of 1999, which allowed commercial banks to again participate in investment banking activities and insurance underwriting. As a result, United States banks were allowed to be "universal" banks much like the policies in place in England and Germany. Many politicians, regulators, and others believed that deregulation of financial institutions would lead to greater competition with consumers benefiting by resulting by more financial product choices and costs.

Dodd-Frank Wall Street Reform and Consumer Protection Act

Dodd-Frank Wall Street Reform and Consumer Protection Act promotes financial stability of the United States by improving accountability and transparency in the financial system

The 2007–2008 financial crisis and the 2008–2009 Great Recession led to politicians, regulators, and others to call for major changes in the regulation of financial institutions. The result was passage of the **Dodd-Frank Wall Street Reform and Consumer Protection Act** in 2010, which was designed "to promote the financial stability of the United States by improving accountability and transparency in the financial system." Other components of the Act included ending the "too big to fail" argument, ending bailouts of financial institutions and other business organizations, and providing consumer protection from abusive financial services practices. In part due to the comprehensiveness of the legislation, much of the implementation and consequences of the Act are still to be determined.

THE SAVINGS AND LOAN CRISIS

During the last half of the 1980s and the first half of the 1990s, well over 2,000 S&Ls were closed or merged into other organizations. Why did this happen? The bottom line is that S&Ls failed because of mismanagement and greed that led to fraudulent activities on the part of some of the institutions' officers.

The S&L business has historically been a difficult one. S&Ls borrow short-term by accepting the deposits of savers and paying interest on the savings. S&Ls, in turn, provide long-term mortgage loans to help finance homes. As long as short-term and long-term interest rates remain relatively the same, S&Ls are concerned primarily with illiquidity due to lending long term but borrowing short term. In situations when many depositors want their money back, S&Ls may be forced to liquidate their mortgage loans even at unfavorable prices. When short-term interest rates rise, as they did in the late 1980s, S&Ls may find themselves paying higher interest rates to depositors than they are earning on their mortgage loans. Unfortunately, S&L managements handled the illiquidity and rising short-term interest rate developments badly.

To make matters worse, S&L managements were ill prepared for the consequences of deregulation. Authorization in the early 1980s to invest funds in a wide range of higher-yielding investments permitted many S&Ls to run wild by supporting speculative office buildings and other commercial ventures. This resulted in overbuilding at inflated costs and in S&L insolvency as the promoters were unable to honor the terms of their loan contracts. Deregulation permitted S&Ls to invest in "junk" bonds, which are low-quality, high-risk bonds issued by businesses. Many of the issuers defaulted on these bonds, resulting in greater pressures on S&L operations.

ETHICAL ISSUES

Mismanagement was a major reason for the collapse of much of the S&L industry. This problem was exacerbated by greed, which led to fraudulent behavior on the part of some S&L officers and managers. Depositors' funds were used to pay exorbitant salaries, purchase expensive automobiles and yachts for personal use, and so forth. Top officers borrowed excessively from their own S&Ls, and in at least one instance, S&L presidents of two associations made loans to each other using depositors' funds.

No evidence suggests the S&L industry was run by unethical individuals prior to the 1980s. Apparently, deregulation provided the opportunity for unscrupulous individuals from outside the industry to pursue personal greed by becoming officers and managers of S&Ls. Of course, the opportunity for greed associated with deregulation resulted in some existing S&L officers behaving unethically and committing fraud. Individuals who acted illegally were prosecuted, some served prison terms, and reputations were lost. Failure to treat depositors and other constituents honestly and fairly resulted in lost confidence and trust and surely contributed to the demise of many S&Ls.

The Federal Savings and Loan Insurance Corporation (FSLIC) had insured the deposits of most S&L depositors since the early 1930s. However, because of the number and size of the S&L failures, the FSLIC was bankrupt by early 1988. As a result, the Financial Institutions Reform, Recovery, and Enforcement Act (FIRREA) was passed in 1989. FIRREA provided for the termination of the FSLIC and the formation of the Savings Association Insurance Fund (SAIF). Also, the Office of Thrift Supervision (OTS) took over the regulation of S&Ls from the Federal Home Loan Bank Board (FHLBB). The Act required S&Ls to commit more of their assets to home loans, restricted S&Ls from holding junk bonds, and allowed commercial banks to purchase S&Ls.

Congress created the Resolution Trust Corporation (RTC) in 1988 to take over and dispose of the assets of failed associations by finding acquirers or through liquidations. For some failed S&Ls, deposit transfers were made to sound organizations for a fee without requiring the assumption of any of the defunct S&L's poor-quality assets. Some risky assets of failed S&Ls, such as junk bonds, were purchased at deep discount prices by the RTC and later resold. Assets of failed S&Ls that acquiring firms did not want were disposed of by the RTC. In 1995, Congress shut down the RTC.

Commercial banks have suffered some of the same difficulties as the S&Ls. However, losses from international loans, agricultural loans, and from loans to the petroleum industry have been more significant for commercial banks, and many banks had to be merged with other banks. Savings banks and credit unions experienced some difficulties as well but to a lesser extent.

PROTECTION OF DEPOSITORS' FUNDS

As a result of bank "runs," caused by many depositors trying to retrieve their deposited funds at the same time, during the late 1920s and early 1930s, insurance protection laws for deposits at depository institutions were passed to restore the confidence of depositors. The Federal Deposit Insurance Corporation (FDIC) was created in 1933 to protect deposits in banks. This was followed by federal legislation that created the Federal Savings and Loan Insurance Corporation (FSLIC) and the National Credit Union Share Insurance Fund (NCUSIF) to protect deposits in S&Ls and credit unions, respectively. Of course, as previously noted, the S&L crisis of the 1980s led to the insolvency of the FSLIC and its replacement with SAIF, which is the insuring agency for S&Ls.

Over the years, the limitation on deposit account insurance was increased until, by 1980, it was set at $100,000 per account. Today, deposit account insurance is $250,000 per account.

The pool of funds available to the FDIC for covering insured depositors is called the Bank Insurance Fund, which collects annual insurance premiums from commercial banks. Prior to 1991, all banks paid the same premium rate on their deposits. Thus, riskier banks were being subsidized by safer banks. The Federal Deposit Insurance Corporation Improvement Act of 1991 (FDICIA) was enacted, in part, to address this problem. The FDICIA provided for differences in deposit premiums based on the relative riskiness of banks.

One of the special problems of insuring bank losses has been the practice and assumption that some banks are "too big to fail", too big in the sense that the problems created by losses may extend far beyond the failed bank. On this basis, depositors have typically received 100 percent coverage of their funds even though coverage of only the first $250,000 deposited is guaranteed by law. This practice tended to reduce the incentive for large depositors to exercise market discipline and created an incentive for large deposits to be shifted to "too big to fail" banks. Congress addressed this issue with the FDICIA, which generally requires that failed banks be handled in such a way as to provide the lowest cost to the FDIC. Limited exceptions, however, were provided if serious adverse effects on economic conditions could be expected as a result of failure of big banks.

Deposit insurance will likely continue to exist. Changes will have to be made if we are to avoid future burdens on taxpayers resulting from deposit insurance programs. Suggestions for solving these problems include eliminating all deposit insurance, reducing insurable deposits limits to protect only the small deposits, levying higher premiums on depository institutions for the insurance, and having more strict regulatory and supervisory control.

CONCEPT CHECK

What were the two main provisions of the Depository Institutions Deregulation and Monetary Control Act of 1980, also known as the Monetary Control Act?

What were the reasons for the savings and loan crisis?

How are depositors' funds in commercial banks and S&Ls protected today?

STRUCTURE OF BANKS

Bank structure is characterized by how a bank is established, the extent to which branching takes place, and whether a holding company organizational structure is used. We will address each of these structural characteristics in terms of commercial banks, as well as comment on how the other three depository institutions are structured.

BANK CHARTERS

To start and operate a bank or other depository institution, a charter must be obtained that spells out the powers of the institution. Commercial banks may obtain charters from the federal government or from a state government, making the United States a *dual banking system*. While there are many similarities between federal and state charters, federally chartered banks must include *national* in their titles while state chartered banks cannot use the word. Federally chartered banks must be members of the Federal Reserve System and the Federal Deposit Insurance Corporation. State-chartered banks are not required to join the Fed or the FDIC although almost all banks are covered by federal deposit insurance.

dual banking system allows commercial banks to obtain charters from the federal government or a state government

There about 8,000 commercial banks insured by the FDIC. Roughly 30 percent of these banks hold national charters, and 70 percent are state chartered. Fewer than 20 percent of the state banks are members of the Fed. For some time, concern was expressed that the Fed might not be able to administer monetary policy effectively if it could not regulate nonmember state banks. This concern disappeared at the beginning of the 1980s when reserve requirements set by the Fed for member banks were extended to state nonmember banks.

S&Ls and credit unions can obtain federal or state charters. Savings banks are state chartered. There are about 1,500 savings institutions that are insured by the FDIC. Approximately 60 percent of these savings institutions hold federal charters, and 40 percent have state charters. Credit unions are not insured by the FDIC. While S&Ls, credit unions, and savings banks are important components of the banking system, we will continue to focus on commercial banks because of their dominant role in the banking system.

DEGREE OF BRANCH BANKING

Commercial banks wanting to operate branches away from their home offices are restricted by state laws as to the number of offices they are permitted as well as where the offices may be located.

unit banking
exists when a bank can have only one full-service office

limited branch banking
allows additional banking offices within a geographically defined distance of a bank's main office

statewide branch banking
allows banks to operate offices throughout a state

Unit banking means that a bank can have only one full-service office. Back in the 1960s, about one-third of the states were unit banking states. Today, there are no unit banking states. Colorado was the last unit banking state before it began permitting some form of limited branching in 1991.

In addition to unit banking, there is limited banking and statewide banking. States with **limited branch banking** permit banks under their jurisdiction to locate offices within a geographically defined (e.g., within a county) distance of their main office. **Statewide branch banking** means, as the name implies, that banks can operate offices throughout the state. Back in the 1960s, about one-third of the states permitted limited branching, and about one-third permitted statewide branching. Today, statewide branching is permitted in most states.

One of the particular merits of branch banking is that these systems are less likely to fail than independent unit banks. In a branch banking system, a wide diversification of investments can be made. Therefore, the temporary reverses of a single community are not as likely to cause the complete failure of an entire banking chain. This is true primarily of those branch systems that operate over wide geographical areas rather than in a single metropolitan area.

The independent bank cannot rely on other banks to offset local economic problems. It is on this point that branch banking operations appear to have their strongest support. The record of bank failures in the United States is one of which the banking system as a whole cannot be proud. However, opponents of branch banking have pointed out that the failure of a system of banks, although less frequent, is far more serious.

The pros and cons of branch banking among bank customers have conflicting points of view. The placement of branches in or near shopping centers, airports, and other centers of activity is convenient for consumers. The ability to make deposits or to withdraw funds at a branch is a special advantage for the elderly. Businesses may satisfy large borrowing requirements by dealing with a bank that has been able to grow to a substantial size through its branch operations.

BANK HOLDING COMPANIES

one-bank holding companies (OBHCs)
permits a firm to own and control one bank

multibank holding companies (MBHCs)
permits a firm to own and control two or more banks

A bank may be independently owned by investors, or it may be owned by a holding company. As the name suggests, a holding company owns and controls other organizations or firms. **One-bank holding companies (OBHCs)** own only one bank. **Multibank holding companies (MBHCs)** own and control two or more banks. OBHCs and MBHCs may own other businesses permitted by law. The policies of banks controlled by a holding company are determined by the parent company and coordinated for the purposes of that organization. The holding company may or may not engage in direct banking activities. The banks controlled by the holding company may operate branches.

There was little control over bank holding companies until the depression years of the early 1930s. Bank holding companies did not come under the jurisdiction of state or federal control unless they engaged directly in banking operations. The Banking Act of 1933 and the Securities Acts of 1933 and 1934 imposed limited control on bank holding companies, but it remained for the Bank Holding Company Act of 1956 to establish clear authority over these operations.

The Bank Holding Company Act defined a bank holding company as one that directly or indirectly owns, controls, or holds the power to vote 25 percent or more of the voting shares of each of two or more banks. Thus, the Act regulated MBHCs but not OBHCs. MBHCs were not permitted to engage in nonfinancial activities, and financial activities were restricted primarily to direct banking activities. As a result, during the 1960s while the MBHCs were heavily restricted in terms of their nonbanking activities, the OBHCs diversified widely into nonfinancial areas, including manufacturing, retailing, and transportation.

The Bank Holding Company Amendments of 1970 allowed bank holding companies to acquire companies with activities closely related to banking, such as credit card operations, insurance, and data processing services. The 1970 amendments brought the OBHCs under the provisions of the 1956 act. Thus, while MBHCs were granted more flexibility in terms of banking-related activities, OBHCs had to divest their nonfinancial holdings. Today, bank holding companies control over three-fourths of the banks in the United States and most of the banking assets.

The liberalization of regulations relating to interstate banking is as significant as the liberalization of branch banking within states. All states currently permit the acquisition of banks by out-of-state bank holding companies. In contrast, only one state permitted interstate banking before

CONCEPT CHECK
How are banks chartered in the United States and what types of branch banking are permitted?

What is the difference between an OBHC and an MBHC?

1982. However, while some state laws still limit entry to banking organizations from nearby states, called regional reciprocal, states are increasingly permitting entry on a nationwide basis, known as national reciprocal or open entry. Today, nationwide banking systems are common in the United States.

THE BANK BALANCE SHEET

A balance sheet indicates an organization's financial position at a particular point. In other words, the balance sheet represents a "snapshot" of its assets, liabilities, and owners' capital. Assets are the financial and physical items owned by the bank. Liabilities are the financial debts and obligations owed by the bank. Owners' capital is the financial equity capital supplied by the bank's owners. Since the term *balance sheet* is used, total assets must equal the sum of the bank's liabilities and its owners' capital. Figure 3.5 shows a representative composite balance sheet for FDIC-insured commercial banks. Here we continue to focus on commercial banks because of their dominant role in the banking system, and while the balance sheets of the three other types of depository institutions differ somewhat in terms of weights for individual accounts, the account categories are similar.

FIGURE 3.5

Representative Composite Balance Sheet for Commercial Banks

	PERCENT OF TOTAL ASSETS		PERCENT OF TOTAL ASSETS
ASSETS:		**LIABILITIES AND**	
CASH & BALANCES DUE		**OWNERS' CAPITAL:**	
FROM DEPOSITORY	7%	**DEPOSITS**	68%
INSTITUTIONS			
		Transaction accounts	
Vault cash and cash items		Demand deposits	
in process of collection		NOW accounts	
Balances due from depository		Nontransactional accounts	
institutions		Time deposits	
Balances due from Federal		Savings deposits	
Reserve Banks		Foreign deposits	
SECURITIES	18	**OTHER LIABILITIES**	24
U.S. government securities		Federal funds purchased	
State and local government		Other borrowed money	
securities		& liabilities	
Other debt securities			
Equity securities		**OWNERS' CAPITAL**	8
		Common stock	
LOANS	59	Surplus	
Loans secured by real estate		Undivided profits	
Loans to depository			
institutions		**TOTAL LIABILITIES**	
Commercial and industrial		**& CAPITAL**	*100%*
loans			
Loans to individuals			
Other loans			
OTHER ASSETS	16		
Bank premises and fixed			
assets			
Assets held in trading			
accounts			
All other assets			
TOTAL ASSETS	*100%*		

ASSETS

The principal assets of banks and other depository institutions are cash assets, securities owned assets, loans, and bank fixed assets.

Cash and Balances Due from Depository Institutions

"Cash and balances due from depository institutions" account for fewer than 10 percent of FDIC-insured commercial bank assets. "Currency plus cash items in the process of collection" is the most important component and represents about one-half of the total for this account. "Balances due from depository institutions" is a large component, with "balances due from Federal Reserve Banks" being a relatively small portion of this account.

A certain minimum of vault cash is needed to meet the day-to-day currency requirements of customers. The amount of cash required may be small compared to total resources because the typical day's operation will result in approximately the same amount of cash deposits as cash withdrawals. A margin of safety, however, is required to take care of those periods when for one reason or another withdrawals exceed deposits.

The appropriate amount of cash a bank should carry depends largely on the character of its operations. For example, a bank that has some large accounts might be expected to have a larger volume of unanticipated withdrawals (and deposits) than a bank that has only small individual accounts. An unpredictable volume of day-to-day withdrawals requires, of course, a larger cash reserve.

"Balances due from depository institutions" reflect, in large part, the keeping of substantial deposits with correspondent banks. Correspondent banks typically are located in large cities, and these relationships can help speed the check clearing process, as discussed earlier in the chapter.

"Balances due from Federal Reserve Banks" reflect reserves held at Federal Reserve Banks. Bank and other depository institutions are required to keep a percentage of their deposits as reserves with the Reserve Bank in their districts or in the form of vault cash. As noted, the Monetary Control Act requires uniform reserve amounts for all depository institutions to enhance monetary control and competitive fairness. As withdrawals are made and total deposit balances decrease, the amount of the required reserves decreases. The vault cash reserves that have been freed may be used to help meet withdrawal demands.

Securities

Securities are the second major group of bank assets and account for about one-fifth of total assets. Securities issued by the U.S. Treasury and by U.S. government corporations and agencies account for about three-fourths of the total securities held by banks. Commercial banks hold debt securities issued by state and local governments, as well as other types of debt instruments.

CAREER OPPORTUNITIES IN FINANCE
Financial Institutions

Opportunities
Financial institutions, such as banks, S&Ls, and credit unions, assist businesses and individuals with the flow of funds between borrowers. Financial intermediary jobs provide the chance to work with individuals, small businesses, and large corporations on a variety of financial matters, and, therefore, provide invaluable business world experience. In addition, individuals interested in finance may find numerous entry-level jobs with strong advancement opportunities.

Jobs
Loan analyst
Loan officer
Financial economist

Responsibilities
A loan analyst evaluates loan applicants in terms of their creditworthiness and ability to repay. Since these types of loans are usually for

one or more years, the loan analyst must monitor and reevaluate outstanding loans on a periodic basis.

A loan officer is responsible for generating new loan business and managing existing loans. As such, a loan officer must have the ability to address the needs of existing clients while identifying and actively pursuing new clients.

A financial economist analyzes business conditions over time and prepares forecasts of economic activity and employment trends. This information is crucial for lending institutions so that they do not make unwise loans.

Education
The level of education needed varies among different jobs. However, all of these jobs require a solid background in economics and finance, as well as experience with computers, statistics, and communication.

FIGURE 3.6
Bank Prime Rate Changes, 1980–2012

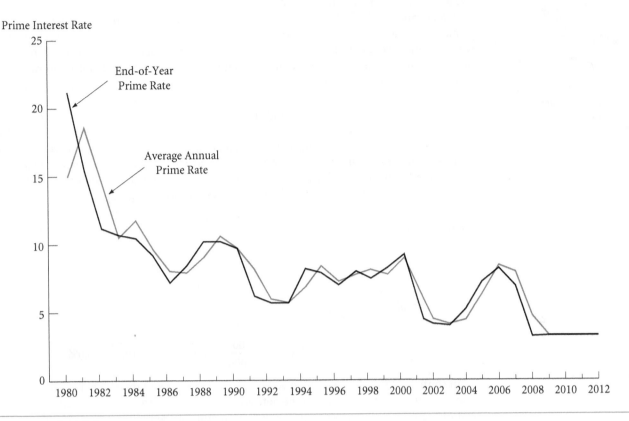

Source: www.stlouisfed.org.

Equity securities include investments in mutual funds and other equity securities, such as the holding of capital stock in a Federal Reserve Bank. Member banks of the Fed must hold shares of stock in the Federal Reserve Bank in their district.

Loans

Loans account for about three-fifths of bank assets, making this the most important account category. Loans secured by real estate comprise about two-fifths of total bank loans and represent one-fourth of total bank assets. In a **secured loan**, specific property is pledged as collateral for the loan. In the event the borrower fails to repay the loan, the lending institution will take the assets pledged as collateral for the loan. In all cases, the borrower is required to sign a note specifying the details of the indebtedness, but unless specific assets are pledged for the loan, it is classified as unsecured.

The second most important loan category is composed of commercial and industrial loans, which represent a little more than one-fourth of all bank loans. These are loans made to businesses, and they may be secured or unsecured. An **unsecured loan** represents a general claim against the assets of the borrower. The interest rate charged by banks for short-term unsecured loans to their highest-quality business customers is referred to as the **prime rate**. This represents, in theory, the lowest business loan rate available at a particular point and is sometimes called the floor rate.[2] Less qualified business borrowers will be charged a higher rate, for example, prime plus two percentage points. If the prime rate is 8 percent, then the financially weaker business borrower would be charged 10 percent (8 percent prime plus 2 percentage points more).

Figure 3.6 shows changes in the prime rate from 1980 to 2012. The average annual and end-of-year prevailing rates are graphed. Notice that the prime rates during the early 1980s were at historically high levels. Since then, prime rates have been in a generally consistent decline with secondary peaks in 1990, 2000, and 2006, with the 2006 rate peaking at 8.25 percent. During the

secured loan
loan backed by collateral

unsecured loan
loan that is a general claim against the assets of the borrower

prime rate
interest rate charged by banks for short-term unsecured loans to a bank's highest-quality business customers

---

2. We say that "in theory" the prime rate is the lowest borrowing rate for unsecured loans because almost everything is negotiable. In fact, many instances have occurred in which large corporate borrowers have negotiated bank loans at interest rates below the prevailing prime rate.

INTERNET ACTIVITY

Go to the Chase Corporation Web site, http://www.chase. com. Find information on types of personal loans and their costs.

2007–2008 financial crisis, the prime rate declined to about 7 percent at the end of 2007 and down to 3.25 percent at the end of 2008. The prime rate continued at 3.25 percent during the 2008–2009 Great Recession and on through 2012.

A loan customarily includes a specified rate of interest such as the prevailing prime rate or prime plus some percentage point amount. For short-term loans, the interest often is paid along with the principal amount of the loan when the loan contract matures. In some instances, a discount loan or note is offered. With a discount loan, the interest is deducted from the stated amount of the note at the time the money is lent. The borrower receives less than the face value of the note but repays the full amount of the note when it matures.

A given discount rate results in a higher cost of borrowing than an interest loan made for the same rate. This is true because, under the discount arrangement, actual money received by the borrower is less although the amount paid for its use is the same. For example, if $5,000 is borrowed on a loan basis at an interest rate of 10 percent for one year, at maturity $5,000 plus $500 interest must be repaid. In general terms, the annual percent cost of borrowing for a one-year loan with interest paid annually is determined in the following way:

Standard Loan:

$$\text{Percent Annual Rate} = \frac{\text{Interest Paid}}{\text{Amount Borrowed}} \times 100 \tag{3.1}$$

For our example, we have:

$$\text{Percent Annual Rate} = \frac{\$500}{\$5,000} \times 100 = .10 \times 100 = 10.0\%$$

In contrast, if the $5,000 is borrowed on a discount basis and the rate is 10 percent, a deduction of $500 from the face value of the note is made and the borrower receives only $4,500. At the end of the year, the borrower repays the face amount of the note, which is $5,000. In general terms, the percent annual rate on a one-year discount loan is calculated as follows:

Discount Loan:

$$\text{Percent Annual Rate} = \frac{\text{Discount Amount}}{\text{Amount Borrowed} - \text{Discount Amount}} \times 100 \tag{3.2}$$

INTERNET ACTIVITY

Go to the St. Louis Federal Reserve Bank's Web site for financial and economic data (referred to as FRED), http:// www.stlouisfed.org, and find current information on the prime rate charged by commercial banks. Click on the Research & Data tab to the right. Click on the FRED Economic Data tab.

For our example, we have:

$$\text{Percent Annual Rate} = \frac{\$500}{\$5,000 - \$500} \times 100 = \frac{\$500}{\$4,500} \times 100 = .111 \times 100 = 11.1\%$$

In the first case, the borrower has paid $500 for the use of $5,000; in the second case, $500 has been paid for the use of only $4,500. The effective rate of interest, therefore, on the discount basis is approximately 11.1 percent compared with the 10 percent paid when the $5,000 was borrowed on a loan basis.

Loans to individuals are an important category for commercial bank lending. Loans to individuals constitute about one-fifth of all bank loans. Credit cards and related loan plans comprise less than half of all bank loans to individuals.

Other Bank Assets

Other bank assets represent about 16 percent of total bank assets. They include bank premises and fixed assets, assets held in trading accounts, and all other assets, including other real estate owned and intangible assets.

As noted, about three-fifths of the assets of commercial banks are in the form of loans, with about one-fourth of assets being held in the form of real estate loans. In contrast, S&Ls and savings banks have about three-quarters of their assets in the form of real estate mortgages and mortgage-backed securities. The assets of credit unions are largely consumer loans with a small percentage in government securities. Some credit unions make home mortgage loans although such mortgage financing typically constitutes a small percentage of their total assets.

LIABILITIES AND OWNERS' CAPITAL

Banks and other depository institutions acquire their capital funds and liabilities from two major sources. Owners' capital or equity represents the initial investment and retained earnings of the owners of the institutions. Liabilities represent the funds owed to depositors and others from whom the bank has borrowed. The most important liability of a depository institution consists of its deposits of various kinds, but you should understand the other liabilities.

Deposits

As can be seen in Figure 3.5, deposits represent about two-thirds of FDIC-insured commercial bank liabilities and owners' capital. Deposits are separated into transactional accounts, which include demand (checking account) deposits and NOW accounts, and nontransactional accounts. Transactional accounts constitute about one-fifth of total deposits, and demand deposits represent over three-fourths of transactional account deposits. Nontransactional accounts comprise three-fifths of total deposits. The remaining components are nondomestic or foreign deposits. Nontransactional accounts are in the form of time and savings deposits, each being about one-half of the total. Money market deposit accounts (MMDAs) represent the largest component of savings accounts.

Most time deposits are **certificates of deposit (CDs)** that have a stated maturity and pay a fixed rate of interest or are sold at a discount. Although records reveal that commercial banks issued certificates of deposit as early as 1900, a major innovation in the early 1960s resulted in a tremendous growth in their importance. Large-denomination CDs for deposits of $100,000 or more were issued in negotiable form, which meant they could be bought and sold. In Chapter 2, we discussed negotiable certificates of deposit (negotiable CDs). The vastly increased use of negotiable CDs in the 1960s caused a secondary market for them to develop. Today, CDs issued by banks and other depository institutions are purchased and sold in the money markets as readily as most forms of debt obligations.

Other Liabilities

The second category of liabilities is represented by items that when combined have smaller dollar significance than that of deposits. Included are federal funds purchased or borrowed from other banks. As discussed in Chapter 2, federal funds are short-term (usually overnight) loans from banks with excess reserves to banks that need to borrow funds to meet minimum reserve requirements. Other borrowed money and liabilities include longer-term notes and debt issues, as well as taxes, interest, and wages owed.

Owners' Capital

The owners' equity capital includes stock, surplus, and undivided profits or retained earnings. At the time a bank is formed, stock is purchased by the owners of the bank or by the public. In the case of credit unions, the members buy shares. Occasionally, additional stock may be sold to accommodate bank expansion. A bank's common stock account reflects the number of shares of stock outstanding times a "par" or stated value per share. The surplus account is used to record separately the difference between the sales price of the stock and the stock's par value.

BANK MANAGEMENT

Banks are managed to make profits and increase the wealth of their owners. However, bank management must consider the interests of depositors and bank regulators. Profitability often can be increased when bank managers take on more risk at the expense of bank safety. The lower the level of bank safety, the greater the likelihood of bank failure. Bank managers must trade off higher profitability objectives against the desire of depositors to maintain the safety of their deposits. Bank regulators try to ensure that bank managers are prudent in their trade-off decisions between profitability and risk or safety.

Banks can fail because of inadequate liquidity or by becoming insolvent. **Bank liquidity** reflects the ability to meet depositor withdrawals and to pay off other liabilities when they come due. The inability to meet withdrawal and debt repayments results in bank failure. **Bank solvency** reflects the ability to keep the value of a bank's assets greater than its liabilities. When the value of a bank's liabilities exceeds its assets, the bank is insolvent and, thus, has failed. However, from a technical standpoint, failure does not take place until depositors or creditors are not paid and, consequently, take legal action. Figure 3.7 illustrates the trade-off involving

certificates of deposit (CDs)
time deposits with a stated maturity and pay a fixed rate of interest or are sold at a discount

CONCEPT CHECK

Which is the largest category of bank assets, and what are some of the components of that category?

Which is the largest category of bank liabilities, and what are some of the components of that category?

bank liquidity
reflects the ability to meet depositor withdrawals and to pay off other liabilities when they come due

bank solvency
reflects the ability to keep the value of a bank's assets greater than its liabilities

FIGURE 3.7

Trade-Off of Profitability Objective Against Bank Liquidity and Bank Solvency

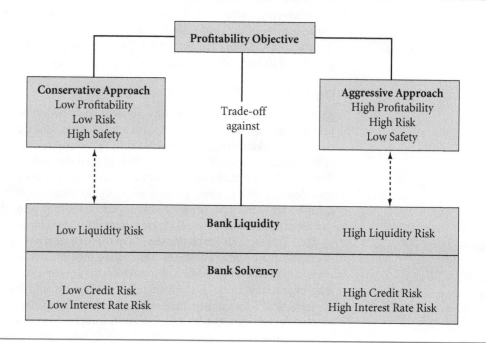

profitability and bank safety or risk. Bank managers manage their bank's riskiness in terms of bank liquidity and bank solvency. We will first discuss bank liquidity management and then cover the issue of bank solvency in terms of capital adequacy management.

LIQUIDITY MANAGEMENT

liquidity risk
likelihood that a bank will be unable to meet its depositor withdrawal demands and/or other liabilities when they are due

Liquidity management is the management of a bank's *liquidity risk*, which is the likelihood that the bank will be unable to meet its depositor withdrawal demands and/or other liabilities when they are due. Figure 3.7 shows that lower liquidity risk is associated with higher bank safety and generally lower bank profits. The opposite is the case when bank managers choose to take on greater liquidity risk to improve profits. In deciding on how much liquidity risk is appropriate, bank managers make asset management and liability management decisions.

Asset Management

A bank needs cash assets to meet depositor withdrawal requests when demanded. However, cash assets do not earn interest for the bank. Thus, the more cash assets are held, the lower the profitability and vice versa. In contrast, banks earn higher interest on loans and on longer-maturity securities investments. However, these types of assets are not easily converted into cash assets, and if converted, the conversion costs can be high. For example, if a loan is sold to another investor, the loan may have to be discounted, sold well below its face value.

primary reserves
vault cash and deposits held at other depository institutions and at Federal Reserve Banks

Let's return to the aggregate bank balance sheet depicted in Figure 3.4. The cash assets of the firm included under the heading "cash and balances due from depository institutions" are considered to be the bank's *primary reserves* to meet liquidity requirements. Vault cash and deposits held at other depository institutions and at Federal Reserve Banks are immediately available. Cash items in process of collection, while not immediate cash, are being converted into cash on an ongoing basis. However, primary reserves do not earn interest, and thus, bank managers want to minimize the amount of primary reserves they hold. FDIC-insured commercial banks hold primary reserves that amount to about 7 percent of total bank assets.

secondary reserves
short-term securities held by banks that are quickly converted into cash at little cost to the banks

To supplement their primary reserves, banks hold secondary reserves to help meet depositor withdrawal demands and other liabilities as they come due. *Secondary reserves* are short-term securities held by banks that are quickly converted into cash at little cost to the banks. For example, the holding of U.S. Treasury bills is an important source of secondary reserves for most banks. Banks would prefer to hold secondary reserves over primary reserves because interest is earned on secondary reserves. On the other hand, secondary reserves are less liquid than cash assets and, thus, provide a little more liquidity risk than do primary reserves. In Figure 3.4, short-term securities and long-term securities are grouped under the heading "securities." As a consequence, we cannot readily estimate the average amount of secondary reserves held by banks.

Remember, banks are in business to make profits for the bank owners. Banks accept deposits from savers and, in turn, make loans to businesses and individuals. Figure 3.4 shows that nearly three-fifths of bank assets are in the form of loans. Bank loans are generally less liquid and have higher risks of default than other bank assets. As a consequence, bank loans offer higher potential profit than do other securities. Thus, after setting primary reserve and secondary reserve targets, banks concentrate on meeting loan demand by individuals and businesses. **Credit (default) risk** is the likelihood that borrowers will not make interest and principal payments. Higher interest rates can be charged to riskier borrowers, but such customers are more likely to default on their loans. Bank managers must trade off the size of their loan portfolios against the amount of credit risk they are willing to assume. The acceptance of higher credit risk increases the likelihood of insolvency.

After primary reserve and secondary reserve targets have been set, loan demand has been met, and bank fixed asset decisions have been made, remaining funds are invested in longer-maturity securities. Included would be U.S. government notes and bonds, state and local government debt securities, and other securities. These are riskier than the short-term securities held as secondary reserves and, thus, offer higher potential profitability that is second only to the potential profitability of bank loans.

credit (default) risk
the likelihood that borrowers will not make interest and principal payments

Liability Management

A bank's liabilities can be managed to help the bank maintain a desired level of liquidity. This is possible because certain types of bank liabilities are sensitive to changes in interest rates. Included would be negotiable certificates of deposit (negotiable CDs), commercial paper, and federal funds. For example, if a bank needs cash to meet unexpected depositor withdrawals, it could immediately attract more liabilities by raising short-term interest rates it will pay on negotiable CDs or by issuing commercial paper at acceptable interest rates being demanded in the marketplace. Likewise, the bank could borrow federal funds from other banks that have excess reserves as long as it is willing to pay that day's interest rate. Recall that federal funds are overnight loans, and the bank may have to reborrow each day for several days to offset liquidity pressures.

Time and savings deposits generally are less sensitive to immediate changes in interest rates and receive less focus from a liability management standpoint. Longer-term debt and bank capital do not work well in terms of liquidity management because of the time it takes for debt and equity securities to be issued or sold.

Liability management is meant to supplement asset management in managing bank liquidity. In banks incurring severe liquidity problems, bank managers may find they are unable to sell their negotiable CDs or commercial paper. Furthermore, if banks pay higher interest rates to sell negotiable CDs, they must find assets to invest in that will provide returns higher than the cost of funds. Otherwise, profitability will suffer.

CONCEPT CHECK

What is meant by asset management by a bank?

How does a bank conduct liability management?

CAPITAL MANAGEMENT

Adequate capital is necessary to ensure banks remain solvent, meet depositor demands, and pay their debts as they come due. A bank is considered solvent as long as its assets are worth more than its liabilities. Let's return to Figure 3.5. Since we know that total assets must equal total liabilities plus owners' capital, the difference between total assets and total liabilities is owners' capital, which reflects the degree of solvency.

What can cause a bank to become insolvent? One reason is that excessive credit risk could result in nonrepayment of loans. For example, if businesses default on the loans they owe to a bank, that bank's assets will decline by the amount of the defaults. If a bank's assets decline enough relative to its liabilities, the bank could become insolvent. In addition to credit risk reasons, a bank may become insolvent because of **interest rate risk**, which is the risk associated with changing market interest rates on the value of underlying debt instruments.[3] For example, let's assume a bank

interest rate risk
the risk associated with changing market interest rates on the value of underlying debt instruments

---

3. There is an inverse relationship between the price or value of debt instruments and interest rates. When market interest rates increase, debt instruments go down in value, and vice versa.

purchases $100 million of long-term U.S. government bonds when interest rates are 6 percent. If interest rates rise, the value of the bonds held as assets will decline. If the decline in the bond value causes the bank's assets to be less than its liabilities, the bank would be insolvent.

Adequate bank capital represents an important cushion against credit risk and interest rate risk as they affect bank solvency. Bank regulators set minimum capital ratio requirements for the banks and other depository institutions that they regulate. A basic equity capital ratio could be defined as owners' or equity capital divided by total assets.

$$\text{Equity Capital Ratio} = \frac{\text{Equity Capital}}{\text{Total Assets}} \times 100 \qquad (3.3)$$

The Equity Capital Ratio for a bank with owners' equity of $3 million and total assets of $50 million would be the following:

$$\text{Equity Capital Ratio} = \$3\text{million} / \$50 \text{ million} = 6\%$$

Bank regulators use other capital ratios. Adjustments often are made to exclude intangible assets such as goodwill, which is created in mergers and acquisitions. A broader view of capital is often used. Banks sometimes hold securities that count as equity capital called trust-preferred securities and provide for loan-loss reserves in the event that loans have to be written off. Tier 1 capital is composed of common equity plus trust-preferred securities minus intangible assets. Tier 2 capital is a bank's loan-loss reserve amount plus other qualifying securities (e.g., subordinated debt and preferred stock) plus net unrealized gains on marketable securities. Total capital is the sum of Tier 1 and Tier 2 capital.

The central banks and other national supervisory authorities of major industrialized countries met in Basel, Switzerland, in mid-1988 (Basel I Accord), in 2003 (Basel II Accord), and again in 2010 (Basel III Accord). The objectives were to improve risk measurement and management of large internationally involved banks and to improve the transparency of bank riskiness to customers and other constituencies. As a result, the Bank for International Settlements (BIS) established capital adequacy requirements for banks with international operations based on the use of risk-weighted assets. The weightings were established as follows:

BANK ASSETS	RISK-WEIGHT (%)
Cash and equivalents	0%
Government securities	0
Interbank loans	20
Mortgage loans	50
Ordinary loans	100
Standby letters of credit	100

INTERNET ACTIVITY

Go to the Board of Governors of the Federal Reserve System's Web site, http://www. federalreserve.gov, and find information on regulation and operations of the banking system. (For starters, click on the Banking Information & Regulation tab.)

Two capital ratios (Tier 1 and Total Capital) are calculated using risk-adjusted assets. They are defined as:

$$\text{Tier 1 Ratio} = \frac{\text{Tier 1 Capital}}{\text{Risk-Adjusted Assets}} \times 100 \qquad (3.4)$$

$$\text{Total Capital Ratio} = \frac{\text{Tier 1 + Tier 2 Capital}}{\text{Risk-Adjusted Assets}} \times 100 \qquad (3.5)$$

Let's assume that a bank has owners' capital of $3 million, trust-preferred securities of $.5 million, and a $1 million loan-loss reserve account. Intangible assets (goodwill) amount to $2 million. In terms of other assets: cash and equivalents = $1 million; government securities = $2 million; interbank loans = $5 million; mortgage loans = $20 million; ordinary loans = $18 million; and standby letters of credit = $2 million.

Tier 1 capital = $3 million in owners' equity + $.5 million in trust-preferred securities − $2 million in intangible assets, or $1.5 million. Total capital = Tier 1 capital of $1.5 million + $1.0 million in loan-loss reserves, or $2.5 million. Risk-adjusted assets are the following:

INTERNET ACTIVITY

Go to the Small Business Administration's Web site, http://www.sba.gov. Find information about small business lending in the United States and write a brief summary.

Cash and equivalents	=	$1 million	×	0.00	=	$0 million
Government securities	=	$2 million	×	0.00	=	$0 million
Interbank loans	=	$5 million	×	0.20	=	$1 million
Mortgage loans	=	$20 million	×	0.50	=	$10 million
Ordinary loans	=	$18 million	×	1.00	=	$18 million
Standby letters of credit	=	$2 million	×	1.00	=	$2 million
Risk-adjusted assets	=					$31 million

The Tier 1 and Total Capital ratios are calculated as follows:

$$\text{Tier 1 Ratio} = \frac{\$1.5 \text{ million}}{\$31 \text{ million}} \times 100 = .0484 \times 100 = 4.84\%$$

$$\text{Total Capital Ratio} = \frac{\$2.5 \text{ million}}{\$31 \text{ million}} \times 100 = .0806 \times 100 = 8.06\%$$

CONCEPT CHECK

How are the primary capital and the total capital ratios calculated?

What are the Basel Accords?

How does the FDIC use risk-based capital ratios?

To be considered to be "adequately capitalized," a bank needs to have a 4 percent Tier 1 capital ratio and an 8 percent Total Capital (Tier 1 plus Tier 2) ratio. U.S. bank regulatory authorities adopted these ratio requirements.

Bank managers have a strong incentive to meet minimum capital ratio requirements. Banks that are classified as being undercapitalized by the FDIC must submit plans to the FDIC indicating how they intend to become adequately capitalized. Significantly undercapitalized banks may be required to replace their managers and even their board of directors, as well as restructure their balance sheets. Critically undercapitalized banks must restructure and may be seized by the FDIC.

The 2007–2008 financial crisis impacted many countries throughout the world causing great concern that the international financial system might collapse, Underperforming mortgages and mortgage-related securities became referred to as "troubled assets" or "toxic assets." Banks and other holders of these securities were forced to "write down" the values of these assets to reflect their new market values. This, in turn, reduced their bank capital ratios to unacceptable levels.

As a result, global banking regulators passed Basel III in late 2010 that requires banks throughout the world to keep much larger capital reserves to be held to protect against possible losses. Basel III provides for the current Tier 1 capital ratio to increase from 2 percent to 7 percent by 2019 with initial increases slated to begin in 2013. However, due to the unknown impact of such large increases in bank capital requirements, delays are occurring in the implementation of Basel III.

INTERNATIONAL BANKING AND FOREIGN SYSTEMS

Banks with headquarters in one country may open offices or branches in other countries. When banks operate in more than one country, we call this *international banking*. European banks dominated international banking until the 1960s when world trade began expanding rapidly and multinational corporations increased in number and size. As a response to these and other developments involving international trade, American banks began opening offices in foreign countries and establishing correspondent banking arrangements with foreign banks. In essence, as U.S. corporations began expanding their operations in other countries, the American banks with which they were working followed them. Likewise, the growing importance of the U.S. dollar in international transactions and the movement by foreign corporations to invest in the United States resulted in foreign banks opening offices in the United States. Today, U.S. banks are actively involved throughout the world with major operations in Europe, Asia, and Latin America, and foreign banks have opened hundreds of offices in the United States.

GLOBAL DISCUSSION

international banking when banks operate in more than one country

Banking in the United States has traditionally been highly regulated to protect depositor funds and to maintain citizen confidence in the U.S. banking system. European and most other countries generally have adopted less restrictive approaches to bank regulation. This led to a competitive disadvantage for U.S. domestic banks relative to foreign-owned banks. The result was the passage of the International Banking Act (IBA) of 1978, which was intended to provide a level playing field for all banks. Some of the provisions included restricting foreign banks in terms of their U.S. interstate banking activities and giving authority to the Fed to impose reserve requirements on foreign banks. Rules against nonbanking operations for U.S. banks were extended to foreign banks operating in the United States. Congress strengthened regulations relating to foreign banks by enacting the Foreign Bank Supervision Enhancement Act in 1991. This Act requires that the Fed give its approval before foreign banks can open offices in the United States and requires that the Fed examine U.S. offices of foreign banks each year.

While most countries have central banking systems that operate much like the U.S. Federal Reserve System, some countries allow their banks to engage in commercial and investment banking. This is called *universal banking*. As noted earlier in the chapter, Germany is a universal banking country. Its largest banks participate in both types of banking. The United Kingdom does not restrict its banks from engaging in commercial and investment banking. However, British banks traditionally have been either "clearing banks," which are similar to U.S. commercial banks, or "merchant banks," which are similar to U.S. investment banks. In recent years, some British clearing banks have formed subsidiaries to perform a wide range of investment banking activities. Likewise, merchant banks are expanding beyond investment banking. As a result, banking consolidations are taking place, and the United Kingdom is moving more toward universal banking. Commercial banking and investment banking are separated in Japan much as in the United States.

German banks are allowed to own shares of stock in German firms and are permitted to vote those shares. Japanese banks are allowed to own common stock in their business customer firms, as well as to engage in various cross holdings of stock involving other Japanese firms and banks. United Kingdom banks are not actively involved with the firms they conduct business with. While stock ownership in business firms by banks is not restricted in the United Kingdom, British banks are generally risk averse to ownership of common stock.

CONCEPT CHECK

What is international banking, and why has it grown in importance?

What is universal banking, and which country has important universal banks?

APPLYING FINANCE TO. . .

INSTITUTIONS AND MARKETS

Commercial banks, insurance companies, pension funds, and mutual funds play important roles in getting the savings of individuals into the hands of business firms so investments can be made to maintain and grow the businesses. Thrift institutions (savings and loans, savings banks, and credit unions) along with commercial banks comprise the banking system and help with the financial functions of creating money and transferring money, which is conducted largely through a highly efficient check processing or clearing system. In contrast with commercial banks, while thrift institutions accept the savings of individuals, they focus on lending to individuals, who want to purchase durable goods and homes.

INVESTMENTS

Bank loans to businesses and other debt obligations such as small CDs originate in the primary debt obligations market. However, since they are specific arrangements with business borrowers and depositors, these debt obligations do not trade in a secondary debt obligations market. Rather, business loans and small CDs are usually held to maturity, and loans are repaid and depositors redeem their CDs. Investment banking firms and brokerage houses help businesses market their new debt and equity securities issues so funds can be raised in addition to those provided by banks.

FINANCIAL MANAGEMENT

Financial managers borrow from commercial banks and depend on the banking system to help support day-to-day operating activities involving producing and selling their products and services. Materials must be purchased from suppliers and are usually paid for by writing checks. Sales made to consumers are often paid by check. Business firms depend on the banking system having a highly efficient check clearing system so cash outflows and inflows can be reasonably balanced. Financial managers rely on mutual funds, insurance companies, and pension funds to buy their new security issues.

SUMMARY

This chapter began with a review of the financial institutions that currently play major roles in the financial system. We provided an overview of the banking system followed by a comparison of commercial banking, investment banking, and universal banking. We discussed the five current functions of banks and the banking system: accepting deposits, granting loans, issuing checkable deposit accounts, clearing checks, and creating deposit money. A sixth function, investment banking, was added when the United States moved to universal banking.

We presented a review of the historical development of the U.S. banking system. Banking prior to the Civil War was described first, followed by how and when thrift institutions entered the banking system. Legislation passed to govern the banking system and to protect depositors' funds was then covered.

Our attention turned to the structure and operation of U.S. banks. Banks may obtain state or federal charters, which makes the United States a dual banking system. Individual states have the authority to decide whether banks can operate branches in their states. Today, most states permit statewide branching although a few states have limited branch banking laws that restrict branching to a specified geographical area such as a county. Banks may be independently owned or owned by either a one-bank holding company (OBHC) or a multibank holding company (MBHC).

A bank's balance sheet is composed of assets that equal its liabilities and owners' capital. Bank assets are primarily in the form of cash and balances due from depository institutions, securities, loans, and fixed assets. Most assets are held in the form of loans.

A bank's liabilities are primarily in the form of deposits that may take the form of transaction accounts, such as demand deposits or nontransactional accounts, which are time and savings deposits. Owners' capital is provided through the purchase of common stock or by retaining profits in the bank.

Bank management involves the trade-off of potential profitability against bank safety. Banks can fail because of inadequate bank liquidity or because of bank insolvency. Bank liquidity is the ability to meet depositor withdrawals and to pay debts as they come due. Bank solvency reflects the ability to maintain the value of the bank's assets above the value of its liabilities. Liquidity management is practiced in terms of asset management and liability management. Capital management focuses on maintaining adequate bank capital relative to assets to protect the bank against insolvency and liquidity risk.

The development of international banking and some examples of foreign banking systems compared to the U.S. banking system were described in the last section of the chapter.

KEY TERMS

bank liquidity	financial intermediations	mutual fund
bank solvency	Glass-Steagall Act of 1933	one-bank holding companies (OBHCs)
banking system	Gramm-Leach-Bliley Act of 1999	pension funds
brokerage firms	insurance companies	primary reserves
certificates of deposit (CDs)	interest rate risk	prime rate
commercial bank	international banking	savings bank
contractual savings organizations	investment bank	savings and loan associations (S&Ls)
credit (default) risk	investment banking firms	secondary reserves
credit unions	investment companies	secured loan
depository institutions	limited branch banking	securities firms
Dodd-Frank Wall Street Reform and Consumer Protection Act	liquidity risk	statewide branch banking
	mortgage	thrift institutions
dual banking system	mortgage-backed security	unit banking
finance companies	mortgage banking firms	universal bank
finance firms	multibank holding companies (MBHCs)	unsecured loan

DISCUSSION QUESTIONS

1. Discuss how and why banks suffered financial difficulties during the financial crisis.

2. Describe the major financial institutions engaged in getting the savings of individuals into business firms that want to make investments to maintain and grow their firms.

3. Compare commercial banking with investment banking. What is universal banking?

4. Describe the functions of banks and the banking system.

5. Describe the three basic ways for processing or collecting a check in the United States.

6. How did the First Bank of the United States serve the nation? Briefly describe why the Second Bank of the United States was chartered.

7. Briefly describe why and when thrift institutions were founded.

8. Why was it considered necessary to create the Federal Reserve System when we had the benefits of the National Banking Act?

9. Comment on the objectives of the Depository Institutions Deregulation and Monetary Control Act of 1980 (DIDMCA).

10. Why was the Garn-St. Germain Depository Institutions Act thought to be necessary?

11. Why was the Dodd-Frank Wall Street Reform and Consumer Protection Act passed?

12. Describe the reasons for the savings and loan crisis that occurred during the 1980s.

13. Briefly describe the purpose of the Financial Institutions Reform, Recovery, and Enforcement Act (FIRREA) of 1989. Indicate the purpose of the Resolution Trust Corporation (RTC).

14. How are depositors' funds protected today in the United States?

15. Describe the structure of banks in terms of bank charters, branch banking, and bank holding companies.

16. What are the major asset categories for banks? Identify the most important category. What are a bank's major liabilities and which category is the largest in size?

17. What is meant by bank liquidity and bank solvency?

18. Describe how assets are managed in terms of a bank's liquidity risk. Briefly describe how liquidity management is used to help manage liquidity risk.

19. Describe what is meant by liquidity risk, credit risk, and interest rate risk.

20. Define and describe the following terms: equity capital ratio, tier 1 ratio, and total capital ratio. How are these used by bank regulators?

21. What are the Basel Accords, and what is their purpose?

22. Define international banking. Describe how some foreign banking systems differ from the U.S. banking system.

EXERCISES

1. Go to http://www.stlouisfed.org and identify sources and uses of funds for commercial banks. (Try typing "commercial banks" in the Search box.)

2. You are the treasurer of a midsize industrial manufacturer. Your firm's cash balances vary between $300,000 and $1,000,000. During the last three board meetings, a board member has asked how you protect this cash while it is being lodged in banks or other temporary facilities. Your problem is to satisfy the board member, obtain some income from the cash or cash equivalent balances, and have funds available for immediate payout if required. What course of action do you follow?

3. You and three other staff members of the U.S. Office of Comptroller of the Currency (OCC) have been assigned identical projects. You are to review the articles that have been written, the speeches made, and in general, the suggestions that have been offered to revamp the structure of the FDIC to render it more stable and financially able to withstand adverse events. Based on the few suggestions offered in this chapter and your own ideas, what is your conclusion?

4. You are the mayor of a community of 12,000 people. You are active in nearly all of the civic activities of the town, and as such, your opinion is solicited on political, economic, sociological, and other factors. You have been asked by one of the civic groups to comment on the implications for the community of a prospective purchase of

the largest local commercial bank by an out-of-state bank holding company. What is your response?

5. Banks provide checking account services, accept savings deposits, and lend to borrowers. In other words, they are in the money business. We all have heard stories of banks or their partner firms "misplacing" or "losing" bags of money. Lending rates are subject to change periodically. Both of these situations can produce ethical dilemmas or decisions. How would you react to the following scenarios?

a. You are walking down the street and see a large money bag with "First National Bank" printed on it. The bag is sitting on the sidewalk in front of a local office of First National Bank. You are considering whether to pick up the bag, check its contents, and find the owner. Alternatively, you could pick up the money bag and take it to the local police station or return it directly to the bank. What would you do?

b. You are a loan officer of First National Bank. The owner of a small business has come into the bank today and is requesting an immediate $100,000 loan for which she has appropriate collateral. You know the bank is going to reduce its lending interest rate to small businesses next week. You could make the loan or inform the small business owner she could get a lower rate if the loan request is delayed. What would you do?

PROBLEMS

1. The following three one-year "discount" loans are available to you:

Loan A: $120,000 at a 7 percent discount rate
Loan B: $110,000 at a 6 percent discount rate
Loan C: $130,000 at a 6.5 percent discount rate

a. Determine the dollar amount of interest you would pay on each loan and indicate the amount of net proceeds each loan would provide. Which loan would provide you with the most upfront money when the loan takes place?

b. Calculate the percent interest rate or effective cost of each loan. Which one has the lowest cost?

2. Assume that you can borrow $175,000 for one year from a local commercial bank.

a. The bank loan officer offers you the loan if you agree to pay $16,000 in interest plus repay the $175,000 at the end of one year. What is the percent interest rate or effective cost?

b. As an alternative you could get a one-year, $175,000 discount loan at 9 percent interest. What is the percent interest rate or effective cost?

c. Which one of the two loans would you prefer?

d. At what discount loan interest rate would you be indifferent between the two loans?

3. ABE Banc has the following asset categories:

Cash	$1 million
Securities	$4 million
Loans	?
Other assets	$2 million
Total assets	?

a. What would be the bank's total assets if loans were twice the size of the amount of securities?

b. If total assets were $12 million, what would be the amount of the loans?

c. If total assets were $11 million and $1 million of securities were sold with the proceeds placed in the cash account, what would be the amount of the loans?

4. ATM Banc has the following liabilities and equity categories:

Deposits	$9 million
Other liabilities	$4 million
Owners' capital	?
Total liabilities and capital	?

a. What would be the bank's total liabilities and capital if owners' capital were half the size of other liabilities?

b. If total liabilities and capital were $15.5 million, what would be the amount of the owners' capital?

c. If total liabilities and capital were $14 million and $1 million of deposits were withdrawn from the bank, what would be the amount of the owners' capital?

5. The following are selected balance sheet accounts for Third State Bank: vault cash = $2 million; U.S. government securities = $5 million; demand deposits = $13 million; nontransactional accounts = $20 million; cash items in process of collection = $4 million; loans to individuals = $7 million; loans secured by real estate = $9 million; federal funds purchased = $4 million; and bank premises = $11 million.

a. From these accounts, select only the asset accounts and calculate the bank's total assets.

b. Calculate the total liabilities for Third State Bank.

c. Based on the totals for assets and liabilities, determine the amount in the owners' capital account.

6. A bank's assets consist of the following:

Cash	$1.5 million
Loans	$10 million
Securities	$4.5 million
Fixed assets	$2 million

In addition, the bank's owners' capital is $1.5 million.

a. Calculate the equity capital ratio.

b. If $2 million in bad loans were removed from the bank's assets, show how the equity capital ratio would change.

7. Rearrange the following accounts to construct a bank balance sheet for Second National Bank. What are the total amounts that make the bank's balance sheet balance?

Demand deposits: $20 million	Government securities owned: $7 million
Cash assets: $5 million	Bank fixed assets: $14 million
Loans secured by real estate: $30 million	Time and savings deposits: $40 million
Commercial and industrial loans: $18 million	Federal funds purchased: $6 million
Owners' capital: $6 million	Other long-term liabilities: $2 million

8. Use the data from Problem 7 for Second National Bank and calculate the equity capital ratio.

9. Tenth National Bank has common stock of $2 million, retained earnings of $5 million, loan loss reserves of $3 million, and subordinated notes outstanding in the amount of $4 million. Total bank assets are $105 million. Calculate the equity capital ratio.

10. Let's assume you have been asked to calculate risk-based capital ratios for a bank with the following accounts:

Cash = $5 million
Government securities = $7 million

Mortgage loans = $30 million
Other loans = $50 million
Fixed assets = $10 million
Intangible assets = $4 million
Loan-loss reserves = $5 million
Owners' equity = $5 million
Trust-preferred securities = $3 million

Cash assets and government securities are not considered risky. Loans secured by real estate have a 50 percent weighting factor. All other loans have a 100 percent weighting factor in terms of riskiness.

a. Calculate the equity capital ratio.

b. Calculate the Tier 1 Ratio using risk-adjusted assets.

c. Calculate the Total Capital Ratio using risk-adjusted assets. (Total capital = Tier 1 plus Tier 2.)

11. **Challenge Problem** This problem focuses on bank capital management and various capital ratio measures. The following are recent balance sheet accounts for Prime First National Bank.

Cash assets	$17 million	Demand deposits	$50 million
Loans secured by real estate	40	Time & savings deposits	66
Commercial loans	45	Federal funds purchased	15
Government securities owned	16	Trust-preferred securities	2
Goodwill	5		
Bank fixed assets	15	Owners' capital	5
Total assets	$138 million	Total liabilities and owners' capital	$138 million

Note: The bank has loan-loss reserves of $10 million. The real estate and commercial loans shown on the balance sheet are net of the loan-loss reserves.

a. Calculate the equity capital ratio. How could the bank increase its equity capital ratio?

b. Risk-adjusted assets are estimated using the following weightings process: cash and government securities = .00; real estate loans = .50; commercial and other loans = 1.00.

Calculate the risk-adjusted assets amount for the bank.

c. Calculate the Tier 1 Ratio based on the information provided and the risk-adjusted assets estimate from Part b.

d. Calculate the Total Capital Ratio based on the information provided and the risk-adjusted assets estimate from Part b. (Total capital = Tier 1 plus Tier 2.)

e. What actions could the bank management team take to improve the bank's Tier 1 and Total Capital ratios?

• CHAPTER 4 •

The Federal Reserve System

Chapter Learning Objectives . . .

AFTER STUDYING THIS CHAPTER, YOU SHOULD BE ABLE TO DO THE FOLLOWING:

- Discuss how the Federal Reserve responded to the recent financial crisis and Great Recession.
- Identify three weaknesses of the national banking system that existed before the Federal Reserve System.
- Describe Federal Reserve membership in terms of who must join and who may join.
- Describe the composition of the Fed's Board of Governors.
- Discuss how the Fed uses reserve requirements to carry out monetary policy.
- Discuss how discount rate policy is employed by the Fed.
- Describe the Fed's use of open-market operations to alter bank reserves.
- Describe the ways in which the Reserve Banks accommodate the clearance and collection of checks.
- Discuss structural characteristics of central banks located in selected foreign countries.

Where We Have Been . . .

In Chapter 3, we discussed the types and roles of financial institutions that have evolved in the United States to meet the needs of individuals and businesses and help the financial system operate efficiently. We described the traditional differences between commercial banking and investment banking followed by coverage of the functions of banks (all depository institutions) and the banking system. By now you should have an understanding of the structure and chartering of commercial banks, the availability of branch banking, and the use of bank holding companies. You should have a basic understanding of the bank balance sheet and how the bank management process is carried out in terms of liquidity and capital management. We provided selected information on international banking and several foreign banking systems.

Where We Are Going . . .

The last two chapters in Part 1 address the role of policy makers in the financial system and how international trade and finance influence the U.S. financial system. In Chapter 5, you will have the opportunity to review economic objectives that direct policy-making activities. We will briefly review fiscal policy and how it is administered through taxation and expenditure plans. This is followed by a discussion of the policy instruments employed by the U.S. Treasury and how the Treasury carries out its debt management activities. You will see how the money supply is changed by the banking system, as well as develop an understanding of the factors that affect bank reserves. We will also describe and discuss the monetary base and the money multiplier. Chapter 6 focuses on how currency exchange rates are determined and how international trade is financed.

How This Chapter Applies to Me . . .

Actions taken by the Fed impact your ability to borrow money and the cost or interest rate on that money. When the Fed is taking an easy monetary stance, the availability of money and its cost will be lower. Such an action, in turn, will likely result in lower interest rates on your credit card, your new automobile loan, and possibly your interest rate on a new mortgage loan. Actions by the Fed influence economic activity and the type and kind of job opportunities that may be available to you. For example, a tightening of monetary policy in an effort to control inflation may lead to an economic slowdown.

While many individuals know that the Federal Reserve System (Fed) is the central bank of the United States, what the Fed does and how it operates are less clear. Stephen H. Axilrod comments:

> There must be almost as many images of the Fed as an institution and of the wellsprings of its actions as there are viewers. Mine, born of a particular experience, is a generally benign one. It is of an unbiased, honest, straightforward institution that quite seriously and carefully carries out its congressionally given mandates. . . . It is of course through the window of monetary policy that the public chiefly sees and judges the Fed.[1]

This chapter focuses on understanding the structure and functions of the Fed. Chapter 5 describes how the Fed administers monetary policy in cooperation with fiscal policy and Treasury operations to carry out the nation's economic objectives.

FINANCIAL CRISIS

Federal Reserve System (Fed)
U.S. central bank that sets monetary policy and regulates banking system

Federal National Mortgage Association (Fannie Mae)
created to support the financial markets by purchasing home mortgages from banks and thus freeing the proceeds that could be lent to other borrowers.

Government National Mortgage Association (Ginnie Mae)
created to issue its own debt securities to obtain funds that are invested in mortgages made to low-income to moderate-income home purchasers.

Federal Home Loan Mortgage Corporation (Freddie Mac)
formed to aid mortgage markets by purchasing and holding mortgage loans.

U.S. CENTRAL BANK RESPONSE TO THE FINANCIAL CRISIS AND GREAT RECESSION

As previously noted, the 2007–2008 financial crisis and the 2008–2009 Great Recession combined to create a "perfect financial storm." Many government officials, politicians, financial institution executives, and business professionals felt during the midst of the financial storm in 2008 that the U.S. and world financial systems were on the verge of collapse. The **Federal Reserve System (Fed)**, the central bank of the United States, is responsible for setting monetary policy and regulating the banking system. Direct actions and involvement by the Fed were critical in government and related institutional efforts to avoid financial collapse.

The federal government has historically played an active role in encouraging home ownership by supporting liquid markets for home mortgages. If banks and other lenders originate home mortgages and then "hold" the mortgages, new mortgage funds are not readily available. However, when banks and other lenders are able to sell their mortgages in a secondary mortgage market to other investors, the proceeds from the sales can be used to make new mortgage loans. In 1938, the president and Congress created the **Federal National Mortgage Association (FNMA or Fannie Mae)** to support the financial markets by purchasing home mortgages from banks and thus freeing funds that could be lent to other borrowers. Fannie Mae was converted to a government-sponsored enterprise (GSE), or "privatized," in 1968 by making it a public, investor-owned company. The **Government National Mortgage Association (GNMA or Ginnie Mae)** was created in 1968 as a government-owned corporation. Ginnie Mae issues its own debt securities to obtain funds that are invested in mortgages made to low-income to moderate-income home purchasers. The **Federal Home Loan Mortgage Corporation (FHLMC or Freddie Mac)** was formed in 1970 also as a government-owned corporation to aid the mortgage markets by purchasing and holding mortgage loans. In 1989, Freddie Mac also became a GSE when it became a public, investor-owned company.

Ginnie Mae and Fannie Mae issue mortgage-backed securities to fund their mortgage purchases and holdings. Ginnie Mae purchases Federal Housing Administration (FHA) and Veterans Affairs (VA) federally insured mortgages, packages them into mortgage-backed securities, which are sold to investors. Ginnie Mae guarantees the payment of interest and principal on the mortgages held in the pool. Fannie Mae purchases individual mortgages or mortgage pools from financial institutions and packages or repackages them into mortgage-backed securities as ways to aid development of the secondary mortgage markets. Freddie Mac purchases and holds mortgage loans.

As housing prices continued to increase, these mortgage activities by Ginnie Mae, Fannie Mae, and Freddie Mac aided the government's goal of increased home ownership. However, after the housing price bubble burst in mid-2006 and housing-related jobs declined sharply, the ability of mortgage borrowers to meet interest and principal payments became more difficult causing the values of mortgage-backed securities to decline sharply. Fannie Mae and Freddie Mac held large amounts of low quality, subprime mortgages which had higher likelihoods of loan defaults and worsened housing-related developments. As default rates on these mortgage loans increased,

---

1. Stephen H. Axilrod, *Inside the Fed*, Cambridge: The MIT Press, 2009, p. 159.

Fannie Mae and Freddie Mac suffered cash and liquidity crises. To avoid a meltdown, the Federal Reserve provided rescue funds in July 2008 and, in September 2008, the U.S. government assumed control of both firms.

The Fed, sometimes along with the help of the U.S. Treasury, helped a number of financial institutions (on the verge of failing because of the collapse of the values of mortgage-backed securities) merge with other firms. Examples included the Fed's efforts in aiding the March 2008 acquisition of Bear Stearns by the JP Morgan Chase & Co. bank and the 2008 sale of Merrill Lynch to Bank of America . However, Lehman Brothers, a major investment bank, was allowed to fail in September 2008. Shortly after the Lehman bankruptcy and the Merrill sale, American International Group (AIG), the largest insurance firm in the United States, was "bailed out" by the Federal Reserve with the U.S. government receiving an ownership interest in AIG. Like Merrill Lynch, Fannie Mae, and Freddie Mac, AIG was considered "too big to fail" due to its potential impact on the global financial markets.

In addition to direct intervention, the Fed engaged in quantitative easing actions to help avoid a financial system collapse in 2008 and to stimulate economic growth after the 2008–2009 Great Recession. We will discuss the Fed's quantitative easing actions later in the chapter.

CONCEPT CHECK

Who are some of the institutional participants in the mortgage markets?

What actions did the Fed take to help avoid a financial system collapse?

THE U.S. BANKING SYSTEM PRIOR TO THE FED

In Chapter 1, when we discussed the characteristics of an effective financial system, we said that one basic requirement was the need for a monetary system that efficiently carried out the financial functions of creating and transferring money. While we have an efficient monetary system today, this was not always the case. To understand the importance of the Federal Reserve System (Fed), we will briefly review the weaknesses of the banking system that gave rise to the establishment of the Fed. National Banking Acts passed in 1863 and 1864 provided for the National Banking System. Banks could receive national charters, capital and reserve requirements on deposits and banknotes were established, and banknotes could be issued only against U.S. government securities owned by the banks but held with the U.S. Treasury. These banknotes, backed by government securities, were supposed to provide citizens with a safe and stable national currency. Improved bank supervision was provided for with the establishment of the Office of the Comptroller of the Currency (OCC) under the control of the U.S. Treasury.

WEAKNESSES OF THE NATIONAL BANKING SYSTEM

Although the National Banking System overcame many of the weaknesses of the prior systems involving state banks, it lacked the ability to carry out other central banking system activities that are essential to a successful operating financial system. Three essential needs or requirements include an efficient national payments system, an elastic or flexible money supply that can respond to changes in the demand for money, and a lending/borrowing mechanism to help alleviate liquidity problems when they arise. The first two requirements relate directly to the transferring and creating money functions. The third requirement relates to the need to maintain adequate bank liquidity. Recall from Chapter 3 that we referred to bank liquidity as the ability to meet depositor withdrawals and to pay other liabilities as they come due. All three of these needs were deficient until the Fed was established.

INTERNET ACTIVITY

Go to the Federal Reserve Board of Governors' Web site, http://www.federalreserve.gov. Click on Economic Research & Data. Click on Data Download Program (under Interactive Tools and Guides) and click on "All statistical releases" near the top left. Identify the amount of bank reserves and note any recent changes.

The payments system under the National Banking Acts was based on an extensive network of banks with correspondent banking relationships. It was costly to transfer funds from region to region, and the check clearing and collection processes sometimes were quite long. Checks written on little-known banks located in out-of-the-way places often were discounted or were redeemed at less than face value. For example, let's assume that a check written from an account at a little-known bank in the western region of the United States was sent to pay a bill owed to a firm in the eastern region. When the firm presented the check to its local bank, the bank might record an amount less than the check's face value in the firm's checking account. The amount of the discount was to cover the cost of getting the check cleared and presented for collection to the bank located in the western region. Today, checks are processed or cleared quickly and with little cost throughout the U.S. banking system. Recall from Chapter 3 that the current U.S. payments system allows checks to be processed directly or indirectly. The indirect clearing process can involve the use of bank clearinghouses as discussed in Chapter 3 or a Federal Reserve Bank. The role of the Fed in processing checks is discussed in this chapter.

A second weakness of the banking system under the National Banking Acts was that the money supply could not be easily expanded or contracted to meet changing seasonal needs and/or changes in economic activity. As noted, banknotes could be issued only to the extent that they were backed by U.S. government securities. Note issues were limited to 90 percent of the par value, as stated on the face of the bond, or the market value of the bonds, whichever was lower. When bonds sold at prices considerably above their par value, the advantage of purchasing bonds as a basis to issue notes was eliminated.[2]

For example, if a $1,000 par value bond was available for purchase at a price of $1,100, the banks would not be inclined to make such a purchase since a maximum of $900 in notes could be issued against the bond, in this case 90 percent of par value. The interest that the bank could earn from the use of the $900 in notes would not be great enough to offset the high price of the bond. When government bonds sold at par or at a discount, on the other hand, the potential earning power of the note issues would be quite attractive and banks would be encouraged to purchase bonds for note issue purposes. The volume of national banknotes, and thus the money supply, depended on the government bond market rather than the seasonal or cyclical needs of the nation for currency.

A third weakness of the National Banking System involved the arrangement for holding reserves and the lack of a central authority that could lend to banks when they had temporary liquidity problems. A large part of the reserve balances of banks was held as deposits with large city banks, in particular with large New York City banks. Banks outside of the large cities were permitted to keep part of their reserves with their large city bank correspondents. Certain percentages of deposits had to be retained in their own vaults. These were the only alternatives for holding reserve balances. During periods of economic stress, the position of these large city banks was precarious because they had to meet the demand for deposit withdrawals by their own customers as well as by the smaller banks. The frequent inability of the large banks to meet such deposit withdrawal demands resulted in hardship for the smaller banks whose reserves they held. A mechanism for providing loans to banks to help them weather short-term liquidity problems is crucial to a functional banking system.

THE MOVEMENT TO CENTRAL BANKING

central bank
federal government agency that facilitates the operation of the financial system and regulates money supply growth

A ***central bank*** is a government-established organization responsible for supervising and regulating the banking system and for creating and regulating the money supply. While central bank activities may differ somewhat from country to country, central banks typically play an important role in a country's payments system. A central bank commonly lends money to its member banks, holds its own reserves, and is responsible for creating money.

Even though the shortcomings of the National Banking System in terms of the payments system, inflexible money supply, and illiquidity were known, opposition to a strong central banking system still existed in the United States during the late 1800s. The vast western frontiers and the local independence of the southern areas during this period created distrust of centralized financial control. This distrust deepened when many of the predatory practices of large corporate combinations were being made public by legislative commissions and investigations around the turn of the century.

CONCEPT CHECK

What were the three main deficiencies associated with the national banking system prior to the establishment of the Fed?

What types of functions and activities do central banks usually perform?

The United States was one of the last major industrial nations to adopt a permanent system of central banking. However, many financial and political leaders had long recognized the advantages of such a system. These supporters of central banking were given a big boost by the 1907 financial panic. The central banking system, adopted by the United States under the Federal Reserve Act of 1913 was a compromise between the system of independently owned banks in this country and the single central bank systems of such countries as Canada, Great Britain, and Germany. This compromise took the form of a series of central banks, each representing a specific region of the United States. The assumption was that each central bank would be more responsive to the particular financial problems of its region.

---

2. A bond's price will differ from its stated or face value if the interest rate required in the marketplace is different from the interest rate stated on the bond certificate. In Chapter 10, we will discuss bond valuation calculations.

STRUCTURE OF THE FEDERAL RESERVE SYSTEM

The Federal Reserve System (Fed) is the central bank of the United States and is responsible for setting monetary policy and regulating the banking system. The Fed did not replace the system that existed under the National Banking Acts of 1863 and 1864 but rather was superimposed on the National Banking System created by these acts. Certain provisions of the National Banking Acts, however, were modified to permit greater flexibility of operations.

The Fed system consists of five components:

1. Member banks
2. Federal Reserve District Banks
3. Board of Governors
4. Federal Open Market Committee (FOMC)
5. Advisory committees

These five components are depicted in Figure 4.1.

MEMBER BANKS

The Federal Reserve Act of 1913 provided that all national banks were to become members of the Fed. In addition, state-chartered banks were permitted to join the system if they could show evidence of a satisfactory financial condition. The Federal Reserve Act required that all member banks purchase capital stock of the Federal Reserve Bank (Reserve Bank) of their district up to a maximum of 6 percent of their paid-in capital and surplus. In practice, however, member banks

FIGURE 4.1
Organization of the Federal Reserve System

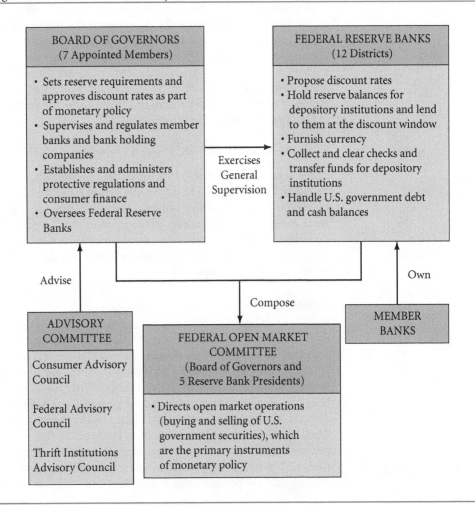

SMALL BUSINESS PRACTICE
Commercial Banks as Providers of Small Business Credit

The 1980s and 1990s were difficult for the banking industry in the United States. Many savings and loan associations (S&Ls) failed, and many mergers involving S&Ls and commercial banks occurred. Furthermore, many of the consolidations involved small commercial banks that traditionally tended to specialize in small business lending. As a result, concern has been expressed about where, or even whether, small businesses will able to obtain loans and other forms of business credit.

In contrast, the first part of the decade of the 2000s was characterized by Fed monetary policy that emphasized liquidity and low interest rates in an effort to stimulate economic recovery after the dot.com and the tech bubbles burst at the beginning of the decade and in reaction to the September 11, 2001, terrorist attack. Even after the U.S. economy began recovering, the Fed maintained an easy monetary policy. Then came the real estate housing price bubble burst, followed by the 2007–2008 financial crisis and 2008–2009 Great Recession. During the crisis, the availability of bank loans for small businesses nearly dried up. There now is an ongoing effort to encourage banks to increase the availability of loan funds to small businesses.

have had to pay only 3 percent; the remainder is subject to call at the discretion of the Fed. Member banks are limited to a maximum of 6 percent dividends on the stock of the Reserve Bank that they hold. The Reserve Banks, therefore, are private institutions owned by the many member banks of the Fed.

State-chartered banks are permitted to withdraw from membership with the Fed six months after written notice has been submitted to the Reserve Bank of their district. In such cases, the stock originally purchased by the withdrawing member is canceled and a refund is made for all money paid in.

Approximately 3,500, or about one-third, of the nation's commercial banks are members of the Fed. This includes all commercial banks with national charters plus roughly one-fifth of the state-chartered banks. These member banks hold approximately three-fourths of the deposits of all commercial banks. National banks control about three-fifths of the total assets of all FDIC-insured commercial banks, and the state-chartered banks that belong to the Fed control another one-fourth of total assets. Even these figures understate the importance of the Federal Reserve in the nation's financial system. As indicated in Chapter 3, the Depository Institutions Deregulation and Monetary Control Act of 1980 generally eliminated distinctions between banks that are members of the Fed and other depository institutions by applying comparable reserve and reporting requirements to all these institutions.

FEDERAL RESERVE DISTRICT BANKS

The Federal Reserve Act of 1913 provided for the establishment of twelve Federal Reserve districts. Each district is served by a Reserve Bank. Figure 4.1 indicates that district banks have a wide range of responsibilities, including holding reserve balances for depository institutions and lending to them at the prevailing discount (interest) rate. The district banks issue new currency and withdraw damaged currency from circulation, as well as collect and clear checks and transfer funds for depository institutions. The boundaries of the districts and the cities where district banks are located are shown in Figure 4.2.

Directors and Officers

Each Reserve Bank has corporate officers and a board of directors. The selection of officers and directors is unlike that of other corporations. Each Reserve Bank has on its board nine directors, who must be residents of the district in which they serve. The directors serve terms of three years, with appointments staggered so that three directors are appointed each year. To ensure the various economic elements of the Federal Reserve districts are represented, the nine members of the board of directors are divided into three groups: Class A, Class B, and Class C.

Class A and Class B directors are elected by the member banks of the Federal Reserve district. The Class A directors represent member banks of the district, and the Class B directors represent nonbanking interests. These nonbanking interests are commerce, agriculture, and industry. The Class C directors are appointed by the Board of Governors (BOG or Board) of the Fed. These persons may not be stockholders, directors, or employees of existing banks.

FIGURE 4.2
The Federal Reserve System

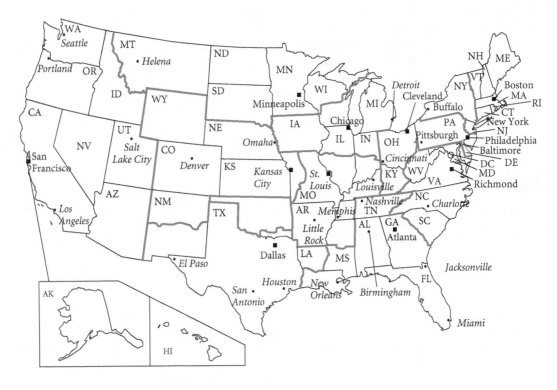

○ Board of Governors of the Federal Reserve System
■ Federal Reserve Bank cities
· Federal Reserve Branch cities

Source: Board of Governors of the Federal Reserve System.

The majority of the directors of the Reserve Banks are elected by the member banks of each district. However, the three nonbanking members of each board appointed by the Board are in a more strategic position than the other board members. One member appointed by the Board is designated chairperson of the board of directors and Federal Reserve agent, and a second member is appointed deputy chairperson. The Federal Reserve agent is the Board's representative at each Reserve Bank. He or she is responsible for maintaining the collateral that backs the Federal Reserve notes issued by each Reserve Bank.

Each Reserve Bank has a president and first vice president, who are appointed by its board Board of directors and approved by the Board of Governors. A Reserve Bank may have several additional vice presidents. The president is responsible for executing policies established by the board of directors and for the general administration of Reserve Bank affairs. All other officers and personnel of the Reserve Bank are subject to the authority of the president.

Federal Reserve Branch Banks

In addition to the twelve Reserve Banks, twenty-five branch banks have been established. These branch banks are for the most part in geographical areas not conveniently served by the Reserve Banks. For this reason, the geographically large western Federal Reserve districts have most of the branch banks. The San Francisco district has four, the Dallas district has three, and the Atlanta district has five branch banks. The New York Federal Reserve district, on the other hand, has only one branch bank, while the Boston district has no branches. The cities in which Reserve Banks and their branches are located are also shown in Figure 4.2.

BOARD OF GOVERNORS

Fed's Board of Governors
seven-member board of the
Federal Reserve that sets
monetary policy

The **Fed's Board of Governors**, or formally the Board of Governors (BOG or Board) of the Fed, is composed of seven members and is responsible for setting monetary policy. Each member is appointed for a term of fourteen years. The purpose of the fourteen-year term undoubtedly was to reduce political pressure on the board. Board members can be of any political party, and no specific provision concerns the qualifications a member must have. All members are appointed by the president of the United States with the advice and consent of the Senate. One member is designated as the chairperson and another as the vice chairperson.

The appointive power of the president and the ability of Congress to alter its structure make the Board a dependent political structure. However, it enjoys much independence in its operations. The Board is, in fact, one of the most powerful monetary organizations in the world. The chair of the Board plays an especially influential role in policy formulation. Because the Board attempts to achieve its goals without political considerations, disagreement between the administration in power and the Board is common. From time to time, pressures from Congress or the president have undoubtedly influenced the Board's decisions, but its semi-independence generally prevails.

INTERNET ACTIVITY

Go to the Federal Reserve
Board of Governors' Web site,
http://www.federalreserve.gov.
Click on Banking Information
& Regulation and find the
Fed's list of regulations by
clicking on Regulations along
the left-hand side. Write a brief
summary about the materials
on Regulation Z

Figure 4.1 illustrates how the Board establishes monetary policy. The Board sets reserve requirements and reviews and approves the discount rate actions of the twelve district banks. The Board operates through the Federal Open Market Committee (FOMC) to control the money supply as a means of meetings monetary policy objectives. We will explore these monetary policy instruments in more detail later in the chapter.

In addition to setting the nation's monetary policy, the Board directs and coordinates the activities of the twelve Reserve Banks under its jurisdiction. The Board is responsible for approving the applications of state-chartered banks applying for membership in the system and for recommending the removal of officers and directors of member banks when they break rules established by the Fed and other regulatory authorities. In addition, the Board implements many of the credit control devices that have come into existence since the mid-1960s, such as the Truth in Lending Act (TILA), the Equal Credit Opportunity Act, and the Home Mortgage Disclosure Act.

The Board publishes the *Federal Reserve Bulletin*, which carries articles of current interest and offers a convenient source of the statistics compiled by the Fed. The Board and all twelve of the Reserve Banks engage in intensive research in monetary matters.

FEDERAL OPEN MARKET COMMITTEE (FOMC)

As early as 1922, efforts were made to coordinate the timing of purchases and sales of securities by the Reserve Banks to achieve desirable national monetary policy objectives. The Federal Open Market Committee (FOMC), with the additional powers granted to it by the Banking Act of 1935, has full control over all open-market operations of the Reserve Banks. As noted in Figure 4.1, this committee consists of the seven members of the board plus five presidents (one of whom must be from New York) of Reserve Banks. The FOMC conducts open-market operations through the process of buying and selling U.S. government securities. These activities represent the primary method for carrying out monetary policies.

CONCEPT CHECK

Which type of commercial
bank must belong to the Fed,
and which type can choose to
join?

What is the number of Reserve
Banks, and how many branch
banks operate in the Fed?

How many individuals serve
on the Board, and what is the
Board responsible for?

ADVISORY COMMITTEES

Figure 4.1 indicates that the Fed has three major advisory committees. The Federal Advisory Council provides advice and general information on banking-related issues to the Board. Each of the twelve Reserve Districts elects one member to serve on the council. The membership of the Consumer Advisory Council is composed of representatives from depository institutions and their customers and, as the committee title suggests, provides advice relating to consumer issues. The Thrift Institutions Advisory Council consists of members from savings and loans associations, savings banks, and credit unions and provides advice on issues that directly affect thrift institutions.

ROLE OF THE CHAIR OF THE FED BOARD OF GOVERNORS

ETHICAL ISSUES

Special authority attaches to the chairperson of any board. The chair of the Board of Governors (Board or BOG) of the Fed is no exception. The holder of that position is generally recognized as the most powerful influence on monetary policy in the nation. As for any chairperson, the chair's power derives in large measure from the personality, experience, and leadership of the individual.

High moral and ethical standards are a must for the chair of the Board. A successful chair must have the confidence and trust of the president and Congress, bank officers, business leaders, foreign officials, and the general public. While the Fed has tried in recent years to make its activities and intentions more transparent, the impact of Fed actions are not often felt for many months afterward. Constituents must trust the chair will do what is right for the economy and society. Unethical behavior on the part of a Board chair would not be tolerated. High-quality reputation matters.

Since the early 1950s, there have been six Fed chairs. The chairs, along with the period served, are the following:

1. William McChesney Martin Jr. (1951–1970)
2. Arthur Burns (1970–1978)
3. G. William Miller (1978–1979)
4. Paul Volcker (1979–1987)
5. Alan Greenspan (1987–2006)
6. Ben Bernanke (2006–present)

William Martin, Jr.'s tenure as chair has been the longest in Fed history. He focused on maintaining the Fed's independence from Congress and the president. The 1970s were a particularly difficult decade from an economic standpoint in the United States. Inflation was increasing at a rapid rate. Oil price shocks occurred in 1973–1974 and again in 1978–1979. Wage and price controls were tried with no success. Arthur Burns served as chair throughout most the 1970s until his term expired in 1978. President Jimmy Carter nominated William Miller as chair, but he served only one year. By 1979, public confidence in Carter was low. Reactions in the financial markets in New York City suggested concern over whether the president could control inflation.

In July 1979, Paul Volcker's name had surfaced as a possible chair of the Fed who could fight inflation in the United States. Volcker was an economist who had served as president of the New York Federal Reserve Bank and was well known on Wall Street. Volcker had served in government positions in the Kennedy, Johnson, and Nixon administrations, as well as in commercial banking with Chase Manhattan.

While Volcker had impressive credentials, some of the comments gathered by the Carter administration included: "rigidly conservative . . . very right-wing . . . arbitrary and arrogant . . . not a team player."[3] While the Fed is legally independent from the White House, it is normal for the Fed chair to work with a president's economic advisors in a joint effort to reach certain economic objectives. Of course, there are times when it might be in the best interest of the people if the Fed pursues its own direction in applying monetary policy to achieve objectives such as lower inflation.

History shows that under Paul Volcker's guidance, a restrictive Fed policy brought down the double-digit inflation of the 1970s and the early 1980s. Volcker dominated the Board during his tenure, and the Federal Open Market Committee consistently responded to his leadership. When Volcker resigned as chairman in June 1987, the financial markets reacted negatively. The U.S. dollar fell relative to other currencies, and U.S. government and corporate bond prices fell. Why? In a word, uncertainty, meaning uncertainty about the future direction of monetary policy. Volcker was a known inflation fighter. In contrast, the policies of the incoming Fed chair, Alan Greenspan, were unknown.

Greenspan was viewed as a conservative economist. He served as an economics advisor to President Gerald Ford and as a business consultant. Greenspan's first big test was the October 1987 stock market crash. He responded by pumping liquidity into the banking system. The result was avoidance of monetary contraction and asset devaluation of the kind that followed the 1929 stock market crash. A reversal of policy occurred in mid-1988 when interest rates were raised to fight increasing inflation. During 1990–1991, a relatively mild recession occurred. However, inflation has been kept below the 3 percent level since then. During Greenspan's service as chair of the Board, the U.S. economy showed real economic growth, interest rates

3. William Greider, *Secrets of the Temple: How the Federal Reserve Runs the Country*, New York: Simon and Schuster, 1987, p. 35

CONCEPT CHECK
Who have been the three chairs of the Board since the beginning of the 1980s?

declined to historic lows, and stock prices reached all-time highs. A 1996 survey of more than two hundred chief executive officers of the largest U.S. corporations gave overwhelming support for the "good job" that Greenspan was doing. The business and financial sectors of the United States maintained their strong support of Greenspan's Fed leadership. In 2004, Greenspan was nominated by President George W. Bush and confirmed by the U.S. Senate for a fifth and final four-year term as chair of the Fed. A Fed policy of high monetary liquidity and low interest rates was established during the early part of the decade of the 2000s in response to an economic downturn that was exacerbated by the September 11, 2001, terrorist attack. This easy money policy was continued through Greenspan's tenure, which lasted through January 2006.

In February 2006, Ben Bernanke became chair of the Board. It was only a few months before the housing price bubble burst and the economy started slowing down. Bernanke was responsible for establishing monetary policy that helped guide the United States through the "perfect storm" involving the 2007–2008 financial crisis, which had placed the U.S. economic system on the verge of collapse,[4] and the subsequent 2008–2009 Great Recession. Ben Bernanke continues to lead the setting of monetary policy as we move into the second decade of the twenty-first century.

MONETARY POLICY FUNCTIONS AND INSTRUMENTS

OVERVIEW OF RESPONSIBILITIES

monetary policy *involves regulating the growth of the money supply and regulating its cost and availability*

The primary responsibility of the Fed is to formulate **monetary policy**, which involves regulating the growth of the money supply, and therefore, regulating its cost and availability. By exercising its influence on the monetary system of the United States, the Fed performs a unique and important function: promoting economic stability. The system's broad powers to affect economic stabilization and monetary control were absent in 1913 when the Fed came into existence. At that time, the system was meant to help the money supply contract and expand as dictated by economic conditions, serve as bankers' banks in times of economic crisis, provide a more effective check clearance system, and establish a more effective regulatory system. Much of these responsibilities initially fell to the twelve Reserve Banks, but as the scope of responsibility for the monetary system was broadened, power was concentrated with the Board. Today, the responsibilities of the Fed may be described as those relating to monetary policy, to supervision and regulation, and to services provided for depository institutions and the government.

dynamic actions *Fed actions that stimulate or repress the level of prices or economic activity*

Public discussions of Fed operations are almost always directed toward **dynamic actions** that stimulate or repress the level of prices or economic activity. However, this area is a minor part of the continuous operation of the Fed. Far more significant in terms of time and effort are the defensive and accommodative responsibilities. **Defensive activities** are those that contribute to the smooth, everyday functioning of the economy. Unexpected developments and shocks occur continually in the economy; unless these events are countered by appropriate monetary actions, disturbances may develop. Large unexpected shifts of capital out of or into the country, along with large financing efforts by big corporations, may alter the reserve positions of the banks. Similarly, buyouts and acquisitions of one corporation by another, supported by bank financing, affect reserve positions. In our competitive market system, unexpected developments contribute to the vitality of our economy. Monetary policy, however, has a special responsibility to absorb these events smoothly and prevent many of their traumatic short-term effects. The **accommodative function** of the nation's monetary system is the one with which we are the most familiar. Meeting the credit needs of individuals and institutions, clearing checks, and supporting depository institutions represent accommodative activities.

defensive activities *Fed activities that contribute to the smooth, everyday functioning of the economy*

accommodative function *Fed efforts to meet credit needs of individuals and institutions, clearing checks, and supporting depository institutions*

The basic policy instruments of the Fed that allow it to increase or decrease the money supply are the following:

- Changing reserve requirements
- Changing the discount rate
- Conducting open-market operations

4. For an interesting personal experience perspective of working with the Fed chairs, see: Stephen H. Axilrod, *Inside the Fed*, Cambridge: The MIT Press, 2009.

In recent years, the Fed has engaged in a non-traditional monetary policy called quantitative easing (QE). We will first cover the traditional policy instruments and then discuss the use of quantitative easing.

The Fed sets reserve requirements for depository institutions (i.e., banks), sets the interest rate at which to lend to banks, and executes open-market operations. By setting reserve requirements, the Fed establishes the maximum amount of deposits the banking system can support with a given level of reserves. The amount of reserves can be affected directly through open-market operations, thereby causing a contraction or expansion of deposits by the banking system. Discount or interest rate policy on loans to banks affects the availability of reserves to banks and influences the way they adjust to changes in their reserve positions. Thus, the Fed has a set of tools that enables it to influence the size of the money supply to attain the Fed's broader economic objectives.

RESERVE REQUIREMENTS

fractional reserve system
a system in which banks are required by the Fed to hold reserves equal to a specified percentage of their deposits

bank reserves
vault cash and deposits held at Reserve Banks

required reserves
the minimum amount of bank reserves that must be held by banks

required reserves ratio
the percentage of deposits that must be held as reserves

excess reserves
when bank reserves are greater than required reserves

The banking system of the United States is a *fractional reserve system* because banks are required by the Fed to hold reserves equal to a specified percentage of their deposits. *Bank reserves* are defined as vault cash and deposits held at the Reserve Banks. *Required reserves* are the minimum amount of bank reserves that must be held by banks. The *required reserves ratio* is the percentage of deposits that must be held as reserves. If a depository institution has reserves in excess of the required amount, it may lend them out. This is how institutions earn a return, and it is how the money supply is expanded. In our system of fractional reserves, control of the volume of checkable deposits depends primarily on reserve management. In Chapter 5, the mechanics of money supply expansion and contraction are explained in detail.

The banking system has *excess reserves* when bank reserves are greater than required reserves. The closer to the required minimum the banking system maintains its reserves, the tighter the control the Fed has over the money creation process through its other instruments. If the banking system has close to the minimum of reserves (that is, if excess reserves are near zero), then a reduction of reserves forces the system to tighten credit to reduce deposits. If substantial excess reserves exist, the pressure of reduced reserves is not felt so strongly. When reserves are added to the banking system, depositories may expand their lending but are not forced to do so. However, since depositories earn no interest on reserves, profit maximizing motivates them to lend out excess reserves to the fullest extent consistent with their liquidity requirements. When interest rates are high, this motivation is especially strong.

The ability to change reserve requirements is a powerful tool the Fed uses infrequently. For a number of reasons, the Fed prefers to use open-market operations to change reserves rather than change reserve requirements. If reserve requirements are changed, the maximum amount of deposits that can be supported by a given level of reserves changes. It is possible to contract total deposits and the money supply by raising reserve requirements while holding the dollar amount of reserves constant. Lowering reserve requirements provides the basis for expanding money and credit.

It has been argued that changing reserve requirements is too powerful a tool and that its use as a policy instrument would destabilize the banking system. The institutional arrangements through which the banking system adjusts to changing levels of reserves might not respond as efficiently to changing reserve requirements. Another advantage of open-market operations is they can be conducted quietly, while changing reserve requirements requires a public announcement. The Fed feels that some of its actions would be opposed if public attention were directed toward them.

Changing reserve requirements has been used as a policy instrument on occasion. In the late 1930s, the nation's banks were in an overly liquid position because of excessive reserves. Banks had large amounts of loanable funds that businesses neither wished nor could qualify to borrow because of the continuing depression. The reserves were so huge that the Fed could no longer resolve the situation through its other policy instruments. Therefore, it increased reserve requirements substantially to absorb excess reserves in the banking system.

Reserve requirements were lowered during World War II to ensure adequate credit to finance the war effort. They were raised again in the postwar period to absorb excess reserves. In the 1950s and early 1960s, reserve requirements were lowered on several occasions during recessions. In each case, the lowering made available excess reserves to encourage bank lending, ease credit, and stimulate the economy. By using this policy tool, the Fed was publicly announcing its intention to ease credit in the hopes of instilling confidence in the economy.

In the late 1960s and 1970s, reserve requirements were selectively altered to restrain credit because the banking system was experimenting with new ways to get around Fed controls. Banks were using more negotiable certificates of deposit (negotiable CDs), Eurodollar borrowings, and other sources of reserve funds. This prompted the Fed to impose restraint on the banks by manipulating the reserve requirements on specific liabilities.

The evolution of the banking system eventually led Congress to pass the Depository Institutions Deregulation and Monetary Control Act of 1980 (DIDMCA), which made significant changes in reserve requirements throughout the financial system. Up to this time, the Fed had control over the reserve requirements of its members only. Nonmember banks were subject to reserve requirements established by their own states, and there was considerable variation among states. As checks written on member banks were deposited in nonmember banks and vice versa, funds moved among banks whose deposits were subject to different reserve requirements. This reduced the Fed's control over the money supply.

The 1980 act applies uniform reserve requirements to all banks with certain types of accounts. For banks that are members of the Fed, these requirements are, in general, lower now than they were prior to the DIDMCA. In general, for approximately the first $50 million of transaction account deposits at a depository institution, the reserve requirement is 3 percent. For deposits over approximately $50 million, the reserve requirement is 10 percent, which was reduced from 12 percent in April 1992. The "break point" between the 3 percent and the 10 percent rates is subject to change each year based on the percentage change in transaction accounts held by all depository institutions. In general, transaction accounts include deposits against which the account holder is permitted to make withdrawals to make payments to third parties or others. Accounts that restrict the amount of withdrawals per month are considered to be savings accounts rather than transaction accounts.

Banks and other depository institutions with large transaction account balances are required to hold a proportionately higher percentage of reserves. Let's illustrate this point under the assumption that the reserve requirement will be 3 percent on the first $50 million of transaction account balances and 10 percent on amounts over $50 million. Assume that First Bank has $50 million in transaction accounts while Second Bank has $100 million. What are the dollar amounts of required reserves for each bank? What percentage of required reserves to total transaction deposits must be held by each bank? Following are the calculations:

BANK	ACCOUNT AMOUNT	RESERVE PERCENTAGE	RESERVE REQUIREMENT AMOUNT
First Bank	$50 million	3%	$1.5 million
	0	10%	0
Total	**$50 million**		**$1.5 million**
Percent	($1.5 million/$50 million) =		3.0%
Second Bank	$50 million	3%	$1.5 million
	50	10%	5.0
Total	**$100 million**		**$6.5 million**
Percent	($6.5 million/$100 million) =		6.5%

While First Bank was required to hold reserves of only 3 percent against its $50 million in transaction account balances, Second Bank had to hold reserves of 6.5 percent of its $100 million in transaction accounts. Depository institutions with even larger transaction account balances will have to hold proportionately higher reserves. As a result, their percentage of reserves to total transactions accounts will be closer to 10 percent.

A change in reserve requirement percentages on large transaction account balances has the most impact. For example, if the reserve requirement for transaction balances greater than $50 million is increased from 10 percent to 12 percent, Second Bank would have reserve requirements of $7.5 million or 7.5 percent of its $100 million in transaction accounts. The required reserves on the second $50 million increase to $6 million, which is the result of multiplying $50 million times 12 percent. Adding the $1.5 million on the first $50 million in transaction accounts and the $6 million on the second $50 million results in total required reserves of $7.5 million, which is 7.5 percent of the total transaction accounts of $100 million. Thus, it should be evident that a small change in reserve requirements can have a major impact on the money supply and economic activity.

CONCEPT CHECK

What is meant by the terms required reserves *and* excess reserves?

Which bank assets are counted as bank reserves for the purpose of meeting reserve requirements?

DISCOUNT RATE POLICY

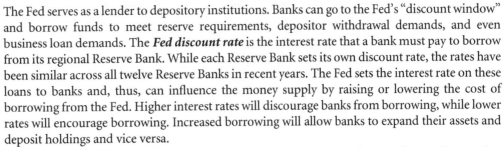

Fed discount rate
interest rate that a bank must pay to borrow from its regional Reserve Bank

The Fed serves as a lender to depository institutions. Banks can go to the Fed's "discount window" and borrow funds to meet reserve requirements, depositor withdrawal demands, and even business loan demands. The **Fed discount rate** is the interest rate that a bank must pay to borrow from its regional Reserve Bank. While each Reserve Bank sets its own discount rate, the rates have been similar across all twelve Reserve Banks in recent years. The Fed sets the interest rate on these loans to banks and, thus, can influence the money supply by raising or lowering the cost of borrowing from the Fed. Higher interest rates will discourage banks from borrowing, while lower rates will encourage borrowing. Increased borrowing will allow banks to expand their assets and deposit holdings and vice versa.

Loans to depository institutions by the Reserve Banks may take two forms. One option allows the borrowing institution to receive an advance, or loan, secured by its own promissory note together with "eligible paper" it owns. In the second option, the borrower may discount—or sell to the Reserve Bank—its eligible paper, which includes securities of the U.S. government and federal agencies, promissory notes, mortgages of acceptable quality, and bankers' acceptances. This discounting process underlies the use of the terms "discount window" and "discount rate policy."

Discount rate policy was originally intended to work in the following fashion. If the Fed wanted to cool an inflationary boom, it would raise the discount rate. An increase in the discount rate would lead to a general increase in interest rates for loans, decreasing the demand for short-term borrowing for additions to inventory and accounts receivable. This would lead to postponing the building of new production facilities and, therefore, to a decreased demand for capital goods. As a consequence, the rate of increase in income would slow down. In time, income would decrease and with it the demand for consumer goods. Holders of inventories financed by borrowed funds would liquidate their stocks in an already weak market. The resulting drop in prices would tend to stimulate the demand for, and reduce the supply of, goods. Thus, economic balance would be restored. A reduction in the discount rate was expected to have the opposite effect.

Discount policy is no longer a major instrument of monetary policy and, in fact, is regarded more as an adjustment or fine-tuning mechanism. As an adjustment mechanism, the discount arrangement does provide some protection to depository institutions in that other aggressive control actions may be temporarily moderated by the ability of banks to borrow. For example, the Fed may take a strong restrictive position through open-market operations. Individual banks may counter the pressure by borrowing from their Reserve Banks. The Reserve Banks are willing to tolerate what appears to be an avoidance of their efforts while banks are adjusting to the pressure being exerted. Failure to reduce their level of borrowing can always be countered by additional Fed open-market actions.

Figure 4.3 shows year-end interest rates charged by the Federal Reserve Bank of New York for "discount window borrowing" or *adjustment credit* over the 1980–2012 period. Interest rates for *adjustment credit* are plotted through 2002 and reflect the rate on short-term loans made available to depository institutions that had temporary needs for funds unavailable through reasonable alternative sources. Beginning in 2003, the discount window interest rate reflects the rate for

INTERNET ACTIVITY

Go to the St. Louis Federal Reserve Bank's Web site, http://www.stlouisfed.org. Click on Research & Data and then click on FRED Economic Data. Find the current discount rate charged by Federal Reserve Banks on loans to depository institutions. Describe recent changes or trends in discount rates.

PERSONAL FINANCIAL PLANNING
The Fed and the Consumer

The Fed affects personal finance in several ways. First, the Fed controls the money supply. Actions that severely restrict the money supply may lead to an economic recession. Too rapid a growth in the money supply may result in inflation and a decrease in purchasing power. Should the Fed act to slow down or reduce the growth rate of the money supply, there will be growing constraints on the ability of banks to lend as their excess reserves decline. This may result in higher loan rates, as loanable funds become scarcer. This could help bank savers, however, as banks and other depository institutions may

raise the interest they pay on saving accounts and CDs to attract more funds they will later lend to others.

The Fed acts in other ways to maintain people's trust and confidence in the banking system. As this chapter discusses, the Fed has supervisory power over many banks to ensure they have adequate capital and reserves and are following regulations. The Fed's Regulation Z requires lenders to tell borrowers the annual percentage rate on the loans they receive. The Fed clears checks by transporting them between banking centers and by debiting and crediting bank balances with the Fed.

FIGURE 4.3

Fed Lending Rate Versus Bank Prime Rate Changes, 1980–2012

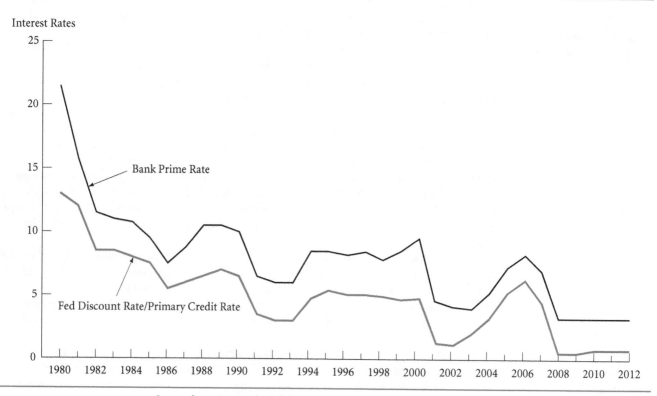

Source: http://www.stlouisfed.org.

primary credit, which replaced the prior adjustment credit designation. Primary credit is available ordinarily for overnight loans to depository institutions in generally sound financial condition.

For comparative purposes, year-end bank prime rates presented in Chapter 3 are plotted in Figure 4.3. The Fed lending rate and the bank prime rate generally "track" each other over time. Both interest rate series peaked at the end of 1980 and remained high during 1981 when inflation rates were high in the United States. In 2003, the Fed changed from a single discount rate to a prime credit rate and a secondary credit rate. Figure 4.3 plots the prime credit rate beginning in 2003. In response to the 2007–2008 financial crisis and the 2008–2009 Great Recession, the bank prime rate and the Fed prime credit rate were reduced. The bank prime rate, which was 8.25 percent at the end of 2006, was decreased to 3.25 percent by the end of 2008 and continued at that level throughout 2012. The Fed's prime credit rate, which was 6.25 percent at the end of 2006, was lowered to 0.50 percent by the end of 2008 and was maintained at that level until 2010 when it was increased slightly to .75 percent.

The Fed's lending rate to depository institutions was consistently lower than the bank prime lending rate throughout the 1980–2012 period. Of course, to make profits, banks must be able to borrow from depositors, and sometimes from the Fed, at rates lower than the rates the banks lend at. The determinants of interest rates will be discussed in detail in Chapter 8.

CONCEPT CHECK

What is meant by the term discount rate, *and how does the Fed use it?*

OPEN-MARKET OPERATIONS

open-market operations *buying and selling of securities in the open market by the Fed through its FOMC to alter bank reserves*

The most used instrument of monetary policy is ***open-market operations***, the buying and selling of securities in the "open market" by the Fed through its FOMC to alter bank reserves. The Fed can purchase securities to put additional reserves at the disposal of the banking system or sell securities to reduce bank reserves. You might ask, "Where does the Fed get securities to sell?" A brief look at the Fed's balance sheet will help provide an answer.

The Fed's assets are primarily held in the form of government and government agency securities, which generally represent over 85 percent of total assets. Coins and cash in the process of collection are about 2 percent of total assets. The remainder is assets that include gold certificates and Fed premises. Federal reserve notes (recall our discussion of fiat money in Chapter 2) represent nearly 90 percent of the Fed's total liabilities and capital. Deposits in the form of depository institution reserves held at the Reserve Banks are about 7 percent of the total. Other liabilities, particularly U.S. Treasury deposits and capital in the form of stock purchased by member banks and surplus earned from operations, make up the remaining total liabilities and capital.

The Federal Reserve Act of 1913 did not provide for open-market operations. However, to maintain stability in the money supply, this policy instrument developed out of Reserve Bank experiences during the early years of Fed operations. Unfortunately, these early efforts were coordinated poorly. Reserve Banks bought government securities with funds at their disposal to earn money for meeting expenses and to make a profit and pay dividends on the stock held by member banks. All twelve Reserve Banks usually bought and sold the securities in the New York market. At times, their combined sales were so large that they upset the market. Furthermore, the funds used to buy the bonds ended up in New York member banks and enabled them to reduce their borrowing at the Federal Reserve Bank of New York. This made it difficult for the Federal Reserve Bank of New York to maintain effective credit control in its area. As a result, an open-market committee was set up to coordinate buying and selling of government bonds. The FOMC was legally established in 1933. In 1935, its present composition was established: the Board plus five of the presidents of the twelve Reserve Banks, who serve on a rotating basis.

Open-market operations have become the most important and effective means of monetary and credit control. These operations can take funds out of the market and raise short-term interest rates and help restrain inflationary pressures, or they can provide for easy money conditions and lowered short-term interest rates. Of course, such monetary ease will not necessarily start business on the recovery road after a recession. When used with discount rate policy, open-market operations are basically an effective way of restricting credit or making it more available.

Open-market operations differ from discount operations in that they increase or decrease bank reserves at the initiative of the Fed, not of the individual banking institutions. The process in simplified form works as follows. If the FOMC wants to buy government securities, it contacts dealers to ask for offers and accepts the best offers that meet its needs. The dealers receive wire transfers of credit for the securities from the Reserve Banks. These credits are deposited with member banks. The member banks receive credit for these deposits with their Reserve Banks, thus adding new bank reserves that form the basis for additional credit expansion. The Fed restricts its purchases to U.S. government securities primarily because of their liquidity and safety.

If the Fed wants to reduce bank reserves, it sells government securities to the dealers. The dealers pay for them by a wire transfer from a depository to a Reserve Bank. The Reserve Bank then deducts the amount from the reserves of the depository institution.

Open-market operations do not always lead to an immediate change in the volume of deposits. This is especially true when bonds are sold to restrict deposit growth. As bonds are sold by the Reserve Banks, some banks lose reserves and are forced to borrow from their Reserve Bank. Since they are under pressure from the Fed to repay the loans, they use funds from maturing loans to repay the Reserve Bank. Thus, credit can be gradually restricted as a result of the adjustments banks must make to open-market operations.

QUANTITATIVE EASING

Quantitative easing (QE) is a non-traditional monetary policy designed to stimulate economic activity when conventional monetary policy methods are ineffective. The Fed engages in purchasing financial assets from banks and other financial institutions with newly created money resulting in larger bank excess reserves and increased money supply and liquidity. In response to the financial crisis and the Great Recession, which has been followed by relatively slow economic growth, the Fed has engaged in three rounds (QE1, QE2, and QE3) of quantitative easing. QE1 was initiated in late 2008 when the Fed began buying large amounts of mortgage-backed securities and Treasury securities from banks. These actions helped avoid a financial system collapse and contributed to the recovery from the Great Recession. However, slowing economic activity in 2010 led to the Fed announcing QE2, which provided for the purchase of an additional $600 billion of Treasury securities. In an effort to provide further monetary liquidity to encourage economic growth, QE3 was initiated in September 2012 when the Fed stated it planned to purchase $85 billion in Treasury and mortgage-backed securities per month for the foreseeable future.

CONCEPT CHECK

What is meant by open-market operations?

quantitative easing (QE) a non-traditional monetary policy designed to stimulate economic activity when conventional monetary policy methods are ineffective

CONCEPT CHECK

What is quantitative easing?

IMPLEMENTATION OF MONETARY POLICY

federal funds rate
rate on overnight loans from banks with excess reserves to banks that have deficit reserves

Monetary policy has traditionally tried to control the rate of change or growth in the money supply (such as M1) or it has targeted a level for a specific type of interest rate. In fact, the Fed often sets interest rate targets for the *federal funds rate*, which is the rate on overnight loans from banks with excess reserves to banks that have deficit reserves. Open-market purchases of securities add to bank reserves and increase the money supply. Sales of securities lower reserves and the money supply. However, when the target is the money supply, interest rates may fluctuate widely because the demand for money may change relative to a specific money supply target. Furthermore, a focus on the money supply might not produce the desired impact on gross domestic product (GDP) because of changes in the velocity of money as we saw in Chapter 2.

In recent years, the Fed has chosen to focus on the level of the federal funds rate as the primary means of carrying out monetary policy. Banks with excess reserves lend to banks that need to borrow funds to meet reserve requirements. Interest rates such as the federal funds rate reflect the intersection of the demand for reserves and the supply of reserves. Open-market purchases of securities causes the federal funds rate to fall, and sales of securities cause the rate to rise.

The Fed uses its open-market operations to provide liquidity to the banking system in times of emergency and distress. For example, the stock market crash on October 19, 1987, caused concern of a possible economic collapse. The Fed, through open-market purchases, increased the money supply. The terrorist attacks on September 11, 2001, caused widespread concern about the near-term ability of stock and other financial markets to function properly with a related possibility of economic collapse. The FOMC provided liquidity to the banking system and encouraged renewed confidence in the financial system by reducing the federal funds rate on September 17, 2001, from 3.5 percent to 3.0 percent.

CONCEPT CHECK

What are the two targets that the Fed can focus on when formulating monetary policy?

In 2001, the Fed lowered the federal funds rate to 2.5 percent on October 2, to 2.0 percent on November 2, and finally to 1.75 percent on December 11. The next rate reduction, to 1.25 percent, occurred on November 6, 2002; that was followed by a reduction to 1.0 percent on June 25, 2003. As the U.S. economy began growing, concern shifted to the possibility of renewed inflation, causing the Fed to begin increasing the federal funds rate in 2004. In reaction to the 2007–2008 financial crisis and the 2008–2009 Great Recession, the federal funds rate was decreased to historical lows. From 5.25 percent at the end of 2006, the federal funds rate was reduced to 0.15 percent by the end of 2008 and has been kept below 0.25 percent through 2012.

With recent federal funds rates near zero and economic activity not growing rapidly, the Fed engaged in a non-traditional monetary activity called quantitative easing (QE) beginning in late 2008. QE takes the form of purchasing mortgage-backed securities and Treasury securities from banks and other financial institutions, which provides more monetary liquidity in the financial system. As of early 2013, the Fed indicated it intended to keep short-term interest rates near zero until the unemployment rate drops to 6.5 percent and inflation expectations don't exceed 2.5 percent.

FED SUPERVISORY AND REGULATORY FUNCTIONS

A strong and stable banking system is vital to the growth and the stability of the entire economy. The supervision of commercial banks and other depository institutions is primarily concerned with the safety and soundness of individual institutions. It involves oversight to ensure that depository institutions are operated carefully. Depository institution regulation relates to the issuance of specific rules or regulations that govern the structure and conduct of operations.

SPECIFIC SUPERVISORY RESPONSIBILITIES

INTERNET ACTIVITY

Each of the twelve Federal Reserve Banks has its own Web site and tries to specialize in specific types of information. Go to the Federal Reserve Bank of San Francisco's Web site (http://www.frbsf.org) and the Federal Reserve Bank of Minneapolis's Web site (http://www.minneapolisfed.org), and identify the types of consumer and economic information they provide.

On-site examination of commercial banks is one of the Fed's most important responsibilities. This function is shared with the federal Office of the Comptroller of the Currency (OCC), the Federal Deposit Insurance Corporation (FDIC), and state regulatory agencies. Although the Fed is authorized to examine all member banks, in practice it limits itself to state-chartered member banks and all bank holding companies. It cooperates with state examining agencies to avoid overlapping examining authority. The OCC directs its attention to nationally chartered banks, and the FDIC supervises insured nonmember commercial banks.

In addition to these three federal banking supervisory agencies, two federal agencies are primarily responsible for supervising and regulating depository institutions that are not commercial banks. The National Credit Union Administration (NCUA) supervises and regulates credit unions, and the Office of Thrift Supervision (OTS) oversees S&Ls and other savings institutions. The examination generally entails five steps:

1. An appraisal of the soundness of the institution's assets
2. An evaluation of internal operations, policies, and management
3. An analysis of key financial factors, such as capital and earnings
4. A review for compliance with all banking laws and regulations
5. An overall determination of the institution's financial condition

The Federal Reserve conducts on-site inspections of parent bank holding companies and their nonbank subsidiaries. These inspections include a review of nonbank assets and funding activities to ensure compliance with the Bank Holding Company Act of 1956.

The Fed has broad powers to regulate the overseas activities of member banks and bank holding companies. Its aim is to allow U.S. banks to be competitive with institutions of host countries in financing U.S. trade and investment overseas. Along with the OCC and the FDIC, the Fed has broad oversight authority to supervise all federal and state-licensed branches and agencies of foreign banks operating in the United States.

SPECIFIC REGULATORY RESPONSIBILITIES

The Fed has legal responsibility for the administration of the Bank Holding Company Act of 1956, the Bank Merger Act of 1960, and the Change in Bank Control Act of 1978. Under these acts, the Fed approves or denies the acquisitions of banks and other closely related nonbanking activities by bank holding companies. Furthermore, it permits or rejects changes of control and mergers of banks and bank holding companies.

The Fed is responsible for writing rules or enforcing a number of major laws that offer consumers protection in their financial dealings. In 1968, Congress passed the ***Consumer Credit Protection Act***, which requires the clear explanation of consumer credit costs and garnishment procedures (taking wages or property by legal means) and prohibits overly high-priced credit transactions. ***Regulation Z***, which was drafted by a Federal Reserve task force, enacts the Truth in Lending section of the act. The purpose of the law and Regulation Z is to make consumers aware of and able to compare the costs of alternate forms of credit. Regulation Z applies to consumer finance companies, credit unions, sales finance companies, banks, S&Ls, residential mortgage brokers, credit card issuers, department stores, automobile dealers, hospitals, doctors, dentists, and any other individuals or organizations that extend or arrange credit for consumers.

The law requires a breakdown of the total finance charge and the annual percentage rate of charge. The finance charge includes all loan costs, including not only interest or discount but service charges, loan fees, finder fees, insurance premiums, and points (an additional loan charge). Fees for such items as taxes not included in the purchase price, licenses, certificates of title, and the like may be excluded from the finance charge if they are itemized and explained separately. Figure 4.4 lists the Truth in Lending Act (TILA) and other consumer protection acts that fall under Fed jurisdiction.

In addition to consumer protection laws, the Federal Reserve, through the Community Reinvestment Act of 1977 (CRA), encourages depository institutions to help meet the credit needs of their communities for housing and other purposes while maintaining safe and sound operations. This is particularly true in neighborhoods of families with low or moderate income.

FED SERVICE FUNCTIONS

The Reserve Banks provide a wide range of important services to depository institutions and to the U.S. government. The most important of these services is the payments mechanism, a system whereby billions of dollars are transferred each day. Other services include electronic funds transfers (ETFs), net settlement facilities, safekeeping and transfer of securities, and serving as fiscal agent for the United States.

CONCEPT CHECK

What federal agencies are responsible for conducting on-site examinations of commercial banks?

What federal agencies are responsible for regulating depository agencies that are not commercial banks?

Consumer Credit Protection Act

requires the clear explanation of consumer credit costs and garnishment procedures (taking wages or property by legal means) and prohibiting overly high-priced credit transactions

Regulation Z

enacts the Truth in Lending section of the Consumer Credit Protection Act with the intent to make consumers aware of and able to compare costs of alternate forms of credit

CONCEPT CHECK

What is Regulation Z?

FIGURE 4.4

Consumer Protection Responsibilities of the Federal Reserve System

- The *Truth in Lending* section of the *Consumer Credit Protection Act* requires disclosure of the finance charge and the annual percentage rate of credit along with certain other costs and terms to permit consumers to compare the prices of credit from different sources. This act also limits liability on lost or stolen credit cards.

- The *Fair Credit Billing Act* sets up a procedure for the prompt correction of errors on a revolving charge account and prevents damage to credit ratings while a dispute is being settled.

- The *Equal Credit Opportunity Act* prohibits discrimination in the granting of credit on the basis of sex, marital status, race, color, religion, national origin, age, or receipt of public assistance.

- The *Fair Credit Reporting Act* sets up a procedure for correcting mistakes on credit records and requires that records be used only for legitimate business purposes.

- The *Consumer Leasing Act* requires disclosure of information to help consumers compare the cost and terms of one lease of consumer goods with another and to compare the cost of leasing versus buying on credit or for cash.

- The *Real Estate Settlement Procedures Act* requires disclosure of information about the services and costs involved at the time of settlement when property is transferred from seller to buyer.

- The *Electronic Fund Transfer Act* provides a basic framework regarding the rights, liabilities, and responsibilities of consumers who use electronic transfer services and of the financial institutions that offer them.

- The *Federal Trade Commission Improvement Act* authorizes the Federal Reserve Board to identify unfair or deceptive acts or practices on the part of banks and to issue regulations to prohibit them.

Source: *The Federal Reserve System Purposes & Functions,* Board of Governors of the Federal Reserve System, Washington, D.C.

THE PAYMENTS MECHANISM

An efficient payments mechanism is necessary for the monetary system to carry out the financial function of transferring money, which is a requirement for an effective financial system. Figure 4.5 provides a review of how checks have traditionally been processed through the banking system. Recall from Chapter 3 that banks can clear checks either directly with one another or indirectly through bank clearinghouses. Checks can be processed or cleared through the Fed. The payments mechanism administered by the Fed includes providing currency, coin, and ETFs.

Electronic forms of payment are replacing the check, as a payment method. Included alternatives are credit cards, debit cards, and online account transfers. Furthermore, instead of transporting and sorting paper checks, more banks process the checks they receive electronically.

Coin and Currency

Even though the movement toward a cashless society continues, the United States remains highly dependent on currency and coin to conduct transactions. The Fed is responsible for ensuring that the economy has an adequate supply of cash to meet the public's demand. Currency and coin are put into or retired from circulation by the Reserve Banks, which use depository institutions for this purpose. Nearly all currency in circulation is in the form of Federal Reserve notes. These notes are printed by the U.S. Treasury Department, Bureau of Engraving and Printing.

Check Clearance and Collection

One of the Fed's important contributions to the smooth flow of financial interchange is to facilitate the clearance and collection of checks of the depository institutions of the nation (see Figure 4.5). Each Reserve Bank serves as a clearinghouse for all depository institutions in its

FIGURE 4.5

Traditional Method for Processing Checks Through the Banking System

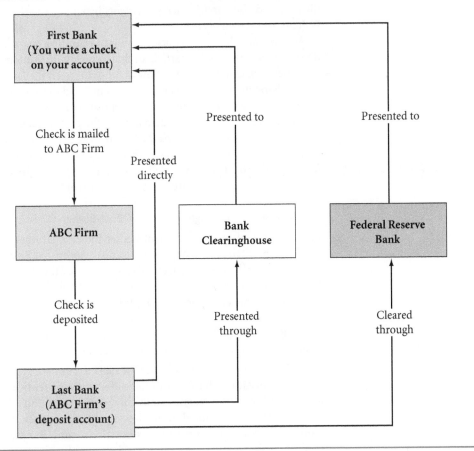

district, provided they agree to pay the face value on checks forwarded to them for payment. Today, nearly all the checks processed for collection by Reserve Banks are received as electronic check images.

Let's illustrate how the check clearing process traditionally took place through Reserve Banks. Assume the owner of a business in Sacramento, California, places an order for merchandise with a distributor in San Francisco. The order is accompanied by a check drawn on the owner's bank in Sacramento. The distributor deposits the check with its bank in San Francisco, at which time the distributor receives a corresponding credit to its account with the bank. The distributor's bank will send the check to the Reserve Bank of its district, located in San Francisco. The Reserve Bank will forward the check to the bank in Sacramento on which the check was drawn. The adjustment of accounts is accomplished at the Reserve Bank through an alternate debit and credit to the account of each bank involved in the transaction. The San Francisco bank, which has honored the check of its customer, will receive an increase in its reserves with the Reserve Bank, and the bank in Sacramento will have its reserves decreased by a corresponding amount. The bank in Sacramento will reduce the account of the business on which the check was written. Notice that the exchange takes place without any transfer of currency.

Check Clearance among Federal Reserve Districts

If an order was placed by the Sacramento firm with a distributor of goods in Chicago, the check would be subject to an additional step in being cleared through the Fed. The Chicago distributor, like the San Francisco distributor, deposits the check with the bank of its choice and in turn receives an increase in its account. The Chicago bank deposits the check for collection with the Federal Reserve Bank of Chicago, which forwards the check to the Federal Reserve Bank of San Francisco. The Reserve Bank of San Francisco then presents the check for payment to the bank on which it was drawn. Thus, check clearance has two routes: the *intradistrict settlement*, in which the transaction takes place entirely within a single Federal Reserve district, and the *interdistrict settlement*, in which relationships exist between banks of two Federal Reserve districts.

As described, Reserve Banks are able to minimize the actual flow of funds by increasing or decreasing reserves of the participating depository institutions. In the same way, the Interdistrict Settlement Fund eliminates the flow of funds between the Reserve Banks needed to make interdistrict settlements. The Interdistrict Settlement Fund in Washington, D.C., has a substantial deposit from each of the Reserve Banks. These deposit credits are increased or decreased, depending on the clearance balance of the day's activities on the part of each Reserve Bank. At a certain hour each day, each Reserve Bank informs the Interdistrict Settlement Fund by direct wire of the amount of checks it received the previous day that were drawn upon depository institutions in other Federal Reserve districts. The deposit of each Reserve Bank with the Interdistrict Settlement Fund is increased or decreased according to the balance of the day's check clearance activities.

Check Clearance through Federal Reserve Branch Banks

Branch banks of the Reserve Banks enter into the clearance process in an important way. If a check is deposited with a depository located closer to a Reserve Branch Bank than to a Reserve Bank, the branch bank, in effect, takes the place of the Reserve Bank. The Federal Reserve facilitates the check clearing services of the reserve banks and their branches by maintaining a small group of regional check processing centers.

Check Routing

In the past, a many employees at the twelve Reserve Banks were engaged in check clearing. Fundamental to the clearance process was the need to read the system of symbols and numerals shown in Figure 4.6. Although these symbols differ from conventional numbers, they are easily read and are referred to as the magnetic ink character recognition (MICR) line. Information about the clearance process is printed on the lower part of the check. In addition to the clearance symbol, banks include a symbol for each customer's account. Banks continue to include the older check routing symbol in the upper right-hand corner of their checks. Today, banks can keep an image of a check and process payment electronically through automated clearinghouses (ACHs). Banks have several ways to clear checks.

TRANSFER OF CREDIT

The Fed provides for the transfer of hundreds of millions of dollars in depository balances around the country daily. The communication system called Fedwire may be used by depository institutions to transfer funds for their own accounts, to move balances at correspondent banks, and to send funds to another institution on behalf of customers.

OTHER SERVICE ACTIVITIES

A large portion of Fed employees hold jobs directly related to the Fed's role as a *fiscal agent* for the U.S. government. The services include holding the Treasury's checking accounts; assisting in the collection of taxes; transferring money from one region to another; and selling, redeeming, and paying interest on federal securities. The federal government makes most of its payments to the public from funds on deposit at the Reserve Banks. The Fed acts as a fiscal agent for foreign central banks and international organizations such as the International Monetary Fund (IMF).

CONCEPT CHECK

How are checks cleared between Federal Reserve districts?

GLOBAL DISCUSSION

CENTRAL BANKS IN OTHER COUNTRIES

Central banks in other developed countries, like the U.S. Fed, are responsible for regulating the country's money supply, safeguarding the country's currency, and carrying out the country's monetary policy. Most other countries have a single central bank with branches that differ from the Fed's twelve Reserve Banks. Of course, the Board has effectively centralized control of U.S. monetary policy.

FIGURE 4.6

Traditional use of Check Routing Symbols

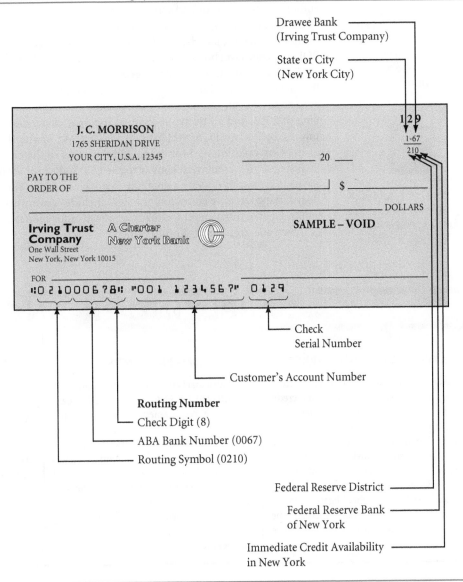

Drawee Bank
(Irving Trust Company)

State or City
(New York City)

Check
Serial Number

Customer's Account Number

Routing Number

Check Digit (8)

ABA Bank Number (0067)

Routing Symbol (0210)

Federal Reserve District

Federal Reserve Bank
of New York

Immediate Credit Availability
in New York

INTERNET ACTIVITY

Go to the European Central Bank's Web site, http://www. ecb.int. Click on European Central Bank, and find information on how it is structured and how it operates.

Empirical evidence shows a link between central bank independence from government intervention and inflation and economic growth rates. In countries where central banks are relatively independent from their governments, there have generally been lower inflation rates and higher economic growth rates than in countries where central banks are closely tied to their governments.

Three economically important foreign central banks are those from the United Kingdom (UK), Japan, and the European Monetary Union. The central bank in the United Kingdom is the Bank of England (BOE). It was created well before the formation of the Fed in 1913. The BOE is managed by a governor and five additional officers, all of whom are appointed for five-year terms. The BOE governor reports to the chancellor, who has final responsibility for setting monetary policy. In contrast with the United States, commercial banks in the UK are not required to hold reserves at the Bank of England. Also recall from Chapter 3 that the UK does not legally separate commercial banking and investment banking activities.

European Central Bank (ECB)

conducts monetary policy for the European countries that have joined the European Monetary Union and adopted the euro as their common currency

CONCEPT CHECK

What are three major central banks in addition to the Fed?

The central bank of Japan, called the Bank of Japan (BOJ), was created in 1947. The top official of the BOJ is the governor, who heads the Policy Board, which is the central decision-making authority. The governor and some members of the board are appointed by the Japanese equivalent of the U.S. Congress, and other board members are appointed by the finance minister. Japanese commercial banks, like their U.S. counterparts, are required to hold reserves on deposit with the BOJ, and banks can borrow at an official discount rate from the BOJ.

The ***European Central Bank (ECB)*** conducts monetary policy for the European countries that have joined the European Monetary Union. In 1999, twelve countries initially adopted the euro as their common currency. Euro notes and coins were officially introduced at the beginning of 2002, and all twelve individual national currencies were withdrawn as legal tender by July 1, 2002. The ECB, which is headquartered in Frankfurt, Germany, is responsible for controlling inflation and for managing the value of the euro relative to other currencies. The ECB structure is somewhat similar to the U.S. Fed's in that the twelve national central banks of the euro countries operate much like the twelve Federal Reserve District Banks. Like the Fed's Board, the governing council of the ECB includes governors from some of the national central banks. Each national central bank is responsible for managing payment systems and furnishing currency and credit in its home country.

APPLYING FINANCE TO . . .

INSTITUTIONS AND MARKETS

Depository institutions, commercial banks, savings and loans, savings banks, and credit unions comprise the banking system. The Fed is the U.S. central bank, which supervises and regulates the banking system. The Fed, along with depository institutions, creates and transfers money. Monetary policy actions of the Fed affect the primary financial markets for debt obligations, influencing the availability of bank loans and the interest rates that must be paid on those loans.

INVESTMENTS

Securities markets, primary and secondary, are affected by Fed actions. An increase in reserve requirements will restrict the amount of individual savings that would be available to make loans. Other Fed actions may cause banks to raise loan interest rates and cause the economy to slow down and security prices to decline. When the Fed raises the discount rate, banks react to protect their profit margins by raising their lending rates to individuals and businesses.

FINANCIAL MANAGEMENT

Financial management activities are directly affected by Fed monetary policy actions. A tightening of monetary policy makes it more difficult and costly for businesses to borrow funds. To the extent that economic activity also declines, it is more difficult for financial managers to sell new stocks and bonds in the primary securities markets. Of course, an easing of monetary policy will make it easier for financial managers to raise financial capital and they will be able to do so at lower interest rates.

SUMMARY

This chapter began with a discussion of the U.S. banking system prior to the establishment of the Fed. The national banking system suffered from an inflexible money supply, liquidity problems, and payment transfer problems. While the movement to a central banking system in the United States was a slow process, the Federal Reserve Act was finally passed in 1913. Coverage focused on the organization and structure of the Fed in terms of membership, Reserve Banks, the Board, and the FOMC. National banks must belong to the Federal Reserve System, while state-chartered banks and other depository institutions can elect to join the Fed.

The Fed has dynamic, defensive, and accommodative responsibilities. Dynamic activities attempt to influence economic activity by controlling the money supply. Defensive activities attempt to smooth changes in day-to-day economic operations. Accommodative activities provide credit and checking-related services to individuals and institutions.

The basic policy instruments of the Fed include setting reserve requirements, lending to depository institutions at the discount rate, and conducting open-market operations involving the purchase and sale of U.S. government securities. Open-market operations are the primary method used today for carrying out traditional monetary policy objectives. Since late 2008, the Fed has used QE to try to stimulate economic activity.

The Fed performs supervisory, regulatory, and service functions. Supervision of commercial banks is shared by the Fed with the OCC and the FDIC. Service functions performed by the Fed include providing and supporting a national payments mechanism, publishing research results, and other activities. Payments mechanism activities involve providing currency and coin, clearing and collecting checks, and electronic funds transfer.

The last section of the chapter described some of the characteristics of central banks in the United Kingdom, Japan, and the European Monetary Union.

KEY TERMS

accommodative function

bank reserves

central bank

Consumer Credit Protection Act

defensive activities

dynamic actions

European Central Bank (ECB)

excess reserves

Fed Board of Governors (Board or BOG)

Fed discount rate

federal funds rate

Federal Home Loan Mortgage Corporation (FHLMC or Freddie Mac)

Federal National Mortgage Association (FNMA or Fannie Mae)

Federal Reserve System (Fed)

fractional reserve system

Government National Mortgage Association (GNMA or Ginnie Mae)

monetary policy

open-market operations

quantitative easing (QE)

Regulation Z

required reserves

required reserves ratio

DISCUSSION QUESTIONS

1. Identify some of the institutional participants in the mortgage markets.

2. What actions did the Fed take to help avoid a financial system collapse in 2008–2009?

3. Describe the weaknesses of the national banking system that was in place prior to passage of the Federal Reserve Act of 1913.

4. What functions and activities do central banks usually perform?

5. Describe the organizational structure of the Federal Reserve System in terms of its five major components.

6. Explain how the banking interests of large, medium, and small businesses are represented on the board of directors of each Reserve Bank.

7. What is a Reserve Branch Bank? How many such branches exist, and where are most of them located?

8. How are members of the Board appointed? To what extent are they subject to political pressures?

9. Discuss the structure, the functions, and the importance of the FOMC.

10. Identify the six individuals who served as chairs of the Board since the early 1950s. Indicate each individual's approximate time and length of service as chair.

11. Distinguish among the dynamic, defensive, and accommodative responsibilities of the Fed.

12. Identify and briefly describe the three traditional instruments that may be used by the Fed to set monetary policy.

13. Describe what is meant by quantitative easing by the Fed.

14. Reserve Banks have at times been described as bankers' banks because of their lending powers. What is meant by this statement?

15. Describe the two "targets" that the Fed can use when establishing monetary policy. Which target has the Fed focused on in recent years?

16. Explain the usual procedures for examining national banks. How does this process differ from the examination of member banks of the Fed holding state charters?

17. What federal agencies are responsible for supervising and regulating depository institutions that are not commercial banks?

18. Describe the objectives of the Consumer Credit Protection Act of 1968. What is the Truth in Lending section of the act? What is Regulation Z?

19. Explain the process by which the Reserve Banks provide the economy with currency and coin.

20. Describe how a check drawn on a commercial bank but deposited for collection in another bank in a distant city might be cleared through the facilities of the Fed.

21. What is the special role of the Fed's Interdistrict Settlement Fund in the check clearance process?

22. In what way do the Reserve Banks serve as fiscal agents for the U.S. government?

23. Briefly describe and compare the central banks in the United Kingdom, Japan, and Economic Monetary Union.

EXERCISES

1. You are a resident of Seattle, Washington, and maintain a checking account with a bank in that city. You have just written a check from that bank to pay your tuition. Describe the process by which the banking system enables your college to collect the funds from your bank.

2. As the executive of a bank or thrift institution, you are faced with an intense seasonal demand for loans. Assuming that your loanable funds are inadequate to take care of the demand, how might your Reserve Bank help you with this problem?

3. The Board has decided to ease monetary conditions to counter early signs of an economic downturn. Because price inflation has been a burden in recent years, the Board is eager to avoid any action that the public might interpret as a return to inflationary conditions.

How might the Board use its various powers to accomplish the objective of monetary ease without drawing unfavorable publicity to its actions?

4. An economic contraction (recession) is occurring, and the Fed plans to use all facilities at its command to halt the decline. Describe the measures that it may take.

5. You have recently retired and are intent on extensive travel to many of the exotic lands you have only read about. You will be receiving a pension check, a Social Security check, and dividends and interest from several corporations. You are concerned about the deposit of these checks during your several months of absence, and you have asked your banker if an arrangement is available to solve this problem. What alternative might the banker suggest?

6. The prime rate, and other interest rates, offered by banks often change in the same direction as a change in the Fed's target for the federal funds rate. As an employee of a Federal Reserve District Bank, you have been told that your District Bank will be increasing its discount rate early next week. Expectations are that an increase in the discount rate will lead to an increase in the federal funds rate, which will lead to an increase in the prime rate and other bank lending rates. You have been thinking about buying a new automobile for the past couple of months. Given this information of a planned discount rate increase, you are considering buying your new automobile before the end of the week. What are the ethical issues, if any, involved in this scenario? What would you do?

PROBLEMS

1. A new bank has vault cash of $1 million and $5 million in deposits held at its Federal Reserve District Bank.

   a. If the required reserves ratio is 8 percent, what dollar amount of deposits can the bank have?

   b. If the bank holds $65 million in deposits and currently holds bank reserves such that excess reserves are zero, what required reserves ratio is implied?

2. Assume a bank has $5 million in deposits and $1 million in vault cash. If the bank holds $1 million in excess reserves and the required reserves ratio is 8 percent, what level of deposits are being held?

3. A bank has $110 million in deposits and holds $10 million in vault cash.

   a. If the required reserves ratio is 10 percent, what dollar amount of reserves must be held at the Reserve Bank?

   b. How would your answer in Part (a) change if the required reserves ratio was increased to 12 percent?

4. A bank has $10 million in vault cash and $110 million in deposits. If total bank reserves were $15 million with $2 million considered to be excess reserves, what required reserves ratio is implied?

5. The Friendly National Bank holds $50 million in reserves at its Federal Reserve District Bank. The required reserves ratio is 12 percent.

   a. If the bank has $600 million in deposits, what amount of vault cash would be needed for the bank to be in compliance with the required reserves ratio?

   b. If the bank holds $10 million in vault cash, determine the required reserves ratio that would be needed for the bank to avoid a reserves deficit.

   c. If the Friendly National Bank experiences a required reserves deficit, what actions can it take to be in compliance with the existing required reserves ratio?

6. Assume that banks must hold a 2 percent reserve percentage against transaction account balances up to and including $40 million. For transaction accounts above $40 million, the required reserve percentage is 8 percent. Assume that Dell National Bank has transaction account balances of $200 million.

   a. Calculate the dollar amount of required reserves that Dell National Bank must hold.

   b. What percentage of Dell's total transaction account balance must be held in the form of required reserves?

7. Assume that the Fed decides to increase the required reserve percentage on transaction accounts above $40 million from 8 percent to 10 percent. All other information remains the same as given in Problem 6, including the transaction account balances held by Dell National Bank.

   a. What would be the dollar amount of required reserves?

   b. What percentage of total transaction account balances held by Dell would be held as required reserves?

8. Show how your answers in Problem 6 would change if the Fed lowered the cut-off between the 2 percent rate and the 8 percent rate from $40 million in transaction account balances down to $20 million.

9. **Challenge Problem** You have been asked to assess the impact of possible changes in reserve requirement components on the dollar amount of reserves required. Assume the reserve percentages are set at 2 percent on the first $50 million of traction account amounts, 4 percent on the second $50 million, and 10 percent on transaction amounts over $100 million. First National Bank has transaction account balances of $100 million, while Second National Bank's transaction balances are $150 million and Third National Bank's transaction balances are $250 million.

   a. Determine the dollar amounts of required reserves for each of the three banks.

   b. Calculate the percentage of reserves to total transactions accounts for each of the three banks.

   c. The Central Bank wants to slow the economy by raising the reserve requirements for member banks. To do so, the reserve percentages will be increased to 12 percent on transaction balances above $100 million. Simultaneously, the 2 percent rate will apply on the first $25 million. Calculate the reserve requirement amount for each of the three banks after these changes have taken place.

   d. Show the dollar amount of changes in reserve requirement amounts for each bank. Calculate the percentage of reserve requirement amounts to transaction account balances for each bank.

   e. Which of the two reserve requirement changes discussed in (c) causes the greatest impact on the dollar amount of reserves for all three of the banks?

   f. Now assume that you could either (1) lower the transactions account amount for the lowest category from $50 million down to $25 million or (2) increase the reserve percentage from 10 percent to 12 percent on transactions account amounts over $200 million. Which choice would you recommend if you wanted to achieve a moderate slowing of economic activity?

• CHAPTER 5 •

Policy Makers and the Money Supply

Chapter Learning Objectives . . . AFTER STUDYING THIS CHAPTER, YOU SHOULD BE ABLE TO DO THE FOLLOWING:

- Discuss the objectives of national economic policy and the conflicting nature of these objectives.
- Identify the major policy makers and briefly describe their primary responsibilities.
- Discuss how the U.S. government responded to the 2007–2009 perfect financial storm.
- Identify the policy instruments of the U.S. Treasury and briefly explain how the Treasury manages its activities.
- Describe U.S. Treasury tax policy and debt management responsibilities.
- Discuss how the expansion of the money supply takes place in the U.S. banking system.
- Briefly summarize the factors that affect bank reserves.
- Explain the meaning of the monetary base and money multiplier.
- Explain what is meant by the velocity of money and give reasons why it is important to control the money supply.

Where We Have Been . . . In Chapter 4, we discussed the role of the Federal Reserve System (Fed) as the central bank in the U.S. banking system. Money must be easily transferred, checks must be processed and cleared, banks must be regulated and supervised, and the money supply must be controlled. The Fed assists or directly performs all of the activities that are necessary for a functioning financial system. You learned about the characteristics and requirements of Fed membership and the composition of the Fed Board of Governors (Board). You were introduced to the Fed's monetary policy functions: its open-market operations, the administration of reserve requirements, and the setting of interest rates on loans to depository institutions. We also discussed Fed supervisory and regulatory functions.

Where We Are Going . . . The last chapter in Part 1 focuses on how currency exchange rates are determined and how international trade is financed. We begin by discussing what is meant by currency exchange rates and foreign exchange markets. This is followed by a discussion of factors that determine exchange rate relationships and changes in those relationships over time. You will then learn how the financing of international trade takes place, including how exporters finance with a draft or bill of exchange. Financing by the importer and the use of a commercial letter of credit and a trust receipt are covered. The last section will introduce you to the importance of balancing international transactions or what is referred to as international financial equilibrium. In Part 2, our focus will be on investments, including the securities and other financial markets needed to market and transfer financial assets.

How This Chapter Applies to Me . . . The opportunity to vote gives you a way of influencing economic and political developments in this country. The president and members of Congress are policy makers elected by the people. After reading this chapter, you should have a better understanding of the national economic policy objectives in the United States and how government officials and the Fed influence the economy. You will be in a more knowledgeable position to make informed economic decisions about activities that may influence your life and career.

Government and private policy makers often are maligned in the press and sometimes even by themselves. For example, President Ronald Reagan in 1986 said this:

> *The government's view of the economy could be summed up in a few short phrases: If it moves, tax it. If it keeps moving, regulate it. And if it stops moving, subsidize it.*[1]

While this statement is somewhat humorous to most of us, it serves to start us thinking about what should be the country's broad-based economic objectives and what mechanisms are needed for achieving these objectives. We need a system of checks and balances to ensure that policy makers will operate in the best interests of the people of the United States. The president and Congress pass laws and set fiscal policy, while the Fed sets monetary policy and attempts to regulate the supply of money and the availability of credit.

NATIONAL ECONOMIC POLICY OBJECTIVES

Ernest Hemingway said the following:

> *The first panacea for a mismanaged nation is inflation of the currency; the second is war. Both bring a temporary prosperity; both bring a permanent ruin. Both are the refuge of political and economic opportunists.*[2]

Most of us would agree with Hemingway that currency inflation and war are unacceptable economic objectives. While people with differing views debate the proper role of government, there is broad agreement that decisions by government policy makers to levy taxes and make expenditures significantly affect the lives of each of us. In addition to the checks and balances offered by two political parties, the Fed is expected to operate independently of the government but also in the best interests of the country and its people. There is a strong tradition in the United States that national economic objectives should be pursued with minimum interference to the economic freedom of individuals.

The *Employment Act of 1946* and the *Full Employment and Balanced Growth Act of 1978*, typically referred to as the *Humphrey-Hawkins Act*, spell out the role of the U.S. government in carrying out the economic goals of economic growth and stable prices. Most of us also would agree that economic growth is good if it leads to improved living standards for the people. However, for this to occur, economic growth must be accompanied by stable prices and high and stable employment levels. The relationship between the money supply and demand affects the level of prices and economic activity in our market economy. Therefore, the process by which the money supply is increased and decreased is an important factor to the success of the economy. Since we live in a global environment, our economic well-being also depends on achieving a reasonable balance in international trade and other transactions. To summarize, our country's economic policy actions are directed toward these four general goals:

1. Economic growth
2. High employment
4. Price stability
5. Balance in international transactions

Accompanying these economic goals is a desire for stability in interest rates, financial markets, and foreign exchange markets.

ECONOMIC GROWTH

The standard of living of U.S. citizens has increased dramatically during the history of the United States as a result of the growth of the economy and its productivity. Of course, growth means more than merely increasing total output. It requires that output increase faster than the population so that the average output per person expands. Growth is a function of two components: an increasing stock of productive resources—the labor force and stock of capital—and improved technology and skills.

---

1. Address, White House Conference on Small Business, August 15, 1986.
2. "Notes on the Next War: A Serious Topical Letter," *Esquire*, September, 1935.

gross domestic product (GDP)

the output of goods and services in an economy

The output of goods and services in an economy is referred to as the **gross domestic product (GDP)**. The United States began the 1980s with a double-dip recession or economic downturn in "real" terms (i.e., after price changes have been factored out). A mild economic decline occurred in 1980, followed by a deeper decline that lasted from mid-1981 through most of 1982. The GDP then grew in real terms throughout the remainder of the 1980s before a mild downturn began in mid-1990 and lasted through the first quarter of 1991. Although some industries underwent substantial downsizing and restructuring, the economy continued to grow in real terms throughout the 1990s. As we moved into the twenty-first century, economic growth slowed domestically and worldwide resulting in a U.S. recession in 2001. Economic recovery began in 2002 and economic growth continued for a number of years until the United States entered into the Great Recession of 2008–2009.

HIGH EMPLOYMENT

Unemployment represents a loss of potential output and imposes costs on the entire economy. The economic and psychological costs are especially hard on the unemployed. While there is some disagreement over what we should consider full employment, it is a stated objective of the U.S. government to promote stability of employment and production at levels close to the national potential. This aim seeks to avoid large changes in economic activity, minimizing the hardships that accompany loss of jobs and output.

The U.S. unemployment rate reached double-digit levels during the early 1980s with a peak at about 11 percent near the end of 1982. As the economy began expanding, unemployment levels declined throughout the remainder of the 1980s until the rate fell below 5.5 percent. The recession that began in mid-1990, along with other job dislocations associated with corporate downsizing and restructuring, resulted in an unemployment rate exceeding 7.5 percent in 1992. The remainder of the 1990s was characterized by a steady decline in the unemployment rate to a level below 4.5 percent. As the country entered the twenty-first century, economic activity slowed and the unemployment level began rising. With an economic recovery beginning in 2002, employment opportunities improved for a period of years. However, the economy slowed in 2007 and entered into a steep decline in 2008, causing the unemployment rate to exceed the 10 percent level. Even with economic recovery beginning during the second half of 2009, the unemployment rate remained at the 10 percent level as the decade of the 2000s came to a close.

PRICE STABILITY

inflation

occurs when a rise or increase in the price of goods or services is not offset by increases in the quality of those goods and services

In recent decades, the importance of stable prices has become well accepted but difficult to achieve. Consistently stable prices help create an environment in which the other economic goals are more easily reached. **Inflation** occurs when a rise or increase in the prices of goods and services is not offset by increases in the quality of those goods and services. Inflation discourages investment by increasing the uncertainty about future returns. Therefore, high inflation rates are no longer considered acceptable as a price to pay for high levels of employment.

Inflation was at double-digit levels during the early 1980s, and this was reflected in record high interest rates. However, as the economy turned down in the 1981–1982 recession, inflation rates declined and continued declining until inflation fell below 3 percent. After a brief rise at the beginning of the 1990s, inflation steadily declined to 2 percent and continued at low levels in the early years of the twenty-first century. However, the Fed began expressing concern in 2004 about possible rising inflation and reacted by increasing the federal funds rate. Inflation remained low throughout the remainder of the decade of the 2000s even though the Fed reduced its target for the federal funds rate to historically low levels in response to the financial and economic pressures faced in the United States.

BALANCE IN INTERNATIONAL TRANSACTIONS

The increasing importance of international trade and international capital markets has resulted in a new emphasis on worldwide financial affairs. The U.S. economy is so large that the actions taken with respect to the country's own national affairs influence the economies of other nations. Economic policy makers, therefore, must always maintain a worldview rather than a narrow nationalistic approach.

CONCEPT CHECK

What are the four goals or objectives of economic policy?

Nations that produce and sell (export) more than they buy (import) will have a net capital inflow or surplus and vice versa. For example, Japan has used its large surplus of exports over imports with the United States to make investments in the United States. Nations that continually operate with international trade deficits will become increasingly weaker economically, while those with consistent surpluses will become economically stronger. Therefore, movement toward international financial equilibrium over time is in the best interests of worldwide trade and economic growth.

During the 1980s, 1990s, and the first decade of the 2000s, the United States consistently operated with a large negative trade balance. In other words, its imports of goods and services have consistently exceeded its exports of goods and products. U.S. service exports are generally larger than its service imports. However, the much larger negative merchandise trade or goods balance results in a negative overall trade balance. This negative trade balance remains of great concern to policy makers today. Unfortunately, throughout the first part of the twenty-first century, the negative trade balances, particularly with China, have been increasing in size.

FOUR POLICY MAKER GROUPS

Four groups of policy makers are actively involved in achieving the nation's economic policy objectives:

1. Federal Reserve System
2. The president
3. Congress
4. U.S. Treasury

Figure 5.1 illustrates how the four groups use monetary and fiscal policies, supported by debt management practices, to carry out the four economic objectives of economic growth, stable prices, high employment, and balance in international transactions.

As discussed in Chapter 4, the Fed establishes monetary policy including managing the supply and cost of money. We will see later in this chapter how the money supply is changed. *Fiscal policy* involves setting the annual national budget and reflects government influence on economic activity through taxation and expenditure plans. Fiscal policy is carried out by the president and Congress. The U.S. Treasury supports economic policy objectives through its debt management practices.

fiscal policy
involves setting the annual national budget and reflects government influence on economic activity through taxation and expenditure plans

ETHICAL BEHAVIOR IN GOVERNMENT

Since World War II, twelve individuals have served as president of the United States. The decade of the 1990s included George H. W. Bush and Bill Clinton. The decade of the 2000s was primarily under the direction of George W. Bush and Barack Obama. One would expect that the leader of the United States should and would exhibit a high level of moral and ethical behavior. We expect the people of our nation to practice sound ethical behavior by treating others fairly and honestly. Certainly, the president has the opportunity to lead by example.

Two recent presidents, Richard Nixon (who served as president during 1969–1974) and Bill Clinton (who served as president during 1993–2001), were each accused of unethical behavior while president. Nixon resigned on August 9, 1974, before he was about to be impeached

ETHICAL ISSUES

FIGURE 5.1
Policy Makers and Economic Policy Objectives

Policy Makers	Types of Policies or Decisions	Economic Objectives
Federal Reserve System The President Congress U.S. Treasury	Monetary Policy Fiscal Policy Debt Management	Economic Growth High Employment Price Stability International Balance

because of the Watergate scandal involving office break-ins. In 1998, Clinton became the second president to be impeached by the House of Representatives. Clinton's handling of personal indiscretions with a White House intern led to his trial in the Senate. He was found not guilty and completed his second term.[3]

Unethical behavior in government has not been limited to presidents. There have been numerous accounts of unethical behavior on the part of members of Congress. Some individuals have been impeached and others have been sent to prison. With this said, the vast majority the Congress and past presidents have practiced high ethical behavior, including treating their constituents fairly and honestly. The other good news is that the U.S. government and society have overcome the isolated unethical behavior of a few leaders.

GLOBAL DISCUSSION

POLICY MAKERS IN THE EUROPEAN ECONOMIC UNION

As in the United States, European governments use monetary and fiscal policies to achieve similar economic goals such as economic growth and price stability. In December 1991, the members of the *European Union (EU)* signed the *Maastricht Treaty* in Maastricht, Netherlands. The objective was to converge their economies, fix member country exchange rates, and introduce the euro as a common currency at the beginning of 1999. Monetary and fiscal policy actions of each country were to focus on maintaining price stability, keeping government budget deficits below 3 percent of gross domestic product (GDP) and total government debt below 60 percent of GDP, and maintaining stability in relative currency exchange rates. Twelve members of the EU ratified the Maastricht Treaty and adopted the euro as their common currency. They are known as the *European Monetary Union (EMU)*.

It is striking that twelve countries with widely different applications of monetary and fiscal policies in the past could agree on similar economic and financial objectives. While each country continues to formulate its own fiscal policies today, the *European Central Bank (ECB)* focuses on maintaining price stability across the twelve euro member countries. The sheer size of the EMU means that European policy makers and U.S. policy makers must work together in achieving the worldwide goals of economic growth and price stability.

GOVERNMENT REACTION TO THE PERFECT FINANCIAL STORM

FINANCIAL CRISIS

As we briefly discussed in earlier chapters, a "perfect financial storm" developed in the midst of the 2007–2008 financial crisis and the 2008–2009 Great Recession. In 2008, the U.S. economy was on the verge of financial collapse. The housing price bubble burst in 2006, and home prices began a sharp and prolonged decline. Stock market prices peaked in 2007 and fell sharply until mid-2009.

SMALL BUSINESS PRACTICE
Government Financing Assistance for Small Businesses

Small businesses can seek financing help from the federal and state or from the local levels. The Small Business Administration (SBA) was created in 1953 by the federal government. The SBA provides financial assistance to small firms that are unable to obtain loans from private lenders at reasonable terms and interest costs. In Chapter 16, we will discuss the SBA in greater detail.

Small business investment companies (SBICs) are chartered and regulated by the SBA. SBICs help finance small businesses by making both equity investments and loans. SBICs get their funds (to be lent or invested in small businesses) from privately invested

capital and long-term bonds purchased or guaranteed by the SBA. These bonds typically have ten-year maturities. A small business is currently defined as a firm with less than $6 million in net worth or net income of less than $2 million.

At the state and local level, sources of financing exist for small businesses. For example, most states have Small Business Development Centers (SBDCs) that can help small businesses find sources of financing. Small businesses may find sources of financing help by contacting their state's Department of Economic Development or Department of Commerce.

---

3. For a further discussion of past U.S. presidents, see Frank Freidel and Hugh S. Sidey, *The Presidents of the United States of America*, Willard, OH: R.R. Donnelley and Sons, 1996.

The economy slowed in 2007 followed by economic contraction in early 2008. The resulting 2008–2009 recession turned out to be the steepest U.S. recession since the Great Depression of the 1930s. Individuals were defaulting on their home mortgages in increasing numbers due to falling home prices and increasing unemployment. Business firms and financial institutions, which had borrowed heavily during years of easy money and low interest rates, were faced with their own financial difficulties as economic activity slowed markedly. Many of the debt securities issued and backed by home mortgage loans, called mortgage-backed securities, became difficult to value and became known as "troubled" or "toxic" assets.

Many major financial institutions and business corporations were on the verge of collapse or failure. Some of the largest financial institutions were deemed as being "too big to fail" because their failure would cause cascading negative repercussions throughout the United States and many foreign economies. As discussed in Chapter 4, the Fed moved to increase liquidity in the monetary system and reduced its target federal funds rate to a below .25 percent level. The Fed worked with the U.S. Treasury to facilitate the merger of financially weak institutions with institutions that were financially stronger. For example, in March 2008, the Fed and Treasury assisted in the acquisition of Bear Stearns by JPMorgan Chase & Co.

The Federal National Mortgage Association (FNMA or Fannie Mae) and the Federal Home Mortgage Association (FHLMC or Freddie Mac), briefly discussed in Chapter 4 as being major participants in the secondary mortgage markets, were on the verge of financial insolvency and possible collapse in mid-2008. Fannie Mae was actively creating and packaging mortgage-backed securities, many of which became troubled assets as home owners began defaulting on the underlying mortgages. Freddie Mac purchased home mortgages, including lower-quality subprime mortgages, attempting to support the mortgage markets and home ownership. In an attempt to avoid a meltdown, the Fed provided rescue funds in July 2008 and the U.S. government assumed control of Fannie Mae and Freddie Mac in September 2008.

In addition to the efforts of the Fed and the Treasury, the U.S. Congress and the president responded with the passage of the *Economic Stabilization Act of 2008* in early October of that year. A primary focus of this legislation, which became known as the *Troubled Asset Relief Program (TARP)*, was to allow the U.S. Treasury purchase up to $700 billion of troubled or toxic assets held by financial institutions. Then, in an effort to stimulate economic activity, Congress and the president passed the $787 billion *American Recovery and Reinvestment Act of 2009*, in February 2009, with the funds to be used to provide tax relief, appropriations, and direct spending. In part, as a result of these actions, economic activity in the United States began recovering in the second half of 2009. However, as the decade of the 2000s came to a close, the unemployment rate remained at the 10 percent level and has continued at high levels since then resulting in the Fed engaging in quantitative easing (QE) as discussed in Chapter 4.

As it turned out, the U.S. Treasury purchase of troubled bank-held assets developed slowly. In fact, passage of the *Dodd-Frank Wall Street Reform and Consumer Protection Act of 2010* amended the *Emergency Economic Stabilization Act of 2008*. Title XIII, known as the "Pay It Back Act," reduced the availability of TARP funds from $700 billion to $475 billion and mandated that any unused funds could not be used in new programs.

GOVERNMENT INFLUENCE ON THE ECONOMY

CONCEPT CHECK

How did the U.S. government respond to the perfect financial storm?

The federal government plays a dual role in the economy. In its traditional role, it provides services that cannot be provided as efficiently by the private sector. In this role, it acts like a firm, employing resources and producing a product. The magnitude of this role and its influence on economic activity has led to its more modern role: guiding or regulating the economy. The decisions of a number of policy-making entities must be coordinated to achieve the desired economic objectives.

A government raises funds to pay for its activities in three ways:

1. Levies taxes
2. Borrows
3. Prints money for its own use

Because the last option has tempted some governments, with disastrous results, Congress delegated the power to create money to the Fed. Our federal government collects taxes to pay for most of its spending, and it borrows, competing for funds in the financial system, to finance its deficits.

To illustrate the complex nature of the government's influence on the economy, consider the many effects of a federal deficit. To finance it, the government competes with other borrowers in the financial system. This absorbs savings, and it may raise interest rates. Private investment may be reduced if it becomes more difficult for firms to borrow the funds needed. On the other hand, a deficit stimulates economic activity. The government is spending more, collecting less in taxes, or both, leaving more income for consumers to spend. The larger the deficit, the more total spending, or aggregate demand, will be available. In some circumstances, this stimulation of the economy generates enough extra income and savings to finance the deficit and additional investment by firms.

Furthermore, the Fed may buy government securities, financing some of the deficit and providing additional reserves to the banking system, thus increasing the money supply. This process is known as ***monetizing the debt***. The Fed has at times monetized some of the deficit, especially during World Wars I and II. It does not do so now since that would be counter to current monetary policy and would have a significant impact on the financial markets. The competition for funds would make it more difficult for some borrowers to meet their financing needs. The characteristics and maturities of debt sold by the Treasury would determine which sectors were most affected.

The decisions of policy makers enter this process at a number of points. The president and the Council of Economic Advisors (CEA) formulate a *fiscal policy*: the relationship of the Treasury's tax plans to its expenditure plans to influence the economy of the nation. Congress must pass legislation authorizing the Treasury's plan or a variation of it. The Treasury is responsible for collecting taxes and disbursing funds and for the huge task of debt management, which includes financing current deficits and refinancing the outstanding debt of the government. As discussed in the previous chapter, the Fed contributes to the attainment of the nation's economic goals by formulating monetary policy. It uses its powers to regulate the growth of the money supply and, thus, to influence interest rates and the availability of loans.

The principal responsibilities of these policy makers have not always been the same. When the Fed was established in 1913, most of the power to regulate money and credit was placed in its hands. However, as the public debt grew during World War I, the Great Depression of the 1930s, and World War II, the Treasury became interested in credit conditions. Policies that affect interest rates and the size of the money supply affect the Treasury directly since it is the largest borrower in the nation. Therefore, the U.S. Treasury took over primary responsibility for managing the federal debt. In managing the large public debt and various trust funds placed under its jurisdiction, the Treasury has the power to influence the money market materially. The Fed came back into its own in the 1950s and has become the chief architect of monetary policy.

When it is felt that the Fed is not being responsive to the needs of the economy, the president will usually exercise pressure. The president formulates budgetary and fiscal policy, but Congress must pass legislation to implement these policies. Congress exercises its authority to modify presidential proposals before passing legislation. In short, there is much overlap of influence among those who make policy decisions. All three types of policies, however, are directed toward achieving the four objectives: economic growth, high employment, price stability, and a balance in international transactions.

It should not be surprising that the policy instruments of the policy makers at times put them at cross purposes. A long-standing debate continues over the balance between full employment and price stability. A particular policy that leads toward one may make the other more difficult to achieve, yet each objective has its supporters. As with all governmental policy, economic objectives are necessarily subject to compromise and trade-offs.

Recent legislative efforts to stimulate economic activity in the United States have their own cost or price. For example, the $787 billion *American Recovery and Reinvestment Act of 2009* provided for tax relief, appropriation expenditures, and direct spending. The bottom line was a shortfall between tax receipts and spending of $1.4 trillion in fiscal 2009. The fiscal 2010 and 2011 budgets were similar with spending of $3.6 trillion accompanied by a deficit of $1.3 trillion in each year. For fiscal 2012, spending was $3.5 trillion with a deficit of $1.1 trillion.

monetizing the debt
the Fed buys government securities, financing some of the deficit and providing additional reserves to the banking system, thus increasing the money supply

CONCEPT CHECK
What is fiscal policy?
What is monetizing the debt?

POLICY INSTRUMENTS OF THE U.S. TREASURY

The Treasury has vast power to affect the supply of money and credit. The magnitude of Treasury operations, however, dictates that it must play as defensive or neutral a role as possible. Since the power to regulate the money supply has been placed primarily in the hands of the Fed, close cooperation between the Treasury and the Fed must exist if Treasury operations are not to disrupt the money supply.

Consider the impact on monetary affairs of a massive withdrawal of taxes from the banking system without offsetting actions. The decrease in bank deposits would result in a temporary breakdown of the system's ability to serve the credit needs of the public. Yet the federal government periodically claims taxes without significant impact on lending institutions. In like manner, borrowing by the government or the refunding of maturing obligations could be traumatic in their effect on money and credit, but such is not the case. In short, the Fed manages these dynamic aspects of money and credit, while the Treasury largely limits its actions to taxing, borrowing, paying bills, and refunding maturing obligations. The Treasury carries out these functions with as little interference with the conduct of monetary affairs as possible. This is a major challenge.

MANAGING THE TREASURY'S CASH BALANCES

Treasury operations involve spending over $1 trillion a year. Maintaining a large cash balance is necessary since Treasury receipts and payments do not occur on a regular basis throughout the year. Because of this, the Treasury must handle its cash balances in such a way that it will not create undesirable periods of credit ease or tightness. To affect bank reserves as little as possible, the Treasury has developed detailed procedures for handling its cash balances.

Treasury Tax and Loan Accounts

INTERNET ACTIVITY

Go to the U.S. Treasury's Web site, http://www.treas.gov, click on the About tab, and identify the mission and goals of the U.S. Department of the Treasury. Write a brief summary.

The Treasury's primary checkable deposit accounts for day-to-day operations are kept at Reserve Banks. Most cash flows into the Treasury through Treasury Tax and Loan Accounts (Tax and Loan Accounts) of banks, S&Ls, and credit unions (referred to here as *banks,* for short). Employers deposit the income taxes, Social Security, and railroad retirement taxes they withheld in their Treasury Tax and Loan Accounts. They have the option of depositing these government receipts with Reserve Banks or one of the other banks. Most employers make their payments to the latter.

The Treasury may pay income and eligible profits taxes in Tax and Loan Accounts. Many excise taxes may be paid to a Reserve Bank or to a qualified bank with a Tax and Loan Account. The proceeds from a large portion of the sales of new government securities flow into Tax and Loan Accounts. If the Treasury feels its balances at the Reserve Banks are too large, it can transfer funds to its accounts at the banks.

Treasury Receipts and Outlays

The Treasury tries to handle its cash receipts, outlays, and balances to avoid large changes in bank reserves. To do this, the Treasury tries to keep balances in its accounts at the Reserve Banks relatively stable. Almost all Treasury disbursements are made by checks drawn against its deposits at the Reserve Banks. Most Treasury receipts are deposited in Tax and Loan Accounts at the various banks, but some are deposited directly in the Treasury accounts at the Reserve Banks. The Treasury adjusts its withdrawals to keep its balances at the Reserve Banks as stable as possible. This means the funds shifted from banks and the funds deposited directly in Reserve Banks must closely correspond to the volume of Treasury checks that are likely to be presented to the Reserve Banks.

CONCEPT CHECK

Where does the Treasury keep its primary checkable deposits?

If the Treasury accounts at the Reserve Banks are kept at about the same level, bank reserves are unchanged. This is possible only if accurate forecasts are made of the daily receipts and spending from the Treasury account so funds from the Tax and Loan Accounts may be shifted in the right amounts at the right time. If the forecasts were not worked out with a reasonable degree of success, Treasury operations would cause bank reserves to change a great deal over short periods. Despite these precautions, the Treasury's account frequently does fluctuate by as much as several billion dollars from day to day. The Fed closely monitors the Treasury account and takes any changes into consideration in conducting daily open-market operations to minimize the effect on bank reserves.

POWERS RELATING TO THE FEDERAL BUDGET AND TO SURPLUSES OR DEFICITS

The government may influence monetary and credit conditions indirectly through taxation and expenditure programs, especially by having a significant cash deficit or surplus. Budget-making decisions rest with Congress and are usually based on the needs of the government and on political considerations, without giving much weight to monetary and credit effects. Because of the magnitude of the federal budget, government income and spending may be one of the most important factors in determining credit conditions.

General Economic Effects of Fiscal Policy

Economic activity depends largely on aggregate demand or on total spending in the economy. An increase in aggregate demand will generally cause an increase in production and employment but may cause prices to rise. If the economy is close to full employment, increases in aggregate demand will likely increase prices more than output. Similarly, decreases in aggregate demand will result in lower employment and reduced prices.

Fiscal policy affects aggregate demand and economic activity. Government spending is a large component of aggregate demand, and any change in government spending has a multiplied effect on aggregate demand. An increase in government spending increases employment and incomes and, thus, increases consumer spending. In a downturn, spending decreases and tax receipts of all types—including those for Social Security—decreases when fewer people are at work because these taxes are based on payrolls. Changes in taxes directly affect disposable income and affect aggregate demand through consumer spending.

Various federal government programs act to stabilize disposable income and economic activity in general. Some act on a continuing basis as **automatic stabilizers**. Other government fiscal actions, such as actions to continue federal programs that stabilize economic activity, are discretionary and depend on specific congressional actions. Automatic stabilizers include the following:

> *automatic stabilizers*
> *federal government programs that act on a continuing basis to stabilize disposable income and economic activity in general*

- Unemployment insurance program
- Welfare payments
- Pay-as-you-go progressive income tax

The unemployment insurance program is funded largely by the states. Under this program, payments are made to workers who lose their jobs, providing part of their former incomes. Another stabilizer is welfare payments under federal and state aid programs. Unemployment and welfare benefits are examples of **transfer payments**, or income payments for which no current productive service is rendered.

> *transfer payments*
> *income payments for which no current productive services is rendered*

Another important automatic stabilizer is the pay-as-you-go progressive income tax. Pay-as-you-go refers to the requirement that tax liabilities of individuals and institutions be paid on a continuing basis throughout the year. The progressive nature of our income tax means that as income increases to various levels, the tax rate increases. In other words, as incomes increase, taxes increase at a faster rate. The reverse is true: At certain stages of decreased income, the tax liability decreases more quickly. The result is generally immediate since, for most wages subject to withholding taxes, tax revenues change almost as soon as incomes change.

These programs are a regular part of our economy. In times of severe economic fluctuations, Congress can stabilize disposable income. Income tax rates have been raised to lower disposable income and to restrain inflationary pressures; they have been lowered during recessions to increase disposable income and spending. Government spending can be increased during recessions to increase disposable income. Likewise, it could be cut during prosperity to reduce disposable income, but for political reasons, attempts to do this have not been successful.

When a recession is so severe that built-in stabilizers or formulas are not adequate to promote recovery, there is seldom a complete agreement on the course of action to take. A decision to change the level of government spending and/or the tax rates must be made. Increased spending or a comparable tax cut would cost the same number of dollars initially, but the economic effects would differ. When income taxes are cut, disposable income is increased almost immediately under our system of tax withholding. This provides additional income for all sectors of the economy and for an increase in demand for many types of goods.

Congress may decide to increase government spending, but the effects of increased government spending occur more slowly than those of a tax cut since it takes time to get programs started and put into full operation. The increased income arises first in those sectors of the economy where the money is spent. Thus, the initial effect is on specific areas of the economy rather than on the economy as a whole.

The secondary effects of spending resulting from a tax cut or from increased government spending depend on how and what proportion the recipients spend. To the extent that they spend it on current consumption, aggregate demand is further increased in the short run. The goods on which recipients spend the income determine the sectors of the economy that receive a boost. If they invest the added income and use it to purchase capital goods, spending is increased. In this case, however, a time lag occurs, and different sectors of the economy are affected. If the money is saved and therefore added to idle funds available for investment, there is no secondary effect on spending.

The effects must be considered if economic activity is to be restrained by a decrease in government spending or by a tax increase. A decrease in spending by the government will cut consumer spending by at least that amount; the secondary effects may cut it further. A tax increase may not cut spending by a like amount since some taxpayers may maintain their level of spending by reducing current saving or by using accrued savings. A tax increase could, however, cut total spending more if it should happen to discourage specific types of spending, such as on home building or on credit purchases of consumer durable goods. This could lead to a spending cut that is greater than the amount of money taken by the higher taxes.

Effects of Tax Policy

The **tax policy** and tax program of the federal government have a direct effect on monetary and credit conditions that may work in several ways. The level of taxes in relation to national income may affect the volume of saving and thus the funds available for investment without credit expansion. The tax structure determines whether saving is done largely by upper-income groups, middle-income groups, or all groups. This can affect the amount of funds available for different types of investment. Persons in middle-income groups may be more conservative than those with more wealth. They tend to favor bonds or mortgages over equity investments. Persons in high tax brackets, on the other hand, tend to invest in securities of state and local governments because income from these investments is not subject to income taxes. They may invest for capital gains since taxes on the gains may be deferred until the asset is sold.

Changes in corporate tax rates may affect the amount of funds available for short-term investment in government bonds and the balances kept in bank accounts. The larger the tax payments, the less a corporation has available for current spending. Also, if tax rates are raised with little warning, a corporation may be forced to use funds it had been holding for future use. Businesses that are short of funds may be forced to borrow to meet their taxes. In either case, a smaller amount of credit is available for other uses.

Effects of Deficit Financing

The government spending program affects the overall economy and monetary and credit conditions. When the spending rate is faster than the collection of taxes and other funds, **deficit financing** will affect the monetary and banking system. The effect will depend on how the deficit is financed. Budgetary deficits result in government competition for private investment funds. When credit demands are great, there may be a threat of **crowding out** private borrowers from the capital markets. When credit demands are slack, the sale of Treasury obligations puts idle bank reserves to use. When deficit financing is so large that the private sector cannot or will not absorb the Treasury obligations offered, the Fed may purchase a significant portion of the issues.

Annual deficits exceeded $1 trillion in fiscal 2009, 2010, and 2011. The reported deficit was $1.1 trillion in fiscal 2012. Recovery from the financial crisis and the Great Recession has been a costly endeavor.

RECENT FINANCIAL CRISIS-RELATED ACTIVITIES

The U.S. Treasury, under the leadership of Treasury Secretary Henry Paulson, played an important role in helping the U.S. survive the 2007–2008 financial crisis and the subsequent recession. The Treasury, working closely with the Fed, helped the acquisition of Bear Stearns by JPMorgan Chase & Co. in March 2008. Under the leadership of Henry Paulson, the Treasury was actively involved in

CONCEPT CHECK

What are automatic stabilizers?

What are transfer payments?

tax policy
sets the level and structure of taxes to affect the economy

deficit financing
affects the monetary and banking system when the spending rate is faster than the collection of taxes and other funds

crowding out
lack of funds for private borrowing caused by the sale of government obligations to cover large federal deficits

FINANCIAL CRISIS

helping financial institutions on the brink of collapse find help through mergers with financially stronger institutions. In September 2008, Bank of America acquired Merrill Lynch. However, during the same month, Lehman Brothers declared bankruptcy when no viable financial alternatives surfaced. Shortly thereafter, American International Group (AIG) was "bailed out" by the Federal Reserve and Treasury efforts with the U.S. government receiving an ownership interest in AIG.

The Emergency Economic Stabilization Act of 2008 provided the Treasury with funds to purchase troubled or toxic assets held by financial institutions. However, much of the Troubled Asset Relief Program (TARP) funds were used to invest capital in banks with little equity in their balance sheets, as well as to rescue "too big to fail" financial institutions and large nonfinancial business firms—such as General Motors (GM) and Chrysler—who were on the verge of failing.

national debt
total debt owed by a government

AMOUNT OF NATIONAL DEBT AND DEBT MANAGEMENT

The *national debt*, which is sometimes referred to as the government or public debt, is the total debt owed by a government. Annual government expenditures have exceeded annual tax receipts in every fiscal year since the end of the 1960s, except for fiscal 1998. As noted earlier, recent annual deficits have exceeded $1 trillion. In the effort to recover from the financial crisis and the great depreciation, the fiscal 2009 budget deficit was $1.8 trillion and the fiscal 2010 deficit was $1.3 trillion. Deficits remained at the $1.3 trillion level in fiscal 2011 and a $1.1 trillion deficit occurred in fiscal 2012. The cumulative effect of these large annual deficits has resulted in the U.S. national debt exceeding $16 trillion.

debt management
includes determining the types of refunding to carry out, the types of securities to sell, the interest rate patterns to use, and decisions to make on callable issues

Debt management includes determining the types of refunding to carry out, the types of securities to sell, the interest rate patterns to use, and decisions to make on callable issues. Since World War II, federal debt management has become an important Treasury function affecting economic conditions in general and money markets in particular. The economy and the money markets are affected in several ways by the large government debt. First, interest must be paid on government securities that are issued to finance the national debt. Interest payments do not transfer resources from the private to the public sector, but they do represent a transfer of funds from taxpayers in general to security holders. When the debt is widely held, little or no redistribution of income occurs among groups. However, the taxes levied to pay the interest may decrease taxpayer incentive and so affect economic activity. This could lead to less risk-taking and slow economic growth.

CONCEPT CHECK
What is deficit financing?

One of the basic objectives of debt management is to handle it in such a way as to establish an economic climate that encourages orderly growth and stability. To avoid inflation in boom periods, large numbers of individuals have been encouraged to save and to buy bonds. During recessions, the Treasury can borrow in ways that are least likely to compete with private demands for funds. For instance, the Treasury can sell short-term securities to attract idle short-term funds, especially idle bank reserves. Thus, there will be no restriction of credit for business and individuals. Credit will be available in larger amounts to the extent that bank purchases of bonds lead to credit expansion.

INTERNET ACTIVITY
Go to the U.S. Treasury's Web site, http://www.treas.gov. Click on the Resource Center tab. In the drop-down menu, click on FAQs. Then click on Markets, followed by National Debt. Find information on the size of the national debt and how the national debt is financed. Write a brief summary.

Another objective of debt management policy is to hold down Treasury interest costs. The influence of Treasury policies may tend to reduce all interest rates. Lower interest rates tend to stimulate home building, the construction of business plant and equipment, commercial building, and so forth. This objective of lower interest rates and lower Treasury interest costs, however, may conflict at times with the need for higher interest rates to help restrain inflationary pressures.

A lesser Treasury objective is to maintain satisfactory conditions in the government securities market by maintaining investor confidence. It tries to discourage wide price swings and maintain orderly buying and selling.

CONCEPT CHECK
What is debt management?

Among the more technical objectives are the following: issuing securities to fit the needs of various investor groups, obtaining an evenly spaced scheduling of debt maturities to ease debt retirement if funds are available, and allowing for refunding when that is necessary. Our heavy dependence on foreign investors to purchase new issues in recent years has added a special dimension to the U.S. debt management problem. The terms of new issues must be geared to the special needs of foreign investors from all parts of the world, including a particular need to focus on investors from Japan and China.

CHANGING THE MONEY SUPPLY

As we saw in Chapter 2, the M1 definition of the money supply consists of currency (including coins), demand deposits, other checkable deposits, and traveler's checks. Currency is in the form of Federal Reserve notes and is backed by gold certificates, *Special Drawing Rights (SDRs)*, eligible paper, or U.S. government and agency securities. SDRs are a form of reserve asset, or "paper gold," created by the International Monetary Fund (IMF). Their purpose is to provide worldwide monetary liquidity and to support international trade. Eligible paper, in the form of business notes and drafts, provides little collateral today. Instead, Federal Reserve notes have been increasingly backed by government securities.

Demand deposits and other checkable deposits at commercial banks, S&Ls, savings banks, and credit unions comprise about one-half of the M1 money supply and are collectively termed *checkable deposits*. To simplify further discussion of money supply's expansion and contraction, we will refer to checkable deposits simply as *deposits* in the *banking system*, which includes all of the depository institutions. The word *bank* is used generically to refer to a depository institution.

The banking system of the United States can change the volume of deposits as the need for funds by individuals, businesses, and governments change. This ability to alter the size of the money supply is based on the use of a ***fractional reserve system***. In our fractional reserve system, banks must hold with the Fed reserves equal to a certain percentage of their deposits. To understand the deposit expansion and contraction process, one must study the operations of banks as units in a banking system and the relationship of bank loans to deposits and to bank reserves.

In analyzing deposit expansion, it is helpful to distinguish between primary deposits and derivative deposits. For example, the deposit of a check drawn on the Fed is a ***primary deposit*** because it adds new reserves to the bank where deposited and to the banking system. A ***derivative deposit*** occurs when reserves created from a primary deposit are made available to borrowers through bank loans. Borrowers then deposit the loans so they can write checks against the funds. When a check is written and deposited in another bank, the total reserves of the banking system remains the same. The increase in reserves at the bank where the check is deposited is offset by a decrease in reserves at the bank on which the check is drawn. Banks must keep reserves against primary and derivative deposits.

CHECKABLE DEPOSIT EXPANSION

When reserves were first required by law, the purpose was to assure depositors that banks had the ability to handle withdrawals of cash. This was before the establishment of the Fed, which made it possible for a healthy bank to obtain additional funds in time of need. Depositor confidence is based on deposit insurance and more complete and competent bank examinations by governmental agencies. Today, the basic function of reserve requirements is to provide a means for regulating deposit expansion and contraction.

Deposit creation takes place as a result of the operations of the whole system of banks, but it arises out of the independent transactions of individual banks. To explain the process, therefore, we will consider the loan activities of a single bank. First, we will focus on the bank itself; then, we

fractional reserve system
reserves held with the Fed that are equal to a certain percentage of bank deposits

primary deposit
the deposit of a check drawn on the Fed; it adds new reserves to the bank where deposited and to the banking system

derivative deposit
occurs when reserves created from a primary deposit are made available to borrowers through bank loans

CONCEPT CHECK

What is a fractional reserve system?

How does a primary deposit differ from a derivative deposit?

PERSONAL FINANCIAL PLANNING
How Does the Fed Affect Me?

Suppose you hear on the radio that the Fed has moved to cut interest rates. Such a rate cut affects more than banks or large corporate borrowers; it can have an impact on individuals, too. So, how might a rate cut affect you?

If you have savings at a depository institution, the effect may be negative. Attempts to lower interest rates in the economy may lead to lower interest rates on your interest-on-checking account, your savings account, or the next CD you invest in.

Of course, there is a potential benefit on the borrowing side. An attempt to lower rates can lead to lower loan rates for a car loan,

student loan, home equity loan, or a home mortgage. If someone has a variable or adjustable rate mortgage, his or her interest payments may fall as rates decline. Some interest rates on credit card balances are linked to a market interest rate, so as market interest rates fall, the interest rates on credit card balances will fall, too.

Lower interest rates can help investors in stocks and bonds, too. As we will see in Chapter 10, an economic environment with lower interest rates can lead to increases in stock and bond prices, thus increasing the value of an investor's stock and bond holdings.

will examine its relationship to a system of banks. This approach is somewhat artificial since a bank practically never acts independently of the actions of other banks, but it has been adopted to clarify the process. Furthermore, it helps explain the belief of some bankers that they cannot create deposits since they only lend funds placed on deposit in their banks by their depositors. This analysis shows how a system of banks, in which each bank is carrying on its local activities, can do what an individual banker cannot do.

For illustration, let us assume a bank receives a primary deposit of $10,000 and it must keep reserves of 20 percent against deposits. The $10,000 becomes a cash asset to the bank as well as a $10,000 liability since it must stand ready to honor a withdrawal of the money. The bank statement, ignoring all other items, would then show the following:

ASSETS		LIABILITIES	
Reserves	$10,000	Deposits	$10,000

Against this new deposit of $10,000, the bank must keep required reserves of 20 percent, or $2,000. Therefore, it has $8,000 of excess reserves available. Excess reserves are reserves above the level of required reserves.

It may appear that the banker could proceed to make loans for $40,000 since a 20 percent reserve is all that is needed against the resulting checkable deposits. If this were attempted, however, the banker would soon be in a difficult situation. Since bank loans are usually obtained before a demand for funds, checks would likely be written against the deposit accounts almost at once. Many of these checks would be deposited in other banks, and the bank would be faced with a demand for cash as checks were presented for collection. This demand could reach the full $40,000. Since the bank has only $8,000 to meet it, it could not follow such a course and remain in business.

The amount that the banker can safely lend is the $8,000 of excess reserves. If more is lent, the banker runs the risk of not being able to make payments on checks. After an $8,000 loan, the books would show the following:

ASSETS		LIABILITIES	
Reserves	$10,000	Deposits	$18,000
Loans	$ 8,000		

If a check were written for the full amount of the derivative deposit ($8,000) and sent to a bank in another city for deposit, the lending bank would lose all of its excess reserves. This may be seen from its books, which would appear as follows:

ASSETS		LIABILITIES	
Reserves	$2,000	Deposits	$10,000
Loans	$8,000		

In practice, a bank may be able to lend somewhat more than the $8,000 in this example because banks frequently require customers to keep an average deposit balance of about 15 to 20 percent of the loan. The whole of the additional $1,500 to $2,000 cannot be lent safely because an average balance of $1,500 to $2,000 does not prevent the full amount of the loan from being used for a period of time. With an average balance in each derivative deposit account, however, not all accounts will be drawn to zero at the same time. Therefore, some additional funds will be available for loans.

It may be argued a banker will feel sure that some checks written against the bank will be redeposited in the same bank, and therefore, larger sums can be lent. However, because any bank is only one of thousands, the banker cannot usually count on such redepositing of funds. Banks cannot run the risk of being caught short of reserves. Thus, when an individual bank receives a new primary deposit, it cannot lend the full amount of that deposit but only the amount available as excess reserves. From the point of view of an individual bank, therefore, deposit creation appears impossible. Because a part of every new deposit cannot be lent out because of reserve requirements, the volume of additional loans is less than new primary deposits.

Recognize that *what cannot be done by an individual bank can be done by the banking system.* This occurs when many banks are expanding loans and derivative deposits at the same time. To illustrate this point, assume we have an economy with two banks, A and B. This example can be realistic if we assume that Bank A represents one bank in the system and Bank B represents all other banks combined. Bank A, as in our previous example, receives a new primary deposit of $10,000 and is required to keep reserves of 20 percent against deposits. Therefore, its books would appear as follows:

BANK A

ASSETS		**LIABILITIES**	
Reserves	$10,000	Deposits	$10,000

A loan for $8,000 is made and credited as follows:

BANK A

ASSETS		**LIABILITIES**	
Reserves	$10,000	Deposits	$18,000
Loans	$ 8,000		

Assume that a check is drawn against this primary deposit almost immediately and deposited in Bank B. The books of the two banks would show the following:

BANK A

ASSETS		**LIABILITIES**	
Reserves	$2,000	Deposits	$10,000
Loans	$8,000		

BANK B

ASSETS		**LIABILITIES**	
Reserves	$8,000	Deposits	$8,000

The derivative deposit arising out of a loan from Bank A has been transferred by check to Bank B, where it is received as a primary deposit. Bank B must set aside 20 percent as required reserves and may lend or reinvest the remainder. Its books after such a loan (equal to its excess reserves) would appear as follows:

BANK B

ASSETS		**LIABILITIES**	
Reserves	$8,000	Deposits	$14,400
Loans	$6,400		

Assume a check is drawn against the derivative deposit of $6,400 that was created due to the loan by Bank B. This reduces its reserves and deposits as follows:

BANK B

ASSETS		**LIABILITIES**	
Reserves	$1,600	Deposits	$8,000
Loans	$6,400		

The check for $6,400 will most likely be deposited in a bank, in our example in Bank A or B, since we have assumed that only two banks exist. In the U.S. banking system, it may be deposited in one of the thousands of banks or other depository institutions.

Deposit expansion, as when a bank makes a loan, can take place in the same way when it buys securities. Assume, as we did in the case of a bank loan, the following situation:

BANK A			
ASSETS		**LIABILITIES**	
Reserves	$10,000	Deposits	$10,000

Securities costing $8,000 are purchased and the proceeds credited to the account of the seller, giving the following situation:

BANK A			
ASSETS		**LIABILITIES**	
Reserves	$10,000	Deposits	$18,000
Investments	$ 8,000		

Assume that a check is drawn against the seller's deposit and is deposited in Bank B. The books of the two banks would show the following:

BANK A			
ASSETS		**LIABILITIES**	
Reserves	$2,000	Deposits	$10,000
Investments	$8,000		

BANK B			
ASSETS		**LIABILITIES**	
Reserves	$8,000	Deposits	$8,000

As in the case of a loan, the derivative deposit has been transferred to Bank B, where it is received as a primary deposit.

At each stage in the process, 20 percent of the new primary deposit becomes required reserves, and 80 percent becomes excess reserves that can be lent out. In time, the whole of the original $10,000 primary deposit will have become required reserves, and $50,000 of deposits will have been credited to deposit accounts, of which $40,000 will have been lent out.

Table 5.1 further illustrates the deposit expansion process for a 20 percent reserve ratio. A primary deposit of $1,000 is injected into the banking system, making excess reserves of $800 available for loans and investments. Eventually, $5,000 in checkable deposits will be created.

Multiple expansion in the money supply created by the banking system through its expansion of checkable deposits can be expressed in the following formula:

$$\text{Change in checkable deposits} = \frac{\text{Increase in excess reserves}}{\text{Required reserves ratio}} \tag{5.1}$$

We define the terms *excess reserves* and the *required reserves ratio* in the next section. For our purposes, the maximum increase in the amount of checkable deposits is determined by dividing a new inflow of reserves into the banking system by the percentage of checkable deposits that must be held in reserves.

In the example in Table 5.1, the maximum expansion in the checkable deposits component of the money supply, which is the same as the final stage figure shown for checkable deposit liabilities, would be the following:

$$\text{Change in checkable deposits} = \$1,000 \div .20 = \$5,000$$

The maximum increase in deposits (and money supply) that can result from a specific increase in excess reserves is can be referred to as a *money multiplier*. In our basic example, the money

TABLE 5.1

Multiple Expansion of Deposits—20 Percent Reserve Ratio

	ASSETS				LIABILITIES
	RESERVES				
	TOTAL	REQUIRED	EXCESS	LOANS AND INVESTMENTS	CHECKABLE DEPOSITS
Initial Reserves	$1,000	$200	$800	$0	$1,000
Stage 1	1,000	360	640	800	1,800
Stage 2	1,000	488	512	1,440	2,440
Stage 3	1,000	590	410	1,952	2,952
Stage 4	1,000	672	328	2,362	3,362
Stage 5	1,000	738	262	2,690	3,690
Stage 6	1,000	790	210	2,952	3,952
Stage 7	1,000	832	168	3,162	4,162
Stage 8	1,000	866	134	3,330	4,330
Stage 9	1,000	893	107	3,464	4,464
Stage 10	1,000	914	86	3,571	4,571
.	.	.	.	.	.
.	.	.	.	.	.
.	.	.	.	.	.
Final Stage	$1,000	$1,000	$0	$4,000	$5,000

CONCEPT CHECK

How can an increase in excess reserves produce a larger increase in checkable deposits?

multiplier (*m*) is equal to 1 divided by the required reserves ratio, or $m = 1 \div .20 = 5$. However, in the complex U.S. economy, several factors or "leakages" reduce the ability to reach the maximum expansion in the money supply depicted in this simplified example. We will discuss a more realistic money multiplier ratio in the last section of this chapter.

OFFSETTING OR LIMITING FACTORS

Deposit creation can go on only to the extent that the activities described occur. If, for any reason, the proceeds of a loan are withdrawn from the banking system, no new deposit will arise to continue the process. A new deposit of $10,000 permits loans of $8,000 under a 20 percent required reserve; if this $8,000 were used in currency transactions without being deposited in a bank, no deposit could be created. The custom of doing business by means of checks makes deposit creation possible.

In the examples above, no allowance was made for cash leakage or currency withdrawal from the system. In actual practice, as the volume of business in the economy increases, some additional cash is withdrawn for hand-to-hand circulation and to meet the needs of business for petty cash.

Money may be withdrawn from the banking system to meet the demand for payments to foreign countries, or foreign banks may withdraw some of the money they are holding on deposit in U.S. banks. The U.S. Treasury may withdraw funds it has on deposit in banks. All of these factors reduce the multiplying capacity of primary deposits.

Furthermore, this process can go on only if excess reserves are being lent by the banks. This means banks must be willing to lend the full amount of their excess reserves and that acceptable borrowers who have a demand for loans must be available.

The nonbank public's decisions to switch funds between checkable deposits and time or savings deposits will influence the ability to expand the money supply and credit. This is explored later in the chapter.

CONTRACTION OF DEPOSITS

When the need for funds by business decreases, deposit expansion can work in reverse. Expansion takes place as long as excess reserves exist and the demand for new bank loans exceeds the repayment of old loans. Deposit contraction takes place when old loans are being repaid faster than new loans are being granted and banks are not immediately investing these excess funds.

Assuming that Bank A has no excess reserves, let us see the effect of a loan being repaid. Before the borrower built up deposits to repay the loan, the bank's books showed:

BANK A			
ASSETS		LIABILITIES	
Reserves	$2,000	Deposits	$10,000
Loans	$8,000		

The borrower of the $8,000 must build up his or her deposit account by $8,000 to be able to repay the loan. This is reflected on the books as follows:

BANK A			
ASSETS		LIABILITIES	
Reserves	$10,000	Deposits	$18,000
Loans	$ 8,000		

After the $8,000 is repaid, the books show the following:

BANK A			
ASSETS		LIABILITIES	
Reserves	$10,000	Deposits	$10,000

If no new loan is made from the $10,000 of reserves, deposit contraction will result. This is true because $8,000 of funds have been taken out of the banking system to build up deposits to repay the loan and are being held idle by Bank A as excess reserves. Furthermore, taking out $8,000 of reserves from the banking system may be cumulative on the contraction side as it was during expansion.

FACTORS AFFECTING BANK RESERVES

The level of a bank's excess reserves determines the extent to which deposit expansion (or contraction) takes place. This is true for an individual bank and for the banking system as a whole. Therefore, the factors that affect the level of bank reserves are significant in determining the size of the money supply. **Bank reserves** in the banking system consist of reserve balances and vault cash used to meet reserve requirements. Reserve balances are deposits held at the Reserve Banks by commercial banks and other depository institutions. Vault cash is currency, including coin, held on the premises of these institutions.

Total bank reserves can be divided into two parts. The first, **required reserves**, is the minimum amount of total reserves that a depository institution must hold. The percentage of deposits that must be held as reserves is called the **required reserves ratio**. The second part of total reserves is **excess reserves**, the amount by which total reserves exceed required reserves. If required reserves are larger than the total reserves of an institution, the difference is called **deficit reserves**.

Two kinds of factors affect total reserves: those that affect the currency holdings of the banking system and those that affect deposits at the Fed. Currency flows in response to changes in the demand for it by households and businesses. Reserve balances are affected by a variety of transactions involving the Fed and banks that may be initiated by the banking system, the Fed, the Treasury, or other factors. Although the Fed does not control all of the factors that affect the level of bank reserves, it does have the ability to offset increases and decreases. Thus, it has broad control over the total reserves available to the banking system. Figure 5.2 provides a summary of the transactions that affect bank reserves. Discussion of these transactions follows.

CHANGES IN THE DEMAND FOR CURRENCY

Currency flows into and out of the banking system affect the level of reserves of the banks receiving the currency for deposit. Let's assume that an individual or a business finds it has excess currency of $100 and deposit it in Bank A. Deposit liabilities and the reserves of Bank A

CONCEPT CHECK

What causes deposit contraction to take place?

bank reserves
reserve balances and vault cash used to meet reserve requirements

required reserves
the minimum amount of total reserves that a depository institution must hold

required reserves ratio
the percentage of deposits that must be held as reserves

excess reserves
the amount by which total reserves exceed required reserves

deficit reserves
the amount by which required reserves are larger than total reserves of an institution

FIGURE 5.2

Transactions Affecting Bank Reserves

PUBLIC	SYSTEM	U.S. TREASURY
Change in the non-bank public's demand for currency to be held outside the banking system	Change in reserve ratio Open-market operations (buying and selling government securities) Change in bank borrowings Change in float Change in foreign deposits held in Reserve Banks Change in other Federal Reserve accounts	Change in Treasury spending out of accounts held at Reserve Banks Change in Treasury cash holdings

CONCEPT CHECK

What is the definition of bank reserves?

What is the difference between required reserves and excess reserves?

What is the required reserves ratio?

INTERNET ACTIVITY

Go to the St. Louis Federal Reserve Bank's Web site, http://www.stlouisfed.org, and access the FRED database within the Research & Data tab. Find the MB, MS, and GDP data. Calculate m and the velocity of money.

CONCEPT CHECK

Why does the demand for currency change around the end of the calendar year?

are increased by $100. The bank has excess reserves of $80, assuming a 20 percent level of required reserves. These reserves can be used by the banking system to create $400 in additional deposits. If the bank does not need the currency but sends it to its Reserve Bank, it will receive a $100 credit to its account. The volume of Federal Reserve notes in circulation is decreased by $100. These transactions may be summarized as follows:

1. Deposits in Bank A are increased by $100 ($20 in required reserves and $80 in excess reserves).
2. Bank A's deposit at its Reserve Bank is increased by $100.
3. The amount of Federal Reserve notes is decreased by $100.

The opposite takes place when the public demands additional currency. Let us assume a customer of Bank A needs additional currency and cashes a check for $100. The deposits of the bank are reduced by $100, and this reduces required reserves by $20. If the bank has no excess reserves, it must take steps to get an additional $80 of reserves by borrowing from its Reserve Bank, demanding payment for a loan, not renewing one that comes due, or selling securities. When the check is cashed, the reserves of the bank are reduced by $100. If the bank has to replenish its supply of currency from its Reserve Bank, its reserve deposits are reduced by $100. These transactions may be summarized as follows:

1. Deposits in Bank A are reduced by $100 ($20 in required reserves and $80 in excess reserves).
2. Bank A's deposit at its Reserve Bank is reduced by $100.
3. The amount of Federal Reserve notes in circulation is increased by $100.

Changes in the components of the money supply traditionally have occurred during holiday periods, with the most pronounced change taking place during the year-end holiday season. These changes are beyond the immediate control of the Fed, which must anticipate and respond to them to carry out possible money supply growth targets. Generally, an increase in currency outstanding occurs between November and December and a subsequent partial reversal occurs during January. An increase in circulating currency prior to the Christmas holidays requires adjustment by the Fed to control the money supply. As large amounts of cash are withdrawn from depository institutions, deposit contraction might occur unless the Fed moves to offset it by purchasing government securities in the open market.

Also demand deposits traditionally see an increase between November and December and a subsequent decline in demand deposits during the early part of the next year. This seems to reflect the public's surge in spending during the Christmas holiday season and the payment for many of the purchases early in the next year by writing checks on demand deposit accounts. The Fed, in its effort to control bank reserves and the money supply, must take corrective actions to temper the impact of these seasonal swings in currency and checking account balances. Of course, the increasing use of credit cards and debit cards continues to alter the use of currency and the writing of checks.

FEDERAL RESERVE SYSTEM TRANSACTIONS

Transactions of banks with the Fed and changes in reserve requirements by the Fed affect the level of total reserves or the degree to which deposits can be expanded with a given volume of reserves. Such transactions are initiated by the Fed when it buys or sells securities, by a depository

CAREER OPPORTUNITIES IN FINANCE
Government or Not-for-Profit Organizations

Opportunities

The federal government is the largest employer in the United States. In addition, state and local governments hire thousands of workers across the nation. Not-for-profit organizations, such as hospitals, employ numerous workers with backgrounds in business and finance. Many job seekers, however, never consider that government and not-for-profit organizations need the same financial services as businesses do. Therefore, jobs available in this field often go unnoticed. All federal and state jobs are listed at your local state employment services office and online at https://my.usajobs.opm.gov/, which is the federal government's official jobs site. You may also contact your state or regional Federal Employment Information Center for more information on federal jobs (your state or federal representative will know how to get in touch with these offices).

Jobs

Financial manager
Financial analyst
Financial planner

Responsibilities

A financial manager manages cash funds, makes asset acquisition decisions, controls costs, and obtains borrowed funds. A financial manager with a government or a not-for-profit organization must stay abreast of current legislation and public and private grant opportunities.

A financial analyst assesses the short-term and long-term financial performance of a government or not-for-profit organization.

A financial planner uses financial analysis to develop a financial plan.

Education

Knowledge of economics and finance is necessary for these jobs, and an understanding of the executive and legislative process is helpful. In addition, a primary way in which government and not-for-profit groups obtain funds is by getting grants. Therefore, strong research and writing skills for grant proposals also are essential.

---

institution when it borrows from its Reserve Bank, or by a change in Federal Reserve float. These are examined here, and the effect of a change in reserve requirements is described. Finally, we will look at Treasury transactions, which can affect reserves in the banking system.

Open-Market Operations

When the Fed, through its open-market operations, purchases securities such as government bonds, it adds to bank reserves. The Fed pays for the bonds with a check. The seller deposits the check in an account and receives a deposit account credit. The bank presents the check to the Reserve Bank for payment and receives a credit to its account. When the Fed buys a $1,000 government bond, the check for which is deposited in Bank A, the transactions may be summarized as follows:

1. Bank A's deposit at its Reserve Bank is increased by $1,000. The Reserve Bank has a new asset: a bond worth $1,000.
2. Deposits in Bank A are increased by $1,000 ($200 in required reserves and $800 in excess reserves).

The opposite takes place when the Fed sells securities in the market.

In contrast to the other actions that affect reserves in the banking system, the Fed conducts all open-market operations. For this reason, they are the most important policy tool the Fed has to control reserves and the money supply. Open-market operations are conducted nearly every business day to smooth out ups and downs caused by other transactions and to implement changes in the money supply called for by the Federal Open Market Committee (FOMC).

Depository Institution Transactions

When a bank borrows from its Reserve Bank, it is borrowing reserves; so, reserves are increased by the amount of the loan. Similarly, when a loan to the Reserve Bank is repaid, reserves are reduced by that amount. The transactions when Bank A borrows $1,000 from its Reserve Bank may be summarized as follows:

1. Bank A's deposit at its Reserve Bank is increased by $1,000. The assets of the Reserve Bank are increased by $1,000 by the note from Bank A.
2. Bank A's excess reserves have been increased by $1,000. It aso has a new $1,000 liability, its note to the Reserve Bank.

This process is reversed when a debt to the Reserve Bank is repaid.

CONCEPT CHECK

Who is responsible for conducting open-market operations?

Federal Reserve Float

Federal Reserve float
temporary increase in bank
reserves that results when
checks are credited to the
reserve account of the
depositing bank before they
are debited from the account
of the banks on which they
are drawn

Changes in the Federal Reserve float affect bank reserves. A *float* arises out of the process of collecting checks handled by Reserve Banks. A **Federal Reserve float** is the temporary increase in bank reserves that results when checks are credited to the reserve account of the depositing bank before they are debited from the account of the banks on which they are drawn. Checks drawn on nearby banks are credited almost immediately to the account of the bank in which they were deposited and debited to the account of the bank on which the check was drawn. Under Fed regulations, all checks are credited one or two days later to the account of the bank in which the check was deposited. It may take longer for the check to go through the collection process and be debited to the account of the bank upon which it is drawn. When this happens, bank reserves are increased, and this increase is called a *float*. The process by which a $1,000 check drawn on Bank B is deposited in Bank A and credited to its account before it is debited to the account of Bank B may be summarized in the following way:

1. Bank A transfers $1,000 from its Cash Items in the Process of Collection to its account at the Reserve Bank. Its reserves are increased by $1,000.
2. The Reserve Bank takes $1,000 from its Deferred Availability Account and transfers it to Bank A's account.

Thus, total reserves of banks are increased temporarily by $1,000. They are reduced when Bank B's account at its Reserve Bank is reduced by $1,000 a day or two later.

Changes in reserve requirements change the amount of deposit expansion that is possible with a given level of reserves. With a reserve ratio of 20 percent, excess reserves of $800 can be expanded to $4,000 of additional loans and deposits. If the reserve ratio is reduced to 10 percent, it is possible to expand $800 of excess reserves to $8,000 of additional loans and deposits. When the reserve ratio is lowered, additional expansion takes place because part of the required reserves becomes excess reserves. This process is reversed when the reserve ratio is raised.

Bank reserves are affected by changes in the level of deposits of foreign central banks and governments at the Reserve Banks. These deposits are maintained with the Reserve Banks at times as part of the monetary reserves of a foreign country and may be used to settle international balances. A decrease in such foreign deposits with the Reserve Banks increases bank reserves; an increase in them decreases bank reserves.

CONCEPT CHECK

What is the meaning of the term Federal Reserve float?

Treasury Transactions

Bank reserves are affected by the transactions of the Treasury. They are increased by spending and making payments and decreased when the Treasury increases the size of its accounts at the Reserve Banks. The Treasury makes almost all of its payments out of its accounts at the Reserve Banks, and such spending adds to bank reserves. For example, the recipient of a check from the Treasury deposits it in a bank. The bank sends it to the Reserve Bank for collection and receives a credit to its account. The Reserve Bank debits the account of the Treasury. When a Treasury check for $1,000 is deposited in Bank A and required reserves are 20 percent, the transactions may be summarized as follows:

1. The deposits of Bank A are increased by $1,000, its required reserves by $200, and excess reserves by $800.
2. Bank A's reserves at the Reserve Bank are increased by $1,000.
3. The deposit account of the Treasury at the Reserve Bank is reduced by $1,000.

Treasury funds from tax collections or the sale of bonds are generally deposited in its accounts in banks. When the Treasury needs payment funds from its accounts at the Reserve Banks, it transfers funds from commercial banks to its accounts at the Reserve Banks. This process reduces bank reserves. When $1,000 is transferred from the account in Bank A and required reserves are 20 percent, transactions may be summarized as follows:

1. The Treasury deposit in Bank A is reduced by $1,000, required reserves by $200, and excess reserves by $800.
2. The Treasury account at the Reserve Bank is increased by $1,000, and the account of Bank A is reduced by $1,000.

CONCEPT CHECK

Bank reserves are decreased when the Treasury takes what actions?

The Treasury is the largest depositor at the Fed. The volume of transfers between the account of the Treasury and the reserve accounts of banks is large enough to cause significant changes in reserves in the banking system. For this reason, the Fed closely monitors the Treasury's account and often uses open-market operations to minimize its effect on bank reserves. This is accomplished by purchasing securities to provide reserves to the banking system when the Treasury's account increases and selling securities when the account of the Treasury falls to a low level.

The effect on bank reserves is the same for changes in Treasury cash holdings as it is for changes in Treasury accounts at the Reserve Banks. Reserves are increased when the Treasury decreases its cash holdings, and reserves are decreased when it increases such holdings.

THE MONETARY BASE AND THE MONEY MULTIPLIER

Earlier in this chapter, we examined the deposit multiplying capacity of the banking system. Recall that, in the example shown in Table 5.1, excess reserves of $1,000 were introduced into a banking system having a 20 percent required reserves ratio, resulting in a deposit expansion of $5,000. This can be viewed as a money multiplier of 5.

In our complex financial system, the money multiplier is not quite so straightforward. It will be useful to focus on the relationship between the monetary base and the money supply to better understand the complexity of the money multiplier. The **monetary base** (MB) is defined as banking system reserves plus currency held by the public. More specifically, the monetary base consists of reserve deposits held in Reserve Banks, vault cash or currency held by depository institutions, and currency held by the nonbank public. The **money multiplier** is the number of times the monetary base can be expanded or magnified to produce a given money supply level. Conceptually, the M1 definition of the money supply is the monetary base (MB) multiplied by the money multiplier (m). In equation form, we have:

$$M1 = MB \times m \tag{5.2}$$

The size and stability of the money multiplier are important because the Fed can control the monetary base but it cannot directly control the size of the money supply. Changes in the money supply are caused by changes in the monetary base, in the money multiplier, or in both. The Fed can change the size of the monetary base through open-market operations or changes in the reserve ratio. The money multiplier changes. It fluctuates over time depending on actions taken by the Fed as well as by the nonbank public and the U.S. Treasury.

At the end of December 2012, the money multiplier was approximately .89, as determined by dividing the $2,459.6 billion M1 money stock by the $2,760.7 billion monetary base.[4] Taking into account the actions of the nonbank public and the Treasury, the formula for the money multiplier in today's financial system can be expressed in this way:[5]

$$m = \frac{(1 + k)}{[r(1 + t + g) + k]} \tag{5.3}$$

where

r = the ratio of reserves to total deposits (checkable, noncheckable time and savings, and government)

k = the ratio of currency held by the nonbank public to checkable deposits

t = the ratio of noncheckable deposits to checkable deposits

g = the ratio of government deposits to checkable deposits

Let's illustrate how the size of the *money multiplier* is determined by returning to our previous example of a 20 percent reserve ratio. Recall that in a more simple financial system, the *money multiplier* would be determined as $1 \div r$ or $1 \div .20$, which equals 5. However, in our complex system we also need to consider leakages into currency held by the nonbank public, noncheckable

---

monetary base (MB)
banking system reserves plus currency held by the public

money multiplier (m)
number of times the monetary base can be expanded or magnified to produce a given money supply level

---

4. Federal Reserve Bank of St. Louis, *Federal Reserve Economic Database (FRED)*, http://stlouisfed.org. As the 2007–2008 financial crisis worsened, this ratio dropped below 1.0 in late 2008 and has continued below 1.0.

5. The reader interested in understanding how *m* is derived will find a discussion in most financial institutions and markets textbooks.

time and savings deposits, and government deposits. Let's further assume that the reserve ratio applies to total deposits, a k of 40 percent, a t of 15 percent, and a g of 10 percent. The money multiplier would be estimated as the following:

$$m = \frac{(1 + .40)}{[.20(1 + .15 + .10) + .40]} = \frac{1.40}{.65} = 2.15$$

Of course, if a change occurred in any of the components, the money multiplier would adjust accordingly as would the size of the money supply.

In Chapter 2, we briefly discussed the link between the money supply and economic activity. You should be able to recall that the money supply (M1) is linked to the gross domestic product (GDP) via the velocity or turnover of money. More specifically, the **velocity of money (VM)** measures the rate of circulation of the money supply. It is expressed as the average number of times each dollar is spent on purchases of goods and services and is calculated as nominal GDP (GDP in current dollars) divided by M1. Changes in the growth rates for money supply (M1g) and money velocity (M1Vg) affect the growth rate in real economic activity (RGDPg) and the rate of inflation (Ig) and can be expressed in equation form as follows:

$$M1_g + M1V_g = RGDP_g + I_g \tag{5-4}$$

For example, if the velocity of money remains relatively constant, then a link between money supply and the nominal GDP should be observable. Likewise, after nominal GDP is adjusted for inflation, the resulting real GDP growth can be examined relative to M1 growth rates. Changes in money supply have been found in the past to lead to changes in economic activity. However, a relationship between money supply and economic activity has been questioned during the recent perfect financial storm. In an effort to thwart a possible collapse of the financial system, recall that the Fed moved to force short-term interest rates to near zero and provided massive amounts of money liquidity. Furthermore, the Fed introduced the use of a non-traditional monetary tool called quantitative easing to further support the economic recovery efforts after the 2007–2008 financial crisis and the 2008–2009 Great Recession. These efforts have distorted the traditional money multiplier and velocity of money relationships.

velocity of money
the average number of times each dollar is spent on purchases of goods and services and is calculated as nominal GDP (GDP in current dollars) divided by M1

CONCEPT CHECK

What is the monetary base?

What does the velocity of money measure?

APPLYING FINANCE TO...

INSTITUTIONS AND MARKETS

Policy makers pass laws and implement fiscal and monetary policies. A recent change in law, as noted in Chapter 3, allows U.S. commercial banks again to engage in commercial and investment banking activities and to become universal banks. Policy makers influence and change the types of financial institutions and their operations. The operations of depository institutions are directly influenced by monetary policy decisions relating to reserve requirements and Fed discount rates. The ability of financial institutions to carry out the savings-investment process is affected by the actions of policy makers.

INVESTMENTS

The prices of securities typically reflect economic activity and the level of interest rates. Real growth in the economy, accompanied by high employment and low interest rates, makes for attractive investment opportunities. Individual and institutional investors usually find the values of their investments rising during periods of economic prosperity. However, there are times when policy makers fear that the loss of purchasing power associated with high inflation outweighs the value of economic expansion. During these times, securities prices suffer.

FINANCIAL MANAGEMENT

The operations of businesses are directly affected by policy makers. Fiscal and monetary policies that constrain economic growth make it difficult for businesses to operate and make profits. Financial managers must periodically raise financial capital in the securities markets. Actions by policy makers to constrain the money supply and to make borrowing more costly will give financial managers many sleepless nights. On the other hand, expansive monetary policy accompanied by low inflation usually is conducive to business growth, lower interest rates, and higher stock prices—making it easier for financial managers to obtain, at reasonable costs, the financial capital needed to grow their businesses.

The Fed continues to emphasize easy money with short-term interest rates near zero and proposes to continue to do so until the unemployment rate reaches 6.5 percent and inflation is not expected to exceed 2.5 percent. Of course, economic activity is affected by government actions concerning government spending, taxation, and the management of our public debt. Thus, monetary and fiscal policy must work together to achieve the United States' national economic policy objectives.

SUMMARY

This chapter began with a discussion of the four national policy objectives: economic growth, stable prices, high levels of employment, and a balance in international transactions. The Federal Reserve System (Fed), the president, Congress, and the U.S. Treasury were identified as major policy makers. The Fed formulates monetary policy, and Congress and the president sets fiscal policy. The Treasury helps administer and carry out fiscal policy, and the Treasury is responsible for financing the national debt.

The remainder of the chapter focused on several aspects of the money supply. First, the mechanics of deposit expansion and contraction within the banking system were covered. Deposit expansion (and contraction) can take place in the banking system because only a small fraction of the dollar amount of deposits must be held as reserves. Thus, when an individual bank receives a new deposit, a portion of the deposit must be held as reserves while the remainder can be lent out to businesses or individuals. This was followed by a discussion of the factors that affect bank reserves. For example, changes in the demand for currency, the Fed's open-market operations, and Treasury transactions can affect the level of bank reserves. Finally, the terms monetary base (MB) and money multiplier (m) were defined and the importance of controlling the money supply was discussed.

KEY TERMS

automatic stabilizers	Federal Reserve float	national debt
bank reserves	fiscal policy	primary deposit
crowding out	fractional reserve system	required reserves
debt management	gross domestic product (GDP)	required reserves ratio
deficit financing	inflation	tax policy
deficit reserves	monetary base	transfer payments
derivative deposit	monetizing the debt	velocity of money
excess reserves	money multiplier	

DISCUSSION QUESTIONS

1. List and describe briefly the economic policy objectives of the nation.

2. Describe the relationship among policy makers, types of policies, and policy objectives.

3. Describe how the U.S. government responded to the perfect financial storm.

4. Describe the effects of tax policy on monetary and credit conditions.

5. Federal government deficit financing may have a great influence on monetary and credit conditions. Explain.

6. Discuss the various objectives of debt management.

7. Explain how Federal Reserve notes are supported or backed in our financial system.

8. Why are the expansion and contraction of deposits by the banking system possible in our financial system?

9. Trace the effect on its accounts of a loan made by a bank that has excess reserves available from new deposits.

10. Explain how deposit expansion takes place in a banking system consisting of two banks.

11. Explain the potential for deposit expansion when required reserves average 10 percent and $2,000 in excess reserves are deposited in the banking system.

12. Trace the effect on bank reserves of a change in the amount of cash held by the public.

13. Describe the effect on bank reserves when the Federal Reserve sells U.S. government securities to a bank.

14. Summarize the factors that can lead to a change in bank reserves.

15. What is the difference between the monetary base and total bank reserves?

16. Briefly describe what is meant by the money multiplier (m) and indicate the factors that affect its magnitude or size.

17. Define the velocity of money (VM), and explain why it is important to anticipate changes in money velocity.

18. Why does it seem to be important to regulate and control the supply of money?

EXERCISES

1. Go to the St. Louis Federal Reserve Bank's website at http://www.stlouisfed.org, and access current economic data via the Research & Data tab.

　a. Find M1 and the monetary base, and estimate the money multiplier.

　b. Determine the nominal gross national product (GNP in current dollars). Estimate the velocity of money using M1 from (a) and nominal GNP.

　c. Indicate how the *money multiplier* and the velocity of money have changed between two recent years.

2. Important policy objectives of the federal government include economic growth, high employment, price stability, and a balance in international transactions. The achievement of these objectives is the responsibility of monetary policy, fiscal policy, and debt management carried out by the Fed, the president, Congress, and the U.S. Treasury. Describe the responsibilities of the various policy makers in trying to achieve the four economic policy objectives.

3. An economic recession has developed, and the Federal Reserve's Board of Governors has taken several actions to retard further declines in economic activity. The U.S. Treasury wishes to take steps to assist the Fed in this effort. Describe the actions the Treasury might take.

4. The president and members of Congress are elected by the people and are expected to behave ethically. Let's assume that you are a recently elected member of Congress. A special-interest lobbying group is offering to contribute funds to your next election campaign in the hope that you will support legislation being proposed by others that will help the group achieve its stated objectives. What would you do?

PROBLEMS

1. Assume that Banc One receives a primary deposit of $1 million. The bank must keep reserves of 20 percent against its deposits. Prepare a simple balance sheet of assets and liabilities for Banc One immediately after the deposit is received.

2. Assume that Bank A receives a primary deposit of $100,000 and that it must keep reserves of 10 percent against deposits.

　a. Prepare a simple balance sheet of assets and liabilities for the bank immediately after the deposit is received.

　b. Assume Bank A makes a loan in the amount that can be safely lent. Show what the bank's balance sheet of assets and liabilities would look like immediately after the loan.

　c. Assume that a check in the amount of the derivative deposit created in (b) was written and sent to another bank. Show what Bank A's (the lending bank's) balance sheet of assets and liabilities would look like after the check is written.

3. Rework Problem 2 assuming Bank A has reserve requirements that are 15 percent of deposits.

4. Assume two banks, A and Z, exist in the banking system. Bank A receives a primary deposit of $600,000, and it must keep reserves of 12 percent against deposits. Bank A makes a loan in the amount that can be safely lent.

　a. Show what Bank A's balance sheet of assets and liabilities would look like immediately after the loan.

　b. Assume that a check is drawn against the primary deposit made in Bank A and is deposited in Bank Z. Show what the balance sheet of assets and liabilities would look like for each of the two banks after the transaction has taken place.

　c. Assume that Bank Z makes a loan in the amount that can be safely lent against the funds deposited in its bank from the transaction described in (b). Show what Bank Z's balance sheet of assets and liabilities would look like after the loan.

5. The SIMPLEX financial system is characterized by a required reserves ratio of 11 percent; initial excess reserves are $1 million, and there are no currency or other leakages.

　a. What would be the maximum amount of checkable deposits after deposit expansion, and what would be the money multiplier?

　b. How would your answer in (a) change if the reserve requirement had been 9 percent?

6. Assume a financial system has a monetary base (MB) of $25 million. The required reserves ratio is 10 percent, and no leakages are in the system.

　a. What is the size of the money multiplier *(m)*?

　b. What will be the system's money supply?

7. Rework Problem 6 assuming the reserve ratio is 14 percent?

8. The BASIC financial system has a required reserves ratio of 15 percent; initial excess reserves are $5 million, cash held by the public is $1 million and is expected to stay at that level, and no other leakages or adjustments are in the system.

　a. What would be the *money multiplier* and the maximum amount of checkable deposits?

　b. What would be the money supply amount in this system after deposit expansion?

9. Rework Problem 8, assuming that the cash held by the public drops to $500,000 with an equal amount becoming excess reserves and the required reserves ratio drops to 12 percent.

10. The COMPLEX financial system has these relationships: The ratio of reserves to total deposits is 12 percent, and the ratio of noncheckable deposits to checkable deposits is 40 percent. In addition, currency held by the nonbank public amounts to 15 percent of checkable deposits. The ratio of government deposits to checkable deposits is 8 percent, and the monetary base is $300 million.

　a. Determine the size of the M1 money multiplier and the size of the money supply.

　b. If the ratio of currency in circulation to checkable deposits were to drop to 13 percent while the other ratios remained the same, what would be the impact on the money supply?

　c. If the ratio of government deposits to checkable deposits increases to 10 percent while the other ratios remained the same, what would be the impact on the money supply?

　d. What would happen to the money supply if the reserve requirement increased to 14 percent while noncheckable deposits to checkable deposits fell to 35 percent? Assume the other ratios remain as originally stated.

11. **Challenge Problem** ABBIX has a complex financial system with the following relationships: The ratio of required reserves to total deposits is 15 percent, and the ratio of noncheckable deposits to checkable deposits is 40 percent. In addition, currency held by the nonbank public amounts to 20 percent of checkable deposits. The ratio of government deposits to checkable deposits is 8 percent. Initial excess reserves are $900 million.

a. Determine the M1 multiplier and the maximum dollar amount of checkable deposits.

b. Determine the size of the M1 money supply.

c. What will happen to ABBIX's money multiplier value if the reserve requirement decreases to 10 percent while the ratio of noncheckable deposits to checkable deposits falls to 30 percent? Assume the other ratios remain as originally stated.

d. Based on the information in (c), estimate the maximum dollar amount of checkable deposits, as well as the size of the M1 money supply.

e. Assume that ABBIX has a target M1 money supply of $2.8 billion. The only variable you have direct control over is the required reserves ratio. What would the required reserves ratio have to be to reach the target M1 money supply amount? Assume the other original ratio relationships hold.

f. Now assume that currency held by the nonbank public drops to 15 percent of checkable deposits and that ABBIX's target money supply is changed to $3.0 billion. What would the required reserves ratio have to be to reach the new target M1 money supply amount? Assume the other original ratio relationships hold.

• CHAPTER 6 •

International Finance and Trade

Chapter Learning Objectives . . .

AFTER STUDYING THIS CHAPTER, YOU SHOULD BE ABLE TO DO THE FOLLOWING:

- Explain how the international monetary system evolved and how it operates today.
- Describe the efforts undertaken to achieve economic unification of Europe.
- Describe how currency or foreign exchange markets are organized and operate.
- Explain how currency exchange rates are quoted.
- Describe the factors that affect currency exchange rates.
- Describe how the world banking systems facilitate financing of sales by exporters and purchases by importers.
- Identify recent developments in the U.S. balance of payments.

Where We Have Been . . .

In Chapter 5, you learned how the Federal Reserve System (Fed) operates in conjunction with governmental policy makers (the president, Congress, and the U.S. Treasury) in the common effort of achieving the goals of economic growth, high and stable employment levels, price stability, and a balance in international transactions. You now understand policy instruments of the Treasury and how the national debt is managed. You learned how the money supply is expanded and contracted and the importance of the monetary base and money multiplier in setting monetary policy.

Where We Are Going . . .

In Part 2, we focus on developing a better understanding of the area of investments including how securities are valued and how securities markets operate. Chapter 7 examines how savings are directed into various investments, and Chapter 8 discusses how interest rates, or the "price" of money, are determined in the financial markets. Chapter 9 introduces "time" as a factor when determining rates of return on investments. In the remaining chapters, you will learn about the characteristics of bonds and stocks and how they are priced or valued, how securities markets work, and the need to consider risk versus return trade-offs when investing in securities.

How This Chapter Applies to Me . . .

You live in a global environment. You likely have purchased products grown or manufactured in foreign countries and sold in the United States. For example, you may purchase fresh fruit during the winter that was grown in and shipped from South America. You may have purchased a Swiss-made watch from a retail store in the United States. You may have had to convert U.S. dollars into a foreign currency such as euros for a direct product purchase from a manufacturer in Germany. You may have traveled internationally and needed to exchange your dollars for that country's currency. You may even live and work outside the United States in the future. Thus, a basic understanding of international trade and factors that affect currency exchange rates will be useful knowledge to have.

It is important to have an "open view" of other countries from the perspective of what they do and why they do it. Maria Mitchell, a U.S. astronomer, probably summed it up best when she stated the following:

> *I have never been in any country where they did not do something better than we do it, think some thoughts better than we think, catch some inspiration from heights above their own.*[1]

---

1. *Life, Letters, and Journals*, by Maria Mitchell, 1896.

Interactions among countries are complex. Philosophical, cultural, economic, and religious differences exist. These differences jointly establish the basis for international relations and help us understand the practice of internationalism by specific countries. Differences in philosophies, cultures, economic models, and religion often provide the basis for establishing a nation's foreign policy. At the same time, nearly everyone would agree that, in the best interests of worldwide economic growth and productivity, countries must work together in facilitating international trade and the flow of financial capital. While this chapter focuses on the economics of international trade and finance, we recognize the importance of being willing to understand the basis for differences among countries in terms of philosophies, cultures, economic models, and religions.

GLOBAL DISCUSSION

international monetary system
a system of institutions and mechanisms to foster international trade, manage the flow of financial capital, and determine currency exchange rates

GLOBAL OR INTERNATIONAL MONETARY SYSTEM

In the first five chapters of Part 1, we focused on covering the role of the U.S. financial system, the monetary system, and monetary policy. When viewed in a global context, responsibilities become more complex. The global or *international monetary system* is a system of institutions and mechanisms to foster world trade, manage the flow of financial capital, and determine currency exchange rates. We first begin with a brief discussion of the historical development of international trade and finance. Then we turn our attention to how the international monetary system has changed or evolved over the past couple of centuries.

DEVELOPMENT OF INTERNATIONAL FINANCE

International finance probably began about 5,000 years ago when Babylonian cities rose to importance as centers of trading between the Mediterranean Sea and civilizations in the East. Gold was used for transactions and as a store of value probably beginning around 3000 B.C., when the pharaohs ruled Egypt. Centers of international finance shifted to the Greek city of Athens around 500 B.C. and to the Roman Empire and Rome around 100 B.C.[2] It appears that whenever international trade developed, financial institutions came into existence and international bankers followed.

Instruments and documents similar to those in use today were designed to control movement of cargo, insure against losses, satisfy government requirements, and transfer funds. Financial centers shifted to the northern European cities during the 1500s and, in more recent years, to London, New York, and Tokyo. Today, international trade takes place and international claims are settled around the clock. It is no longer necessary to have a physical center, such as a city, in which to carry out international financial operations.

HOW THE INTERNATIONAL MONETARY SYSTEM EVOLVED

Before World War I

gold standard
a standard in which currencies of countries of major countries are convertible into gold at fixed exchange rates

Prior to the start of World War I in 1914, the international monetary system operated mostly under a *gold standard* whereby the currencies of major countries were convertible into gold at fixed exchange rates. For example, 1 ounce of gold might be worth 20 U.S. dollars, or $1 would be worth one-twentieth (or .05) of an ounce of gold. At the same time, 1 ounce of gold might be worth 5 French francs (FF), or FF1 would be worth one-fifth (or .20) of an ounce of gold. Since $20 could be converted into 1 ounce of gold that could then be used to purchase 5 FF, or 20 U.S. dollars, the exchange rate between the dollar and franc would be 20 to 5, or 4 to 1. Alternatively, .20 ÷ .05 equals 4 to 1.

CONCEPT CHECK

When did international finance begin?

What is meant by being on a gold standard?

Recall from Chapter 1 that the American colonies relied primarily on the Spanish dollar to conduct business transactions prior to the 1800s. In 1792, the first U.S. monetary act was enacted and provided for a *bimetallic standard* based on gold and silver. A standard based solely on gold was not adopted until 1879. In those days, coins were *full-bodied money* in that their metal content was worth the same as their face values. Paper money then was *representative full-bodied money* because the paper money was backed by an amount of precious metal equal to the money's face value.

---

2. For a more detailed look at the early development of international finance, see Robert D. Fraser, *International Banking and Finance,* 6th ed., Washington, DC: R&H Publishers, 1984, ch. 2.

INTERNET ACTIVITY

Go to the International Monetary Fund Web site, http://www.imf.org using the Search box, and find information about "special drawing rights" (SDRs) and how they are used as reserve assets.

During the 1800s, most other developed countries had their own currencies tied to gold, silver, or both. By the end of the 1800s, most countries had adopted the gold standard. However, coinciding with the start of World War I, most countries went off the gold standard. For example, the Federal Reserve Act of 1913 provided for the issuance of Federal Reserve Notes, called *fiat money* because they were not backed by gold or silver. Recall from Chapter 1 that the government decreed the notes to be "legal tender" for purposes of making payments and discharging public and private debts. Fiat money has value that is based solely on confidence in the U.S. government's being able to achieve economic growth and maintain price stability. Most foreign governments moved to monetary systems based on fiat money.

A major criticism of the gold standard was that as the volume of world trade increased over the years, the supply of "new" gold would fail to keep pace. Thus, without some form of supplementary international money, the result would be international deflation. A second criticism of the gold standard was a lack of an international organization to monitor and report whether countries were deviating from the standard when it was in their own best interests.

World War I through World War II: 1915–1944

During the interwar period from 1915 through 1944, which encompassed most of World War 1, the period in between, and World War II, an attempt was made to go back onto the gold standard. Many nations returned to the gold standard during the 1920s only to go off it again in the early 1930s because of financial crises associated with the Great Depression. A series of bank failures and continued outflow of gold caused the United States to abandon the gold standard in 1933.

Bretton Woods Fixed Exchange Rate System: 1945–1972

In mid-1944, authorities from all major nations met in Bretton Woods, New Hampshire, to formulate a post-World War II international monetary system. The *International Monetary Fund (IMF)* was created to promote world trade through monitoring and maintaining fixed exchange rates and by making loans to countries facing balance of trade and payments problems. The International Bank for Reconstruction and Development or *World Bank* was created to help economic growth in developing countries.

The most significant development of the conference was the exchange rate agreement commonly called the *Bretton Woods system*, in which individual currencies would be tied to gold through the U.S. dollar via fixed or pegged exchange rates. One ounce of gold was set equal to $35. Each participating country's currency was then set at a "par" or fixed value in relation to the U.S. dollar. For example, one French franc might be one-seventh of a U.S. dollar or $.1429. Thus, a franc would "indirectly" be worth $5 in gold (i.e., $35 ÷ 7). In essence, one franc could be exchanged for $.1429, which could be exchanged for $5 in gold (.1429 × $35).

Countries adopting the Bretton Woods system could hold their reserves in gold or U.S. dollars because the dollar was the only currency on the gold standard. This eliminated one of the criticisms associated with all currencies being on a gold standard system in that world economic growth was restricted to the rate of increase in new gold production since gold was the only monetary reserve. Since the Bretton Woods System allowed for the holding of gold and U.S. dollars as foreign exchange reserves, this new monetary system allowed for less restrictive world economic growth. The negative side of the Bretton Woods System was that the U.S. government had to produce balance-of-payments deficits so foreign exchange reserves would grow.

Unfortunately, by the 1960s, the value of the U.S. gold stock was less than the amount of foreign holdings of dollars. This caused concern about the viability of the Bretton Woods System. To help keep the System operating, in 1970, the International Monetary Fund (IMF) created a new reserve asset called *special drawing rights (SDRs)*, a basket or portfolio of currencies that could be used to make international payments. At first, the SDRs comprised a weighted average of sixteen currencies. At the beginning of the 1980s, the SDR basket was reduced to include only five major currencies. The current SDR basket includes the U.S. dollar (45 percent weight), euro (29 percent weight), Japanese yen (15 percent weight), and British pound (11 percent weight).

Attempts were made to save the Bretton Woods System in 1971 when representatives of major central banks met at the Smithsonian Institution in Washington, D.C., and raised the price of gold to $38 per ounce. In early 1973, the price of gold was increased to $42 per ounce. However, the end of fixed exchange rates was at hand.

International Monetary Fund (IMF)
created to promote world trade through monitoring and maintaining fixed exchange rates and by making loans to countries facing balance of trade and payments problems

World Bank
created to help economic growth in developing countries (also called the International Bank for Reconstruction and Development)

Bretton Woods system
a system in which individual currencies would be tied to gold through the U.S. dollar via fixed or pegged exchange rates

Special Drawing Rights (SDRs)
reserve assets created by the IMF and consisting of a basket or portfolio of currencies that could be used to make international payments

flexible exchange rates
a system in which currency
exchange rates are
determined by supply and
demand

CONCEPT CHECK

What was the Bretton Woods
System of exchange rates?

What exchange rate system is
in use today?

GLOBAL DISCUSSION

European Union (EU)
organization established to
promote trade and economic
development among
European countries

eurozone members
countries that have adopted
the euro as their common
currency

euro
official currency of the
eurozone member countries

CONCEPT CHECK

What is the European Union
(EU)?

What are eurozone members?

What is a euro?

What financial crises have
some EU countries been facing
recently?

Flexible Exchange Rate System: 1973–Present

Beginning in March 1973, major currencies were allowed to "float" against one another. By the mid-1970s, gold was abandoned as a reserve asset, and IMF members accepted a system of *flexible exchange rates*, in which currency exchange rates are determined by supply and demand. A primary objection to flexible exchange rates is the possibility of wide swings in response to changes in supply and demand, with a resulting uncertainty in world trade. Evidence indicates that exchange rates indeed have been more volatile since the collapse of the Bretton Woods System compared to when the System was in place.

Today, many countries allow their currencies to float against others, including Australia, Japan, Canada, the United States, and the United Kingdom (UK). The European Monetary Union (EMU) allows the euro to float freely. In contrast, India, China, and Russia employ semifloating or managed floating systems involving active government intervention. China, for example, pegs its currency to the dollar, with adjustments being related to monetary targets. Thus, the current exchange rate system is a composite of flexible or floating exchange rates, managed floating exchange rates, and pegged exchange rates.

EUROPEAN UNIFICATION

EUROPEAN UNION

The *European Union (EU)* was established to promote trade and economic development among European countries. Economic integration was to be achieved by eliminating barriers that previously restricted the flow of labor, goods, and financial capital among countries. The European Union's history can be traced back to the early 1950s. Six European countries signed the Treaty of Rome that established the *European Economic Community (EEC)* in 1957. The EEC became the *European Community (EC)* in 1978.

In late 1991, members of the European Community met in Maastricht, Netherlands, to draft a treaty. The resulting *Treaty on European Union*, referred to as the *Maastricht Treaty*, was signed by twelve European members in 1992. The *Maastricht Treaty* created the European Union, provided for economic convergence, the fixing of member country exchange rates, and the planned introduction of the euro as the common currency. By 1995, the fifteen EU members were Austria, Belgium, Denmark, Finland, France, Germany, Greece, Ireland, Italy, Luxembourg, Netherlands, Portugal, Spain, Sweden, and the United Kingdom. The European Union grew to a total of twenty-five members with the addition of Cyprus, Czech Republic, Estonia, Hungary, Latvia, Lithuania, Malta, Poland, Slovakia, and Slovenia in 2004. Bulgaria and Romania were added to the European Union in 2007. Croatia joined the EU in mid-2013, resulting in a union of twenty-eight independent states.

EUROZONE MEMBERS

The *European Monetary Union (EMU)* began as a twelve-member subset of the original fifteen members of the EU. EU members Denmark, Sweden, and the United Kingdom chose not to join the EMU. By ratifying the Maastricht Treaty, the EMU agreed to have overall monetary policy set by the *European Central Bank (ECB)* and adopted the euro as its common currency. It is common practice today to refer to the subset of EU members that have adopted the euro as their common currency as *eurozone members.* Slovenia became a eurozone member in 2007, Cyprus and Malta in 2008, Slovakia in 2009, Estonia in 2011, and Latvia in 2014, bringing eurozone membership to 18 countries.

THE EURO

On January 1, 1999, the official currency of the twelve *European Monetary Union* members became the *euro*, a paper currency consisting of seven denominations from 5 to 500. Coins were designed and minted separately. At the beginning of 2002, individual EMU countries' currencies began being phased out; only the euro coin and currency were legal tender by July 2002.

Designing the euro paper currency was a difficult task. It could not include images (e.g., the Eiffel Tower) that could be associated with a single country. Likewise, portraits of individuals (e.g., royalty, military leaders) could not be used. Ultimately, the euro was designed to include "gates" and "windows" for the front of the bills "to symbolize the future"; "bridges" were chosen

SMALL BUSINESS PRACTICE
Finding Foreign Customers

To conduct business in a foreign country, a domestic firm must export to that country or produce goods or offer services in that country. Exporting may take place indirectly or directly. Indirect exporting by U.S. companies involves U.S.-based exporters. These exporters may sell for manufacturers, buy for overseas customers, buy and sell for their own account, and/or buy on behalf of intermediaries or wholesalers.

Exporters that sell for manufacturers usually are manufacturers' export agents or export management companies. A manufacturer's export agent usually represents several noncompeting domestic manufacturers. An export management company acts as an export department for a number of noncompeting domestic firms. Exporters that purchase for overseas customers are called export commission agents since they are paid a commission by foreign purchasers to buy on their behalf.

Small businesses usually find it necessary to use indirect exporting. Direct exporting uses manufacturers' agents, distributors, and retailers

located in the countries where they are conducting business. Only large domestic firms are able to engage in direct exporting.

Various forms of government assistance are available to help businesses in their exporting efforts. Many states have government "trade export" departments that assist firms in their export activities. At the federal level, the Export-Import Bank of the United States was founded in 1934 to aid domestic businesses in finding foreign customers and markets for their products. Export credit insurance also is available to help exporters. The Foreign Credit Insurance Association (FCIA) provides credit insurance policies to U.S. exporters to protect against nonpayment by foreign customers.

In some instances, "countertrading" is used to foster sales to foreign customers. Under such an arrangement, a U.S. exporter sells its goods to a foreign producer in exchange for goods produced by that foreign company. Simple kinds of countertrading take the form of a barter arrangement between a domestic firm and a foreign firm.

---

for the back of the bills. The paper currency uses multicolored ink, watermarks, and three-dimensional holographic images to thwart counterfeiting efforts.

FINANCIAL CRISIS

EUROPEAN UNION FINANCIAL CRISES

The European Union suffered many of the economic problems that the United States went through in the 2007–2008 financial crisis involving the fear of a worldwide financial system collapse. However, while the U.S. was able to recover from its 2008–2009 Great Recession, the economies of many European Union countries continue to face economic development uncertainties and high levels of unemployment. Tax receipts often have been less than government expenditures in many of the EU countries causing national debts to grow rapidly. Rising interest rates have made it increasingly more costly to service interest payments on large amounts of government debt.

Some EU countries have been forced into austerity government expenditure plans at a time of no economic growth and high unemployment, causing in some instances social unrest. Greece has been experiencing difficult economic trade-offs and concern has been expressed as to whether the country will remain a eurozone member. Concern also has been expressed about the financial viability of Spain, Portugal, and Italy.

Efforts are underway to establish a "banking union" to help oversee eurozone efforts to assist members to emerge from their debt crises. The European Central Bank also has committed to buying bonds issued by eurozone countries having financial troubles to help stabilize the costs of government debt financing. Most observers believe that other EU actions will be necessary to solve member country debt crises and to recover from economic recession levels.

GLOBAL DISCUSSION

CURRENCY EXCHANGE MARKETS AND RATES

CURRENCY EXCHANGE MARKETS

currency exchange markets (foreign exchange markets) electronic markets where banks and institutional traders buy and sell currencies on behalf of businesses, other clients, and themselves

We ordinarily think of a market as a specific place or institution, but this is not always so. **Currency exchange markets**, also called foreign exchange markets, are electronic markets where banks and institutional traders buy and sell various currencies on behalf of businesses, other clients, and themselves. The major financial centers of the world are connected electronically so that when an individual or firm engaged in a foreign transaction deals with a local bank, that individual or firm is, in effect, dealing with the exchange markets of the world. Transactions throughout the world may be completed in only a few minutes by virtue of the effective communications network serving the various financial institutions, including central banks of every nation.

INTERNET ACTIVITY

Go to the European Central Bank Web site, http://www. ecb.int click on the The €uro tab, and find information about the history of the euro.

CONCEPT CHECK

What are currency exchange markets?

TABLE 6.1

Selected Foreign Exchange Rates, Late February, 2013

COUNTRY	CURRENCY	FOREIGN CURRENCY IN U.S. DOLLARS (DIRECT METHOD)	FOREIGN CURRENCY PER U.S. DOLLAR (INDIRECT METHOD)
Australia	Dollar	1.0227	0.9778
Brazil	Real	0.5065	1.9743
Canada	Dollar	0.9713	1.0296
China	Yuan	0.16074	6.2214
European	Euro	1.3075	0.7648
Hong Kong	Dollar	0.1289	7.7555
India	Rupee	0.01832	54.5750
Japan	Yen	0.010795	92.6350
Mexico	Peso	0.0784	12.7560
Russia	Ruble	0.0327	30.5865
Singapore	Dollar	0.8084	1.2370
South Africa	Rand	0.1109	9.0150
Switzerland	Franc	1.0700	0.9346
United Kingdom	Pound	1.5175	0.6590

Sources: www.money.cnn.com and www.reuters.com

---

currency exchange rate
value of one currency relative to another currency

direct quotation method
indicates the value of one unit of a foreign currency in terms of a home country's currency

indirect quotation method

indicates the number of units of a foreign currency needed to purchase one unit of the home country's currency

INTERNET ACTIVITY

Go to the CNNMoney Web site, http://money.cnn.com. Click on the Markets tab and then on the Currencies tab, and find current currency exchange rates for the U.S. dollar relative to the Australian dollar, British pound, and Canadian dollar. Find either the direct or indirect exchange rate and calculate the other one.

EXCHANGE RATE QUOTATIONS

A *currency exchange rate* indicates the value of one currency relative to another currency. Table 6.1 shows the currency exchange rates for a variety of foreign currencies relative to the U.S. dollar during February 2013. Currency exchange rates are stated in two basic ways. The *direct quotation method* indicates the value of one unit of a foreign currency in terms of a home country's currency. For illustration purposes, let's focus on the U.S. dollar as the domestic or home country's currency relative to the European euro. Notice in Table 6.1 that the "U.S. dollar equivalent" of one euro was $1.3075; or, stated differently, it took $1.3075 to buy one euro. The *indirect quotation method* indicates the number of units of a foreign currency needed to purchase one unit of the home country's currency. Again, turning to Table 6.1, we see that it takes .7648 euros to purchase one U.S. dollar.

Table 6.1 shows the value of other major currencies in U.S. dollar terms in late February 2013. An Australia dollar was worth $1.0227, a United Kingdom (British) pound had a value $1.5175, a Swiss franc equaled $1.0700, and a Japanese yen was worth $.0108. The corresponding indirect quotations in units relative to one U.S. dollar were as follows: Australia dollar = 0.9778, United Kingdom pound = 0.6590, Swiss franc = 0.9346, and Japanese yen = 92.635. Finding the other quotation is easy if we know the direct or indirect quotation. For example, the indirect quotation can be calculated as follows:

$$\text{Indirect Quotation} \atop \text{(foreign currency units)} = \frac{1}{\text{Direct Quotation} \atop \text{(home currency value)}} \qquad (6.1)$$

For illustration purposes, let's use the euro versus U.S. dollar relationships previously noted. A euro was worth $1.3075 and represents a direct quotation where the United States is the home country. To find the indirect quotation, we would calculate the following:

$$\text{Indirect Quotation} = \frac{1}{\$1.3075} = .7648 \text{ euros}$$

Of course, if we knew that the indirect quotation for the euro relative to the dollar was .7648 euros per U.S. dollar, we could divide that value into 1 to get the direct quotation value: $1 \div .7648 = 1.3075$ or $1.3075.

Table 6.2 shows the "crossrates" amongst several major currencies: the U.S. dollar, the British pound, the yen, and the euro. It is possible to calculate the exchange rate between the yen and the euro by first knowing each of their values relative to the U.S. dollar. For example, a yen was

TABLE 6.2
Selected Foreign Exchange Crossrates, Late February, 2013

CURRENCY	U.S. DOLLAR	EURO	YEN	BRITISH POUND
U.S. Dollar	1.0	0.7648	92.6357	0.6590
Euro	1.3075	1.0	121.1209	0.8616
Yen	0.010795	0.008256	1.0	0.006897
British Pound	1.5175	1.1606	140.574	1.0

Sources: www.money.cnn.com and www.reuters.com

CONCEPT CHECK

What is the difference between the direct and indirect quotation methods for stating currency exchange rates?

worth $.010795 and a euro $1.3075 in late February 2013. Dividing .010795 by 1.3075 gives a value of one yen in euros as 0.008256 euros. Since Table 6.2 shows the crossrates between the yen and the euro, we can read the value of one yen in terms of euros as 0.008256 euros. Of course, if we wanted to know the value of a Brazilian real in euros, we would have to return to Table 6.1 and make the calculation directly. In late February 2013, the U.S. dollar value of a Brazilian real was $.5065 and the value of a euro was $1.3075. Dividing .5065 by 1.3075 indicates that one real was worth .3874 euros.

Electronic and newspaper exchange rate quotes are for large unit transfers within the currency exchange markets. Consequently, individuals buying foreign currencies would not get the same ratio. The currency exchange prices for an individual always favor the seller, who makes a margin of profit.

The balance in the foreign account of a U.S. bank is subject to constant drain as the bank sells foreign currency claims to individuals who import goods or obtain services from other countries. These banks may reestablish a given deposit level in their correspondent banks through selling dollar claims in the foreign countries concerned or by buying claims from another dealer in the foreign exchange.

FACTORS THAT AFFECT CURRENCY EXCHANGE RATES

spot exchange rate
current rate being quoted for delivery of the currency on the spot

forward exchange rate
negotiated exchange rate for the purchase or sale of a currency where delivery will take place at a future date

Each currency exchange rate shown in Table 6.1 is said to be a *spot exchange rate*, or the current rate being quoted for delivery of the currency "on the spot." Actually, it is common practice to have up to two days for delivery after the trade date. It is also possible to enter into a contract for the purchase or sale of a currency when delivery will take place at a future date. In this case, the negotiated exchange rate is referred to as a *forward exchange rate*.

Supply and Demand Relationships

The supply and demand relationship involving two currencies is said to be in "balance" or equilibrium at the current or spot exchange rate. Demand for a foreign currency derives from the demand for the goods, services, and financial assets of a country (or group of countries, such as the eurozone members). For example, U.S. consumers and investors demand a variety of eurozone member goods, services, and financial assets, most of which must be paid for in euros. The supply of European euros comes from eurozone member demand for U.S. goods, services, and financial assets. A change in the relative demand for euros versus U.S. dollars will cause the spot exchange rate to change. Currency exchange rates depend on relative inflation rates, relative interest rates, and political and economic risks.

Figure 6.1 illustrates how exchange rates are determined in a currency exchange market. Graph A depicts a supply and demand relationship between the U.S. dollar and the euro (€). The market, in our example, is in balance when one euro is worth $1.31. This price reflects the market clearing price that equates the demand (D_1) for euros relative to the supply (S_1) of euros.

Now, assume Americans increase their demand for products and services from eurozone member countries, such as Germany and France. These products and services would be priced in euros. Americans will need to exchange their dollars for euros to pay for their purchases. The consequence is an increase or shift in demand for euros from D_1 to D_2 as depicted in Graph B of Figure 6.1. The supply of euros reflects demand by eurozone member countries for U.S. products and services, and as long as there is no change, S_1 will remain unchanged. As a consequence of this scenario, the increased demand for euros results in a new higher equilibrium price of $1.32.

CONCEPT CHECK

What factors determine currency exchange rates?

FIGURE 6.1

Exchange Rate Determination in the Currency Exchange Market

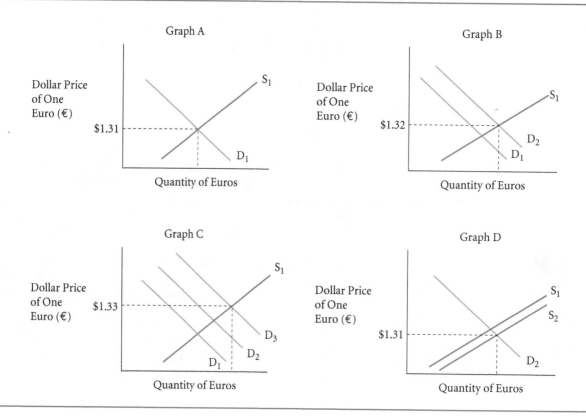

An increased demand for the goods and services from eurozone member countries could cause the dollar price or value of one pound to increase more. Graph C in Figure 6.1 depicts such an increase as a shift from D_2 to D_3. Again, with no change in the supply of euros, the new market clearing price of a pound might be $1.33. As the euro's dollar value increases, the prices of euro-zone member products increase. At some point, as eurozone member products become more costly, and U.S. demand for these foreign goods declines. Graph D depicts this cutback in U.S. demand for euros as a shift downward from D_3 in Graph C to D_2. In a similar fashion, the higher dollar value of the euro in Graph C makes U.S. goods and services less costly to eurozone members, and thus, the supply of euros might increase or shift from S_1 to S_2. The net result could be a new equilibrium exchange rate in which the dollar price of a euro is $1.31.

A change in the demand for one country's financial assets relative to another country's financial assets will cause the currency exchange rate between the two countries to change to a new equilibrium price. For example, a nation with a relatively strong stock market will attract investors who seek out the highest returns on their investment funds, much as a nation with a higher relative economic growth rate attracts capital investments. For example, if the stock market in the United States is expected to perform poorly relative to the stock markets in eurozone member countries, investors will switch or move their debt investments denominated in U.S. dollars into euro-denominated debt investments. This increased demand for euros relative to U.S. dollars will cause the euro's dollar value to increase.

Let's turn our attention to what happens if changes occur in relative nominal (observed) interest rates and inflation rates between two countries. Recall that the nominal interest rate for government debt securities is composed of a "real rate" plus an inflation expectation.[3] The higher (lower) the inflation rate, the higher (lower) will be the nominal interest rate. A nation with a relatively lower inflation rate will have a relatively stronger currency. For example, if inflation declines in the United States relative to eurozone member countries, eurozone member products

---

3. We will cover the factors that determine interest rates in detail in Chapter 8.

of comparable quality will become more expensive. Americans will find it less expensive to buy American products as will eurozone members. The result will be fewer eurozone member imports into the United States and greater U.S. exports to eurozone member countries, causing an appreciation of the dollar relative to the euro. For example, the euro might decline in value from $1.31 to, say, and $1.29.

Inflation, Interest Rates, and Other Factors

purchasing power parity (PPP)

states that a country with a relatively higher expected inflation rate will have its currency depreciate relative to a country (or group of countries using a single currency) with a relatively lower inflation rate

Purchasing power parity (PPP) states that a country with a relatively higher expected inflation rate will have its currency depreciate relative to a country (or group of countries using a single currency) with a relatively lower inflation rate. For example, if the U.S. inflation rate is expected to be 6 percent next year and the eurozone member inflation rate is expected to be 3 percent, we would expect the U.S. dollar to depreciate and the euro to appreciate over the next year. Let's assume that the United States is the home country (hc), the eurozone members represent the foreign country (fc), and the expected inflation rate is designated as InfR. In general equation form we can say that the current or spot rate (SR_0) is equal to the future or forward rate in one year (FR_1) times the expected relative inflation rates:

$$FR_1 = SR_0 \times \frac{1 + InfR_{hc}}{1 + InfR_{fc}} \tag{6.2}$$

For our example, let's assume that the spot rate for a euro is $1.31. We estimate the forward rate as follows:

$$FR_1 = \$1.31 \times \frac{1.06}{1.03}$$

And

$$FR_1 = \$1.31 \times 1.0291 = \$1.35$$

Thus, based on relative expected inflation rates, we expect the euro to appreciate from $1.31 to $1.35 over the next year.

interest rate parity (IRP)

states that a country with a relatively higher nominal interest rate will have its currency depreciate relative to a country with a relatively lower nominal interest rate

Interest rate parity (IRP) states that a country with a relatively higher nominal interest rate will have its currency depreciate relative to a country with a relatively lower nominal interest rate. For example, let's assume that the interest rate (IntR) on a one-year U.S. government debt security is 9 percent while the interest rate on a comparable one-year eurozone government debt security is 6 percent. We can use an equation similar to the one for PPP to calculate the forward rate based on IRP:

$$FR_1 = SR_0 \times \frac{1 + IntR_{hc}}{1 + IntR_{fc}} \tag{6.3}$$

political risk

the risk associated with the possibility that a national government might confiscate or expropriate assets held by foreigners

For consistency, let's assume that the spot rate for a euro is $1.31. We estimate the forward rate as follows:

$$FR_1 = \$1.31 \times \frac{1.09}{1.06}$$

And

$$FR_1 = \$1.31 \times 1.0283 = \$1.35$$

economic risk

risk associated with possible slow or negative economic growth, as well as variability in economic growth

Thus, based on relative one-year government interest rates, we expect the euro to appreciate from $1.31 to $1.35 over the next year.[4]

Political risk is the risk associated with the possibility that a national government might confiscate or expropriate assets held by foreigners. A nation with lower political risk will generally have a stronger currency. ***Economic risk*** is the risk associated with the possibility of slow or negative

4. The PPP and IRP will provide different estimates of the one-year forward rate if we extend the decimal places beyond two. This is because the ratios of 1.06/1.03 and 1.09/1.06 differ slightly.

economic growth, as well as variability in economic growth. A nation with a higher economic growth rate, along with growth stability, will generally have a stronger currency. Furthermore, a nation with a stronger economic growth rate will attract more capital inflows relative to a nation growing more slowly. For example, a stronger U.S. economy relative to the British economy will cause investors in both countries to switch from pound investments to dollar investments.

CURRENCY EXCHANGE RATE APPRECIATION AND DEPRECIATION

The change (appreciation or depreciation) of a foreign currency (FC) relative to a domestic or home currency is typically expressed on a percentage basis:

$$\%FC\ Change = \frac{FC's\ New\ Value - FC's\ Old\ Value}{FC's\ Old\ Value} \tag{6.4}$$

Let's use an example where the demand for eurozone member financial assets increases relative to the demand for U.S. financial assets, causing the U.S. dollar value of the euro to increase from $1.31 to $1.34. The associated percent euro change would be the following:

$$\%Euro\ Change = \frac{\$1.34 - \$1.31}{\$1.31} = \frac{\$0.03}{\$1.31} = 2.3\%$$

In other words, the euro would have appreciated by 2.3 percent relative to the dollar.

Previously, we discussed the possibility that the value of a European euro might drop from $1.31 to $1.29 if the inflation rate in the United States is lower than the inflation rate for the eurozone member countries. The percent change in the euro would be calculated this way:

$$\%Euro\ Change = \frac{\$1.29 - \$1.31}{\$1.31} = \frac{-\$0.02}{\$1.31} = -1.5\%$$

Thus, the euro has depreciated by 1.5 percent relative to the U.S. dollar because of the new and relatively higher eurozone member inflation rate.

The amount of U.S. dollar ($US) appreciation or depreciation can be easily calculated since the value of one currency is the inverse of the other currency. For example, when the dollar price of a euro is $1.31, one $US is worth €0.7634 (i.e., 1 ÷ $1.31). Similarly, when the dollar price of a euro declines to $1.29, one $US is worth 1 ÷ $1.29, or €0.7752. When the dollar value of the euro increases, one dollar can be exchanged for fewer euros and vice versa.

PERSONAL FINANCIAL PLANNING
Investing Overseas

People living in the United States are affected by international finance at least two ways. First, the growth or recession of overseas economies affects jobs in the United States. If foreign economies go into recession (as the Japanese and other Asian economies did in the mid-to late 1990s), there will be less export demand for U.S. goods and services. Thus, a worker's personal financial status can be imperiled by a layoff or reduced working hours.

The second effect on individuals is perhaps less clear to see: the effect of foreign investors on U.S. financial markets and interest rates. Stock and bond prices are affected, as is any other price, by supply and demand. Foreign inflows of capital into U.S. financial markets can help raise U.S. stock and bond prices, giving U.S. investors better returns on their own investment. Of course, money can flow out, too. If foreign investors sell their U.S. security holdings, this can lead to lower security prices and lower, even create negative, returns to U.S. investors.

Pessimism about the strength of the U.S. dollar can lead to higher U.S. interest rates on everything from Treasury bills to home mortgages. Here's how this can happen using a Japanese investor as

an example. A Japanese investor will compare U.S. and Japanese interest rates before deciding to buy Japanese government debt or U.S. Treasury bonds for example. In addition to looking at U.S. interest rates, the Japanese investor will consider the expected change in the U.S. dollar exchange rate with the Japanese yen. If the U.S. dollar is expected to weaken against the yen, this means the Japanese investor's U.S. dollar investment may lose value by the time it is converted back to yen at maturity. To be attractive, U.S. interest rates will have to be higher to compensate the Japanese investor for the falling dollar.

Suppose interest rates in Japan are 4 percent and economists predict the U.S. dollar will fall in value against the yen by 3 percent in the next year. That means Japanese investors will not find U.S. bonds attractive unless their interest rate is at least 4 percent (the Japanese interest rate) + 3 percent (the expected loss in the value of the U.S. dollar) or 7 percent. If the dollar is expected to fall by 5 percent, U.S. interest rates will have to be 9 percent (4 percent + 5 percent) to attract Japanese investors. A falling or weaker dollar puts upward pressure on interest rates throughout the U.S. economy.

INTERNET ACTIVITY

Go to the CNNMoney Web site, http://money.cnn.com. Click on the Markets tab and then on the Currencies tab and find current currency exchange rates for the U.S. dollar relative to the Japanese yen, euro, and the Swiss franc. Find the direct or indirect exchange rate and calculate the other one.

arbitrage

the simultaneous, or nearly simultaneous, purchasing of commodities, securities, or bills of exchange in one market and selling them in another where the price is higher

An appreciation (or depreciation) of a home currency (HC) relative to a foreign currency (FC) can be expressed on a percentage basis as follows:

$$\%HC\ Change = \frac{1/FC's\ New\ Value\ -\ 1/FC's\ Old\ Value}{1/FC's\ Old\ Value} \qquad (6.5)$$

Using the preceding data for the relative interest rate example involving the American dollar and the European euro, we have the following:

$$\%\$US\ Change = \frac{1/\$1.29\ -\ 1/\$1.31}{1/\$1.31} = \frac{€0.7752\ -\ €0.7634}{€0.7634} = \frac{0.0118}{0.7634} = 1.5\%$$

The U.S. dollar, in this example, appreciated by 1.5 percent relative to the euro, which is the mirror opposite of the −1.5 percent decline (depreciation) of the euro from $1.31 to $1.29.

ARBITRAGE

Arbitrage is the simultaneous, or nearly simultaneous, purchasing of commodities, securities, or bills of exchange in one market and selling them in another where the price is higher. In international exchange, variations in quotations among countries at any time are quickly brought into alignment through the arbitrage activities of international financiers. For example, if the exchange rate was reported in New York at €1 = $1.34 and in Brussels, Belgium, at €1 = $1.33, alert international arbitrageurs would sell claims to euros in New York at the rate of $1.34 and would have Brussels correspondents sell claims on U.S. dollars in Brussels at the rate of $1.33 for each euro. Such arbitrage would be profitable only when dealing in large sums. Under these circumstances, if an arbitrageur sold a claim on €100 million in New York, $134 million would be received. The corresponding sale of claims on American dollars in Brussels would be at the rate of €100 million for $133 million. Hence, a profit of $1 million would be realized on the transaction. A quotation differential of as little as one-sixteenth of one cent may be sufficient to encourage arbitrage activities.

The ultimate effect of large-scale arbitrage activities on exchange rates is the elimination of the variation between the two markets. The sale of large amounts of claims to American dollars in Brussels would drive up the price for euros, and in New York the sale of claims to euros would force the exchange rate down.

EXCHANGE RATE DEVELOPMENTS FOR THE U.S. DOLLAR

The dollar continues to be an important currency for international commercial and financial transactions. Because of this, the United States and the rest of the world benefit from a strong and stable U.S. dollar. Its strength and stability depend directly on the ability of the United States to pursue noninflationary economic policies. In the late 1960s and the 1970s, the United States failed to meet this objective. Continuing high inflation led to a dollar crisis in 1978, which threatened the stability of international financial markets.

Figure 6.2 shows the strength of the dollar relative to an index of major currencies that trade widely outside the United States for 1980 through 2012. As inflation was brought under control in the early 1980s and economic growth accelerated after the 1981–1982 recession, the dollar rose against other major currencies until it reached record highs in 1985. As discussed, higher economic growth and relatively lower inflation rates lead to a stronger currency. These economic developments, coupled with a favorable political climate, caused the value of the dollar to rise sharply.

However, the renewed strength of the dollar contributed to a worsening of the trade imbalance because import prices were effectively reduced while exported U.S. goods became less cost competitive. Beginning in 1985, United States economic growth slowed relative to economic growth in other developed countries. Also, the belief that the U.S. government wanted the dollar to decline on a relative basis so as to reduce the trade deficit contributed to a decline in the desirability of holding dollars. This resulted in a major shift toward holding more foreign assets and fewer U.S. assets. As a consequence, the dollar's value declined by 1987 to levels below those in place when flexible exchange rates were reestablished in 1973. Between 1987 and 2000, the value of the dollar in international exchange fluctuated within a fairly narrow range compared to the 1980–1987 period.

FIGURE 6.2

U.S. Dollar Value Relative to an Index of Major Currencies

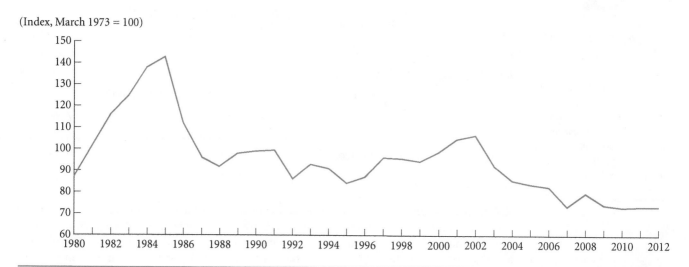

(Index, March 1973 = 100)

Source: http://www.federalreserve.gov/releases/.

FINANCIAL CRISIS

The U.S. dollar appreciated relative to other currencies in 2001 and 2002. Stock prices peaked in 2000 and then began declining rapidly as the Internet and tech bubbles burst. Declining stock prices were followed by a recession in 2001 and the terrorist attack on September 11, 2001. After first raising interest rates, the Federal Reserve System (Fed) reduced interest rates and provided liquidity in the financial markets. The Fed continued its high liquidity, low interest rate environment throughout the remainder of the decade. This financial markets environment was accompanied by large amounts of borrowing by business firms, financial institutions, and individuals.

Housing prices peaked in 2006, stock prices peaked in 2007, the financial crisis developed in 2007–2008, and the U.S. economy entered the Great Recession in 2008–2009. Debt-heavy individuals began defaulting on their home mortgages, financial institutions were finding it difficult to remain solvent, and business firms were failing during this "perfect financial storm." These economic developments were accompanied by the U.S. dollar declining rapidly against an index of major currencies beginning in 2003. Figure 6.2 shows this decline continuing through 2007 before stabilizing at a relatively low level during the 2010–2012 period.

In contrast, a stronger dollar leads to concern about the deficit in the U.S. trade balance, but at the same time it offers hope of lower inflation. A stronger dollar results in more imports of foreign merchandise since it requires fewer dollars for purchase. Just as a U.S. tourist abroad finds it cheaper to travel when the dollar is strong, importers find prices lower when their dollars increase in relative strength. When the dollar weakens, inflation may follow, countered by a reduced balance of trade deficit. We discuss balance of trade and balance of payments implications in the last section of this chapter.

CONDUCTING BUSINESS INTERNATIONALLY

MANAGING FOREIGN EXCHANGE RISK

CONCEPT CHECK

What actions can firms that have foreign sales take to reduce foreign exchange risk?

Firms that have foreign sales must be concerned with the stability of the governments and changing values of currency in the countries in which they do business. They must pay attention to commodity price changes and other uncertainties related to monetary systems.

Large firms usually have special departments that handle international transactions. These firms may engage in foreign exchange speculation as opportunities arise, but risk reduction is their primary goal. Among the possible actions of skilled foreign exchange specialists are hedging, adjusting accounts receivable and payable procedures, cash management, and borrowing and lending activities. Existing or anticipated variations in the value of foreign currencies guide all these actions. For example, a seller with a claim for payment within ninety days may anticipate a possible decline in the currency value of his customer's country. The seller can hedge by entering into a futures contract for the delivery of that currency at the existing exchange rate on the day of the contract.[5] By so doing, a loss in the collection process is offset by a gain in the delivery process ninety days hence. The fee for the futures contract becomes a cost of the transaction.

Large multinational companies enjoy special opportunities for risk reduction and speculation since they can move cash balances from one country to another as monetary conditions warrant. For example, if a decline in the value of a particular currency is expected, cash in the branch in that country may be moved back to the United States, or a firm may borrow funds in a foreign market and move them immediately to the United States (or to another country) with the expectation of repaying the loan at a reduced exchange rate. This is speculation rather than a risk reduction activity. An expected decline in a currency may lead to an attempt to accelerate collection of accounts receivable, with funds transferred quickly to another country. Payments on accounts payable may be delayed in the expectation of a decline in exchange rates. If, on the other hand, a foreign currency is expected to increase in relative value, the preceding actions would be reversed.

New career opportunities have developed with the increasing importance of multinational financial management. Some corporations maintain special departments to study foreign business activities and their prospective profitability; to analyze governmental attitudes, tax rates, and duties; and to determine how foreign operations are to be financed. In addition, to protect bank balances and other investments, almost constant attention must be given to day-to-day exchange rate changes.

ETHICAL ISSUES

ETHICAL CONSIDERATIONS

The concept of acceptable ethical behavior differs across cultures and countries. In some primarily developing countries, it seems to be acceptable practice for government officials and others to request "side" payments and even bribes as a means for foreign companies to do business in these countries. This is morally wrong. In addition, the Foreign Corrupt Practices Act (FCPA) prohibits U.S. firms from bribing foreign officials. For violators of the FCPA, the U.S. Justice Department may impose monetary penalties and criminal proceedings may be brought against violators. Government actions may result in lost reputations and firm values.

For example, Titan Corporation had its proposed 2004 sale to Lockheed Martin Corporation implode because it could not promptly resolve a bribery investigation brought by the U.S. Justice Department. Another example was the 2004 indictment of two former HealthSouth Corporation executives for conspiracy in a bribery scheme involving a Saudi Arabian hospital. An attempt was made to conceal the bribery by setting up a bogus consulting contract for the director general of the Saudi foundation that owned the hospital. The former HealthSouth Corporation executives were indicted after a U.S. Justice Department investigation alleged they had violated the *U.S. Travel Act* by using interstate commerce when making the bribes and had violated the FCPA by falsely reflecting the bogus bribe payments as legitimate consulting expenses on HealthSouth Corporation's financial statements.

When conducting business activities in certain foreign countries, business executives are sometimes faced with extortion demands by organized criminals. Most of us would agree that extortion payments are morally wrong. Paying organized criminals is the same as paying corrupt government officials.

GLOBAL DISCUSSION

FINANCING INTERNATIONAL TRADE

One of the substantial financial burdens of any industrial firm is the manufacture process. When a U.S. manufacturer exports goods to distant places such as India or Australia, funds are tied up for the period of manufacture and for a lengthy period of transportation. To reduce costs, manufacturers may require the foreign importer to pay for the goods as soon as they are on the way to their destination. In this way, a substantial financial burden is transferred to the importer.

---

5. We discuss futures contracts in the Learning Extension at the end of Chapter 11.

draft (bill of exchange)
an unconditional written order, signed by the party drawing it, requiring the party to whom it is addressed to pay a certain sum of money to order or to bearer

sight draft
an instrument requiring immediate payment

time draft
an instrument requiring payment at a later date

documentary draft
draft that is accompanied by an order bill of lading along with other papers such as insurance receipts, certificates of sanitation, and consular invoices

order bill of lading
represents the written acceptance of goods for shipment by a transportation company and the terms under which the goods are to be transported to their destination

clean draft
a draft that is not accompanied by any special documents and is generally used when the exporter has confidence in the importer's ability to meet the draft when presented

FINANCING BY THE EXPORTER

If the exporter has confidence in foreign customers and is in a financial position to sell to them on an open-book account, then sales arrangements should operate much as in domestic trade, subject to the complex nature of any international transaction.

Sight and Time Drafts

As an alternative to shipping merchandise on open-account financing, the exporter may use a collection draft. A **draft** (**bill of exchange**) is an unconditional written order, signed by the party drawing it, requiring the party to whom it is addressed to pay a certain sum of money to order or to bearer. A draft may require immediate payment by the importer upon its presentation, meaning on demand, or it may require only acceptance on the part of the importer, providing for payment at a specified future time. An instrument requiring immediate payment is classified as a **sight draft**; one requiring payment later is a **time draft**. A draft may require remittance, or payment, in the currency of the country of the exporter or of the importer, depending on the transaction's terms. An example of a sight draft form is shown in Figure 6.3.

Drafts may be documentary or clean. A **documentary draft** is accompanied by an order bill of lading along with other papers such as insurance receipts, certificates of sanitation, and consular invoices. The **order bill of lading** (see Figure 6.4) represents the written acceptance of goods for shipment by a transportation company and the terms under which the goods are to be transported to their destination. In addition, the order bill of lading carries title to the merchandise being shipped, and only its holder may claim the merchandise from the transportation company. The documentary sight draft is generally referred to as a documentary payments draft (D/P draft), and the documentary time draft is referred to as a documentary acceptance draft (D/A draft).

A **clean draft** is one that is not accompanied by any special documents and is generally used when the exporter has confidence in the importer's ability to meet the draft when presented. Once the merchandise is shipped to the importer, it is delivered by the transportation company, regardless of any actions by the importer in terms of the draft.

Bank Assistance in the Collection of Drafts

An importer will generally avoid paying for a purchase before the goods are shipped because several days or perhaps weeks may elapse before the goods arrive. But the exporter is often unwilling to send the draft and documents directly to the importer. Therefore, the exporter usually works through a commercial bank.

A New York exporter dealing with an importer in Portugal with whom there has been little experience may ship goods on the basis of a documentary draft that has been deposited for collection with the local bank. That bank, following the specific instructions regarding the manner of collection, forwards the draft and the accompanying documents to its correspondent bank in Lisbon. The correspondent bank holds the documents until payment is made in the case of a sight draft or until acceptance is obtained if a time draft is used. When collection is made on a sight draft, it is remitted to the exporter.

FIGURE 6.3
Sight Draft or Bill of Exchange

$ 2,500.00   New Orleans, Louisiana, August 15, 20-

At sight -
_____ PAY TO THE

ORDER OF   Mervin J. Mansfield

Two thousand five hundred no/100 - - - - - -
_____ DOLLARS

VALUE RECEIVED AND CHARGE TO ACCOUNT OF

TO _____ Brazilian Import Company   NEW ORLEANS EXPORT COMPANY

No. _____ 11678 Rio de Janeiro, Brazil   *Theresa M. Jones*

CONCEPT CHECK

What is meant by a draft or bill of exchange?

What is an order bill of lading?

FIGURE 6.4
Order Bill of Lading

UNITED STATES LINES CO.

(SPACES IMMEDIATELY BELOW FOR SHIPPERS MEMORANDA– NOT PART OF BILL OF LADING)

FORWARDING AGENT – REFERENCES John Doe Shipping Co., #E6776 F.M.B. #9786	EXPORT DEC. No. X67-90687

DELIVERING CARRIER TO STEAMER: Penn Central Company	CAR NUMBER – REFERENCE 876528

BILL OF LADING
(SHORT FORM)

(NOT NEGOTIABLE UNLESS CONSIGNED "TO ORDER")

SHIP American Banker	FLAG	PIER	PORT OF LOADING
PORT OF DISCHARGE FROM SHIP Liverpool (Where goods are to be delivered to consignee or On-carrier) If goods to be transhipped beyond Port of Discharge, show destination Here —► To	AM.	61 N.R. THROUGH BILL OF LADING	NEW YORK

SHIPPER _____ Midwest Printing Company

CONSIGNED TO: ORDER OF _____ M.T. Wilson & Co.

ADDRESS ARRIVAL NOTICE TO _____ Same at 15 Dock St., Liverpool, E.C. 3

PARTICULARS FURNISHED BY SHIPPER OF GOODS				
MARKS AND NUMBERS	NO. OF PKGS.	DESCRIPTION OF PACKAGES AND GOODS	MEASUREMENT	GROSS WEIGHT IN POUNDS
M. T. W. & Co. Liverpool	56	Books		10,145
		SPECIMEN		

FREIGHT PAYABLE IN   NEW YORK

(10,145) @ _____ PER 2240 LBS.....$ _____	
_____ @ _____ PER 100 LBS.......$ _____	
_____ FT. @ _____ PER 40 CU. FT....$ _____	
545 FT. @ $1.05 PER CU. FT.......$ _____	572	25
_____ $ _____	
_____ $ _____	
_____ $ _____	
_____ $ _____	
TOTAL............$ _____	

(TERMS OF THIS BILL OF LADING CONTINUED FROM REVERSE SIDE HEREOF)

IN WITNESS WHEREOF,
THE MASTER OR AGENT OF SAID VESSEL HAS SIGNED........**3**

BILLS OF LADING, ALL OF THE SAME TENOR AND DATE, ONE OF WHICH
BEING ACCOMPLISHED, THE OTHERS TO STAND VOID.

UNITED STATES LINES COMPANY

BY _____ *J.H.*
     FOR THE MASTER

B/L No.   ISSUED AT NEW YORK, N.Y.

M-105

January   12   20--
  MO.   DAY   YEAR

Financing Through the Exporter's Bank

Recognize that, throughout the preceding transaction, the banking system only provided a service to the exporter and in no way financed the transaction. The exporter's bank, however, may offer financing assistance by allowing the exporter to borrow against the security of a documentary draft. Such loans have the financial strength of the exporter and the importer to support them since documents for taking possession of the merchandise are released after the importer has accepted the draft.

The amount the exporter can borrow is less than the face amount of the draft and depends mainly on the credit standing of the exporter and the importer. When the exporter is financially strong enough to offer suitable protection to the bank, a substantial percentage of the draft may be advanced even though the importer may not be known to the exporter's bank. In other cases, the advance may be based on the importer's financial strength.

The character of the goods shipped has an important bearing on the amount lent since the goods offer collateral security for the advance. Goods that are not breakable or perishable are better as collateral; goods for which there is a ready market are preferable to those with a limited market.

FINANCING BY THE IMPORTER

Like the exporter, the importer may arrange payment for goods without access to bank credit. When an order is placed, payment in full may be made or a partial payment offered. The partial payment gives some protection to the exporter and the importer. It protects the exporter against rejection of the goods for no reason, and it gives the importer some bargaining power in the event the merchandise is damaged in shipment or does not meet specifications. When the importer is required to make full payment with an order but wants some protection in the transaction, payment is sent to a bank in the exporter's country. The bank is instructed not to release payment until certain documents are presented to the bank to prove shipment of the goods according to the terms of the transaction. The bank, of course, charges a fee for this service.

Financing Through the Importer's Bank

In foreign trade, because of language barriers and the difficulty in obtaining credit information about companies in foreign countries, the use of the banker's acceptance is common. The *banker's acceptance* is a draft drawn on and accepted by a bank rather than the importing firm. An example of a banker's acceptance is shown in Figure 6.5. The importer must, of course, make arrangements with the bank in advance. The exporter must know before shipment is made whether or not the bank in question has agreed to accept the draft. This arrangement is facilitated by the use of a ***commercial letter of credit***, a bank's written statement to an individual or firm guaranteeing acceptance and payment of a draft up to a specified sum if the draft is presented according to the terms of the letter (see Figure 6.6).

commercial letter of credit
a bank's written statement to an individual or firm guaranteeing acceptance and payment of a draft up to a specified sum if the draft is presented according to the terms of the letter

Importer Bank Financing: An Example

The issue of a commercial letter of credit and its use in international finance are shown in this example. The owner of a small exclusive shop in Chicago wishes to import expensive perfumes from Paris. Although the shop is known locally, its financial reputation is not known widely enough to permit it to purchase from foreign exporters on the basis of an open-book account or drafts drawn on the firm. Under these circumstances, the firm would substitute the bank's credit for its own credit through the use of a letter of credit. Upon application by the firm, the bank issues the letter if it is satisfied that its customer is in a satisfactory financial condition.

The letter of credit is addressed to the French exporter of perfumes. The exporter, upon receipt of the commercial letter of credit, would not be concerned about making the shipment. Although

FIGURE 6.5
Banker's Acceptance

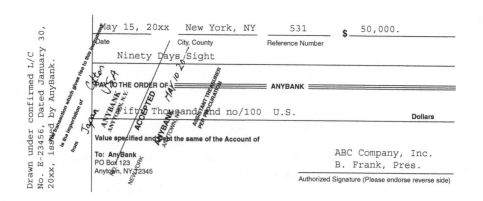

FIGURE 6.6:
Irrevocable Commercial Letter of Credit

Irrevocable Commercial Letter Of Credit	AnyBank P.O. Box 123 Anytown, New York 12345	**AnyBank**	Cable Address: AnyBank	Letter Of Credit Division

May 2, 20-- $50,000.

> Drafts drawn hereunder must be marked
> "Drawn under AnyBank Anytown
> L/C Ref. E-23456   "and indicate the date hereof

    ABC Company, Inc.

    B. Frank, President

SPECIMEN

Gentlemen:
We hereby authorize you to draw on AnyBank, Anytown

by order of   J. R. Doe & Company, New York, N.Y.

and for account of   J. R. Doe & Company

up to an aggregate amount of   Fifty Thousand Dollars U.S. Currency

available by your drafts at 90 days sight, for full invoice value, in duplicate
accompanied by Commercial Invoice in triplicate . . .
                Consular Invoice in duplicate . . .
                Full set of onboard Bills of Lading to order of AnyBank,
Anytown, marked Notify J. R. Doe & Company, New York,N.Y., and bearing
a separate onboard endorsement signed by the Master and also marked
freight collect at port of destination . . . .

Relating to shipment of Cotton.

. . . Any charges for negotiation of the draft(s) are for your account.
. . . Marine and war risk insurance covered by buyers.

Drafts must be drawn and negotiated not later than   October 2, 20--

The amounts thereof must be endorsed on this Letter Of Credit.
We hereby agree with the drawers, endorsers, and bonafide holders of all drafts drawn under and in compliance
with the terms of this credit, that such drafts will be duly honored upon presentation to the drawee.
This letter of credit is subject to the Uniform Customs and Practice for Documentary Credits (1974 Revision) International Chamber Of Commerce Publication No. 290.

Yours very truly,

D. E. Price

D. E. Price
Vice President
Authorized Signature

---

the exporter may not have heard of the Chicago firm, the bank issuing the commercial letter of credit may be known to the exporter or to his bank. (International bank directories provide bank credit information.) The French exporter ships the perfumes and, at the same time, draws a draft in the appropriate amount on the bank that issued the letter of credit. The draft and the other papers required by the commercial letter of credit are presented to the exporter's bank. The bank sends the draft and the accompanying documents to its New York correspondent, who forwards them to the importer's bank in Chicago. The importer's bank thoroughly inspects the papers that accompany the draft to ensure all provisions of the letter of credit have been met. If the bank is satisfied, the draft is accepted and the appropriate bank officials sign it. The accepted draft, now a banker's acceptance, may be held until maturity by the accepting bank or returned to the exporter on request. If the acceptance is returned to the exporter, it may be held until maturity and sent to the accepting bank for settlement or it may be sold to other investors. An active market for bankers' acceptances exists in the world's money centers.

After having accepted the draft, the Chicago bank notifies its customer that it has the shipping documents and that arrangements should be made to take them over. As the shop sells the perfume, it builds up its bank account with daily deposits until it is sufficient to retire the acceptance. The bank can then meet its obligation on the acceptance without having advanced its other funds at any time.

In releasing shipping documents to a customer, some banks prefer to establish an agency arrangement between the firm and the bank whereby the bank retains title to the merchandise. The instrument that provides for this is called a ***trust receipt***. Should the business fail, the bank would not be in the position of an ordinary creditor trying to establish its claim on the business assets. Rather, it could repossess, or take back, the goods and place them with another agent for sale since title had never been transferred to the customer. As the merchandise is sold under a trust receipt arrangement, generally the business must deposit the proceeds with the bank until the total amount of the acceptance is reached.

In summary, the banker's acceptance and the commercial letter of credit involve four principal parties: the importer, the importer's bank, the exporter, and the exporter's bank. Each benefits to a substantial degree through this arrangement. The importer benefits by securing adequate credit. The importer's bank benefits because it receives a fee for issuing the commercial letter of credit and for the other services provided in connection with it. The exporter benefits by being assured that payment will be made for the shipment of merchandise. Thus, a sale is made that might otherwise have been rejected because of lack of guaranteed payment. Finally, the exporter's bank benefits if it discounts the acceptance since it receives a high-grade credit instrument with a definite, short-term maturity. Acceptances held by commercial banks provide a low, but certain, yield, and banks can liquidate them quickly if funds are needed for other purposes.

BANKER'S ACCEPTANCES

The Federal Reserve System's Board of Governors (Board) authorizes member banks to accept drafts that arise in the course of certain types of international transactions. These include the import and export of goods, the shipment of goods between foreign countries, and the storage of highly marketable staple goods in any foreign country. A ***banker's acceptance*** is a promise of future payment issued by a firm and guaranteed by a bank. The maturity of a banker's acceptance arising out of international transactions may not exceed six months. This authority to engage in banker's acceptance financing is intended to encourage banks to participate in financing international trade and to strengthen the U.S. dollar abroad.

Bankers' acceptances are used to finance international transactions on a wide variety of items, including coffee, wool, rubber, cocoa, metals and ores, crude oil, jute, and automobiles. Because of the growth of international trade and the increasing competition in foreign markets, banker's acceptances have become increasingly important. Exporters have had to offer more liberal terms on their sales to compete. The banker's acceptance permits them to do so without undue risk.

The cost of financing an international transaction with the banker's acceptance involves the interest cost involved in the exporter's discounting the acceptance and involves the commission charge of the importer's accepting bank. Foreign central banks and commercial banks regard banker's acceptances as attractive short-term funds commitments. In recent years, foreign banks have held more than half of all dollar-denominated banker's acceptances, with most of the remainder held by domestic banks. Nonfinancial corporations have played a small role as investors in acceptances. Few firms deal in banker's acceptances. These dealers arrange nearly simultaneous exchanges of purchases and sales.

OTHER AIDS TO INTERNATIONAL TRADE

The Export-Import Bank

The ***Export-Import Bank*** was authorized in 1934 and, in 1945, became an independent agency of the government. The bank's purpose has been to help finance and facilitate exports and imports between the United States and other countries. It is the only U.S. agency engaged solely in financing foreign trade.

The Export-Import Bank is a government-owned corporation with capital of $1 billion in nonvoting stock paid in by the U.S. Treasury. It may borrow from the Treasury on a revolving basis and sell short-term discount promissory notes. It pays interest on these loans and dividends on the capital stock. In performing its function, the bank makes long-term loans to private enterprises and governments abroad to finance the purchase of U.S. equipment, goods, and services. The Export-Import

---

trust receipt
an instrument through which a bank retains title to goods until they are paid for

CONCEPT CHECK

What is meant by a commercial letter of credit?

What is a trust receipt?

---

banker's acceptance
a promise of future payment issued by a firm and guaranteed by a bank

CONCEPT CHECK

What are bankers' acceptances and how are they used?

Export-Import Bank
bank established to help finance and facilitate exports and imports between the United States and other countries

Bank aids substantially in the economic development of foreign countries by giving emergency credits to assist them in maintaining their level of U.S. imports during temporary balance-of-payments difficulties. In addition, the bank finances or guarantees the payment of medium-term commercial export credit extended by exporters and, in partnership with private insurance companies, offers short-term and medium-term credit insurance. It lends and guarantees only where repayment is reasonably assured and avoids competition with sources of private capital.

CONCEPT CHECK

What is the Export-Import Bank, and what does it do?

Traveler's Letter of Credit

A firm's buyer who is traveling abroad may not know in advance from which individuals or firms purchases will be made, for example, an art buyer touring several countries. The buyer could carry U.S. currency, but this involves possible physical loss of the money and sometimes a substantial discount for its conversion into the local currency. A traveler's letter of credit is a convenient and safer method for travelers who need large amounts of foreign currency.

traveler's letter of credit issued by a bank in one country and addressed to a list of foreign banks, which have agreed to purchase sight drafts presented to them by persons with appropriate letters of credit

The ***traveler's letter of credit*** is issued by a bank in one country and addressed to a list of foreign banks. These banks are usually correspondents of the issuing bank and have agreed to purchase sight drafts presented to them by persons with appropriate letters of credit. When a bank issues a letter of credit, it sends a copy of the signature of the person to whom the letter is issued to each of its foreign correspondent banks. When someone presents a draft for payment in foreign currency to one of these correspondent banks, his or her signature is compared with the signature the bank has. The bank may ask the individual for supplementary identification.

As with a commercial letter of credit, a maximum total draft amount is stated in a traveler's letter of credit. So that an individual with such a letter does not exceed authorized withdrawals, each bank to which the letter is presented enters on it the amount of the draft it has honored.

CONCEPT CHECK

What is a traveler's letter of credit and how is it used internationally?

Traveler's Checks

Traveler's checks, which are offered by banks and other financial intermediaries in the United States, are generally issued in denominations of $10, $20, $50, and $100. These checks, generally purchased by an individual before leaving for a foreign country, promise to pay on demand the even amounts indicated on the face of the checks. Each check must be signed by the purchaser twice, once when it is bought and again in the presence of a representative of the business, hotel, or financial institution where it is presented for payment. This allows the person cashing a traveler's check to determine whether the signature is authentic.

The use of traveler's checks is widespread and offers several advantages to the traveler, including protection in the event of loss and almost certain acceptance when they are presented for payment. Traveler's checks are usually sold for their face amount plus a charge of 1 percent. They can be purchased in the United States in major foreign currency denominations, for example, British pounds. This eliminates a traveler's exposure to varying exchange rates and the extra amount that is often charged (in the form of a less favorable exchange rate than the official rate) when U.S. dollar checks are cashed in a foreign country.

CONCEPT CHECK

What are the advantages associated with the use of traveler's checks?

GLOBAL DISCUSSION

BALANCE IN INTERNATIONAL TRANSACTIONS GOAL

Just as monetary policy plays an important role in the nation's stability, growth, interest rates, and price levels, it helps keep international financial relationships in balance. Since the dollar is widely held as a medium of international exchange, U.S. monetary policy has especially significant effects on the world economy. No nation is a world unto itself, nor can a nation pursue whatever policies it desires without regard to other nations. Policy makers of all economies must recognize the interdependence of their actions in attempting to maintain a balance in international transactions that is sometimes referred to as international financial equilibrium.

Briefly, the nations of the world attempt to achieve international financial equilibrium by maintaining a balance in their exchange of goods and services. In general, international trade benefits all countries involved. Consumers benefit by getting lower-cost goods since the goods come from the country where they are produced most efficiently. Producers benefit by expanding their markets. Over one-tenth of the U.S. national income comes from selling goods to foreigners, and a like amount of our needs are met through imports. However, individuals and firms make the decisions to import and export, and problems arise if they are out of balance over time.

INTERNET ACTIVITY

*Go to the CNNMoney Web
site, http://money.cnn.com.
Click on the Markets tab and
then on the Currencies tab and
find current currency exchange
rates for the euro relative to the
British Pound, and the
Japanese yen. Find the direct
and indirect currency exchange
quotations.*

balance of payments
*involves all of its
international transactions,
including foreign investment,
private and government
grants, U.S. military
spending overseas, and many
other items besides the
buying and selling of goods
and services*

balance of trade
*the net balance of exports
and imports of goods and
services*

**merchandise trade
balance**
*the net difference between a
country's import and export
of goods*

NATURE OF THE PROBLEM

Exports are sales to foreigners; they are a source of income to domestic producers. Imports divert spending to foreign producers and, therefore, represent a loss of potential income to domestic producers. When the two are in balance, there is no net effect on total income in the economy. However, an increase in exports over imports tends to expand the economy just as an increase in investment or government spending does. An excess of imports tends to contract the economy.

As in the domestic economy, goods and services are not exchanged directly in international trade; payment flows through monetary or financial transactions. Methods of making payments and financing international trade were discussed previously. Other short-term and long-term lending and investment are conducted across national boundaries on a large scale. In addition, government grants for military and civilian purposes are sources of international financial flows. These flows can have an important impact on domestic economies and may affect monetary policy.

Since producers, consumers, and investors in different countries use different currencies, the international financial system requires a mechanism for establishing the relative values, or exchange rates, among currencies and for handling their actual exchange. Under the system of *flexible exchange rates* that began in 1973, rates are determined in the process of exchange: by supply and demand in the foreign exchange market. This system reduces the impact of international financial transactions on domestic money supplies. Still, changes in exchange rates do affect imports and exports and can, thus, affect domestic production, incomes, and prices. International financial markets strongly influence domestic interest rates and vice versa, so that domestic monetary policy still involves international considerations.

In short, domestic economies are linked to one another in a worldwide economic and financial system. The United States has played a leading role in the development and growth of that system. Before we take a closer look at that role, we should examine the accounting system used to keep track of international financial transactions.

BALANCE-OF-PAYMENTS ACCOUNTS

The U.S. **balance of payments** involves all of its international transactions, including foreign investment, private and government grants, U.S. military spending overseas, and many other items besides the buying and selling of goods and services. The most important element of the balance of payments is the **balance of trade**, which is the net balance of exports and imports of goods and services. A more narrow view considers only the import and export of goods and is termed the **merchandise trade balance.** The merchandise trade balance was consistently favorable between the 1950s and the beginning of the 1970s. However, imports of goods have exceeded exports since the latter part of the 1970s.

The following are exports, imports, and balance on goods amounts in billions of dollars for selected years beginning with 1980 and ending in 2010:

YEAR	EXPORTS	IMPORTS	BALANCE ON GOODS
1980	$224.3	−$249.8	−$25.5
1990	387.4	−498.4	−111.0
2000	772.0	−1,224.4	−452.4
2005	894.6	−1,677.4	−782.8
2010	1,288.7	−1,934.6	−645.9

Source: *Economic Report of the President*, 2012, Table B-106.

As recorded in the preceding table, exports of goods increased nearly six times from $224.3 billion in 1980 to $1,288.7 billion in 2010. However, over the same period, imports of goods increased nearly eight times, from $249.8 billion in 1980 to $1,934.6 billion in 2010, and the balance on goods grew from −$25.5 billion in 1980 to −$645.9 billion in 2010.

Factors that impact international trade balances include the exchange value of the U.S. dollar relative to other currencies, relative inflation rates, and economic growth. A relatively stronger U.S. economy means that more will be spent on imports, while the weaker foreign economy means that less will be spent on U.S. exports. A weaker real exchange rate, where the nominal exchange rate is adjusted for inflation differences, makes for a weaker U.S. dollar, which lowers the dollar cost of U.S. goods relative to foreign goods.

We can better understand the U.S. balance of payments by examining the current account and capital account balances information shown in Table 6.3. An annual balance of trade (goods and services) deficit of $599.9 billion occurred in 2011 and reflects the net of merchandise trade, service transactions, and military transactions. We find the current account balance by adjusting the goods and services balance for net income flows that come primarily from investments and from unilateral, or one-way, transfers. These transfers include remittances, pensions, private gifts and grants, and U.S. government grants (excluding military). Thus, the *current account balance* shows the flow of income into and out of the United States during a specified period. For 2011, the current account balance showed a deficit of $465.9 billion.

The *capital account balance* includes all foreign private and government investment in the United States netted against U.S. investments in foreign countries. Deficits or surpluses in the current account must be offset by changes in the capital account. That is, changes in the current account and the capital account must be equal except for statistical discrepancies caused by measurement errors and the inability to keep track of all international transactions. According to Table 6.3, the balance on the capital account for 2011 was a surplus of $516.1 billion. Since this amount was more than the current account deficit of $465.9 billion, the difference reflects a statistical discrepancy of –$50.2 billion for 2011.

The first item in the capital account section, changes in U.S. government assets other than official reserve assets, represents an outflow of $103.7 billion and includes government ownership of assets in foreign countries, gold, and the reserve position in the International Monetary Fund (IMF). The second item, changes in U.S. private assets abroad, reflects private investments abroad and represents an outflow of capital which was $364.1 billion in 2011.

The third and fourth items reflect foreign ownership changes, both government and private, in investments in the United States. Among those changes are increases in bank deposits, purchases of government and corporate securities, loans, and direct investment in land and buildings. Both of these items give rise to inflows of capital with $211.8 billion coming from an increase in foreign official assets and $789.2 billion from foreign private assets in 2011. The fifth item reflects a decrease in U.S. official reserve assets of $15.9 billion in 2011. Capital account transactions (net) reflected payments of $1.2 billion in 2011 for debt forgiveness and the disposition of certain assets.

From an international monetary management point of view, U.S. government ownership of foreign assets is of special interest. Under the current system of flexible exchange rates, a country's central bank does not have to redeem its currency. However, it may want to control its exchange

---

current account balance shows the flow of income into and out of the United States during a specified period

capital account balance includes foreign government and private investment in the United States netted against U.S. investment in foreign countries

CONCEPT CHECK

What is the U.S. balance of payments?

What are the differences between the current account balance and the capital account balance?

TABLE 6.3
U.S. Balance of Payments in 2011 ($ Billions)

	INCOME (+)	PAYMENTS (−)	NET
Current Account			
Goods and services			
Exports	$2,103,4		
Imports		$2,663,3	
Balance on goods and services			−$599.9
Income, net			227.0
Unilateral current transfers, net			−133.0
Balance on current account			−$465.9
Capital Account			
Changes in U.S. government assets other than official reserve assets		−103.7	
Changes in U.S. private assets abroad		−364.1	
Changes in foreign official assets in U.S.	211.8		
Changes in foreign private assets in U.S.	789.2		
Changes in U.S. official reserve assets		−15.9	
Capital account transactions, net		−1.2	
Balance on capital account			$ 516.1
Statistical discrepancy (calculated)		−50.2	
Adjusted balance on capital account			$ 465.9

Source: http://www.federalreserve.gov/econresdata/releases/intlsumm/

INSTITUTIONS AND MARKETS

Commercial banks play an important role in financing international trade. Banks provide commercial letters of credit that guarantee acceptance and payment of drafts. Bankers' acceptances, promises of future payment issued by a firm and guaranteed by a bank, are important financial instruments that facilitate international trade. Banks throughout the world are important participants in the electronic currency exchange markets. Traveler's letters of credit and traveler's checks are provided by financial institutions to help travelers purchase products and cover living expenses while in foreign countries.

INVESTMENTS

Individuals and businesses interested in investing in securities issued by foreign corporations may need to use the currency exchange markets to convert U.S. dollars into the currencies of the countries where those corporations are located. Individuals traveling internationally will need to convert their U.S. dollars into the local currencies through the aid of financial institutions. Investors may speculate on the relative future movements of currencies through the use of spot and forward markets.

FINANCIAL MANAGEMENT

Financial managers use currency exchange markets to hedge against currency exchange risk associated with possible changes in the exchange rates between currencies. Financial managers may hedge in the forward markets or seek the aid of banks to sell unneeded currencies or to purchase currencies needed to conduct business operations. Financial managers rely on banks and other financial institutions to aid them in their international transactions as importers and as exporters.

rate by entering the foreign exchange market to buy or sell that currency, thus adding to demand or supply. Intervention by central banks in the flexible exchange rate system is called a *managed float*.

Under a pure flexible system in which central banks do not enter the foreign exchange market at all, there would be no change in the official government ownership of foreign assets. However, the rest of the accounts would still balance. Any surplus or deficit in current accounts would be balanced by the capital accounts. For example, a trade deficit might be balanced partly by an increase in foreign assets in the United States, including deposits in U.S. banks.

SUMMARY

In this chapter, we discussed the development of international finance and the international monetary system as it evolved from a gold standard system to a system of flexible exchange rates. We covered the developments toward European economic unification through the creation of the European Union (EU), which currently has twenty-eight countries as members. In addition, eighteen members of the EU are eurozone members, who are European countries that have adopted the euro as their common currency and the European Central Bank (ECB) as their central monetary policy-making authority. The banking system, along with the arbitrage activities of international financiers, support and facilitate international transactions and activities. Management of foreign exchange is particularly important to multinational corporate financial managers as they attempt to protect their international claims against currency fluctuations.

Foreign exchange markets are electronic communication systems that connect major financial centers throughout the world. Numerous factors determine exchange rates: supply and demand relationships, relative interest rate levels, relative inflation rates, political risk, and economic risk. Alternatives to effect the settlement of purchase and sale claims were explored, along with the instruments available to exporters and importers for financing their international activities.

Nations of the world want to maintain a balance in their exchange of goods and services, as well as in their payments balances. When international financial equilibrium does not exist, exchange rates usually adjust to reflect these imbalances. Furthermore, when the current account shows a surplus or deficit in the flow of income into and out of the United States, changes in the capital account must offset the current account imbalance. This is accomplished by a change in the relationship between foreign private and government investment in the United States relative to U.S. investment in foreign countries.

KEY TERMS

arbitrage

balance of payments

balance of trade

bankers' acceptances

Bretton Woods System

capital account balance

clean draft

commercial letter of credit

currency exchange markets

currency exchange rate

current account balance

direct quotation method

documentary draft

draft (bill of exchange)

economic risk

euro

European Union (EU)

eurozone members

Export-Import Bank

flexible exchange rates

foreign exchange markets

forward exchange rate

gold standard

indirect quotation method

interest rate parity (IRP)

International Monetary Fund (IMF)

international monetary system

merchandise trade balance

order bill of lading

political risk

purchasing power parity (PPP)

sight draft

special drawing rights (SDRs)

spot exchange rate

time draft

traveler's letter of credit

trust receipt

World Bank (International Bank for Reconstruction and Development)

DISCUSSION QUESTIONS

1. What is the purpose of an international monetary system?

2. What is meant by the statement that the international monetary system has operated mostly under a "gold standard"? What are the major criticisms associated with being on a gold standard?

3. Describe the Bretton Woods System for setting currency exchange rates. What are special drawing rights (SDRs) and how are they used to foster world trade?

4. What is an international monetary system based on "flexible exchange rates"?

5. Describe the international monetary system currently in use.

6. What is the European Union (EU)? How did it develop? Who are the current members of the EU?

7. What is meant by the term eurozone members? Which countries are eurozone members?

8. What is the euro? Identify some of its distinguishing characteristics.

9. What types of financial crises have some countries in the EU faced in recent years?

10. What are currency or foreign exchange markets?

11. Explain the role of supply and demand in establishing exchange rates between countries.

12. Describe the activities and economic role of the arbitrageur in international finance.

13. What is meant by the statement that foreign exchange quotations may be given in terms of sight drafts, cable orders, and time drafts?

14. Describe the various ways by which an exporter may finance an international shipment of goods. How may commercial banks assist the exporter in collecting drafts?

15. How do importers protect themselves against improper delivery of goods when they are required to make payment as they place an order?

16. Describe the process by which an importing firm may substitute the credit of its bank for its own credit in financing international transactions.

17. How may a bank protect itself after having issued a commercial letter of credit on behalf of a customer?

18. Describe the costs involved in connection with financing exports through banker's acceptances.

19. Describe the ultimate sources of funds for export financing with banker's acceptances. How are acceptances acquired for investment by these sources?

20. Explain the role played in international trade by the Export-Import Bank. Do you consider this bank to be in competition with private lending institutions?

21. Commercial letters of credit, traveler's letters of credit, and traveler's checks play an important role in international finance. Distinguish among these three types of instruments.

22. Briefly indicate the problems facing the United States in its attempt to maintain international financial equilibrium.

23. The U.S. international balance of payments position is measured in terms of the current account balance. Describe the current account balance and indicate its major components.

24. Discuss the meaning of the capital account balance and identify its major components.

EXERCISES

1. You are the owner of a business that has offices and production facilities in several foreign countries. Your product is sold in all these countries, and you maintain bank accounts in the cities in which you have offices. At present, you have short-term notes outstanding at most of the banks with which you maintain deposits. This borrowing is to support seasonal production activity. One of the countries in which you have offices is strongly rumored to be on the point of devaluation, or lowering, of its currency relative to that of the rest of the world. What actions might this rumor cause you to take?

2. Explain the concept of "balance" as it relates to a nation's balance of payments.

3. As an exporter of expensive electronic equipment, you have a substantial investment in the merchandise that you ship. Your foreign importers are typically small or medium-size firms without a long history of operations. Although your terms of sales require payment upon receipt of the merchandise, you are concerned about the possible problem of nonpayment and the need to reclaim merchandise that you have shipped. How might the banking system assist and protect you in this situation?

4. As an importer of merchandise, you depend on the sale of the merchandise for funds to make payment. Although customary terms of sale are ninety days for this type of merchandise, you are

not well-known to foreign suppliers because of your recent entry into business. Furthermore, your suppliers require almost immediate payment to meet their own expenses of operations. How might the banking systems of the exporter and importer accommodate your situation?

5. As a speculator in the financial markets, you notice that, for the last few minutes, Swiss francs are being quoted in New York at a price of $0.5849 and in Frankfurt at $0.5851.

    a. Assuming that you have access to international trading facilities, what action might you take?

    b. What would be the effect of your actions and those of other speculators on these exchange rates?

6. You manage the cash for a large multinational industrial enterprise. As a result of credit sales on ninety-day payment terms, you have a large claim against a customer in Mexico City. You have heard rumors of the possible devaluation of the Mexican peso. What actions, if any, can you take to protect your firm against the consequences of a prospective devaluation?

7. Assume, as the loan officer of a commercial bank, that one of your customers has asked for a commercial letter of credit to enable his firm to import a supply of well-known French wines. This customer has a long record of commercial success yet has large outstanding debts to other creditors. In what way might you accommodate the customer and at the same time protect your bank?

8. For the entire year, the nation's balance of trade with other nations has been in a substantial deficit position, yet as always, the overall balance of payments will be in "balance." Describe the various factors that accomplish this overall balance in spite of the deficit in the balance of trade.

9. Assume you are the international vice president of a small U.S.-based manufacturing corporation. You want to expand your business in several developing countries but are aware that some business practices are considered to be "acceptable" in these countries but not necessarily in the United States. How would your react to the following situations?

    a. You met yesterday with a government official from one of the countries in which you would like to make sales. He said that he could speed up the process for acquiring the necessary licenses for conducting business in his country if you would pay him for his time and effort. What would you do?

    b. You want to make a major sale of your firm's products to the government of a foreign country. You have identified the key decision maker. You are considering offering the official a monetary payment if she would recommend buying your firm's products. What would you do?

    c. Your firm has a local office in a developing country where you want to increase business opportunities. Representatives from a local crime syndicate have approached you and have offered to provide "local security" in exchange for a monthly payment to them. What would you do?

PROBLEMS

1. Exchange rate relationships between the U.S. dollar and the euro have been volatile. When the euro began trading at the beginning of 1999, it was valued at 1.17 U.S. dollars. By late-2000, a euro was worth only $.83 and peaked at $1.60 in mid-2008. Calculate the percentage changes in the value of a euro from its initial value to its late-2000 value and to its high mid-2008 value.

2. Over a two-year period, the U.S. dollar equivalent of a euro increased from $1.3310 to $1.4116. Using the indirect quotation method, determine the currency per U.S. dollar for each of these dates.

3. Over a two-year period, the U.S. dollar equivalent of a euro increased from $1.3310 to $1.4116. Determine the percentage change of the euro between these two dates.

4. A few years ago, the U.S. dollar equivalent of a foreign currency was $1.2167. Today, the U.S. dollar equivalent of a foreign currency is $1.3310. Using the indirect quotation method, determine the currency per U.S. dollar for each of these dates.

5. A few years ago the U.S. dollar equivalent of a foreign currency was $1.2167. Today, the U.S. dollar equivalent of a foreign currency is $1.3310. Determine the percentage change of the euro between these two dates.

6. If the U.S dollar value of a British Pound is $1.95 and a euro is $1.55, calculate the implied value of a euro in terms of a British Pound.

7. Assume a U.S. dollar is worth 10.38 Mexican Pesos and .64 euros. Calculate the implied value of a Mexican Peso in terms of a euro.

8. Assume that five years ago a euro was trading at a direct method quotation of $.8767. Also assume that this year the indirect method quotation was .8219 euros per U.S. dollar.

    a. Calculate the euro "currency per U.S. dollar" five years ago.

    b. Calculate the "U.S. dollar equivalent" of a euro this year.

    c. Determine the percentage change (appreciation or depreciation) of the U.S. dollar value of one euro between five years ago and this year.

    d. Determine the percentage change (appreciation or depreciation) of the euro currency per U.S. dollar between five years ago and this year.

9. Assume that last year the Australian dollar was trading at $.5527, the Mexican peso at $.1102, and the British Pound was worth $1.4233. By this year, the U.S. dollar value of an Australian dollar was $.7056, the Mexican peso was $.0867, and the British pound was $1.8203. Calculate the percentage appreciation or depreciation of each of these three currencies between last year and this year.

10. Assume that the Danish krone (DK) has a current dollar ($US) value of $0.18.

    a. Determine the number of DK that can be purchased with one $US.

    b. Calculate the percentage change (appreciation or depreciation) in the Danish krone if it falls to $0.16.

    c. Calculate the percentage change (appreciation or depreciation) in the U.S. dollar if the DK falls to $0.16.

11. Assume the U.S. dollar ($US) value of the Australian dollar is $0.73 while the U.S. dollar value of the Hong Kong dollar is $0.13.

    a. Determine the number of Australian dollars that can be purchased with one $US.

    b. Determine the number of Hong Kong dollars that can be purchased with one $US.

    c. In $US terms, determine how many Hong Kong dollars can be purchased with one Australian dollar.

12. Assume one U.S. dollar ($US) can currently purchase 1.316 Swiss francs. However, it has been predicted that one $US soon will be exchangeable for 1.450 Swiss francs.

   a. Calculate the percentage change in the $US if the exchange rate change occurs.

   b. Determine the dollar value of one Swiss franc at both of the above exchange rates.

   c. Calculate the percentage change in the dollar value of one Swiss franc based on the preceding exchange rates.

13. Assume inflation is expected to be 3 percent in the United States next year compared with 6 percent in Australia. If the U.S. dollar value of an Australian dollar is currently $0.500, what is the expected exchange rate one year from now based on purchasing power parity?

14. Assume inflation is expected to be 8 percent in New Zealand next year compared with 4 percent in France. If the New Zealand dollar value of a euro is $0.400, what is the expected exchange rate one year from now based on purchasing power parity?

15. Assume the interest rate on a one-year U.S. government debt security is currently 9.5 percent compared with a 7.5 percent on a foreign country's comparable maturity debt security. If the U.S. dollar value of the foreign country's currency is $1.50, what is the expected exchange rate one year from now based on interest rate parity (IRP)?

16. Assume the interest rate in Australia on one-year government debt securities is 10 percent and the interest rate on Japanese one-year debt is 5 percent. Assume the current Australian dollar value of the Japanese yen is $0.0200. Using interest rate parity (IRP), estimate the expected value of the Japanese yen in terms of Australian dollars one year from now.

17. **Challenge Problem** Following are currency exchange "crossrates" between pairs of major currencies. Currency crossrates include direct and indirect methods for expressing relative exchange rates.

	U.S. DOLLAR	U.K. POUND	SWISS FRANC	JAPANESE YEN	EUROPEAN EURO
European Monetary Union	1.1406	?	0.6783	0.0087	—
Japan	130.66	185.98	77.705	—	114.60
Switzerland	1.6817	2.3936	—	0.0129	?
United Kingdom	?	—	0.4178	?	0.6162
United States	—	1.4231	?	0.0077	0.8767

   a. Fill in the missing exchange rates in the crossrates table.

   b. If the inflation rate is expected to be 3 percent in the European Monetary Union(EMU) and 4 percent in the United States next year, estimate the forward rate of one euro in U.S. dollars one year from now.

   c. If the one-year government interest rate is 6 percent in Japan and 4 percent in the United Kingdom, estimate the amount of yen that will be needed to purchase one British Pound one year from now.

   d. Based solely on purchasing power parity (PPP), calculate the expected one-year inflation rate in the United States if the Swiss inflation rate is expected to be 3.5 percent next year and the one-year forward rate of a Swiss franc is $.6100.

   e. Assume the U.S. dollar is expected to depreciate by 15 percent relative to the euro at the end of one year from now and the interest rate on one-year government securities in the EMU is 5.5 percent. What would be the current U.S. one-year government security interest rate based solely on the use of interest rate parity to forecast forward currency exchange rates?

PART 2

INVESTMENTS

INTRODUCTION

The field of finance is composed of three areas:—institutions and markets, investments, and financial management. These areas are illustrated in the accompanying diagram. Part 2 focuses on the investments area of finance. Investments involve the sale or marketing of securities, the analysis and valuation of securities and other financial claims, and the management of investment risk through holding diversified portfolios. Money flows into the financial markets from households' and firms' retained earnings. Funds flow into financial institutions such as banks and life insurance companies, which, in turn, invest the funds in various securities such as stocks and bonds, as well as other financial claims. Financial claims are anything that has a debt or equity claim on income or property, such as a car loan, a mortgage, or an equity investment in a small partnership. Financial institutions facilitate the work of the financial markets by directing funds from savers to those individuals, firms, or governments who need funds to finance current operations or growth.

Part 1 dealt with the operations of the financial markets in general within the context of the financial system. The financial crisis and Great Recession of 2007–2009, sometimes referred to as the "perfect financial storm," tested the workings of the U.S. financial system to an extent not seen since the 1930s Great Depression. Although some evidence suggested that the U.S. financial system was on the verge of collapse in late 2008, efforts on the part of policy makers, business leaders, and individuals set the stage for economic recovery and a return to financial stability as the decade of the 2000s came to an end.

Part 2 introduces many of the important concepts and tools that financial institutions and investors use in the financial markets. For example, no one would want to invest (except perhaps altruistically) $100 now and expect to receive only their $100 back after one year. Because they give up the use of their money, investors expect a return on their investments. Thus we say that money has a "time value." Having one dollar today is of greater value to us than the promise of receiving one dollar in the future.

How much can we expect to receive for our $100 investment? The answer is determined in the financial markets. As with any other market, the financial markets consider demand and supply forces to determine the "price" of money, namely the interest rate or the expected return on an investment. The amount of interest received on a certificate of deposit or a bond, or the expected return on a common stock investment, all depends on the workings of the financial markets and the marketplace's evaluation of the investment opportunity.

Through the investing process, institutions, firms, and individual investors come together. Firms and governments go to the financial markets, seeking investors and institutions to whom they can sell financial securities. Investors and institutions participate in the financial markets, seeking profitable investments to help meet their goals. For an investor, the goal may be a comfortable retirement or funds accumulation to purchase a car or house. For financial institutions, the higher the returns they earn on prudent investments, the greater will be their profits and the stronger their competitive position. A financial institution that prudently earns higher returns in the financial markets will be able to offer current and potential customers higher interest rates on their deposits than a competitor whose financial market returns are lower.

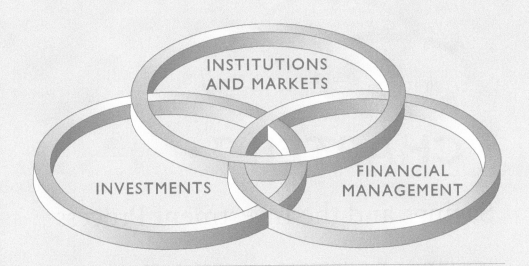

INSTITUTIONS AND MARKETS

INVESTMENTS

FINANCIAL MANAGEMENT

Part 2 introduces us to the process of investing and to the tools that can be used to evaluate financial market securities. Chapter 7 examines the work of financial markets to direct savings into various investments. Chapter 8 discusses influences that affect the financial market's determination of the price of money, or the interest rate or expected return on an investment. Chapter 9 examines the effect of interest rates more closely by introducing the concept of time value of money. This chapter shows us how we can compare different dollar amounts of cash over time to determine whether an investment is attractive or not. Chapter 10 introduces us to bonds and stocks. We review their characteristics, and we use the time value concepts from Chapter 9 in a pragmatic manner to see how we can estimate their value. We also learn in Chapter 10 how to read and interpret information about bonds and stocks from the financial pages of papers such as *The Wall Street Journal*.

Chapter 11 delves deeper into the workings of the securities markets. It focuses on the processes that institutions and firms use to issue securities and the process that investors use when buying or selling securities. Chapter 12 completes our overview of investing in the securities markets by examining the trade-off between risk and expected return: To have an incentive to invest in higher-risk securities, investors must have higher returns. Chapter 12 introduces us to the tools that investors and securities market participants use to evaluate and to control investment risk.

• CHAPTER 7 •

Savings and the Investment Process

Chapter Learning Objectives:

AFTER STUDYING THIS CHAPTER, YOU SHOULD BE ABLE TO DO THE FOLLOWING:

- Identify and describe the major components of the gross domestic product (GDP).
- Describe how the balance between exports and imports affects the GDP.
- Discuss recent developments in the level of personal and corporate savings.
- Describe the principal sources of federal government revenues and expenditures.
- Identify the major sources of savings in the United States.
- Identify and describe the factors that affect savings.
- Describe major capital market securities that facilitate the savings and investment process.
- Describe the types of mortgage loans available to individuals and how the mortgage markets facilitate home ownership.
- Discuss the role of individuals in the recent financial crisis.

Where We Have Been...

Part 1 of this book introduced you to how the U.S. financial system works. In Chapter 1, you learned about the role of finance and were able to answer the question: What is finance? Chapter 2 provided you with information about the development of the U.S. monetary system, and Chapter 3 covered the importance of commercial banks and other financial institutions in helping the financial system operate smoothly. In Chapter 4, you learned about the Federal Reserve System (Fed) and its monetary policy functions and instruments. After reading Chapter 5, you should have a better understanding of who the U.S. policy makers are and how they carry out monetary policy, fiscal policy, and debt management to achieve the nation's economic objectives. Chapter 6 showed how international trade is conducted and how currency exchange markets support international trade.

Where We Are Going...

Part 2 focuses on the area of finance called investments. In Chapter 8, you will be introduced to the structure of interest rates. You will learn about the supply and demand for loanable funds and the determinants of nominal or market interest rates. Characteristics of U.S. Treasury debt obligations, which are considered to be free of default risk, will be discussed. Our attention then turns to the term or maturity structure of interest rates. Next, we cover inflation premiums and price movements. The last section of the chapter examines default risk premiums. The remainder of Part 2 includes Chapter 9 on the time value of money, Chapter 10 on the characteristics and valuations of bonds and stocks, Chapter 11 on securities markets, and Chapter 12 on financial return and risk concepts.

How This Chapter Applies to Me...

Every day you are faced with deciding whether to consume more or to save. For example, after buying dinner at a restaurant, you may still have a few dollars left in the form of extra income, possibly from a part-time job while you are in college. What will you do with the money? You might buy a new CD or take a friend to the movie theater. Alternatively, you might decide to place the money in a savings account at a bank. The process of intermediation moves your discretionary money from savings into investment. Of course, saving is not costless. Each time you make a decision to save, you are foregoing current consumption. This action on your part not to immediately consume all of your income helps the economy grow.

Our parents and other "experts" have likely provided similar advice to each of us about the importance of saving for a "rainy day." Of course, they were telling us not to consume all of our current income but rather to put some aside for an unexpected financial need, that is, a rainy day. Such an action of saving provides protection against unanticipated future expenditures for the individual, and it allows for investment. You are probably not a saver at this stage in your life. We say this because most individuals are spenders of their parents' earnings and savings during their formative years from birth through college. At the time of college graduation, most individuals have little or no savings but possess "earning power." As earnings exceed expenditures, individuals have the opportunity to save in a variety of ways ranging from short-term money market investments (considered to be cash) to long-term real estate investments in the form of home ownership.

As you move through your life cycle, you likely will have the opportunity to invest in stocks and bonds. Likewise, having an understanding of the types of financial assets that are used by businesses to finance and grow their businesses will be of value to those of you who pursue business careers.

GROSS DOMESTIC PRODUCT AND CAPITAL FORMATION

Recall from Chapter 5 our discussion of the national economic policy objectives of economic growth, high employment, price stability, and balance in international transactions. Economic growth and employment are reflected in the output of goods and services by a nation, as well as the nation's ability to build buildings, roads, inventories, and other infrastructure.

capital formation
process of constructing real property, manufacturing producers' durable equipment, and increasing business inventories

All of a nation's output of goods and services may be consumed, or a portion of them may be saved. Individuals consume by making expenditures on durable and nondurable goods and services. Governments consume by purchasing goods and services. If all output is not consumed, savings can be invested to construct residential and commercial structures, manufacture producers' durable equipment, and increase business inventories. This process is termed **capital formation** and results in economic growth.

GDP COMPONENTS

Recall that *gross domestic product (GDP)* is a nation's output of goods and services achieved over a specified period such as one year. Increases in GDP over time measure the extent of economic growth, which is one of the country's national economic policy objectives. In Chapter 2, we focused on the relationship between GDP and monetary policy in terms of the money supply and velocity.

GDP is composed of consumption and investment components, as well as the net export of goods and services. More specifically, GDP consists of four components:

1. Personal consumption expenditures (PCE)
2. Government expenditures (GE) including gross investment
3. Gross private domestic investment (GPDI)
4. Net exports (NE) of goods and services

personal consumption expenditures (PCE)
expenditures by individuals for durable goods, nondurable goods, and services

Personal consumption expenditures (PCE) indicate expenditures by individuals for durable goods, nondurable goods, and services. We all like to eat, buy clothes, have roofs over our heads, enjoy the comforts of heating and cooling, benefit from interior lighting, own automobiles and televisions, receive education, travel, and get haircuts and other services. The fact is we consume throughout our lives. Depending on where we are in our life cycles, we typically meet our consumption desires by spending our parents' earnings and savings during our formative years from birth through college graduation, generating our own earnings during our working lives, and spending our own savings during our retirement years.

government expenditures (GE)
expenditures for goods and services plus gross investments by federal, state, and local governments

Government expenditures (GE) include expenditures for goods and services plus gross investments by the federal, state, and local governments. The federal government spends over one-half of its total expenditures on direct payments to individuals in the form of health, Social Security, and income security support. This should not be a surprise since some would argue that the elected representatives of the people run the U.S. government for the benefit of the people.

INTERNET ACTIVITY

Go to the Web site of the Federal Reserve Bank of St. Louis, http://www. stlouisfed.org. Access the Federal Reserve Economic Database (FRED), and find the current size of the U.S. gross domestic product (GDP) and its major components.

TABLE 7.1

Gross Domestic Product Consumption, Investment, and International Components ($ Billions)

	2006	2009	2012
Total gross domestic product	**$13,253.9**	**$14,258.7**	**$15,681.5**
Personal consumption expenditures	**9,270.8**	**10,092.6**	**11,120.9**
Durable goods	1,071.3	1,034.4	1,219.1
Nondurable goods	2,716.0	2,223.3	2,564.2
Services	5,483.6	6,835.0	7,337.6
Gross private domestic investment	**2,218.4**	**1,622.9**	**2,058.6**
Fixed investment	2,165.0	1,747.9	2,000.9
Nonresidential	1,397.9	1,386.6	1,618.0
Structures	411.6	480.7	460.5
Equipment and software	986.2	906.0	1,157.6
Residential structures	767.1	361.3	382.8
Change in private inventories	53.4	−125.0	57.7
Net exports of goods and services	**−761.8**	**−390.1**	**−560.8**
Exports	1,466.2	1,560.0	2,182.6
Imports	2,228.0	1,950.1	2,743.3
Government consumption expenditures and gross investment	**2,526.4**	**2,933.3**	**3,062.9**
Federal	926.4	1,144.9	1,214.3
State and local	1,600.0	1,788.4	1,848.6

Source: *Survey of Current Business* and http://www.bea.gov.

gross private domestic investment (GPDI)

measures fixed investment in residential and nonresidential structures, producers' durable equipment, and changes in business inventories

net exports (NE)

exports of goods and services minus imports

Gross private domestic investment (GPDI) measures fixed investment in residential and nonresidential structures, producers' durable equipment, and changes in business inventories. The final component of GDP is the **net exports (NE)** of goods and services, or exports minus imports.

In equation form, we have the following:

$$GDP = PCE + GE + GPDI + NE \qquad (7.1)$$

Consumption is reflected by the sum of personal consumption expenditures and government purchases of goods and services. Savings used for capital formation produce the gross private domestic investment. In addition, if the exports of goods and services exceed imports, GDP will be higher.

Table 7.1 contains a breakdown of these four GDP components for the United States in 2006, 2009, and 2012. For 2012, the GDP was $15.7 trillion. This compares with domestic output of about $13.3 trillion GDP in 2006 and $14.3 trillion for 2009. However, the rate of increase over the decade of the 2000s slowed during the latter part of the decade, which coincided with the 2007–2008 financial crisis and the 2008–2009 Great Recession.

Personal consumption expenditures of $11.1 trillion in 2012 accounted for about 71 percent of GDP. This percentage relationship has been stable throughout the decade of the 2000s and shows the importance of the individual in sustaining and improving the standard of living as reflected in GDP growth over time. However, in dollar terms, personal consumption expenditures for durable goods and nondurable goods declined from the 2006 to 2009 levels as the economy began slowing in 2007 and entered into the 2008–2009 Great Recession before recovering by 2012. However, individual expenditures for services increased between 2006 and 2009 and between 2009 and 2012 to more than offset the decline in expenditures for goods over the three measurement years.

Government expenditures, in the form of consumption and gross investment, amounted to $3.0 trillion in 2012. Continued increases occurred in federal, state, and local government expenditures over the three years shown in Table 7.1. Capital formation measured in terms of gross private domestic investment dropped sharply from $2.2 trillion in 2006 to $1.6 trillion in 2009 before recovering to $2.1 trillion in 2012. Fixed investment declined sharply between 2006 and 2009 largely due to a dramatic decline in residential structures and reflects the housing price bubble that burst in 2006, resulting in a steep decline in home prices that was still continuing through 2009. The change in private inventories for 2009 was –$125 billion, reflecting the severity of the financial crisis of 2007–2008 and the 2008–2009 Great Recession.

GLOBAL DISCUSSION

IMPLICATIONS OF INTERNATIONAL PAYMENT IMBALANCES

Table 7.1 shows that imports of goods and services exceeded exports by about $761.8 billion in 2006, $390.1 billion in 2009, and 560.8 billion in 2012. To place this in perspective, net exports were about 6 percent of the U.S. GDP in 2006, fell to about 3 percent in 2009, and rose to about 4 percent in 2012. Dollar amounts of exports increased across the three years depicted in Table 7.1. In contrast, while the dollar amount of imports fell between 2006 and 2009, they increased rapidly by 2012. These developments reflect the impact of the 2007–2008 financial crisis and the 2008–2009 Great Recession, as well as the weakening of the U.S. dollar relative to other major currencies as the decade of the 2000s came to a close.

Of course, the consequences of negative balances of goods and services caused by imports exceeding exports were GDPs lower than what would have occurred, other things being equal, if an export and import equilibrium had existed.

The importance of achieving a balance in international transactions was discussed in Chapter 6. Recall that when completing the accounting transactions for the U.S. balance of payments, a deficit balance on goods and services in the *current account* is offset in the *capital account* by a net increase in foreign government and private ownership of U.S. assets. When the U.S. operates at a *balance-of-payments* deficit, the Fed must reduce its reserve assets or borrow from foreign central banks. *Reserves* are in the form of gold, foreign exchanges (currencies), special drawing rights (SDRs), and reserves credit in the International Monetary Fund (IMF). Foreign exchanges (currencies) accounts represent the vast majority of all international reserve assets with the U.S. dollar comprising over half of these currency assets. Thus, the U.S. dollar has been the most important reserve currency for conducting world trade although in recent years the value of the U.S. dollar relative to the euro has been declining.

While the negative net exports over imports reflects an aggregate of trade with many countries, the United States has been running large trade deficits in goods and services with Japan and China in recent years. This means that the United States has been buying more from Japan and China than those countries have been buying from the United States. One consequence is that Japan and China could have been investing more in the United States by purchasing U.S financial and real assets relative to U.S. investments in Japan and China. However, if the Japanese decide to hold relatively fewer claims on U.S. assets, the exchange rate between the yen and the dollar must change. In contrast, the Chinese renminbi (which is the currency foreigners can hold, or yuan, the currency within China) is a more politically controlled currency that is pegged within a narrow range to the U.S. dollar.

Recall from Chapter 6 that an equilibrium exchange rate between the currencies of two countries is established by the supply and demand for those currencies. A U.S. trade deficit in goods and services with Japan means that the demand for yen by Americans will be greater than the supply of yen from the Japanese. That is, Americans will demand more yen to pay for their purchases of Japanese goods and services relative to the supply of yen reflected in the demand by Japanese for American goods and services. The result will be a stronger yen and a weaker dollar unless offsetting actions occur, such as a willingness of the Japanese to invest more in U.S. assets or government intervention in the foreign exchange markets to support the dollar.

In 1990, one U.S. dollar could be exchanged for more than 150 yen. By late 1995, the exchange rate was about 100 yen per dollar. In other words, the dollar value of one yen had increased from roughly $0.007 (1 ÷ 150) to $0.01 (1 ÷ 100). In early 2013, the exchange rate was about 93 yen per dollar. Of course, in a worldwide market economy, at some point a lower dollar should lead to fewer imports of Japanese goods and services (because of their higher cost in terms of dollars) by Americans. At the same time, the Japanese should find American goods and services to be less costly because of the stronger yen, and American exports to Japan should increase. Of course, if the U.S. dollar rises relative to the yen, the opposite trade relationships would exist.

LINK BETWEEN SAVING AND INVESTMENT

Table 7.2 shows the link between saving and investment in the United States. For 2011 (data for 2012 were not yet available), gross saving was $1.8 trillion. Gross saving is composed of net saving and consumption of fixed private and government capital. Net saving was –$99.3 billion in 2011.

TABLE 7.2
Saving and Investment in the United States ($ Billions)

	2006	2008	2011
Gross saving	**$2,174.4**	**$1,824.1**	**$1,837.5**
Net saving	**513.7**	**−23.0**	**−99.3**
Net private saving	666.5	659.8	1,240.1
Personal saving	235.0	286.4	489.4
Undistributed corporate profits	644.7	480.7	777.9
Inventory valuation adjustment	−38.0	−38.2	−62.6
Capital consumption adjustment	−176.4	−64.1	35.4
Wage accruals less disbursements	1.3	−5.0	0.0
Net government saving	−152.7	−682.7	−1,339.4
Federal	−203.8	−642.6	−1,237.4
State and local	51.0	−40.2	−102.0
Consumption of fixed capital	**1,660.7**	**1,847.1**	**1,936.8**
Private	1,391.4	1,536.2	1,587.4
Domestic business	1,123.3	1,252.3	1,339.1
Households and institutions	268.1	283.9	308.8
Government	269.3	310.9	363.9
Federal	106.6	119.8	141.5
State and local	162.7	191.2	222.4
Gross domestic investment	**$2,752.2**	**$2,632.4**	**2,335.1**
Gross private domestic investment	2,327.2	2,136.1	1,854.9
Gross government investment	425.1	496.3	480.2
Capital account transactions	4.2	−.4	1.7
Net lending or borrowing (−)	−802.6	−706.8	−467.4

Source: *Survey of Current Business* and http://www.bea.gov.

This is because net private saving of $1,240.1 billion was more than offset by net government dissaving of $1,339.4 billion due to a large federal government deficit. In comparison, gross saving was nearly $2.2 trillion in 2006 with net saving being about $514 billion. For 2008, net saving was a –$23 billion due to net private saving of about $660 billion while net government saving was –$683 billion. These differing results between 2006 and 2008 reflect the 2007–2008 financial crisis and the 2008–2009 Great Recession.

Personal saving by individuals provided about $286 billion in net savings in 2008, which represented about 43 percent of net private saving. Corporate profits that were not distributed to owners amounted to almost $481 billion in 2008. Total corporate saving is composed of undistributed corporate profits plus adjustments for corporate inventory valuation and capital consumption. Inventory valuation adjustment amounted to –$38 billion in 2008. *Capital consumption adjustment*, also called depreciation, is the estimate of the "using up" of plant and equipment assets for business purposes. These allowances amounted to –$64 billion in 2008. The combined total of the three sources of corporate saving amounted to slightly more than $378 billion in 2008. By comparison, undistributed corporate profits were about $645 billion in 2006 with a net for corporate savings of $430 billion. The slowing economy between 2006 and 2008 are shown in these data.

Personal saving was about $489 billion in 2011 or a 71 percent increase over the 2008 level of $286 billion. Net corporate saving were about $751 billion in 2011, which was about a 99 percent increase over the $378 billion in 2008. For 2011, undistributed corporate profits were almost $778 billion, with the inventory valuation adjustment being about –$63 billion, and capital consumption adjustments at $35 billion.

As Table 7.2 shows, the consumption of fixed capital comes primarily from the private sector. In 2008, consumption of fixed capital was slightly more than $1.8 trillion with the private sector consumption being about $1.5 trillion and the government sector only about $311 billion. Domestic business accounted for about 82 percent of private consumption in 2008 with households and institutions making up the remainder of private consumption. For 2011, the consumption of fixed capital was over $1.9 trillion with private sector consumption being over $1.5 trillion while the government sector contributed only about $364 billion.

CONCEPT CHECK

What are personal consumption expenditures (PCE)?

What is meant by gross private domestic investment (GPDI)?

When the U.S. dollar declines in value relative to the Japanese yen, what is the likely impact of exports and imports between the two countries?

What are capital consumption allowances?

SMALL BUSINESS PRACTICE
Typical Life Cycle Patterns for the Small Venture Firm

A successful entrepreneurial firm will typically progress through several stages of financing. The first stage is called the "seed" or development stage. Here, a firm works on an idea, development of a concept, or prototype product and may conduct some preliminary market research. If the firm is successful in producing a product or delivering a service, it moves into the startup stage. Financing will be needed for "working capital" investments in inventories and to extend trade credit to customers. A manufacturing "startup" will need to invest in plant and equipment.

A third stage can be viewed as the *breakeven* stage, when the firm is generating enough revenues to cover its operating costs. A fourth stage represents the *recovery of investment* stage. If the firm continues to be successful, the fifth stage results in the *maximum*

generation of profits. This occurs because cash flows from operations exceed new capital expenditure requirements, as well as additional investment in working capital. A sixth stage may be viewed as *maturity or stability.*

Timmons and Spinelli report that it takes an average of two and a half years for a firm to break even from an operating standpoint and over six years on average to recover initial equity investments.* Of course, some firms will recover initial their investment more rapidly, while others will fail or not progress beyond the startup stage. Ultimately, a plan is needed for how the successful entrepreneur will "exit" or leave the business. For example, the firm could be sold or merged with another firm.

*Jeffry A. Timmons and Stephen Spinelli, *New Venture Creation*, 7th Edition (New York: McGraw-Hill/Irwin, 2007), pp. 390–391.

Gross savings leads to gross investment. Table 7.2 shows that most of the gross domestic investment of $2.3 trillion in 2011 was in the form of nearly $1.9 trillion in gross private domestic investment. Personal saving and undistributed corporate profits accounted for most of the net private savings of $1.2 trillion.

FEDERAL GOVERNMENT RECEIPTS AND EXPENDITURES

THE BUDGET

Beginning in 1970 and continuing until fiscal year 1998, the federal government operated with an annual budget deficit. The government was willing to spend more than it received in the form of taxes and other revenues for more than twenty-five consecutive fiscal years. Surplus budgets lasted for only four fiscal years, with annual budget deficits again being the norm beginning in fiscal 2002 with deficits exceeding $1 trillion annually for fiscal years 2009, 2010, 2011, and 2012. On the one hand, fiscal policy can use a deficit budget to stimulate economic activity. On the other hand, recent large annual deficits have resulted in a national debt that currently exceeds $16 trillion.

The federal government relies primarily on tax revenues to support its various expenditure programs. In addition, revenues for general expenditures are received for specific services benefiting the persons charged. Examples of these revenues include postal receipts, rental receipts from federal housing projects, and food and housing payments collected from some government employees. The federal government receives substantial insurance trust revenues from contributions to such programs as Medicare and Social Security. In turn, it makes large disbursements from these revenues. The federal government relies on borrowing to bridge the gap between revenues and expenditures.

Figure 7.1 provides a graphic illustration of the percentage breakdown of revenues (income) and expenditures (outlays) for fiscal year 2011. The major income sources are personal income taxes (30 percent) and social insurance receipts (Social Security, Medicare, and unemployment and other retirement taxes), which accounted for 23 percent of receipts. Corporate taxes accounted for 5 percent of income. Excise, customs, estate, gift, and miscellaneous taxes contributed 6 percent of income. The remaining income of 36 percent came from borrowing to cover the deficit.

The primary expenditures for fiscal year 2011 were in the form of Social Security, Medicare, and other retirement outlays and accounted for 37 percent of the total outlays. Outlays for national defense, veterans, and foreign affairs activities amounted to 24 percent of outlays. The third most important outlays category was for social programs (Medicaid, food stamps, temporary assistance for needy families, supplemental security income, etc.) and accounted for 23 percent of fiscal 2011 expenditures. The remaining outlays were for physical, human, and community development (8 percent), net interest on the debt (6 percent), and law enforcement and general government activities (2 percent).

FIGURE 7.1
The Federal Government Dollar, Fiscal Year 2011

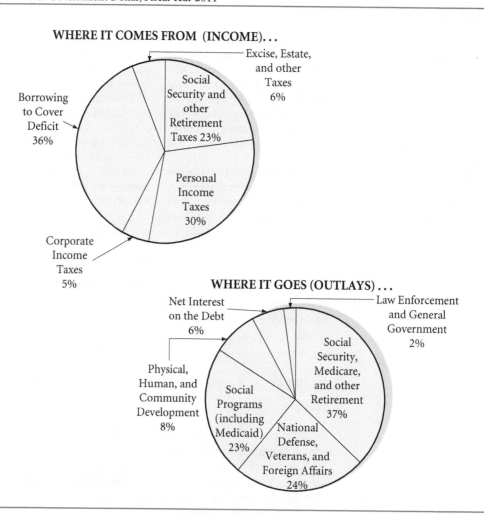

WHERE IT COMES FROM (INCOME)...

Excise, Estate, and other Taxes 6%

Social Security and other Retirement Taxes 23%

Borrowing to Cover Deficit 36%

Personal Income Taxes 30%

Corporate Income Taxes 5%

WHERE IT GOES (OUTLAYS)...

Net Interest on the Debt 6%

Law Enforcement and General Government 2%

Social Security, Medicare, and other Retirement 37%

Physical, Human, and Community Development 8%

Social Programs (including Medicaid) 23%

National Defense, Veterans, and Foreign Affairs 24%

Source: Department of the Treasury, Internal Revenue Service, http://www.irs.gov.

Local governments depend heavily on property taxes for their revenues, while state governments depend largely on sales taxes and special taxes, such as those on motor fuel, liquor, and tobacco products. In contrast, the federal government relies primarily on individual income taxes, social insurance taxes, and corporate income taxes for its revenues.

ETHICAL ISSUES

FISCAL POLICY MAKERS

In Chapter 5, we noted that Congress and the president determine the nation's fiscal policy. These individuals are elected by the people under the belief that they are to serve the people. Decisions relating to taxing and spending, and the resulting impact on whether federal budgets will be surpluses or deficits, are important to voters. Voters expect their elected politicians to behave ethically by acting honestly and fairly with their constituencies.

For the most part, our elected federal politicians seemed to have acted ethically and with integrity. However, there have been some examples of unethical and illegal behavior. *Impeachment* is a formal legislative process in which charges of "high crimes and misdemeanors" are brought against high-level officials. The House of Representatives votes on whether to impeach an official; if it does impeach, a trial is held in the Senate. In the United States, only two presidents out of forty-four have been impeached. They were Andrew Johnson, the seventeenth president, and Bill Clinton, the forty-second president. Both were acquitted. Former President Richard Nixon resigned before being impeached.

Occasionally, members of Congress have engaged in illegal activities. Some have been convicted in criminal court. Since the mid-1970s, at least twelve members have received prison sentences for

PERSONAL FINANCIAL PLANNING
Develop a Personal Financial Plan

Developing a personal financial plan is necessary to increase the chances for reaching your financial goals. Goals in business, life, and finances rarely are met by accident. With a bewildering array of investment choices and confusing tax laws, more people are turning to an investment professional for help and guidance. An important step in creating a personal financial plan is to develop a policy statement. A policy statement contains basic information to help guide future financial decisions. A policy statement will describe an investor's objective. An objective will have two components: a return goal (capital gain, income, or both) and information about the investor's risk tolerance. Investors who cannot handle the ups and downs of the stock market will not want to place as much of their savings in stocks as someone who is willing to take on the additional risk.

In addition to an objective, the policy statement needs to include information about the five sets of constraints faced by every investor:

1. Liquidity needs. Does the investor need to be able to sell assets and obtain cash quickly?

2. Time horizon. Over what time horizon can be funds be invested? Two years? Ten? Thirty years or more?

3. Taxes. The investor's tax situation is an important consideration as investing goals should focus on after-tax returns. Capital gains and losses, income, IRA accounts, 401(k) plans, and taxable versus nontaxable securities all lead to decision-making complications.

4. Legal and regulatory factors. Investment decisions are affected by rules and regulations. Even something as basic as investing money in a bank certificate of deposit (bank CD) often carries with it the warning: "substantial interest penalty upon early withdrawal."

5. Unique needs and preferences. This constraint can include wanting to exclude certain investments because of personal preference or social consciousness reasons. For example, an investor may not want to own stock or bonds issued by firms that produce or sell pornography, tobacco, or alcoholic beverages.

---

such activities as accepting bribes, taking part in kickback schemes, extortion, illegal sex offenses, and mail fraud. While the activities of these individuals have tainted Congress, by far most members behave personally and professionally ethically when representing the people who elected them.

DEBT FINANCING

budgetary deficit
when tax and other general revenues fail to meet expenditures

federal statutory debt limits
limits on the federal debt set by Congress

As we have observed, the federal government obtains funds for expenditures primarily through tax revenues. When these tax and other general revenues fail to meet expenditures, a **budgetary deficit** is incurred. Until recent years, these deficits have been of modest size compared to total government expenditures. However, their cumulative impact has created a vast increase in the total federal debt. Although Congress had set **federal statutory debt limits**, it has been necessary to increase the limits several times in recent years due to continuing large federal government budget deficits.

U.S. citizens and financial institutions hold or own a large portion of the outstanding U.S. federal debt. Part of our debt is due to our role as a creditor nation from 1918 until 1985. Until World War I, the United States depended heavily on foreign investment, and it was not until 1985 that liabilities to foreign creditors again exceeded claims against foreign creditors. Our return to being a debtor nation was due in large measure to relatively high domestic interest rates, relative political stability in the world arena, and the development of an extremely unfavorable balance of trade. The nation's excess of imports relative to exports has continued to be large since 1964. To the extent that foreign claims resulting from a surplus of imports are invested in federal obligations, foreign ownership of the federal debt increases.

Nowhere in the economy is the significance of a smoothly functioning financial system more apparent than in connection with the federal debt. Not only does the financial system accommodate the federal government by financing its frequent budgetary deficits, but it also provides for the smooth transition from old debt issues that mature to the new issues that replace them. The financial markets face a greater challenge in such refunding of government issues than in absorbing net new debt. Just as the nation's industrial development depended on an equally efficient development of financial institutions, many of the financial activities of modern government depend on these same institutions.

CONCEPT CHECK

What are the major revenues and expenditures in the federal budget?

What is meant by a budgetary deficit?

Public borrowing is a relatively modern development. During the Middle Ages, governments borrowed from wealthy merchants and others on an individual basis. Often, crown jewels were offered as collateral for such advances. Large public borrowing by governments, as for businesses, became possible only when monetary systems were refined and efficient financial institutions developed that could facilitate the transfer of monetary savings.

HISTORICAL ROLE AND CREATION OF SAVINGS

As the size of U.S. businesses expanded, the importance of accumulating and converting large amounts of financial capital to business use increased. The corporate form of organization provided a convenient and flexible legal arrangement for bringing together available financial capital. These advantages of the corporation over sole proprietorship, private ownership, and partnership are described in Chapter 13.

Developments in public transportation were often too costly and speculative for private promoters to undertake. The magnitude of early canal, turnpike, and railroad construction was such that the government undertook much of the financing of these projects. In fact, until the end of the nineteenth century, governmental units contributed more funding to these efforts than did private interests. Since this government financing was accomplished largely through bond issues rather than current revenues, the ultimate source of funds was the savings of individuals who bought the bonds.

FOREIGN SOURCES OF SAVINGS

Foreign investors purchased large amounts of the securities sold by government and private promoters to develop the United States. In particular, foreign capital played a decisive role in the development of the nation's early transportation system.

The huge role foreign capital played in the economic development of the United States is found in the developing nations of today. These nations face many of the financial problems the United States experienced during its early years. Private savings in many of these countries are negligible because almost all current income must be used for immediate consumption. Individual nations and such international organizations as the World Bank supply large amounts of capital to the developing nations of the world to increase their productive capacity.

The flow of development capital stimulates economic expansion in these countries and makes their capital more efficient. For example, speedier transportation reduces the amount of goods in transit, thus releasing working capital for other purposes. In due time, as internal capital formation increases, it is hoped that the need for foreign capital will be eliminated and these countries can then enjoy an independent capital formation process.

DOMESTIC SUPPLY OF SAVINGS

As capital formation accelerated after the Civil War, the demand for funds also increased. Wealthy Americans and foreign investors could no longer provide funds at a rapid enough rate. Britain was investing heavily in India because of political commitments, and the other European countries were not large or wealthy enough to continue supplying funds in quantities adequate to sustain U.S. growth. The American family soon took over the function of providing savings for the capital formation process. Per capita income rose to a level at which American families could afford luxuries beyond the subsistence level and could save part of what they had earned. Thus, the United States developed to the stage where it could generate sufficient capital to finance its own expansion. Ultimately the result was a change in the country's status from a debtor nation to a creditor nation.

CREATION OF SAVINGS

Today, the U.S. financial system is viewed as comprising three basic economic units: individuals, business firms (including financial institutions), and governments (federal, state, and local). **Savings** occur when all of an economic unit's income is not consumed and are represented by the accumulation of cash and other financial assets. **Savings surplus** occurs when an economic unit, such as individuals taken as a group, has current income that exceeds its direct investment in real assets. These surplus savings are made available to savings deficit units. For example, business firms as a group are often unable to meet all their plant and equipment investment needs out of **undistributed profits** or earnings retained in the business, which are profits remaining after taxes and, in the case of corporations, after the cash dividends are paid to stockholders. When

CONCEPT CHECK

How were the savings of individuals important in the early development of the United States?

savings

occur when all of an economic unit's income is not consumed and are represented by the accumulation of cash and other financial assets

savings surplus

occurs when an economic unit, such as individuals taken as a group, has current income that exceeds its direct investment in real assets

undistributed profits
(earnings retained in the business)

profits remaining after taxes and, in the case of corporations, after the cash dividends are paid to stockholders

savings deficit
a situation in which it becomes necessary to acquire funds from a savings surplus unit

CONCEPT CHECK
What is the difference between savings surplus and savings deficit units?

personal saving
savings of individuals equal to personal income less personal current taxes less personal outlays

voluntary savings
savings in the form of financial assets held or set aside for use in the future

contractual savings
savings accumulated on a regular schedule for a specified length of time by prior agreement

CONCEPT CHECK
What are the differences between voluntary savings and contractual savings?

INTERNET ACTIVITY
Go to the Web site of the Federal Reserve Bank of St. Louis, http://www.stlouisfed.org. Access the Federal Reserve Economic Database (FRED, and find current information on the size of disposable personal income and personal savings.

expenditures on real assets exceed current income, a **savings deficit** situation exists and it becomes necessary to acquire funds from a savings surplus unit.

MAJOR SOURCES OF SAVINGS

An important savings sector in the economy is the savings of individuals called **personal saving**. In equation form, we have the following:

$$\text{Personal saving} = \text{personal income} - \text{personal current taxes} - \text{personal outlays} \quad (7.2)$$

Personal income includes compensation of employees, personal income of persons with capital consumption adjustment, personal interest and dividend income, and net government social benefits to persons. Personal income less personal current taxes equals disposable personal income. Then, subtracting personal outlays (personal consumption expenditures, personal nonmortgage interest payments, and personal current transfer payments made primarily to the government) equals personal saving.

Voluntary savings are savings in the form of financial assets held or set aside for use in the future. **Contractual savings** are savings accumulated on a regular schedule for a specified length of time by prior agreement. An example is the accumulation of reserves in insurance and pension funds. Contractual savings are not determined by current decisions. They are disciplined by previous commitments that the saver has some incentive to honor.

Most financial intermediaries accumulate capital from individuals, who as a group, consistently represent a savings surplus unit. Corporations also represent an important source of savings. However, their large demand for investment funds, as is the case for unincorporated business firms, generally results in a net need for external funds. While financial intermediaries can save, their primary role in the U.S. financial system is to aid the savings-investment process. The U.S. government, on balance, has operated as a savings-deficit unit in recent years. Thus, the ability to provide adequate funds to meet investment needs primarily depends on the savings of individuals and corporations.

PERSONAL SAVINGS

Table 7.3 shows personal savings amounts in the United States in 2006, 2009, and 2012. Personal income rose from nearly $11.3 trillion in 2006 to about $12.1 billion in 2009 and to $13.4 trillion in 2012. Personal current taxes decreased between 2006 and 2009 before increasing in 2012. Disposable personal income increased in 2009 and 2012. Individuals increased their personal outlays from about $10.5 trillion in 2009 to nearly $11.5 trillion in 2012. Personal savings amounted to $235.0 billion in 2006, increased to $502.7 billion in 2009, and declined to $470.1 billion in 2012. The personal savings rate in the United States, which is personal savings as a percentage of disposable personal income, was 2.4 percent in 2006, increased to 4.6 percent in 2009, and was 3.9 percent in 2012. The U.S. savings rate continues to lag the personal savings rates in Japan and Western Europe.

TABLE 7.3
Personal Savings in the United States ($ Billions)

	2006	2009	2012
Personal income	$11,268.1	$12,072.1	$13,405.9
Less: personal current taxes	1,352.4	1,107.6	1,474.7
Disposable personal income	9,915.7	10,964.5	11,931.2
Less: personal outlays	9,680.7	10,461.8	11,461.2
Personal savings	235.0	502.7	470.1
Savings rate (personal savings/disposable personal income)	2.4%	4.6%	3.9%

Sources: *Survey of Current Business* and www.bea.gov.

U.S. personal savings rates were higher in the past. For example, historical savings rates for each five-year interval from 1960 through 2010 were the following:

YEAR	SAVINGS RATES (%)	YEAR	SAVINGS RATES (%)
1960	5.8	1990	4.3
1965	7.0	1995	4.8
1970	8.1	2000	1.0
1975	9.2	2005	1.4
1980	7.1	2010	5.1
1985	4.5		

The savings rate increased from slightly below 6 percent in 1960 to more than 9 percent by 1975. Tax reform in the form of lower personal income tax rates in the mid-1960s and in the 1970s may have contributed to this higher personal savings rate. However, the savings rate declined to less than 5 percent in 1985, 1990, and 1995. The savings rate was 1.0 percent in 2000 and 1.4 percent in 2005, before returning to the 5.1 percent level in 2010.

Individuals maintain savings for a number of reasons. They set aside a part of their current income to make mortgage payments on loans used to purchase homes. They save to acquire costly durable consumer goods, such as cars and appliances. Savings are set aside by individuals to meet unforeseeable financial needs. These savings are not set aside for specific future consumption; instead, they represent emergency or rainy-day funds. Individuals may save for long-term foreseeable spending, such as children's college education or retirement. For short periods, people may save a portion of current income simply because desirable goods and services are unavailable for purchase.

A number of media are available in which to maintain savings, ranging in liquidity from cash balances to stocks and bonds. Three factors usually influence a person's choice of medium: liquidity, degree of safety, and return. Various types of financial instruments and securities that individuals may hold are discussed later in this chapter.

CORPORATE SAVINGS

Table 7.4 shows nonfinancial corporate savings in the United States for 2006, 2008, and 2011 (data for 2012 were unavailable). Corporate profits before taxes declined from $923.9 billion in 2006 to $711.6 billion in 2008. Between 2006 and 2008, nonfinancial corporate tax liabilities decreased from $307.6 billion to $237.8 billion. The net result was a decline in after-tax profits from $616.2 billion in 2006 to $473.8 billion in 2008. This decline coincided with the 2007–2008 financial crisis and the 2008–2009 Great Recession. Profits before taxes in 2011 exceeded the 2006 level. Even though tax liabilities were higher in 2011 relative to 2006, profits after taxes exceed $1.0 trillion in 2011.

Corporations save by producing profits after taxes and then not paying all profits to investors in the form of dividends. The proportion of after-tax profits retained in the organization is referred to as undistributed profits. Corporate profits that were not distributed to owners amounted to $145.1 billion in 2006, dropped to $64.5 billion in 2008, and increased to $455.0 billion in 2011.

TABLE 7.4

Nonfinancial Corporate Savings in the United States ($ Billions)

	2006	2008	2011
Profits before taxes (with IVA and CCAdj)	$923.9	$711.6	$1,388.1
Less: tax liabilities	307.6	237.8	379.0
Profits after taxes	616.2	473.8	1,009.0
Less: dividends	471.1	409.3	554.0
Undistributed profits	145.1	64.5	455.0
Retention rate (undistributed profits/profits after taxes)	23.5%	13.6%	45.1%
Addenda:			
Profits before taxes (without IVA and CCAdj)	1,117.9	806.7	1,415.2
Inventory valuation adjustment (IVA)	−38.0	−38.2	−62.6
Capital consumption adjustment (CCAdj)	−156.0	−56.8	35.4

Source: *Survey of Current Business* and www.bea.gov.

Retention rates (undistributed profits divided by profits after taxes) were 23.5 percent in 2006, 13.6 percent in 2008, and 45.1 percent in 2011. Corporate profitability suffered during the 2007–2008 financial crisis and the 2008–2009 Great Recession but rebounded sharply by 2011.

Table 7.4 refers to nonfinancial corporate profits before taxes and includes an inventory valuation adjustment (IVA) and a capital consumption adjustment (CCAdj). Inventory values may increase or decrease in a given year and, thus, can affect nonfinancial corporate profits before taxes. **Capital consumption adjustment**, also called depreciation, is the estimate of the "using up" of plant and equipment assets for business purposes. By subtracting the IVA and CCAdj amounts from the profits before taxes (including IVA and CCAdj), the results were adjusted profits before taxes of $1,179.9 billion in 2006, $806.7 billion in 2008, and $1,415.2 billion in 2011.

Corporate saving for short-term working capital purposes is by far the most important reason for accumulating financial assets. Seasonal business changes create an uneven demand for corporate operating assets, such as inventories and accounts receivable. Because of these seasonal changes, cash inflow is seldom in the right amount and at the right time to accommodate the increased levels of operating assets. Quarterly corporate income tax liabilities also impose the necessity of accumulating financial assets.

The short-term accumulation of financial assets on the part of business corporations does not add to the level of long-term savings of the economy as a whole. However, these funds do enter the monetary stream and become available to users of short-term borrowed funds. As such, these short-term savings serve to meet a part of the demand for funds of consumers, government, and other businesses. A corporation typically holds this type of savings in the form of checkable deposits with commercial banks, short-term obligations of the federal government, commercial paper, and certificates of deposit (CDs) issued by commercial banks. These financial assets meet the requirements of safety and liquidity.

Corporations engage in the savings process to meet planned spending in the future. Reserves are often set up to provide all or part of the cost of construction, purchase of equipment, or major maintenance and repairs to existing facilities. Savings committed to these purposes are often invested in securities that have longer maturities and higher yields than those held for short-term business purposes. These securities include the debt obligations of corporations and government and include, to a limited extent, corporate stock.

FACTORS AFFECTING SAVINGS

Several factors influence the total amount of savings in any given period:

- Levels of income
- Economic expectations
- Cyclical influences
- Life stage of the individual saver or corporation

The precise relationship between savings and consumption is the subject of much debate and continuing study; however, we will limit our observations here to broad generalizations.

LEVELS OF INCOME

For our purposes, savings have been defined as current income minus tax payments and consumption spending. Keeping this definition in mind, let us explore the effect of changes in income on the levels of savings of individuals. As income falls, the individuals attempt to maintain their present standard of living as long as possible. In so doing, the proportion of their consumption spending increases and total savings diminish. As income is further reduced, the individuals may be forced to curtail consumption spending, which results in a lower standard of living. Such reduction is reasonably limited, however, since the basic needs of the individuals or family units must be met. Personal savings will be eliminated when income is drastically reduced, and the individual may **dissave**, that is, spend accumulated savings rather than further reduce consumption spending.

As income increases, the individual will again be in a position to save. However, the saving may not begin immediately, as the individuals may desire to buy the things that they could not afford during the low-income period. The amount of this need, notably for durable consumer goods, largely determines the rate of increase in savings during periods of income recovery.

capital consumption adjustment (depreciation)
the estimate of the "using up" of plant and equipment assets for business purposes

CONCEPT CHECK

What are capital consumption adjustments?

How do corporations save?

dissave
spend accumulated savings rather than further reduce consumption spending

On the whole, income levels are closely associated with levels of employment. Changes in business activity, in turn, influence employment levels. Downturns in the economy during 1980, 1981–1982, 1990, 2001, and 2008 resulted in declines in employment levels and correspondingly lowered levels of income. Post-World War II unemployment highs of the early 1980s exceeded 10 percent. During the decade of the 1990s, unemployment averaged less than 5 percent, with deviations resulting in higher levels in the 1990 and 2001 recessions. The 2007–2008 financial crisis and the 2008–2009 Great Recession, led to unemployment levels exceeding 10 percent.

ECONOMIC EXPECTATIONS

The anticipation of future events has a significant effect on savings. If individuals believe their incomes will decrease in the near future, they may curtail their spending to establish a reserve for the expected period of low income. For example, a worker anticipating a protracted labor dispute may increase current savings as partial protection against the financial impact of a strike.

Expectations of a general increase in price levels may have a strong influence on the liquidity that savers want to maintain. The prospect of price increases in consumer durable goods may cause an increase in their sales as individuals buy before prices increase. Savings are thus quickly converted to consumer spending. Corporate savings may also be reduced as a result of price increase expectations. In addition to committing funds to plant and office equipment before price increases take place, corporations typically increase their inventory positions. As for the individual, the prospect of an interruption in the supply of inventory because of a labor strike or other cause often results in a rapid stockpiling of raw materials and merchandise. The prospect of price decreases and of large production capacity has the opposite effect: The liquidity and financial assets of a business increase relative to its operating assets.

Unprecedented price increases during the inflationary 1970s led many individuals to develop a "buy it now because it will cost more later" philosophy. This resulted in a classic example of the impact of price increase expectations on the spend-save decisions of individuals. Inflation peaked at double-digit levels at the beginning of the 1980s. However, after some upward pressure in the form of price increases at the end of the 1980s, inflation during the 1990s and the early years of the twenty-first century has generally been in the 2 percent to 3 percent range.

ECONOMIC CYCLES

Cyclical movements in the economy are the primary cause of changes in levels of income. Cyclical movements affect the amounts and the types of savings. Economic cycles may be viewed in terms of the two-year to four-year traditional business cycle or in terms of much longer cycles that correspond with generations of people.

Let's begin with a discussion that concentrates on the traditional business cycle. In general, interest rates on securities with short maturities are lower than interest rates on long-term maturities.[1] However, when economic activity is peaking; short-term interest rates are higher than long-term interest rates. Generally, interest rates are high because inflation rates are high, and the Fed raises short-term interest rates higher to slow economic activity and reduce inflation. As a recession deepens, short-term interest rates fall faster than long-term interest rates. Finally, when interest rates get low enough, businesses will find it attractive to borrow and grow. The savings rate usually goes down in a recessionary period and savers emphasize liquidity and safety when they do save. When the economy is growing, individuals usually save more and may hold their savings in riskier short-term securities.

Harry Dent, Jr., discusses much longer cycles based on *generation waves*, with the largest generation wave in the history of the United States being the baby boom wave.[2] In his view, a generation wave consists of birth wave, innovation wave, spending wave, and organization wave components or stages. These components correspond with birth, coming of age, adulthood, and maturity. For the baby boom generation, the birth wave peaked in the early 1950s. The innovation wave peaked in the 1980s. This was a period of rapid introduction of new technologies, and the country began the movement from a production economy to an information economy. According to Dent, the spending wave, in turn, which will peak early in this century, has driven the economic successes of the 1990s. The last stage will peak when the baby boomers reach age sixty-five in

---

1. We discuss the term or maturity structure of interest rates in detail in Chapter 8.

2. Harry Dent, Jr., *The Great Boom Ahead*, New York: Hyperion, 1993. Also see Harry Dent, Jr., *The Roaring 2000s*, New York: Simon & Schuster, 1998.

CONCEPT CHECK

What are general factors that affect savings?

roughly 2025. While a lot of economists are skeptical about broad-based generalizations made by Harry Dent, Jr., and others, all will agree that the economic clout of a large number of individuals moving through their life cycles at about the same time can influence the economy and the securities markets.

LIFE STAGES OF THE INDIVIDUAL SAVER

The pattern of savings over an individual's life span follows a somewhat predictable pattern when viewed over the total population. A successful individual life cycle would have the following stages:

- Formative/education developing
- Career starting/family creating
- Wealth building
- Retirement enjoying

Individuals save little during their formative and education developing stage because little income is produced. They typically consume a portion of their parents' earnings and savings, which is substantial if they attend college. As they enter their career starting and family creating stage, they possess little savings but have large earning power potential. Their income increases. However, expenses increase during these early family-forming years. Saving and investing typically focus on purchasing a home and accruing life and disability insurance.

By the time individuals reach their wealth building stage, two new factors result in increased savings. First, income is typically higher than at any previous time; second, the expense of raising and educating children has been reduced or eliminated. Thus, this group typically saves the most. At the retirement enjoying stage, the individuals' income is sharply reduced. They may begin the process of dissaving. Pension fund payments along with accumulated savings are drawn upon for current living expenses.

CONCEPT CHECK

How does the pattern of savings usually differ over an individual's lifetime?

The level of savings of individuals is, therefore, a function of the age composition of the population as a whole. A population shift to a large proportion of individuals in the productive middle-age years would result in a greater savings potential. These views of the life stages of the individual saver are consistent with the generation wave approach described by Harry Dent, Jr. That is, if a large number of individuals are moving through their individual life cycles at approximately the same time, their combined efforts will have a major impact on the overall economy. On a collective basis, they spend at about the same time and are likely to save at about the same time. Spending has kept the U.S. economy in almost continual growth since the early 1980s, and saving and investing in retirement plans and directly in mutual funds (which, in turn, buy bonds and stocks) helped the stock market perform well during the 1990s. Stock prices peaked in 2007, fell sharply by early 2009, and then reached record highs in mid-2013.

LIFE STAGES OF THE CORPORATION

As the financial savings of individuals are governed partly by age, so the financial savings generated by a business firm are a function of its life stage. The following are the life cycle stages of a successful business firm:

- Startup stage
- Survival stage
- Rapid growth stage
- Maturity stage

INTERNET ACTIVITY

Go to the Web Site of the Federal Reserve Board of Governors of the Federal Reserve System, http://www. federalreserve.gov, and identify current interest rates on U.S. Treasury bills and bonds.

Not all business firms proceed through a fixed life cycle stage. To the extent, however, that a firm experiences the typical pattern of starting up, surviving, vigorous growth, and ultimate maturity, its flow of financial savings may experience a predictable pattern.

During the development of the business idea and starting the business stage, the firm is spending cash rather than building cash. The business firm typically continues to burn cash as it tries to find a successful operating niche. During the early part of the expansion years (rapid growth stage) of a successful business, the volume of physical assets typically increases rapidly. So rapid is this growth that the firm is unable to establish a strong position with respect to its financial assets. Indeed, it is during these years of the corporate life cycle that there is a large need for borrowed capital. At this time, the corporation is typically a heavy user of financial assets rather than a provider.

CONCEPT CHECK

What are some of the stages in a typical corporate life cycle?

As the firm reaches the second part of its rapid growth stage, it builds surplus or "free" cash flow and increases the firm's value. Free cash is money available after funds have been reinvested in the firm to sustain its growth. As the enterprise matures and its growth slows to a long, sustainable growth rate, it reaches its peak of savings. Earnings and cash flows are high, and commitment of funds to increased operating assets is reduced. The maturity stage can last almost indefinitely as long as the firm remains competitive in its industry. Of course, sometimes a firm's products or services are no longer competitive or needed by consumers, and the firm again starts consuming more cash than it brings in. Such firms will eventually cease to exist.

CAPITAL MARKET SECURITIES

Financial markets play an important role in the marketing and transferring of financial assets and thus are an integral part of the savings and investment process. In Chapter 1, we defined *money markets* as markets where debt securities of one year or less are issued or traded. In Chapter 2, we discussed *money market securities*, which are debt instruments or securities with maturities of one year or less. The major securities that trade in the money markets are Treasury bills, negotiable certificates of deposit (negotiable CDs), commercial paper, banker's acceptances, repurchase agreements, and federal funds. Treasury bills and negotiable CDs are short-term investment vehicles available to individuals. These two short-term investments as well as commercial paper, banker's acceptances, and repurchase agreements are investments used by business firms. Federal funds are used by depository institutions with excess funds lending to depository institutions that have a need for funds.

In Chapter 1, we also defined *capital markets* as markets where debt securities with maturities longer than one year and corporate stocks are issued or traded. **Capital market securities** are debt securities with maturities longer than one year and corporate stocks. Capital markets are important to individuals who seek to finance home purchases. Capital markets are important to corporations who raise funds to finance their operations. Individuals and corporations with excess funds also invest in capital market securities.

Figure 7.2 identifies the basic securities that are issued and traded in capital securities markets. In Chapter 3 we initially defined a mortgage. We review the definition here as part of our discussion of capital market securities. A **mortgage** is a loan backed by real property in the form of buildings and houses. In the event the debt is not repaid, the lender can use proceeds from the sale of the real property to extinguish any remaining loan interest or principal balance. Individuals rely heavily on residential mortgages to assist them in owning their own homes. Businesses also often find it worthwhile to borrow against the real property they own.

Bonds are long-term debt instruments issued by government units and business corporations. A **Treasury bond**, sometimes referred to as a *note* for shorter securities, is a debt instrument or security issued by the U.S. federal government with a typical maturity ranging from five to twenty years. Treasury bonds are sold to raise funds needed to reconcile longer-term imbalances between

capital market securities
debt securities with maturities longer than one year and corporate stocks

mortgage
loan backed by real property in the form of buildings and houses

Treasury bond
a debt instrument or security issued by the U.S. federal government with a typical maturity ranging from five to twenty years

FIGURE 7.2
Major Capital Market Securities

SECURITIES	TYPICAL MATURITIES	ISSUERS	INVESTORS	SECONDARY MARKET
Mortgages	Up to 30 years	Financial intermediaries	Individuals, business firms, and institutions	High activity
Treasury bonds	Up to 30 years	U.S. government	Individuals, business firms, and institutions	High activity
Municipal bonds	Up to 30 years	State/local governments	Individuals, business firms, and institutions	Moderate activity
Corporate bonds	Up to 30 years	Corporations	Individuals, business firms, and institutions	Moderate activity
Corporate stocks	None	Corporations	Individuals, business firms, and institutions	High activity

tax receipts and government expenditures. These bonds have low risks of default, and investors know they are easily marketable in the secondary securities market. For example, if an investor initially purchases a twenty-year federal government bond and later identifies another investment opportunity, the bond can be easily sold in the secondary capital market. A ***municipal bond*** is a debt instrument or security issued by a state or local government. Maturities on state and local government bonds, like Treasury bonds, often are in the five-year to twenty-year range. However, municipal bonds issued to build airports or bridges may have their maturities set approximately equal to the expected lives of the assets being financed. Some investors find municipal bonds to be attractive investments because the interest paid on these securities is exempt from federal income taxes and because these bonds can be sold in a secondary market.

Corporations issue financial instruments or securities, called debt and equity, to raise funds to acquire real assets to support the operations of their firms. Corporate debt instruments are bonds and equity securities are stocks. A ***corporate bond*** is a debt instrument issued by a corporation to raise long-term funds. Corporate bonds are typically issued with five- to twenty-year maturities and may be secured by the pledge of real property, plant, or equipment or they may be issued with only the backing of the general credit strength of the corporation.[3] A share of ***common stock*** represents an ownership interest in a corporation. Corporations often issue new shares of their common stocks to raise funds for capital expenditures and investments in inventories. Active secondary markets exist for trading the common stocks of larger corporations after the stocks are initially issued. Corporations can issue various classes of common stock, another type of stock called *preferred stock*, and even securities that are convertible into shares of common stock, as will be discussed later.

Corporations can use derivative securities to insure or hedge against various financial risks. A ***derivative security*** is a financial contract that derives its value from the value of another asset, such as a bond or stock. The use of derivative securities is explored in the Learning Extension to Chapter 11.

MORTGAGE MARKETS

An important element of the savings-investment process is the availability of financing to purchase homes. Since most individuals do not have the funds to purchase their home outright, they must rely on mortgage loans. ***Mortgage markets*** are markets in which mortgage loans are created to purchase buildings and houses and are originated in primary markets and traded in secondary markets.[4] Mortgage debt is typically divided into farm loans, nonfarm, nonresidential loans that include commercial property, and residential property loans. Mortgage loans on residential property also are typically divided into multifamily loans and one- to four-family loans. Residential mortgages account for the largest portion of outstanding mortgage debt and thus receive emphasis in this text. Furthermore, because residential mortgage-related developments contributed to the recent financial crisis, we discuss mortgage markets fundamentals now.

Mortgage loans are federally insured or conventional mortgages. In the event a borrower defaults on a mortgage, federal insurance guarantees the loan repayment to the bank making the mortgage loan. The Federal Housing Administration (FHA) and the Veterans Administration (VA) provide insurance on FHA and VA mortgage loans. Lenders making conventional mortgage loans may assume the risk that the borrower may default or purchase private insurance to protect against borrower default.

TYPES OF MORTGAGES AND MORTGAGE-BACKED SECURITIES

The purchase of houses in the United States traditionally has been financed with fixed interest rate, long-term loans. A ***fixed-rate mortgage*** typically has a fixed interest rate and constant monthly payments over the life of the loan, which is typically 15 or 30 years. A loan that is repaid in equal payments over a specified time period is referred to as an *amortized* loan. We will discuss amortized loans in Chapter 9. The traditional fixed-rate residential mortgage loan required a sizeable down payment, typically 20 percent of the house purchase price, at the time the loan was made.

---

municipal bond
debt instrument issued by a state or local government

corporate bond
debt instrument issued by a corporation to raise long-term funds

common stock
ownership interest in a corporation

derivative security
financial contract that derives its value from the value of another asset, such as a bond or stock

CONCEPT CHECK
What financial instruments typically have maturities up to one year?

What financial instruments and securities typically have maturities in excess of one year?

mortgage markets
markets in which mortgage loans are created to purchase buildings and houses and are originated in primary markets and traded in secondary markets

fixed-rate mortgage
fixed interest rate with constant monthly payments over the life of the loan, which is typically 15 or 30 years

---

3. Various types of corporate bonds and their characteristics are discussed in Chapter 10.
4. Primary and secondary markets for corporate bonds and stocks will be discussed in Chapter 11.

Holders of fixed-rate mortgages benefited by knowing their monthly mortgage payment would not change over the loan's life, and thus they could plan and budget for the contractual monthly payment amounts. As a result, the *default rate*, or failure to make timely periodic payments, was low on fixed-rate mortgage loans. However, the benefits of fixed-rate mortgages were offset, in part, by the fact that only a portion of the U.S. population could qualify to purchase their own houses.

During the past couple of decades, a period of generally high fixed-rate mortgage loan interest rates and a time in which it was desired to extend housing ownership to more individuals in the United States, the use of adjustable-rate mortgages grew. An ***adjustable-rate mortgage (ARM)*** has an interest rate that changes or varies over time with market-determined interest rates on a U.S. Treasury bill or other debt security. The interest rate on an ARM is often adjusted annually to reflect changes in U.S. Treasury bill rates (or other interest rate benchmark). Lenders typically offer ARMs with variable interest rates for one to five years with a provision to switch to a fixed rate over the remaining life of the ARM.

Because ARMs typically offer lower initial interest rates and lower monthly payments, more individuals can qualify for home ownership. However, because of possible changing market-determined interest rates and potential changeovers to fixed interest rates, individuals who were able to make initially low monthly mortgage payments may find themselves unable to meet their mortgage payments if interest rates are adjusted upward.

Mortgage loans are originated in the primary mortgage markets by mortgage brokers, mortgage companies, and depository financial institutions, which include banks, savings and loan associations (S&Ls), savings banks, and credit unions. Mortgage brokers and mortgage companies typically sell the mortgage loans they originated in the secondary mortgage markets. Commercial banks, which are the dominant type of depository institution that originate mortgage loans, hold and collect the periodic payments by borrowers on the loans they originated or they sell the loans in the secondary mortgage markets.

In some instances, banks and other mortgage lenders "pool" together loans they originated into securities. Other financial intermediaries "repackage" mortgage loans into securities. ***Securitization*** is the process of pooling and packaging mortgage loans into debt securities. A ***mortgage-backed security*** is a debt security created by pooling together a group of mortgage loans whose periodic payments belong to the holders of the security. Some mortgage-backed securities "pass through" the interest and principal payments to the owners of the securities. Payments on the underlying mortgages are made to the financial institution that created the mortgage-backed security. The institution, in turn, pays or passes through the payments to the investors or owners of the securities. In some mortgage-backed securities, the issuer separates or "strips" the interest and principal payment streams into separate securities. Cash flows from interest and principal payments are dependent on continued mortgage payments by the borrowers on the underlying mortgage loans. The uncertainty of mortgage payments is further increased when mortgages are prepaid during periods of declining interest rates.

CREDIT RATINGS AND SCORES

A ***credit rating*** indicates the expected likelihood that a borrower will miss interest or principal payments and possibly default on the debt obligation in the form of a loan, mortgage, or bond. Credit ratings are prepared by private organizations on individuals, financial institutions, business firms, and government entities.

A credit rating for an individual is typically expressed in terms of a ***credit score***, which is a number that indicates an individual's creditworthiness or likelihood that a debt will be paid according to the terms that were initially agreed to. Creditworthiness reflects an individual borrower's capacity to pay, collateral or security to the lender, and character. Some borrowers have the capacity to pay but may be insufficiently trustworthy that they will pay. Credit scores are based on an individual's credit history as reflected in credit report information (e.g., payments on credit cards, auto loans, mortgages) and public records (e.g., bankruptcies, tax liens).

While many different credit score systems are in use, each attempts to differentiate among high quality, moderate quality, and low quality borrowers. For example, a credit scoring system may range from 500 to 1,000 in 100-point increments. Mortgage loans issued to borrowers with credit scores above 700 might be viewed as prime mortgage loans. A ***prime mortgage*** is a home loan to a borrower with relatively high creditworthiness indicating a relatively high likelihood that mortgage payments will be made when due. Of course, the higher the credit score, the higher the borrower's credit quality with scores above 900 reflecting the highest credit quality classification.

---

adjustable-rate mortgage (ARM)
has an interest rate that changes or varies over time with market-determined interest rates on a U.S. Treasury bill or other debt security

securitization
Process of pooling and packaging mortgage loans into debt securities

mortgage-backed security
a debt security created by pooling together a group of mortgage loans whose periodic payments belong to the holders of the security

CONCEPT CHECK

What is a mortgage loan?

What are the primary types of mortgages?

What are mortgage-backed securities?

credit rating
indicates the expected likelihood that a borrower will miss interest or principal payments and possibly default on the debt obligation in the form of a loan, mortgage, or bond

credit score
a number that indicates an individual's creditworthiness or likelihood that a debt will be paid according to the terms that were initially agreed to

prime mortgage
a home loan to a borrower with relatively high creditworthiness indicating a relatively high likelihood that mortgage payments will be made when due

subprime mortgage
home loan made to a
borrower with a relatively
poor credit score indicating a
higher likelihood that the
borrower will miss mortgage
payments when due

Mortgage loan borrowers with credit scores of 700 or below, for example, might be considered to be subprime borrowers. A **subprime mortgage** is a home loan to a borrower with a relatively poor credit score indicating a higher likelihood that the borrower will miss mortgage payments when due. Making mortgage loans to subprime borrowers is a risky business in that an event such as an economic downturn in the form of a recession could result in a large percentage of subprime mortgage borrowers missing their mortgage payments and even defaulting on their home loans.

MAJOR PARTICIPANTS IN THE SECONDARY MORTGAGE MARKETS

As previously discussed, banks and other financial institutions originate mortgage loans and sometimes package mortgages to create mortgage-backed securities that often are sold in the secondary mortgage markets. Recall that the federal government has played an active role in the development of secondary mortgage markets. The Federal National Mortgage Association (FNMA or Fannie Mae) was created in 1938 to support the financial markets by purchasing home mortgages from banks so the resulting funds could be lent to other borrowers. The Government National Mortgage Association (GNMA or Ginnie Mae) was created in 1968. Ginnie Mae issues its own debt securities to obtain funds that are invested in mortgages made to low-income to moderate-income home purchasers. The Federal Home Loan Mortgage Corporation (FHLMC or Freddie Mac) was formed in 1970 to purchase and hold mortgage loans. Freddie Mac acquired prime mortgages and subprime mortgages over time.

Ginnie Mae and Fannie Mae issue mortgage-backed securities to fund their mortgage purchases and holdings. The securitization of mortgage loans by pooling and packaging the loans into mortgage-backed securities by Ginnie Mae and Fannie Mae aided in the development of the secondary mortgage markets.

As default rates on mortgage loans and mortgage-backed securities increased sharply after the housing price bubble burst, Ginnie Mae and Freddie Mac suffered liquidity problems. In mid-2008, in an effort to avoid a financial meltdown, the Fed provided rescue funds for Ginnie Mae and Freddie Mac and the federal government took over control of both organizations.

CONCEPT CHECK

What is a credit rating and what is a credit score?

How do prime and subprime mortgages differ?

CONCEPT CHECK

What are Ginnie Mae, Fannie Mae, and Freddie Mac?

A FURTHER LOOK AT THE 2007–2008 FINANCIAL CRISIS

EARLY FACTORS

FINANCIAL CRISIS

The "seeds" that culminated in the 2007–2008 financial crisis were sown in the 2001 recession. Businesses emphasized cost cutting and improved operating efficiencies in the latter part of the 1980s. These efforts, coupled with a nearly decade-long economic growth in the 1990s left the United States awash with vast amounts of unused financial capital. The U.S. economy benefited further from large expenditures to hopefully minimize the so-called "Year 2000 (or Y2K)" problem associated with the fact that many computer programs used only two digits to indicate the year. For example, 1901 was coded as 01 and 1999 as 99. No one was sure what would happen when the first year of the new century was designated as 00. As a result, large precautionary expenditures were incurred to hopefully minimize potential problems.

The late 1990s saw the Internet "bubble" in the stock market; stock prices rose out of proportion from the ability of firms to generate earnings or cash flows. In particular, "high-flying" stocks included Internet or tech-oriented stocks. Some forecasted the end of long-standing business models and the genesis of new ways of doing business using the Internet and information as tools to gain profits. However, the movement from "brick and mortar" firms to e-commerce firms did not pave the way to a "new economic world," and the Internet and tech bubbles burst.

Stock prices peaked in 2000 and began a rapid decline. The falling stock market, coupled with a slowing post-Y2K economy and recession in 2001, encouraged the Fed to lower interest rates to stimulate spending, borrowing, and economic growth. The terrorist attacks of September 11, 2001, added concern and uncertainty about the economy. To assist the economy, the Fed maintained liquidity of the financial sector and continued to lower interest rates. The Fed was covered in Chapter 4, and we discussed the role of the Federal Reserve's Board of Governors as a major policy maker group in Chapter 5.

Fiscal policy became stimulative, with increased government spending and the passage of tax cuts in 2002. Fiscal policy influences economic activity through taxation and expenditure plans and is carried out by the president and Congress with the support of the U.S. Treasury.

We discussed the role of fiscal policy in Chapter 5. Overall, the setting of low interest rates, fiscal policy stimulation, and the resulting growing economy helped create an environment conducive for excessive spending and borrowing.

A BORROWING-RELATED CULTURAL SHIFT

On the whole, U.S. consumers used to limit their use of debt, but over time the American psyche changed to wanting sooner, if not instant, gratification with respect to buying large-ticket items. Rather than saving and waiting to purchase expensive items, the use of credit cards rose. Borrowing replaced "save now, buy later" as a spending philosophy. The U.S. savings rate was typically about 7–8 percent from the mid 1960s through the early 1980s. Since then, the U.S. savings rate fell to below the 2 percent level during most of the decade of the 2000s. However, probably as a result of the onset of the 2007–2008 financial crisis and the 2008–2009 Great Recession, individuals increased their savings rate to over 5 percent of their disposable income in 2010. The 2012 personal savings rate was about 4 percent.

The cultural shift that allowed the public to "spend now and pay later" (rather than their parents' or grandparents' philosophy of "save now, spend later") also affected household budgets. In addition to carrying a home mortgage and/or car loan or lease payments, the average American household continues to carry large amounts of unpaid credit card debt. The growing use of debt during most of the first decade of the 2000s resulted in a larger portion of U.S. household budgets going toward debt service, repaying borrowing funds with principal and interest.

U.S. government officials engaged in efforts to expand home ownership by encouraging lenders to make mortgage loans available to a broader spectrum of individuals during the 1990s and the first decade of the 2000s. The typical, traditional home loan has been a 30-year, fixed interest rate amortized loan involving a constant monthly payment that would result in a zero loan balance at maturity. These traditional home loans typically required a 20 percent down payment. To increase the number of individuals who could qualify for home ownership, alternative mortgage loan instruments were developed and in some instances credit standards were lowered.

As discussed earlier in this chapter, the traditional fixed-rate mortgage was often replaced by an adjustable-rate mortgage (ARM). Mortgage lenders often offered initial below market interest rates on ARMs as well as offered subprime mortgages to borrowers with relatively low credit scores, which suggested that the likelihood that loan payments might be missed when due. Soon after the housing price bubble burst in mid-2006 and the economy began slowing in 2007, poorly qualified borrowers began defaulting on their mortgages. Developments in the mortgage markets were major contributors to the severity of the 2007–2008 financial crisis and contributed to the 2008–2009 Great Recession. Of course, while individuals were responsible for entering into risky home mortgages, they were encouraged to do so by government officials, government-supported agencies, and mortgage originators and financial institution lenders.

As the United States moves into the second decade of the twenty-first century, individuals and businesses have been using less financial leverage, i.e., they have been de-leveraging. More prudent use of credit seems to be occurring. These use of credit developments, accompanied by indications of economic growth and the beginning of the recovery of housing markets suggest that the 2007–2008 financial crisis and the 2008–2009 Great Recession are behind us.

CONCEPT CHECK

What early factors contributed to the 2007–2008 financial crisis?

What cultural shift occurred on the part of individuals that contributed to the 2007–2008 financial crisis?

SUMMARY

This chapter focused on how savings are created and how they are converted into investments. The major components of gross domestic product (GDP) were identified and discussed in terms of consumption, investment, and the net exports balance of goods and services.

The three basic economic units were identified as individuals, business firms (including financial intermediaries), and governments. The federal government has been primarily a savings deficit unit over the past several decades. This produced many annual budget deficits and a large national debt. Major sources of savings in the United States come from individuals and business firms. These savings may

be directly invested and accumulated in financial institutions and then loaned or invested.

Factors that affect the level of savings were then discussed. This was followed by a discussion of capital market securities used by issuers and investors that help the savings and investment process work efficiently. Specific attention was directed to the mortgage markets including the types of real estate mortgages that are available to individuals in the primary markets and how mortgages are traded in the secondary markets. Characteristics of the 2007–2008 financial crisis involving individuals and their pursuit of home ownership were discussed.

APPLYING FINANCE TO...

INSTITUTIONS AND MARKETS	INVESTMENTS	FINANCIAL MANAGEMENT
Savings of individuals are accumulated in a number of ways by financial institutions that, in turn, make pooled savings available to businesses so they can maintain and grow their operations. Savings are gathered by commercial banks and other depository institutions. Insurance companies collect premium payments and pension funds, gather contributions, and invest these funds until needed. Mutual funds play a major role in attracting the savings of individuals and then investing the pooled funds in securities.	Governments issue debt securities to finance their needs, and corporations issue debt and equity securities to maintain and grow their businesses. The savings of individuals are the primary source for raising financial capital by governments and corporations. Capital market securities were covered with specific attention given to mortgage loans and mortgage markets. Financial institutions gather savings and make the savings available to governments and corporations in the primary securities markets. The process of determining interest rates for borrowing financial capital and pricing new stock issues will be covered as we progress through Part 2.	Financial managers often must raise additional amounts of debt and equity funds to finance the plans for their firms. While they may depend somewhat on loans from banks, they may need to attract financial capital by selling bonds or stocks privately or publicly. A decision to raise funds must be accompanied with the willingness to pay the required interest rates established in the marketplace or selling stock at a market-determined price.

KEY TERMS

adjustable-rate mortgage (ARM)	dissave	personal saving
budgetary deficit	federal statutory debt limits	prime mortgage
capital consumption adjustment	fixed-rate mortgage	savings
capital formation	government expenditures (GE)	savings deficit
capital market securities	gross private domestic investment (GPDI)	savings surplus
common stock	mortgage	securitization
contractual savings	mortgage-backed security	subprime mortgage
corporate bond	mortgage markets	Treasury bond
credit rating	municipal bond	voluntary savings
credit score	net exports (NE)	undistributed profits
derivative security	personal consumption expenditures (PCE)	

DISCUSSION QUESTIONS

1. What is capital formation?

2. Describe the major components of gross domestic product (GDP).

3. Identify the major components of net saving and describe their relative contributions in recent years.

4. Identify the various sources of revenues in the federal budget.

5. Identify the major expense categories in the federal budget.

6. Describe whether the federal government has been operating with surplus or deficit budgets in recent years.

7. Briefly describe the historical role of savings in the United States.

8. Compare savings surplus and savings deficit units. Indicate which economic units are generally of one type or the other.

9. Define personal saving.

10. Also, differentiate between voluntary and contractual savings.

11. Describe the recent levels of savings rates in the United States.

12. How and why do corporations save?

13. Describe the principal factors that influence the level of savings by individuals.

14. How do economic cycle movements affect the media or types of savings by businesses?

15. What are the life cycle stages of individuals?

16. How does each life cycle stage relate to the amount and type of individual savings?

17. What are the life cycle stages of corporations and other business firms?

18. Explain how financial savings generated by a business a function of its life cycle stage.

19. What are the two types of maturity-related financial markets?

20. Identify and briefly describe the major securities that are originated or traded in capital securities markets.

21. What is a mortgage? What is meant by the term *mortgage markets*?

22. Identify and briefly describe the two major types of residential real estate mortgages.

23. What is meant by the term *securitization*? What is a mortgage-backed security?

24. Briefly describe credit ratings and credit scores.

25. Identify and describe the roles of several major participants in the secondary mortgage markets.

26. What role did individuals play in the development of the 2007–2008 financial crisis?

EXERCISES

1. Go to the U.S. Department of Commerce, Bureau of Economic Analysis Web site at http://www.bea.gov, click on the National tab, and determine the following:

   a. The current personal savings rate in the United States.

   b. The amount of current corporate savings as reflected in the amount of undistributed profits.

2. Assume you are an elected member of Congress. A lobbying group has agreed to provide financial support for your reelection campaign next year. In return for the group's support, you have been asked to champion their self-interests in the form of a spending bill that is being considered by Congress. What would you do?

3. Match the following financial instruments and securities with their issuers.

Instruments/Securities	Issuers
a. corporate stocks	1. commercial banks
b. Treasury bonds	2. corporations
c. municipal bonds	3. U.S. government
d. negotiable certificates of deposit	4. state/local governments

4. Match the following financial instruments and securities with their typical maturities.

Instruments/Securities	Maturities
a. corporate stocks	1. less than one year
b. Treasury bills	2. no maturity
c. mortgages	3. up to about 30 years
d. commercial paper	4. up to one year

PROBLEMS

1. A small country's gross domestic product (GDP) is $12 million.

   a. If government expenditures amount to $7.5 million and gross private domestic investment is $5.5 million, what will be the amount of net exports of goods and services?

2. How would your answer change in Problem 1 if the gross domestic product (GDP) had been $14 million?

3. Personal income amounted to $17 million last year. Personal current taxes amounted to $4 million, and personal outlays for consumption expenditures, nonmortgage interest, and so forth were $12 million.

   a. What was the amount of disposable personal income last year?

   b. What was the amount of personal saving last year?

   c. Calculate personal saving as a percentage of disposable personal income.

4. Assume personal income was $28 million last year. Personal outlays were $20 million, and personal current taxes were $5 million.

   a. What was the amount of disposable personal income last year?

   b. What was the amount of personal saving last year?

   c. Calculate personal saving as a percentage of disposable personal income.

5. The components that comprise a nation's gross domestic product (GDP) were identified and discussed in this chapter. Assume the following accounts and amounts were reported by a nation last year. Government expenditures (purchases of goods and services) were $5.5 billion; personal consumption expenditures were $40.5 billion; gross private domestic investment amounted to $20 billion; capital consumption allowances were $4 billion; personal savings were estimated at $2 billion; imports of goods and services amounted to $6.5 billion; and the exports of goods and services were $5 billion.

   a. Determine the nation's gross domestic product (GDP).

   b. How would your answer change if the dollar amounts of imports and exports were reversed?

6. Assume that some of the data provided in problem 5 change next year. Specifically, government expenditures increase by 10 percent; gross private domestic investment declines by 10 percent; and imports of goods and services drop to $6 billion. Assume the other information as given remains the same next year.

   a. Determine the nation's gross domestic product (GDP) for next year.

   b. How would your answer change in (a) if personal consumption expenditures are only $35 billion next year and capital consumption allowances actually increase by 10 percent?

7. A nation's gross domestic product (GDP) is $600 million. Its personal consumption expenditures are $350 million, and government expenditures are $100 million. Net exports of goods and services amount to $50 million.

   a. Determine the nation's gross private domestic investment.

   b. If imports exceed exports by $25 million, how would your answer to (a) change?

8. A nation's gross domestic product (GDP) is stated in U.S. dollars at $40 million. The dollar value of one unit of the nation's currency (FC) is $0.25.

   a. Determine the value of GDP in FCs.

   b. How would your answer change if the dollar value of one FC increases to $0.30?

9. A country in Southeast Asia states its gross domestic product (GDP) in terms of yen. Assume that last year its GDP was 50 billion yen when one U.S. dollar could be exchanged for 120 yen.

   a. Determine the country's GDP in terms of U.S. dollars for last year.

   b. Assume the GDP increases to 55 billion yen for this year, while the dollar value of one yen is now $0.01. Determine the country's GDP in terms of U.S. dollars for this year.

   c. Show how your answer in (b) would change if one U.S. dollar could be exchanged for 110 yen.

10. **Challenge Problem** (This exercise requires knowledge of probabilities and expected values.) Following are data relating to a nation's operations last year:

Capital consumption allowances	$150 million
Undistributed corporate profits	40 million
Personal consumption expenditures	450 million
Personal savings	50 million
Corporate inventory valuation adjustment	25 million
Federal government deficit	230 million

Government expenditures	10 million
State and local governments surplus	1 million
Net exports of goods and services	22 million
Gross private domestic investment	200 million

   a. Determine the nation's gross domestic product (GDP).

   b. How would your answer change in (a) if exports of goods and services were $5 million and imports were 80 percent of exports?

   c. Show how the GDP in (a) would change under the following three scenarios:

   Scenario 1 (probability of .20): The GDP components would be 120 percent of their values in (a).

   Scenario 2 (probability of .50): The GDP component values used in (a) would occur.

   Scenario 3 (probability of .30): The GDP components would be 75 percent of their values in (a).

   d. Determine the nation's gross savings last year.

   e. Show how your answer in (d) would change if each account simultaneously increases by 10 percent.

   f. Show how your answer in (d) would change if each account simultaneously decreases by 10 percent.

   g. Show how your answer in (d) would have changed if capital consumption allowances had been 10 percent less and personal consumption expenditures had been $400 million.

INSTITUTIONS
AND MARKETS

INVESTMENTS

FINANCIAL
MANAGEMENT

• CHAPTER 8 •

Interest Rates

Chapter Learning Objectives . . .

AFTER STUDYING THIS CHAPTER, YOU SHOULD BE ABLE TO DO THE FOLLOWING:

- Describe how interest rates change in response to shifts in the supply and demand for loanable funds.
- Identify major historical movements in interest rates in the United States.
- Describe the loanable funds theory of interest rates.
- Identify the major determinants of market interest rates.
- Describe the types of U.S. Treasury marketable securities and indicate who owns them.
- Explain the term or maturity structure of interest rates.
- Identify and briefly describe the three theories used to explain the term structure of interest rates.
- Identify broad historical price level changes in the United States and other economies and discuss their causes.
- Describe the various types of inflation and their causes.
- Discuss the effect of default risk premiums on the level of long-term interest rates.

Where We Have Been . . .

In Chapter 7, you learned about the savings and investment process as it takes place in the United States. The gross domestic product (GDP) and capital formation were discussed. GDP is composed of personal consumption expenditures, government purchases, gross private domestic investment, and the net export of goods and services. The historical role of savings and how financial assets and liabilities are created was covered. You should have a basic understanding of the federal government's source of receipts and where expenditures are allocated. You should also understand the major sources of savings, how the major financial institutions direct funds from savings into investment, and factors that affect savings.

Where We Are Going . . .

Chapter 9 focuses on the time value of money. By saving and investing, money can "grow" over time through the compounding of interest. We first cover simple interest and then turn to compounding of current investments (determining future values) and discounting of future cash receipts (finding present values). You will be introduced to annuities, which are investments that involve constant periodic payments or receipts of cash. Chapter 10 focuses on the characteristics and valuations of bonds and stocks. In Chapter 11, you will learn about the characteristics and operation of primary and secondary securities markets. Part 2 concludes with Chapter 12, which focuses on helping you learn and understand concepts relating to financial returns and risks associated with investing in stocks and bonds.

How This Chapter Applies to Me . . .

It is nearly impossible to get through the day without seeing some reference to interest rates on saving or borrowing money. You may see interest rates being offered on savings accounts by depository institutions, interest rates on new and used automobiles, and even the rate at which you could borrow for a loan to pay your tuition or to purchase a home. Your cost of borrowing will generally be higher when you are starting your working career and your credit quality has not yet been established. Understanding the factors that determine the level of interest rates should help you make more informed decisions concerning when to spend, save, and borrow.

173

We all have been tempted by the advertisements for goods and services that suggest we should "buy now and pay for it later." These advertisements are hoping that we will decide that the value of "more" current consumption is worth the added interest we will have to pay on the funds that we must borrow to finance this consumption.

Sometimes individuals like to consume more even though they don't have the money to pay for this consumption. For example, you may see a pair of shoes in a store window "that you have to have right now." Maybe you don't have the money to pay for the shoes. Don't despair for if you have a credit card, the credit card issuer may lend you the money to pay for the shoes. In return, you will have to pay back the amount borrowed plus interest on the loan.

You might be considering making a current investment in your future by borrowing money to go to college. In this case, you hope your current education will lead to an increase in your future earning power, out of which you will have to repay your student loan. When you purchased your shoes on credit, you decided to consume now and pay later for this current consumption. When you decide to invest in your education, you expect that future earnings will be larger, making it easier to repay the student loan. Businesses borrow to make investments in inventory, plant, and equipment that will earn profits sufficient to pay interest, repay the amount borrowed, and provide returns to equity investors. In this chapter, we focus on the cost or price of borrowing funds. An understanding of interest rates, meaning what causes them to change and how they relate to changes in the economy, is of fundamental importance in the world of finance.

SUPPLY AND DEMAND FOR LOANABLE FUNDS

Lenders are willing to supply funds to borrowers as long as lenders can earn a satisfactory return on their loans (i.e., an amount greater than that which was lent). Borrowers will demand funds from lenders as long as borrowers can invest the funds so as to earn a satisfactory return above the cost of their loans. Actually, the supply and demand for loanable funds will take place as long as lenders and borrowers have the expectation of satisfactory returns. Of course, returns received may differ from those expected because of inflation, failure to repay loans, and poor investments. Return experiences will, in turn, affect future supply and demand relationships for loanable funds.

interest rate
basic price that equates the demand for and supply of loanable funds in the financial markets

The basic price that equates the demand for and supply of loanable funds in the financial markets is the ***interest rate***. Figure 8.1 depicts how interest rates are determined in the financial markets. Graph A shows the interest rate (r) that clears the market by bringing the demand (D_1) by borrowers for funds in equilibrium with the supply (S_1) by lenders of funds. For illustrative purposes, we have chosen a rate of 5 percent as the cost or price that makes savings equal to investment (i.e., where the supply and demand curves intersect).

Interest rates may move from an equilibrium level if an unanticipated change or "shock" changes the demand for, or supply of, loanable funds. For example, an increase in the desire to invest in business assets because of an expanding economy might cause the demand for loanable funds to increase or shift upward (i.e., from D_1 to D_2). The result, depicted in Graph B, will be an increase or rise in interest rates to, say, 6 percent, assuming no immediate adjustment in the supply of funds. Of course, as higher interest rates become available to savers, savings may increase, which could cause the supply of loanable funds to increase. A decline in business activity would be expected to have the opposite impact on interest rates.

Graph C depicts an unanticipated increase in inflation, which leads lenders (suppliers) to require a higher rate of interest. This is shown by the shift in supply from S_1 to S_2, which for illustrative purposes shows an increase in the interest rate from 5 percent to 7 percent. At this point, we have not taken into consideration that borrowers may adjust their demand for loanable funds because of the likelihood of more costly loans. Graph D depicts the situation that borrowers (users) may cut back on their demand for loanable funds from D_1 to D_3 because of the unanticipated increase in inflation. For example, this would occur if borrowers felt their higher borrowing costs could not be passed on to their customers, and thus, the returns on their investments would be adversely affected by the higher inflation rates. Instead of the unanticipated increase in inflation shock causing the interest rate to rise to 7 percent, the new equilibrium rate where supply equals demand (investment) might be only 6 percent.

CONCEPT CHECK
How are interest rates determined in the financial markets?

FIGURE 8.1

Interest Rate Determination in the Financial Markets

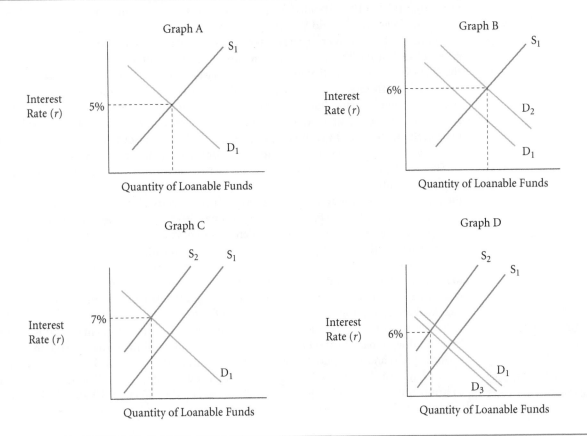

HISTORICAL CHANGES IN U.S. INTEREST RATE LEVELS

Interest rates for loanable funds have varied throughout the history of the United States as the result of shifting supply and demand. Since after the Civil War, there have been four periods of rising or relatively high long-term interest rates and four periods of falling or relatively low interest rates on long-term loans and investments.

The four periods of increasing/high long-term interest rates were the following:

1. 1864–1873
2. 1905–1920
3. 1927–1933
4. 1946–1982

The rapid economic expansion after the Civil War caused the first period of rising interest rates from 1864 to 1873. The second period, from 1905 to 1920, was based on large-scale prewar expansion and the inflation associated with World War I. The third period, from 1927 to 1933, was due to the economic boom from 1927 to 1929 and the unsettled conditions in the securities markets during the early part of the Great Depression, from 1929 to 1933. The rapid economic expansion following World War II led to the last period, from 1946 to 1982.

The four periods of decreasing/low long-term interest rates were the following:

1. 1873–1905
2. 1920–1927
3. 1933–1946
4. 1982–present

The first period of falling interest rates was from 1873 to 1905. As the public debt was paid off and funds became widely available, the supply of funds grew more rapidly than the demand for them. Prices and interest rates fell even though the economy was moving forward. The same general factors were at work in the second period, 1920 to 1927. The third period of low interest rates, from 1933 to 1946, resulted from the government's actions in fighting the Great Depression and continued during World War II, when interest rates were pegged or set.

Beginning in 1966, interest rates entered a period of unusual increases, leading to the highest rates in U.S. history. This increase in rates began as a result of the Vietnam War. It continued in the 1970s because of a policy of on-again, off-again price controls and increased demands for capital arising from ecological concerns and the energy crisis. Furthermore, several periods of poor crops coupled with sharp price increases for crude oil caused worldwide inflation. Interest rates peaked at the beginning of the 1980s, with short-term rates above 20 percent and long-term rates in the high teens. In summary, double-digit inflation, a somewhat tight monetary policy, and heavy borrowing demand by business contributed to these record levels.

The fourth period of declining long-term interest rates began in 1982, when rates peaked, and the decline continues today. Inflation rates dropped dramatically from double-digit levels during the beginning of the 1980s to below 3 percent since the early 1990s. Low inflation rates generally in the 2 to 3 percent range have continued through 2012. The decline in inflation rates seems to have been a primary reason long-term interest rates have moved downward.

Short-term interest rates generally move up and down with the business cycle. Therefore, they show more periods of expansion and contraction. Long-term and short-term interest rates tend to rise in prosperity periods during which the economy is expanding rapidly. A major exception was during World War II, when interest rates were pegged. During this period, the money supply increased rapidly, laying the base for postwar inflation.

Today, short-term and long-term interest rates are at historical lows in the United States This has been due, in part, to the Fed's efforts to avoid a financial meltdown during the 2007–2008 financial crisis and to support economic recovery from the 2008–2009 Great Recession. Recall from Chapter 4 that the Fed has recently employed non-traditional monetary policy actions called quantitative easing (QE). QE 1 was implemented in 2008, QE2 began in 2010, and QE3 was initiated in 2012.

LOANABLE FUNDS THEORY

CONCEPT CHECK

What do short-term interest rates generally move with?

loanable funds theory holds that interest rates are a function of the supply of and demand for loanable funds

CONCEPT CHECK

What is the loanable funds theory?

The **loanable funds theory** holds that interest rates are a function of the supply of and demand for loanable funds. This is a flow theory in that it focuses on the relative supply and demand of loanable funds during a specified period. How the supply of and the demand for loanable funds interact determines the interest rate and the quantity of funds that flows through the financial markets during any period. If the supply of funds increases, holding demand constant, interest rates will tend to fall. Likewise, an increase in the demand for loans will tend to drive up interest rates. This is depicted in Graph B of Figure 8.1.

Sources of Loanable Funds

Two basic sources of loanable funds exist: current savings and expansion of deposits by depository institutions.

The supply of savings comes from all sectors of the economy, and most of it flows through U.S. financial institutions. Individuals may save part of their incomes as voluntary savings or through contractual savings programs, such as purchasing whole life or endowment insurance policies or repaying installment or mortgage loans. Governmental units and not-for-profit institutions sometimes have funds in excess of current expenditures. Corporations may have savings available because they are not paying out all their earnings as dividends. Depreciation allowances that are not being used currently to buy new capital equipment to replace older equipment may be available for lending.

Governmental and private pension funds provide another source of saving. These funds, which are building up large reserves to meet future commitments, are available for investment.

Some savings are invested as ownership equity in businesses either directly in single proprietorships or partnerships or by buying stock in corporations. This is, however, only a small part of total savings. The bulk of the total savings each year is available as loanable funds. Funds may be loaned directly, for example, when someone lends money to a friend to enable the friend to expand business operations. However, most savings are loaned through financial institutions, one of whose basic functions is the accumulation of savings.

SMALL BUSINESS PRACTICE
The Family Business or Venture

Family businesses continue to be popular in the United States. For publicly held firms, corporate goals may differ in part from the goals of managers. For closely held firms that are not family owned, the business goals and the personal goals of owner/managers are closely aligned. For family-owned or family-controlled firms, a third set of goals—family goals—must be considered. When family goals are aligned with the business and manager goals, the business can benefit from family sharing and closeness. However, when family goals differ from business and/or manager goals, conflict and an argumentative environment may prevail. In such instances, family-controlled businesses often fail or the family is forced to sell.

Jeffry Timmons lists several problems unique to family businesses or ventures.* First, problems of control, fairness, and equity often exist. For example, family members may have different ideas as to how

the business should be run. Fairness and equity issues relate to the division of work and relative contributions to running the business. Second is the issue of credibility, whereby founding parents find it difficult to believe that their children can perform in a manner comparable to their own.

The third potential problem relates to family dynamics. Since separating business operations from family life is difficult, tensions in one area often spill over into the other area. Fourth is the problem of deciding succession. If succession is to involve a next-generation family member, the founder must disengage his or her ownership rights and delegate an increased level of responsibility to the new person in control. For succession to succeed, the founder must be willing to assume the role of advisor to the family member who was selected to run the firm in the future.

*Jeffry Timmons, *New Venture Creation*, 4th Edition (Boston: Irwin/McGraw-Hill, 1994). Also see Jeffry A. Timmons and Stephen Spineilli, *New Venture Creation*, 8th Edition (New York: McGraw-Hill/Irwin, 2009), Chapter 18.

CONCEPT CHECK

What are the basic sources of loanable funds?

The other basic source of loanable funds is that created by the banking system. Banks and other depository institutions channel savings to borrowers and create deposits, which are the most widely used form of money in the U.S. economy. This process was discussed in Chapter 3. Net additions to the money supply are a source of loanable funds; during periods when the money supply contracts, the flow of loanable funds drops below the level of current savings.

Loanable funds can be grouped in several ways. They may be divided into short-term funds and long-term funds. We can also group funds in two other ways:

1. Use, such as business credit, consumer credit, agricultural credit, and government credit
2. The institutions supplying each type

Factors Affecting the Supply of Loanable Funds

Many factors affect the supply of loanable funds. Both sources of funds have some tendency to increase as interest rates rise. However, this effect is often small compared to other factors that limit or otherwise affect the volume of savings or the ability of the banking system to expand deposits.

Volume of Savings

The major factor that determines the volume of savings, corporate as well as individual, is the level of national income. When income is high, savings are high; when it is low, savings are low. The pattern of income taxes (i.e., the level of the tax and the tax rates in various income brackets) also influences savings volume. Furthermore, the tax treatment of savings influences the amount of income saved. For example, the tax deferral on (or the postponement of) savings placed in individual retirement accounts (IRAs) increases the volume of savings.

The age of the population has an important effect on the savings volume. As we discussed in Chapter 7, little saving is done during the formative and education-building stage or during the family-forming stage. Therefore, an economy with a large share of young couples with children will have less total savings than one with more people in the older wealth-building stage.

The volume of savings depends on the factors that affect indirect savings. The more effectively the life insurance industry promotes the sale of whole life and endowment insurance policies, the larger the volume of savings. The higher the demand for private pension funds, which accumulate contributions during working years to make payments on retirement, the larger the volume of savings. The effect of interest rates on such savings is often the opposite of the normal effect of price on supply. As interest rates decrease, more money must be paid for insurance for the same amount of coverage because a smaller amount of interest will be earned from the reinvestment of premiums and earnings. Inversely, as interest rates rise, less money needs to be put into reserves to get the same objectives. The same is true of the amount of money that must be put into annuities and pension funds.

When savings result from the use of consumer credit, the effect of interest rates is delayed. For example, assume a car is bought with a three-year loan. Savings, in the form of repaying the loan, must go on for three years regardless of changes in interest rates. There may even be an opposite effect in the case of a mortgage because, if interest rates drop substantially, the loan can be refinanced. At the lower interest rate, the same dollar payments provide a larger amount for repayment of principal, that is, for saving.

Expansion of Deposits by Depository Institutions

The amount of short-term credit available depends largely on the lending policies of commercial banks and other depository institutions and on the policies of the Federal Reserve System (Fed). Lenders are influenced by such factors as present business conditions and future prospects. However, the Fed has great control over the ability of the banking system to create new deposits, as discussed in Chapter 4.

How much long-term credit of different types is available depends on the policies of the different credit suppliers. Since depository institutions do not play a major role in this field, the money supply is not expanded directly to meet long-term credit demands. Indirectly, however, their policies and those of the Fed are important: If the banking system expands the money supply to meet short-term needs, a larger proportion of the supply of loanable funds can be used for long-term credit.

Liquidity Attitudes

How lenders see the future has a significant effect on the supply of long-term and short-term loanable funds. Lenders may feel that the economic outlook is so uncertain that they are reluctant to lend their money. This liquidity preference can be so strong that large amounts of funds lie idle, as they did during the Great Depression in the 1930s. Lenders may prefer liquidity because they expect interest rates to go up in the near future or opportunities for direct investment to be more favorable. Thus, liquidity attitudes may result in keeping some funds idle that would normally be available for lending.

Effect of Interest Rates on the Demand for Loanable Funds

The demand for loanable funds comes from all sectors of the economy. Businesses borrow to finance current operations and to buy plant and equipment. Farmers borrow to meet short-term and long-term needs. Institutions, such as hospitals and schools, borrow primarily to finance new buildings and equipment. Individuals finance the purchase of homes with long-term loans and purchase durable goods or cover emergencies with intermediate-term and short-term loans. Governmental units borrow to finance public buildings, bridge the gap between expenditures and tax receipts, and meet budget deficits. The factors affecting the demand for loanable funds are different for each borrower type. We have considered such factors in detail when analyzing the various credit types. Therefore, this discussion covers only how interest rates affect the major types of borrowing.

Historically, one of the biggest borrowers has been the federal government, and Congress generally gives little consideration to interest rates in its spending programs. Minor changes in interest rates do not affect short-term business borrowing. However, historical evidence shows that large increases in short-term interest rates do decrease the demand for bank loans and other forms of short-term business borrowing.

Changes in long-term interest rates affect long-term business borrowing. Most corporations put off long-term borrowing when rates are up if they expect rates to go down in the near future.

Likewise, minor changes in interest rates have little effect on consumer borrowing. For short-term installment loans, the monthly repayments of principal are so large compared to the interest cost that the total effect on the repayment schedule is small. However, larger interest rate changes have strongly influenced consumer borrowing in the past. This happened during periods when home mortgage rates reached historically high levels and new housing starts declined sharply.

CONCEPT CHECK

How do interest rates influence the demand for loanable funds?

Roles of the Banking System and of the Government

While the effect of interest rates on loanable funds varies, the supply of and the demand for loanable funds are affected by the actions of the banking system and the government. When depository institutions expand credit by increasing the total volume of short-term loans, the supply of loanable funds increases. When credit contracts, the supply of loanable funds decreases. The actions of the Fed in setting discount rates, buying securities in the open market, and changing reserve requirements affect the supply of loanable funds. In fact, all actions that affect the level of banking system reserves and creation of checkable deposits affect the supply of loanable funds in the market.

Government borrowing has become a major influence on demand for funds and will remain so for the foreseeable future. Government surpluses or deficits make funds available in the market or take them out of the market in substantial amounts. Treasury debt management policies affect the supply and demand relationships for short-term, intermediate-term, and long-term funds.

Therefore, financial markets are under the influence of the Treasury, and the Fed strongly influences the supply of funds. The Treasury, through tax policies and other government programs, plays a role on this side of the market. However, the Treasury's major influence is on the demand for funds, as it borrows heavily to finance federal deficits.

International Factors Affecting Interest Rates

Interest rates in the United States are influenced by more than domestic factors. The large trade surpluses with China and Japan, with their accumulation of funds to invest, have had important influences on the rates the federal government pays in issuing new securities. This international influence adds to the critical need to balance the national budget and to avoid the frequency of financing. As production has shifted to many other countries, investment has shifted. In short, the Treasury and the Fed must carefully consider the influence of international movements of funds on domestic interest rates.

CONCEPT CHECK

What are the major factors that affect the supply of loanable funds?

DETERMINANTS OF MARKET INTEREST RATES

In addition to supply and demand relationships, interest rates are determined by a number of specific factors. First, the interest rate (r) that we observe in the marketplace is called a **nominal interest rate** because it includes a premium for expected inflation. Second, a nominal interest rate that is not free from the risk of default by the borrower will have a default risk premium. Thus, in its simplest form, the nominal interest rate can be expressed as the following:

$$r = RR + IP + DRP \tag{8.1}$$

RR is the real rate of interest, IP is an inflation premium, and DRP is the default risk premium.

The **real rate of interest** is the interest rate on a risk-free financial debt instrument when no inflation is expected. The **inflation premium** is the average inflation rate expected over the life of the instrument.

The **default risk premium** (DRP) indicates compensation for the possibility that the borrower will not pay interest and/or will repay principal according to the financial instrument's contractual arrangements. The DRP reflects the application of the risk/return principle of finance presented in Chapter 1. In essence, "higher returns are expected for taking on more risk." This is a higher "expected" return because the issuer may default on some of the contractual returns. Of course, the actual "realized" return on a default risky debt investment could be substantially less than the expected return. At the extreme, the debt security investor could lose all of his or her investment. The DRP is discussed further in the last section of this chapter. The risk/return finance principle to stock investments and to portfolios of securities is further extended in Chapter 12. Instead of a default risk premium, the concentration is on stock risk premiums and market risk premiums.

To cover short-term and long-term debt instruments, two additional premiums are frequently added to the equation that explains nominal interest rates. This expanded version can be expressed this way:

$$r = RR + IP + DRP + MRP + LP \tag{8.2}$$

nominal interest rate
interest rate that is observed in the marketplace and that includes a premium for expected inflation

real rate of interest
interest rate on a risk-free debt instrument when no inflation is expected

inflation premium
average inflation rate expected over the life of the instrument

default risk premium
indicates compensation for the possibility that the borrower will not pay interest and/or will not repay principal according to the financial instrument's contractual arrangements

maturity risk premium
the added return expected by lenders or investors because of interest rate risk on instruments with longer maturities

interest rate risk
reflects the possibility of changes or fluctuations in market values of fixed-rate debt instruments as market interest rates change over time

liquidity premium
compensation for those financial debt instruments that cannot easily be converted to cash at prices close to their estimated fair market values

CONCEPT CHECK

What is the nominal interest rate, and what is the real rate of interest?

What are the definitions of the following: default risk premium, maturity risk premium, and liquidity premium?

What is interest rate risk?

risk-free rate of interest
the combination of real rate of interest and the inflation premium, which in the United States is represented by U.S. Treasury debt instruments or securities

MRP is the maturity risk premium, and LP is the liquidity premium on a financial instrument.

The ***maturity risk premium*** is the added return expected by lenders or investors because of interest rate risk on instruments with longer maturities. ***Interest rate risk*** reflects the possibility of changes or fluctuations in market values of fixed-rate debt instruments as market interest rates change over time. There is an inverse relationship in the marketplace between debt instrument values or prices and nominal interest rates. For example, if interest rates rise from 5 percent to 6 percent because of a previously unanticipated inflation rate increase, the values of outstanding debt instruments will decline. Furthermore, the longer the remaining life until maturity, the greater the reductions in a fixed-rate debt instrument's value to a given interest rate increase. These concepts with numerical calculations are explored in Chapter 10.

The ***liquidity premium*** is the compensation for those financial debt instruments that cannot be easily converted to cash at prices close to their estimated fair market values. For example, a corporation's low-quality bond may be traded infrequently. As a consequence, a bondholder who wishes to sell tomorrow may find it difficult to sell except at a large discount in price.

Those factors that influence the nominal interest rate are discussed throughout the remainder of this chapter, beginning with the concept of a risk-free interest rate and a discussion of why U.S. Treasury securities are used as the best estimate of the risk-free rate. Other sections focus on the term or maturity structure of interest rates, inflation expectations and associated premiums, and default risk and liquidity premium considerations.

RISK-FREE SECURITIES: U.S. TREASURY DEBT OBLIGATIONS

By combining the real rate of interest and the inflation premium, we have the ***risk-free rate of interest***, which in the United States is represented by U.S. Treasury debt instruments or securities. It is generally believed that even with the large national debt, the U.S. government is not going to renege on its obligations to pay interest and repay principal at maturity on its debt securities. Thus, we view U.S. Treasury securities as being free of default risk. Technically, a truly risk-free financial instrument has no liquidity risk or maturity risk (as reflected by interest rate risk). Treasury marketable securities are considered to have almost no liquidity risk, and only longer-term Treasury securities have maturity or interest rate risk associated with changes in market-determined interest rates that occur over time.

Economists have estimated that the annual real rate of interest in the United States and other countries has averaged about 2 to 3 percent in past years. One way of looking at the risk-free rate is to say this is the minimum rate of interest necessary to get individuals and businesses to save. There must be an incentive to invest or save idle cash holdings. One such incentive is the expectation of some real rate of return above expected inflation levels. For illustrative purposes, let's assume 2 percent is the current expectation for a real rate of return. Let's also assume that the nominal interest rate is currently 4 percent for a one-year Treasury security.

Given these assumptions, we can turn to Equation 8.1 to determine the average inflation expectations of holders or investors as follows:

$$4\% = RR + IP + DRP$$
$$4\% = 2\% + IP + 0\%$$
$$IP = 4\% - 2\% - 0\% = 2\%$$

Thus, investors expect a 2 percent inflation rate over the next year; and if they want a real rate of return of 2 percent, the nominal interest rate must be 4 percent.

Let's use the expanded equation to explain nominal interest rates as expressed in Equation 8.2. However, since this is a Treasury security, there is no liquidity premium and no maturity risk premium if we are planning to hold the security until its maturity at the end of one year. Thus, Equation 8.2 would be used as follows to find the average expected inflation rate:

$$4\% = RR + IP + DRP + MRP + LP$$
$$4\% = 2\% + IP + 0\% + 0\% + 0\%$$
$$IP = 4\% - 2\% - 0\% - 0\% - 0\% = 2\%$$

Of course, the answer has not changed and remains 2 percent since no risk premiums were added. The impact of a maturity risk premium is introduced after a discussion of the types of marketable securities issued by the Treasury.

CONCEPT CHECK
What is the risk-free rate of interest?

marketable government securities
securities that can be purchased and sold through customary market channels

MARKETABLE OBLIGATIONS

Marketable government securities, as the term implies, are securities that can be purchased and sold through customary market channels. Large commercial banks and securities dealers maintain markets for these obligations. In addition, nearly all other securities firms and commercial banks, large or small, will help their customers purchase and sell federal obligations by routing orders to institutions that do maintain markets in them. The investments of institutional investors and large personal investors in federal obligations are centered almost exclusively in the marketable issues. These marketable issues are bills, notes, and bonds, the difference among them being their maturity at time of issue. Although the maturity of an obligation is reduced as it remains in effect, the obligation continues to be called by its original descriptive title. Thus, a twenty-year Treasury bond continues to be described in the quotation sheets as a bond throughout its life.

Treasury Bills

Treasury bills
federal obligations issued with maturities up to one year

Treasury bills are issued with maturities up to one year and, thus, are the shortest maturities of federal obligations. They are typically issued for 91 days, with some issues carrying maturities of 182 days. Treasury bills with a maturity of one year are issued at auction every four weeks. Issues of Treasury bills are offered each week by the Treasury to refund the part of the total volume of bills that matures. In effect, the 91-day Treasury bills mature and are rolled over in thirteen weeks. Each week, approximately one-thirteenth of the total volume of such bills is refunded.

When the flow of cash revenues into the Treasury is too small to meet expenditure requirements, additional bills are issued. During those periods of the year when revenues exceed expenditures, Treasury bills are allowed to mature without being refunded. Treasury bills, therefore, provide the Treasury with a convenient financial mechanism to adjust for the lack of a regular revenue flow into the Treasury. The volume of bills may be increased or decreased in response to general surpluses or deficits in the federal budget from year to year.

Treasury bills are issued on a discount basis and mature at par. Each week, the Treasury bills to be sold are awarded to the highest bidders. Dealers and other investors submit sealed bids. Upon being opened, these bids are arrayed from highest to lowest. Those bidders asking the least discount (offering the highest price) are placed high in the array. The bids are accepted in the order of their position in the array until all bills are awarded. Bidders seeking a higher discount (offering a lower price) may fail to receive any bills that particular week. Investors interested in purchasing small volumes of Treasury bills ($10,000 to $500,000) may submit their orders on an average competitive price basis. The Treasury deducts these small orders from the total volume of bills to be sold. The remaining bills are allotted on the competitive basis described above. Then these small orders are executed at a discount equal to the average of the successful competitive bids for large orders.

Investors are not limited to purchasing Treasury bills on their original issue. Because Treasury bills are issued weekly, a wide range of maturities in the over-the-counter market is available. The Treasury bonds, notes, and bills section of *The Wall Street Journal* shows available maturities from one week to one year. The bid and ask quotations are shown in terms of annual yield equivalents. The prices of the various issues obtained from a dealer would reflect a discount based on these yields. Because of their short maturities and their absence of risk, Treasury bills provide the lowest yield available on taxable domestic obligations. Although some business corporations and individuals invest in Treasury bills, by far the most important holders of these obligations are commercial banks.

Treasury Notes

Treasury notes
federal obligations usually issued for maturities of one to ten years

Treasury notes are issued at specified interest rates usually for maturities ranging from one to ten years. These intermediate-term federal obligations are held largely by commercial banks.

Treasury Bonds

Treasury bonds
federal obligations issued
with original maturities in
excess of ten years, often
issued for twenty and
sometimes even thirty years

Treasury bonds typically have original maturities in excess of ten years and often are issued for twenty and sometimes even thirty years. These bonds bear interest at stated rates. Many issues of these bonds are callable, or paid off, by the government several years before their maturity. For example, a twenty-year bond issued in 2010 may be described as having a maturity of 2030–2035. This issue may be called for redemption at par as early as 2030 but no later than 2035. The longest maturity of Treasury bonds is thirty years. Dealers maintain active markets for the purchase and sale of Treasury bonds and the other marketable securities of the government.

All marketable obligations of the federal government, with the exception of Treasury bills, are offered to the public through the Federal Reserve Banks at prices and yields set in advance. Investors place their orders for new issues, and these orders are filled from the available supply of the new issue. If orders are larger than available supply, investors may be allotted only a part of the amount they requested.

Treasury bonds, because of at least initial long-term maturities, are subject to maturity or interest rate risk. Treasury notes with shorter maturities are affected to a lesser extent. For illustrative purposes, let's assume that the nominal interest rate on ten-year Treasury bonds is 5 percent. Let's further assume that investors expect the inflation rate will average 2 percent over the next ten years and they expect a real rate of return of 2 percent annually. By applying Equation 8.2, we can find the maturity risk premium to be the following:

$$5\% = RR + IP + DRP + MRP + LP$$
$$5\% = 2\% + 2\% + 0\% + MRP + 0\%$$
$$MRP = 5\% - 2\% - 2\% - 0\% - 0\% = 1\%$$

CONCEPT CHECK

How do Treasury bills, Treasury notes, and Treasury bonds differ?

Our interpretation is that the holders or investors require a 1 percent maturity risk premium (MRP) to compensate them for the possibility of volatility in the price of their Treasury bonds over the next ten years. If market-determined interest rates rise and investors are forced to sell before maturity, the bonds will be sold at a loss. Furthermore, even if these investors hold their bonds to maturity and redeem them with the government at the original purchase price, the investors would have lost the opportunity of the higher interest rates being paid in the marketplace. This is what is meant by interest rate risk. Of course, if market-determined interest rates decline after the bonds are purchased, bond prices will rise above the original purchase price.

DEALER SYSTEM

dealer system
composed of a closely linked
network of dealers and
brokers in government
securities with an effective
marketing network
throughout the United
States

The **dealer system** for marketable U.S. government securities occupies a central position in the nation's financial markets. The smooth operation of the money markets depends on a closely linked network of dealers and brokers. Bank and nonbank dealers report their daily activity in U.S. government securities to the Federal Reserve Bank of New York. New dealers are added when they can demonstrate a satisfactory responsibility and volume of activity. The dealers buy and sell securities for their own account, arrange transactions with their customers and other dealers, and purchase debt directly from the Treasury for resale to investors. Dealers do not typically charge commissions on their trades. Rather, they hope to sell securities at prices above the levels at which they were bought. The dealers' capacity to handle large Treasury financing has expanded enough in recent years to handle the substantial growth in the government securities market. In addition to the dealers' markets, new issues of federal government securities may be purchased directly at the Federal Reserve Banks.

TAX STATUS OF FEDERAL OBLIGATIONS

CONCEPT CHECK

What is the dealer system for marketable U.S. government securities?

Until March 1941, interest on all obligations of the federal government was exempt from all taxes. The interest on all federal obligations is subject to ordinary income taxes and tax rates. The Public Debt Act of 1941 terminated the issuance of tax-free federal obligations. Since that time, all issues previously sold to the public have matured or have been called for redemption. Income from the obligations of the federal government is exempt from all state and local taxes. Federal obligations, however, are subject to federal and state inheritance, estate, or gift taxes.

PERSONAL FINANCIAL PLANNING
Home Mortgages

Interest rates on home mortgages are affected by the influences discussed in this chapter. A typical thirty-year fixed-rate mortgage incorporates the factors that affect a thirty-year Treasury bond (real rate + inflation expectations + maturity risk premium + liquidity premium), along with other factors, such as default risk premium (since the typical homeowner is a higher risk than the U.S. government) and security premium (lowers the mortgage interest rate since the lender can take possession of the borrower's house and sell it to recoup the amount lent in case of a default). Homeowners can play the short end of the term structure, too. Adjustable-rate mortgages (ARMs) or variable-rate mortgages

rise and fall in line with a specified short-term interest rate, usually a Treasury security. The interest rate paid by the homeowner equals the short-term rate plus a premium, to reflect the homeowner's higher degree of default risk. The danger of buying a home with an ARM is an inflation scare or some other reason may cause a rapid rise in short-term rates, whereas the rate on a fixed-rate loan does not fluctuate. Since short-term rates usually are less than long-term rates, an ARM is an attractive financing possibility for those willing to take the risk of fluctuating short-term rates or those who expect to own their home for only three to five years before they move out of it.

OWNERSHIP OF PUBLIC DEBT SECURITIES

nonmarketable government securities *securities that cannot be transferred to other persons or institutions and can be redeemed only by being turned in to the U.S. government*

The U.S. national debt must be financed and refinanced through the issuance of nonmarketable and marketable government securities. **Nonmarketable government securities** are those securities that cannot be transferred to other persons or institutions and can be redeemed only by being turned in to the U.S. government. The sheer size of the national debt, over $14.8 trillion in September 2011, makes the financing process a difficult one. In fact, the United States must rely on the willingness of foreign and international investors to hold a substantial portion of the outstanding interest-bearing public debt securities issued to finance the national debt.

The ownership of public debt securities, by group or category, is shown in Table 8.1. Private investors, who owned approximately 48 percent of the total outstanding federal debt securities in 2006, increased their ownership to nearly 51 percent by 2008 and to 57 percent by 2011. The percentage of federal debt held by U.S. government accounts (agencies and trust funds) and Federal Reserve Banks dropped from about 52 percent in 2006, to 49 percent in 2008, and down to about 43 percent in 2011. During the time period depicted in Table 8.1, foreign and international investors increased their holdings of total public debt from about 25 percent in 2006, to 28 percent in 2008, and to about 32 percent in 2011. This shows the continuing importance of foreign and international investors in financing the U.S. national debt. All other categories of private investors held less than 6 percent (except for the miscellaneous investor category) of the total federal debt outstanding in 2011.

CONCEPT CHECK
What are nonmarketable government securities?

TABLE 8.1
Ownership of Public Debt of U.S. Treasury Securities (% of Total Debt)

	2006 (SEPT)	2008 (JUNE)	2011 (SEPT)
Federal Reserve and government accounts	52.1%	49.4%	42.8%
Private investors			
Foreign and international investors	25.1	27.9	31.6
State and local governments	5.5	5.5	3.2
U.S. savings bonds	2.4	2.1	1.2
Depository institutions	1.3	1.2	2.0
Insurance companies	1.9	4.7	1.7
Mutual funds	2.8	4.1	4.7
Pension funds	3.8	3.8	5.9
Other miscellaneous groups of investors*	5.1	1.3	6.9
Total private investors	**47.9%**	**50.6%**	**57.2%**
Total U.S. agencies and private investors	**100.0%**	**100.0%**	**100.0%**
Dollar Amount of Public Debt ($ Trillions)	$8.5	$9.5	$14.8

*Includes individuals, corporate and other businesses, dealers and brokers, government-sponsored agencies, bank personal trusts and estates, and other investors.

Source: Economic Report of the President (selected issues).

During the last half of the 1980s, the annual increase in foreign ownership was due primarily to the flow of Japanese capital to this country. Japanese investment in real estate and corporate securities has been publicized. However, as the dollar declined relative to the Japanese yen and other major foreign currencies, investment in U.S. assets became less attractive after interest and other returns were converted back into the foreign currencies. In recent years, interest on the part of Europeans and Chinese has increased. The large trade surpluses China has had with the United States have resulted in the Chinese holding increasing amounts of U.S. financial assets.

MATURITY DISTRIBUTION OF MARKETABLE DEBT SECURITIES

The various types of marketable obligations of the federal government have been described in this section. However, the terms of bills, notes, and bonds describe the general maturity ranges only at the time of issue. To determine the maturity distribution of all obligations, it is necessary to observe the remaining life of each issue regardless of its class. The maturity distribution and average length of marketable interest-bearing federal obligations are shown in Table 8.2. Notice that the average maturity decreased from four years and nine months in 2006 to three years and ten months in November 2008 before returning to four years and eleven months in 2011.

The heavy concentration of debt in the short maturity range (within one year) increased from about 32 percent in 2006 to about 48 percent of the total amount outstanding in late 2008 before dropping back to 32 percent in 2011. This heavy concentration in short-term maturities poses a special problem for the Treasury. This is a problem for the securities markets because the government is constantly selling additional securities to replace those that mature.

The heavy concentration of short-term maturities will not necessarily change by issuing a larger number of long-term obligations. Like all institutions that seek funds in the financial markets, the Treasury has to offer securities that will be accepted by the investing public. Furthermore, the magnitude of federal financing is such that radical changes in maturity distributions can upset the financial markets and the economy in general. The management of the federal debt has become an especially challenging financial problem, and much time and energy are spent in meeting the challenge.

If the Treasury refunds maturing issues with new short-term obligations, the average maturity of the total debt is reduced. As time passes, longer-term issues are brought into shorter-dated categories. Net cash borrowing, which results from budgetary deficits, must take the form of maturities that are at least as long as the average of the marketable debt if the average maturity is not to be reduced. The average length of the marketable debt reached a low level of two years and five months in late 1975. Since that time, progress has been made in raising the length of maturities (although the average maturity continues to be slightly under five years) by selling long-term obligations.

One of the new debt management techniques used to extend the average maturity of the marketable debt without disturbing the financial markets is *advance refunding*. This occurs when the Treasury offers the owners of a given issue the opportunity to exchange their holdings in advance of the holdings' regular maturity for new securities of longer maturity.

In summary, the Treasury is the largest and most active borrower in the financial markets. The Treasury is continuously in the process of borrowing and refinancing. Its financial actions are

CONCEPT CHECK

What is the average maturity of U.S. marketable debt securities?

TABLE 8.2

Average Length and Maturity Distribution of Marketable Interest-Bearing Federal Obligations (% of Total Marketable Debt)

MATURITY CLASS	2006	2008 (NOV)	2011 (DEC)
Within 1 year	32.1%	47.8%	32.2%
1–5 years	37.3	28.1	39.6
5–10 years	17.8	14.3	18.4
10–20 years	8.0	6.7	3.5
20 years and over	4.8	3.1	6.3
Total	100.0%	100.0%	100.0%
Average maturity of all marketable issues:	4 years, 9 months	3 years, 10 months	4 years, 11 months

Source: *Economic Report of the President* (selected issues).

tremendous in contrast with all other forms of financing, including those of the largest business corporations. Yet the financial system of the nation is adapted to accommodate its needs smoothly. Indeed, the existence of a public debt of this magnitude is predicated on the existence of a refined monetary and credit system.

TERM OR MATURITY STRUCTURE OF INTEREST RATES

term structure
indicates the relationship between interest rates or yields and the maturity of comparable quality debt instruments

yield curve
graphic presentation of the term structure of interest rates at a given point in time

INTERNET ACTIVITY

Go to the Web site of the Federal Reserve Bank of St. Louis, http://www.stlouisfed. org. Click on the Research & Data tab, followed by the FRED Economic Data tab. Find current interest rates for different maturities of U.S. Treasury securities, and construct the yield curve.

The **term structure** of interest rates indicates the relationship between interest rates or yields and the maturity of comparable quality debt instruments. This relationship is typically depicted through the graphic presentation of a **yield curve**. A properly constructed yield curve must first reflect securities of similar default risk. Second, the yield curve must represent a particular point in time, and the interest rates should reflect yields for the remaining time to maturity. That is, the yields should include stated interest rates and must consider that instruments and securities could be selling above or below their redemption values. (The process for calculating yields to maturity is shown in Chapter 9.) Third, the yield curve must show yields on a number of securities with differing lengths of time to maturity.

U.S. government securities provide the best basis for constructing yield curves because Treasury securities are considered to be risk free, as previously noted in terms of default risk. Table 8.3 contains interest rates for Treasury securities at selected dates and for various maturities. In early 1980, the annual inflation rate was in double digits. As a result, interest rates were high even though the economy was in a mild recession. Longer-term interest rates were higher in March 1982 even though the economy was in a deep recession. Apparently, investors were expecting the high levels of inflation to continue. However, by the latter part of the 1980s, interest rates had dropped because of reduced inflation. Interest rates on one-year Treasury bills were at 6 percent in March 1991, compared with 14 percent in March 1980. Interest rates declined further as the economy began expanding from a mild recession at the beginning of the 1990s.

By November 1998, after the Fed first pushed up short-term interest rates in an effort to head off possible renewed inflation and then lowered rates in an effort to avoid a recession during the mid-1990s, interest rates were relatively flat across different maturities. The Fed lowered its discount rate many times during the first years of the twenty-first century due to concern about an economic downturn and the terrorist attack in New York City on September 11, 2001. By November 2001, one-year Treasury interest rates had dropped to about 2 percent. Short-term interest rates continued to fall and were at about 1 percent in November 2003. However, in an effort to keep inflation under control, the Fed forced short-term interest rates higher so that one-year rates reached about 5 percent in October 2006.

The Fed moved quickly in 2008 to help avoid a collapse in the financial system by first using its traditional open-market operations to increase monetary liquidity by purchasing government securities. Then, the Fed engaged in a new non-traditional monetary policy action termed quantitative easing (which became known as QE1) in late 2008 in response to the 2007–2008 financial crisis and the 2008–2009 Great Recession. As Table 8.3 shows, the yield on one-year Treasury securities declined to 0.4 percent by October 2008. Because of a relatively slow economic recovery from the Great Recession, QE2 was implemented by the Fed in late 2010, and QE3 followed in late 2012. As a result of massive monetary easing efforts, the interest rates on Treasury securities

TABLE 8.3

Term Structure of Interest Rates for Treasury Securities at Selected Dates (%)

TERM TO MATURITY	MARCH 1980	MARCH 1982	NOVEMBER 2001	OCTOBER 2006	OCTOBER 2008	DECEMBER 2012
6 months	15.0%	12.8%	1.9%	4.9%	0.2%	0.11%
1 year	14.0	12.5	2.2	5.0	0.4	0.16
5 years	13.5	14.0	4.0	4.7	2.3	0.72
10 years	12.8	13.9	4.7	4.7	3.4	1.78
20 years	12.5	13.8	5.3	4.9	4.2	2.54
30 years	12.3	13.5	5.1	4.9	4.2	2.95

Source: *Selected Interest Rates*, Board of Governors of the Federal Reserve System, http://www.federalreserve.gov.

FIGURE 8.2

Yield Curves for Treasury Securities at Selected Dates

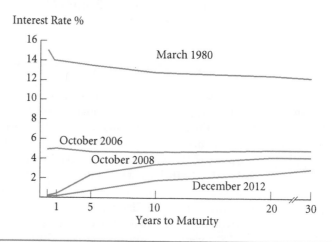

Source: *Selected Interest Rates*, Board of Governors of the Federal Reserve System, http://www.federalreserve.gov.

were forced to historic lows as shown in Table 8.3. The rate on one-year Treasury bills was only 0.16 percent and five-year Treasury securities were yielding only 0.72 percent at the end of December 2012.

Figure 8.2 shows yield curves for March 1980, October 2006, October 2008, and December 2012 reflecting the plotting of the corresponding data in Table 8.3. Because of high inflation rates and monetary policy wanting to constrain economic activity, the March 1980 yield curve was downward sloping and at high overall interest rate levels. Although not plotted, the yield curve for November 2001 was upward sloping and much lower overall due to lower expected inflation rates and efforts by monetary policy to stimulate economic activity.

By October 2006, the yield curve was nearly flat across all maturities with a variation only between about 4.7 percent and 5.0 percent. This flattening of the yield curve was attributable primarily to the Fed's effort to raise short-term interest rates as a way of combating the possibility of increases in inflation rates. As the financial crisis of 2007–2008 developed and was followed by the 2008–2009 Great Recession, short-term interest rates were forced to low levels as depicted for October 2008. The yield curve for December 2012 shows interest rates on Treasury securities at historically low levels due to the monetary easing policies of the Fed including its quantitative easing efforts.

CONCEPT CHECK

What is meant by term structure of interest rates?

What is the definition of a yield curve?

RELATIONSHIP BETWEEN YIELD CURVES AND THE ECONOMY

Historical evidence suggests that interest rates generally rise during periods of economic expansion and fall during economic contraction. Therefore, the term structure of interest rates as depicted by yield curves shifts upward or downward with changes in economic activity. Interest rate levels generally are the lowest at the bottom of a recession and the highest at the top of an expansion period. Furthermore, when the economy begins to recover from a recession, the yield curve typically slopes upward. The curve begins to flatten out during the latter stages of an expansion and typically starts sloping downward when economic activity peaks. As the economy turns downward, interest rates begin falling and the yield curve again goes through a flattening phase to become upward sloping when economic activity again reaches a low point.

TERM STRUCTURE THEORIES

expectations theory states that the shape of the yield curve reflects investor expectations about future inflation rates

Three theories are commonly used to explain the term structure of interest rates. The ***expectations theory*** contends that the shape of a yield curve reflects investor expectations about future inflation rates. If the yield curve is flat, expectations are that the current short-term inflation rate will remain essentially unchanged over time. When the yield curve is downward sloping, investors expect inflation rates to be lower in the future. Recall from Figure 8.2 that the shape of the yield curve in March 1980 was downward sloping. Thus, investors believed that the double-digit inflation rates prevailing in 1980 were expected to decline in the future. In contrast, the relatively flat yield curve in November 1998 suggested that investors expected the low inflation rates in late 1998 to remain at low levels in the future and that the economy would continue to grow at a moderate rate.

The upward-sloping yield curve in November 2001 occurred at the end of the 2001 recession. The yield curve continued to be upward sloping in November 2003 as economic activity continued to increase. A flattening of the yield curve by October 2006 caused some concern about the possibility of a slowdown in economic activity and preceded the 2007–2008 financial crisis and the 2008–2009 Great Recession. By October 2008, the yield curve, while at historically low interest rates for short maturities, was upward sloping, suggesting hope for future recovery. However, due to a slow economic recovery, further monetary easing activities resulted in the low yield curve depicted for the end of December 2012.

To differentiate yield curve shapes in terms of Equations 8.1 and 8.2, recall that the liquidity and the default risk premiums (DRPs) are zero for Treasury securities. Thus, Equation 8.2 for Treasury securities becomes Equation 8.1 plus a maturity risk premium (MRP). However, the expectations theory in its purest form assumes the MRP to be zero. Given this assumption, we have reduced Equation 8.2 to Equation 8.1 such that the yield curve reflects only the real rate (RR) of interest plus the expectation for an inflation premium (IP) over the life of the security.

Let's assume that the current rates of interest or yields are the following: one-year Treasury bills = 4 percent; two-year Treasury notes = 5 percent; and ten-year Treasury bonds = 5 percent. Using a 2 percent real rate of return, we have the following relationships:

Maturity	r	=	RR	+	IP
1-year	4%	=	2%	+	2%
2-year	5%	=	2%	+	3%
10-year	6%	=	2%	+	4%

Thus, the inflation rate is expected to be 2 percent over the next year. However, the inflation rate is expected to average 3 percent per year over the next two years; if inflation is 2 percent the first year, then the rate for the second year will have to be more than 3 percent. Working with simple averages, 3 percent average inflation times two years means that the total inflation will be 6 percent. Thus, 6 percent less 2 percent means that inflation in the second year must be 4 percent.

For years three through ten, inflation must exceed 4 percent annually to average 4 percent over the ten-year period. We can find the average by starting with inflation being at 40 percent (4 percent times 10 years) over the full ten-year period, and 40 percent less the 6 percent for the first two years means that cumulative inflation for the last eight years will be 34 percent. Then, dividing 34 percent by eight means that inflation will have to average 4.25 percent over years three through ten. In summary, we have the following:

TIME PERIOD	AVERAGE INFLATION		NUMBER OF YEARS		CUMULATIVE INFLATION
Year 1	2%	×	1	=	2%
Year 2	4%	×	1	=	4%
Years 3–10	4.25%	×	8	=	34%
Total inflation					**40%**
Total years					**10**
Average inflation (40% ÷ 10 years)					4%

These are arithmetic averages. Technically, we have ignored the impact of the compounding of inflation rates over time. The concept of compounding is presented in Chapter 9, which focuses on the time value of money.

The *liquidity preference theory* holds that investors or debt instrument holders prefer to invest short term so they have greater liquidity and less maturity or interest rate risk. Lenders prefer to lend for the short term because of the risk of higher inflation rates and greater uncertainty about default risk in the future. Borrowers prefer to borrow for the long term so they have more time to repay loans. The net result is a willingness to accept lower interest rates on short-term loans as a trade-off for greater liquidity and lower interest rate risk.

liquidity preference theory holds that investors or debt instrument holders prefer to invest short term so they have greater liquidity and less maturity or interest rate risk

CONCEPT CHECK

What is the expectations theory in terms of the term structure of interest rates?

What is the liquidity preference theory?

What is the market segmentation theory?

market segmentation theory
holds that securities of different maturities are not perfect substitutes for one another

The ***market segmentation theory*** holds that securities of different maturities are not perfect substitutes for one another. For example, commercial banks concentrate their activities on short-term securities because of their demand and other deposit liabilities. On the other hand, the nature of insurance company and pension fund liabilities allows these firms to concentrate holdings in long-term securities. Thus, supply and demand factors in each market segment affect the shape of the yield curve. In some time periods, interest rates on intermediate-term Treasury securities may be higher (or lower) than those for short-term and long-term treasuries.

INFLATION PREMIUMS AND PRICE MOVEMENTS

inflation
an increase in the price of goods or services that is not offset by an increase in quality

Actions or factors that change the value of the money unit or the supply of money and credit affect the whole economy. The change affects first the supply of loanable funds and interest rates and, later, the demand for and the supply of goods in general. ***Inflation***, as previously defined, is an increase in the price of goods or services that is not offset by an increase in quality. Recall than when investors expect higher inflation rates, they will require higher nominal interest rates so a real rate of return will remain after the inflation. A clearer understanding of investor expectations about inflation premiums can be had by reviewing past price movements followed by exploring possible types of inflation.

HISTORICAL INTERNATIONAL PRICE MOVEMENTS

GLOBAL DISCUSSION

Changes in the money supply or in the amount of metal in the money unit have influenced prices since the earliest records of civilization. The money standard in ancient Babylon was in terms of silver and barley. The earliest available price records show that one shekel of silver was equal to 240 measures of grain. At the time of Hammurabi (about 1750 B.C.), a shekel in silver was worth between 150 and 180 measures of grain, while in the following century it declined to 90 measures. After Persia conquered Babylonia in 539 B.C., the value of the silver shekel was recorded as between 15 and 40 measures of grain.

Alexander the Great probably caused the greatest inflationary period in ancient history when he captured the large gold hoards of Persia and took them to Greece. Inflation was high for some years, but twenty years after Alexander's death, a period of deflation began and lasted over fifty years.

The first recorded cases of deliberate currency debasement (lowering the value) occurred in the Greek city-states. The government would debase currency by calling in all coins and issuing new ones containing less of the precious metals. This must have been a convenient form of inflation, for there are many such cases in the records of Greek city-states.

Ancient Rome

During the Punic Wars, devaluation led to inflation as the heavy bronze coin was reduced in stages from one pound to one ounce. Similar inflation occurred in Roman history. Augustus brought so much precious metal from Egypt that prices rose and interest rates fell. From the time of Nero, debasements were frequent. The weight of gold coins was reduced, and silver coins had baser metals added to them so they were finally only 2 percent silver. Few attempts were made to arrest or reverse this process of debasement of coins as the populace adjusted to the process. When Aurelian tried to improve the coinage by adding to its precious metal content, he was resisted so strongly that armed rebellion broke out.

The Middle Ages Through Modern Times

During the Middle Ages, princes and kings debased the coinage to get more revenue. The rulers of France used this ploy more than others, and records show that profit from debasement was sometimes greater than the total of all other revenues.

An important example of inflation followed the arrival of Europeans in America. Gold and silver poured into Spain from Mexico and Peru. Since the riches were used to buy goods from other countries, they were distributed over the continent and to England. Prices rose in Spain and in most of Europe but not in proportion to the increase in gold and silver stocks because trade increased and many people hoarded the precious metals.

Paper money was little used until the end of the seventeenth century. The first outstanding example of inflation due to the issuing of an excessive amount of paper money was in France.

CONCEPT CHECK

What do we mean by the term inflation?

What was the first example of rapid inflation after paper money began being used?

In 1719, the government gave Scottish banker, John Law, a charter for a bank that could issue paper money. The note circulation of his bank amounted to almost 2,700 million livres (the monetary unit in use at that time in France), against which he had coin of only 21 million livres and bullion of 27 million livres. Prices went up rapidly but fell as quickly when Law's bank failed. Afterward, the money supply was again restricted.

The next outstanding period of inflation was during the American Revolutionary War (1775–1783) and French (1789–1799) Revolution. For example, France's revolutionary government issued paper currency in huge quantities. This currency, called assignats, declined to 0.5 percent of its face value.

Spectacular inflation also took place in Germany in 1923, when prices soared to astronomical heights. During World War II, runaway inflation took place in China and Hungary, as well as in other countries.

INFLATION IN THE UNITED STATES

Monetary factors have often affected price levels in the United States, especially during major wars.

Revolutionary War

The war that brought the United States into being was financed mainly by inflation. The Second Continental Congress had no real authority to levy taxes and found it difficult to raise money. As a result, the congress decided to issue notes for $2 million. It issued more notes until the total rose to over $240 million. The individual states issued $200 million more. Since the notes were crudely engraved, counterfeiting was common, adding to the total of circulating currency. Continental currency depreciated in value so rapidly that the expression "not worth a continental" became a part of the American language.

War of 1812

During the War of 1812, the government tried to avoid repeating the inflationary measures of the Revolutionary War. However, since the war was unpopular in New England, it was impossible to finance it by taxation and borrowing. Paper currency was issued in a somewhat disguised form: bonds of small denomination bearing no interest and having no maturity date. The wholesale price index, based on 100 as the 1910–1914 average prices, rose from 131 in 1812 to 182 in 1814. Prices declined to about the prewar level by 1816 and continued downward as depression hit the economy.

Civil War

The Mexican War (1846–1848) did not involve the total economy to any extent and led to no inflationary price movements. The Civil War (1861–1865), however, was financed partly by issuing paper money. In the war's early stages, the U.S. Congress could not raise enough money by levying taxes and borrowing to finance all expenditures; therefore, it resorted to inflation by issuing U.S. Notes with no backing, known as greenbacks. In all, $450 million was authorized. Even though this was but a fraction of the cost of the war, prices went up substantially. Wholesale prices on a base of 100 increased from 93 in 1860 to 185 in 1865. Attempts to retire the greenbacks at the end of the war led to deflation and depression in 1866. As a result, the law withdrawing greenbacks was repealed.

World War I

Although the U.S. government did not print money to finance World War I, it did practice other inflationary policies. About one-third of the cost of the war was raised by taxes and two-thirds of the cost by borrowing. The banking system provided much of this credit, which added to the money supply. People were even persuaded to use Liberty Bonds as collateral for bank loans to buy other bonds. The wholesale price index rose from 99 in 1914 to 226 in 1920. Then, as credit expansion was restricted in 1921, it dropped to 141 in 1922.

World War II and the Postwar Period

The government used fewer inflationary policies to finance World War II. Nevertheless, the banking system took up large sums of bonds. By the end of the war, the debt of the federal government had increased by $207 billion. Bank holdings of government bonds had increased by almost $60 billion. Prices went up by about one-third during the war because they were held in check after the first year by price and wage controls. Then, they rose rapidly when the controls were lifted after the war. In 1948, wholesale prices had risen to 236 from a level of 110 in 1939.

Wholesale prices increased during the Korean War and again during the 1955–1957 expansion in economic activity as the economy recovered from the 1954 recession. Consumer goods prices continued to move upward during most of the entire postwar period, increasing in those years in which wholesale prices hardly changed.

Recent Decades

INTERNET ACTIVITY

Go to the Web site of the Council of Economic Advisors, http://www.whitehouse.gov/ cea/pubs.html. Click on the Economic Report tab and click on the 2013 Economic Report of the President. Next, click on the "download as pdf" under Appendix B. Find current inflation rates based on the consumer price index for all items and when food and energy prices are excluded.

Figure 8.3 shows the consumer price index (CPI) for all items, and a related consumer price measure when food and energy are excluded, since the end of the 1970s. Although not depicted, wholesale consumer goods prices increased substantially when the Vietnam War escalated after mid-1965. Prices continued upward after American participation in the Vietnam War was reduced in the early 1970s. After American participation in the war ended in 1974, prices rose at the most rapid levels since World War I. Inflation was worldwide in the mid-1970s; its effects were much worse in many other industrial countries than in the United States.

As the 1970s ended, economists realized the full impact of a philosophy based on a high inflation rate. Many economists thought high inflation could keep unemployment down permanently even though history has shown that it does not. The government's efforts to control interest rates by increasing the money supply created doubts that such policies would reduce inflation and high interest rates. By October 1979, the Fed abandoned this failed approach to interest rate control and adopted a policy of monetary growth control. The result was twofold. First, there was a far greater volatility in interest rates as the Fed concentrated on monetary factors. Second, during the first three quarters of 1980, some monetary restraint was exercised. This monetary restraint depressed production and employment. The Fed backed off from this position of restraint, and by the end of 1980, a far greater level of monetary stimulus had driven interest rates to new peaks.

By this time, the prime rate had risen to 21.5 percent and three-month Treasury bills had doubled in yield from their midyear lows. These high interest rates had a profound negative effect on such interest-sensitive industries as housing and automobiles. The Fed reversed the rapid growth of money supply throughout 1981 until late in 1982. Unemployment climbed as the effects of monetary restraint were imposed on the economy, but the back of inflation was broken. By the end of 1982, economic recovery was in place, along with an easing of monetary restraint.

Figure 8.3 shows that inflation stayed at moderate levels beginning in 1983 and continuing through most of the remainder of the 1980s until the end of the decade. After peaking in 1990 above a 6 percent annual rate, the CPI stayed at about 3 percent until 1997, when the inflation

FIGURE 8.3
Consumer Price Index

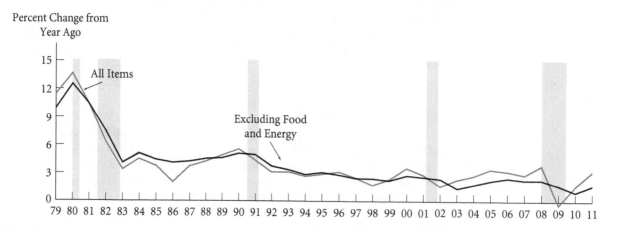

Source: *Economic Report of the President* (selected issues).

CONCEPT CHECK

What happened to inflation in the United States during the 1980s and the 1990s?

What happened to inflation in the United States during the first part of the twenty-first century?

rate dropped further. In early 1994, the Fed moved toward a tighter monetary policy in an effort to keep inflation from rising. As the country finished the 1990s and moved into the early twenty-first century, inflation rates remained at relatively low levels. For 2008, the CPI for all items was 3.8 percent, reflecting a record high price of oil. The alternative CPI measure, adjusted to exclude food and energy, was 2.3 percent for 2008. Since then, the CPI has declined, and inflation has remained at historically low levels throughout the 2009-2011 period.

TYPES OF INFLATION

Inflation may be associated with a change in costs, a change in the money supply, speculation, and so-called administrative pressures.

Price Changes Initiated by a Change in Costs

The price level can sometimes increase without the original impulse coming from the money supply or its velocity. If costs rise faster than productivity increases, as when wages go up, businesses with some control over prices will try to raise them to cover the higher costs. Such increases are likely to be effective when the demand for goods is strong compared to the supply. The need for more funds to meet production and distribution at higher prices usually causes the money supply and velocity to increase. This type of inflation is called *cost-push inflation,* as this rise in prices comes from the cost side, not from increases in the money supply. Prices may not go up, however, if the monetary authorities restrict credit expansion. In that case, only the most efficient businesses will have enough demand to operate profitably. As a result, some resources will be unemployed.

Cost-push inflation is different from inflation caused by an increase in the money supply, which is called *demand-pull inflation* and may be defined as an excessive demand for goods and services during periods of economic expansion as a result of large increases in the money supply. In practice, both aspects of inflation may occur at the same time since cost-push inflation can occur only in industries in which labor negotiations are carried out industry-wide and in which management has the ability to increase prices.

Demand-pull inflation may also be caused by changes in demand in particular industries. The demand for petroleum, for example, may be greater than demand in general, so prices rise in this industry before they rise generally. The first rise is likely to be in the basic materials themselves, leading to increased profits in the industries that produce them. Labor will press for wage increases to get its share of the total value of output, and thus labor costs rise. Price rises in basic industries lead to price increases in the industries that use their products. Wage increases in one major industry are also likely to lead to demands for similar increases in other industries and among the nonorganized workers in such industries. The process set into motion can lead to general changes in prices, provided the monetary authorities do not restrict credit so as to prevent it.

Price Changes Initiated by a Change in the Money Supply

The way in which factors that affect prices relate to one another is complex. The following discussion considers the adjustments that take place when the primary change is in the money supply or its velocity. Of course, more complex relationships arising out of changes in the money supply and the goods side of the equation during business cycles could take place.

An increase in the supply or velocity of money can cause several types of inflation. Inflation may result when the supply of purchasing power increases. Government deficits financed by creating deposits or private demands for funds may initiate this type of inflation. If this happens when people and resources are not fully employed, the volume of trade will go up and prices will be only slightly affected at first. As unused resources are brought into use, however, prices will rise. When resources such as metals become scarce, their prices will rise. As any resource is used up, the expectation of future price rises will force prices up because attempts to buy before such price rises will increase demand above current needs. Since some costs will lag, such as interest costs and wages set by contract, will lag, profits will rise, increasing the demand for capital goods.

Once resources are fully employed, the full effect of the increased money supply will be felt on prices. Prices may rise out of proportion for a time as expectations of higher prices lead to faster spending and so raise the velocity of money. The expansion will continue until trade and prices

cost-push inflation
occurs when prices are raised to cover rising production costs, such as wages

demand-pull inflation
an excessive demand for goods and services during periods of economic expansion relative to supply

are in balance at the new levels of the money supply. Velocity will probably drop somewhat from those levels during the period of rising prices since the desire to buy goods before the price goes up has disappeared.

Even if the supply of money is increased when people and resources are fully employed, prices may not go up proportionately. Higher prices increase profits for a time and so lead to a demand for more capital and labor. Thus, previously unemployed spouses, retired workers, and similar groups enter the labor force. Businesses may use capital more fully by having two or three shifts use the same machines.

Demand-pull inflation traditionally exists during periods of economic expansion when the demand for goods and services exceeds the available supply of such goods and services. A second version of inflation associated with increases in the money supply occurs because of monetization of the U.S. government debt. Recall from Chapter 5 that the Treasury finances government deficits by selling U.S. government securities to the public, commercial banks, or the Fed. When the Fed purchases U.S. government securities, reserves must be created to pay for the purchases. This, in turn, may lead to higher inflation because of an increase in money supply and bank reserves.

Speculation and Administrative Inflation

speculative inflation
caused by the expectation
that prices will continue to
rise, resulting in increased
buying to avoid even higher
future prices

When an increased money supply causes inflation, it can lead to the additional price pressure called ***speculative inflation***. Since prices have risen for some time, people believe that they will keep on rising. Inflation becomes self-generating for a time because, instead of higher prices resulting in lower demand, people may buy more to get goods before their prices go still higher as happened in the late 1970s. This effect may be confined to certain areas as it was to land prices in the 1920s Florida land boom or to security prices in the 1928–1929 stock market boom. Such a price rise leads to an increase in velocity as speculators want to turn over their funds as rapidly as possible and many others want to buy ahead of needs before there are further price rises.

For three decades, until the early 1980s, price pressures and inflation were continual despite occasional policies of strict credit restraint. During this long period, prices continued upward in recession periods though at a slower rate than in prosperity periods. The need to restrain price rises hampered the Fed's ability to promote growth and fight recessions. Prices and other economic developments during this period led many to feel that the economy had developed a long-run *inflationary bias*. However, the continued low inflation rates in the late 1980s and the 1990s may have curtailed these beliefs for a while.

administrative inflation
the tendency of prices, aided
by union-corporation
contracts, to rise during
economic expansion and to
resist declines during
recessions

Those economists who believe that long-run inflationary bias will continue do so based on two factors. First, prices and wages tend to rise during periods of boom in a competitive economy. This tendency is reinforced by wage contracts that provide escalator clauses to keep wages in line with prices and by wage increases that are sometimes greater than increases in productivity. Second, during recessions, prices tend to remain stable rather than decrease because major unions have long-run contracts calling for annual wage increases no matter what economic conditions are at the time. The tendency of large corporations to rely on nonprice competition (advertising, and style and color changes) and to reduce output rather than cut prices keeps prices stable. Furthermore, if prices do decline drastically, the government will likely step in with programs to help take excess supplies off the market. Prices would probably decline in a severe and prolonged depression, and the government would take action to counter resulting unemployment, however, before the economy reached such a level. Thus, we no longer experience the downward price pressure of a depression.

The inflation resulting from these factors is called ***administrative inflation***. This is to distinguish it from the type of inflation that happens when demand exceeds the available supply of goods because demand is increasing faster than supply in the early stages of a recovery period or because demand from monetary expansion by the banking system or the government exceeds available supply.

CONCEPT CHECK

What is the difference between cost-push inflation and demand-pull inflation?

What is meant by the terms speculative inflation *and* administrative inflation?

Traditional monetary policy is not wholly effective against administrative inflation. If money supplies are restricted enough, prices can be kept in line; this will lead to long-term unemployment and slow growth. New firms and small growing firms will have trouble getting credit since lending policies are likely to be conservative. The government must develop new tools to deal with administrative inflation effectively.

FINANCE PRINCIPLE

default risk
risk that a borrower will not
pay interest and/or repay the
principal on a loan or other
debt instrument according to
the agreed contractual terms

DEFAULT RISK PREMIUMS

Investors are said to be "risk averse"; that is, they expect to be compensated with higher returns for taking on more risk in the form of greater uncertainty about return variability or outcome. This is the pillar of finance, known as the risk/return principle, or "higher returns are expected for taking on more risk" principle. *Default risk* is the risk that a borrower will not pay interest and/or repay the principal on a loan or other debt instrument according to the agreed contractual terms. The consequence may be a lower-than-expected interest rate or yield or even a complete loss of the amount originally lent. The premium for default risk will increase as the probability of default increases.

To examine default risk premiums for debt securities, it is necessary to hold some of the other risk premiums constant. By referring to Equation 8.2, we can develop a procedure for measuring that portion of a nominal interest rate (r) attributable to default risk. Recall that the nominal interest rate is a function of a real interest rate, an inflation premium, a default risk premium, a maturity risk premium, and a liquidity risk premium.

First, we constrain our analysis to the long-term capital markets by considering only long-term Treasury bonds and long-term corporate bonds. By focusing on long-term securities, the maturity risk will be the same for all the bonds and can be set at zero for analysis purposes. We have also said the liquidity premium is zero for Treasury securities because the securities can be sold without requiring a substantial price discount. Corporate securities are less liquid than Treasury securities. However, we can minimize any possible liquidity premiums by considering the bonds of large corporations. This allows us to set the liquidity premium at zero for analysis purposes.

For the following example, assume the real rate is 2 percent, inflation averages 3 percent, the nominal interest rate is 5 percent for long-term Treasury bonds, and high-quality corporate bonds have a 6 percent nominal interest rate. Using Equation 8.2, we have the following results:

$$r = \text{RR} + \text{IP} + \text{DRP} + \text{MRP} + \text{LP}$$
$$6\% = 2\% + 3\% + \text{DRP} + 0\% + 0\%$$
$$\text{DRP} = 6\% - 2\% - 3\% - 0\% - 0\% = 1\%$$

Since the 5 percent Treasury bond represents the risk-free rate of interest, subtracting the 2 percent real rate results in a long-term average annual inflation premium of 3 percent. Another way of looking at the default risk premium (DRP), assuming zero maturity risk and liquidity premiums, is that it is the difference between the interest rates on the risky (corporate) and risk-free (Treasury) securities. In our example, we have the following:

$$\text{DRP} = 6\% - 5\% = 1\%$$

Thus, investors require a 1 percent premium to hold or invest in the corporate bond instead of the Treasury bond.

Another corporate bond with a higher default risk may carry an interest rate of 8 percent. If the other assumptions used above are retained, the DRP would be the following:

$$8\% = 2\% + 3\% + \text{DRP} + 0\% + 0\%$$
$$\text{DRP} = 8\% - 2\% - 3\% - 0\% - 0\% = 3\%$$

Alternatively, we could find DRP as follows:

$$\text{DRP} = 8\% - 5\% = 3\%$$

So, to get investors to invest in these riskier corporate bonds, a default risk premium of 3 percentage points must be offered above the interest rate or yield on Treasury bonds.

The examination of actual DRPs in Table 8.4 shows long-term interest rates for Treasury bonds and two corporate bonds with different degrees of default risk. The characteristics of corporate bonds will be discussed in Chapter 10, but here, one way potential default risk is measured is through bond ratings. The highest rating, Aaa, indicates the lowest likelihood of default. Investors in these bonds require a small default risk premium over Treasury bonds. Baa-rated

investment grade bonds
ratings of Baa or higher that
meet financial institution
investment standards

INTERNET ACTIVITY

*Go to the Web site of the
Federal Reserve Bank of
St. Louis, http://www.
stlouisfed.org. Click on the
Research & Data tab, followed
by the FRED Economic Data
tab. Find current interest rates
for long-term Treasury bonds,
as well as Aaa and Baa
corporate bonds, and indicate
the size of default risk
premiums.*

ETHICAL ISSUES

**high-yield bonds (junk
bonds)**
with ratings lower than Baa,
bonds that have a substantial
probability of default

CONCEPT CHECK

What is default risk?

*What is a default risk
premium and how is it
calculated?*

bonds have higher default risks but are considered to be of reasonably high quality. **Investment grade bonds** have ratings of Baa or higher and meet financial institution (banks, pension funds, insurance companies, etc.) investment standards.

In March 1980, the DRP on corporate Aaa bonds over twenty-year Treasuries was 0.5 percentage point (i.e., 13.0% − 12.5%). The DRP of the highest-quality corporate bonds over Treasury bonds generally falls in the range of 0.5 to 0.75 percentage point. In fact, the DRP was about 0.8 percentage point in March 1982 when the economy was in a deep recession. The DRP on Aaa-rated corporate bonds had increased to unusually high 1.7 percentage points in November 2001, reflecting an economic downturn and concerns about terrorism in the United States. The October 2006 risk premium for Aaa-rated bonds remained low at a 0.6 percentage point differential over twenty-year Treasury bonds. By October 2008, when the U.S. was in the midst of the 2007–2008 financial crisis and the 2008–2009 recession, the risk premium for Aaa-rated bonds had increased to 1.0 percentage point. As of December 2012, the Aaa-rated corporate bond risk premium was about 1.1 percent.

The DRPs on Baa corporate bonds are generally better indicators of investor pessimism or optimism about economic expectations than are those on Aaa-rated bonds. More firms fail or suffer financial distress during periods of recession than during periods of economic expansion. Thus, investors tend to require higher premiums to compensate for default risk when the economy is in a recession or is expected to enter one. In Table 8.4, the risk premium on Baa-rated bonds was 2 percentage points in March 1980 (14.5% − 12.5%), and it increased to 3 percentage points in March 1982 when a deep recession existed. The DRP on Baa-rated bonds was 2.5 percentage points in November 2001 and reflected concerns about the slowing of economic activity in the United States and continued uncertainty after the terrorist attack on September 11, 2001. As of October 2006, the risk premium on Baa-rated corporate debt was 1.5 percentage points over the interest rate on twenty-year Treasury bonds. The Baa-rated bond risk premium increased to 2.1 percentage points by October 2008 due to the financial difficulties in the United States. While interest rates on Treasury bonds and corporate Baa-rated bonds dropped sharply by December 2012, the risk premium remained at about the 2.1 percent level.

Sometimes corporations issue bonds with ratings lower than Baa. These are called **high-yield bonds (junk bonds)** because they have a substantial probability of default. While many institutional investors are restricted to investing in only investment-grade (Baa-rated or higher) corporate debt, others are permitted to invest in high-yield, high-risk corporate debt. Recall the discussion in Chapter 3 about the savings and loan associations (S&Ls) crisis that was caused in part by corporate defaults on high-yield or junk bonds that they held. Michael Milken, who was at Drexel, Burnham, Lambert at the time, was instrumental in getting those S&Ls and other institutions allowed to purchase junk bonds to do so. Some individuals would argue that the purchasers of junk bonds were sophisticated enough to make rational risk/return decisions; *caveat emptor*—let the buyer beware. Other individuals charged that unethical and illegal behavior on the part of the marketers of junk bonds contributed to the failure of many of the issuers of the bonds as well as the purchasers (particularly S&Ls) of the bonds. In 1989, Milken was sent to prison, and Drexel Burnham Lambert went bankrupt.

TABLE 8.4

Default Risk Premiums on Corporate Bonds at Selected Dates (%)

	MARCH 1980	MARCH 1982	NOV. 2001	OCT. 2006	OCT. 2008	DEC. 2012
Aaa-rated corporate bonds	13.0	14.6	7.0	5.5	5.2	3.67
Less: 20-year Treasury bonds	12.5	13.8	5.3	4.9	4.2	2.54
Equals: default risk premium on Aaa bonds	.5	.8	1.7	.6	1.0	1.13
Baa-rated corporate bonds	14.5	16.8	7.8	6.4	6.3	4.63
Less: 20-year Treasury bonds	12.5	13.8	5.3	4.9	4.2	2.54
Equals: default risk premium on Baa bonds	2.0	3.0	2.5	1.5	2.1	2.09

Source: *Selected Interest Rates*, Board of Governors of the Federal Reserve System, http://www.federalreserve.gov.

APPLYING FINANCE TO...

INSTITUTIONS AND MARKETS

Depository institutions make profits by achieving a spread between the interest rates they pay individuals on savings accounts and the interest rates they charge businesses and other individuals for loans. Interest rates are important to financial institutions, such as insurance companies and pension funds, that accumulate premiums and contributions and invest these proceeds in government and corporate securities for the benefit of their policy-holders and employees. The government depends on financial institutions holding or owning an important portion of the U.S. Treasury securities issued to finance the national debt.

INVESTMENTS

Interest rates are set in the financial markets based on the supply and demand for loanable funds. The cost or price of home mortgage loans depends on the supply and demand for such loans in the mortgage markets. Interest rates offered on Treasury debt securities reflect a real rate of interest and an expected inflation premium. Corporate bond borrowers must pay a default risk premium (DRP) above the interest rate being offered on government debt securities. Corporate issuers of high-quality investment-grade bonds pay lower DRPs relative to issuers of lower-quality bonds. Observed interest rates may reflect a maturity risk premium (MRP) and/or a liquidity premium(LP).

FINANCIAL MANAGEMENT

The prevailing level of interest rates is important to financial managers. When interest rates are high, businesses will find it less profitable to borrow from financial institutions or in the securities markets because investment in inventories, plant, and equipment will look less attractive. Likewise, when interest rates are relatively low, loans are generally available and stock prices are usually high. Thus, financial managers often find it attractive to grow their businesses during periods when funds to finance the expansion activities can be borrowed at low interest rates or when they can issue new shares of their common stocks at high prices.

SUMMARY

This chapter began by illustrating how interest rates change given shifts in demand and/or supply curves. The loanable funds theory for explaining interest rates was presented. The following determinants of market interest rates were discussed: real rate of interest, inflation premium, default risk premium (DRP), maturity risk premium (MRP), and liquidity premium (LP).

Three types of U.S. Treasury securities (bills, notes, and bonds) were identified and described. The term structure of interest rates was defined and depicted with a yield curve graph. Next, the three theories used to explain the term structure, expectations, liquidity preference, and market segmentation. Major price movements were identified. We described the types of inflation: cost-push, demand-pull, speculative, and administrative. The final topic focused on how default risk premiums are estimated and what causes them to change over time.

KEY TERMS

administrative inflation

cost-push inflation

dealer system

default risk

default risk premium (DRP)

demand-pull inflation

expectations theory

high-yield bonds (junk bonds)

inflation

inflation premium

interest rate

interest rate risk

investment grade bonds

liquidity preference theory

liquidity premium (LP)

loanable funds theory

market segmentation theory

marketable government securities

maturity risk premium (MRP)

nominal interest rate

nonmarketable government obligations

real rate of interest

risk-free rate of interest

speculative inflation

term structure

Treasury bills

Treasury bonds

Treasury notes

yield curve

DISCUSSION QUESTIONS

1. What is the interest rate, and how is it determined?

2. Describe how interest rates may adjust to an unanticipated increase in inflation.

3. Identify major periods of rising interest rates in U.S. history, and describe some of the underlying reasons for these interest rate movements.

4. How did the Federal Reserve System (Fed) contribute to the recent historically low interest rates?

5. How does the loanable funds theory explain the level of interest rates?

6. What are the main sources of loanable funds? Indicate and briefly discuss the factors that affect the supply of loanable funds.

7. Indicate the sources of demand for loanable funds, and discuss the factors that affect the demand for loanable funds.

8. What are the factors, in addition to supply and demand relationships, that determine market interest rates?

9. What are the types of marketable obligations issued by the Treasury?

10. Explain the mechanics of issuing Treasury bills, indicating how the price of a new issue is determined.

11. Describe the dealer system for marketable U.S. government obligations.

12. What is the tax status of income from federal obligations?

13. Describe any significant changes in the ownership pattern of federal debt securities in recent years.

14. What have been the recent developments in the maturity distribution of marketable interest-bearing federal debt?

15. Describe the process of advance refunding of the federal debt.

16. What is the term structure of interest rates, and how is it expressed?

17. Identify and describe the three basic theories used to explain the term structure of interest rates.

18. Describe the process by which inflation took place before modern times.

19. Discuss the early periods of inflation based on the issue of paper money.

20. What was the basis for inflation during World Wars I and II?

21. Discuss the causes of the major periods of inflation in American history.

22. Explain the process by which price changes may be initiated by a general change in costs.

23. How can a change in the money supply lead to a change in the price level?

24. What is meant by the speculative type of inflation?

25. What is meant by a default risk premium (DRP)?

26. How can a DRP change over time?

EXERCISES

1. Go to the Federal Reserve Bank of St. Louis website at http://www.stlouisfed.org. Click on the Research and Data tab, followed by the FRED Economic Data tab, and find interest rates on U.S. Treasury securities and on corporate bonds with different bond ratings.

   a. Prepare a yield curve or term structure of interest rates.

   b. Identify existing default risk premiums between long-term Treasury bonds and corporate bonds.

2. As an economist for a major bank, you are asked to explain a substantial increase in the price level when neither the money supply nor the velocity of money has increased. How can this occur?

3. As an advisor to the U.S. Treasury, you have been asked to comment on a proposal for easing the burden of interest on the national debt. This proposal calls for the elimination of federal taxes on interest received from Treasury debt obligations. Comment on the proposal.

4. As one of several advisors to the secretary of the U.S. Treasury, you have been asked to submit a memo in connection with the average maturity of the obligations of the federal government. The basic premise is that the average maturity is far too short. As a result, issues of debt are coming due with great frequency and need constant reissue. On the other hand, the economy shows signs of weakness. It is considered unwise to issue long-term obligations and absorb investment funds that might otherwise be invested in employment-producing construction and other private-sector support. Based on these conditions, what course of action do you recommend to the secretary of the U.S. Treasury?

5. Assume a condition in which the economy is strong, with relatively high employment. For one reason or another, the money supply is increasing at a high rate, with little evidence of money creation slowing down. Assuming the money supply continues to increase, describe the evolving effect on price levels.

6. Assume you are employed as an investment advisor. You are working with a retired individual who depends on her income from her investments to meet her day-to-day expenditures. She would like to find a way of increasing the current income from her investments. A new high-yield bond (junk bond) issue has come to your attention. If you sell these high-yield bonds to a client, you will earn a higher-than-average fee. You wonder whether this would be a win-win investment for your retired client, who is seeking higher current income, and for you, who would benefit in terms of increased fees. What would you do?

PROBLEMS

1. Assume investors expect a 2.0 percent real rate of return over the next year. If inflation is expected to be 0.5 percent, what is the expected nominal interest rate for a one-year U.S. Treasury security?

2. A one-year U.S. Treasury security has a nominal interest rate of 2.25 percent. If the expected real rate of interest is 1.5 percent, what is the expected annual inflation rate?

3. A ten-year U.S. Treasury bond has a 3.5 percent interest rate, while an identical maturity corporate bond has a 5.25 percent interest rate. Real interest rates and inflation rate expectations would be the same for the two bonds. If a default risk premium of 1.50 percentage points is estimated for the corporate bond, determine the liquidity premium for the corporate bond.

4. A thirty-year U.S. Treasury bond has a 4.0 percent interest rate. In contrast, a ten-year Treasury bond has an interest rate of 3.7 percent. If inflation is expected to average 1.5 percentage points over the next ten years and thirty years, determine the maturity risk premium (MRP) for the thirty-year bond over the ten-year bond.

5. A thirty-year U.S. Treasury bond has a 4.0 percent interest rate. In contrast, a ten-year Treasury bond has an interest rate of 2.5 percent. A maturity risk premium (MRP) is estimated to be 0.2 percentage points for the longer maturity bond. Investors expect inflation to average 1.5 percentage points over the next ten years.

   a. Estimate the expected real rate of return on the ten-year U.S. Treasury bond.

b. If the real rate of return is expected to be the same for the thirty-year bond as for the ten-year bond, estimate the average annual inflation rate expected by investors over the life of the thirty-year bond.

6. You are considering an investment in a one-year government debt security with a yield of 5 percent or a highly liquid corporate debt security with a yield of 6.5 percent. The expected inflation rate for the next year is expected to be 2.5 percent.

   a. What would be your real rate earned on either of the two investments?

   b. What would be the default risk premium (DRP) on the corporate debt security?

7. Inflation is expected to be 3 percent over the next year. You desire an annual real rate of return of 2.5 percent on your investments.

   a. What nominal rate of interest would have to be offered on a one-year Treasury security for you to consider making an investment?

   b. A one-year corporate debt security is being offered at 2 percentage points over the one-year Treasury security rate that meets your requirement in (a). What would be the nominal interest rate on the corporate security?

8. Find the nominal interest rate for a debt security given the following information: real rate = 2 percent, liquidity premium = 2 percent, default risk premium = 4 percent, maturity risk premium = 3 percent, and inflation premium = 3 percent.

9. Find the default risk premium for a debt security given the following information: inflation premium = 3 percent, maturity risk premium = 2.5 percent, real rate = 3 percent, liquidity premium = 0 percent, and nominal interest rate = 10 percent.

10. Find the default risk premium (DRP) for a debt security given the following information: inflation premium = 2.5 percent, maturity risk premium = 2.5 percent, real rate = 3 percent, liquidity premium = 1.5 percent, and nominal interest rate = 14 percent.

11. Assume that the interest rate on a one-year Treasury bill is 6 percent. and the rate on a two-year Treasury note is 7 percent.

   a. If the expected real rate of interest is 3 percent, determine the inflation premium on the Treasury bill.

   b. If the maturity risk premium (MRP) is expected to be zero, determine the inflation premium on the Treasury note.

   c. What is the expected inflation premium for the second year?

12. A Treasury note with a maturity of four years carries a nominal rate of interest of 10 percent. In contrast, an eight-year Treasury bond has a yield of 8 percent.

   a. If inflation is expected to average 7 percent over the first four years, what is the expected real rate of interest?

   b. If the inflation rate is expected to be 5 percent for the first year, calculate the average annual rate of inflation for years 2 through 4.

   c. If the maturity risk premium (MRP) is expected to be zero between the two Treasury securities, what will be the average annual inflation rate expected over years 5 through 8?

13. The interest rate on a ten-year Treasury bond is 9.25 percent. A comparable maturity Aaa-rated corporate bond is yielding 10

percent. Another comparable maturity, but lower-quality, corporate bond has a yield of 14 percent, which includes a liquidity premium of 1.5 percent.

   a. Determine the default risk premium (DRP) on the Aaa-rated bond.

   b. Determine the DRP on the lower-quality corporate bond.

14. A corporate bond has a nominal interest rate of 12 percent. This bond is not liquid and requires a 2 percent liquidity premium (LP). The bond is of low quality and, thus, has a default risk premium (DRP) of 2.5 percent. The bond has a remaining life of twenty-five years, resulting in a maturity risk premium (MRP) of 1.5 percent.

   a. Estimate the nominal interest rate on a Treasury bond.

   b. What would be the inflation premium on the Treasury bond if investors required a real rate of interest of 2.5 percent?

15. **Challenge Problem** Following are some selected interest rates:

MATURITY OR TERM	RATE	TYPE OF SECURITY
1 year	4.0%	Corporate loan (high quality)
1 year	5.0%	Corporate loan (low quality)
1 year	3.5%	Treasury bill
5 years	5.0%	Treasury note
5 years	6.5%	Corporate bond (high quality)
5 years	8.0%	Corporate bond (low quality)
10 years	10.5%	Corporate bond (low quality)
10 years	8.5%	Corporate bond (high quality)
10 years	7.0%	Treasury bond
20 years	7.5%	Treasury bond
20 years	9.5%	Corporate bond (high quality)
20 years	12.0%	Corporate bond (low quality)

   a. Plot a yield curve using interest rates for government default risk-free securities.

   b. Plot a yield curve using corporate debt securities with low default risk (high quality) and a separate yield curve for low-quality corporate debt securities.

   c. Measure the amount of default risk premiums (DRPs), assuming constant inflation rate expectations and no maturity or liquidity risk premiums on any of the debt securities for high-quality and low-quality corporate securities based on information from (a) and (b). Describe and discuss why differences might exist between high-quality and low-quality corporate debt securities.

   d. Identify the average expected inflation rate at each maturity level in (a) if the real rate is expected to average 2 percent per year and if there are no maturity risk premiums (MRPs) expected on Treasury securities.

   e. Using information from (d), calculate the average annual expected inflation rate over years 2 through 5. Calculate the average annual expected inflation rates for years 6 through 10 and for years 11 through 20.

   f. Based on the information from (e), reestimate the MRPs for high-quality and low-quality corporate debt securities. Describe what seems to be occurring over time and between differences in default risks.

INSTITUTIONS AND MARKETS

INVESTMENTS

FINANCIAL MANAGEMENT

• CHAPTER 9 •

Time Value of Money

Chapter Learning Objectives... AFTER STUDYING THIS CHAPTER, YOU SHOULD BE ABLE TO DO THE FOLLOWING:

- Recall the six principles of finance.
- Explain what is meant by the time value of money.
- Describe the concept of simple interest and the process of compounding.
- Describe discounting to determine present values.
- Find interest rates and time requirements for problems involving compounding or discounting.
- Describe the meaning of an ordinary annuity.
- Find interest rates and time requirements for problems involving annuities.
- Calculate annual annuity payments.
- Make compounding and discounting calculations using time intervals that are less than one year.
- Describe the difference between the annual percentage rate and the effective annual rate.
- Describe the meaning of an annuity due (in the Learning Extension).

Where We Have Been... In Chapter 8, you learned how interest rates are determined in the financial markets. The supply of and demand for loanable funds were discussed along with the determinants of market or "nominal" interest rates. You should recall that the determinants are the real rate of interest, an inflation premium, and a default risk premium for risky debt. A maturity risk premium adjusts for differences in lives or maturities, and there may be a liquidity premium. You learned about the characteristics of U.S. government debt securities and the term or maturity structure of interest rates. You should know how inflation premiums and price movements affect interest rates, as well as why default risk premiums exist and how they are measured.

Where We Are Going... Chapter 10 will focus on the characteristics and valuations of bonds and stocks. You will learn about the long-term external financing sources available to and used by businesses. You will then explore the characteristics and features of both debt and equity capital. Next, the general principles of valuation, which build on the time value of money (covered in this chapter), and how bonds and stocks are valued will be covered. Calculating rates of return is the last topic in Chapter 10. In Chapter 11, you will focus on the characteristics and operation of primary and secondary securities markets. Chapter 12, the last chapter in Part 2, will focus on financial return and risk concepts.

How This Chapter Applies to Me... You probably have experienced the need to save money to buy an automobile or pay for your tuition. Your savings grow more rapidly when you can earn interest on previously earned interest in addition to interest on the starting amount of your savings. This is known as compounding and means the longer you save, the faster your savings will grow and the larger will be your down payment on your automobile purchase or the more money you will have for your tuition. An understanding of compounding will be useful to you when investing in stocks and bonds and planning for eventual retirement.

Most of us would agree that if other things are equal:

More money is better than less money.

Most of us also would agree that:

Money today is worth more than the same amount of money received in the future.

Of course, the value of an additional dollar is not necessarily the same for all individuals. For example, a person subsisting at the poverty level would likely find an added dollar to be worth more in "economic terms" than would an extra dollar to a millionaire or billionaire. Having an added dollar today probably has more "economic worth" to you or us than it would to Bill Gates, the founder and former CEO of Microsoft. At the same time, his personal desire or drive for accumulating more dollars is likely to be greater than your desire.

This chapter makes no attempt to consider the economic or psychic values of more money to a specific individual. Rather, it concentrates on the principle of finance, initially presented in Chapter 1, stating that "money has a time value." The focus here is on how money can grow or increase over time as well as how money has a lower worth today if one has to wait to receive the money sometime in the future. This occurs because one loses the opportunity of earning interest on the money by not being able to save or invest the money.

Financial calculators or spreadsheet software programs will perform the calculations and procedures discussed in this chapter. However, the calculation procedures are first described in detail to enhance the understanding of the logic involved in the concepts of the time value of money. By learning to work the problems the "long way," using step-by-step calculations, following the steps given for financial calculators, spreadsheet programs, and tables-based calculations should make more sense. Students are encouraged to explore using multiple problem-solving methods.

FINANCE PRINCIPLE

PRINCIPLES OF FINANCE

In Chapter 1, we identified six principles of finance. These principles serve as the foundation of finance:

1. Money has a time value.
2. Higher returns are expected for taking on more risk.
3. Diversification of investments can reduce risk.
4. Financial markets are efficient in pricing securities.
5. Manager and stockholder objectives may differ.
6. Reputation matters.

time value of money
math of finance whereby a
financial return is earned
over time by saving or
investing money

The pricing and valuation of financial securities including bonds, stocks, and real asset investments are best understood in the context of the finance principles. The ***time value of money*** is the math of finance whereby a financial return (e.g., interest) is earned over time by saving or investing money.

In addition to investors requiring compensation or a financial return for lending or investing their financial capital, they want to be compensated with higher expected returns for taking on more financial risk. For example, we explored in Chapter 8 the concept of default risk premiums (DRPs) for investing in corporate bonds relative to investing in Treasury bonds. Higher DRPs are required by investors in corporate bonds relative to government bonds because there is a higher likelihood or probability that corporations are more likely to miss paying their interest and principal payment obligations on time. Risk/return trade-offs will be addressed in greater detail in future chapters. The ability to diversify away some investment risk through the holding of diversified portfolios of securities is important to investors when making investment decisions.

CONCEPT CHECK
What are the six principles of finance?

The actions of individuals to seek to find undervalued and overvalued investment opportunities contribute to making financial markets reasonably efficient, meaning current prices reflect the underlying intrinsic valuations of real and financial assets. We know that management objectives may differ from owner objectives. Methods for getting managers to manage for the best interests of equity investors will be discussed during Part 3 of this textbook. The final principle is based on the belief that "reputation matters" and reflects the ethical behavior of individuals and organizations as to how others are treated legally, fairly, and honestly.

BASIC CONCEPTS

We will concentrate on the *time value of money* financial principle in this chapter. Money can increase or grow over time if we can save (invest) it and earn a return on our savings (investment). Let's begin with a savings account illustration. Assume you have $1,000 to save or invest; this is your *principal*. The **present value** of a savings or an investment is its amount or value today. For our example, this is your $1,000.

A bank offers to accept your savings for one year and agrees to pay to you an 8 percent interest rate for use of your $1,000. This amounts to $80 in interest (0.08 × $1,000). The total payment by the bank at the end of one year is $1,080 ($1,000 principal plus $80 in interest). This $1,080 is referred to as the future value or value after one year. The **future value** of a savings amount or investment is its value at a specified time or date in the future. In general word terms, we have the following equation:

$$\text{Future value} = \text{Present value} + (\text{Present value} \times \text{Interest rate})$$

or

$$\text{Future value} = \text{Present value} \times (1 + \text{Interest rate})$$

In our example, we have this result:

$$\text{Future value} = \$1,000 + (\$1,000 \times 0.08)$$
$$= \$1,080$$

or

$$\text{Future value} = \$1,000 \times 1.08$$
$$= \$1,080$$

Let's now assume that your $1,000 investment remains on deposit for two years but that the bank pays only **simple interest**, which is interest earned only on the investment's principal. In word terms, we have the following equation:

$$\text{Future value} = \text{Present value} \times \left[1 + (\text{Interest rate}) \times (\text{number of periods})\right]$$

For our example, this becomes the following result:

$$\text{Future value} = \$1,000 \times \left[1 + (0.08 \times 2)\right]$$
$$= \$1,000 \times 1.16$$
$$= \$1,160$$

Another bank will pay you a 10 percent interest rate on your money. Thus, you would receive $100 in interest ($1,000 × 0.10) or a return at the end of one year of $1,100 ($1,000 × 1.10) from this second bank. While the $20 difference in return between the two banks ($1,100 versus $1,080) is not great, it has some importance to most people. For a two-year deposit for which simple interest is paid annually, the difference increases to $40. The second bank would return $1,200 ($1,000 × 1.20) to you versus $1,160 from the first bank. If the funds were invested for ten years, we would accumulate $1,000 × [1 + (0.08 × 10)] or $1,800 at the first bank. At the second bank, we would have $1,000 × [1 + (0.10 × 10)] or $2,000, a $200 difference. This interest rate differential between the two banks will become more important when we introduce the concept of compounding.

Of course, interest rates paid by banks and other financial institutions are low, partly due to the Fed's easy monetary policy during the 2007–2008 financial crisis and the 2008–2009 Great Recession. The Fed has since tried to stimulate economic growth.

COMPOUNDING TO DETERMINE FUTURE VALUES

Compounding is an arithmetic process whereby an initial value increases or grows at a *compound interest* rate over time to reach a value in the future. **Compound interest** involves earning interest on interest in addition to interest on the principal or initial investment. To understand compounding, let's assume you leave the investment with a bank for more than one year. For example, the first bank accepts your $1,000 deposit, adds $80 at the end of one year, retains the $1,080 for the second year, and pays you interest at an 8 percent rate. The bank returns your

---

present value
amount or value today of a savings or an investment

future value
value of a savings amount or an investment at a specified time or date in the future

simple interest
interest earned only on the investment's principal

CONCEPT CHECK

What is the time value of money?

What do we mean by present value and future value?

What is simple interest?

compounding
arithmetic process whereby an initial value increases or grows at a compound interest rate over time to reach a value in the future

compound interest
involves earning interest on interest in addition to interest on the principal or initial investment

initial deposit plus accumulated interest at the end of the second year. How much will you receive as a future value? In word terms, we have the following calculation:

$$\text{Future value} = \text{Present value} \times \big[(1 + \text{Interest rate}) \times (1 + \text{Interest rate})\big]$$

For our two-year investment example, we have the following calculation:

$$\begin{aligned}
\text{Future value} &= \$1,000 \times (1.08) \times (1.08) \\
&= \$1,000 \times 1.1664 \\
&= \$1,166.40 \\
&= \$1,166 \text{ (rounded)}
\end{aligned}$$

A timeline can be used to illustrate this two-year example as follows:

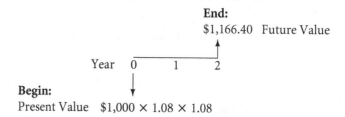

Thus, for a one-year investment, the return would be $1,080 ($1,000 $\times$ 1.08), which is the same as the return on a simple interest investment as was previously shown. However, a two-year investment at an 8 percent compound interest rate will return $1,166.40, compared to $1,160 using an 8 percent simple interest rate.

The compounding concept can be expressed as the following equation:

$$FV_n = PV(1 + r)^n \tag{9.1}$$

FV is the future value, PV is the present value, r is the interest rate, and n is the number of periods in years. For our $1,000 deposit, 8 percent, two-year example, we have the following calculation:

$$\begin{aligned}
FV_2 &= \$1,000(1 + 0.08)^2 \\
&= \$1,000(1.1164) \\
&= \$1,166.40 \\
&= \$1,166 \text{ (rounded)}
\end{aligned}$$

If we extend the time period to ten years, the $1,000 deposit would grow to the following amount:

$$\begin{aligned}
FV_{10} &= \$1,000(1 + 0.08)^{10} \\
&= \$1,000(2.1589) \\
&= \$2,158.90 \\
&= \$2,159 \text{ (rounded)}
\end{aligned}$$

Texas Instruments (TI) and Hewlett Packard (HP) make two popular types of financial calculators. However, they are programmed differently.[1] Reference is made to the use of TI and HP calculators when discussing calculator solutions throughout the remainder of this chapter. Other available financial calculators are usually programmed like the TI or HP calculators. If you are going to use a financial calculator to solve time value of money problems, you must understand how your calculator works.

Most financial calculators are programmed to find future values (FVs). Typically, financial calculators will have a present value (PV) key, a future value (FV) key, a number of time periods (N) key, an interest rate key (usually designated %i), and a Compute key (usually designated as CPT). If you have a financial calculator, you can verify the FV result for the ten-year example.

First, clear any values stored in the calculator's memory. Next, enter 1000 and press the PV key. (Some financial calculators require that you enter the PV amount as a minus value because it is an investment or outflow.) Then, enter 8 and press the %i key (most financial calculators are

---

1. For problems involving present values (PVs) and future values (FVs), HP calculators require one of the values to be entered as a negative. In contrast, PVs and FVs are entered as positive values in TI calculators, and the internal program makes one of the values negative for calculation purposes. Other TI and HP differences when entering data are noted later in this chapter.

programmed so you enter whole numbers rather than decimals for the interest rate). Next, enter 10 for the number of time periods (usually years) and press the N key. Finally, press the CPT key followed by the FV key to calculate the future value of 2,158.93, which rounds to $2,159. Actually, financial calculators are programmed to calculate answers to twelve significant digits.

Financial Calculator Solution:

Inputs:	10	8	1000
	N	%i	PV
Press:	CPT	FV	
Solution:	2158.93		

Computer spreadsheet programs are available for finding future values. Following is the same problem solved using Excel spreadsheet program. For presentation purposes, the solution only for the two-year version of the problem is shown. That is, how much would you accumulate after two years if you invested $1,000 at an 8 percent interest rate with annual compounding?

Spreadsheet Solution:

	A11 ▼	fx		
	A	B	C	D
1	Interest Rate	0.08		
2	Time Period	0	1	2
3	Cash Flow	1000		
4	Future Value (FV)		1080.00	1166.40
5				
6	Cash Flow fx Calc	-1000	0	0
7	Financial Function			
8	FV Solution			$1,166.40

We set up our spreadsheet with descriptive labels in cells A1 through A4. We then solve the compound interest problem by placing the interest rate in decimal form (0.08) in Cell B1. The time periods are placed on Row 2, beginning with period 0 (the current period) in Cell B2 and so forth. The cash flow of 1000 (an investment) is listed in cell B3. In this simple problem, we replicate the basic "by hand" calculations in spreadsheet format and the FV calculations beginning in C4 and continuing to D4.

In Cell C4, we place the formula = B3*(1+B1), which reflects compounding the $1,000 investment at 8 percent interest for one year. Cell D4 shows compounding of the investment at

SMALL BUSINESS PRACTICE
Calculating Rates of Return for Venture Capitalists and Other Investors

Venture capitalists represent an important source of financing for small businesses. Venture capitalists, of course, are in the business of providing financial capital to small businesses with the expectation of earning a return on their investments commensurate with the risks associated with those investments. A typical "exit strategy" of venture capitalists is to maintain an investment in a firm for approximately five years and, if the investment is successful, sell the firm to another company or take the firm public in an initial public offering (IPO).

A venture capitalist usually will invest in a small business by taking a direct ownership position in the form of common stock or by accepting the firm's bond plus an "equity kicker" or the right to purchase a certain portion of the firm (e.g., 50 percent). For example, let's assume that a venture capitalist invests $5 million in a firm. In return, the venture capitalist receives shares of stock representing

50 percent ownership in the firm. Let's assume the firm can be sold for $40 million at the end of five years. What will be the rate of return that the venture capitalist will earn on the $10 million investment? The present value (PV) is $5 million and the future value (FV) is $20 million (i.e., $40 million times .5, or 50 percent). Since, we know the time period is five years, we solve for the interest rate *r*. Using a financial calculator results in a compound interest rate (%i) of 32.0 percent.

What would have been the venture capitalist's rate of return if the firm had been sold for $40 million at the end of six years instead of at the end of five years? Again, the PV is $5 million, the FV is $20 million, and the time period is six years. Solving for the interest rate yields 26.0 percent. Thus, if the sale of the firm is delayed by one year, the compound rate of return on the venture capitalist's investment drops 6 percentage points from 32 percent down to 26 percent.

8 percent for a second year and can be calculated as C4*(1+B1), so compounding at an 8 percent interest rate results in an FV of $1,166.40 after two years. Of course, we could have made the FV calculation in one step as = B3*(1+B1)^2, which produces 1,166.40.

Excel and other spreadsheet programs have built-in financial functions so spreadsheet solutions do not have to be calculated the long way. The bottom portion of the spreadsheet solution example illustrates the use of the financial function for future value. Here we enter the cash flow in time period zero as −1000 to reflect an outflow and a present value. Click on the Excel financial wizard (*fx*) icon, then Financial, then FV, and OK to bring up the dialogue box where the FV components for the problem at hand are requested. The equation is FV(Rate, Nper, Pmt, PV, Type). The Rate is 0.08; Nper is the number of time periods (2 in the preceding example); Pmt is 0 since no periodic payments exist; PV is –1000; and Type is 0, reflecting that payments occur at the end of the period. Thus, we would have: FV(0.08,2,0,−1000,0). Clicking OK results in an FV of $1,166.40, or $1,166 rounded. Of course, rather than inserting numbers, one could insert specific cell references in the FV function.

If the investment had been compounded for ten years, the FV function inputs would have been FV(0.08,10,0,–1000,0). Clicking OK would result in an answer of $2,158.92, or $2.159 rounded.

In addition, tables have been prepared to simplify the calculation effort if financial calculators or spreadsheet programs are unavailable. Equation 9.1 can be rewritten as follows:

$$FV_n = PV(FVIF_{r,n})$$ (9.2)

The $(1 + r)^n$ part of Equation 5.1 is replaced by a future value interest factor (FVIF) corresponding to a specific interest rate and a specified time period.

Table 9.1 shows FVIF values carried to three decimal places for a partial range of interest rates and time periods. (Table 1 in the Appendix is a more comprehensive FVIF table.) Let's use Table 9.1 to find the FV of $1,000 invested at an 8 percent compound interest rate for a ten-year period; at the intersection of the 8 percent column and ten years, we find an FVIF of 2.159. Putting this information into Equation 9.2 gives the following solution.

Table-based Solution:

$$FV_{10} = \$1,000(2.159)$$
$$= \$2,159$$

INTERNET ACTIVITY

Go to the Chase Bank Web site, http://www.chase.com. Under the Products & Services drop-down menu, select "Savings & CDs" and click on Savings & CDs Overview. Identify the interest rates being paid on certificates of deposit (CDs) of various maturities and amounts.

Further examination of Table 9.1 shows how a $1 investment grows or increases with various combinations of interest rates and time periods. For example, if another bank offers to pay you a 10 percent interest rate compounded annually, the FVIF at the intersection of 10 percent and ten years would be 2.594, making your $1,000 investment worth $2,594 ($1,000 × 2.594). The difference between the 8 percent and 10 percent rates is more significant at $435 ($2,594 − $2,159) than the $200 difference that occurred with simple compounding over ten years. Thus, we see the advantage of being able to compound at higher interest rates over a period of years.

The compounding or growth process can be depicted in graphic form. Figure 9.1 shows graphic relationships among FVs, interest rates, and time periods. For example, notice how $1 will grow differently over a ten-year period at 5 percent versus 10 percent interest rates. Of course, if no

TABLE 9.1

Future Value Interest Factor (FVIF) of $1

YEAR	5%	6%	7%	8%	9%	10%
1	1.050	1.060	1.070	1.080	1.090	1.100
2	1.102	1.124	1.145	1.166	1.188	1.210
3	1.158	1.191	1.225	1.260	1.295	1.331
4	1.216	1.262	1.311	1.360	1.412	1.464
5	1.276	1.338	1.403	1.469	1.539	1.611
6	1.340	1.419	1.501	1.587	1.677	1.772
7	1.407	1.504	1.606	1.714	1.828	1.949
8	1.477	1.594	1.718	1.851	1.993	2.144
9	1.551	1.689	1.838	1.999	2.172	2.358
10	1.629	1.791	1.967	2.159	2.367	2.594

FIGURE 9.1
Future Value, Interest Rate, and Time Period Relationships

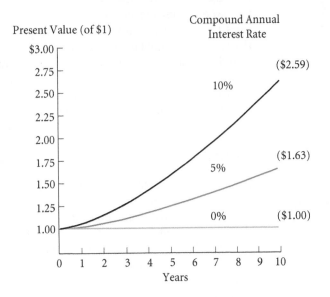

interest is being earned, then the initial $1 investment will remain at $1 no matter how long the investment is held. At a 10 percent interest rate, the initial $1 grows to $2.59 (rounded) after ten years. This compares with $1.63 (rounded) after ten years if the interest rate is only 5 percent. The FV increases at an increasing rate as the interest rate increases and as the time period is lengthened.

In recent years, the benefits of compounding have been tempered because of historically low interest rates. Recall, that the Federal Reserve System (Fed) has employed a policy of monetary easing through its open-market operations and the non-traditional monetary policy tool of quantitative easing (QE).

INFLATION OR PURCHASING POWER IMPLICATIONS

The compounding process described in the preceding section does not say anything about the purchasing power of the initial $1 investment at some point in the future. As seen, $1 growing at a 10 percent interest rate would be worth $2.59 (rounded) at the end of ten years. With zero inflation, you could purchase $2.59 of the same quality of goods after ten years relative to what you could purchase now. However, if the stated or *nominal* interest rate is 10 percent and the inflation rate is 5 percent, then in terms of increased purchasing power, the "net" or differential compounding rate would be 5 percent (10 percent − 5 percent) and $1 would have an inflation-adjusted value of $1.63 after ten years. This translates into an increased purchasing power of $0.63 ($1.63 − $1.00).

Also note that if the compound inflation rate is equal to the compound interest rate, the purchasing power would not change. For example, if in Figure 9.1 the inflation and interest rates were 5 percent, the purchasing power of $1 would remain the same over time. Thus, to make this concept operational, subtract the expected inflation rate from the stated interest rate and compound the remaining (differential) interest rate to determine the change in purchasing power over a stated time period. For example, if the interest rate is 10 percent and the inflation rate is 3 percent, the savings or investment should be compounded at a differential 7 percent rate. Turning to Table 9.1, we see that $1 invested at a 7 percent interest rate for ten years would grow to $1.967 ($1.97 rounded) in terms of purchasing power. Of course, the actual dollar value would be $2.594 ($2.59 rounded).

GLOBAL DISCUSSION

Financial contracts (e.g., savings deposits and bank loans) in countries that have experienced high and volatile inflation rates sometimes have been linked to a consumer price or similar inflation index. Such actions are designed to reduce the exposure to inflation risk for savers and lenders. Since the interest rate they receive on their savings deposits will vary with the rate of inflation, savers receive purchasing power protection. As inflation rises, so will the rate of interest individuals receive on their savings deposits such that purchasing power will be maintained.

CONCEPT CHECK

What is compounding?

What is compound interest?

Bank lenders are similarly protected against changing inflation rates since the rates they charge on their loans will vary with changes in inflation rates. At least in theory, banks will be able to maintain a profit spread between the interest rates they pay to savers and the higher interest rates they lend to borrowers because inflation affects both financial contracts. Of course, if the borrowers are business firms, they need to be able to pass on higher prices for their products and services to consumers to be able to maintain profit margins when interest rates are rising along with increases in inflation.

Inflation in the United States has been generally from 2 percent to 3 percent during the first part of the twenty-first century. However, some economists are concerned that the Fed's continued emphasis on monetary liquidity through its QE1, QE2, and QE3 quantitative easing efforts will result in much higher inflation rates in the future.

DISCOUNTING TO DETERMINE PRESENT VALUES

Most financial management decisions involve present values (PVs) rather than future values (FVs). For example, a financial manager who is considering purchasing an asset wants to know what the asset is worth rather than in the future. An asset has value because it will produce a stream of future cash benefits. To determine its value now in time period zero, we have to discount or reduce the future cash benefits to their present value. *Discounting* is an arithmetic process whereby a future value (FV) decreases at a compound interest rate over time to reach a present value (PV).

discounting

arithmetic process whereby a future value (FV) decreases at a compound interest rate over time to reach a present value (PV)

Let's illustrate discounting with a simple example involving an investment. Assume that a bank or other borrower offers to pay you $1,000 at the end of one year in return for using $1,000 of your money now. If you are willing to accept a zero rate of return, you might make the investment. Most of us would not jump at an offer like this. Rather, we would require some return on our investment. To receive a return of 8 percent, you would invest less than $1,000 now. The amount to be invested would be determined by dividing the $1,000 that is due at the end of one year by one plus the interest rate of 8 percent. This results in an investment amount of $925.93 ($1,000 ÷ 1.08), or $926 rounded. Alternatively, the $1,000 could have been multiplied by 1 ÷ 1.08, or 0.9259 (when carried to four decimal places) to get $925.90, or $926 rounded.

Let's assume you will not receive the $1,000 for two years and the compound interest rate is 8 percent. What dollar amount (PV) would you be willing to invest? In word terms, we have the following equation:

Present value = Future value × {[1 ÷ (1 + Interest rate)] × [1 ÷ (1 + Interest rate)]}

For our two-year investment example, we get the following value:

$$\text{Present value} = \$1,000 \times (1 \div 1.08) \times (1 \div 1.08)$$
$$= \$1,000 \times (0.9259) \times (0.9259)$$
$$= \$1,000 \times 0.8573$$
$$= \$857.30$$

A timeline can be used to illustrate this two-year example as follows:

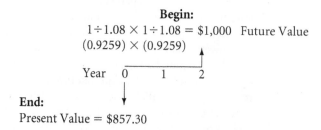

Thus, for a one-year investment, the PV would be $925.90 ($1,000 × 1 ÷ 1.08, or 0.9259). A two-year investment would have a PV of $857.30 ($1,000 × 0.9259 × 0.9259).

The discounting concept can be expressed in equation form:

$$PV = FV_n \div (1 + r)^n$$

or

$$PV = FV_n \left[1 \div (1 + r)^n \right] \tag{9.3}$$

The individual terms are the same as those defined for the future value (FV) equation. The FV equation has simply been rewritten to solve for the present value (PV). For the $1,000, 8 percent, two-year example, we have the following answer:

$$\begin{aligned} PV &= \$1,000\left[1 \div (1 + 0.08)^2\right] \\ &= \$1,000(1 \div 1.1164) \\ &= \$1,000(0.8573) \\ &= \$857.30 \\ &= \$857 \text{ (rounded)} \end{aligned}$$

If we extend the time period to ten years, the $1,000 FV would decrease to the following:

$$\begin{aligned} PV &= \$1,000\left[1 \div (1 + 0.08)^{10}\right] \\ &= \$1,000(1 \div 2.1589) \\ &= \$1,000(0.4632) \\ &= \$463.20 \\ &= \$463 \text{ (rounded)} \end{aligned}$$

Most financial calculators are programmed to readily find present values (PVs). As noted, financial calculators typically have a PV key, an FV key, a number of time periods (N) key, an interest rate (%i) key, and a compute (CPT) key. If you have a financial calculator, you can verify the PV result for the ten-year example. First, clear the calculator. Enter 1000 (or −1000 for some calculators to find a positive PV) and press the FV key. Enter 8 and press the %i key. Enter 10 and press the N key. Finally, press the CPT key followed by the PV key to calculate the PV of 463.19, which rounds to $463.

Financial Calculator Solution:

Inputs:	10	8	1000
	N	%i	FV
Press:	CPT	PV	
Solution:	463.19		

Excel or another spreadsheet program can be used to find present values (PVs). For a simple PV problem, we show the calculation by hand in spreadsheet format as well as using the preprogrammed PV financial function. What would be the PV of receiving $1,000 two years from now if the annual discount rate is 8 percent?

Spreadsheet Solution:

	A	B	C	D
	D1 ▼		*fx*	
1	Interest Rate .	0.08		
2	Time Period	0	1	2
3	Cash Flow	0	0	1000
4	Present Value	857.34	925.93	
5				
6	Cash Flow fx Calc	0	0	-1000
7	Financial Function			
8	PV Solution:	$857.34		

When making the calculation by hand, we enter 0.08 as the interest rate in Cell B1, then the time periods beginning with 0 in Cell B2 and so forth, and a cash flow of 1000 in Cell D3. In Cell C4, we insert the equation = D3/(1+B1)^1 and get 925.93. In Cell B4, we enter the equation = C4/(1+B1)^1, with the result being 857.34. Of course, we could have solved for the PV in one step by entering in Cell B4 the equation = D3/(1+B1)^2 and found 857.34 directly.

The bottom portion of the spreadsheet solution example illustrates the use of the Excel's financial function called present value (PV). To get a positive PV value, we enter −1000 as the cash flow in time period 2. Click on the Excel financial wizard (*fx*) icon, click on Financial, click on PV, and then press OK to bring up the dialogue box where the PV components for the problem at hand are requested. The equation is PV(Rate, Nper, Pmt, FV, Type). The Rate is 0.08; Nper is the number of time periods, or 2 in this example; Pmt is zero since no periodic payments exist; FV is −1000; and Type is 0, reflecting that payments occur at the end of the period. This equates to PV(0.08,2,0,−1000,0). Pressing OK results in a PV of $857.34, or $857 rounded. Because the PV function in Excel is programmed to give a negative number when there is a positive FV, much like the PV solutions on most calculators, we entered the FV as a negative number to get a positive present value (PV). Of course, rather than inserting numbers, one could insert specific cell references in the PV function.

If the investment had been discounted for ten years, the PV function inputs would have been: PV(0.08,10,0,−1000,0). Pressing OK would result in an answer of $463.19, or $463 rounded.

In addition, tables have been prepared to simplify the calculation effort if financial calculators or computer programs are unavailable. Equation 9.3 can be rewritten this way:

$$PV = FV_n (PVIF_{r,n}) \qquad (9.4)$$

The $1 \div (1 + r)^n$ part of Equation 9.3 is replaced by a present value interest factor (PVIF) corresponding to a specific interest rate and a specified time period.

Table 9.2 shows PVIF values for a range of interest rates and time periods. (Table 2 in the Appendix is a more comprehensive PVIF table.) Let's use Table 9.2 to find the PV of $1,000 invested at an 8 percent compound interest rate for a ten-year period. At the intersection of the 8 percent column and ten years, we find a PVIF of 0.463. Putting this information in Equation 9.4 gives the following.

Table-based Solution:

$$PV = \$1,000(0.463)$$
$$= \$463$$

Further examination of Table 9.2 shows how a $1 investment decreases with various combinations of interest rates and time periods. For example, if another bank offers to pay interest at a 10 percent compound rate, the PVIF at the intersection of 10 percent and ten years would be 0.386, resulting in your $1,000 FV being worth an investment of $386 ($1,000 × 0.386). The difference in required investments needed to accumulate $1,000 at the end of ten years between 8 percent and 10 percent interest rates is $77 ($463 − $386). In essence, the PV of an FV decreases as the interest rate increases for a specified time period.

The discounting process can be depicted in graphic form. Figure 9.2 shows graphic relationships among present values (PVs), interest rates, and time periods. For example, notice how a $1 future value (FV) will decrease differently over a ten-year period at 5 percent versus 10 percent interest rates. Of course, at a zero interest rate, the PV remains at $1 and is not affected by time. If no interest is being earned, the $1 FV will have a PV of $1 no matter how long the investment is held. At a 5 percent interest rate, the PV of $1 declines to $0.61 (rounded) if an investor has to wait ten years to receive the $1. This compares with a PV of $1 of only $0.39 (rounded) if the interest rate is 10 percent and the investor must wait ten years to receive $1. Notice that the PV decreases at an increasing rate as the interest rate is increased and as the time period is lengthened.

CONCEPT CHECK

What is discounting?

TABLE 9.2

Present Value Interest Factor (PVIF) of $1

YEAR	5%	6%	7%	8%	9%	10%
1	.952	.943	.935	.926	.917	.909
2	.907	.890	.873	.857	.842	.826
3	.864	.840	.816	.794	.772	.751
4	.823	.792	.763	.735	.708	.683
5	.784	.747	.713	.681	.650	.621
6	.746	.705	.666	.630	.596	.564
7	.711	.665	.623	.583	.547	.513
8	.677	.627	.582	.540	.502	.467
9	.645	.592	.544	.500	.460	.424
10	.614	.558	.508	.463	.422	.386

FIGURE 9.2
Present Value, Interest Rate, and Time Period Relationships

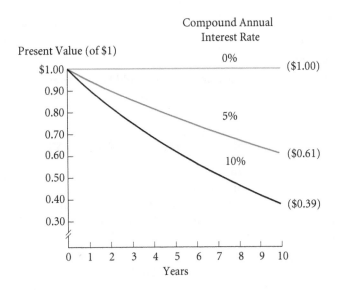

EQUATING PRESENT VALUES AND FUTURE VALUES

Notice that Equations 9.1 and 9.3 are two ways of looking at the same process involving compound interest rates. That is, if we know the future value (FV) of an investment, we can find its present value (PV) and vice versa. For example, an initial investment of $1,000 will grow to $1,116.40 at the end of two years if the interest rate is 8 percent. To reduce the impact of rounding errors, we are carrying our calculations here to four decimal places:

$$FV_2 = \$1,000(1 + 0.08)^2$$
$$= \$1,000(1.1664)$$
$$= \$1,166.40$$

PERSONAL FINANCIAL PLANNING
So You Want to Be a Millionaire?

A million dollars can be acquired in a number of ways. Probably the easiest legal way is to inherit it. Those of us who won't benefit that way must save a portion of our disposable personal income and live long enough to take advantage of compounding interest. For example, if you could invest $10,000 now (at the end of time period zero), the following combinations of annual compound interest rates and time periods would make you a millionaire.

INTEREST RATE (%)	TIME (YEARS)
5	94.4
10	48.3
15	33.0
20	25.3

At a 5 percent compound rate it would take more than ninety-four years to accumulate $1 million. This is probably unacceptable (or possible) for most of us. Even if we could compound our interest at a 20 percent annual rate, it would take a little more than twenty-five years to become a millionaire.

An alternative approach would be to create an investment annuity of $10,000 per year. Now let's show the time required to become a millionaire under the assumption of an ordinary annuity where the first investment will be made one year from now:

INTEREST RATE (%)	TIME (YEARS)
5	36.7
10	25.2
15	19.8
20	16.7

With this approach the time required, particularly at higher interest rates, is more feasible. Compounding at 5 percent would still require making annual investments for nearly thirty-seven years to accumulate $1 million. At 10 percent, it would take a little more than twenty-five years to attain that goal. Of course, the most critical factor, which might be easier said than done, is the ability to come up with $10,000 per year out of disposable personal income. Good luck.

CONCEPT CHECK

How do present values and future values relate or equate to each other?

Now, what is the PV of a $1,166.40 FV is if we must wait two years to receive the FV amount and if the interest rate is 8 percent? The solution would be the following:

$$PV = \$1,166.40[1 \div (1 + 0.08)^2]$$
$$= \$1,166.40(1 \div 1.1664)$$
$$= \$1,166.40(0.8573)$$
$$= \$1.000$$

Thus, an investor should be indifferent about receiving a $1,000 PV now or a $1,166 FV two years from now if the compound interest rate is 8 percent.

FINDING INTEREST RATES AND TIME REQUIREMENTS

Recall the four variables from the future value (9.1 and 9.2) and present value (9.3 and 9.4) equations: PV = present value, FV = future value, r = interest rate, and n = number of periods. As long as we know the values for any three of these variables, we can solve for the fourth or unknown variable. This is accomplished by using a financial calculator, a financial function in a spreadsheet program, or tables.

SOLVING FOR INTEREST RATES

INTERNET ACTIVITY

Go to the Citibank Web site, http://www.citibank.com. Click on Personal and then interest rates on credit cards. Identify the types of credit cards available to individuals and the prevailing interest rates on the credit cards.

Assume that the present value (PV) of an investment is $1,000, the future value (FV) is $1,403, and the time period is five years. What compound interest rate would be earned on this investment?

This problem can be solved using a financial calculator. If a financial calculator is used, enter PV = 1000, FV = 1403, N = 5, and press CPT followed by the %i key to find an interest rate (r) of 7.01, or 7 percent rounded (some calculators may require the PV entry or FV entry to be negative).

Financial Calculator Solution:

Inputs:	5		1000		1403
	N		PV		FV
Press:	CPT		%i		
Solution:	7.01				

A second way of solving for the interest rate is with a spreadsheet program using a financial function. Excel has a financial function called RATE that makes it possible to solve the interest rate quickly. Click on the financial wizard (*fx*), click on Financial, and click on RATE. Entering the requested data and clicking OK gives the following solution:

Spreadsheet Solution:

$$= RATE(Nper, Pmt, PV, FV, Type)$$
$$= RATE(5, 0, -1000, 1403, 0)$$
$$= 7.01\%$$

The number of periods (Nper) is 5, there are zero periodic payments (Pmt), the present value (PV) is entered as −1000, the future value (FV) is 1403, and the Type is zero since cash flows occur at the end of a time period.

Table-based Solution:

The interest rate answer can be found by setting up the problem using Equation 9.2 and Table 9.1 as follows:

$$FV_5 = PV(FVIF_{r,5})$$
$$\$1,403 = \$1,000(FVIF_{r,5})$$
$$FVIF_{r,5} = 1.403$$

Since we know the number of time periods is five, we can turn to Table 9.1 and read across the year-five row until we find future value interest factor (FVIF) of 1.403. This occurs under the 7 percent column, indicating that the interest rate r is 7 percent.

We can work the problem using Equation 9.4 and Table 9.2 as follows:

$$PV = FV_5(PVIF_{r,5})$$
$$\$1,000 = \$1,403(PVIF_{r,5})$$
$$PVIF_{r,5} = 0.713$$

Turning to Table 9.2, we read across the year-five row until we find the present value interest factor (PVIF) of 0.713. This occurs under the 7 percent column, indicating that the interest rate r is 7 percent.

SOLVING FOR TIME PERIODS

Let's assume an investment has a present value (PV) of \$1,000, a future value (FV) of \$1,403, and an interest rate of 7 percent. What length of time does this investment involve?

This problem can be solved using a financial calculator and entering PV = 1000 (or −1000), FV = 1403, and %i = 7. Pressing the Compute (CPT) key followed by the N key gives us an n of 5.01, or 5 years rounded.

Financial Calculator Solution:

Inputs:	7	1000	1403
	%i	PV	FV
Press:	CPT	N	
Solution:	5.01		

Spreadsheet Solution:

The number of time periods can be determined by using the Excel financial function called NPER. Following the sequence described and clicking on the NPER financial function we have the following answer:

$$= NPER(Rate,Pmt,PV,FV,Type)$$
$$= NPER(.07,0,-1000,1403,0)$$
$$= 5.00$$

The interest rate is 7 percent, there are no payments, the PV is −1000, the FV is 1403, and type is zero.

Table-based Solution:

The answer can be found by using Equation 9.2 and Table 9.1 as follows:

$$FV_n = PV(FVIF_{7\%,n})$$
$$\$1,403 = \$1,000(FVIF_{7\%,n})$$
$$FVIF_{7\%,n} = 1.403$$

Since we know the interest rate is 7 percent, we can turn to Table 9.1 and read down the 7 percent column until we find the future value interest factor (FVIF) of 1.403. Notice that this occurs in the year-five row, indicating that the time period n is five years.

We can work the problem using Equation 9.4 and Table 9.2 as follows:

$$PV = FV_n(PVIF_{7\%,n})$$
$$\$1,000 = \$1,403(PVIF_{7\%,n})$$
$$PVIF_{7\%,n} = .713$$

Turn to Table 9.2, we read down the 7 percent column until we find the PVIF of 0.713. This occurs at the year-five row, indicating that the time period n is five years.

RULE OF 72

Investors often ask, "How long will it take for my money to double in value at a particular interest rate?" Table 9.1 illustrates the process for answering this question. We pick a particular interest rate and read down the table until we find a future value interest factor (FVIF) of 2.000. For example, at an 8 percent interest rate, it will take almost nine years (note the FVIF of 1.999) for an investment to double in value. At a 9 percent interest rate, the investment will double in about eight years (FVIF of 1.993). An investment will double in a little over seven years (FVIF of 1.949) if the interest rate is 10 percent.

A shortcut method, referred to as the ***Rule of 72***, can be used to approximate the time required for an investment to double in value. This method is applied by dividing the interest rate into the number 72 to determine the number of years it will take for an investment to double in value. For example, if the interest rate is 8 percent, 72 divided by 8 indicates that the investment will double in value in nine years. This is the same conclusion drawn from Table 9.1. Likewise, at an interest rate of 10 percent it will take approximately 7.2 years (72 ÷ 10) for an investment to double in value. At low or high interest rates, the Rule of 72 does not approximate the compounding process as well, and a larger estimation error occurs in the time required for an investment to double in value.

> *Rule of 72*
> *a shortcut method used to approximate the time required for an investment to double in value*

CONCEPT CHECK
How is the *Rule of 72* used?

FUTURE VALUE OF AN ANNUITY

The previous discussion focuses on cash payments or receipts that occurred only as lump sum present values (PVs) and future values (FVs). However, many finance problems involve equal payments or receipts over time, referred to as *annuities*. More specifically, an **annuity** is a series of equal payments (receipts) that occur over a number of time periods.

An ***ordinary annuity*** exists when the equal payments (receipts) occur at the end of each time period.[2] For example, suppose you want to invest $1,000 per year for three years at an 8 percent interest rate. However, since you will not make your first payment until the end of the first year, this will be an ordinary annuity.

This problem also can be illustrated using a timeline as follows:

> *annuity*
> *a series of equal payments (receipts) that occur over a number of time periods*

> *ordinary annuity*
> *equal payments (receipts) occur at the end of each time period*

> *annuity due*
> *exists when equal periodic payments start at time period zero or, in other words, the beginning of each time period*

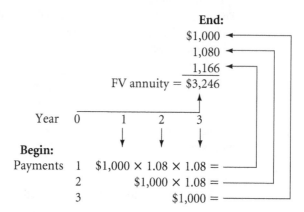

To calculate the future value (FV) of this ordinary annuity we must add the FVs of the first payment ($1,166), the second payment ($1,080), and the third payment ($1,000). This results in an FV of $3,246. To summarize, since the first payment is made at the end of the first year, it is compounded for two years. The second payment is compounded for one year, and the third payment earns zero interest since the payment is made at the end of the third year.

The FV of this annuity can be determined by making the following computations:

$$
\begin{aligned}
\text{FV ordinary annuity} &= \$1{,}000(1.08)^2 + \$1{,}000(1.08)^1 + \$1{,}000(1.08)^0 \\
&= \$1{,}000(1.166) + \$1{,}000(1.080) + \$1{,}000(1.000) \\
&= \$1{,}000(3.246) \\
&= \$3{,}246
\end{aligned}
$$

---

2. An ***annuity due*** exists when equal periodic payments start at the end of time period zero or, in other words, at the beginning of each time period. Annuity due problems are discussed in Learning Extension 9.

While the computational process was easy for the three-year ordinary annuity example, the required calculations become more cumbersome as the time period is lengthened. As a result, the following equation was derived for finding the FV of an ordinary annuity (FVA):

$$FVA_n = PMT\{[(1 + r)^n - 1] \div r\} \tag{9.5}$$

PMT is the periodic equal payment, r is the compound interest rate, and n is the total number of periods. Inserting the data from the preceding three-year annuity example results in the following answer:

$$\begin{aligned}
FVA_3 &= \$1{,}000\{[(1 + 0.08)^3 - 1] \div 0.08\} \\
&= \$1{,}000[(1.2597 - 1) \div 0.08] \\
&= \$1{,}000(3.246) \\
&= \$3{,}246
\end{aligned}$$

Most financial calculators are programmed to find FVs of annuities. In addition to the previously identified keys, financial calculators also will have a payments (PMT) key for purposes of working problems involving ordinary annuities. The result for the three-year ordinary annuity can be verified using a financial calculator.

First, clear the calculator. Enter –1000 (for both TI and HP calculators) and press the PMT key. Enter 8, press the %i key, enter 3, and press the N key. Finally, press the CPT key and then the FV key to calculate the FVA of 3246.40, which rounds to $3,246. Because this problem involves a periodic outflow of $1,000, most financial calculators require that the payment be entered as a negative number to solve for a positive FVA.

Financial Calculator Solution:

Inputs:	3	8	−1000
	N	%i	PMT
Press:	CPT	FV	

Solution: 3246.40

Spreadsheet programs are available for finding FVs of annuities. Following is a solution using an Excel spreadsheet and future value (FV). The difference here is that we have a constant periodic payment.

Spreadsheet Solution:

	A	B	C	D	E
1	Interest Rate	0.08			
2	Time Period	0	1	2	3
3	Cash Flow	0	-1000	-1000	-1000
4					
5	Financial Function				
6	FV Solution:				$3,246.40

We solve for the future value of the annuity as follows:

$$\begin{aligned}
&= FV(Rate, Nper, Pmt, PV, Type) \\
&= FV(.08, 3, -1000, 0, 0) \\
&= \$3{,}246.40
\end{aligned}$$

In addition, tables have been prepared to simplify the calculation effort if financial calculators or computer programs are unavailable. Equation 9.5 can be rewritten in the following way:

$$FVA_n = PMT(FVIFA_{r,n}) \tag{9.6}$$

The $[(1 + r)^n - 1] \div r$ part of Equation 9.5 is replaced by a future value interest factor of an annuity (FVIFA) corresponding to a specific interest rate and a specified time period.

TABLE 9.3
Future Value Interest Factor (FVIFA) for a $1 Ordinary Annuity

YEAR	5%	6%	7%	8%	9%	10%
1	1.000	1.000	1.000	1.000	1.000	1.000
2	2.050	2.060	2.070	2.080	2.090	2.100
3	3.152	3.184	3.215	3.246	3.278	3.310
4	4.310	4.375	4.440	4.506	4.573	4.641
5	5.526	5.637	5.751	5.867	5.985	6.105
6	6.802	6.975	7.153	7.336	7.523	7.716
7	8.142	8.394	8.654	8.923	9.200	9.487
8	9.549	9.897	10.260	10.637	11.028	11.436
9	11.027	11.491	11.978	12.488	13.021	13.579
10	12.578	13.181	13.816	14.487	15.193	15.937

Table-based Solution:

Table 9.3 shows FVIFA values for a partial range of interest rates and time periods. (Table 3 in the Appendix is a more comprehensive FVIFA table.) Let's use Table 9.3 to find the future value of an ordinary annuity (FVA) involving annual payments of $1,000, an 8 percent interest rate, and a three-year time period. At the intersection of the 8 percent column and three years, we find a FVIFA of 3.246. Putting this information into Equation 9.6 gives the following answer:

$$FVA_3 = \$1,000(3.246)$$
$$= \$3,246$$

CONCEPT CHECK

What is an annuity?

What is an ordinary annuity?

Further examination of Table 9.3 shows how a $1 annuity grows or increases with various combinations of interest rates and time periods. For example, if $1,000 is invested at the end of each year (beginning with year one) for ten years at an 8 percent interest rate, the FVA would be $14,487 ($1,000 × 14.487). If the interest rate is 10 percent for ten years, the FVA would be $15,937 ($1,000 × 15.937). These results demonstrate the benefits of higher interest rates on the future values of annuities (FVAs).

PRESENT VALUE OF AN ANNUITY

Many present value (PV) problems also involve cash flow annuities. Usually, these are ordinary annuities. Let's assume that we will receive $1,000 per year beginning one year from now for a period of three years at an 8 percent compound interest rate. How much would you be willing to pay now for this stream of future cash flows? Since we are concerned with the value now, this becomes a PV problem.

We can illustrate this problem using a timeline as follows:

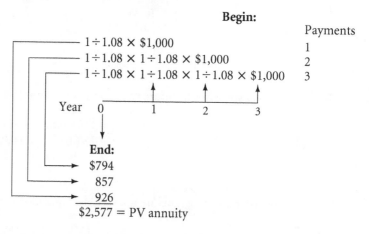

To calculate the present value of this ordinary annuity (PVA) we must sum the present values of the first payment ($794), the second payment ($857), and the third payment ($926). This results in a present value of $2,577.

We can find the present value of this annuity by making the following computations:

$$
\begin{aligned}
\text{PV ordinary annuity} &= \{\$1,000[1 \div (1.08)^1]\} + \{\$1,000[1 \div (1.08)^2]\} \\
&\quad + \{\$1,000[1 \div (1.08)^3]\} \\
&= [\$1,000(0.926)] + [\$1,000(0.857)] + [\$1,000(0.794)] \\
&= \$1,000(2.577) \\
&= \$2,577
\end{aligned}
$$

While the computational process was easy for the preceding three-year ordinary annuity example, the required calculations become more cumbersome as the time period is lengthened. As a result the following equation was derived for finding the present value of an ordinary annuity (PVA):

$$
\text{PVA}_n = \text{PMT}\{[1 - (1 \div (1 + r)^n)] \div r\} \tag{9.7}
$$

The various inputs are the same as previously defined. Inserting the data from the preceding three-year annuity example results in the following answer:

$$
\begin{aligned}
\text{PVA}_3 &= \$1,000\{[1 - (1 \div (1 + 0.08)^3)] \div 0.08\} \\
&= \$1,000[(1 - 0.7938) \div 0.08] \\
&= \$1,000(0.2062 \div 0.08) \\
&= \$1,000(2.577) \\
&= \$2,577
\end{aligned}
$$

Most financial calculators are programmed to find present values of annuities. The result for the three-year PVA problem can be verified with a financial calculator. First, clear the calculator. Enter 1000 for a TI calculator (or –1000 for an HP calculator) and press the payments (PMT) key. Enter 8, press the %i key, enter 3, and press the N key. Finally, press the CPT key followed by the PV key to calculate the PVA of 2577.10, which rounds to $2,577.

Financial Calculator Solution:

Inputs:	3	8	1000
	N	%i	PMT
Press:	CPT	PV	
Solution:	2577.10		

Spreadsheet programs are available for finding present values of annuities. The following is an Excel spreadsheet solution.

Spreadsheet Solution:

	A	B	C	D	E
1	Interest Rate	0.08			
2	Time Period	0	1	2	3
3	Cash Flow	0	-1000	-1000	-1000
4					
5	Financial Function				
6	PV Solution:	$2,577.10			

Use the previously described present value (PV) financial function provided by Excel as follows:

$$
\begin{aligned}
&= \text{PV(Rate,Nper,Pmt,FV,Type)} \\
&= \text{PV}(.08, 3, -1000, 0, 0) \\
&= \$2,577.10
\end{aligned}
$$

In addition, tables have been prepared to simplify the calculation effort if financial calculators or computer programs are unavailable. Equation 9.7 can be rewritten in the following way:

$$
\text{PVA}_n = \text{PMT}(\text{PVIFA}_{r,n}) \tag{9.8}
$$

The $\{1 - [1 \div (1 + r)^n]\} \div r$ part of Equation 9.7 is replaced by a present value interest factor of an annuity (PVIFA) corresponding to a specific interest rate and a specified time period.

Table-based Solution:

Table 9.4 shows PVIFA values for a partial range of interest rates and time periods. (Table 4 in the Appendix is a more comprehensive PVIFA table.) Let's use Table 9.4 to find the PVA involving annual payments of $1,000, an 8 percent interest rate, and a three-year time period. Notice that at the intersection of the 8 percent interest rate column and three years, we find a PVIFA of 2.577. Putting this information into Equation 9.8 gives the following:

$$PVA_3 = \$1,000(2.577)$$
$$= \$2,577$$

CONCEPT CHECK

How do we find the present value of an annuity?

Further examination of Table 9.4 shows how the present value (PV) of a $1 annuity decreases with various combinations of interest rates and time periods. For example, if $1,000 is paid at the end of each year (beginning with year one) for ten years at an 8 percent interest rate, the PVA would be $6,710 ($1,000 × 6.710). If the interest rate is 10 percent for ten years, the PVA would be $6,145 ($1,000 × 6.145). These results demonstrate the costs of higher interest rates on the present values of annuities.

INTEREST RATES AND TIME REQUIREMENTS FOR ANNUITIES

How to find or solve for interest rates or time periods for problems involving a lump sum present value (PV) or future value (FV) was discussed previously in this chapter. That originally involved working with four variables: PV = present value, FV = future value, r = interest rate, and n = number of periods. A fifth variable is added to reflect payments (PMT) involving annuities.

SOLVING FOR INTEREST RATES

Assume the future value of an ordinary annuity (FVA) is $5,751, the annual payment is $1,000, and the time period is five years. What is the interest rate for this problem?

A financial calculator could be used to solve this problem if the FV of an ordinary annuity (FVA) or the PV of an ordinary annuity (PVA) is known. If you have a financial calculator and you know the FV, enter FV = 5751, PMT = –1000 (for TI and HP calculators), and N = 5. Press the Compute (CPT) key followed by the %i key to find an r of 7 percent. (Some financial calculators will give an error message if the 1000 PMT is entered as a positive number. If the PVA is known instead of the FV, the preceding procedure would be followed except that PV = 4100 would be entered instead of the FV amount.)

Financial Calculator Solution:

Inputs:	5	−1000	5751
	N	PMT	FV
Press:	CPT	%i	
Solution:	7.00		

TABLE 9.4

Present Value Interest Factor (PVIFA) for a $1 Ordinary Annuity

YEAR	5%	6%	7%	8%	9%	10%
1	0.952	0.943	0.935	0.926	0.917	0.909
2	1.859	1.833	1.808	1.783	1.759	1.736
3	2.273	2.673	2.624	2.577	2.531	2.487
4	3.546	3.465	3.387	3.312	3.240	3.170
5	4.329	4.212	4.100	3.993	3.890	3.791
6	5.076	4.917	4.767	4.623	4.486	4.355
7	5.786	5.582	5.389	5.206	5.033	4.868
8	6.463	6.210	5.971	5.747	5.535	5.335
9	7.108	6.802	6.515	6.247	5.995	5.759
10	7.722	7.360	7.024	6.710	6.418	6.145

Spreadsheet Solution:

Excel's RATE financial function can be used to solve this interest rate of an annuity problem, much as the function was used elsewhere in this chapter for problems without periodic payments. The financial function solution would be the following:

$$= \text{RATE(Nper,Pmt,PV,FV,Type)}$$
$$= \text{RATE}(5, -1000, 0, 5751, 0)$$
$$= 7.00\%$$

Table-based Solution:

The answer can be found by setting up the problem using Equation 9.6 and Table 9.3 as follows:

$$FVA_5 = PMT(FVIFA_{r,5})$$
$$\$5,751 = \$1,000(FVIFA_{r,5})$$
$$FVIFA_{r,5} = 5.751$$

Since we know that the number of time periods is five, we can turn to Table 9.3 and read across the year-five row until we find the FVIFA of 5.751. This occurs under the 7 percent column, indicating that the interest rate r is 7 percent.

Let's assume we know the present value of the preceding ordinary annuity is $4,100. We could then find the interest rate for the problem using present value annuity tables as follows:

$$PVA_5 = PMT(PVIFA_{r,5})$$
$$\$4,100 = \$1,000(PVIFA_{r,5})$$
$$PVIFA_{r,5} = 4.100$$

Turning to Table 9.4, we read across the year-five row until we find the PVIFA of 4.100. This occurs under the 7 percent column, indicating that the interest rate r is 7 percent.

SOLVING FOR TIME PERIODS

Let's assume that the future value of an ordinary annuity (FVA) is $5,751, the annual payment is $1,000, and the interest rate is 7 percent. How long would it take for your $1,000 annual investments to grow to $5,751?

Financial Calculator Solution:

We can solve this problem using a financial calculator. We know that the FVA is $5,751, so enter FV = 5751, PMT = –1000, %i = 7, and press the CPT key followed by the N key to find an n of five years. If we knew the present value of the annuity instead of the FV, we could work the problem by substituting the PV for the FV.

Inputs:	7		–1000	5751
	%i		PMT	FV
Press:	CPT		N	
Solution:	5.00			

Spreadsheet Solution:

Excel's NPER financial function can be used to solve for the number of periods in an annuity problem, much as we used the function earlier for problems without periodic payments. The financial function solution would be the following:

$$= \text{NPER(Rate,Pmt,PV,FV,Type)}$$
$$= \text{NPER}(.07, -1000, 0, 5751, 0)$$
$$= 5.00$$

Table-based Solution:

The problem can be set up by using Equation 9.6 and Table 9.3 as follows:

$$FVA_n = PMT(FVIFA_{7\%,n})$$
$$\$5,751 = \$1,000(FVIFA_{7\%,n})$$
$$FVIFA_{7\%,n} = 5.751$$

Since we know the interest rate is 7 percent, we can turn to Table 9.3 and read down the 7 percent column until we find FVIFA of 5.751. This occurs in the year-five row, indicating that the *n* time period is five years.

If we knew the present value of the above ordinary annuity was $4,100, we could work the problem using Equation 9.8 and Table 9.4 as follows:

$$PVA_n = PMT(PVIFA_{7\%,n})$$
$$\$4,100 = \$1,000(PVIFA_{7\%,n})$$
$$PVIFA_{7\%,n} = 4.100$$

Turning to Table 9.4, we read down the 7 percent column until we find PVIFA of 4.100. This occurs at the year-five row, indicating that the *n* time period is five years.

DETERMINING PERIODIC ANNUITY PAYMENTS

EXAMPLES INVOLVING ANNUAL PAYMENTS

In many instances, you must determine the periodic equal payment required for an annuity. For example, you may wish to accumulate $10,000 at the end of five years from now by making equal annual payments beginning one year from now. If you can invest at a compound 6 percent interest rate, what will be the amount of each of your annual payments?

Financial Calculator Solution:

This is a future value of an ordinary annuity (FVA) problem. Using a financial calculator, the annual payments (PMT) would be found as follows:

Inputs	6	5	10000
	%i	N	FV
Press	CPT	PMT	
Solution	1773.96		

Spreadsheet Solution:

Excel's PMT financial function can be used to solve for the annual payment amount. The financial function solution would be the following:

$$= PMT(Rate,Nper,PV,FV,Type)$$
$$= PMT(.06,5,0,-10000,0)$$
$$= \$1,773.96$$

Table-based Solution:

Equation 9.6 and Table 9.3 can be used as follows:

$$FVA_n = PMT(FVIFA_{r,n})$$
$$\$10,000 = PMT(FVIFA_{6\%,5})$$
$$\$10,000 = PMT(5.637)$$
$$PMT = \$1,773.99$$
$$= \$1,774 \text{ (rounded)}$$

The future value interest factor of an annuity (FVIFA) factor of 5.637 is taken from Table 9.3 at the intersection of the 6 percent column and the year-five row.

As another example, we might want to find the equal payment necessary to pay off, or *amortize,* a loan. An **amortized loan** is repaid in equal payments over a specified time period. Let's assume

CONCEPT CHECK

What is the process for solving for either interest rates or time period requirements for annuities?

amortized loan
a loan repaid in equal payments over a specified time period

that a lender offers you a $20,000, 10 percent interest rate, three-year loan that is to be fully amortized with three annual payments. The first payment will be due one year from the loan date, making the loan an ordinary annuity. How much will you have to pay each year?

This is a present value (PV) problem because the $20,000 is the value or amount of the loan now. The annual payment can be found with a financial calculator, a financial function in a spreadsheet program, or with a table-based approach using Equation 9.8 and Table 9.4 as follows:

$$PVA_n = PMT(PVIFA_{10\%,3})$$
$$\$20,000 = PMT(2.487)$$
$$PMT = \$8,041.82$$
$$= \$8,042 \text{ (rounded)}$$

The PVIFA factor of 2.487 is taken from Table 9.4 at the intersection of the 10 percent column and the year-three row.

Table 9.5 illustrates the repayment process with a ***loan amortization schedule***, which shows the breakdown of each payment between interest and principal, as well as the remaining balance after each payment. Since the interest rate is 10 percent, the first year interest will total $2,000 ($20,000 × 0.10). Subsequent interest payments are based on the remaining loan balances, which are smaller each year (referred to as the *declining balance*). Since $6,042 ($8,042 − $2,000) of the first year's $8,042 payment is used to repay part of the principal, the second year's interest payment will be $1,396 ($13,958 × 0.10). The third and last payment covers the final year's interest of $731 plus the remaining principal balance.

loan amortization schedule
a schedule of the breakdown of each payment between interest and principal as well as the remaining balance after each payment

FINANCIAL CRISIS

REAL ESTATE MORTGAGE LOANS WITH MONTHLY PAYMENTS

We discussed characteristics of home mortgages in Chapter 7. The traditional residential real mortgage loan has been a 30-year fixed interest rate mortgage loan requiring equal monthly payments that would pay off or amortize the loan over its life. Let's assume you want to borrow $100,000 for 30 years, and the current interest rate is 6 percent. The mortgage requires you to make equal monthly payments so the loan will be paid in full at maturity. What will be your monthly payment? We begin by first determining you will have to make 360 (12 times 30 years) monthly payments. Since the annual interest rate is 6 percent, you will pay .50 percent (6 percent divided by 12) interest per month. With this information, we can calculate your monthly payment using a financial calculator as follows:

Financial Calculator Solution:

Inputs	.50	360	−100000
	%i	N	PV
Press	CPT	PMT	
Solution	599.55		

You would need to make a $599.55 monthly payment.

Of course, Excel's PMT financial function can be used to solve for the monthly payment amount.

TABLE 9.5
Sample Loan Amortization Schedule

YEAR	ANNUAL PAYMENT	INTEREST PAYMENT	PRINCIPAL REPAYMENT	LOAN BALANCE
0	—	—	—	$20,000
1	$8,042	$2,000	$6,042	13,958
2	8,042	1,396	6,646	7,312
3	8,042	731	7,311*	0

*Because of rounding, the final principal repayment is off by $1.

Spreadsheet Solution:

The financial function solution would be the following:

$$= \text{PMT(Rate,Nper,PV,FV,Type)}$$
$$= \text{PMT}(.005, 360, -100000, 0, 0)$$
$$= 599.55$$

Unfortunately, due to rapidly rising housing prices during the decade prior to 2006, many home buyers needed increasingly larger loans to make their real property purchases. For example, a $200,000 fixed-rate mortgage loan would result in a much higher monthly payment compared to a $100,000 loan. Rework the above financial calculator and spread sheet solutions using a present value (PV) of –200000. The resulting doubling of the monthly payment to $1,199.10 means that fewer potential home buyers could qualify for these larger loans.

While the need for larger loans was increasing, many lenders, partly encouraged by government officials, were willing to make subprime mortgage loans to individuals with poor credit scores or ratings to increase home ownership. These developments encouraged the increasing use of adjustable-rate mortgages (ARMs). Recall that an ARM typically has an interest rates tied to the bank prime rate or the Treasury bill rate, either of which normally is lower than long-term interest rates on fixed-rate mortgage loans, making it easier for borrowers with low credit scores and/or those wanting to borrow larger amounts to get mortgage loans.

Some lenders further offered initial below-market "teaser" rates such as 1 or 2 percent for the first year or so on their ARM mortgage loans. Of course, when the "teaser" rate period ends, the ARM interest rate adjusts to the current market rate causing the possibility of a dramatic increase in monthly payments. Clearly, lenders lent (and individuals borrowed) mortgage loans characterized by high default risks.

CONCEPT CHECK

What is an amortized loan?

What is a loan amortization schedule?

As of the end of 2012, interest rates on home mortgage loans were at historically low levels. This translates to lower monthly mortgage payments for a specified mortgage loan of, say, $200,000 suggesting it would be easier for potential home buyers to qualify for mortgage loan financing. However, because of recent mortgage loan defaults and mortgage loans that are underwater (i.e., the mortgage loan is greater than the value of the home) associated with the bursting of the housing price bubble in mid-2006, lenders are requiring larger equity down payments on new mortgage loans.

MORE FREQUENT COMPOUNDING OR DISCOUNTING INTERVALS

In many situations, compounding or discounting may occur more often than annually. For example, recall from the beginning of this chapter the $1,000 that could be invested at one bank at an 8 percent annual interest rate for two years. Remember that the future value (FV) at the end of two years was the following:

$$FV_2 = \$1,000(1.08)^2$$
$$= \$1,000(1.166)$$
$$= \$1,166.40$$

Now let's assume that another bank offers the same 8 percent interest rate but with semiannual (twice a year) compounding. We can find the FV of this investment by modifying Equation 9.1 as follows:

$$FV_n = PV(1 + r \div m)^{n \times m} \tag{9.9}$$

The *m* value is the number of compounding periods per year. For this problem, we find the following answer:

$$FV_2 = \$1,000(1 + 0.08 \div 2)^{2 \times 2}$$
$$= \$1,000(1.04)^4$$
$$= \$1,000(1.1699)$$
$$= \$1,169.90$$

Thus, by compounding semiannually, the FV would increase by $3.50. The more-frequent-than-annual compounding process can be described operationally as follows. Divide the annual interest rate of 8 percent by the number of times compounding is to take place during the year (0.08 ÷ 2 = 0.04).

We need to increase the total number of periods to reflect semiannual compounding. To do this, multiply the number of years for the loan by the frequency of compounding within a year (2 years × 2 = 4 periods).

Previously in this chapter, it was shown that a $1,000 investment at an 8 percent interest rate would grow to $2,158.92 or $2,159 (rounded) at the end of ten years. However, if semiannual compounding had been available, the FV of the $1,000 investment would have been the following:

$$FV_{20} = \$1,000(1.04)^{20}$$
$$= \$1,000(2.1911)$$
$$= \$2,191.10$$

The following subsection shows how the financial calculator solution would be found.

Financial Calculator Solution:

Inputs: 20   4   1000
               [N]   [%i]   [PV]

Press: [CPT]   [FV]

Solution: 2191.12

Spreadsheet Solution:
The Excel FV function inputs would be the following:

$$= FV(0.04, 20, 0, -1000, 0)$$
$$= \$2,191.12$$

CONCEPT CHECK

What is the process for compounding or discounting more frequently than annually?

Table-based Solution:
The future value interest factor (FVIF) can be found in Table 1 in the Appendix. When a three-decimal place table is used, the factor is 2.191 with an FV of $2,191 (rounded). Semiannual compounding will result in $32 more than the $2,159 earned with annual compounding. It follows that more frequent compounding, such as quarterly or monthly, produces higher earnings.

The process described also applies to discounting problems when discounting occurs more frequently than annually. The use of financial calculators and spreadsheet programs are more expedient as the frequency of compounding or discounting within a year increases.

COST OF CONSUMER CREDIT

UNETHICAL LENDERS

ETHICAL ISSUES

usury
the act of lending money at an excessively high interest rate

History has shown many examples of individuals being charged exorbitant interest rates on loans. There is a word, *usury,* for this type of action. **Usury** is the act of lending money at an excessively high interest rate. Lenders who exhibited such unethical behavior were sometimes referred to as "loan sharks." Lenders, of course, are in the business of making a rate of return on the money they have to lend. Without question, lenders deserve to earn a fair rate of return to compensate them for their time and the risk that the borrower will not repay the interest and/or principal on time or in full.

In Chapter 8, we defined this added compensation as a risk premium above the prevailing risk-free rate. Good ethical behavior is consistent with treating borrowers honestly and fairly. However, because of the existence of unethical lenders, various laws have made usury illegal. While it is illegal to charge usurious rates of interest, some unscrupulous lenders still behave unethically when making loans to consumers. Congress passed the *Consumer Credit Protection Act of 1968,* which prohibits excessively high-priced credit transactions. Regulation Z enacts the Truth in Lending section of the act, whereby the Federal Reserve System (Fed) has the responsibility of making consumers aware of the costs of alternative forms of credit. Lenders must disclose all loan costs (interest amounts, service charges, loan and finder fees, etc.), as well as the *annual percentage rate* (APR) of charge or interest. It is unfortunate but a fact of life that, because of the unethical behavior of some lenders, laws must be enacted to protect consumers.

APR VERSUS EAR

annual percentage rate (APR)
determined by multiplying the interest rate charged per period by the number of periods in a year

Banks, finance companies, and other lenders are required by the Truth in Lending law to disclose their lending interest rates on credit extended to consumers. Such a rate is called a contract or stated rate, or more frequently, an **annual percentage rate (APR)**. The method of calculating the APR on a loan is set by law. The APR is the interest rate r charged per period multiplied by the number of periods in a year m:

$$\text{APR} = r \times m \qquad (9.10)$$

Thus, a car loan that charges interest of 1 percent per month has an APR of 12 percent (i.e., 1 percent × 12 months). An unpaid credit card balance that incurs interest charges of 1.5 percent per month has an APR of 18 percent (1.5 × 12 months).

However, the APR misstates the true interest rate. The **effective annual rate (EAR)**, sometimes called the *annual effective yield*, is the true opportunity cost measure of the interest rate as it considers the effects of periodic compounding. For example, say an unpaid January balance of $100 on a credit card accumulates interest at the rate of 1.5 percent per month. The interest charge is added to the unpaid balance; if left unpaid, February's balance will be $101.50. If the bill remains unpaid through February, the 1.5 percent monthly charge is levied based on the total unpaid balance of $101.50. In other words, interest is assessed on previous months' unpaid interest charges. Thus, since interest compounds, the APR formula will *understate* the true or effective interest cost. This will always be true except in the special case where the number of periods is one per year, meaning in annual compounding situations.

effective annual rate (EAR)
measures the true interest rate when compounding occurs more frequently than once a year

If the periodic interest charge r is known, the EAR is found by using Equation 9.11:

$$\text{EAR} = (1 + r)^m - 1 \qquad (9.11)$$

The m value is the number of periods per year. If the APR is known instead, divide the APR by m and use the resulting number for r in Equation 9.11.[3]

As an example of the EAR concept, let's find the true annual interest cost of a credit card that advertises an 18 percent APR. Since credit card charges are typically assessed monthly, m (the number of periods per year) is 12. Thus, the monthly interest rate is the following:

$$r = \text{APR} \div m = 18\% \div 12 = 1.5\%$$

From Equation 9.11, the EAR is the following:

$$(1 + 0.015)^{12} - 1 = 1.1956 - 1 = 0.1956, \text{ or } 19.56\%$$

INTERNET ACTIVITY

Go to the Board of Governors of the Federal Reserve Web site, http://www.federalreserve. gov, click on the Consumer Information tab and then click on Consumer's Guide: Credit Reports and Credit Scores. Describe some of the resources and tools that are available to consumers.

The true interest charge on a credit card with an 18 percent APR is really 19.56 percent.

When the annual stated rate stays the same, more frequent interest compounding helps savers earn more interest over the course of a year. For example, is it better to put your money in an account offering (option 1) 8 percent interest per year, compounded quarterly, or (option 2) 8 percent interest per year, compounded monthly?

Compounding interest quarterly means that the bank is paying interest four times a year to its depositors. Option 1 involved four periods per year and a periodic interest rate r of 8 percent divided by 4, or 2 percent. Every dollar invested with option 1 will grow to $1.0824 [$1(1 + 0.02)^4$] after one year's time. Another way of expressing this is that the EAR of 8 percent compounded quarterly is 8.24 percent.

Under option 2, the relevant time period is one month and the periodic interest rate is 8 percent ÷ 12, or 0.67 percent. Every dollar invested under option 2 will grow to $1.0830 [$1(1 + 0.0067)^{12}$]. Thus, the EAR of 8 percent compounded monthly is 8.30 percent.

As option 2 gives the depositor more interest over the course of a year, depositors should choose it over option 1. This example illustrates that, for the same APR or stated rate, more frequent compounding increases the future value (FV) of an investor's funds more quickly.

CONCEPT CHECK

What is the annual percentage rate (APR) on a loan?

What is the effective annual rate (EAR) on a loan?

---

3. Some financial calculators are preprogrammed with an "interest rate conversion" function, with which one can easily switch between an EAR (sometimes called EFF% for the "effective" rate) and the APR.

APPLYING FINANCE TO...

INSTITUTIONS AND MARKETS

Depository institutions offer savings accounts and certificates of deposit (CDs) to individual savers. To entice individuals to save with them, these financial institutions often state annual percentage rates (APRs) but compound the interest more frequently than once a year. The result is that the effective annual rate (EAR) is higher than the stated annual percentage rate (APR). Of course, since most financial institutions depend on the spread between their cost of obtaining funds and their lending rates, they must balance the EARs at which they borrow and lend. Credit card loans typically provide for monthly compounding so that the EAR is higher than the annual percentage rate (APR).

INVESTMENTS

Most financial decisions are based on the rate at which an investment is compounded or a future value is discounted. Savers are interested in growing or compounding their savings over time and know the longer an investment can compound, the more rapidly it will grow in value at a specified interest rate. Investors make plans, based on the compound rates of return they expect to earn on their investments, when they can buy a home, when they can send their children to college, and when they can retire. The ability to compound interest more than once a year means that investors can reach their goals sooner or at lower interest rates.

FINANCIAL MANAGEMENT

Financial managers borrow from banks and issue debt to raise funds to maintain and grow their firms. While some business loans are simple interest loans, others take the form of fully amortized loans, whereby annuity payments are composed of a declining interest portion and a rising principal repayment portion over the life of the loan. Investors, of course, expect to earn compound rates of return on their debt and equity investments held for more than a year. Accordingly, financial managers must invest funds in capital projects that will generate excess cash flows sufficient in amount to provide investors with their expected rates of return.

SUMMARY

This chapter has introduced the reader to the concept of the time value of money, which is the basis of many financial applications and one of the six financial principles. It began with an explanation and illustration of simple interest, whereby one starts with a present value (PV) amount as it grows to a future value (FV) in one time period. Then, compounding interest over several time periods to determine future values was discussed. This was followed with a discussion and illustrations of the concept of discounting to determine PVs and a discussion of how to find interest rates and time requirements were covered in problems involving FVs and present values.

Future value (FV) problems involving ordinary annuities were described and the calculation process illustrated. This was followed with a section on how to calculate the present value of an ordinary

annuity (PVA). Solving for either interest rates or time periods was then discussed in problems involving annuities. The next section focused on how to determine annual annuity payments. This is particularly useful for finding periodic payments for loans, such as traditional fixed-rate home mortgages, that are amortized (repaid in equal payments) over their lives.

The last two sections of the chapter addressed how to handle more frequent compounding or discounting intervals and a comparison of two interest rate concepts, the annual percentage rate (APR) versus the effective annual rate (EAR).

The Learning Extension that follows covers the meaning of an annuity due and will illustrate some annuity due problems.

KEY TERMS

amortized loan

annual percentage rate (APR)

annuity

annuity due

compounding

compound interest

discounting

effective annual rate (EAR) (annual effective yield)

future value (FV)

loan amortization schedule

ordinary annuity

present value (PV)

Rule of 72

simple interest

time value of money

usury

DISCUSSION QUESTIONS

1. Identify the six principles of finance.

2. Briefly describe the time value of money.

3. Explain simple interest.

4. Describe the process of compounding and the meaning of compound interest.

5. Briefly describe how inflation or purchasing power impacts stated or nominal interest rates.

6. What is discounting? Give an illustration.

7. Briefly explain how present values (PVs) and future values (FVs) are related.

8. Describe the process for solving for the interest rate in PV and FV problems.

9. Describe the process for solving for the time period in PV and FV problems.

10. How can the Rule of 72 be used to determine how long it will take for an investment to double in value?

11. What is an ordinary annuity?

12. Briefly describe how to solve for the interest rate or the time period in annuity problems.

13. Describe the process for determining the size of a constant periodic payment that is necessary to fully amortize a loan such as a home mortgage.

14. Describe compounding or discounting that is done more often than annually.

15. What is usury, and how does it relate to the cost of consumer credit?

16. Explain the difference between the annual percentage rate and the effective annual rate.

EXERCISES

1. Go to the Federal Reserve Web site, http://www.federalreserve.gov. Click on the Consumer Information tab, and research consumer credit in the various hyperlinks. Find average interest rates charged by commercial banks on new automobile loans, personal loans, and credit card plans.

   a. Compare the average level of interest rates among the three types of loans.

   b. Click on the Economic Research & Data tab, click on the "Statistics: Releases and Historical Data" hyperlink and then "Consumer Credit," and compare trends in the cost of consumer credit provided by commercial banks over the past three years.

2. Go to the Federal Reserve Web site, http://www.federalreserve.gov. Click on the Consumer Information tab and access "Recent Statistical Releases" and then "Consumer Credit." Determine current interest rates charged by auto finance companies on new automobile loans. Also compare the trend in the cost of loans from auto finance companies over the past three years.

3. Assume that you and your partner are in the consumer lending business. A customer, talking with your partner, is discussing the possibility of obtaining a $10,000 loan for three months. The potential borrower seems distressed and says he needs the loan by tomorrow or several of his relatively new appliances will be repossessed by the manufacturers. You overhear your partner saying that to process the loan within one day there will be a $1,000 processing fee so that $11,000 in principal will have to be repaid to have $10,000 to spend now. Furthermore, because the money is needed now and is for only three months, the interest charge will be 6 percent per month. What would you do?

PROBLEMS

1. Find the future value (FV) one year from now of a $7,000 investment at a 3 percent annual compound interest rate. Also, calculate the FV if the investment is made for two years.

2. Find the FV of $10,000 invested now after five years if the annual interest rate is 8 percent.

   a. What would be the FV if the interest rate is a simple interest rate?

   b. What would be the FV if the interest rate is a compound interest rate?

3. Determine the future values (FVs) if $5,000 is invested in each of the following situations:

   a. 5 percent for ten years

   b. 7 percent for seven years

   c. 9 percent for four years

4. You are planning to invest $2,500 today for three years at a nominal interest rate of 9 percent with annual compounding.

   a. What would be the future value (FV) of your investment?

   b. Now assume that inflation is expected to be 3 percent per year over the same three-year period. What would be the investment's FV in terms of purchasing power?

   c. What would be the investment's FV in terms of purchasing power if inflation occurs at a 9 percent annual rate?

5. Find the present value (PV) of $7,000 to be received one year from now assuming a 3 percent annual discount interest rate. Also calculate the PV if the $7,000 is received after two years.

6. Determine the present values (PVs) if $5,000 is received in the future (i.e., at the end of each indicated time period) in each of the following situations:

   a. 5 percent for ten years

   b. 7 percent for seven years

   c. 9 percent for four years

7. Determine the present value (PV) if $15,000 is to be received at the end of eight years and the discount rate is 9 percent. How would your answer change if you had to wait six years to receive the $15,000?

8. Determine the future value (FV) at the end of two years of an investment of $3,000 made now and an additional $3,000 made one year from now if the compound annual interest rate is 4 percent.

9. Assume you are planning to invest $5,000 each year for six years and will earn 10 percent per year. Determine the future value (FV) of this annuity if your first $5,000 is invested at the end of the first year.

10. Determine the present value (PV) now of an investment of $3,000 made one year from now and an additional $3,000 made two years from now if the annual discount rate is 4 percent.

11. What is the present value (PV) of a loan that calls for the payment of $500 per year for six years if the discount rate is 10 percent and the first payment will be made one year from now? How would your answer change if the $500 per year occurred for ten years?

12. Determine the annual payment on a $500,000, 12 percent business loan from a commercial bank that is to be amortized over a five-year period.

13. Determine the annual payment on a $15,000 loan that is to be amortized over a four-year period and carries a 10 percent interest rate. Prepare a loan amortization schedule for this loan.

14. You are considering borrowing $150,000 to purchase a new home.

  a. Calculate the monthly payment needed to amortize an 8 percent fixed-rate 30-year mortgage loan.

  b. Calculate the monthly amortization payment if the loan in (a) was for 15 years.

15. Assume a bank loan requires an interest payment of $85 per year and a principal payment of $1,000 at the end of the loan's eight-year life.

  a. At what amount could this loan be sold for to another bank if loans of similar quality carried an 8.5 percent interest rate? That is, what would be the present value (PV) of this loan?

  b. Now, if interest rates on other similar quality loans are 10 percent, what would be the PV of this loan?

  c. What would be the PV of the loan if the interest rate is 8 percent on similar quality loans?

16. Use a financial calculator or computer software program to answer the following questions:

  a. What would be the future value (FV) of $15,555 invested now if it earns interest at 14.5 percent for seven years?

  b. What would be the FV of $19,378 invested now if the money remains deposited for eight years and the annual interest rate is 18 percent?

17. Use a financial calculator or computer software program to answer the following questions:

  a. What is the present value (PV) of $359,000 that is to be received at the end of twenty-three years if the discount rate is 11 percent?

  b. How would your answer change in (a) if the $359,000 is to be received at the end of twenty years?

18. Use a financial calculator or computer software program to answer the following questions:

  a. What would be the future value (FV) of $7,455 invested annually for nine years beginning one year from now if the annual interest rate is 19 percent?

  b. What would be the present value (PV) of a $9,532 annuity for which the first payment will be made beginning one year from now, payments will last for twenty-seven years, and the annual interest rate is 13 percent?

19. Use a financial calculator or computer software program to answer the following questions.

  a. What would be the future value (FV) of $19,378 invested now if the money remains deposited for eight years, the annual interest rate is 18 percent, and interest on the investment is compounded semiannually?

  b. How would your answer for (a) change if quarterly compounding were used?

20. Use a financial calculator or computer software program to answer the following questions.

  a. What is the present value (PV) of $359,000 that is to be received at the end of twenty-three years, the discount rate is 11 percent, and semiannual discounting occurs?

  b. How would your answer for (a) change if monthly discounting were used?

21. What would be the present value (PV) of a $9,532 annuity for which the first payment will be made beginning one year from now, payments will last for twenty-seven years, the annual interest rate is 13 percent, quarterly discounting occurs, and $2,383 is invested at the end of each quarter?

22. Answer the following questions.

  a. What is the annual percentage rate (APR) on a loan that charges interest of .75 percent per month?

  b. What is the effective annual rate (EAR) on the loan described in (a)?

23. You have recently seen a credit card advertisement stating that the annual percentage rate (APR) is 12 percent. If the credit card requires monthly payments, what is the effective annual rate (EAR) of interest on the loan?

24. A credit card advertisement states that the annual percentage rate (APR) is 21 percent. If the credit card requires quarterly payments, what is the effective annual rate (EAR) of interest on the loan?

25. **Challenge Problem** (A computer spreadsheet software program or a financial calculator that can handle uneven cash flow streams will be needed to solve the following problems.) The following cash flow streams are expected to result from three investment opportunities:

YEAR	INVESTMENT STABLE	INVESTMENT DECLINING	INVESTMENT GROWING
1	$20,000	$35,000	$10,000
2	20,000	30,000	15,000
3	20,000	20,000	20,000
4	20,000	5,000	30,000
5	20,000	0	50,000

  a. Find the present values (PVs) at the end of time period zero for each of these three investments if the discount rate is 15 percent. Find the PVs for each investment using 10 percent and 20 percent discount rates.

  b. Find the future values (FVs) of these three investments at the end of year-five if the compound interest rate is 12.5 percent. Find the FVs for each investment using 2.5 percent and 22.5 percent compound rates.

  c. Find the PVs of the three investments using a 15 percent annual discount rate but with quarterly discounting. Find the PVs for semiannual and monthly discounting for a 15 percent stated annual rate.

  d. Find the FVs of the three investments using a 12.5 percent annual compound rate but with quarterly compounding. Find the FVs for semiannual and monthly compounding for a 12.5 percent stated annual rate.

  e. Assume that the PV for each of the three investments is $75,000. What is the annual interest rate (%i) for each investment?

  f. Show how your answers would change in (e) if quarterly discounting takes place.

  g. Assume that the FV for each of the three investments is $150,000. What is the annual interest rate (%i) for each investment? (Remember that (e) and (g) are independent of each other.)

  h. Show how your answers would change in (g) if quarterly compounding takes place.

LEARNING EXTENSION 9

Annuity Due Problems

FUTURE VALUE OF AN ANNUITY DUE

In contrast with an ordinary annuity, an *annuity due* exists when the equal periodic payments occur at the beginning of each period. Let's return to the example used in the "Future Value of an Annuity" section in this chapter. Recall that the problem involved a three-year annuity, $1,000 annual payments, and an 8 percent interest rate. However, let's assume the first payment is made at the beginning of the first year, namely at time zero. This will allow the first $1,000 payment to earn interest for three years, the second payment to earn interest for two years, and the third payment to earn interest for one year.

The calculation process to find the future value (FV) of this annuity due problem can be demonstrated as follows:

$$
\begin{aligned}
\text{FV annuity due} &= \$1,000(1.08)^3 + \$1,000(1.08)^2 + \$1,000(1.08)^1 \\
&= \$1,000(1.260) + \$1,000(1.166) + \$1,000(1.080) \\
&= \$1,000(1.260 + 1.166 + 1.080) \\
&= \$1,000(3.506) \\
&= \$3,506
\end{aligned}
$$

By making the first payment now, the FV of this annuity at the end of three years will be $3,506. This contrasts with an FV of $3,246 if payments are delayed by one year, as would be the case with an ordinary annuity.

Table-based Solution:

Equation 9.6 can be easily modified to handle annuity due problems as follows:

$$ \text{FVAD}_n = \text{PMT}(\text{FVIFA}_{r,n})(1 + r) \qquad \text{(LE9.1)} $$

FVAD is the future value of an annuity due and the $(1 + r)$ factor effectively compounds each payment by one more year to reflect that payments start at the beginning of each period. In this problem, the annual payment is $1,000, the time period is three years, and the interest rate is 8 percent. Using Equation LE9.1, the FV of this annuity due would be the following:

$$
\begin{aligned}
\text{FVAD}_3 &= \$1,000(\text{FVIFA}_{8\%,3})(1 + 0.08) \\
&= \$1,000(3.246)(1.08) \\
&= \$1,000(3.506) \\
&= \$3,506
\end{aligned}
$$

The future value interest factor of an annuity (FVIFA) of 3.246 comes from Table 9.3 at the intersection of the 8 percent interest rate column and the year-three row.

Annuity due problems can be solved with financial calculators. In fact, most financial calculators have a DUE key (or a switch) for shifting payments from the end of time periods to the beginning of time periods. If you have a financial calculator, you can verify the FVAD result for the three-year annuity problem. First, clear the calculator. Enter −1000 (for TI and HP calculators) and press the PMT key. Enter 8, press the %i key, enter 3, and press the N key. Finally, instead of pressing the CPT key, press the DUE key followed by the FV key to find the FVAD of 3506.11, which rounds to $3,506.

Financial Calculator Solution:

Inputs:	3	8	−1000
	N	%i	PMT
Press:	DUE	FV	
Solution:	3506.11		

Spreadsheet Solution:

The future value of an annuity due (FVAD) problem is solved by again using Excel's future value (FV) financial function but adjusting for when the cash flows occur as follows:

$$= FV(Rate,Nper,Pmt,PV,Type)$$
$$= FV(.08,3,-1000,0,1)$$
$$= \$3,506.11$$

The "Type" value was given a "1" to indicate the beginning of period cash flows. Previously, we used a "0" value in "Type" to reflect cash flows occurring at the end of each time period.

PRESENT VALUE OF AN ANNUITY DUE

Occasionally, you will have to do present value annuity due (PVAD) problems. For example, leasing arrangements often require the person leasing equipment to make the first payment at the time the equipment is delivered. Let's illustrate this by assuming lease payments of $1,000 will be made at the beginning of each year for three years. If the appropriate interest rate is 8 percent, what is the PVAD leasing problem?

The calculation process to find the PVAD problem can be demonstrated as follows:

$$PVAD = \$1,000\left[1 \div (1.08)^0\right] + \$1,000\left[1 \div (1.08)^1\right] + \$1,000\left[1 \div (1.08)^2\right]$$
$$= \$1,000(1.000) + \$1,000(0.926) + \$1,000(0.857)$$
$$= \$1,000(2.783)$$
$$= \$2,783$$

By making the first payment now, the present value of this annuity is $2,783. This contrasts with a present value (PV) of $2,577 if payments are delayed by one year, as would be the case with an ordinary annuity.

Table-based Solution:

Equation 9.8 can be easily modified to handle annuity due problems as follows:

$$PVAD_n = PMT(PVIFA_{r,n})(1 + r) \qquad \text{(LE9.2)}$$

PVAD is the present value of an annuity due and the $(1 + r)$ factor effectively compounds each payment by one more year to reflect that payments start at the beginning of each period.

In the preceding problem, the annual payment is $1,000, the time period is three years, and the interest rate is 8 percent. Using Equation LE9.2, the PVAD would be the following:

$$PVAD_3 = \$1,000\left[(PVIFA_{8\%,3})(1 + 0.08)\right]$$
$$= \$1,000\left[(2.577)(1.08)\right]$$
$$= \$1,000(2.783)$$
$$= \$2,783$$

The present value interest factor of an annuity (PVIFA) of 2.577 comes from Table 9.4 at the intersection of the 8 percent interest rate column and the year-three row. Present value annuity due (PVAD) problems can be solved with computer software programs and financial calculators.

If you have a financial calculator, you can verify the PVAD result for the preceding three-year annuity problem. First, clear the calculator. Enter 1000 for TI calculators (or −1000 for HP calculators) and press the payments (PMT) key. Enter 8, press the %i key, enter 3, and press the N key. Finally, instead of pressing the Compute (CPT) key, press the DUE key followed by the PV key to find the PVAD of 2783.26, which rounds to $2,783.

Financial Calculator Solution:

Inputs:	3	8	1000
	N	%i	PMT
Press:	DUE	PV	
Solution:	2783.26		

Spreadsheet Solution:

The present value of an annuity due (PVAD) problem is solved by again using Excel's present value (PV) financial function but adjusting for when the cash flows occur as follows:

$$= PV(Rate,Nper,Pmt,FV,Type)$$
$$= PV(.08,3,-1000,0,1)$$
$$= \$2,783.26$$

The "Type" value was given a "1" to indicate beginning of period cash flows. Previously, we used a "0" value in "Type" to reflect cash flows occurring at the end of each time period.

INTEREST RATES AND TIME REQUIREMENTS FOR ANNUITY DUE PROBLEMS

Tables containing future value interest factor of an annuity (FVIFA) and present value interest factor of an annuity (PVIFA) factors are unavailable for annuity due problems. Thus, it is better to use a spreadsheet program or a financial calculator when finding the interest rate for an annuity due problem. Let's assume that the future value of an annuity due (FVAD) problem is $6,153, each payment is $1,000, and the time period is five years. What is the interest rate on this problem? If you have a financial calculator, enter FV = 6153, PMT = −1000, and N = 5. Press the DUE key and the %i key to find an r of 7 percent.

Financial Calculator Solution:

Inputs:	5	−1000	6153
	N	PMT	FV
Press:	DUE	%i	
Solution:	7.00		

Spreadsheet Solution:

Excel's RATE financial function can be used to solve for the interest rate involving an annuity due problem. The process is similar to the one used for an ordinary annuity problem, except that a "1" value in "Type" is entered to indicate that cash flows occur at the beginning of each time period. The financial function solution would be the following:

$$= RATE(Nper,Pmt,PV,FV,Type)$$
$$= RATE(5,-1000,0,6153,1)$$
$$= 7.00\%$$

The n time periods involved in an annuity due problem can be determined using a computer software program or a financial calculator. For example, in the preceding problem, let's assume we know the interest rate is 7 percent, the future value (FV) is $6,153, and the payment is $1,000 (entered as –1000). What we don't know is the number of time periods required. We can solve for N as follows:

Financial Calculator Solution:

Inputs:	7		–1000	6153
	%i		PMT	FV
Press:	DUE		N	
Solution:	5.00			

Spreadsheet Solution:

Excel's NPER financial function can be used to solve for the number of periods in an annuity due problem. However, in contrast with an ordinary annuity, a value of "1" for "Type" must be entered to indicate that the cash flows occur at the beginning of the time periods. The financial function solution would be the following:

$$= \text{NPER(Rate,Pmt,PV,FV,Type)}$$
$$= \text{NPER(.07,} - 1000,0,6153,1)$$
$$= 5.00$$

Of course, the same process could be used for finding interest rates or the number of time periods if the present value of the annuity due (PVAD) instead of the future value were known. This would be done by substituting the present value (PV) for the future value (FV) in financial calculator or spreadsheet calculations.

PROBLEMS

1. Assume you are planning to invest $100 each year for four years and will earn 10 percent per year. Determine the future value (FV) of this annuity due problem if your first $100 is invested now.

2. Assume you are planning to invest $5,000 each year for six years and will earn 10 percent per year. Determine the future value (FV) of this annuity due problem if your first $5,000 is invested now.

3. What is the present value (PV) of a five-year lease arrangement with an interest rate of 9 percent that requires annual payments of $10,000 per year with the first payment being due now?

4. Use a financial calculator to solve for the interest rate involved in the following future value of an annuity due (FVAD) problem. The future value (FV) is $57,000, the annual payment is $7,500, and the time period is six years.

5. **Challenge Problem** (This problem requires access to a spreadsheet software package or a financial calculator that can handle uneven cash flows.) The following are the cash flows for three investments (originally presented in end-of-chapter problem 25) that occur at the beginning of each year rather than at the end of each year.

YEAR	INVESTMENT STABLE	INVESTMENT DECLINING	INVESTMENT GROWING
1	$20,000	$35,000	$10,000
2	20,000	30,000	15,000
3	20,000	20,000	20,000
4	20,000	5,000	30,000
5	20,000	0	50,000

a. Find the present values (PVs) at the end of time period zero for each of these three investments if the discount rate is 15 percent.

b. Find the future values (FVs) of these three investments at the end of year five if the compound interest rate is 12.5 percent.

c. Assume that the PV for each of the three investments is $75,000. What is the annual interest rate (%i) for each investment?

d. Assume that the FV for each of the three investments is $150,000. What is the annual interest rate (%i) for each investment? (Note: (c) and (d) are independent of each other.)

• CHAPTER 10 •

Bonds and Stocks: Characteristics and Valuations

Chapter Learning Objectives...

AFTER STUDYING THIS CHAPTER, YOU SHOULD BE ABLE TO DO THE FOLLOWING:

- Identify the major sources of external long-term financing for corporations.
- Describe major characteristics of corporate bonds.
- Identify the reasons why investors seek stocks for an investment vehicle.
- Describe major characteristics of preferred stock and common stock.
- Describe the process for issuing dividends by a firm.
- Explain how financial securities are valued in general and specifically for bonds and stocks.

Where We Have Been...

The financial system is composed of a number of participants, such as banks, insurance companies, credit unions, and individuals, among others. Some borrow or lend funds; others seek to sell or purchase ownership rights, or common stock, in firms. We've seen how investors are willing to give up their money in the expectation of receiving a return that will exceed the inflation rate and will reward them for the risk of their investment. Time-value-of-money principles (present value, future value) help borrowers and lenders determine items such as how much to borrow, repayment schedules, and the return on an investment.

Where We Are Going...

Bonds and stocks are traded in securities markets, which will be the topic of Chapter 11. We tie together the concepts of expected return, risk, and valuation in Chapter 12 when we discuss financial risk and return concepts. In Chapter 16, we will discuss additional sources of funds for business financing.

How This Chapter Applies to Me...

Time value of money is one of the most important concepts in finance. Here, we will see applications of time value concepts to the investor and how an investor can evaluate a firm's prospects and estimate appropriate prices for its securities. Greater depth and detail will be presented in an investments course. Many investors lack the time or ability to analyze securities, so they will purchase a mutual fund, which is a professionally managed investment pool. As a financial manager, this chapter will introduce you to various types of capital market securities and their features, so you will know more about the financing choices facing firms.

Mark Twain had a quote about financial markets:

> *October. That month is especially dangerous for investing in stocks. Other dangerous months include August, January, June, March, November, July, February, April, December, May, and September.*[1]

That pretty much covers them all. In this chapter we'll begin to learn about financial markets and the characteristics of stocks and bonds.

---

1. Mark Twain. *Pudd'nhead Wilson*. Hartford, Conn: American Publishing Company, 1897. Print.

Borrowing money brings with it the obligation to repay the debt. Individuals and firms who do not repay their borrowing may find themselves unable to borrow again in the future and, worse yet, filing for bankruptcy. Prudent use of debt by issuers can help finance the purchase of capital, equipment, houses, and so forth. We'll learn more about the corporate decision to borrow in a future chapter. In this chapter, we'll begin to learn about the characteristics of bonds from an investor's perspective.

Investing in the stock market is, for many, the best means available for enjoying the benefits of corporate wealth creation. As firms grow in size, the profitability, market share, market value, and the value of the shares of stock many times grow, too. This helps investors meet their financial goals, such as preparing to meet the needs of paying for the college education of their child or their own retirement. In this chapter, we'll discuss common stock, preferred stock, and principles behind how to value equity.

financial assets
claims against the income or
assets of individuals,
businesses, and governments

In Chapter 2, we described *financial assets* as claims against the income or assets of individuals, businesses, and governments. Businesses obtain long-term external financial capital either by borrowing or by obtaining equity funds. Long-term borrowing can be privately negotiated or can be obtained by issuing debt obligations called bonds. Equity capital may be obtained by finding new partners with financial capital to invest or through the public markets by issuing shares. This chapter describes the characteristics of bonds and applies the time-value-of-money techniques from Chapter 9 to see how to value bonds. Later in the chapter, we'll discuss the characteristics of stocks and tools used to value them.

LONG-TERM EXTERNAL FINANCING SOURCES FOR BUSINESSES

Businesses obtain long-term financing from internal funds, which are generated from profits, and from external funds, which are obtained from capital markets. Some firms will have little need for external funds. They may be able to generate sufficient internal funds to satisfy their need for capital, or they may require little investment in fixed assets (for example, firms operating in service industries). Other businesses, such as high-tech firms that experience rapid growth, cannot generate enough internal funds for their capital needs and may be forced to seek financing, often from the capital markets.

The proportion of internal to external financing varies over the business cycle. During periods of economic expansion, firms usually rely more on external funds because the funds needed for investment opportunities outstrip the firms' ability to finance them internally. During periods of economic contraction, the reverse is true. As profitable investment opportunities become fewer, the rate of investment is reduced and reliance on external capital markets decreases.

INTERNET ACTIVITY

Examine recent financing activity and data at the Federal Reserve Board and Securities Exchange Commission Web sites, http://www.federalreserve.gov *and* http://www.sec.gov.

Long-term funds are obtained by issuing corporate bonds and stocks. Table 10.1 shows that the total of new security issues amounted to more than $2,600 billion in 2006 but to about $1,000 billion annually in 2008–2011 due to a steep recession and financial market anxiety. Most of the annual funds raised from security issues come from corporate bond sales. In fact, corporate bonds accounted for approximately 90 percent of total new security issues from 1995 to 2011. Firms issue more bonds than equities for two basic reasons. First, as we will see in Chapter 18, borrowing is cheaper than raising equity financing. Second, bonds and other loans have a maturity date when they expire or come due; at times, new bonds are sold to repay maturing ones. On the other hand, equity never matures. Firms can repurchase their outstanding stock, or the shares of one firm may be merged or acquired by another firm. That is the reason the "net issues" line for common stocks shows negative numbers. Over the time period covered in the table, corporations have been net repurchasers, rather than net issuers, of new equity.

Table 10.1 further shows that corporations have been annually raising approximately 90 percent of their publicly held long-term debt funds by selling their bonds through public issues in the United States. The second important method of raising long-term debt funds is through private sales or placements in the United States. Public security issues are offered for sale to all investors, must be approved by the Securities and Exchange Commission (SEC), and are accompanied by public disclosure of the firm's financial statements and other information. Private placements are sold to specific qualified investors, do not go through SEC scrutiny, and do not require public disclosure of company information. Since private sales are "private," we do not have good data on these sales over time.

TABLE 10.1
Public Offerings of Bonds and Stocks ($ billions) 2006–2011

	2006		2007		2008		2009		2010		2011		2006–2011
	AMOUNT	PERCENT	AMOUNT	PERCENT	AMOUNT	PERCENT	AMOUNT	PERCENT	AMOUNT	PERCENT	AMOUNT	PERCENT	AVERAGE PERCENTAGE
New Security Issues													
Corporate Bonds	2500.8	95.5%	2220.5	92.9%	865.6	80.7%	970.7	93.9%	893.7	87.2%	909.10	87.5%	89.6%
Public offerings, Corporate Stocks	118.6	4.5%	168.6	7.1%	206.8	19.3%	63.0	6.1%	131.1	12.8%	129.5	12.5%	10.4%
Total	**2619.4**	**100.0%**	**2389.1**	**100.0%**	**1072.4**	**100.0%**	**1033.7**	**100.0%**	**1024.80**	**100.0%**	**1038.60**	**100.0%**	**100.0%**
Bonds by Type of Offering													
Public, domestic	2296.5	91.8%	2002.7	90.2%	748.7	86.5%	784.3	80.8%	879.90	98.5%	880.70	96.9%	90.8%
Sold Abroad	204.2	8.2%	217.8	9.8%	116.9	13.5%	186.4	19.2%	13.80	1.5%	28.40	3.1%	9.2%
Total	**2500.7**	**100.0%**	**2220.5**	**100.0%**	**865.6**	**100.0%**	**970.7**	**100.0%**	**893.70**	**100.0%**	**909.10**	**100.0%**	**100.0%**
Stocks by Type of Offering													
Common shares issued	118.6		168.6		206.8		63.0		131.1		129.5		
Common shares repurchased	721.3		999.8		587.6		126.3		409.1		602.2		
Net issues	−602.7		−831.2		−380.8		−63.3		−278.0		−472.7		
Retained earnings (internal financing) by corporations	497.5		403.4		440.0		488.0		650		708		
Net long term financing raised by corporations	2,395.6		1,792.7		924.8		1,395.4		1,265.7		1,144.4		
Net percent from bonds		104.4%		123.9%		93.6%		69.6%		70.6%		79.4%	90.2%
Net percent from common stock		−25.2%		−46.4%		−41.2%		−4.5%		−22.0%		−41.3%	−30.1%
Net percent from internal financing		20.8%		22.5%		47.6%		35.0%		51.4%		61.9%	39.8%
		100.0%		100.0%		100.0%		100.0%		100.0%		100.0%	100.0%

Source: *Federal Reserve Bulletin (tables 1.46, 1.57), Economic Report of the President (Table B-90)*, various issues

FIGURE 10.1

Net Percent of Financing from Bonds, New Stock Issues, and Retained Earnings, 1995–2011

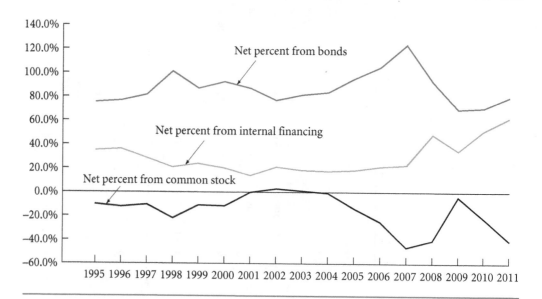

GLOBAL DISCUSSION

CONCEPT CHECK

Which security is more frequently issued, stocks or bonds?

Why would a U.S. firm issue bonds overseas?

How important are internal equity and external equity as a financing source for U.S. corporations?

U.S. firms may borrow funds overseas. This percentage varies over this time frame, from 1.5 percent in 2010 to over 19 percent in 2009. There are four reasons why U.S. firms raise funds outside of the United States. First, if they have overseas plants or factories, it may make financial sense to raise funds in the country in which the plant is built. Second, financing costs, such as interest rates, are sometimes lower overseas although the recent downtrend in overseas financing may be due to lower interest rates in the United States. Third, if securities are issued outside of the United States, the issuer avoids the costly and time-consuming SEC approval process. Fourth, the growing number of large bond offerings (issues of $1 billion or more at one time) causes issuers to seek access to the global capital markets to find buyers.[2]

The bottom of Table 10.1 and Figure 10.1 show the mix between external (bonds and stocks) and internal (retained profits) financing for U.S. corporations. Because of merger, acquisition, and stock buyback activity, external public equity has fallen in recent years as this trend began in the 1980s. To make up for the shortfall, publicly issued bonds have increased relative to retained earnings as a funding source. But since the Great Recession, firms have become more "tight-fisted," seeking to retain more earnings and build up liquidity in the face of a weak economy and an uncertain regulatory environment.

DEBT CAPITAL

A debt agreement is a contract between lenders and the firm. As such, holders of debt capital have certain rights and privileges not enjoyed by the firm's owners (those holding shares of common stock) in a corporation. A debt holder may force the firm to abide by the terms of the debt contract even if the result is reorganization or bankruptcy of the firm. The periodic interest payments due to the holders of debt securities must be paid or else the creditors can force the firm into bankruptcy. Table 10.2 summarizes important characteristics of bonds, which we'll be reviewing in this section.

Except for rarely issued perpetuities[3], all debt issues have maturity dates when issuers are obligated to pay the bond's principal (***par value*** or ***face value***) to bondholders. In the United States, par value is usually $1,000 for corporate bonds. All but zero-coupon issues pay interest, called coupon payments. If a bond has an 8 percent coupon and a par value of $1,000, it pays annual

par value (face value)
principal amount that the issuer is obligated to repay at maturity

---

2. Gregory Zuckerman, "Cautious Bond Investors Have Issuers Thinking Big," *Wall Street Journal* (July 27, 1998), pp. C1, C23.

3. A perpetuity is a bond without a maturity date. Its owners and heirs receive interest payments in perpetuity as long as the firm exists.

TABLE 10.2

Common Elements of Bonds

•	Represent borrowed funds
•	Contractual agreement between a borrower and lender (indenture)
•	Senior claim on assets and cash flow
•	No voting rights
•	Par value
•	Having a bond rating improves the issue's marketability to investors
•	Covenants

•	Interest:	Tax deductible to the issuing firm
		Usually fixed over the issue's life but can be variable as the indenture allows coupon rate on new issues affected by market interest rates and bond rating
•	Maturity:	Usually fixed; can be affected by convertibility, call and put provisions, sinking fund, extendibility features in the indenture
•	Security:	Can have senior claim on specific assets pledged in case of default or can be unsecured (debenture or subordinated [junior claim] debenture)

GLOBAL DISCUSSION

interest of 8 percent of $1,000 or $0.08 \times \$1,000 = \$80$. A bond with a 10 percent coupon would pay interest of $100 per year. Eurobonds pay a single annual coupon interest payment. In the United States, bonds pay interest semiannually; an 8 percent coupon will pay interest of $40 every six months during the life of the bond.

Bondholders have the legal status as creditors, not owners, of the firm. As such, they have priority claims on the firm's cash flows and assets. This means that bondholders must receive their interest payments before the firm's owners receive their dividends. In case of bankruptcy, the debt holders must receive the funds owed to them before funds are distributed to the firm's owners. Because of this first claim on a firm's cash flow and assets, debt is a less risky investment than equity.

Offsetting the advantages of owning debt is its lower return. The interest payments creditors receive usually are considerably less over a period of years than the returns received by equity holders. Also, as long as the corporation meets its contractual obligations, the creditors have little choice in its management and control except for those formal agreements and restrictions that are stated in the loan contract.

Long-term corporate debt securities fall into two categories: secured obligations and unsecured obligations. A single firm can have many types of debt contracts outstanding. Although ownership of many shares of stock may be evidenced by a single stock certificate, the bondholder has a separate security for each bond owned. Bonds can be registered bonds or bearer bonds. Bonds currently issued in the United States are **registered bonds** in that the issuer knows the bondholders' names and interest payments are sent directly to the bondholder. **Bearer bonds** have coupons that are "clipped" from the side of the bond certificate and presented, like a check, to a bank for payment. Thus, the bond issuer does not know who is receiving the interest payments. Bearer bonds are more prevalent outside of the United States. Regulations prevent their issuance in the United States, primarily because unscrupulous investors may evade income taxes on the clipped coupons.

Bonds can be sold in the public market, following registration with the SEC, and traded by investors. There is a "private" market, too; bonds can be sold in a private placement to qualified investors, typically institutional investors such as insurance companies and wealthy individuals. Other forms of debt capital exist in addition to bonds. Businesses can borrow from banks; a popular source of debt financing are commercial finance companies, which will be further discussed in Chapter 16.

ETHICAL ISSUES

registered bonds
bonds issued in the United States and for which the issuer knows the names of the bondholders and the interest payments are sent directly to the bondholder

bearer bonds
have coupons that are "clipped" and presented, like a check, to the bank for payment; the bond issuer does not know who is receiving the interest payments

WHO BUYS BONDS?

The U.S. Treasury has a Treasury Direct program to sell Treasury securities directly to individual investors, but the main buyers of Treasury bonds are large institutions, such as pension funds or insurance companies, which hold them for investment purposes; others, such as investment banks, may purchase them and then resell them to smaller investors.

Similarly, corporate debt markets are oriented toward the large institutional investor who can purchase millions of dollars of bonds at a time. But several innovative firms, such as Ally Financial

SMALL BUSINESS PRACTICE
Financing Sources for the Start-Up Firm

So you want to start your own business? All businesses require some initial financial capital to carry out the firm's operations. A service business requires less financial capital than would a manufacturing business. Both need working capital in the form of inventories and possibly accounts receivable if sales are made on credit terms. In addition, a manufacturing business requires fixed assets to manufacture the products that are to be sold.

Now that you have decided to start a new business, where are you going to get the necessary financial capital? First, you can use your own assets. You may have some accumulated savings to use and or have some financial assets in the form of stocks and bonds that can be sold. Second, you can turn to family and friends for financial support. You can borrow from family members and friends or you can offer them a partial ownership (equity) position in the firm.

A small business can sometimes get outside financing from business angels or venture capitalists. Angels are wealthy individuals who provide financial capital to small businesses, usually during their early development. Venture capitalists organize partnerships that specialize in providing debt and equity capital to small businesses in their development and early expansion stages. The partners in a venture capital pool typically include insurance companies, endowment funds, and other institutional investors.

After a firm begins operations, some financing may be obtained from customers and/or suppliers. Large customers may be willing to "lend" to you in the form of advance "partial payments" on products that have not yet been completed. Suppliers often will give small businesses credit, in some cases for several months, on purchases of materials and supplies. Bank financing is another source of possible outside financing for the small business once operations have begun. The federal government through the Small Business Administration (SBA) provides an additional source of financing for small businesses. Many states and local communities also provide financing assistance to small businesses.

INTERNET ACTIVITY

Learn more about these financing options by visiting http://www.treasurydirect.gov, http://www.ally.com/about/ investor/term-notes/, and http://www.incapital.com.

trust indenture
an extensive document and details the various provisions and covenants of the loan arrangement

ETHICAL ISSUES

trustee
represents the bondholders to ensure the bond issuer respects the indenture's provisions

covenants
impose restrictions or extra duties on the firm

(formerly GMAC), IBM, United Parcel Service (UPS), Caterpillar, and GE Capital, initiated programs in recent years to sell $1,000 par value bonds directly to the retail, or individual, investor. Called SmartNotes, medium-term notes, or direct access notes (depending on the issuer and the investment banker selling them), the programs target small investors who have only a few thousand rather than millions to invest in bonds.

BOND COVENANTS

The **trust indenture** is an extensive document and details the various provisions and covenants of the loan arrangement. A **trustee** represents the bondholders to ensure the bond issuer respects the indenture's provisions. In essence, the indenture is a contract between the bondholders and the issuing firm. The indenture details the par value, maturity date, and coupon rate of the issue. A bond indenture may include **covenants**, which can impose restrictions or extra duties on the firm.

Examples of covenants include stipulations that the firm maintain a minimum level of net working capital,[4] keep pledged assets in good working order, and send audited financial statements to bondholders. Others include restrictions on the amount of the firm's debt, its dividend payments, the amount and type of additional covenants it may undertake, and asset sales.

These examples illustrate the purpose of covenants: to protect the bondholders' stake in the firm. Bonds have value, first, because of the firm's ability to pay coupon interest and, second, because of the value of the assets or collateral backing the bonds in case of default. Without proper covenant protection, the value of a bond can decline sharply if a firm's liquidity and assets depreciate or if its debt grows disproportionately to its equity. These provisions affect the issue's bond rating (discussed below) and the firm's financing costs since bonds giving greater protection to the investor can be sold with lower coupon rates. The firm must decide if the restrictions and duties in the covenants are worth the access to lower-cost funds.

Covenants are important to bondholders. Holders of RJR Nabisco bonds owned high-quality, A-rated bonds prior to the firm's takeover in 1988 by a leveraged buyout. After the buyout, large quantities of new debt were issued; RJR Nabisco's original bonds were given a lower rating and fell by 17 percent in value. Lawsuits by disgruntled bondholders against the takeover were unfruitful. The courts decided that the bondholders should have sought protection against such increases in the firm's debt load by seeking appropriate covenant language before investing,

---

4. This is a measure of a firm's ability to repay short-term bills as they come due. Net working capital will be discussed further in Chapters 15 and 16.

CONCEPT CHECK

Why are bond returns expected to be lower than stock returns?

Are covenants important to bond investors? Why or why not?

bond ratings
assess both the collateral underlying the bonds as well as the ability of the issuer to make timely payments of interest and principal

ETHICAL ISSUES

rather than running to the courts to correct their mistake. Covenants are the best way for bondholders to protect themselves against dubious management actions or decisions. For example, some bonds allow the investor to force the firm to redeem them if the credit rating falls below a certain level; others, such as Deutsche Telekom's $14.5 billion issue in 2000, increase the coupon rate (in this case by fifty basis points or 0.50 percentage points) if the bond rating falls below an "A" rating. We'll discuss bond ratings in the next section.

BOND RATINGS

Most bond issuers purchase **bond ratings** from one or more agencies such as Standard & Poor's (S&P), Moody's, or Fitch. For a one-time fee, the rater examines the credit quality of the firm (e.g., its ability to pay the promised coupon interest), the indenture provisions, covenants, and the expected trends of firm and industry operations. From its analysis and discussions with management, the agency assigns a bond rating (as shown in Table 10.3) that indicates the likelihood of default (nonpayment of coupon or par value, or violation of the bond indenture) on the bond issue.[5] In addition, the rating agency commits to continually reexamine the issue's risk. For example, should the financial position of the firm weaken or improve, S&P may place the issue on its *Credit Watch* list with negative or positive implications. After that, S&P will downgrade, upgrade, or reaffirm the original rating.

Despite the initial cost and the issuer's concern of a lower-than-expected rating, a bond rating makes it much easier to sell the bonds to the public. The rating acts as a signal to the market that an independent agency has examined the qualities of the issuer and the bond issue and has determined the credit risk of the bond issue justifies the published rating. An unrated bond issue will likely obtain a cool reception from investors. Investors may have good reason to wonder, "What

TABLE 10.3

Examples of Bond Rating Categories

MOODY'S	STANDARD & POORS	FITCH	
Aaa	AAA	AAA	Best quality, least credit risk
Aa1	AA+	AA+	High quality, slightly more risk than a top-rated bond
Aa2	AA	AA	
Aa3	AA–	AA–	
A1	A+	A+	Upper-medium grade, possible future credit quality difficulties
A2	A	A	
A3	A–	A–	
Baa1	BBB+	BBB+	Medium-quality bonds
Baa2	BBB	BBB	
Baa3	BBB–		
Ba1	BB+	BB+	Speculative issues, greater credit risk
Ba2	BB	BB	
Ba3	BB–	BB-	
B1	B+	B+	Very speculative, likelihood of future default
B2	B	B	
B3	B–	B–	
Caa	CCC	CCC	Highly speculative, in default or high likelihood of going into default
Ca	CC	CC	
C	C	C	
	D	DDD	
		DD	
		D	

---

5. In 2012, the minimum fee for a bond rating was about $75,000. Moody's and S&P set the fee at about 5 basis points (or 0.05%) of the issue size. See http://www.bloomberg.com/news/2011-11-15/credit-rating-fees-rise-faster-than-inflation-as-governments-fret-expenses.html. For a review of S&P's rating process, see G. Hessol, "Financial Management and Credit Ratings," *Midland Corporate Finance Journal* (Fall 1985), pp. 49–52.

is the firm trying to hide? If this was an attractive bond issue, the firm would have rated it." In addition, certain types of investors, such as pension funds and insurance companies, may face restrictions against purchasing unrated public debt.

A bond's security or collateral provisions (discussed below) affect its credit rating. Bonds with junior or unsecured claims receive lower bond ratings, leading investors to demand higher yields to compensate for the higher risk. Thus, bond issues of a single firm can have different bond ratings if their security provisions differ.

Viewing Table 10.3, investment-grade bonds are those with ratings of Baa3, BBB–, or better. They are called "investment-grade" as historically investors (individuals and managed funds, such as bank trust department portfolios and pension funds) were allowed to invest in such bonds. Bonds below an investment-grade rating were deemed too risky for such conservative portfolios and were not allowed to be held.

Times and regulations change, however, and bonds that are below investment grade, meaning they have ratings of Ba1, BB+, or lower, have gained a spot in many investment portfolios. Known as **junk bonds** or (euphemistically) **high-yield bonds**, they have more risk but offer higher expected returns and have benefits in lowering unsystematic risk in diversified portfolios. Formerly, issuing companies would seek the highest bond rating possible for new issues for two reasons. First, having high-rated debt added prestige to the company; an AAA-rated firm was viewed as being managed well, financially stable, and strong. In addition, such bonds gave the appearance of a safe investment, and as they had an investment-grade rating, they would find demand by investors such as trust departments and pension funds. The second main reason for seeking a high bond rating is that the higher rating saves the firm interest expense as coupon rates on highly rated bonds are lower than lower-rated bonds because of the risk-expected return tradeoff.

The growth of the high-yield sector of the bond market has attracted investors and issuers. Some firms prefer to issue debt rather than dividend-paying common stock as interest payments are tax-deductible to the issuer. Others, as part of the firm's financial strategy, have issued bonds and used the funds to repurchase shares of common stock. Investors have noted that having junk bonds in a portfolio offers potential return enhancements and may diversify risk.

Over time, the stigma attached to junk bonds has diminished. Issuers and investors are more amenable to these securities. For example, in 1980, fewer than a third of S&P-rated bonds were not investment-quality and many of those were "fallen angels," that is, bonds that were originally issued with an investment-grade rating but whose rates fell into the junk category because the issuing firm ran into financial difficulty.

By the late 1980s, more than half of rated debt was in the high-yield category, and by 2007, over 70 percent of S&P-rated firms had junk bonds outstanding. The number of AAA-rated and AA-rated companies fell from 17 percent of issuers in 1980 to 2 percent in 2007; B-rated bonds, on the other hand, have grown from 7 percent of issues in 1980 to over 40 percent of issues in 2007. Only four nonfinancial firms had an AAA rating in 2013: Automatic Data Processing, ExxonMobil, Johnson & Johnson, and Microsoft.[6]

BONDHOLDER SECURITY

An important attribute of a bond issue that affects its rating is the security, collateral, or assets that are pledged to back the bond issue. In case the bond issuer defaults and misses a payment of coupon interest or principal, the collateral can be sold and distributed to the bond investors. It makes their investment in the issue more secure. There are a number of different types of bonds, each offering different levels of security to their investors.

Mortgage bonds, despite their name, are not secured by home mortgages. Rather, they are backed or secured by specifically pledged property of a firm. As a rule, the mortgage applies only to real estate, buildings, and other assets classified as real property. For a corporation that issues

junk bonds (high-yield bonds)-
bonds with ratings that are below investment grade, that is Ba1, BB+, or lower

INTERNET ACTIVITY

Learn about the rating agencies and their processes at the following Web sites: http://www.standardandpoors. com, http://www.moodys.com, and http://www.fitchratings. com.

6. Reuters, "S&P strips Pfizer's AAA rating on Wyeth acquisition", October 16, 2009, accessed at http://www.reuters.com/article/companyNews/ idUKN1636373320091016 on October 17, 2009; Sereno Ng, "Junk Turns Golden, but May Be Laced With Tinsel, The Wall Street Journal, January 4, 2007, pp. C1, C2; Nicholas Riccio, "The Rise Of 'B' Rated Companies And Their Staying Power As An Asset Class," S&P's *CreditWeek*, January 3, 2007.

first mortgage bonds
backed or secured by
specifically pledged property
of a firm (real estate,
buildings, and other assets
classified as real property)

equipment trust
certificate
a type of mortgage bond that
gives the bondholder a claim
to specific "rolling stock"
(movable assets), such as
railroad cars or airplanes

closed-end mortgage
bond
does not permit future bond
issues to be secured by any of
the assets pledged as security
under the closed-end issue

open-end mortgage bond
allows the same assets to be
used as security in future
issues

debenture bonds
unsecured obligations that
depend on the general credit
strength of the corporation
for their security

subordinate debenture
claims of these bonds are
subordinate or junior to the
claims of the debenture
holders

ETHICAL ISSUES

bonds to expand its plant facilities, the mortgage usually includes a lien, or legal claim, on the facilities to be constructed.

When a parcel of real estate has more than one mortgage lien against it, the first mortgage filed for recording at the appropriate government office, generally the county recorder's office, has priority. The bonds outstanding against the mortgage are known as *first mortgage bonds*. The bonds outstanding against all mortgages subsequently recorded are known by the order in which they are filed, such as second or third mortgage bonds. Because first mortgage bonds have priority with respect to asset distribution if the business fails, they generally provide a lower yield to investors than the later liens. An *equipment trust certificate* is a type of mortgage bond that gives the bondholder a claim to specific "rolling stock" (movable assets), such as railroad cars or airplanes. The serial numbers of the specific items of rolling stock are listed in the bond indenture and the collateral is periodically examined by the trustee to ensure its proper maintenance and repair.

There are two basic types of mortgage bonds. A *closed-end mortgage bond* does not permit future bond issues to be secured by any of the assets pledged as security under the closed-end issue. Alternatively, an *open-end mortgage bond* is one that allows the same assets to be used as security in future issues. As a rule, open-end mortgages usually stipulate that any additional real property acquired by the company automatically becomes a part of the property secured under the mortgage. This provides added protection to the lender.

Debenture bonds are unsecured obligations and depend on the general credit strength of the corporation for their security. They represent no specific pledge of property; their holders are classed as general creditors of the corporation equal with the holders of promissory notes and trade creditors. Debenture bonds are used by governmental bodies and by many industrial and utility corporations. The riskiest type of bond is a *subordinated debenture*. As the name implies, the claims of these bondholders are subordinate, or junior, to the claims of debenture holders. Most junk bonds or high-yield bonds, which we discussed earlier, are subordinated debentures.

Another bond market innovation is "asset securitization." Securitization involves issuing bonds whose coupon and principal payments arise from another existing cash flow stream. Suppose a mortgage lender by virtue of previously issued mortgages has a steady cash flow stream coming into the firm. By selling bonds that use that cash flow stream as collateral, the mortgage banker can receive funds today rather than waiting for the mortgages to be paid off over time.[7] Principal and interest on the newly issued bonds will be paid by homeowners' mortgage payments; in essence, the mortgage payments will "pass through" the original mortgage lender to the investor who purchased the mortgage-backed securities. However, not all the interest payments are passed on; the mortgage lender will be paid a servicing fee from these cash flows to compensate them for collecting the mortgage payments and distributing them to the bond holders.

Securitization allows the original lender to reduce the risk exposure as any homeowner defaults are a risk borne by the investor. In addition, the lender receives new funds, which can, in turn, form the basis for new loans and new issues of mortgage-backed securities. In 2007–2008, the agency issues of this arrangement became clearly known. It led to efforts to encourage loans of questionable quality ("subprime" mortgage loans) as the loans would be packaged and sold to others, and the originator would reap a commission while selling poor-quality loans to others.

Many other cash flow streams are amenable to securitization. Payment streams based on credit card receivables and auto loans have been packaged as bonds and sold to investors. Music artists who collect royalties from past recordings have taken advantage of securitization. In 1997, British rock star David Bowie initiated this trend by his involvement in a $55 million bond deal in which royalty rights from his past recordings were pooled and sold to investors. Interest on the bonds will be paid by the royalty cash flow generated by compact disk, radio playtime and music, and

---

7. Collateralized bonds pledge securities to protect bondholders against loss in case of default. An example of collateralized bonds is collateralized mortgage obligations (CMOs) sold by firms and agencies involved in the housing market. The CMO is backed by a pool of mortgages. Frank J. Fabozzi, *Fixed Income Analysis* (New Hope, PA; Frank J. Fabozzi Associates, 2000) and Frank J. Fabozzi with Steven V. Mann, ed., *The Handbook of Fixed-Income Securities,* 7th edition, (Chicago, IL: McGraw-Hill, 2005).

GLOBAL DISCUSSION

convertible bond
can be changed or converted,
at the investor's option, into
a specific number of shares of
the issuer's common stock

conversion ratio
number of shares into which
a convertible bond can be
converted

conversion value
stock price times the
conversion ratio

callable bonds
can be redeemed prior to
maturity by the issuing firm

call price
price paid to the investor for
redemption prior to
maturity, typically par value
plus a call premium of one
year's interest

call risk
risk of having a bond called
away and reinvesting the
proceeds at a lower interest
rate

call deferment period
specified period of time after
the bond issue during which
the bonds cannot be called

putable bonds
(retractable bonds)
allow the investor to force the
issuer to redeem the bonds
prior to maturity

ringtone downloads.[8] Other innovations include offering bonds backed by pools of insurance contracts. Interest on such bonds is paid from the policy premiums of the contract holders. Many times, however, these bonds have provisions for future payoffs that are affected by the existence of catastrophes such as hurricanes or earthquakes.[9]

TIME TO MATURITY

A straight bond will have a set time to maturity. That is, it will pay coupon interest every six months until the bond matures, at which time the final interest payment is made and the bond's par value is paid to investors. But a variety of features can affect the bond's final maturity.

Geography can play a role. U.S firms routinely issue bonds with ten-year to thirty-year maturities (and even longer in some instances). Bonds in the European market rarely extend their maturity past the seven-to-ten-year range, but this may change as European firms are accessing the capital markets more and are relying on bank debt less for their longer-term financing needs.[10]

A *convertible bond* can be changed or converted, at the investor's option, into a specified number of shares of the issuer's common stock (defined as the bond's *conversion ratio*). The conversion ratio is set initially to make conversion unattractive. If the firm meets with success, however, its stock price will rise and the bond's price will be affected by its *conversion value* (the stock price times the conversion ratio) rather than its value as a straight bond. For example, suppose a firm has issued a $1,000 par value convertible bond. Its conversion ratio is 30 and the stock currently sells for $25 a share. The conversion value of the bond is 30 × $25/share or $750. It makes sense to hold onto the bond rather than convert a bond with a purchase price of about $1,000 into stock that is worth only $750. Should the stock's price rise to $40, the bond's conversion value will be 30 × $40/share or $1,200. Now it may be appropriate for investors to convert their bond into the more valuable shares. Why would a firm issue convertible bonds? Some may do so as way to raise equity at a time when the firm's stock or the overall stock market is out of favor. By selling convertible bonds, they can raise capital and erase the debt from their books when the bonds are converted after the stock price rises.

Callable bonds can be redeemed prior to maturity by the firm. Such bonds will be called and redeemed if, for example, a decline in interest rates makes it attractive for the firm to issue lower coupon debt to replace high-coupon debt. A firm with cash from successful marketing efforts or a recent stock issue also may decide to retire its callable debt.

Most indentures state that, if called, callable bonds must be redeemed at their *call prices*, typically par value plus a call premium of one year's interest. Thus, to call a 12 percent coupon, $1,000 par value bond, an issuer must pay the bondholder $1,120.

Investors in callable bonds are said to be subject to *call risk*. Despite receiving the call price, investors are usually displeased when their bonds are called away. As bonds are typically called after a substantial decline in interest rates, the call eliminates their high coupon payments; investors will have to reinvest the proceeds in bonds that offer lower yields.

To attract investors, callable bonds must offer higher coupons or yields than noncallable bonds of similar credit quality and maturity. Many indentures specify a *call deferment period* immediately after the bond issue during which the bonds cannot be called.

Putable bonds (sometimes called *retractable bonds*) allow investors to force the issuer to redeem them prior to maturity. Indenture terms differ as to the circumstances when an investor can "put" the bond to the issuer prior to the maturity date and receive its par value. Some bond issues can be put only on certain dates. Some can be put to the issuer in case of a bond rating downgrade.[11] The put option allows the investor to receive the full face value of the bond, plus accrued interest. Since this protection is valuable, investors "pay" for it in the form of a lower coupon rate.

8. Karen Richardson, "Bankers Hope For a Reprise of 'Bowie Bonds'" *The Wall Street Journal* (Auguest 23, 2005), pp. C1, C3; anonymous, "Iron Maiden Bank Finishes $30 Million Sale of Bonds," *Wall Street Journal* (February 9, 1999), p. C23.I.S., "Bowie Ch-Ch-Changes the Market," *CFO* (April 1997); see also Patrick McGeehan, "Rock 'n' Roll Bonds Tap Investors' Faith in Future Royalties," *Wall Street Journal* (February 10, 1998), p. C21.

9. Patrick McGeehan, "Investment Banks Are Moving Fast to Offer Securities Backed by Pools of Insurance Policies," *Wall Street Journal* (June 15, 1998), p. C4.

10. Aline van Duyn, "Euro Corporate Bonds Give the Dollar a Run for its Money," *Financial Times* (June 29, 2001), p. 16.

11. Another way to offer protection in the face of a ratings downgrade is for the issues' coupon rate to rise to compensate for the higher credit risk.

extendable notes
have their coupons reset every
two or three years to reflect
the current interest rate
environment and any changes
in the firm's credit quality;
the investor can accept the
new coupon rate or put the
bonds back to the firm

Extendable notes have their coupons reset every two or three years to reflect the current interest rate environment and any changes in the firm's credit quality. At each reset, the investor may accept the new coupon rate (and effectively extend the maturity of the investment) or put the bonds back to the firm.

An indenture may require the firm to retire the bond issue over time through payments to a sinking fund. A *sinking fund* requires the issuer to retire specified portions of the bond issue over time. This provides for an orderly and steady retirement of debt over time. Sinking funds are more common in bonds issued by firms with lower credit ratings. A higher-quality issuer may have only a small annual sinking fund obligation due to a perceived ability to repay investor's principal at maturity.

sinking fund
requirement that the issuer
retire specified portions of the
bond issue over time

INCOME FROM BONDS

A typical bond will pay a fixed amount of interest each year over the bond's life. As we noted above, U.S. bonds pay interest semi-annually while Eurobonds pay interest annually.

Although most bonds pay a fixed coupon rate, some bonds have coupon payments that vary over time. The bond's indenture may tie coupon payments to an underlying market interest rate so that the interest payment will always be a certain level above or will be a specified percentage of a market interest rate, such as the ten-year Treasury note rate. Others, such as the Deutsche Telekom bond issue mentioned above, will have a coupon rate that will increase if the bond's rating falls.

Zero-coupon bonds pay no interest over the life of the bond. The investor buys the bond at a steep discount from its par value; the return to the investor over time is the difference between the purchase price and the bond's par value when it matures. A drawback to taxable investors is that the Internal Revenue Service (IRS) assumes interest is paid over the life of the bond so investors must pay tax on interest they don't receive. Because of these tax implications, zero-coupon bonds are best suited for tax-exempt investment accounts, such as individual retirement accounts (IRAs) or tax-exempt investment organizations, such as pension funds.

Why would an investor purchase a zero-coupon bond? Many bond investors have long-term time horizons before the invested funds are needed (to pay for a child's college education, personal retirement, or other financial goals). Such investors will not spend the bond's coupon interest when it is received; they will re-invest it in other securities. When these investors purchase regular bonds, they face the risk of not knowing what the return will be on the re-invested coupons over the life of the bond. Interest rates may rise, fall, or cycle up and down over the life of the investment. Zero-coupon bonds eliminate this uncertainty by, in essence, locking in the return (the difference between the price paid and the par value) when the bond is purchased.

A large risk faced by bond investors is an unexpected change in inflation. An unexpected increase in inflation can cause lower real returns to an investor as the bond's fixed interest rate does not adjust to varying inflation. In 1997, the U.S. Treasury offered an innovation to investors in U.S. debt: Treasury Inflation Protected Securities.[12] Issued in $1,000 minimum denominations, the principal value of the notes change in accordance with changes in the consumer price index (CPI).[13]

Here's how Treasury Inflation Protected Securities (TIPS) work: Interest payments are computed based upon the inflation-adjusted principal value. In times of rising consumer prices, the principal value and interest payments rise in line with inflation. Should the CPI fall, the principal amount is reduced accordingly. As an example, suppose an inflation-indexed note with a $1,000 par value is sold at a 3 percent interest rate. If inflation over the next year is 4 percent, the principal value rises to $1,000 plus 4 percent or $1,040. The annual interest payment will be 3 percent of $1,040, 0.03 × $1,040, or $31.20. With 4 percent inflation, the principal rises by 4 percent ($1,000 to $1,040) as well as the interest ($30 to $31.20).

Although the principal is not paid until the note matures, the IRS considers the year-by-year change in principal as taxable income in the year in which the change in value is made. In the

---

12. Inflation-adjusted bonds have been offered by other countries for some time. For example, Israel first offered these securities in 1955; the UK in 1981; Australia in 1985; Canada in 1991; and Sweden in 1994.

13. Because of the initial popularity of the inflation-adjusted T-notes, some federal agencies (Federal Home Loan Bank Board, Tennessee Valley Authority) have issued inflation-indexed notes as well.

CONCEPT CHECK

What information does a bond rating give to investors?

How does a collateralized bond differ from a mortgage bond?

Which offer investors greater protection: a mortgage bond, a debenture, or a subordinated debenture? Why?

Explain what a conversion feature does on a bond. What does it mean when a bond is callable?

GLOBAL DISCUSSION

eurodollar bonds
dollar-denominated bonds sold outside the United States

Yankee bonds
dollar-denominated bonds issued in the United States by a foreign issuer

global bonds
bonds that are generally denominated in U.S. dollars and marketed globally

above example, the investor will pay taxes on $71.20, which are the $31.20 in interest received and the $40 increase in principal value. Because of this, these bonds will be most attractive to tax-exempt or tax-deferred investors, such as pension funds and individual IRA accounts.[14] To make the inflation protection more affordable to smaller investors, the U.S. Treasury announced plans in 1998 to offer inflation-protected U.S. savings bonds.[15]

Why are there so many variations in bondholder security, maturity, and income payouts among bond issues? For the same reason why there are different computers, carbonated beverages, and pizza: namely, to meet different needs in the market, or in the case of bonds, to meet the needs of different types of borrowers and lenders. Some borrowers reduce borrowing costs by offering lenders better collateral; others want to maintain flexibility (or they have no collateral to offer), so they issue debentures and pay higher interest rates. From the lenders' perspective, zero-coupon bonds may be attractive as they eliminate reinvestment risk (the risk of reinvesting coupon income at lower interest rates). Similarly, sinking funds or call, put, or convertibility provisions are attractive to different investors in ever-changing market environments.

GLOBAL BOND MARKET

Many U.S. corporations have issued Eurodollar bonds. *Eurodollar bonds* are dollar-denominated bonds that are sold outside the United States. Because of this, they escape review by the SEC, somewhat reducing the expense of issuing the bonds. Eurodollar bonds usually have fixed coupons with annual coupon payments. Most mature in five to ten years, so they are not attractive for firms that want to issue long-term debt. Most Eurodollar bonds are debentures. This is not a major concern to investors, as only the largest, financially strongest firms have access to the Eurobond market. Investors *do* care that the bonds are sold in bearer form because investors can remain anonymous and evade taxes on coupon income. Some researchers believe this is the main reason Eurodollar bond interest rates are low relative to U.S. rates.[16]

U.S. firms aren't the only issuers of securities outside their national borders. For example, foreign firms can issue securities in the United States if they follow U.S. security registration procedures. *Yankee bonds* are U.S. dollar-denominated bonds that are issued in the United States by a foreign issuer. Some issuers find the longer maturities of Yankees attractive to meet long-term financing needs. While Eurodollar bonds typically mature in five to ten years, Yankees may have maturities as long as thirty years. Nonetheless, the euro (€) is becoming a strong competitor to the U.S. dollar for firms that want to raise funds in a currency that has broad appeal to many investors.[17]

Increasingly, the international bond market is ignoring national boundaries. A growing number of debt issues are being sold globally. In 1989, the World Bank was the first issuer of *global bonds.* Global bonds usually are denominated in U.S. dollars. As they are marketed globally, their offering sizes typically exceed $1 billion. In addition to the World Bank, issuers include the governments of Finland and Italy and corporations such as Deutsche Telekom ($14.5 billion raised), Ford Motor Credit ($8.6 billion), Tecnost International Finance (Netherlands) ($8.3 billion), AT&T ($8 billion), Glitnir Bank (Iceland) ($1.25 billion), and Wal-Mart ($5.8 billion).

READING BOND QUOTES

Figure 10.2 shows some of the bond quotation information available in the financial press or Web sites such as http://finance.yahoo.com and http://wsjmarkets.com. The exhibit highlights a bond

14. Gregory Zuckerman, "Inflation-Indexed Bonds Attract Fans," *Wall Street Journal* (May 20, 1999), p. C1; Pu Shen, "Features and Risks of Treasury Inflation Protection Securities," Federal Reserve Bank of Kansas City *Economic Review* (first quarter, 1998), pp. 23–38.

15. In addition, several corporations, such as Merrill Lynch, Morgan Stanley, Household International, Fannie Mae, and Sallie Mae, have issued inflation-protected bonds. Several banks, for example LaSalle Bank and Standard Federal Bank, have inflation-protected certificates of deposit. See Aaron Lucchetti, "Inflation Rears its Head…If Only on New Bond Issues," *Wall Street Journal* (January 28, 2004), pp. C1, C4; Christine Richard, "Corporations, Banks Issue Debt With an Inflation-Wary Hook," *Wall Street Journal* (September 24, 2003), p. C5.

16. W. Marr and J. Trimble, "The Persistent Borrowing Advantage of Eurodollar Bonds: A Plausible Explanation," *Journal of Applied Corporate Finance* (Summer 1988), pp. 65–70.

17. Aline van Duyn, "Euro Corporate Bonds Give the Dollar a Run for its Money," *Financial Times* (June 29, 2001), p. 16.

FIGURE 10.2

Sample Bond Quotation

COMPANY (TICKER)	COUPON	MATURITY	LAST PRICE	LAST YIELD	SPREAD	UST	EST. $ VOL (000S)
Ford Motor Credit (F)	7.000	2018	105.30	6.25	236	5	230,068

quote for a hypothetical bond issued by Ford Motor Credit (Ford Credit), the subsidiary of Ford Motor Company that raises funds to finance car loans and leases.

The ticker symbol (F) refers to Ford's common stock; in stock trading, ticker symbols are used as a shorthand notation rather than full company names. The Ford Credit bond has a coupon rate of 7.000 percent. If its par value is $1,000, as are most corporate bonds, then Ford Credit pays interest of 7 percent of $1,000, or $0.0700 \times 1,000 = \$70.00$ per year or $35.00 every six months. The bond matures (that is, the principal repayment comes due) in 2018. The "Last Price" reports the closing price of the bond, expressed as a percentage of par value. Since its par value is $1,000, a closing price 105.296 percent of par gives a value for the bond of $1,052.96.

A commonly used term that is simple to compute is the current yield of a bond. We calculate current yield by dividing the annual coupon interest by the current price. The Ford Credit bond's current yield is $70.00/$1,052.96 = 6.65 percent. The current yield does not adequately represent the return on a bond investment as it considers income return only and ignores price changes.

The yield to maturity (YTM) is a better measure of investor return on a bond and is shown by the "Last Yield" in Figure 10.2. Yield to maturity represents an estimate of the investor's return on the bond if it was purchased today and held to maturity. We calculate the YTM using the

---

PERSONAL FINANCIAL PLANNING
Investing in Ladders and Barbells

As a first introduction to stocks and bonds, this chapter is filled with applications to personal finance. From knowledge about the different types of stocks and bonds to how to read the stock and bond listings in the paper to basic valuation principles, all these tools and concepts can be used by individual investors as well as professionals.

Let's look at one application for a bond investor. Because of the "seesaw effect," lower interest rates cause bond prices to rise and higher interest rates cause lower bond prices. But the yield curve doesn't just shift up and down over time. Sometimes it twists: This means that short-term rates rise while long-term rates are stable or falling, or long-term rates rise

while short-term rates are stable or falling. To avoid having their holdings hit by sudden moves in short-term or long-term rates, some investors employ a "ladder" strategy.

This strategy invests an equal amount of money in bonds over a range of maturities, so interest rate cycles will average out over the business cycle to reduce the bond investor's risk. Others choose a "barbell" approach, with approximately equal amounts of short-term bonds and long-term bonds purchased. By clumping holdings at either end of the maturity spectrum, investors hope to smooth out the effect of interest rate fluctuations on their bond portfolio.

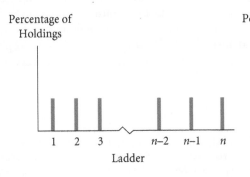

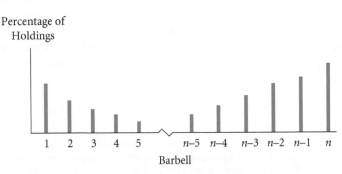

bond's coupon, par value, last price, and time to maturity. Later we will learn to compute a bond's yield to maturity. Here, the yield is presented to us as 6.25 percent.

The "Estimated Spread" is the difference between the YTM on the Ford Credit bond and a similar maturity U.S. Treasury bond. Here, the spread is 236 basis points or 2.36 percent (one basis point represents 0.01 percentage points). The spread is computed from the YTM on a Treasury security that matures in five years, as seen by the number under the "UST" column. Since any corporate bond is riskier than Treasury securities because of default or credit risk, the spread will always be positive. Since the Ford Credit bond has a YTM of 6.25 percent, the five-year Treasury security must have a YTM of about 6.25 percent − 2.36 percent = 3.89 percent.

The "Vol" column represents actual bond trading volume in thousands of dollars for this Ford Credit bond. The market value (quantity traded times last price) of the trading volume is $230,068,000. With a last price of $1,052.96, the approximate number of this type of Ford Credit bond that traded is $230,068,000/$1,052.96 = 218496.

A typical price quote in the financial pages for Treasury bonds is the following:

RATE	MATURITY MO/YR	BID	ASKED	CHG.	ASKED YLD
4.000	Feb 19	100:27	100:28	−1	3.89

INTERNET ACTIVITY

Learn more about the bond market and prices at www.bonds-online.com and www.investinginbonds.com.

The coupon rate for the bond is 4.000 percent of par value, meaning that a $1,000 par value bond will pay $40 of interest annually, in two semi-annual payments of $20. The bond matures in February of 2019. Treasury bond prices are expressed as percentages of par value and in 32nds of a point. The bid price, which is the price received by investors selling bonds, is 100 27/32 percent of par, or $1,008.4375. The ask price, which is paid by investors purchasing the bonds, is 100 28/32 of par or $1,008.75. The bid-ask spread represents dealer profit, or $0.3125 per $1,000 par value bond. Spreads are often an indicator of a security's liquidity; the narrower the bid-ask spread, the greater the liquidity (and, usually, the greater the trading volume). The change in price from the previous day was −1/32 of a percentage point. The YTM, based on the asked price, is 3.89 percent. Note that this is the same bond used as the "UST" bond in the Ford Credit quote in Table 10.1. The five-year Treasury security YTM we estimated above agrees with the data in the Treasury security quote.[18]

CONCEPT CHECK

What is a current yield?

What does the "Est. Spread" mean in the Ford Credit bond quote in Figure 10.2?

corporate equity capital financial capital supplied by the owners of a corporation

stock certificate certificate showing an ownership claim of a specific company

CORPORATE EQUITY CAPITAL

Corporate equity capital is the financial capital supplied by the owners of a corporation. This ownership claim is represented by the **stock certificate**, as shown in Figure 10.3, although today most record-keeping is done electronically. Shares are usually traded 100 shares at a time (called a "round lot") or multiples thereof.

When stockholders sell their shares, the broker forwards the assigned stock certificate to the company and the secretary of the corporation destroys it. A new certificate is issued to the new owner, whose name will then be carried on the stock record. For larger corporations an official transfer agent, generally a trust company or a bank, is appointed for this task. The larger corporations may have an independent stock registrar to supervise the transfer of securities. When an investor sells stock, the stock certificate must be delivered to the stockbroker within three business days (called T + 3). When stock is purchased, adequate funds must be brought to the broker within three business days. As technology advances, so do regulations. In past years, the requirement was T + 5; it is now T + 3; the requirement for T + 1 for settling trades is in the planning stages. Instantaneous settlement, called straight through processing (STP), will occur when all systems are electronically tied together.

---

18. A fine point: the asked yield in the Treasury security quote will slightly understate the true yield to maturity (YTM). It is determined by computing the semi-annual yield given the coupon payments, ask price, and par value and then doubling it. To be exact, we would compound the semi-annual yield over two half-year periods. That is, if the reported Asked Yield is 3.89 percent, the computed semi-annual yield is 3.89/2, or 1.945 percent. Compounding this over two semi-annual periods gives a truer estimate of the YTM, $(1 + 0.01945)^2 − 1$, which equals 3.93 percent.

FIGURE 10.3
Common Stock Certificates

Stock certificates can be kept in the owner's name and in his or her possession. Many investors find it convenient, however, to keep their stock holdings in **street name**. Stock held in street name is kept in the name of the brokerage house, but the broker's accounting system keeps track of dividends, proxy voting, and so on. Some investors find it convenient to keep shares in street name as there is no need for the investor to safeguard the certificates, and delivery of the certificates within the T + 3 time frame is automatic.

Equity securities of the corporation may be grouped broadly into two classes: common stock and preferred stock. We discuss each below.

COMMON STOCK

Common stock (see Table 10.4) represents ownership shares in a corporation. Ownership gives common stockholders certain rights and privileges that bondholders do not have. Common shareholders can vote to select the corporation's board of directors. The board of directors, in turn, exercises general control over the firm. In addition to voting for the board, common shareholders may vote on major issues facing the firm, such as corporate charter changes and mergers.

The common shareholders have a claim on all business profits that remain after the holders of all other classes of debt and equity securities have received their coupon payments or returns. But the firm may wish to retain some of those profits to re-invest in the firm to finance modernization, expansion, and growth. When so declared by the board of directors, owners of a firm's common stock receive dividend payments. The dividend is typically a cash payment that allows shareholders to receive some income from their investment. To many investors, an attractive characteristic of common stock dividends is their potential to increase over time. As a firm achieves success, its profits should grow and the shareholders can expect to see the dollar amount of their dividends rise. Of course, success and growth are not guaranteed. A firm may experience poor earnings or losses, in which case shareholders bear the risk of smaller dividends or the elimination of dividend payments until the firm's financial situation improves.

The common stockholders have the lowest standing when a business venture is liquidated or fails. All creditors, bond holders, and preferred stockholders must, as a rule, be paid in full before

street name
allows stock to be held in the name of the brokerage house

common stock
represents ownership shares in a corporation

TABLE 10.4

Elements of Common Stock

- Represents an ownership claim
- Board of Directors (Board) oversees the firm on behalf of the shareholders and enforces the corporate charter
- Voting rights for Board members and other important issues allowed by the corporate charter
- Lowest claim on assets and cash flow
- Par value is meaningless, and many firms have low or no-par stock
- Dividends: Received only if declared by the firm's Board
              Paid out from after-tax earnings and cash flow; not tax-deductible
              Dividends are taxable when received by the shareholder
              Can vary over time
- Maturity: Never; stock remains in existence until firm goes bankrupt, merges with another firm, or is acquired by another firm

common stockholders receive proceeds from liquidation. As with dividends, all bankruptcy or liquidation proceeds remaining after prior obligations cross-out accrue to the common stockholders, but it is rare when the proceeds of an asset sale from a bankrupt corporation fulfill the claims of creditors and preferred stockholders. Common stockholders generally receive little, if anything, from liquidation proceedings. The common stockholders, therefore, are affected hardest by business failure just as they enjoy the primary benefits of business success.

The common stock of a corporation may be assigned a ***par value***, or stated value, in the certificate of incorporation. It usually bears little relationship to the current price or book value of the stock. It is used mainly for accounting purposes and some legal needs.[19]

Common stock may be divided into special groups, generally Class A and Class B, to permit the acquisition of additional capital without diluting the control of the business. When a corporation issues two classes of common stock, it will often give voting rights to only one class, generally Class B. Except for voting, owners of Class A stock will usually have most or all of the other rights and privileges of common stockholders. Issuing nonvoting equity securities is opposed by some government agencies, including the Securities and Exchange Commission (SEC) because it permits the concentration of ownership control. The New York Stock Exchange (NYSE) refuses to list the common stock of corporations that issue nonvoting classes of common stock.

At times, different stock classes are created following an acquisition of one corporation by another. For example, General Motors' Class E shares and Class H shares were issued in the past to help finance GM's acquisition of Electronic Data Systems (EDS) and Hughes Aircraft, respectively. The dividends on GM's Class E and H shares were related to the earnings of their respective subsidiary.

American depository receipts (ADRs) represent shares of common stock that trade on a foreign stock exchange. The receipts can be traded on U.S. exchanges. We'll learn more about ADRs in Chapter 11, Securities and Markets.

PREFERRED STOCK

Preferred stock (see Table 10.5) is an equity security that has a preference, or senior claim, to the firm's earnings and assets over common stock. Preferred shareholders must receive their fixed dividend before common shareholders can receive a dividend. In liquidation, the claims of the preferred shareholders are to be satisfied before common shareholders receive any proceeds. In contrast with common stock, preferred stock generally carries a stated fixed dividend. The dividend is specified as a percentage of par value or as a fixed number of dollars per year. For example, a preferred stock may be a 9 percent preferred, meaning that its annual dividend is 9 percent of its par or stated value. In such cases, unlike common stock, a preferred stock's par value does have important meaning, much like par value for a bond. The dividend for no-par preferred stock is stated in terms of a dollar amount, for example, preferred as to dividends in the amount of $9 annually. The holder of preferred stock accepts the limitation on the amount of dividends as a fair exchange for the priority held in the earnings and assets of the company.

par value
stated value in the certificate of incorporation; bearing little relationship to the current price or book value of the stock

CONCEPT CHECK

What rights and privileges do common shareholders have that bondholders do not?

What extra risks do shareholders face that bondholders do not?

preferred stock
equity security that has preference, or a senior claim, to the firm's earnings and assets over common stock

---

19. To show further that par value has little significance, consider that most states permit corporations to issue no-par stock.

TABLE 10.5

Elements of Preferred Stock

- Does not represent an ownership claim
- No voting rights unless dividends are missed
- Claim on assets and cash flow lies between those of bondholders (specifically, subordinated debenture holders) and common shareholders
- Par value is meaningful as it can determine the fixed annual dividend
- Dividends: Annual dividends are stated as a dollar amount or as a percentage of par value
  Received only if declared by the firm's board
  Are paid out from after-tax earnings and cash flow; not tax-deductible
  Dividends are taxable when received by the shareholder
  May be cumulative
- Maturity: Unless it has a callable or convertible feature, the stock never matures; it remains in existence until firm goes bankrupt, merges with another firm, or is acquired by another firm

cumulative preferred stock

requires that before dividends on common stock are paid, preferred dividends must be paid for the current period and for all previous periods in which preferred dividends were missed

Thus, unlike with common stock, the par value of a preferred stock is important: Dividends often are expressed as a percentage of par, and the par value represents the holder's claim on corporate assets in case of liquidation. Additionally, when shares of preferred stock are first issued, the initial selling price is frequently close to the share's par value.[20]

Because preferred stocks are frequently nonvoting, many corporations issue them as a means of obtaining equity capital without diluting the control of the current stockholders. Unlike coupon interest on bonds, the fixed preferred stock dividend is not a tax-deductible expense. A major source of preferred stock issues are regulated public utilities, such as gas and electric companies. For regulated firms, the nondeductibility of dividends is not as much of a concern as for other firms because the utilities' tax payments affect the rates they are allowed to charge.

noncumulative preferred stock

makes no provision for the accumulation of past missed dividends

For foreign firms to issue preferred stock, they must do so in the United States. The U.S. security markets are the only public financial markets in which preferred stock is sold.

Preferred stock may have special features. For example, it may be cumulative or noncumulative. *Cumulative preferred stock* requires that before dividends on common stock are paid, preferred dividends must be paid for the current period and for all previous periods in which preferred dividends were missed. Unlike debt holders, the preferred stockholders cannot force the payment of their dividends. They may have to wait until earnings are adequate to pay dividends. Cumulative preferred stock offers some protection for periods during which dividends are not declared.

callable preferred stock

gives the corporation the right to retire the preferred stock at its option

Noncumulative preferred stock, on the other hand, makes no provision for the accumulation of unpaid dividends. The result may be that management may be tempted to declare preferred dividends only when it appears that sufficient earnings are available to pay common stock dividends as well. Practically all modern preferred stock is cumulative.

convertible preferred stock

has a special provision that makes it possible to convert it to common stock of the corporation, generally at the stockholder's option

Callable preferred stock gives the corporation the right to retire the preferred stock at its option. *Convertible preferred stock* has a special provision that makes it possible to convert it to common stock of the corporation, generally at the stockholder's option. This, like many of the special features that preferred stock may have, exists primarily to attract investors to buy securities at times when distribution would otherwise be difficult. Preferred stock that is cumulative and convertible is a popular financing choice for investors purchasing shares of stock in small firms with high growth potential.

participating preferred stock

allows preferred shareholders to receive a larger dividend under certain conditions when common shareholder dividends increase

Participating preferred stock allows preferred shareholders to participate with common shareholders when larger dividend payouts are available. Holders get a larger dividend, if sufficient earnings exist and if common shareholders will be getting a dividend larger than the preferred shareholders. It is a rarely used feature except in some private equity and venture capital investments.

The one tax advantage of preferred stock goes to corporate investors who purchase another firm's preferred. When one corporation buys stock of another firm, 70 percent of the dividend income received by the corporation is exempt from taxes. Thus, for every $100 of dividend income, only $30 is taxable to an investing corporation.

---

20. A recent innovation is *hybrid capital*, a security that is considered equity for accounting purposes but whose payments to security holders are tax-deductible to the firm. Thus, it appears to be a perfect combination of advantages of equity and debt. The details of issuing such capital can be difficult and involve aspects of accounting treatment, securities law, and bank regulation and are, therefore, beyond the scope of our discussion.

CONCEPT CHECK

How is preferred stock similar to a bond? To common stock?

What is meant by the term "cumulative" preferred stock?

READING STOCK QUOTES

Information on stock prices is available for a number of print resources (such as *The Wall Street Journal* and other newspapers with financial sections) and the Internet. Figure 10.4 shows stock quotation information that is available on these print and online resources.

The information from print sources reflects trading that occurred on the previous business day; online information can reflect current trading information but with a 15–20 minute delay in reporting. Information, such as that presented in Figure 10.4, is available on stock prices, recent trends or volatility in prices, the dividend paid by the company, and its earnings per share.

For example, Figure 10.4 shows Microsoft's ticker symbol, MSFT. Tickers are shorthand notation for a stock. Rather than keying in a firm's full name many times only the ticker need be entered to obtain information. Microsoft's stock is traded on the National Association of Securities Dealers Automated Quotation (NASDAQ), an over-the-counter (OTC) exchange we'll discuss in Chapter 11. At the time this information was accessed, the most recent trade for Microsoft stock was for $27.47 a share. If a round lot (100 shares) was purchased at this price the cost of purchasing the shares would be $27.47 × 100 shares = $2,747 plus any commissions. The price of Microsoft stock rose 37 cents from the end of the previous trading day; that means the closing or final price of the previous trading day was 37 cents lower, namely $27.47 − 0.37 = $27.10. If only the price of the final trade of the day is reported (as may be the case for newspaper listings), it will appear under the label of "close" to represent the day's closing price for the stock.

Looking at the information in the second column, we see that Microsoft's stock price has varied from a low of $26.77 to a high of $32.95 over the course of the year (YTD means year to date). Over the past 52 weeks, however, Microsoft's stock has varied from a low price of $25.44 to a high of $32.95. This wide range (about $7, or 30% of the low price) is common. Review for yourself the 52-week ranges of different stocks from a current issue of *The Wall Street Journal*. Many stocks have 52-week ranges where the high price is double that of the low price.

The previous trading day, approximately 36,680,000 shares of Microsoft stock were traded. Many times, the volume is printed in terms of 1,000s (36680) or 100s (366800) to save space.

The column labeled PE gives the price/earnings ratio of the stock. This value is computed by dividing the firm's latest annual earnings per share into its current stock price. Newspaper stock listings report only integer values of PE ratios, so they would list Microsoft's PE ratio as 15. Using the stock's price and the PE ratio, we can compute an estimate Microsoft's earnings per share (EPS):

$$\text{Price/EPS} = 14.9 = (\$27.47)/\text{EPS}; \text{ so our approximation for EPS is } \$1.84$$

INTERNET ACTIVITY

Get stock price quotes online and learn more about stock investing at http://www.fool.com and http://finance.yahoo.com.

Next, the table lists the twelve-month dividend paid by the firm; Microsoft paid $0.92 per share in dividends to its owners over the past twelve months. The final piece of information in the table is the dividend yield of the stock. The dividend yield is calculated as the stock's annual dividend divided by its current price. Since the current price is $27.47, the dividend yield is $0.92/$27.47, or 3.35 percent. In most listings this may be rounded to 3.4 percent.

Dots (...) or "NA" will appear as the dividend or dividend yield for some stocks. This indicates that the firm did not pay dividends in the previous twelve months. Similarly, lack of a number for the firm's PE ratio indicates a firm with a negative net income.

FIGURE 10.4
Stock Quotation Information

FIRM NAME: MICROSOFT	TICKER: MSFT
Market: Nasdaq	YTD range: $26.77–$32.95
Last Trade: $27.47	52 week range: $25.44–$32.95
Change: 0.37	Volume (1000s): 36680
	P/E: 14.9
	Dividend: $0.92
	Dividend Yield: 3.40%

Source: http://finance.yahoo.com, http://www.marketwatch.com, http://moneycentral.msn.com accessed December 23, 2012

As we saw in earlier in this chapter, bonds have different characteristics with respect to time to maturity, coupon income payouts, callable, put options, and so forth. With only a few exceptions, equity has fewer variations. Except for some variations across preferred equity issues (callable, participating, convertible) or different voting rights and dividend rights for common stock, there are not many variations of publicly traded equity issues.

DIVIDENDS AND STOCK REPURCHASES

The process of paying coupon interest on bonds is rather straightforward; it is a legally required payment under the terms of the bond's indenture. Only when a firm contacts the trustee that it will be unable to pay the required interest because of financial difficulty does the process become complex and legalistic.

Dividends, as we've learned, are not a legal obligation of the firm and may be skipped, decreased, increased, stopped, and started according to the collective wisdom of the corporation's board of directors. When they are paid, they are typically paid on a quarterly basis, four times over the course of a year.

Many firms offer shareholders the choice to receive a check for the amount of their dividends or to re-invest the dividends in the firm's stock. ***Dividend reinvestment plans (DRIPS)*** allow shareholders to purchase additional shares automatically with all or part of the investor's dividends. Fractional shares can be purchased and DRIP purchases have no or low commissions.

Suppose an investor owns sufficient shares to receive $10 in dividends on a stock from its quarterly declared dividend. If the stock price is $25, the DRIP program allows the investor to purchase $10/$25 or 0.40 share of the firm's stock. If the stock price is $8, the investor's reinvested dividends will purchase $10/$8 or 1.25 shares of the stock.

If the investor favors the stock and wants to continue holding it, participating in a DRIP is an easy way of purchasing additional shares without any direct cash outlay. It allows income returns to be reinvested to facilitate compounding returns over time. However, as with all dividends, the declared dividend is taxable as income. Whether the dividends are received as cash or reinvested, the investor must pay taxes on them.

HOW DO FIRMS DECIDE ON THE DOLLAR AMOUNT OF DIVIDENDS?

Most firms that issue dividends try to maintain a consistent ***dividend payout ratio***, which is dividends per share divided by earnings per share (EPS). Microsoft's dividend payout ratio, using the information from Figure 10.4 and our calculations, is its dividend of $0.92 per share divided by our calculation of earnings per share, $1.84:

$$\text{Dividend payout ratio} = \$0.92/\$1.84 = 0.50 \text{ or } 50 \text{ percent.}$$

How about the case of a firm that wants to start paying dividends? Microsoft's decision to start paying dividends in 2003 was prompted by its cash balance of $48 billion; its decision to pay a special dividend totaling $30 billion to shareholders in 2004 arose as its cash balance had risen to $60 billion. Suffice it to say, most firms that initiate dividends do not generate as much cash as does Microsoft. Several firms raised dividends or accelerated dividend payments in late 2012 because many feared an increase in dividend tax rates due to the expiration of the Bush tax cuts.[21]

A key component of the "how much?" decision is what level of dividends is sustainable over time? A firm does not want to announce it will begin paying dividends and then have to reduce or eliminate the dividend due to the need to conserve cash. Dividends are thought to send a signal to investors about managements' view of the future cash-generating ability of the firm. Managers and the board of directors have private information about the strategies, competitive responses, and opportunities facing the firm the investing public does not know. Thus, if the firm increases dividends, that is a positive signal or indicator to the financial markets that management believes the future looks stable, or improving, for the firm. A reduction in dividends is taken to be a pessimistic indicator of the firm's future, so firms set dividend levels so future reductions are unlikely given their current perspective on the firm's future.

CONCEPT CHECK

What does the "volume" notation mean in Figure 10.4?

What dividend does Microsoft pay its common shareholders?

What does the PE ratio indicate?

dividend reinvestment plans (DRIPS) allow shareholders to purchase additional shares automatically with all or part of the investor's dividends

dividend payout ratio dividends per share divided by earnings per share (EPS)

21. Dana Mattioli and Alexandra Berzon, "Dividends Come Early To Avoid Fiscal Cliff," *The Wall Street Journal* (November 27, 2012), page B.

target dividend payout policy
a policy of adjusting the dividend payout ratio toward the target dividend payout ratio if the higher earnings appear to be sustainable

special dividend
an extra dividend declared by the firm over and above its regular dividend payout

residual dividend policy
a policy that states that dividends will vary based upon how much excess funds the firm has from year to year

constant payout ratio
a strategy in which the firm pays a constant percentage of earnings as dividends; as earnings rise and fall, so does the dollar amount of dividends

Thus, most firms that start paying dividends will do so at a rather low level, perhaps just a penny a share. The fact that management and the board are sufficiently confident to issue a dividend is a positive signal to the financial markets. As the firm generates more cash, the firm will increase its dollar amount of dividends per share as well as its dividend payout ratio. After a while, the firm will determine a "target" dividend payout ratio that it seeks to maintain over time. However, dividends will not automatically rise along with earnings. If future earnings rise, dividends will not increase until the board feels the higher level of earnings are sustainable. (Remember, firms do not want to ever cut the dollar amount of the dividends per share if they can avoid it.) If the higher earnings appear to be sustainable, the firm will adjust the dividends per share accordingly toward the "target" dividend payout ratio.[22] Some call this the **target dividend payout policy**.

Some firms follow a different dividend strategy of consistently paying a low regular dividend but declaring a **special dividend** when times are particularly good. For a firm in a cyclical industry, with highly variable sales and earnings, this may be a strategy to conserve cash during industry recessions while maintaining the low but stable regular dividend. Shareholders are rewarded when rising earnings allow the company to declare an extra or special dividend. While such a dividend policy may help management control their cash balance, investors, who generally prefer certainty to uncertainty, do not favor such a strategy.

Other dividend payment strategies suffer from the same drawback of creating investor uncertainly due to variable dividend levels. The **residual dividend policy** states that dividends will vary based upon how much excess funds the firm has from year to year. Under a **constant payout ratio** strategy, the firm pays a constant percentage of earnings as dividends; as earnings rise and fall, so does the dollar amount of dividends. Please note that this is not the same as the target payout policy. The firm adjusts dividends around the target over time, depending on earnings sustainability; during some years, the actual payout ratio will exceed the target, and during others, it will be under it in order to have stable, predictable changes in dividends. The constant payout ratio maintains the payout ratio at the expense of varying dollar amount of dividends per share.

The board of directors and management will consider several factors as they examine the level of dividend payout. Some of these factors are the following:

- Ability of the firm to generate cash to sustain the level of dividends. Recall that investors react badly to reductions in dividends. If a dividend level is thought to be unsustainable, the firm's stock price will fall as investors sell the stock.

- Legal and contractual considerations: Dividends, when they are paid, reduce a firm's equity. A firm cannot pay dividends if doing so will reduce the firm's equity below the par value of the common stock. In addition, a bond's indenture (or loan agreement with a bank) may restrict the dollar amount of dividends to ensure adequate cash is available to pay loan interest and principal.

- Growth opportunities. Growing firms require capital, and they will likely want to re-invest all profits into the company to finance expansion and move into new products or markets. Growing firms may seek additional funds from loans, bond issues, and new issues of stock. It is unlikely firms facing growth opportunities will want to initiate or significantly increase their dividends.

- Cost of other financing sources. Dividends are paid, for the most part, from internally generated funds, meaning cash that remains after the firm's bills, interest, and taxes are paid. If a firm has the ability to easily raise low-cost external financing sources, it will be better able to maintain a higher level of dividends. Firms that can raise outside financing, by paying high interest rates or by issuing new shares of stock, will likely have lower levels of dividends.

- Tax rates. Prior to 2003, dividend income was viewed as unattractive by some investors. Why? Because dividend income was taxed as income, at the investors' marginal income

---

22. Discussions of dividend policy theories and practice are available in Julio Brandon and David L. Ikenberry, "Reappearing Dividends," *Journal of Applied Corporate Finance* (Fall 2004), 16 (4), 89–100 and Alon Brav, John R. Graham, Campbell R. Harvey, and Roni Michaely, "Payout Policy in the 21st Century" (April 2003). NBER Working Paper No. W9657. Available at SSRN: http://ssrn.com/abstract=398560 .

tax rate, which exceeded 30% (combined federal and state tax rates) for many. But the Jobs and Growth Tax Relief Reconciliation Act of 2003 reduced the top federal tax rate on dividends from 38% to 15%, the same as the top rate on long-term capital gains. Although surveys of financial officers indicate that tax rates are not a first-order concern when setting dividends, on the aggregate, firms markedly increased dividends after the law was passed. As noted above, President Obama's desire for the top dividend tax rate of 15 percent to rise to 39.6 percent caused some firms to accelerate their early 2013 dividend payments into late 2012.

In addition to giving cash dividends to shareholders, the firm's board of directors can announce other decisions, such as a stock dividend or stock split, that, at first glance, appear to give extra shares and wealth to shareholders. In reality, as we shall see in the next section their effect on the value of a firm's stock and the wealth of shareholders is zero. But the board can make one other decision with respect to the firm's shares that will positively affects shareholders: a stock buy-back or share repurchase program. We'll examine stock dividends, splits, and repurchases next.

STOCK DIVIDENDS AND STOCK SPLITS

A **stock dividend** is what it sounds like: a dividend paid with shares of stock rather than cash. Rather than mention a dollar figure, the announcement will state that the firm is distributing a 5 percent (or "X" percent) stock dividend. But a stock dividend has no net effect on the wealth of the shareholders. To see why, consider the following:

CUL8R Incorporated stock is currently priced at $10 a share, and there are 100,000 shares outstanding; the total market value of the firm is $10 × 100,000 or $1 million. Suppose you own 1,000 shares, meaning you own 1 percent of the shares outstanding and the value of your holdings is $10 × 1,000 shares or $10,000. CUL8R's board has declared a 10 percent stock dividend, so now you own 1,100 shares.

Are you any richer? The answer is no: you still own 1 percent of the shares outstanding, and the value of your CUL8R holdings is still $10,000. You own 1,100 shares, but the number of shares outstanding is 10 percent larger, too. There are 110,000 total shares, and you own 1 percent of this total. Nothing has happened to the value or the earnings ability of the firm with this paper transaction, so the firm's stock price will fall and will equal $1 million / 110,000 shares or approximately $9.09. There are some accounting entries that will affect the firm's equity account, but the total amount of equity in the accounting statements will remain the same.[23] The bottom line is a stock dividend distributes nothing to shareholders and removes nothing from the firm. No value is transferred.

A **stock split** has a similar effect. The firm distributes extra shares for every share owned in a stock split. For example, a firm may announce a two-for-one stock split; this has the effect of doubling the number of shares outstanding and doubling the holdings of each investor, but as in the case of a stock dividend, the net effect on investor wealth is zero. You may own twice as many shares, but the stock price will be cut in half leaving your ownership stake (both in terms of value and percentage owned) the same as it was before the stock split. Occasionally, a firm will announce a "reverse split" in which multiple shares are combined to form one new share. For example, a one-for-four reverse split means four old shares are equal to one new share. When this happens, the stock price will change so again the investor's wealth remains the same.

You may have noted that there is not much of a difference between a stock split and a stock dividend. They involve paper transactions in which the number of shares is increased but prices adjust downward to maintain investor wealth at a constant level. In terms of accounting, a distribution of 5 shares for 4 (a 25 percent stock dividend) is considered to be a stock split; a distribution of less than five for four (less than a 25 percent stock dividend) is considered to be a stock dividend.[24]

CONCEPT CHECK

Why is the decision to reduce dividends not well received by investors?

What policies might a board follow in setting a firm's dividend?

What five influences affect a board's dividend decision?

stock dividend
a dividend in which investors receive shares of stock rather than cash

stock split
a process in which the firms distributes additional shares for every share owned

---

23. The firm's combined value of its par value and additional paid-in capital accounts will rise by the market value of the stock dividend but the firm's retained earnings account will decline by this account, so the firm's equity account remains constant.

24. There is a distinction in what happens to the equity account in the case of a stock split. For a stock split, the only change is to the number of shares outstanding and to the stock's par value (if any). None of the dollar amounts in the equity accounts change. So, if a firm has 100,000 shares outstanding of $1 par value stock and it announces a two-for-one stock split, the number of share outstanding becomes 200,000 and the par value becomes $0.50.

SHARE REPURCHASES

Rather than distribute funds to shareholders in the form of earnings, a firm can repurchase its shares. Why would a firm repurchase its shares of stock? A firm doing small purchases (relative to the total amount of shares outstanding) can acquire shares used in management stock option incentive programs, in which managers can purchase shares of stock at prespecified prices (more will be said about this Chapter 13, Business Organization and Financial Data). Other firms purchase shares of their own stock to use in stock-based acquisitions of other firms. That is, they repurchase shares from current shareholders and then distribute them to owners of a newly acquired firm.

A major reason is to reward longer-term shareholders by enhancing the value of the firm's shares. Increases in stock prices are not taxed until the shares are sold, and if the shares have been held longer than one year, the maximum tax on the increase in value (called a capital gain) is 15 percent for most investors. This tax savings is thought to be a major reason by some researchers for the increase in stock repurchases in recent years.

Another reason for stock repurchases is that the firm has the cash and sees its own stock as one of its most attractive investment alternatives. Rather than investing in expanding the business to new markets, the firm's board of directors and top managers believe the firm's stock is undervalued and offers potential returns. The stock can be purchased at what is perceived to be a low price and re-issued later, after the stock price rises. This is a firm "putting its money where its mouth is." This was a popular reason given for stock repurchases during the 2000–2002 stock market decline. On the other hand, it is an indicator that management is doing a poor job in identifying new corporate strategies for increasing the stock's value.

This section discussed the process of declaring and issuing dividends on equity securities. The following section applies the Chapter 9 time value of money principles to expected cash flows from equity investments. The process of valuation is important to business managers considering ways to issue securities as well as to investors who must make security buy and sell decisions.

CONCEPT CHECK

What is the difference between a stock dividend and a stock split?

What might a firm decide to repurchase shares of its common stock?

What is the tax advantage to investors if funds are used to repurchase shares rather than to pay dividends ?

VALUATION PRINCIPLES

In Chapter 9, we learned how to find the present value (PV) of a series of future cash flows. The present value represents the current worth of the future cash flows (future CF). In other words, it represents the price someone would be willing to pay today to receive the expected future cash flows. For example, we saw an investor would be willing to pay $2,577 to receive a three-year annuity of $1,000 at an 8 percent discount rate.

All securities are valued on the basis of the cash inflows that they are expected to provide to their owners or investors. Thus, mathematically, we have two equations:

$$\text{price} = \left[CF_1/(1 + r)^1 \right] + \left[CF_2/(1 + r)^2 \right] + \cdots + \left[CF_n/(1 + r)^n \right] \tag{10.1}$$

or

$$\text{price} = \sum_{t=1}^{n} \left[CF_t/(1 + r)^t \right] \tag{10.1a}$$

Value or current price should equal the present value of expected future cash flows. Recall from Chapters 8 and 9 that the r represents the appropriate discount rate or the rate of return required by investors. For securities with no default risk (such as Treasury bonds), the r reflects the combination of the real risk-free rate and expected inflation as measured by the nominal risk-free interest rate. For securities with default risk, such as the bonds and stocks issued by corporations, the r represents a nominal risk-free rate plus a premium to reflect default risk.

For illustration purposes, let's assume that a security is expected to pay its owner $100 per year for five years. Let's also assume that investors expect a 10 percent annual compound rate of return on this investment. The 10 percent rate is based on a risk-free rate of 6 percent plus a 4 percent default risk premium. What should be the security's current or present value?

The answer can be determined by using present value (PV) tables, a financial calculator, or a computer software program. For example, using Table 2 (Present Value of $1) in the book's appendix, we can identify the appropriate present value interest factors (PVIF) at 10 percent as follows:

YEAR	CASH FLOW	X	PVIF @ 10%	=	PRESENT VALUE
1	$100		0.909		$ 90.90
2	100		0.826		82.60
3	100		0.751		75.10
4	100		0.683		68.30
5	100		0.621		62.10
				price =	$379.00

Thus, the current or present value of the security at a 10 percent discount rate should be $379.

Notice how the table above resembles a spreadsheet. Indeed, spreadsheets are powerful tools for developing models to evaluate bonds and stocks. Using Excel, we can create a table to do this calculation:

The PVIF formula in cell C6 is: = 1/(1+B2)^A6. In cell C6, the PVIF is computed is 1/(1 + 0.10)^1 or 0.909 (to three decimal places). In cell C7, the interest rate remains the same, but the exponent changes to reflect the fact that the cash flow (CF) is discounted back two years: = 1/(1+B2)^A7. The spreadsheet calculates this as 1/(1 + 0.10)^2 or 0.826. We use the SUM function to add the numbers in cell D11: = SUM(D6:D10).

Of course, since the security's cash flow reflects a $100 five-year annuity, we could have used Table 4 (Present Value of a $1 Ordinary Annuity) in the book's appendix to determine the security's present value (PV) as follows:

$$price = cash\ flow\ annuity \times PVIFA\ @\ 10\%$$
$$= \$100 \times 3.791$$
$$= 379.10$$

PVIFA refers to the present value interest factor of an annuity. Notice that there is a slight rounding error due to the use of three-digit tables.

The security's PV can also be determined by using a financial calculator as follows. First, clear the calculator's memory. Next, enter 100 (or −100 depending on the calculator) using the annuity or payments (PMT) key. Enter 10 and press the %i key. Enter 5 and press the N key. Finally, press the compute (CPT) key followed by the present value (PV) key to calculate the security's current value of $379.08.

Financial Calculator Solution:

Inputs: 5   10   −100

            $\boxed{\text{N}}$ $\boxed{\%\text{i}}$ $\boxed{\text{PMT}}$

Press: $\boxed{\text{CPT}}$ $\boxed{\text{PV}}$

Solution: 379.08

Excel's PV function can compute the present value of an annuity, too. Recall the PV function has the form: PV (periodic interest rate, number of periods, payment, future value, type). To solve for this five-year annuity, we can use the Excel spreadsheet:

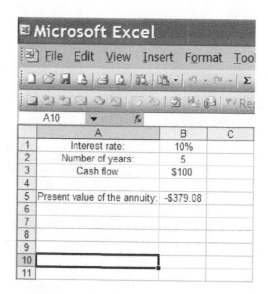

The Excel function in cell B5 will be: = PV(B1,B2,B3,0,0). Cell B1 contains the interest rate; the number of years in the annuity, 5, is found in cell B2; and the periodic annuity payment, $100, is in cell B3. The desired future savings (future value) is zero for the current problem. Since we are computing a regular annuity, we can omit the final item or enter "0" in the final position. The Excel PV function returns a negative number. Recalling the cash flow (CF) diagrams from Chapter 9, if the $100 annuity represents cash inflows to an investor, the present value (PV) must represent an outflow, namely, the price an investor is willing to pay to receive a five-year annuity of $100. By convention, cash outflows are negative numbers and inflows are positive. Should you prefer not to have a negative PV number, simply insert a negative sign before the PV command: = -PV(B1,B2,B3,0,0) so the spreadsheet returns a positive present value:

CONCEPT CHECK

What is the relationship between the present value of future cash flows and the price an investor should be willing to pay for a security?

What does r represent in equation 10.1?

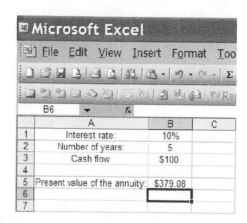

Now we can determine the values of bonds. Conceptually, bond valuation is similar to many of the PV examples covered in Chapter 9.

VALUATION OF BONDS

Corporate and government bonds usually provide for periodic payments of interest plus the return of the amount borrowed or par value when the bond matures. Equation 10-1 can be modified to incorporate these bond cash flows.

DETERMINING A BOND'S PRESENT VALUE

The value of a bond with annual coupon payments can be expressed as follows:

$$
\begin{aligned}
\text{Price} &= \text{PV (expected future cash flows)} \\
&= \left[C_1/(1 + r_b)^1\right] + \left[C_2/(1 + r_b)^2\right] + \cdots \\
&\quad + C_n/(1 + r_b)^n + \left[Par_n/(1 + r_b)^n\right] \tag{10.2}
\end{aligned}
$$

$$
= \sum_{t=1}^{n} \left[C_t/(1 + r_b)^t\right] + \left[Par_n/(1 + r_b)^n\right] \tag{10.2a}
$$

$$
= \text{PV (coupon annuity)} + \text{PV (principal)}
$$

where

Price = the bond's value now or in period zero,

C = the coupon payment,

Par = the bond's principal amount,

r_b = the rate of return required by investors on this quality or risk-class of bonds, given its bond rating; if coupons are paid semi-annually, this is the semiannual required rate of return

In words, we use both equation 9-7 (present value of an annuity) and equation 9-3 (present value of a single amount) to compute a bond's price. We first find the present value of the bond's expected coupon payments. Second, we compute the present value of the bond's principal payment. Third, we add these two present values together to find the bond's price. A point to watch for is the type of bond we are dealing with; Eurobonds pay coupon interest once a year, whereas American bonds pay interest twice a year, delivering one-half of the annual coupon to bondholders every six months. Thus, for American bonds, we need to adjust the calculation of equation 10-2a for semi-annual cashflows. In this circumstance, n, the number of periods, equals

$$n = 2 \times \text{the number of years until maturity}$$

and the required rate of return, r_b, is the semi-annual return. If the market interest rate is given as an annual percentage rate (APR), the semi-annual return is:

$$\text{semi-annual interest rate} = \text{market rate}/2$$

Sometimes the APR is also called a stated annual rate or a nominal rate.

If the market rate is given as 10 percent, stated as the APR, the semi-annual rate is (10 percent/2) or 5 percent.

If the semi-annual interest rate is known, the annual rate is found by doubling it:

$$\text{Annual percentage rate (APR)} = \text{semi-annual rate} \times 2$$

As an example, if we compute or are told that bond's periodic semi-annual return is 3 percent, the APR on the bond is (3 percent × 2) or 6 percent.[25]

---

25. Do you have a credit card? By law, credit card interest rates are quoted on an annual percentage rate (APR) basis. Next time you get your credit card statement, read it over to see the monthly interest rate and the APR. If your monthly interest rate is 1.5 percent, the APR on the credit card is 18 percent (1.5 percent × 12 months). In general, APR = periodic rate × number of periods in a year.

For US bonds, the periodic rate is a semi-annual rate and the number of periods in a year is 2. For a credit card, the periodic rate is a monthly rate and the number of periods in a year is 12.

If you were being charged interest on a weekly basis of 0.5 percent, the APR would be (0.5 percent × 52) which equals 26 percent as we multiply the weekly interest rate by the number of weeks in a year.

Most corporate bonds are issued in $1,000 denominations. To illustrate how a corporate bond's value is calculated, let's assume that a bond with $1,000 face value has a coupon rate of 8 percent and a ten-year life before maturity. Thus an investor will receive $80 ($1,000 × 0.08) annually; for U.S. corporate bonds, half of this annual amount, $40, will be paid every six months with the $1,000 paid at the end of ten years. We determine the bond's present value based on the interest rate required by investors on similar quality bonds. Let's assume investors require an 8 percent rate of return on bonds of similar quality.

With semi-annual coupons, the number of periods is 20 (2 × 10 years) and the periodic (in this case, semi-annual) interest rate is:

$$\text{semi-annual interest rate} = \text{market rate}/2 = 8 \text{ percent}/2 = 4.0 \text{ percent}$$

We need to discount the $40 coupon annuity portion of the bond at the PVIFA at 4 percent for twenty periods, which is 13.590 (see Table 4 in the book's appendix). Since the $1,000 principal will be received only at the end of twenty periods, we use 0.456, the PVIF at 4 percent for twenty years from Table 2 in the Appendix.[26]

Taking these together, we have:

$$\$40 \times 13.590 = \$543.60$$
$$\$1,000 \times 0.456 = \underline{456.00}$$
$$\text{Bond value} = \$999.60$$

Note that an exact answer for the bond's value is $1000; the calculation above is off slightly due to rounding error as the Tables use only 3 decimal places. Had we used 4 or 5 decimal places for the interest factor, the final answer would be closer to $1000. The value of the bond is based upon investors' requirement of a stated annual rate of 8 percent on bonds of this maturity and risk.

Rather than use tables, we can compute bond prices using a financial calculator's functions or with spreadsheets. The spreadsheet format below shows the price of the above bond is $1,000.00:

	A	B	C	D	E
1					
2	Computing Bond Price using APR (annual percentage rate)				
3	Coupon Rate	8.00%			
4	Number of years until maturity	10.00			
5	Number of coupon payments per year	2.00			
6	Par Value	$1,000.00			
7	Market rate	8.00%	(APR)		
8					
9	Compute periodic interest rate:	4.00%	equals B7 / 2		
10	Compute number of periods:	20.00	equals B4 * B5		
11	Compute coupon cash flow:	$40.00	equals (B3 *B6)/B5		
12					
13	Bond price	$1,000.00	equals -PV(B9, B10, B11, B6, 0)		
14					
15					

Suppose that investors required a 10 percent return, or yield, on bonds of similar quality and maturity. The bond must then fall in price to compensate for the fact that only $80 in annual interest is received by the investor. A market return of 10 percent corresponds to a semi-annual

---

26. For bonds paying semi-annual coupons, we must not think in terms of the number of years but rather the number of periods. Because the 4 percent periodic rate of return is a semi-annual rate, we use twenty semi-annual periods of time in both the coupon and par value present value calculations.

return of 10 percent divided by 2, or 5 percent. The appropriate discount factors at 5 percent for twenty years from Tables 2 and 4 in the Appendix would be:

$$40 \times 12.462 = \$498.48$$
$$\$1{,}000 \times 0.377 = \underline{377.00}$$
$$\text{Bond value} = \$875.48$$

Using the above spreadsheet and changing the "market rate" value of cell B7 from 8 percent to 10 percent, we easily find the new price of the bond, $875.38. The spreadsheet's price is more accurate as interest factors from the financial tables are rounded to only three decimal places. The benefit of this calculation with spreadsheets is clear; once we appropriately design the spreadsheet, we can change our inputs or assumptions and see the effect on the bond's price.

	A	B	C	D	E
1					
2	Computing Bond Price using APR (annual percentage rate)				
3	Coupon Rate	8.00%			
4	Number of years until maturity	10.00			
5	Number of coupon payments per year	2.00			
6	Par Value	$1,000.00			
7	Market rate	10.00%	(APR)		
8					
9	Compute periodic interest rate:	5.00%	equals B7 / 2		
10	Compute number of periods:	20.00	equals B4 * B5		
11	Compute coupon cash flow:	$40.00	equals (B3 *B6)/B5		
12					
13	Bond price	$875.38	equals -PV(B9, B10, B11, B6, 0)		
14					
15					

Thus, an investor would be willing to pay about $875 (rounded) for the bond. Although annual coupon payment remains at $80, a new investor would earn a 10 percent return because she or he would pay only $875.38 now and get back $1,000 at the end of ten years. A bond that sells below par value, such as this one, is said to be selling at a *discount* and is called a ***discount bond***. Someone who purchases this discount bond today and holds it to maturity will receive, in addition to the stream of coupon interest payments, a gain of about $125, the difference between the bond's price ($875.38) and its principal repayment ($1,000).

discount bond
bond that is selling below par value

A bond's price will reflect changes in market conditions while it remains outstanding. With its fixed 8 percent coupon rate, this bond will no longer be attractive to investors when alternative investments are yielding 10 percent. The bond's market price will have to fall in order to offer buyers a combined return of 10 percent from the coupon payments and the par value. This is an illustration that bond prices fall as interest rates rise.

If investors required less than a 8 percent (e.g., 6 percent) return for bonds of this quality, then the above-described bond would have a value greater than $1,000; investors would find the bond's 8 percent coupon attractive when other bonds are offering closer to 6 percent. If it was selling to yield a return of 6 percent to investors, the bond's price will rise to $1,149.08 (check this on your own using the Tables; the exact answer from a spreadsheet or financial calculator is $1,148.77). When a bond's price exceeds its par value, it is selling at a *premium*, and it is called a ***premium bond***. The investor who holds the bond until maturity will receive the above-market coupon payments of 8 percent per year, offset by a loss of about $149 (the difference between its purchase price and par value). In most cases where the bond sells at a premium, interest rates have fallen after the bond's issue. This bond's 8 percent coupon rate makes it very attractive to investors; buying pressure increases its price until its overall yield matches the market rate of 6 percent.

premium bond
bond that is selling in excess of its par value

yield to maturity (YTM)
return on a bond if it is held
to maturity

CALCULATING THE YIELD TO MATURITY[27]

Many times, rather than compute price, investors want to estimate the return on a bond investment if they hold it until it matures (this is called the *yield to maturity* or YTM). Financial calculators and computer spreadsheet packages, such as Excel, can be used to find the exact return. An approximate answer for the yield to maturity can be obtained by using the following formula:

$$\text{Approximate yield to maturity} = \frac{\text{Annual interest} + \dfrac{\text{par} - \text{price}}{\text{No. of years until maturity}}}{\dfrac{\text{par} + \text{price}}{2}} \quad (10.3)$$

The numerator of equation 10-3 equals the annual coupon interest plus a straight-line amortization of the difference between the current price and par value. It represents an approximation of the annual dollar return the bondholder expects to receive, as over time the bond's value will rise or fall so it equals its par value at maturity. This estimated annual return is divided by the average of the bond's par value and its current price to give us an approximate yield or percentage return if the bond is held until maturity.

From the example above, we know that if the bond can be purchased for $875, it offers investors a 10 percent return. Let's use equation 10-3 to estimate the approximate yield to maturity if we know the price is $875, annual coupons are $80, and the bond matures in ten years with a par value of $1,000:

$$\text{Approximate yield to maturity} = \frac{\$80 + \dfrac{\$1000 - \$875}{10}}{\dfrac{\$1000 + \$875}{2}}$$

$$= 0.0987 \text{ or } 9.87 \text{ percent}$$

The approximate answer of 9.87 percent is somewhat close to the exact yield to maturity of 10 percent but certainly shows the approximate nature of the formula.

Of course, the use of a financial calculator will give us a precise answer for the yield to maturity. We illustrate the calculation process for a ten-year (or, rather, twenty-period) bond paying interest of $40 per period and a $1,000 principal repayment at maturity. First, we assume the bond is currently trading at $1,000. Second, we assume the price to be $875.48.

Financial Calculator Solution: $1,000 Current Price
(remember to "clear" the time value of money memory before starting any time value calculation!)

Inputs:	20	−1,000	40	1,000
	N	PV	PMT	FV
Press:	CPT	%i		
Solution:	4.00			

Multiply this periodic return of 4 percent by 2 to get the annual percentage rate of 8 percent. Now let's see the yield to maturity when the bond is trading at $875.48:

---

27. The yield to maturity calculation assumes that all coupon cash flows are reinvested at the YTM throughout the bond's life. The realized compound yield (RCY) calculation allows the investor to compute the expected return on a bond using another, perhaps more realistic, return for how the bond's coupons are reinvested. The RCY calculation is done in two steps. First, the future value of all the bond's cash flows is computed using the assumed reinvestment rate. Second, the rate that equates the bond's current price and the future value of cash flows is calculated; this rate is the RCY.

For example, a bond investor may expect interest rates to fall so the reinvestment rate is expected to fall to 6 percent on ten-year bonds. That means the $40 semi-annual coupons are likely to be reinvested at a semi-annual rate of only 3 percent. After ten years (or twenty periods), the future value of the $40 coupons will be $40 x 26.870 (FVIFA factor for 3 percent and twenty years from Table 3 in the Appendix) or $1,074.80. Adding the $1,000 par value we'll receive at that time, the future value of all the bond's cash inflows is $2,074.80. If the current price of the bond is $1,000, the annual RCY is found by solving the future value equation for r: $FV = PV(1 + r)^n = \$2,074.80 = 1,000(1 + r)^{10}$. Solving for r, the realized compound yield is 7.57 percent..

Financial Calculator Solution: $875.48 Current Price

Inputs:	20	−875.48	40	1,000
	N	PV	PMT	FV

Press: CPT   %i

Solution: 5.00

This corresponds to an annual percentage rate of 10 percent.[28]

Given what we know about bonds and our time value of money techniques, the following will be true, if all other influences are kept constant:

- The larger the coupon interest, the higher the bond's price. We've already seen that with a yield to maturity of 8 percent, a ten-year bond that pays annual interest of $80 will have a present value or price of $1,000. A bond that is identical except it has a 10 percent coupon rate will have a price of $50 × 13.590 + $1,000 × 0.456 = $1,135.50.

- The higher the yield to maturity, the lower the price of the bond; the lower the yield to maturity, the higher the bond's price. We have already seen this; when a ten-year bond with an 8 percent coupon sells at an 8 percent yield to maturity, its price is $1,000; when it sells at a 10 percent yield to maturity, its price is $875; its price is $1,149 when the yield to maturity falls to 6 percent. More risky bonds (those with lower bond ratings) will have higher required yields and will sell at lower prices or with higher coupon rates.

CONCEPT CHECK

How do you go about computing a bond's price?

What is a discount bond? A premium bond?

Given two bonds identical in all respects except one pays coupons annually and the other pays coupons semi-annually, which one will have the higher price? Why?

RISK IN BOND VALUATION

Investors in domestic bonds face three types of risk: credit risk, interest rate risk, and reinvestment rate risk. Investors in foreign bonds are subject to two additional risks: political risk and exchange rate risk.

Credit Risk

The cash flows to be received by bond market investors are uncertain; like individuals, corporate debtors may pay interest payments late or not at all. They may fail to repay principal at maturity. To compensate investors for this **credit risk** or **default risk**, rates of return on corporate bonds are higher than those on government securities with the same terms to maturity.

credit risk (default risk) the chance of nonpayment or delayed payment of interest or principal

Government securities are presumed to be free of credit risk. In general, as investors perceive a higher likelihood of default, they demand higher default risk premiums (DRPs). Since perceptions of a bond's default risk may change over its term, the bond's yield to maturity (YTM) may also change even if all else remains constant. Firms, such as Moody's, Standard & Poor's, and Fitch, provide information on the riskiness of individual bond issues through their bond ratings. The bond rating is a measure of a bond's default risk.

The DRP is measured by the difference in the YTM, or spread, of two bonds of equal time to maturity. If a ten-year Treasury note has a yield of 5.4 percent and a ten-year Baa-rated corporate bond has a yield of 7.4 percent, the Baa-Treasury spread of 2.0 percentage points represents the DRP earned by investors who are willing to carry the extra risk of a Baa-rated bond.

Credit risk spreads fluctuate, based upon credit conditions and investors' willingness to take on risk. In good economic times when investors are optimistic, spreads generally narrow; in uncertain times or in a recession, there is a "flight to quality" as investors prefer safer securities and credit spreads widen. Figure 10.5 shows the behavior of spreads between Baa-rated bonds and Treasuries and Aaa-rated bonds and Treasuries over time. During the 2007–2009 financial crisis credit spreads widened to near-record levels. During this time, particular in fall 2008, investors fled from risky securities and sought safety in Treasury securities.

---

28. We can design a spreadsheet to incorporate the inputs and calculation of equation 10-3. We can also use several Excel functions (IRR, YIELD, YIELDMAT) to compute the exact yield to maturity, but their application is too advanced for the current discussion.

FIGURE 10.5

Annual Credit Risk Spreads

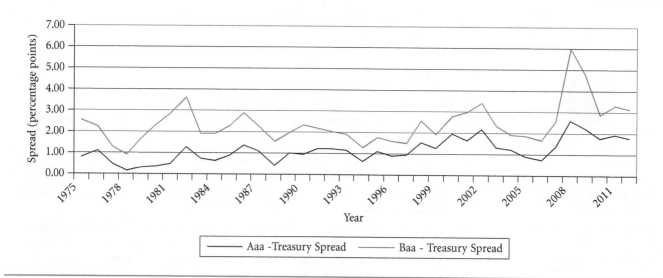

ETHICAL ISSUES

Ethics plays a role in determining a bond's rating. If management, through fraud or accounting gimmickry, make a firm appear more profitable or financially stable, the firm's bonds may have higher bond ratings than they should. After accounting irregularities were discovered at Enron, which at the time was one of the largest energy firms in the United States, its bond rating dropped to "junk" levels and its bank loans came due as a result of failing to meet its loan covenants.

Interest Rate Risk

As we introduced in the discussion of premium and discount bonds, bond prices change in response to changes in interest rates. We know the general level of interest rates in an economy fluctuates. For example, interest rates will change in response to changes in investors' expectations about future inflation rates. In Figure 10.6, we can see the "seesaw effect" means a rise in interest rates renders the fixed coupon interest payments on a bond less attractive, lowering its price. Therefore, bondholders are subject to the risk of capital loss from such interest rate changes should the bonds have to be sold prior to maturity.

A longer term to maturity, all else equal, increases the sensitivity of a bond's price to a given change in interest rates as the discount rate change compounds over a longer time period. Similarly, a lower coupon rate increases the sensitivity of the bond's price to market interest rate changes. This occurs because lower coupon bonds have most of their cash flow occurring further into the future when the par value is paid.

Because of **interest rate risk**, investors will demand a larger risk premium for bonds whose price is especially sensitive to market interest rate changes. Hence, we would expect higher yields to maturity (YTMs) for long-term bonds with low coupon rates rather than for short-term bonds with high coupon rates. The *horizon risk premium* or *horizon spread* is the difference in return

interest rate risk

fluctuating interest rates lead to varying asset prices. In the context of bonds, rising (falling) interest rates result in falling (rising) bond prices

FIGURE 10.6

Relationship Between Current Interest Rates and Bond Prices: The Seesaw Effect

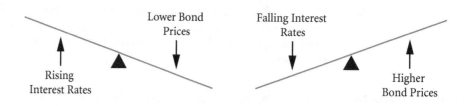

FIGURE 10.7

Horizon (Time) Spreads on Treasury Securities

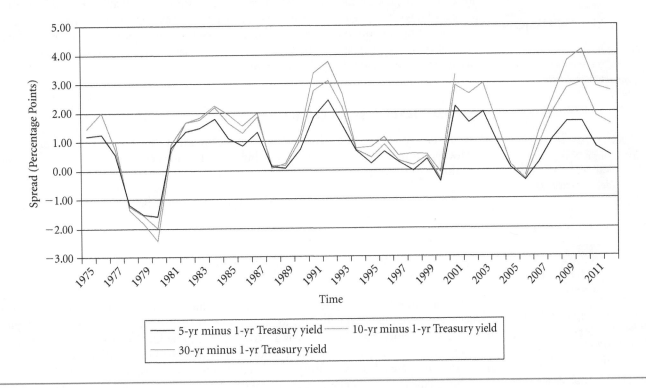

earned by investing in a longer-term bond that has the same credit risk as a shorter-term bond. For example, suppose a five-year Treasury note has a yield of 4.7 percent and a ten-year Treasury note has a yield of 5.4 percent. The difference of 0.7 percentage points is the horizon spread, representing the extra return expected to be earned by investors in the longer-term notes for their exposure to higher levels of interest rate risk. Figure 10.7 shows horizon spreads for five-year, ten-year, and thirty-year Treasury securities, compared with one-year Treasury bills.[29]

The negative spreads around 1979, 2001, and 2006 occurred when the yield curve was inverted and short-term rates exceeded long-term rates. An inverted yield curve typically happens before a recession begins, when short-term rates are rising because of inflationary pressures at the time. In 1983–1985, 1992, and 2009, the yield curve steepened, meaning rates on longer-term Treasury securities rose far above those of short-term Treasury securities. In the cases such as 2008–2009, the financial crisis created a flight to quality even within Treasuries as institutional and corporate funds poured into T-bills, the safest U.S. investment.

Reinvestment Rate Risk

reinvestment rate risk (rollover risk)

fluctuating interest rates cause coupon or interest payments to be reinvested at different interest rates over time

The return an investor receives from a bond investment equals the bond's yield to maturity only if the coupon payments can be reinvested at a rate equal to the bond's yield to maturity. Recall the form of the interest factor in bond price (equation 10-2): $(1 + r_b)^n$. This assumes all the cash flows are reinvested at the periodic rate r_b. If the coupons are reinvested at a lower rate, the investor's actual yield over time will be less than the bond's yield to maturity (YTM). Thus, **reinvestment rate risk** or **rollover risk** occurs when fluctuating interest rates cause coupon payments to be re-invested at different interest rates. Another illustration of reinvestment rate risk occurs when maturing bank CDs are rolled over into new CDs. The risk benefits the investor when the new CD rate is higher than the maturing CD rate; it works against the investor when the new CD rate is lower. It is this risk that zero-coupon securities eliminate as they have no intermediate cash flows requiring reinvestment.

29. The U.S. Treasury did not issue thirty-year securities from 2002 to 2005.

GLOBAL DISCUSSION

political risk
actions by a sovereign nation to interrupt or change the value of cash flows accruing to foreign investments

exchange rate risk
fluctuating exchange rates lead to varying levels of U.S. dollar-denominated cash flows

CONCEPT CHECK

What risks do domestic bond investors face?

What is the seesaw effect?

What special risks do investors in foreign bonds face?

Risks of Nondomestic Bonds

Investors in nondomestic securities face a number of risks beyond those of domestic securities. Among these are political risk and exchange rate risk. *Political risk* can affect a bond investor in a number of ways. A foreign government may block currency exchanges, preventing the investor from repatriating coupon income. Social unrest may lead a foreign corporation to default on its bonds. Of course, exchange rate changes will cause fluctuations in the values of cash flows in terms of U.S. dollars, and this is called *exchange rate risk*.

VALUATION OF STOCKS

All securities are valued on the basis of the cash inflows that they are expected to provide to their owners or investors. We saw the following in the previous chapter and in the above bond discussion:

$$\text{price} = [CF_1/(1 + r)^1] + [CF_2/(1 + r)^2] + \cdots + [CF_n/(1 + r)^n] \tag{10.1}$$

or

$$\text{price} = \sum_{t=1}^{n} \left[CF_t/(1 + r)^t \right] \tag{10.1a}$$

Value or current price should equal the present value (PV) of expected future cash flows. Earlier, we applied this general formula to the case of bond pricing. The cash flows from a typical bond are straightforward: The bond has a known and definite life, has fixed coupon payments paid on a regular basis, pays a known par value or principal when the bond matures, and should have a discount rate (yield to maturity) close to that of bonds with similar credit ratings.

Although the principle for determining an appropriate stock price is the same as that for determining a bond price, equity does not offer the certainty of bond cash flows. Common and preferred stocks are generally assumed to have infinite lives. For common stock, relevant cash flows (dividend payments) will likely vary over time. Finally, determining an appropriate rate at which to discount future dividends is difficult. Despite these difficulties, in this section, we will see that the present value (PV) of all future dividends should equal a stock's current price, and that some simplifying assumptions can make the task of determining stock value easier. Our discussion in this section focuses on common stock. As we will see, the method for valuing preferred stock is a special case of common stock valuation.

It may seem rather strange to treat the stock price as nothing more than the PV of all future dividends. Who buys stock with no intention of ever selling it, even after retirement? Investors generally buy stock with the intention of selling it at some future time ranging from a few hours to thirty years or longer. Despite the length of any one investor's time horizon, the current price of any dividend-paying common stock should equal the PV of all future dividends:[30]

$$\text{price} = \sum_{t=1}^{n} \left[D_t/(1 + r_s)^t \right] \tag{10.4}$$

What if a corporation currently pays no dividends and has no plans to pay dividends in the foreseeable future? The value of this company's stock will not be zero. First, because the firm has no plans to pay dividends does not mean that it never will. To finance rapid growth, young firms

---

30. Here is the intuition behind this statement. A stock is purchased today, in year T, with the plan of selling it in year T + 1. What should its current price be? The current price should equal the present value of dividends over year T and the selling price in year T + 1.

What will be the price of the stock in year T + 1? Suppose another investor plans on buying the stock at the beginning of year T + 1 and selling it a year later in year T + 2. As before, the price of the stock at the beginning of year T + 1 should be the present value of the dividends paid in year T + 1 plus the selling price in year T + 2.

Through substitution, today's price will be the present value of the dividends in year T and T + 1 plus the expected selling price in year T + 2. We can continue extending this exercise through many years: year T + 3, T + 4, and so on. The result is that today's stock price will be the sum of the present value of future dividends.

often retain all their earnings; when they mature, they often pay a portion of earnings as dividends. Second, although the firm may not pay dividends to shareholders, it may be generating cash (or have the potential to do so). The firm's new owner can claim the cash or profits if the firm is acquired or merged, so its current price should reflect this value. Third, at the least, the firm's stock should be worth the per-share liquidation value of its assets; for a going concern, the firm is worth the discounted cash flow value that can be captured by an acquirer.

Estimating all future dividend payments is impractical. Matters can be simplified considerably if we assume that the firm's dividends will remain constant or will grow at a constant rate over time.

VALUING STOCKS WITH CONSTANT DIVIDENDS

If the firm's dividends are expected to remain constant, so that $D_0 = D_1 = D_2...$, we can treat its stock as a perpetuity. We know that preferred stock dividends are constant over time, so this situation is most applicable for valuing shares of preferred stock. The present value (PV) of a perpetuity is the cash flow (CF) divided by the discount rate. For stocks with constant dividends, this means equation 10-4 becomes the following:

$$P_0 = D_0/r_s \qquad (10.5)$$

Many preferred stocks are valued using equation 10-5 since preferred stocks typically pay a constant dollar dividend and do not usually have finite lives or maturities. For example, if the FY Corporation's preferred stock currently pays a $2.00 dividend and investors require a 10 percent rate of return on preferred stocks of similar risk, the preferred stock's present value is the following:

$$P_0 = \$2.00/0.10 = \$20.00$$

For a preferred stock with no stated maturity and a constant dividend, changes in price will occur only if the rate of return expected by investors changes.

VALUING STOCKS WITH CONSTANT DIVIDEND GROWTH RATES

Many firms have sales and earnings that increase over time; their dividends may rise, as well. If we assume that a firm's dividends grow at an annual rate of g percent, next year's dividend, D_1, will be $D_0(1 + g)$; the dividend in two years' time will be $D_0(1 + g)^2$. Generalizing, we have the following:

$$D_t = D_0(1 + g)^t$$

Equation 10-4 can be shown in expanded form in this way:

$$P_0 = [D_0(1 + g)]/(1 + r_s) + [D_0(1 + g)^2]/(1 + r_s)^2 + [D_0(1 + g)^3]/(1 + r_s)^3 + \cdots$$

As long as the dividend growth rate g is less than the discount rate r_s, each future term will be smaller than the preceding term. Although, technically, there are an infinite number of terms, the present value (PV) of dividends received farther into the future will move closer to zero. By accepting that the sum of all these terms is finite, equation 10-4 becomes the following:

$$P_0 = D_1/(r_s - g) \qquad (10.6)$$

Gordon model (constant dividend growth model) a means of estimating common stock prices by assuming constant dividend growth over time

This result is known as the **Gordon model** or the **constant dividend growth model**. The model assumes that a dividend is currently being paid, and this dividend will grow or increase at a constant rate over time. Of course, the assumption of constant growth in dividends may be unrealistic for a firm that is experiencing a period of high growth (or negative growth, that is, declining revenues). Neither constant dividend growth will be a workable assumption for a firm whose dividends rise and fall over the business cycle.

Let's assume the cash dividend per share for XYZ Company for last year was $1.89 and is expected to be $2.05 at the end of this year. This represents a percentage increase of 8.5 percent [($2.05 - $1.89)/$1.89]. If investors expect a 12 percent rate of return, then the estimated current stock value (P_0) would be the following:

$$P_0 = \$1.89(1.085)/(0.12 - 0.085) = (\$2.05/0.035) = \$58.59$$

Thus, if investors believed that the cash dividends would grow at a 8.5 percent rate indefinitely into the future and expected a 12 percent rate of return, they would pay $58.59 for the stock.

A simple spreadsheet can compute stock price using the constant growth assumption:

	A	B	C
1			
2	Constant dividend growth model		
3			
4	Current dividend	$1.89	
5	Expected dividend growth rate	8.50%	
6	Required rate of return	12.00%	
7			
8	Estimated stock price	$58.59	=B4*(1+B5)/(B6-B5)
9			

From this discussion, we can see there are four major influences on a stock's price. First is the firm's earnings per share (EPS), and second is the firm's dividend payout ratio; together, they determine a firm's dollar amount of dividends. The third influence is the firm's expected growth rate in dividends, which will be affected by a number of firm, industry, and economic influences. The fourth is the shareholders' required return; from Chapter 8, we know this return is affected by the real interest rate in the economy, the expected inflation rate, and a risk premium to compensate investors for purchasing risky equities.

We can use the Gordon model to solve for any of the four unknown variables (price, dividends, required return, and growth) as long as we know the other three. For example, rearranging equation 10-4, we can use the market price of the stock to calculate the market's required return for the stock:

$$r_s = D_1/P_0 + g$$

that is, the dividend yield plus the expected growth rate. Similarly, using an estimate for the required return, we can estimate the market's consensus estimate for future dividend growth:

$$g = (P_0 \cdot r - D_0)/(P_0 + D_0)$$

INTERNET ACTIVITY

Examine estimates on the future earnings of firms at http://www.zacks.com and http://www.whispernumber.com. Another great resource of stock analysis is http://www.fool.com.

This is especially valuable as a check against over-optimism on the part of investors when valuing a growth stock, that is, one whose earnings are expected to continue growing at a fast rate over time. At the height of the Internet stock bubble in 1999–2000, stocks of technology firms were priced assuming that 20–30 percent growth or higher was expected indefinitely. Such growth is impossible for long periods of time, so it was only a matter of time that their stock prices tumbled after slower sales resulted in slower earnings and cash flow growth for these firms.

ETHICAL ISSUES

CONCEPT CHECK

What challenges must be faced when determining a value for a firm's common shares?

What risks do shareholders face that can lead to fluctuations in share values?

INTERNET ACTIVITY

Read analyses and expectations of overseas economic activity from sites such as http://www.morganstanley.com (search for "Global Economic Forum") and download exchange rate data from Web sites such as http://www.federalreserve.gov/econresdata/statisticsdata.htm.

GLOBAL DISCUSSION

RISK IN STOCK VALUATION

Investors in common stocks face a number of risks that bondholders do not. This additional risk leads them to require a higher rate of return on a firm's stock than on its debt securities. For example, in the event of corporate failure, the claims of stockholders have lower priority than those of bondholders. So, stockholders face a greater risk of loss than bondholders. Dividends can be variable and omitted, whereas bond cash flows have a legal obligation to be met.

Poor ethical decisions and poor management are another source of risk for stock investors in that such decisions can lower future cash flows and raise the required rate of return demanded by future investors. Accounting gimmickry and decisions by self-serving managers (more will be said about this in Chapter 11) can hurt stock prices as happened with Enron, WorldCom, and Tyco. Poor customer/supplier relations, allegations of poor-quality products, and poor communications, as occurred between Ford Motor Company and one of its tire suppliers, Firestone, hurt both companies and their shareholders.

If the general level of interest rates rises, investors will demand a higher required rate of return on stocks to maintain their risk premium differential over debt securities. This will force stock prices downward. Therefore, stockholders risk losses from any general upward movement of market interest rates.

Also, future dividends, or dividend growth rates, are not known with certainty at the time stock is purchased. If poor corporate performance or adverse general economic conditions lead investors to lower their expectations about future dividend payments, this will lower the present value of shares of the stock, leaving the stockholder with the risk of capital loss. Stock analysts systematically review economic, industry, and firm conditions in great detail to gain insight into corporate growth prospects and the appropriate level of return that an investor should require of a stock.

VALUATION AND THE FINANCIAL ENVIRONMENT

The price of an asset is the present value of future cash flows; the discount rate used in the present value calculation is the required rate of return on the investment. Future cash flows of firms and the required returns of investors are affected by the global and domestic economic environments and the competition faced by firms. Slower sales or higher expenses can harm a firm's ability to pay its bond interest or dividends or to re-invest in its future growth. Besides affecting cash flows, these can affect investors' required rates of return by increasing risk premiums or credit spreads. Inflation pressures and capital market changes influence the level of interest rates and required returns.

GLOBAL ECONOMIC INFLUENCES

Two main overseas influences will affect firms.[31] The first is the condition of overseas economies. Growth in foreign economies will increase the demand for U.S. exports. Similarly, sluggish foreign demand will harm overseas sales and hurt the financial position of firms doing business overseas. The rate of economic growth overseas can affect the conditions faced by domestic firms, too, as growing demand globally may make it easier to raise prices and sluggish demand overseas may lead to intense competition in the U.S. market.

The second influence is the behavior of exchange rates, the price of a currency in terms of another currency. A change in exchange rates over time has two effects on the firm. Changing exchange rates lead to higher or lower U.S. dollar cash flows from overseas sales, more competitively priced import goods, or changing input costs. Thus, changing exchange rates affect profitability by influencing sales, price competition, and expenses. Changing exchange rates also affect the level of domestic interest rates. Expectations of a weaker U.S. dollar can lead to higher U.S. interest rates; to attract capital, U.S. rates will have to rise to compensate foreign investors for expected currency losses because of the weaker dollar.[32] Conversely, a stronger dollar can result in lower U.S. interest rates.

---

31. By "overseas," we refer to events outside of the domestic economy, whether water separates the countries or not. Thus, although we share land borders, to a U.S. firm, the economies of Canada and Mexico are overseas economies.

32. To understand this effect, suppose initially the exchange rate between the U.S. dollar and euro is $1 = €1. Analysts anticipate the dollar will weaken over the year to $1 = €0.95. The European investor who invests 11 for every $1 of investment now expects to receive only €0.95 next year. The investor will require a higher expected return on his U.S. investment to compensate for the effects of the weakening dollar. This is similar to a U.S. investor seeking protection from anticipated inflation by increasing the required rate of return to reflect inflationary expectations.

INTERNET ACTIVITY

The Economic Report of the President is available on the Internet, as are its data tables; see also the Economics Briefing Room of the White House http://www.whitehouse.gov/ economy. Other good sources of domestic economic analysis and data include the Federal Reserve's Web site, http:// www.federalreserve.gov; see especially the Beige Book analysis of economic conditions across the regions of the country. The St. Louis Federal Reserve's Web site, http:// www.stlouisfed.org, has links to the FRED database and to education and analysis sites.

INTERNET ACTIVITY

Some industry analyses and information is available on Web sites such as http:// finance.yahoo.com and www.hoovers.com. Other helpful information on industries is available from trade groups. Use of a Web search engine can help you find these sources.

CONCEPT CHECK

How can the growth of overseas economies affect the value of a U.S. firm's stock?

Why do stock and bond investors need to be aware of expectations in the exchange rate market?

How do fiscal policy, monetary policy, and consumer spending affect the outlook for securities markets?

How does competition affect a firm's profits over time?

DOMESTIC ECONOMIC INFLUENCES

Individuals can spend only what they have (income and savings) or what their future earning capacity will allow them to borrow. Consumption spending (spending by individuals for items such as food, cars, clothes, computers, and so forth) comprises about two-thirds of gross domestic product (GDP) in the United States. Generally, higher disposable incomes (that is, income after taxes) lead to higher levels of consumption spending. Higher levels of spending mean inventories are reduced and companies need to produce more and hire additional workers to meet sales demand. Corporations will spend to obtain supplies and workers based upon expectations of future demand. Similarly, they will invest in additional plant and equipment based upon expected future sales and income. Economic growth results in higher levels of consumer spending and corporate investment, which in turn stimulates job growth and additional demand. Slow or negative growth can lead to layoffs, pessimistic expectations, and reduced consumer and corporate spending. These effects will directly influence company profits and cash flows.

Economic conditions affect required returns, too. Investors will be more optimistic in good economic times and more willing to accept lower risk premiums on bond and stock investments. In poor economic times, credit spreads will rise as investors want to place their funds in safer investments.

Governments shape the domestic economy by fiscal policy (government spending and taxation decisions) and monetary policy. These decisions may affect consumer disposable income (fiscal policy) and the level of interest rates and inflation expectations (monetary policy) and therefore affect the valuation of the bond and stock markets.

Some industry sectors are sensitive to changes in consumer spending. Sales by auto manufacturers, computer firms, and other manufacturers of high-priced items will rise and fall by greater amounts over the business cycle than food or pharmaceutical firms. Changes in interest rates affect some industries more than others, too: banks and the housing industry (and sellers of large household appliances) are sensitive to changes in interest rates more than, say, book and music publishers or restaurants.

INDUSTRY AND COMPETITION

A firm's profits are determined by its sales revenues, expenses, and taxes. We have mentioned taxes and some influences on sales and expenses in our discussion of global and domestic economies, but industry competition and the firm's position within the industry will have a large impact on its ability to generate profits over time. Tight competition means it will be difficult to raise prices to increase sales revenue or profitability. Nonprice forms of competition, such as customer service, product innovation, and the use of technology to the fullest extent in the manufacturing and sales process, may hurt profits by increasing expenses if the features do not generate sufficient sales. Competition may not come only from similar firms; for example, a variety of "entertainment" firms, from music to theater to movies to sports teams, vie for consumers' dollars. Trucking firms and railroads compete for freight transportation; cable and satellite firms compete in the home television markets (and for Internet service, along with telephone service providers). Changes in the cost and availability of raw materials, labor, and energy can adversely affect a firm's competitive place in the market.

The influences of competition and supply ultimately affect a firm's profitability and investors' perceptions of the firm's risk. This, in turn, will affect its bond and stock prices. The most attractive firms for investing will be firms with a competitive advantage over their rivals. They may offer a high-quality product, be the low-cost producer, be innovators in the use of technology, or offer the best customer support. Whatever the source of the advantage, if a firm can build and maintain its advantage over time, it will reap above-normal profits and be an attractive investment.

APPLYING FINANCE TO...

INSTITUTIONS AND MARKETS	INVESTMENTS	FINANCIAL MANAGEMENT
Bond and stock trading occurs in capital markets. Some institutions, such as investment banks, facilitate trading of these securities and develop different variations (e.g., callable, putable) to meet the needs of different kinds of issuers and investors. For other institutions, bonds and stocks are another means of supplying capital in addition to bank loans, private placements, mortgages, and so forth to those needing access to funds.	Bonds and stocks are tools used by investors; they are purchased in an attempt to meet an investor's goals and risk preferences over the investor's time horizon.	These securities are a source of long-term financing for asset acquisition, implementing long-term strategies, and acquiring other firms.

SUMMARY

One purpose of this chapter has been to examine the characteristics of bonds and stocks. A second major purpose has been to determine security values by applying time-value-of-money techniques to the cash flows that investors receive from bond and stock investments. The current price of the securities should equal the present value of future expected cash flows. If security prices are known, these techniques can be used to estimate investment returns.

Stock and debt offerings are major sources of long-term funds for businesses. Bonds offer investors a fixed-income flow and priority in terms of liquidation. Bond covenants, which are found in the indenture, list some of the obligations of the issuer toward the bondholders. Bonds can be secured by corporate assets or be unsecured; unsecured bonds are called debentures. Bond ratings assess the collateral underlying the bonds as well as the ability of the issuers to make timely payments of interest and principal. Bonds can be sold overseas by U.S. issuers; non-U.S. firms can issue bonds in the United States, as long as Securities and Exchange Commission (SEC) requirements are fulfilled.

Most equity offerings are sales of common stock. Preferred stock gives holders preference over common shareholders with respect to dividends and liquidation, but unlike the common shareholders, the (usually) fixed dividend received by preferred shareholders does not allow them to enjoy the benefits of future profit growth. Many investors buy common shares expecting dividends to rise over time.

The financial system and the economic environment are inseparable inputs to analyzing stocks and bonds. Firms' cash flows, and the outlook for their stock and bond issues, are affected by the global economy and domestic economy as growth overseas and at home will affect demand for the firm's products and will affect its costs, too. Industry competition and technological change can make last year's "sure thing" become this year's bankruptcy filing. Changing demand and supply for funds, fluctuating exchange rates, and monetary policy will influence inflationary expectations and required returns on securities. Much of what was learned in economics and in Part 1 of this book has implications for the behavior of the bond and stock market over time.

KEY TERMS

bonds

bond rating

call deferment periods

call price

call risk

callable bond

callable preferred stock

closed-end mortgage bond

collateralized bonds

common stock

constant payout policy

conversion ratio

conversion value

convertible bond

convertible preferred stock

corporate equity capital

coupon payments

covenants

cumulative preferred stock

credit risk (default risk)

debenture bonds

discount bond

dividend payout ratio

dividend reinvestment plan (DRIP)

equipment trust certificate

Eurodollar bonds

exchange rate risk

extendable notes

face value

financial assets

global bonds

Gordon model (constant dividend growth model)

interest rate risk

junk bonds or high-yield bonds

mortgage bonds

noncumulative preferred stock	reinvestment rate risk	stock split
open-end mortgage bond	residual dividend policy	street name
par value	retractable bonds	subordinated debenture
political risk	rollover risk	target dividend payout policy
preferred stock	sinking fund	trustee
premium bond	special dividend	trust indenture
putable bonds	stock certificate	Yankee bonds
registered bonds	stock dividend	yield to maturity (YTM)

DISCUSSION QUESTIONS

1. Describe the relationship between internal and external financing in meeting the long-term financial needs of a firm.

2. What are the major sources of long-term funds available to business corporations? Indicate their relative importance.

3. Why would firms raise capital in markets other than their domestic or home market?

4. Can only large institutional investors purchase bonds? Explain.

5. How does a Treasury Information Protected Securities (TIPS) bond differ from the typical U.S. Treasury security?

6. Describe what is meant by bond covenants.

7. What are bond ratings?

8. Briefly describe the types of bonds that can be issued to provide bondholder security.

9. What is meant by the following terms: convertible bonds, callable bonds, putable bonds, and Eurodollar bonds?

10. Why are investment-grade bonds given that name? Why are junk bonds known as high-yield bonds?

11. Why might a firm want to maintain a high bond rating? What has been happening to bond ratings in recent years?

12. Why might an investor find a zero-coupon bond an attractive investment?

13. Briefly describe how securities are valued.

14. Describe the process for valuing a bond.

15. What is meant by the yield to maturity (YTM) on a bond?

16. Briefly describe the types of risk faced by investors in domestic bonds. Indicate the additional risks associated with nondomestic bonds.

17. What risk does a zero-coupon bond address?

18. According to the behavior of interest rates in Figure 10.5, were investors more concerned or less concerned about risk over the 2002–2006 time period? Explain.

19. What does it mean when the horizon spreads in Figure 10.7 dip below the X-axis? Why do some feel that this was not to be the case in 2006?

20. How do you think credit spreads behave over the course of the economic cycle?

21. What is a "flight to quality?" Under what economic conditions might we see this?

22. Why study stocks if the net amount of stock issues is negative?

23. Why should investors consider common stock as an investment vehicle if they have a long-term time horizon?

24. Why does dividend income growth exceed that of bond income growth over a period of time?

25. What is a capital gain? Is it taxed the same way as dividends?

26. "Taxes on capital gains can be deferred." Explain what this statement means.

27. Explain how a capital loss on the sale of a firm's stock can affect an investor's taxes.

28. What is a round lot of common stock?

29. Describe some of the characteristics of common stock.

30. List and briefly explain the special features usually associated with preferred stock.

31. How do firms decide how much of their earnings to distribute as dividends?

32. Explain how an investor may view a stock dividend, a stock split, and a stock repurchase plan with regards to the value of his stock holdings.

33. Briefly describe how securities are valued.

34. Describe the process for valuing a preferred stock.

35. Describe the process for valuing a common stock when the cash dividend is expected to grow at a constant rate.

36. Discuss the risks faced by common shareholders that are not related to the general level of interest rates.

37. Under what economic forecast would you believe an auto manufacturer would be a good investment? A computer manufacturer?

38. Discuss how changes in exchange rates can affect the outlook for both global and domestic firms.

39. What can looking at data on inventories tell us about the condition of the economy? Data on business expansion or investment plans?

40. Is industry competition good or bad if you are looking for attractive stock investments?

41. Give examples of firms you believe have been successful over time because they are industry leaders in quality; they are the low-cost producer; they are innovative; they offer superior customer service.

42. Energy prices are forecast to go higher. How would this affect your decision to purchase the stocks of

a. ExxonMobil?

b. American Airlines?

c. Ford Motor Company?

d. Archer Daniels Midland, a food processor?

EXERCISES

1. Compute the annual interest payments and principal amount for a Treasury Inflation Protected Security (TIPS) with a par value of $1,000 and a 3 percent interest rate if inflation is 4 percent in year one, 5 percent in year two, and 6 percent in year three.

2. Judy Johnson is choosing between investing in two Treasury securities that mature in five years and have par values of $1,000. One is a Treasury note paying an annual coupon of 5.06 percent. The other is a TIPS which pays 3 percent interest annually.

   a. If inflation remains constant at 2 percent annually over the next five years, what will be Judy's annual interest income from the TIPS bond? From the Treasury note?

   b. How much interest will Judy receive over the five years from the Treasury note? From the TIPS?

   c. When each bond matures, what par value will Judy receive from the Treasury note? The TIPS?

   d. After five years, what is Judy's total income (interest + par) from each bond? Should she use this total as a way of deciding which bond to purchase?

3. Using the regular Treasury note of problem 2:

   a. What is its price if investors' required rate of return is 6.0 percent on similar bonds? Treasury notes pay interest semi-annually.

   b. Erron Corporation wants to issue five-year notes but investors require a credit risk spread of 3 percentage points. What is the anticipated coupon rate on the Erron notes?

4. Assume a $1,000 face value bond has a coupon rate of 8.5 percent, pays interest semi-annually, and has an eight-year life. If investors are willing to accept a 10 percent rate of return on bonds of similar quality, what is the present value or worth of this bond?

5. See Problem 4 to answer these two questions.

   a. By how much would the value of the bond in Problem 4 change if investors wanted an 8 percent rate of return?

   b. A bond with the same par value and coupon rate as the bond in Problem 4 has fourteen years until maturity. If investors will use a 10 percent discount rate to value this bond, by how much should its price differ from the bond in Problem 4?

6. The Garcia Company's bonds have a face value of $1,000, will mature in ten years, and carry a coupon rate of 16 percent. Assume interest payments are made semi-annually.

   a. Determine the present value of the bond's cash flows if the required rate of return is 16 percent.

   b. How would your answer change if the required rate of return is 12 percent?

7. Judith, Inc., bonds mature in eight years and pay a semi-annual coupon of $55. The bond's par value is $1,000.

   a. What is their current price if the market interest rate for bonds of similar quality is 9.2 percent?

   b. A change in Fed policy increases market interest rates 0.50 percentage points from their level in part (a). What is the percentage change in the value of Judith, Inc. bonds from their value in part (a)?

   c. Better profits for Judith, Inc. reduces the market interest rate for its bonds to 9.0 percent. What is the percentage change in the value of Judith, Inc. bonds from the answer in part (b)?

8. Kamins Corporation has two bond issues outstanding, each with a par value of $1,000. Information about each is listed below. Suppose market interest rates rise 1 percentage point across the yield curve. What will be the change in price for each of the bonds? Does this tell us anything about the relationship between time to maturity and interest rate risk?

Bond A: 5 years to maturity, 8 percent coupon, market interest rate is 9 percent

Bond B: 12 years to maturity, 8 percent coupon, market interest rate is 9 percent

9. Billon Corporation has two bond issues outstanding, each with a par value of $1,000. Information about each is listed below. Suppose market interest rates rise 1 percentage point across the yield curve. What will be the change in price for each of the bonds? Does this tell us anything about the relationship between coupon rate and interest rate risk?

Bond A: 10 years to maturity, 0 percent coupon, market interest rate is 9.62 percent.

Bond B: 10 years to maturity, 10 percent coupon, market interest rate is 9.62 percent.

10. Koppen Corporation has two bond issues outstanding, each with a par value of $1,000. Information about each is listed below. Suppose market interest rates rise 1 percentage point across the yield curve. What will be the change in price for each of the bonds? Does this tell us anything about the relationship between frequency of cash flows and interest rate risk?

Bond A: This bond is a Eurobond. It has 10 years to maturity, pays a 7 percent coupon, and the market interest rate is 11.3 percent.

Bond B: This is a issued in the U.S. It has 10 years to maturity, pays a 7 percent coupon, and the market interest rate is 11.3 percent.

11. BVA, Inc., has two bond issues outstanding, each with a par value of $1,000. Information about each is listed below. Suppose market interest rates rise 1 percentage point across the yield curve. What will be the change in price for each of the bonds? Does this tell us anything about the relationship between initial yield to maturity and interest rate risk?

Bond A: 12 years to maturity, pays a 7 percent coupon, and the market interest rate on this BB-rated bond is 12.36 percent.

Bond B: 12 years to maturity, pays a 7 percent coupon, and the market interest rate on this A-rated bond is 10.25 percent.

12. What is the approximate yield to maturity (use formula 10-3) and the exact yield to maturity (use a calculator) for the following bonds? Assume these are bonds issued in the United States.

   a. 10 years to maturity, 6 percent coupon rate, current price is $950.

   b. 16 years to maturity, 0 percent coupon rate, current price is $339.

   c. 25 years to maturity, 8.5 percent coupon rate, current price is $1030.

13. On Thursday, the following bond quotation appears in the newspaper. Interpret each item that appears in the quote and compute its current yield:

COMPANY (TICKER)COUPON	MAT.	LAST PRICE	LAST YIELD	EST SPREAD	EST UST	$VOL (000S)
Wal-Mart Stores						
WMT 4.550	May 1, 2018	99.270	4.649	47	10	66,830

14. Perusing the corporate bond quotations, you write down some summary information:

COMPANY (TICKER) COUPON	MAT.	LAST PRICE	LAST YIELD	EST SPREAD	EST UST	$VOL (000S)
Wal-Mart Stores						
WMT 4.550	10 years	99.270	4.649	47	10	66,830
Wal-Mart Stores						
WMT 4.125	8 years	99.554	4.200	2	10	50,320
Liberty Media						
L 5.700	10 years	102.750	5.314	112	10	26,045
Ford Motor Credit						
F 7.250	8 years	107.407	6.012	183	10	22,863

a. Which company is the riskiest? Why?

b. Which bond has the highest default risk? Why?

c. Why would Wal-Mart have two bonds trading at different yields?

d. Compute the current yield for each of the four bonds.

e. Compute yield to maturity for each of the four bonds.

15. You run across the following bond quotation on a Friday.

RATE	MATURITY MO/YR	BID	ASKED	CHG.	ASKED YLD
7.500	Nov 24	131:06	131:07	−9	5.04

a. What kind of security is it?

b. Interpret the information contained in the quote.

c. Suppose a corporate bond with the same time to maturity has a credit risk spread of 250 basis points. What should be the yield to maturity for the corporate bond?

16. **Challenge Problem** A $1,000 face value bond issued by the Dysane Company currently pays total annual interest of $79 per year and has a thirteen-year life.

a. What is the present value, or worth, of this bond if investors are willing to accept a 10 percent annual rate of return on bonds of similar quality if the bond is a Eurobond?

b. How would your answer in (a) change if the bond is a U.S. bond?

c. How would your answer in (b) change if, one year from now, investors only required a 6.5 percent annual rate of return on bond investments similar in quality to the Dysane bond?

d. Suppose the original bond can be purchased for $925. What is the bond's yield to maturity?

17. **Challenge Problem**

a. You own a two-bond portfolio. Each has a par value of $1,000. Bond A matures in five years, has a coupon rate of 8 percent, and has an annual yield to maturity (YTM) of 9.20 percent. Bond B matures in fifteen years, has a coupon rate of 8 percent and has an annual YTM of 9.20 percent. Both bonds pay interest semi-annually. What is the value of your portfolio? What happens to the value of your portfolio if each YTM rises by one percentage point?

b. Rather than own a five-year bond and a fifteen-year bond, suppose you sell both of them and invest in two ten-year bonds. Each has a coupon rate of 8 percent (semi-annual coupons) and has a YTM of 9.20 percent. What is the value of your portfolio? What happens to the value of your portfolio if the YTM on the bonds rises by one percentage point?

c. Based upon your answers to (a) and (b), evaluate the price changes between the two portfolios. Were the price changes the same? Why or why not?

18. **EXCEL** A bond with a par value of $1,000 has a coupon rate of 7 percent and matures in fifteen years. Using a spreadsheet program, graph its price versus different yields to maturity, ranging from 1 percent to 20 percent. Is the relationship between price and yield linear? Why or why not?

19. Global Cycles (GC) offers investors a dividend reinvestment plan (DRIP) program. An investor purchases 100 shares of GC at a price of $20 per share on January 2. How many shares will the investor own on December 31 if the following dividends are paid and the investor participates in the DRIP program (assume the firm allows fractional shares and accounts for them up to three decimal places)? If the stock's price is $27.50 on December 31, what is the value of her investment in GC?

March 1: dividend paid of $0.50 per share; stock price is $21

June 1: dividend paid of $0.50 per share; stock price is $22.5

September 1: dividend paid of $0.55 per share; stock price is $19

December 1: dividend paid of $0.55 per share; stock price is $25

20. If a stock's earnings per share are $2.00, what will be the dividend per share if the payout ratio is 40 percent? If the following year's earnings per share are $2.10, what will the payout ratio be if the firm wants to maintain dividend growth of 8 percent?

21. You purchased 200 shares of H2O Corporation stock at a price of $20. Consider each of the following announcements separately. What will the price of the stock be after each change? How many shares will you own? What will be the total value of your holdings (value of stock plus any income)?

a. The firm announces a 10 percent stock dividend.

b. The firm announces a two-for-one stock split.

c. The firm announces a $0.50 per share dividend (in your answer use the price of the stock on the ex-dividend date).

d. The firm announces it will repurchase 10 percent of its shares; you do not offer to sell any of your shares.

22. The Fridge-Air Company's preferred stock pays a dividend of $4.50 per share annually. If the required rate of return on comparable quality preferred stocks is 14 percent, calculate the value of Fridge-Air's preferred stock.

23. The Joseph Company has a stock issue that pays a fixed dividend of $3.00 per share annually. Investors believe the nominal risk-free rate is 4 percent and this stock should have a risk premium of 6 percent. What should be the value of this stock?

24. The Lo Company earned $2.60 per share and paid a dividend of $1.30 per share in the year just ended. Earnings and dividends per share are expected to grow at a rate of 5 percent per year in the future. Determine the value of the stock:

a. if the required rate of return is 12 percent.

b. if the required rate of return is 15 percent.

c. Given your answers to (a) and (b), how are stock prices affected by changes in investor's required rates of return?

25. The French Thaler and Company's stock has paid dividends of $1.60 over the past 12 months. Its historical growth rate of dividends has been 8 percent, but analysts expect the growth to slow to 5 percent annually for the foreseeable future.

a. Determine the value of the stock if the required rate of return on stocks of similar risk is 15 percent.

b. If analysts believe the risk premium on the stock should be reduced by 2 percentage points, what is the new required rate of return on French Thaler and Company stock? How much should its price change from the answer you computed in part (a)?

26. Mercier Corporation's stock is selling for $95. It has just paid a dividend of $5 a share. The expected growth rate in dividends is 8 percent.

a. What is the required rate of return on this stock?

b. Using your answer to (a), suppose Mercier announces developments that should lead to dividend increases of 10 percent annually. What will be the new value of Mercier's stock?

c. Again using your answer to (a), suppose developments occur that leave investors expecting that dividends will not change from their current levels in the foreseeable future. Now what will be the value of Mercier stock?

d. From your answers to (b) and (c), how important are investors' expectations of future dividend growth to the current stock price?

27. The common stock of RMW Inc. is selling at $88 a share. It just paid a dividend of $4. Investors expect a return of 15 percent on their investment in RMW Inc. From this information, what is the expected growth rate of future dividends?

28. Lerman Company has preferred stock outstanding. It pays an annual dividend of $10. If its current price is $70, what discount rate will investors be using to value the stock?

29. Interpret the following stock price quote. In addition, what are Sizzler's approximate earnings per share? What was the stock's closing price the previous day?

YTD % CHG	52 WEEKS HI	LO	STOCK	SYM	DIV	YLD %	PE	VOL 100S	LAST	NET CHG
+17.3	7.13	5.00	Sizzlr	SZ	0.16	2.7	25	844	6	−0.25

30. **Challenge Problem** Ritter Incorporated paid a dividend of $2 per share. Its management team has announced a technological breakthrough that is expected to result in a temporary increase in sales, profits, and common stock dividends. Analysts expect the firm's per-share dividends to be $2.50 next year, $3 in two years, and $3.50 in three years. After that, normal dividend growth of 5 percent is expected to resume. If shareholders expect a 15 percent return on their investment in Ritter, what should the firm's stock price be?

31. **Challenge Problem** Tough times have hit the retail store chain of Brador, Inc. Analysts expect its dividend of $1.00 a share to fall by 50 percent next year and another 50 percent the following year before it returns to its normal growth pattern of 3 percent a year. If investors expect a return of 18 percent on their investment in Brador stock, what should its current stock price be?

32. **EXCEL** JW Corp has a dividend of $0.50. The dividend is growing at a 6 percent rate over time. Based on the stock's risk, investors require an 11 percent rate of return.

a. Using the Gordon model, what should the stock's price be?

b. Estimate the firm's dividends for the next ten years and find their present value. What proportion of the stock's price is based upon dividends that are expected to occur more than ten years into the future?

c. What proportion of the firm's price is based upon dividends that are expected to occur more than five years into the future?

33. **EXCEL** A firm's dividends are expected to grow 20 percent a year for the next five years and then trend downward by 3 percentage points per year until they stabilize at a constant growth rate of 5 percent. The current dividend is $0.80 a share and the stock's required rate of return is 13 percent. What should its current price be? If these growth expectations come to pass, what will its price be four years from now? Eight years from now?

LEARNING EXTENSION 10

Annualizing Rates of Return

An investment provides two sources of returns: income and price changes. Bonds pay coupon interest (income), and as we saw in Chapter 10, fluctuating market interest rates can lead to changing bond prices and capital gains or losses. Stocks may pay dividends (a source of investor income) and rise or fall in value over time, leading to capital gains or losses. Such is the case with other investment vehicles such as real estate or mutual funds.

HOLDING PERIOD RETURNS

The dollar return on a single financial asset held for a specific time, or holding period, is given by the following:

$$\text{Dollar return} = \text{Income received} + \text{Price change} \qquad \text{(LE 10-1)}$$

Suppose during the time, Amy held a share of stock, and she received dividends of $2 while the stock price rose from a purchase price of $25 to its current level of $30. Should Amy sell the stock today, her dollar return would be the following:

$$\text{Dollar return} = \text{Income received} + \text{price change}$$

$$= \$2 + (\$30 - \$25)$$

$$\$7 = \$2 + \$5$$

She received $2 in dividends and the value of her investment rose by $5 for a total dollar return of $7. To compare this investment return with others, it is best to measure the dollar return relative to the initial price paid for the stock. This percentage return is the dollar return divided by the initial price of the stock:

$$\text{Percentage return} = (\text{Dollar return}/\text{Initial price}) \qquad \text{(LE 10-2)}$$

Amy's percentage return was the following:

$$\text{Percentage return} = (\text{Dollar return}/\text{Initial price}) = (\$7/\$25) = 0.28 \text{ or } 28 \text{ percent}$$

ANNUALIZED RATES OF RETURN

To compare the returns on one investment with another, they should be measured over equal time periods, such as a year, a month, or a day. By convention, most investors use annual returns as a means by which to compare investments. To *annualize a return* means to state it as the annual return that would result in the observed percentage return. Equation LE 10-3 gives us a formula for determining annualized returns:

$$\text{Annualized return} = (1 + \text{percentage return})^{1/n} - 1 \qquad \text{(LE 10-3)}$$

The n value is the number of years an investment was held. For a one-year example, Amy's annualized return is the same as her percentage return. This can be shown as follows:

$$\text{Annualized return} = (1 + 0.28)^{1/1} - 1$$
$$= (1.28)^{1} - 1 = 1.28 - 1 = 0.28 \text{ or } 28 \text{ percent}$$

The superscript fraction 1/1 indicates that Amy's investment was for one year. When investments are held for longer than one year, the fraction becomes less than one, indicating that the percentage return must be spread over a longer time period. For example, if Amy's investment was purchased two years ago, her annualized return would be the following:

$$\text{Annualized return} = (1 + 0.28)^{1/2} - 1$$
$$= (1.28)^{0.5} - 1 = 1.131 - 1 = 0.131 \text{ or } 13.1 \text{ percent}$$

Also notice that the annualized return is not just the 28 percent total return divided by two years or 14 percent, which would be a simple average annual return. Rather, the annualized return measured by equation LE 10-3 captures the compounding or discounting effects of holding investments longer than one year.

It should now be apparent that as the investment holding period lengthens, the annualized return gets progressively smaller. For example, let's assume Amy earned her 28 percent total return over a period of four years. Her annualized return would be calculated as follows:

$$\text{Annualized return} = (1 + 0.28)^{1/4} - 1$$
$$= (1.28)^{0.25} - 1 = 1.064 - 1 = 0.064 \text{ or } 6.4 \text{ percent}$$

A financial calculator can be used to simplify the calculation effort as follows:

Financial Calculator Solution: 1-Year Investment

Exponent	$1/n = 1/1 = 1$						
Input	1.28	Y^x	then	1	$=$	−1	$=$
Solution	0.28						

Financial Calculator Solution: 2-Year Investment

Exponent	$1/n = 1/2 = 0.5$						
Input	1.28	Y^x	then	0.5	$=$	−1	$=$
Solution	0.131						

Financial Calculator Solution: 4-Year Investment

Exponent	$1/n = 1/4 = 0.25$						
Input	1.28	Y^x	then	0.25	$=$	−1	$=$
Solution	0.064						

Annualized returns can be calculated for investments held for less than one year. Let's assume Amy held her investment for nine months while earning a percentage return of 28 percent. What would be Amy's annualized return under this scenario?

$$\text{Annualized return} = (1 + 0.28)^{1/(9/12)} - 1$$
$$= (1.28)^{1/0.75} - 1 = (1.28)^{1.33} - 1 = 1.389 - 1 = 0.389 \text{ or } 38.9 \text{ percent}$$

Because most individual and institutional investors are interested in comparing annualized returns, you must know how to compute percentage returns and how to annualize them.

PROBLEMS

1. Given the information below, compute annualized returns:

ASSET	INCOME	PRICE CHANGE	INITIAL PRICE	TIME PERIOD
A	$2	$6	$29	15 months
B	0	10	40	11 months
C	50	70	30	7 years
D	3	−8	20	24 months

2. Given the information below, compute annualized returns

ASSET	PURCHASE PRICE	CURRENT PRICE	INCOME RECEIVED	TIME PERIOD
A	$20	$26	$2	75 weeks
B	15	18	0.40	3 months
C	150	130	0	2 years
D	3.50	3.00	0.20	8 months

• CHAPTER 11 •

Securities and Markets

Chapter Learning Objectives . . .

AFTER STUDYING THIS CHAPTER, YOU SHOULD BE ABLE TO DO THE FOLLOWING:

- Describe the processes and institutions used by businesses to distribute new securities to the investing public.
- Outline the recent difficulties and changes in structure of the investment banking industry.
- Describe how securities are traded among investors.
- Identify the regulatory mechanisms by which the securities exchanges and the over-the-counter (OTC) markets are controlled.
- Explain influences that affect broker commissions.

Where We Have Been . . .

For the savings process to work, funds must be routed from savings to the users of funds. Banks and other financial institutions assist with this process; so do securities markets. Chapter 10 introduced us to the characteristics of stocks and bonds, how they can be priced using time value concepts, and the risks that investors face when holding them. Supply and demand forces in financial markets set market prices for securities. Interest rates and asset prices rise and fall based upon investors' and issuers' desires to buy and sell securities.

Where We Are Going . . .

The process of raising funds in securities markets is important for business firms. A firm's ability to raise funds will be the topic of future chapters: long-term fund raising is the focus of Chapter 18's capital structure discussion and short-term financing is discussed in Chapter 16.

How Does This Chapter Apply to Me . . .

Securities markets, typically the secondary markets such as the New York Stock Exchange, are in the news every day. Stock and bond indexes reflect the changing values of securities over time. Investors' decisions and reactions to news events lead to changes in interest rates, bond prices, and stock prices. Movements in market prices affect personal wealth. Many people make decisions through direct investment or through their decisions regarding where to place their 401(k) or individual retirement account (IRA) investments that involve the securities markets. As a financial manager, the trend in your firm's stock price over time, relative to competitors and the overall market, is a reflection of how investors view your firm's prospects.

The goal of every investor is to

> *Buy low and sell high.*

Will Rogers, the famous American humorist, gave his own thoughts in 1929 on how to succeed in investing:

> *Buy a stock that will go up in value. If it doesn't go up, don't buy it!*

Of course, the ability to buy securities at a low price and to sell them at a higher price is the goal of every investor, but it is difficult to do. In this chapter, we'll learn how securities are issued, about the different markets in which they are traded, and how investors can buy and sell securities.

ISSUING SECURITIES: PRIMARY SECURITIES MARKETS

primary market
original issue market in which securities are initially sold

Recall from Chapter 1 that newly created securities are sold in the **primary market** while existing securities are traded in the **secondary market**. The initial sale of newly issued debt or equity securities is called a **flotation**; the initial sale of equity to the public is called an **initial public offering (IPO)**. To raise money, corporations usually use the services of firms called **investment bankers**, or **underwriters**, whose main activity is marketing securities and dealing with the securities markets. Investment bankers act as intermediaries between corporations and the general public when corporations want to raise capital. Investment banks, for the most part, were separate, stand-alone firms. After the 2007–2009 financial crisis. most investment banks either failed (Bear Stearns, Lehman Brothers) or were purchased by stronger financial institutions (such as Bank of America's acquisition of Merrill Lynch). Current investment banking firms include Bank of America (Bank of America Merrill Lynch), Barclays (Barclays Capital), Citigroup, Goldman Sachs, JPMorgan Chase & Co. (JPMorgan), and Morgan Stanley, among others.

secondary market
market in which existing securities are traded among investors

flotation
initial sale of newly issued debt or equity securities

initial public offering (IPO)
initial sale of equity to the public

PRIMARY MARKET FUNCTIONS OF INVESTMENT BANKERS

Although the specific activities of investment bankers differ depending upon their size and financial resources, the functions of investment bankers include originating, underwriting, and selling newly issued securities.

investment bankers (underwriters)
main activity is marketing securities and dealing with the securities markets

Originating

Most of the larger investment banking firms engage in originating securities. As an originator, the investment bank seeks to identify firms that may benefit from a **public offering**, which is a sale of securities to the investing public, or a **private placement**, which is a sale of securities to a small group of private investors. The Securities and Exchange Commission (SEC) regulates the public offering process. The private placement process has fewer regulations, but the securities can only be sold to investors who meet certain SEC-regulated guidelines for wealth and investment knowledge. Most of this section will focus on the role of an investment bank in a public offering.

public offering
sale of securities to the investing public

private placement
sale of securities to a small group of private investors

Once the investment bank identifies a firm that may want to sell securities, the investment bank attempts to sell itself to the issuer as the best investment bank to handle the offering.[1] Once an agreement is reached, the investment bank makes a detailed study (called **due diligence**) of the corporation. The investment bank uses this information to determine the best means of raising the needed funds. The investment banker will recommend the types, terms, and offering price of securities that should be sold.[2] He or she aids the corporation in preparing the registration and informational materials required by the SEC.

due diligence
detailed study of a corporation

prospectus
highly regulated document that details the issuer's operations and finances and must be provided to each buyer of a newly issued security

One important and carefully regulated piece of information is the **prospectus**, which details the issuer's finances and must be provided to each buyer of the security. Some of the questions one chief financial officer (CFO) used to quiz prospective investment banking partners for his firm's IPOs are listed in Table 11.1. These questions cover several of the underwriting, selling, and aftermarket aspects of the going-public process, which we will discuss below.

Another piece of advice the investment bank gives firms who want to have an IPO is when to go public. At times, the investing public is particularly interested in firms operating in certain industries or that develop certain technologies. Firms that go public in "hot" IPO markets, meaning when investors are anxious to buy new issues and prices are bid up, sometimes, to twice or three times their initial offering price, are likely to receive better prices for their shares than if they go public in a "cold" market, when investors are less receptive to new stock issues.

---

1. For one firm's process of selecting an investment banker, see Alix Nyberg, "The Tough Go Shopping," *CFO* (January 2001), pp. 89–93; Orin C. Smith, "Wanted: The Right Investment Banker," *Financial Executive* (November/December 1994), pp. 14–18. Mr. Smith describes his firm's experience of "going public" when he was chief financial officer of Starbucks Coffee Company.

2. Chapter 18, Capital Structure and the Cost of Capital, will detail some of the items a firm and its investment bank will consider before deciding the securities type to be sold.

TABLE 11.1

Selections from One Firm's Quiz for Potential Investment Banking Firms Interested in Doing its IPO

1. How would you position our company in relation to the market and its competition?
2. What companies would you choose as comparable companies from a valuation standpoint? How do you value our company and why?
3. Explain your pricing strategy for our firm's public offering and contrast it with at least four other recent IPOs that you have managed or co-managed.
4. How frequently will research reports be published during the two years following the offering? Present examples of frequency of your research for other IPOs in the last two years.
5. Under what circumstances would you stop research coverage of the company? Have you dropped coverage of any companies you have taken public in the last three years?
6. Please prepare a table that demonstrates your trading performance post-IPO for five or six high-profile IPOs that you have managed in the last 12 to 18 months.

Based upon Alix Nyberg, "The Tough Go Shopping," *CFO* (January 2001), p. 90.

Underwriting

underwriting agreement
contract in which the
investment banker agrees to
buy securities at a
predetermined price and then
resell them to investors

Investment bankers not only help to sell securities to the investing public, but they also sometimes assume the risk arising from the possibility that such securities may not be purchased by investors. This occurs when the investment banker enters into an ***underwriting agreement*** with the issuing corporation. As shown in Figure 11.1, with an underwriting agreement, securities are purchased at a predetermined or "firm commitment" price by the underwriters, who then sell them to investors at the ***offer price***. The difference between the offer price and the price paid by the investment bank is called a ***spread***. The spread is revenue to the investment bank, which is used to cover its expenses and to provide a profit from its underwriting activities.

offer price
price at which the security is
sold to the investors

The issuer has almost no price risk in a firm commitment offering once the offer price is set. The issuer receives the proceeds from the sale immediately, which it can spend on the purposes outlined in the prospectus. The investment bank carries, or underwrites, the risk of fluctuating stock prices. The investment bank carries the risk of loss, or at least the possibility of a smaller spread than expected, should the market's perception of the issuer change or an economic event (such as an unexpected attempt by the Fed to increase interest rates) result in a stock market decline before the investment bank can sell all the securities; but as we shall see in a later section, the phenomenon of "underpricing" or first-day price increases for IPOs is prevalent and reduces the possibility of an investment banker losing money on a firm commitment underwriting.

spread
difference between the offer
price and the price paid by
the investment bank

best-effort agreement
agreement which the
investment bankers try to sell
securities of the issuing
corporation; but they assume
no risk for the possible failure
of the flotation

Another means of offering securities is called best-effort selling. Under a ***best-effort agreement***, investment bankers try to sell the securities of the issuing corporation, but they assume no risk for a possible failure of the flotation. The investment bankers are paid a fee or commission for those securities they sell. The best-effort agreement is typically used when the investment bankers anticipate there may be some difficulty in selling the securities and they are unwilling to assume the underwriting risk. From the perspective of investors, an investment bank putting its money at risk with a firm commitment underwriting agreement would be preferable. Investors should view a best-effort offering with some concern. If the investment banker is not willing to support the firm's security sale, why should other investors?

Firms that are public and wish to raise additional funds have several choices. They can sell additional securities by using the underwriting process as discussed above. They can also

FIGURE 11.1

Diagram of a Firm Commitment Underwriting

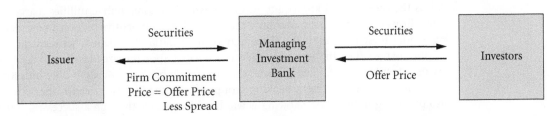

choose to use shelf registration, sell securities to a private party, have a rights offering, or seek competitive bids. We discuss each of these below.

Shelf Registration

The SEC's Rule 415 allows firms to register security issues (debt and equity) and "put them on the shelf" for sale any time over the succeeding two years. Once registered, the securities can be offered for sale by submitting a short statement to the SEC whenever the firm needs the funds or market conditions are attractive. The **shelf registration** process saves issuers time and money. There is no cost or penalty for registering shelf securities and not issuing them. Filing fees are low, and the firm can take some securities from the shelf, sell them immediately through one underwriter, and later sell more with another underwriter. Not every firm can use shelf registration. Firms must meet four size, credit quality, and ethics requirements:

1. The market value of the firm's common stock must be at least $150 million.
2. It must have made no defaults on its debt in the previous three years.
3. The firm's debt must be investment grade (rated BBB or better).
4. The firm must not have been found guilty of violating the Securities Exchange Act of 1934 in the previous three years.

shelf registration allows firms to register security issues (both debt and equity) with the SEC and have them available to sell for two years

ETHICAL ISSUES

Sell Securities to a Private Party

A publicly held firm can choose to sell securities in a private placement. To keep current shareholders from suspecting any "sweetheart deals," privately placed equity is typically sold at a slight premium to the stock's current market price.

Private equity sales may occur if the firm is the rumored or actual target of a hostile takeover. Management may try to stall the takeover or stop it by selling a large block of voting stock to an investor or syndicate that seems friendlier. Occasionally, news stories contain articles of rumored deals involving firms in financial difficulty that are seeking equity infusions to keep them afloat.

Private placements of equity may fulfill a need for an emergency infusion of equity. Since the shares are not being sold in a public offering, the private placement avoids SEC registration and subsequent publicity. The private sale must follow other SEC regulations however. The firm must disclose the sale after it occurs, and the private investors must meet SEC requirements as "accredited investors." Basically, accredited investors are those who are considered knowledgeable enough or sufficiently strong enough financially to invest without the protection provided by the SEC's registration process. Accredited investors can include wealthy individuals with investment experience as well as financial institutions, such as insurance companies and pension funds.

Rights Offerings

Under the charters of some corporations, if additional shares of common stock (or any security that may be converted to common stock) are to be issued, the securities must be offered for sale first to the existing common stockholders. That is, the existing shareholders have *pre-emptive rights* to purchase newly issued securities. The purpose of this regulation is to permit existing stockholders to maintain their proportional share of ownership. Once popular in the United States, rights offerings among public corporations became infrequent during the 1980s and 1990s although they are still used among privately held firms. On the other hand, rights offerings remain popular among public firms in Europe.

Competitive Bidding

State, local, and federal government bond issues, as well as those of governmental agencies, usually require competitive bidding by investment bankers before awarding underwriting agreements. This is the case for debt and equity securities issued by some public utilities. Large, financially strong firms will occasionally announce they are seeking competitive bids on a new security offering. Under these circumstances, there may be little initial negotiation between the investment houses and the issuer. In these cases, the issuer decides upon the size of issue and the type of security that it wishes to sell. Then it invites the investment banking houses to offer bids for handling the securities. The investment banking group offering the highest price for the securities, while also providing information showing it will be able to carry through a successful flotation, will usually be awarded the contract.

A great deal of disagreement has existed about the relative advantages and disadvantages of competitive bidding by investment banking houses. Investment bankers strongly contend that the continuing advice they give is essential to an economical and efficient distribution of an issuer's primary market securities. Others contend that competitive bidding enables corporations to sell their securities at higher prices than would otherwise be the case.

A variation of competitive bidding, usually occuring when issuers seek bids solely from investment banking firms, is the **Dutch auction** bidding process, which allows smaller firms and individual investors to purchase securities. The U.S. Treasury uses a Dutch auction, and some IPOs use the Dutch auction mechanism. Most notable was the 2004 Google stock public offering. The process begins when the issuer and its investment banks determine a price range for the stock. After setting up an account with one of the underwriters, investors place bid prices for the number of shares they want to purchase via Internet, fax, or telephone. Bidders can place bids outside the price range if they believe demand will be high (higher bid price) or weak (lower bid price) than expected by underwriters. At the close of the bidding period, the underwriters determine the highest bid, or clearing price, at which all the offered shares are sold.

For example, suppose a firm, Yoogle, wants to issue 100 million shares in a Dutch auction IPO. Assume only five bids are made:

BIDDER	PRICE	NUMBER OF SHARES
A	$20.50	25 million
B	$20.47	25 million
C	$20.45	25 million
D	$20.43	25 million
E	$20.40	25 million

The clearing price is $20.43; the number of shares to be purchased at that price or higher allows all the offered shares to be sold. Investors A, B, C, and D will be able to purchase their desired number of shares, and investor E will receive no shares in the IPO.

If two or more investors place bids at the clearing price, the offering firm can make one of three choices. First, it can increase the offering size to absorb the extra demand; second, it can sell shares on a pro rata basis to the lowest bidders; and third, it can sell shares on a pro rata basis to all successful bidders. To illustrate, here is what would happen if investors D and E had each placed a bid of $20.43 for 25 million shares. At the clearing price of $20.43, there are orders for 125 million shares, but only 100 million shares are offered. Under the first option, Yoogle can decide (if the prospectus gives Yoogle permission to do so) to increase the offering size to 125 million shares and sell the desired amounts to each investor. With the second option, Yoogle allocates 75 million shares to bidders A, B, and C, and splits the remaining 25 million shares between bidders D and E in proportion to the size of their bids. Since they wanted the same number of shares, the remaining shares are divided evenly with bidders D and E each receiving 12.5 million shares. Under the third option, with 100 million shares to sell and clearing price demand for 125 million, each investor receives 100/125 or 80 percent of their desired number of shares. That is, bidders A, B, C, D, and E will receive 25 million × 0.80 shares, or 20 million shares, each.

Selling

The amount of securities sold in public offerings is large. In 2003, over $5.3 trillion of equity and debt was raised; in 2006, over $7.6 trillion worth of debt and equity securities were sold in the primary market. This fell to about $4.4 trillion in the recessionary market of 2008.[3] To assist the underwriting and best-effort process, the majority of large investment banking houses maintain "retail" outlets throughout the nation. Retail selling is selling to individual investors. There are also many independent retail brokerage outlets not large or financially strong enough to engage in major originating and underwriting functions. These independents may be able to assist the major investment banks in selling new issues. Like the underwriters, they depend upon the resale of securities at a price above their cost to cover expenses and provide profit from operations. A few of the large investment banking houses do not sell to individuals. Rather, they

Dutch auction
a bidding process, which allows smaller firms and individual investors to purchase securities

INTERNET ACTIVITY

Go to http://www.openipo.com to visit a site of an investment bank (W.R. Hambrecht & Co.) that uses Dutch auctions in initial public offerings it underwrites.

---

3. The first issue of *The Wall Street Journal* each year contains a summary of the prior years' largest IPOs and leading underwriting firms.

confine their activities entirely to originating, underwriting, and selling securities to institutional investors. Institutional investors are large investors such as insurance companies, pension funds, investment companies, and other large financial institutions.

Regulatory authorities permit announcements of security offerings to be placed in newspapers and other publications. These announcements, called *tombstones*, are very restricted in wording and must not seem to be soliciting sales. An announcement is shown in Figure 11.2. This tombstone is careful to point out that "This is neither an offer to sell nor a solicitation of an offer to buy any of these securities." The word "tombstone" apparently derives from the small amount of information it provides and the large amount of white space it features. Boston Chicken was seeking to sell 10.35 million shares of common stock at an offer price of $34.50 a share. The underwriters are shown on the bottom of the announcement.

tombstones
announcements of securities offerings to be placed in newspapers and other publications

FIGURE 11.2

A Security Offering Announcement, or Tombstone

This announcement is under no circumstances to be construed as an offer to sell or as a solicitation of an offer to buy any of these securities. The offering is made only by the Prospectus.

New Issue   December 5, 1995

10,350,000 Shares

Boston Chicken, Inc.

Common Stock

Price $34.50 Per Share

Copies of the Prospectus may be obtained from any State or jurisdiction in which this announcement is circulated from only such of the undersigned or other dealers or brokers as may lawfully offer these securities in such State or jurisdiction.

Merrill Lynch & Co.		**Alex. Brown & Sons** Incorporated
Dean Witter Reynolds Inc.	A.G. Edwards & Sons, Inc.	Goldman, Sachs & Co.
Montgomery Securities	Morgan Stanley & Co. Incorporated	Oppenheimer & Co., Inc.
Piper Jaffray Inc.	Prudential Securities Incorporated	Schroder Wertheim & Co.
Smith Barney Inc.		Nesbitt Burns Securities Inc.
Arnhold and S. Bleichroeder, Inc.	J. C. Bradford & Co.	Equitable Securities Corporation
EVEREN Securities, Inc.	Hanifen, Imhoff Inc.	Interstate/Johnson Lane Corporation
Janney Montgomery Scott Inc.	Edward D. Jones & Co.	Ladenburg, Thalmann & Co. Inc.
Legg Mason Wood Walker Incorporated	Principal Financial Securities, Inc.	Pryor, McClendon, Counts & Co., Inc.
Rauscher Pierce Refsnes, Inc.	Wessels, Arnold & Henderson, L.L.C.	Wheat First Butcher Singer

The investment bank or banks chosen to originate and handle a flotation are called the lead bankers. In the issue shown in Figure 11.2, the two firms listed at the top, Merrill Lynch and Alex Brown, are the lead bankers. These lead bankers formed a **syndicate** of several investment banking firms to participate in the underwriting and distribution of the issue. Syndicate members are listed under the lead bankers, in alphabetical order, in the tombstone ad. For large issues, many firms may be part of the syndicate. For an $8 billion Kraft Foods IPO in 2001, about 75 firms, including the lead bankers, were part of the syndicate. Visa's IPO, the largest ever at the time ($17 billion offering) had 15 firms in its syndicate.

The period after a new issue is initially sold to the public is called the **aftermarket**. This period may vary from a few hours to several weeks. During this period, the members of the syndicate may not sell the securities for less than the offering price. Investors who decide to sell their newly purchased securities may depress the market price temporarily, so the syndicate steps in to buy back the securities to prevent a larger price drop. This is called **market stabilization**. Although the Securities Exchange Act of 1934 prohibits manipulation of this sort by all others, underwriters are permitted to buy shares if the market price falls below the offering price. If market stabilization is allowed for a particular issue, it must be stipulated in the prospectus. If part of an issue remains unsold after a period of time, for example thirty days, members may leave the syndicate and sell their securities at whatever price the market will allow. The lead underwriter decides when the syndicate is to break up, freeing members to sell at the prevailing market price.

As an example of underwriting risk, at times the lead banker is left holding many more shares of an offering than it would like.[4] Merrill Lynch and its investment funds once owned over one-half of outstanding shares of First USA Inc., a credit card company, more than three months after its initial public offering (IPO). Bond offerings can turn sour because of unexpected interest rate increases in the economy or credit deterioration by the firm. Convertible bonds are bonds that can be converted to shares of common stock at predetermined prices, and they are sometimes shunned by investors if the conversion and other features are not to their liking. Rumors were that JPMorgan was left owning 80 percent of a convertible bond offering in 2000 for LSI Logic, a semiconductor firm; this was at the peak of the technology bull market. As the bear market continued into 2001, other firms (including CFSB, Salomon Smith Barney, and Merrill Lynch) were holding large stakes of convertible bond issues.[5] But underwriting is a lucrative business, earning firms billions of dollars in fees.

COST OF GOING PUBLIC

One of the drawbacks of going public is its cost. The issuing firm faces direct out-of-pocket costs for accountants' and lawyers' fees, printing expenses, and filing fees.

In addition, the firm faces two additional costs, which together represent the difference between the market value of the firm's shares in the aftermarket and the actual proceeds the firm receives from the underwriters. The first of these costs is the spread, as discussed earlier. The second cost, **underpricing**, represents the difference between the aftermarket stock price and the offering price. Underpricing represents money left on the table or money the firm could have received had the offer price better approximated the aftermarket value of the stock. For example, suppose a firm raises $15 million by selling one million shares at an offer price of $15. By the close of trading on the first day, the firm's stock price is $20. The firm's market value rose $(20 - 15) \times 1$ million shares or $5 million. Had the securities originally been offered at $20, the firm might have received an additional $5 million for the stock. Some would argue that the firm left $5 million "on the table," financing it could have received had the stock been priced better. To view it another way, if the offer price had been $20, the firm could have raised $15 million by selling only 750,000 shares.

Studies of IPOs in the United States find that firms' IPOs are, on average, underpriced more if it is a smaller issue, if it is issued by a technology firm, if the firm has benefited from venture capital financing, and if the issue's underwriters are more prestigious.[6] Underpricing is not only

syndicate
group of several investment banking firms that participate in the underwriting and distributing a security issue

aftermarket
the period after a new issue is initially sold to the public; during this period, members of the syndicate may not sell the securities for less than the offering price

market stabilization
intervention of the syndicate to buy back securities to prevent a larger price drop

INTERNET ACTIVITY
Review recent offerings and position openings at investment banking firms such as Merrill Lynch (http://www.ml.com) and Morgan Stanley (http://www.morganstanley.com).

CONCEPT CHECK
What are the three primary market functions of investment banks?

How does an underwriting agreement differ from a best effort offering?

What is a tombstone ad?

underpricing
represents the difference between the aftermarket stock price and the offering price

4. Alexandra Peers and Craig Torres, "Underwriters Hold Huge Stakes in IPOs," *The Wall Street Journal* (August 12, 1992), p. C1.

5. Suzanne McGee, "First Boston's 'Son of Tyco' Deal Goes Sour," *The Wall Street Journal* (February 15, 2001), pp. C1, C16; Gregory Zuckerman, "Stalled Convertible: J. P. Morgan Is Left Holding $400 Million of LSI Bond Issue," *The Wall Street Journal* (March 2, 2000), pp. C1, C19.

6. For reviews of these studies, see Jay R. Ritter, "Investment Bank and Securities Issuance," in George Constantinides, Milton Harris, and Rene Stulz, editors, *Handbook of the Economics of Finance*, North-Holland (2002).

TABLE 11.2

Average Initial Returns for 49 Countries

COUNTRY	SIZE	TIME PERIOD	AVG. INITIAL RETURN
Argentina	20	1991–1994	4.40%
Australia	1,562	1976–2011	21.80%
Austria	102	1971–2010	6.30%
Belgium	114	1984–2006	13.50%
Brazil	275	1979–2011	33.10%
Bulgaria	9	2004–2007	6.50%
Canada	696	1971–2010	6.70%
Chile	65	1982–2006	8.40%
China	2,102	1990–2010	137.40%
Cyprus	66	1999–2011	20.80%
Denmark	164	1984–2011	7.40%
Egypt	53	1990–2000	8.40%
Finland	162	1971–2006	17.20%
France	697	1983–2010	10.50%
Germany	736	1978–2011	24.20%
Greece	373	1976–2011	50.80%
Hong Kong	1,259	1980–2010	15.40%
India	2,964	1990–2011	88.50%
Indonesia	386	1990–2011	25.70%
Iran	279	1991–2004	22.40%
Ireland	31	1999–2006	23.70%
Israel	348	1990–2006	13.80%
Italy	273	1985–2009	16.40%
Japan	3,100	1970–2010	40.40%
Jordan	53	1999–2008	149.00%
Korea	1,593	1980–2010	61.60%
Malaysia	413	1980–2009	62.60%
Mexico	88	1987–1994	15.90%
Netherlands	181	1982–2006	10.20%
New Zealand	214	1979–2006	20.30%
Nigeria	114	1989–2006	12.70%
Norway	153	1984–2006	9.60%
Philippines	123	1987–2006	21.20%
Poland	224	1991–2006	22.90%
Portugal	28	1992–2006	11.60%
Russia	40	1999–2006	4.20%
Saudi Arabia	76	2003–2010	264.50%
Singapore	591	1973–2011	26.10%
South Africa	285	1980–2007	18.00%
Spain	128	1986–2006	10.90%
Sri Lanka	105	1987–2008	33.50%
Sweden	406	1980–2011	26.10%
Switzerland	159	1983–2008	28.00%
Taiwan	1,312	1980–2006	37.20%
Thailand	459	1987–2007	36.60%
Turkey	355	1990–2011	10.30%
United Kingdom	4,877	1959–2011	16.10%
United States	12,246	1960–2011	16.80%

Source: from Tim Loughran, Jay R. Ritter, and Kristian Rydquist, Initial Public Offerings, International Insights, *Pacific-Basin Finance Journal* (June 1994), vol. 2, pp. 165-199, updated July 6, 2012, available on http://bear.warrington.ufl.edu/ritter/ipodata.htm.

a U.S. occurrence. Table 11.2 shows that studies in many countries find large first-day returns to IPOs, indicating underpricing. Why underpricing occurs is a matter of debate among researchers; it evidently isn't dependent upon a country's security markets, regulations, or trading mechanisms since it occurs in so many different countries. Some theories include cases where some investors have better information (presumably via their own research) than others regarding the attractiveness of an IPO. To give incentive for the uninformed investors to continue to purchase primary market equity offerings, they on average must earn profits via underpricing. Other theories deal with irrational investor behavior: Investors who want to purchase shares but are unable to in the public offering frantically bid up the prices of shares to purchase them from those who did purchase IPO shares.

Together, these three costs (direct costs, the spread, and underpricing) are an IPO's **flotation costs**. The flotation costs of an issue depend upon a number of factors, including the size of the offering, the issuing firm's earnings, its industry, and the condition of the stock market. The flotation costs, relative to the amount raised, are usually lower for a firm commitment offering than a best-effort offering. Best-effort offerings have higher costs for two reasons. First, it is typically higher-risk firms that utilize best-effort offerings, so the banker charges higher fees to compensate for his extra efforts. Second, on average, best-effort offerings raise smaller amounts of money, so the fixed costs of preparing the offering are spread over fewer shares sold. One study found that for U.S. corporations, the average costs for IPOs of equity, not including underpricing, averaged 11.0 percent of the proceeds. For seasoned equity offerings (SEOs), that is, follow-on equity offerings of firms that have public equity outstanding, these costs averaged 7.1 percent. For convertible bonds, the costs averaged 3.8 percent. For straight debt issues, issuing costs average 2.2 percent, although they were sensitive to the credit rating of the issue.[7]

Studies have shown that underpricing varies over time and with IPO volume. In addition, IPO volume is cyclical: periods of frantic IPO activity alternate with periods when few firms go public. There is a close relationship between IPO volume and underpricing. Periods of "hot IPO markets" have heavy IPO volume with large underpricing, and periods of low IPO volume or "cold IPO markets" show less underpricing. The data in Table 11.3 show these patterns since 1975. Note the hot IPO markets in the late 1990s and the cooler markets in the early 1980s, late 1980s, and after the turn of the millennium.

Innovations Among Investment Banking Firms

As we saw in Chapter 10, investment banking firms have tried to meet the needs of issuers and investors by developing many variations of "debt" and "equity." As far as the process of underwriting is concerned, the Internet has had a relatively minor impact on public offerings. Some firms have tried using the Internet as a means to sell securities to small investors and to reduce the amount of underpricing of securities. Most investment banks are large, well-capitalized firms. Investors who receive offering shares in an offering are typically large institutional clients of the investment banks and their favored retail customers (those with large brokerage accounts who do a lot of trading). The Internet has the potential to make investors more equal by allowing them to bid for shares in Dutch auctions. By selling shares to the highest bidders, all investors are treated equally; if small investors bid a higher price than an investment bank, they will receive their requested number of shares first. Second, by seeking bids, the hope is the average price received by the issuing firm will exceed the price they would receive in a firm commitment underwriting. Bond offerings have been made available on the Internet, too. Internotes is a name given to bonds sold via the Internet. Corporations, government agencies, and municipalities have issued bonds using the Internet.[8]

Another means of going public for a private firm to merge with or acquire a public firm. This is how the New York Stock Exchange (NYSE) "went public"; it purchased the publicly held electronic communications network (ECN) firm, Archipelago Holdings.

flotation costs
composed of direct costs, the spread, and underpricing

INTERNET ACTIVITY

Jay Ritter of the University of Florida's Warrington College of Business is a leading academic researcher on IPOs. His Web site, http://bear.warrington.ufl.edu/ritter/index.html, offers data and recent research findings on IPOs

INTERNET ACTIVITY

Web sites of firms involved in the Internet IPO market include W. R. Hambrecht & Co. (http://www.wrhambrecht.com). An information source on public offerings is http://www.ipo.com.

INTERNET ACTIVITY

Visit the site of a firm that facilitates Internet bond offerings: http://www.incapital.com/.

7. Inmoo Lee, Scott Lochhead, Jay Ritter, and Quanshui Zhao, "The Costs of Raising Capital," *Journal of Financial Research*, vol. 19, no. 1 (Spring 1996).

8. Rachel Koning, "Chicago Bonds Go Straight to Buyers," *The Wall Street Journal*, September 15, 2005, page D2; Emily S. Plishner, "E-bonds: Will They Fly?," *CFO* (March 2001), pp. 87–92; Terzah Ewing, "Too Hot an IPO? Andover.net's 252% Pop Raises Questions About Underwriter's 'Dutch Auction,'" *The Wall Street Journal* (December 9, 1999), pp. C1, C23; John Thackray, "A Kinder, Gentler IPO?," *CFO* (October 1999), pp. 41–42; Silvia Ascarelli, "Investment Bank Niche Thrives for Online IPOs," *The Wall Street Journal* (October 18, 1999), p. A431.

TABLE 11.3

Number of Offerings and Average First-Day Returns (Underpricing) Of Initial Public Offerings In 1975–2012

YEAR	NUMBER OF OFFERINGS	AVERAGE FIRST-DAY RETURN
1975	12	−0.2%
1976	26	1.9%
1977	15	3.6%
1978	19	12.6%
1979	39	8.5%
1980	75	13.9%
1981	197	6.2%
1982	81	10.7%
1983	522	9.0%
1984	222	2.5%
1985	214	6.5%
1986	478	6.1%
1987	334	5.7%
1988	127	5.5%
1989	120	7.7%
1990	115	10.5%
1991	294	11.8%
1992	415	10.2%
1993	526	12.7%
1994	411	9.8%
1995	460	21.1%
1996	688	17.2%
1997	485	14.0%
1998	316	20.3%
1999	485	69.8%
2000	382	56.2%
2001	79	14.2%
2002	70	8.6%
2003	67	12.3%
2004	183	12.3%
2005	168	10.1%
2006	162	11.9%
2007	162	13.8%
2008	21	6.4%
2009	43	10.6%
2010	101	9.0%
2011	82	13.2%
2012	103	20.9%

First-day returns are computed as the percentage return from the offering price to the first closing market price.
Source: based on Table 8 of Jay R. Ritter, "Initial Public Offerings: Updated Statistics," unpublished (December 11, 2012), http://bear.warrington.ufl.edu/ritter/

THE FACEBOOK IPO[9]

Few IPOs caught the attention of so many of a firm's customers as the Facebook IPO on May 18, 2012. At its IPO, Facebook's offer price was $38, valuing the social network at $104 billion, the largest ever by a U.S. firm at its initial offering. The IPO was slated to sell $18.4 billion of

9. The section is based on a number of articles, including: S. Raice, A. Das, and J. Letzing, "Facebook Prices IPO at Record Value," *The Wall Street Journal*, May 17, 2012; S. Raice, R. Dezember and J. Bunge, "Facebook's IPO Sputters," *The Wall Street Journal*, May 18, 2012; J. Strasburg, J. Bunge, and G. Chon, "Nasdaq's Facebook Problem," *The Wall Street Journal*, May 21, 2012; J. Bunge, A. Lucchetti, and G. Chon, "Investors Pummel Facebook," *The Wall Street Journal*, May 22, 2012; S. Raice, A. Das, and G. Chon, "Inside Fumbled Facebook Offering," *The Wall Street Journal*, May 23, 2012; B. Philbin, "Morgan Stanley Chief Defends Facebook Handling," *The Wall Street Journal*, May 30, 2012; D. Weidner, "Facebook IPO Facts, Fiction, and Flops," *The Wall Street Journal*, May 30, 2012; M. Langley, A. Das, and A. Lucchetti, "Morgan Stanley Was 'Driver' on Facebook's Wild IPO Ride," *The Wall Street Journal*, May 30, 2012; A. Lucchetti, "Facebook's Next Fight: Suits and More Suits," *The Wall Street Journal*, September 26, 2012; T. Demos and A. Lucchetti, "Facebook's IPO Suits to be Handled in New York," *The Wall Street Journal*, October 5, 2012; R. Winkler, "Facebook's Halloween Trick," *The Wall Street Journal*, October 31, 2012; J. Light, "Facebook's Friends Left Early," *The Wall Street Journal*, November 5, 2012.

common stock, second only to Visa's 2008 offering. The reason for the difference between Facebook's market capitalization or market value at the IPO ($104 billion) and the value of the stock sold ($18.4 billion) is that some private investors and insiders (such as CEO Mark Zuckerberg) did not want to sell all their shares at the IPO or were prevented from doing it. After all, it would look poorly if all the insiders wanted to sell their shares at the IPO. Outside investors would wonder why they were selling and not keeping their shares unless they were pessimistic about the firm's future.

With such a large offering, competition was fierce among investment bankers for who would get to take Facebook public—earning publicity and large fees for the banker. The syndicate had 33 members; Morgan Stanley was selected as the primary or managing underwriter. Other major syndicate members included JPMorgan Chase & Co. and Goldman Sachs. Fees for taking Facebook public totaled $176 million.

During its "road show", when investment bankers were discussing the firm's risk and return potential, the preliminary price range for Facebook's IPO was between $28 and $35 per share. Such a wide range is common; pricing a new issue is full of uncertainty and assumptions, one of which is how potential buyers are pricing the shares and how eager they are to buy the IPO shares. Apparently high demand for Facebook's IPO caused the firm's management and its lead investment banker to increase the offering price range from $34 to $38 per share shortly before the initial public offering (IPO).

Still, demand for the IPO was high as Facebook was a profitable firm. If all of its users, about 900 million at the time of its IPO, lived in the same country, it would be the third most-populated nation in the world: not a bad start for a firm that didn't exist until 2004.

Despite its popularity, there was a flurry of worrisome news prior to the IPO. Facebook's financial news raised concerns. Prior to its May 2012 IPO, Facebook announced the latest quarter's sales revenues were down 6 percent from the prior quarter and profits fell 32 percent over the same time frame. A major supplier of Facebook ads, General Motors (GM), decided to stop placing ads on Facebook as GM determined the ads weren't generating enough new car purchases.

In addition to the underwriters' decision to raise the IPO offering price two days prior to the IPO, they increased the number of shares to be sold by 25 percent. Typically in an IPO, investors request to purchase more shares than they expect to receive, hoping to receive about 50 percent of their order. When the smaller allotment is received, some investors enter the market to purchase additional shares, helping to create the first-trading day price rise. But the late decision to increase the offering by 25% caught some institutional (e.g., hedge funds, pension funds, mutual funds) and some retail (individual) investors by surprise. They received more shares at the IPO than they expected to receive. One hedge fund manager received a half-million more shares than he expected. Some retail investors who didn't expect to receive any shares did receive some. All this helped to reduce demand at the opening of Facebook trading and led to an oversupply of shares that some wanted to sell.

Facebook's IPO on Friday May 18 started well as the price "popped" over 10 percent from the $38 offering price to over $42. The opening suffered from a 30-minute delay from National Association of Securities Dealers Automated Quotation (NASDAQ) computer and trading problems due, in part, to heavy trading volume: 571 million shares were traded by the end of the first day, which is a lot, considering 421 million shares were sold in the IPO. Facebook's price fell back to its $38 offering price, rose to the $41 range, but fell again before the end of the trading day, closing at $38.23, barely above the $38 offering price.

Morgan Stanley, the lead underwriter, had to enter the market to help stabilize the price as the lack of a sustained "pop," computer issues, and delayed trade confirmations (leading to confusion as to whether some investors' orders were executed) resulted in increased selling pressure on the stock.

On the next trading day, Monday May 21, selling pressure continued as investors had the weekend to consider the problems on the first day of trading, and many decided to sell some or all of their holdings. Facebook ended its first full day of trading down $4 from its offering price, closing at $34 per share. On the second full trading day, Tuesday May 22, the stock fell to $31. The stock would gyrate, closing below $18 per share in early September before rising back to the mid-20s by the end of 2012, 30 percent under its offering price.

What happened to Facebook's anticipated IPO? As we noted above, some disappointing news came out shortly before the IPO. In spite of this, the offering price and the number of shares to be offered was increased, something which occurs in a small fraction of initial public offerings

(IPOs). Personnel at the investment banks were having second thoughts, too. Stock analysts at some of the underwriters were informing selected clients they were going to reduce their estimates of Facebook's future earnings.

Another reason for the price decline is basic economics of supply and demand. Although the total number of Facebook shares hasn't changed, the number eligible to be sold and traded increased in the first few months after the IPO. The IPO's "lock up" provisions expired, allowing early investors (when Facebook was a private firm) to sell shares. After its 421 million share IPO, another 271 million shares were eligible to be sold and traded 3 months after the IPO (in August) and another 229 million shares in October. Another 800 million shares became eligible for trading in mid-November. Thus, the public "float" or publicly available shares quadrupled during Facebook's first 6 months of trading. No doubt, some of these early investors opted to sell some of their shares, increasing supply and putting further downward pressure on Facebook's stock price.

In the four months following Facebook's IPO, about 50 lawsuits had been filed. Some investors filed lawsuits against Facebook and its underwriters, claiming the analysts' forecast changes should have been shared with the entire marketplace prior to the IPO. Lawsuits were filed against NASDAQ, too, alleging losses due to the computer and trading malfunctions at the beginning of Facebook's public trading. It will be a while before the last chapter is written on the Facebook IPO.

Although we've focused on the Facebook IPO in this section, Figure 11.3 shows the time frame from late 2011 through 2012 was not kind to most high-tech IPOs. Facebook, Groupon, Yelp, and Zynga finished 2012 below their offering prices. During this time frame, the Standard & Poor's 500 (S&P500) rose over 10 percent. So, while the market was rising, these high-tech IPOs fell in value, in part because of disappointing news about the firms, their sales, and profits.

OTHER FUNCTIONS OF INVESTMENT BANKING FIRMS

Investment banking firms engage in many activities beyond their primary function of distributing long-term security instruments. For example, they have traditionally dominated the commercial paper market. Commercial paper is an important source of short-term financing for business that we will discuss in Chapter 16. Through buying and selling commercial paper, investment bankers assist with the short-term cash flow needs of many businesses. Three investment banking firms dominate commercial paper activities. They are Goldman Sachs, Merrill Lynch, and Credit Suisse.

FIGURE 11.3

Share Price Performance of Selected High-tech IPOs, November 2011 through December 2012

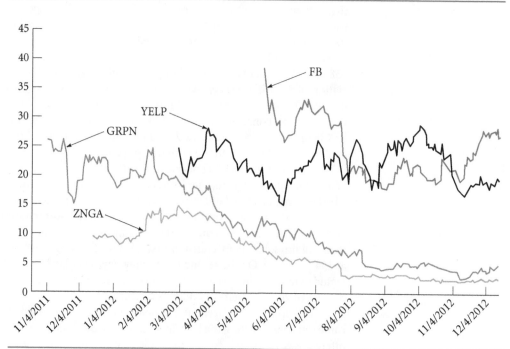

INTERNET ACTIVITY

An overview of various regulations and the Electronic Data Gathering and Retrieval (EDGAR) system for required SEC filings can be found at http://www.sec.gov.

ETHICAL ISSUES

broker

one who assists the trading process by buying or selling securities in the market for an investor

dealer

satisfies the investor's trades by buying and selling securities from his or her own inventory

blue-sky laws

protect the investor from fraudulent security offerings

In recent years, merger and acquisition (M&A) activities have increased in importance for many investment banking firms. Firms with strong M&A departments compete intensely for the highly profitable activity of corporate mergers or acquisitions. Investment banking firms act on behalf of corporate clients in identifying firms that may be suitable for merger. Large fees are charged for this service.

Other activities of investment bankers include the management of pension and endowment funds for businesses, colleges, churches, hospitals, and other institutions. In many cases, officers of investment banking firms are on the boards of directors of major corporations. In this capacity, they can offer financial advice and participate in the financial planning of the firm. Investment bankers also provide financial counseling on a fee basis.

Not all investment bankers engage in every one of these activities. The size of the firm largely dictates the various services it provides. Some firms, known as *boutiques*, specialize in a few activities, such as mergers or underwriting IPOs for high-tech firms.

INVESTMENT BANKING REGULATION

Federal regulation of investment banking is administered primarily under the provisions of the Securities Act of 1933. The chief purposes of the Act are to provide full, fair, and accurate disclosure of the character of newly issued securities offered for sale and to prevent fraud in the sale of such securities. The first purpose is achieved by requiring that the issuer file a registration statement with the Securities and Exchange Commission (SEC) and deliver a prospectus to potential investors. The SEC, however, does not pass judgment on the investment merit of any securities. It is illegal for a seller of securities to represent the SEC's approval of a registration statement as a recommendation of investment quality. The philosophy behind the Securities Act of 1933 is that the most effective regulatory device is the requirement that complete and accurate information be disclosed for securities on which investment decisions may be made. Although the SEC does not guarantee the accuracy of any statement made by an issuer of securities in a registration statement or prospectus, legal action may be taken against officers and other representatives of the issuing company for any false or incorrect statements. Full disclosure is, therefore, instrumental in accomplishing the second purpose, that of fraud prevention.

The Securities Exchange Act of 1934 established the SEC and gave it authority over the securities markets. All brokers and dealers doing business in the organized markets must register with the SEC. A **broker** assists the trading process by buying or selling securities in the market for an investor. A **dealer** satisfies investors' trades by buying and selling securities from his or her own inventory. In addition, attempts to manipulate securities prices were declared illegal.

In addition to federal regulation of investment banking, most states have **blue-sky laws** to protect investors from fraudulent security offerings. Blue-sky laws apparently get their name from the efforts of some unscrupulous operators who, if not restricted, would promise to sell investors pieces of the blue sky. Because state laws differ in their specific regulations, the federal government is the primary regulator of investment banking. The most common violation of state blue-sky laws is that of misrepresenting the financial condition and asset position of companies.

SMALL BUSINESS PRACTICE
Business Angels: Who Are They?

Business angels are private investors who provide startup capital for small businesses. Although they are wealthy individuals, angels seldom invest more that $100,000 in a firm. The annual investment in the angel market is estimated to be $20 billion. In addition to providing financing, angels provide valuable advice and sometimes help with the preparation of business plans. Robert Gaston completed a survey of over 400 angel investors for the Small Business Administration (SBA) and found the following: Angels typically are entrepreneurs and over 80 percent are business owners or managers. Angels will consider small investments, are usually older than the individuals they are helping, and are the largest source of small business financial

capital. Iris Lorenz-Fife in *Financing Your Business* (Prentice-Hall) provides valuable advice on how to attract angels, how to react when angels respond, and a checklist for the small business person to examine in terms of deciding whether angels are right for you.

Angels usually identify small business investment opportunities through word of mouth referrals from bankers, accountants, lawyers, and business consultants. Angels are attracted to individuals who have the drive to succeed. When an angel responds to a business plan, ensure you spell out the amount, timing, and length of the investment. Also, the degree of involvement of the angel in the firm's operations should be spelled out in advance.

CONCEPT CHECK

Describe the costs of "going public" by issuing shares of common stock.

What is the difference between a broker and a dealer?

What are some of the regulations that investment banks must follow?

The Glass-Steagall Act of 1933 ended the ability of commercial banks to act as underwriters of newly issued securities. There were many commercial bank failures during the Great Depression, and there was thought to be evidence that some of the failures resulted from the underwriting activities and poor equity investments of banks. With the passage of the Gramm-Leach-Bliley Act of 1999, the walls between commercial banking and investment banking fell and the traditional boundaries among insurance, commercial banks, investment banks, and other financial institutions have blurred.

TRADING SECURITIES—SECONDARY SECURITIES MARKETS

The primary market, we have learned, is where securities are first issued; the issuer sells the securities in an offering to investors. Any trading of the securities, thereafter, occurs in the secondary market. The secondary markets provide liquidity to investors who wish to sell securities. It is safe to say that, were it not for secondary securities markets for trading between investors, there would be no primary market for the initial sale of securities. Selling securities to investors would be difficult if investors had no easy way to profit from their holdings or no way to sell them for cash. Secondary markets allow investors to shift their assets into different securities and different markets. These markets provide pricing information, thus providing a means to evaluate a firm's management and for management to determine how investors are interpreting its actions. The secondary market for securities has two components: organized security exchanges, which have trading floors, and the over-the-counter (OTC) market, a network of independent dealers and agents who communicate and trade electronically rather than on a trading floor. The NYSE is the prime example of an organized exchange while NASDAQ is an OTC market.

A firm that fares poorly is penalized by pressure placed on the firm's management by its stockholders as market prices of its securities fall in the secondary market. In addition, when such a firm seeks new capital, it will have to provide a higher expected return to investors. The position of a firm's management becomes increasingly vulnerable as business deteriorates. Ultimately the firm's directors may replace management, or the firm may be a target of a takeover attempt.

ORGANIZED SECURITY EXCHANGES

An organized securities exchange is a location with a trading floor where all trading takes place under rules created by the exchange. Organized exchanges in the United States include the New York Stock Exchange (NYSE; this is part of the NYSE-Euronext group following a 2007 merger of a U.S. and European stock exchange) as well as several regional exchanges, such as the Boston, Chicago, Cincinnati, Philadelphia, and Pacific Stock Exchanges. The regionals trade local and national issues, including *dual-listed* stocks, which are those traded on more than one exchange. Another national exchange, the American Stock Exchange (AMEX), was merged into NYSE-Euronext in 2008; it has become part of the larger stock exchange and, in 2009, was renamed NYSE Amex Equities. The "branding" function of marketing works in finance as well as the NYSE-Euronext firm seeks to take advantage of the stature and goodwill of the "NYSE" brand in such renaming.

In late 2012, the IntercontinentalExchange (ICE) made a bid, valued at the time at over $8 billion, to buy NYSE-Euronext. If approved by U.S. and European regulators, it will create the world's largest exchange operator. The iconic "New York Stock Exchange" name, with its global recognition, will likely not change after the acquisition. If approved, a newly formed company, ICE Group, will have two units: NYSE-Euronext will focus on stock trading, and the IntercontinentalExchange (ICE) will a focus on trading futures, options, and other such contracts.

The organized stock exchanges use the latest in electronic communications. This ensures an internally efficient trading mechanism where orders are tracked and processed quickly. It ensures that prices on the different exchanges are identical, so a trader cannot *arbitrage*, or purchase a security on one exchange at one price while selling it on another, at a different price, to lock in a riskless profit. The present methods of transmitting information within cities and between cities are in sharp contrast to the devices used before the introduction of the telegraph in 1844. Quotations were conveyed between New York and Philadelphia through signal flags in the daytime and light signals at night from high point to high point across New Jersey in as little as ten minutes.

Because of its relative importance and because in most respects its operations are typical of those of the other exchanges, the NYSE, sometimes called the "Big Board," will provide the basis for the following description of exchange organization and activities.

STRUCTURE OF THE NEW YORK STOCK EXCHANGE

Like all the stock exchanges in the nation, the objective of the NYSE is to provide a convenient meeting place where buyers and sellers of securities or their representatives may conduct business. In addition, the NYSE provides facilities for the settlement of transactions, establishes rules for the trading processes and the activities of its members, provides publicity for the transactions, and establishes standards for the corporations whose securities are traded on the exchange.

There are three basic types of members: designated market makers, floor brokers, and registered traders. In turn, there are two variations of floor brokers: house brokers and independent brokers.

The largest group of members on the New York Stock Exchange is the house brokers. The key function of **house brokers**, or **commission brokers**, is to act as agents to execute customers' orders for securities purchases and sales. In return, the broker receives a commission for the service. Merrill Lynch owns several seats used by their house brokers. **Independent brokers** handle the house brokers' overflow. When trading volume is particularly heavy, house brokers will ask an independent broker to help them in handling their orders. **Registered traders** are individuals who purchase a seat on the exchange to buy and sell stocks for their own account. Since they do their own trading, they do not pay any commissions. They may also be on retainer from a brokerage house, often a regional firm that does not want its own seat on the exchange.

Designated market markers (DMMs), or assigned dealers, have the responsibility of making a market in an assigned security. Each stock is assigned to a DMM[10], who has a trading post on the exchange floor. DMMs select the opening price at the start of trading each day, based upon the previous day's closing price and the backlog of buy and sell orders that exist. As market makers, DMMs maintain an inventory of the security in question and stands ready to buy or sell to maintain a fair and orderly market. That means they must be ready to purchase shares of their assigned stock when there are many sellers. and they must be willing to sell shares when traders want to buy. Exchange regulations require DMMs to maintain an orderly market, meaning that trading prices should not change by more than a few cents (stocks are traded in decimals, so the smallest difference in price can be one cent). DMMs maintain bid and asked prices for the security, and the margin between the two prices represents the DMMs' potential gross profit. The bid price is that price the buyer is willing to pay for the securities (thus, it represents the investors' selling price). The ask price is the price at which the owner is willing to sell securities (thus, it represents the investors' purchase price). If the current bid price from brokers is 50.00 and the current ask price is 50.05, DMMs may enter a bid of 50.02 or 50.03 or a lower ask price to lower the spread and maintain market order.

A recent innovation to the NYSE is a new set of traders called **Supplemental Liquidity Providers** (SLPs). Their purpose is to help add liquidity to the NYSE trading floor, meaning they supplement the work of DMMs by buying and selling shares throughout the day. To be an SLP, the firm must present the best bid or offer prices in their assigned securities at least 5 percent of the trading day. The NYSE pays the liquidity providers a rebate when they execute a trade. The goal is for the SLPs to generate more bid and ask prices and to lead to tighter bid-ask spreads and greater liquidity in the stock market.

A penny may not seem like much, but an extra penny per share profit on the billion shares traded each day on the NYSE can add to a sizable sum. In the past, trading in listed stocks was supervised by "specialists" rather than DMMs or SLPs. Specialists, which did several of the functions of the current DMMs, had access to order flow information, meaning expected orders, called limit orders that would be forthcoming should prices change (we will discuss limit orders in a few pages). Specialist firms were accused of placing their own interests above that of their customers by "front running." Front running occurred when a specialist traded to take advantage of information they had (but others did not) about large buy or sell orders that would soon be

house brokers (commission brokers)
act as agents to execute customers' orders for securities purchases and sales

independent brokers
handle the commission brokers' overflow

registered traders
individuals who purchase a seat on the exchange to buy and sell stocks for their own account

designated market makers (DMM)
assigned dealers who have the responsibility of making a market in an assigned security

INTERNET ACTIVITY

GETCO LLC is a NYSE designated market maker; their Web site is http://www.getcollc. com. Names of other DMMs, are available on the NYSE Web site, http://usequities.nyx. com/listings/dmms.

Supplemental Liquidity Providers (SLPs)
help add liquidity to the NYSE trading floor, meaning they supplement the work of DMMs by buying and selling shares throughout the day

ETHICAL ISSUES

---

10. The six designated market markers are: Barclay's Capital, GETCO LLC, Knight Capital Group, LLC, Goldman Sachs, J. Streicher & Co. LLC, and Virtu Financial Capital Markets LLC.

INTERNET ACTIVITY

Learn about the different exchanges and their listing requirements at http://www. nyse.com, https://usequities. nyx.com/markets/nyse-mkt-equities, and http://www. nasdaq.com. Many international exchanges are available on the Web, too. See, for example, the Toronto Stock Exchange, http://www.tsx.com; exchanges in the United Kingdom, http://www. londonstockexchange.com; the Tokyo Stock Exchange, http:// www.tse.or.jp/english/index. htm ; and the Frankfort Stock Exchange, http://www. deutsche-boerse.com. Links to many more are available at www.world-exchanges.org (World Federation of Exchanges).

CONCEPT CHECK

How do secondary securities markets assist the function of primary markets?

Describe the four types of members of the New York Stock Exchange.

bid
price offered by a potential buyer

ask
price requested by the seller

spread
difference between the bid and ask prices

market order
an order for immediate purchase or sale at the best possible price

placed. An example would be buying a stock for $23.27 knowing in a few minutes a customer will place a large buy order which will likely push the price higher to $23.30 or $23.32.

Another example of profiting from trades is "negative obligation," that is, when a specialist intervened in a trade when his or her assistance is unnecessary. It occurs when a specialist purchased shares from a seller and then immediately sold them to a buyer at a higher price. The specialist should have allowed the two traders to trade between themselves without the specialist making a profit. In 2004, the NYSE and SEC fined five specialist firms $240 million for such tactics. The NYSE received sanctions, too, from the SEC and was forced to add staff and funds to increase its oversight of regulations and trading. The new DMM structure lessens the chance of such unfair trading activity.

Other exchanges face ethics issues, too. In the late 1990s, two dozen firms involved in NASDAQ trading were accused of setting unfairly high trading commissions and were fined a total of $900 million.

Listing Securities

All securities must be listed before they may be traded on the New York Stock Exchange (NYSE). To qualify for listing its security, a corporation must meet certain requirements regarding profitability, total value of outstanding stock, or stockholder's equity. Over time, the NYSE revamped its listing standards in an attempt to attract more high-growth firms (which had been favoring the NASDAQ OTC market for listings) and more foreign companies.[11] The corporation also pays a fee for the privilege of being listed. The original listing fee ranges from $150,000–$250,000. Continuing annual fees range from $35,000–$500,000, depending on the number of outstanding shares. The acceptance of the security by the exchange for listing on the Big Board does not constitute endorsement of its quality.

Security Transactions

Buying and selling securities is similar to buying and selling other items in a negotiated market. Whether you want to sell a house or a car, you have a price you are asking potential buyers to pay. Buyers of your house or car may not want to pay your price but will offer their own price, a bid, to see if you will agree to sell for a lower price. In security transactions, potential buyers place **bid** prices, as in an auction, and sellers have their **ask** prices. The difference between the lower bid and higher ask is the **spread**. The narrower the spread, the more liquid the market and the quicker a transaction can be made.

Internet sites inform us (with a time delay, unless you purchase access to real-time data) what the bid and ask prices for a security throughout the day. For example, a quote from such a site for Microsoft stock may show the following:

Bid: 30.42 × 50900
Ask: 30.43 × 50800

This means there is demand for 50,900 shares by potential buyers at that point during the day and the highest bid price for Microsoft shares is $30.42. There are 50,800 shares offered for sell at that time and the lowest asking price is $30.43. With trading in pennies, this is the tightest spread possible since only one cent separates the bid and ask prices. This shows that Microsoft stock, at least in this snapshot of time, is quite liquid.

Investors can place a number of different types of orders to buy or sell securities. To execute a trade, they need to contact a stock brokerage firm where they can set up an account. The investor can then specify the type of order to be placed as well as the number of shares to be traded in specific firms. Securities orders to buy and sell can be market, limit, or stop-loss orders.

Market Order

An order for immediate purchase or sale at the best possible price is a **market order**. The brokerage firm that receives an order to trade shares of stock listed on the NYSE at the best price possible transmits the order to its New York office, where the order is transmitted to its commission broker on the floor of the exchange.

11. The listing standards for U.S. firms can be found on the NYSE website: http://usequities.nyx.com/regulation/listed-companies-compliance/listings-standards/us

Limit Order

limit order
maximum buying price (limit buy) or the minimum selling price (limit sell) specified by the investor

In a **limit order,** the maximum buying price (limit buy) or the minimum selling price (limit sell) is specified by the investor. For example, if a commission broker has a limit buy order at 50 from an investor and other brokers have ask prices higher than 50, the order would not be filled at that moment. The broker will wait until a price of 50 or less becomes available. Of course, if the price of the stock progresses upward rather than downward, the order will not be completed. Limit orders may be placed to expire at the end of one day, one week, one month, or on a good-until-canceled basis.

Stop-Loss Order

stop-loss order
order to sell stock at the market price when the price of the stock falls to a specified level

A **stop-loss order** is an order to sell stock at the market price when the price of the stock falls to a specified level. The stockholder may protect gains or limit losses due to a fall in the price of the stock by placing a stop-loss order at a price a few points below the current market price. For example, an investor paying $50 for shares of stock may place a stop-loss order at a price of $45. If the price does fall to $45, the commission broker sells the shares for as high a price as possible. This order does not guarantee a price of $45 to the seller since, by the time the stock is actually sold; a rapidly declining stock price may have fallen to well below $45. On the other hand, if the stock price does not reach the specified price, the order will not be executed.

These orders can be used to protect profits. If the stock increases in price after its purchase, the investor can cancel the old stop-loss order and issue a new one at a higher price.

Short Sale

short sale
sale of securities that the seller does not own

A **short sale** is sale of securities that the seller does not own. An investor will want to short a stock if he or she feels the price will decline in the future. Shares of the stock are borrowed by the broker and sold in the stock market. In the event that a price decline does occur, the short seller covers the resulting short position by buying enough stock to repay the lender. If any dividends are paid during the time the stock is shorted, the short seller must pay the dividends owed on the borrowed shares.

As an example, suppose Amy thinks AT&T's stock price will fall in the future because of intense competition in the telecommunications industry. She contacts her broker, for example, Merrill Lynch, and gives instructions to sell 100 shares of AT&T short. The broker in turn arranges to borrow the necessary stock, probably from another Merrill Lynch investor who has their stock in **street name**, meaning they keep their stock certificates at the brokerage firm rather than taking personal possession of them. Having sold the borrowed stock, the brokerage house keeps the proceeds of the sale as collateral. In our example, if the securities were sold at $40, Merrill Lynch will keep the proceeds from the 100 shares, $4,000, in Amy's account. Let's say the stock drops to a price of $36 and Amy wants to cover her short position. She tells her broker to buy 100 shares, which costs her $3,600. Merrill Lynch returns the newly purchased shares to the account from which they were borrowed. Amy sold $4,000 worth of stock and purchased $3,600 worth of stock after it fell in price; the difference, $400, is Amy's profit, ignoring brokerage commissions. The person from whose account the shares were borrowed will never know that they were borrowed; Merrill Lynch's internal record keeping will keep track of all such transactions.

street name
an investor's stock certificates are kept at the brokerage firm rather than taking personal possession of them

If the price of AT&T stock rises, the short seller must still cover her short position at some future time. If the price rises to $45 a share and the position is closed, Amy will pay $4,500 to purchase 100 shares to cover her position. Amy will suffer a loss of ($4,000 − $4,500) or $500 from her short sale.

Because short sales have an important effect on the market for securities, the SEC regulates them closely. Heavy short sale trades can place undue pressure on a firm's stock price. Among the restrictions on short sales is one relating to selling only on an uptick. This means that a short sale can take place only when the last change in the market price of the stock from transaction-to-transaction was an increase. For example, if the most recent transaction prices were 39.95, 39.95, 40.00, 40.00, 40.00, the short sale would be allowed as the last price change was an increase. A short sale would not be allowed if the most recent transactions prices were, for example, 40.07, 40.01, 40.00 or 40.10, 40.00, 40.00, since the most recent price change was a decrease.

In addition, Federal Reserve System (Fed) and NYSE regulations require the short seller to maintain a margin or deposit of at least 50 percent of the price of the stock with the broker. Loans of stock are callable on 24 hours' notice.

Buying on Margin

Buying on margin means the investors borrow money and invest it along with their own funds in securities. The securities so purchased become collateral for the loan. The **margin** is the minimum percentage of the purchase price that investors must pay in cash. In other words, margin is the ratio of the investor's equity (own money) to the market value of the security. In order to buy on margin, the investor must have a margin account with the brokerage firm, which in turn arranges the necessary financing with banks.

Margin trading is risky; it magnifies the profits as well as the losses from investment positions. For example, suppose an investor borrows $20,000 and combines it with $30,000 of his own money to purchase $50,000 worth of stocks. His initial margin is 60 percent ($30,000 of his own money divided by the $50,000 value of the securities). Should the market value of his stock rise 10 percent to $55,000, the value of his equity rises to $35,000:

Market value of securities:	$55,000
Less: borrowed funds	$20,000
Value of investor's position:	$35,000

This increase in value to $35,000 represents a gain of 16.7 percent ($5,000/$30,000). A 10 percent rise in the stock's value increased the value of the investor's position by 16.7 percent because of the use of margin.

Margin also magnifies losses. If the value of the securities falls by 10 percent to $45,000, the value of the investor's equity would fall to $25,000:

Market value of securities:	$45,000
Less: borrowed funds	$20,000
Value of investor's position:	$25,000

This loss in value to $25,000 represents a loss of 16.7 percent. A 10 percent fall in the stock's value decreased the value of the investor's position by 16.7 percent because of the use of margin.

Should the value of the securities used as collateral in a margin trade begin to decline, the investor may receive a **margin call** from the brokerage firm. The investor will face a choice of either closing out the position or investing additional cash to increase the position's equity or margin. If the market price of the pledged securities continues to decline and the investor fails to provide the new margin amount, the brokerage house will sell the securities. Under current Fed regulations, investors must have an **initial margin** of at least 50 percent when entering into a margined trade. The minimum **maintenance margin** to which the position can fall is 25 percent before the broker will have to close out the position. Depending upon the individual investor's creditworthiness, a brokerage firm can impose more stringent margin requirements.

The combination of falling prices, margin calls, and sales of securities can develop into a downward spiral for securities prices. This kind of spiral played an important role in the stock market crash of 1929. At that time, there was no regulatory restraint on margin sales and, in fact, margins of only 10 percent were common. An outcome of this was the Securities Act of 1933 and the Securities Exchange Act of 1934 to regulate short sales, margin trading, and the process of issuing and trading securities.

Record Keeping

When a trade takes place, the information is sent to a central computer system, which, in turn, sends the information to display screens across the nation. This consolidated report includes all transactions on the New York Stock Exchange (NYSE) as well as those on the regional exchanges and other markets trading NYSE-listed stocks. Trades can be for a **round lot** of 100 shares or an **odd lot,** a trade of fewer than 100 shares.[12] The details of the purchase transaction are sent to the exchange's central office and then to the brokerage office where the order was placed. Trade information is also sent to the registrar of the company whose shares were traded. The company needs this information so new certificates can be issued in the name of the investor or the brokerage firm (if the shares are to be kept in street name). Likewise, records will be updated so dividends, annual reports, and shareholder voting material can be sent to the proper person.

buying on margin
investors borrow money and invest it along with their own funds in securities

margin
the ratio of the investor's equity (own money) to the market value of the security

margin call
the option of either closing out the position or investing additional cash to increase the position's equity or margin

initial margin
initial equity percentage

maintenance margin
minimum margin to which an investment may fall before a margin call will be placed

round lot
sale or purchase of 100 shares

odd lot
sale or purchase of fewer than 100 shares

---

12. For a few high-priced stocks listed on the New York Stock Exchange (NYSE), a round lot is ten shares.

INTERNET ACTIVITY

Examples of how trades are placed can be found on the Web sites of several exchanges, including http://www.nyse.com and http://www.nasdaq.com.

program trading
technique for trading stocks as a group rather than individually; a minimum of 15 different stocks with a minimum value of $1 million are traded

CONCEPT CHECK

How does a limit order differ from a stop order?

How does a short sale work? What does "buying on margin" mean?

A security is bought in *street name* when the brokerage house buys the security in its own name on behalf of the investor. The advantage of this is the investor may sell the securities by phoning the broker without the necessity of signing and delivering the certificates. New regulations imposed in 1995 require stock trades to be settled in three days. Before this regulation, settlement did not have to take place until five days after the trade. This "T+3" requirement means funds to purchase shares or stock certificates of shares that were sold must be presented to the stock broker within three days of the stock trade. This shorter settlement time should make street name accounts more appealing to investors. Plans are underway for a "T+1" (one-day settlement requirement) and hopes exist for an all-electronic process that would make settlement immediate.

Program Trading

Around 1975, stocks began to be traded not only individually but also in packages or programs. **Program trading** is a technique for trading stocks as a group rather than individually; it is defined as the trading for a group of at least fifteen different stocks with a value of at least $1 million. At first, program trades were simply trades of any portfolio of stocks held by an equity manager who wanted to change the portfolio's composition for any number of reasons. Today, the portfolios traded in package form are often made up of the stocks included in a stock index, such as the Standard & Poor's 500. In a typical week, 25 percent of all NYSE trades are program trades; in some weeks, the percentage has risen to over 40 percent. The most active program traders include Morgan Stanley, Merrill Lynch, UBS, Credit Suisse, and Goldman Sachs.

A wide range of portfolio trading strategies is now described as program trading. The best known form of program trading is known as *index arbitrage*, when traders buy and sell stocks with offsetting trades in futures and options to lock in profits from price differences between these different markets.[13] Program traders use computers to keep track of prices in the different markets and to give an execution signal when appropriate. At the moment the signal is given, the orders for the stocks are sent directly to the NYSE trading floor for execution by the proper designated market maker (DMM). The use of computers allows trades to be accomplished more quickly. This can cause problems if price movements trigger simultaneous sales orders by a number of large program traders. A serious plunge in market prices may occur. As a result, efforts have been made to control some aspects of program trading by limiting its use on days when the Dow Jones Industrial Average (DJIA) rises or falls more than 10 percent.

Over-the-Counter Market

In addition to the organized exchanges, the other major secondary market for securities trading is the over-the-counter (OTC) market. The largest OTC market is the NASDAQ system; NASDAQ stands for National Association of Securities Dealers Automated Quotation. Although it trades more than twice as many issues as the NYSE, the OTC is composed mainly of stocks of smaller firms even though companies such as Intel, Microsoft, Novell, and Apple Computer are listed on it.

There are several differences between the organized exchanges and the OTC market. Organized exchanges have a central trading location or floor, such as the NYSE trading floor on Wall Street in New York City. The OTC is a telecommunications network linking brokers and dealers that trade OTC stocks. The organized exchanges have DMMs that make markets and control trading in listed stocks; the OTC has no DMMs. Instead, OTC dealers buy from and sell for their own account to the public, other dealers, and commission brokers. In a sense, they operate in the manner of any merchant. They have an inventory, composed of the securities in which they specialize, that they hope to sell at a price enough above their purchase price to make a profit. The OTC markets argue that theirs is a competitive system, with multiple dealers making a market in a company's stock.

To trade in an OTC stock, investors contact their broker, who then checks a computer listing of dealers for that particular stock. After determining which dealer has the highest bid price or lowest ask price, the broker contacts the dealer to confirm the price and to execute the transaction.

INTERNET ACTIVITY

The NASDAQ Web site is http://www.nasdaq.com.

---

13. Futures and options are discussed in this chapter's Learning Extension.

The OTC market is regulated by the Maloney Act of 1938. This act amended the Securities Exchange Act of 1934 to extend SEC control to the OTC market. The law created the legal basis for OTC brokers and dealers to form national self-regulating trade associations. This was one instance where business requested government regulation. It stemmed from honest dealers in the investment field who had little protection against bad publicity resulting from the unscrupulous practices of a few OTC dealers. Under this provision, the Financial Industry Regulatory Authority (FINRA) was formed.[14] All rules adopted by FINRA must be reported to the SEC. The SEC has the authority to take away any powers of the FINRA.

The FINRA has established a lengthy set of rules and regulations intended to ensure fair practices and responsibility on the part of the association's members. Any broker or dealer engaged in OTC activities is eligible to become a member of the FINRA as long as it can prove a record of responsible operation and the broker or dealer is willing to accept the FINRA code of ethics.

Third and Fourth Security Markets

It should not be surprising that an activity as broad as the security market would give rise to special arrangements. Despite their names, the third and fourth markets are two additional types of secondary markets that have evolved over time.

third market
market for large blocks of listed stocks that operates outside the confines of the organized exchanges

The **third market** is a market for large blocks of listed shares that operates outside the confines of the organized exchanges. In the third market, blocks of stock (units of 10,000 shares) are traded OTC. The participants in the third market are large institutions (such as mutual funds, insurance companies, and pension funds) that often need to trade large blocks of shares. Brokers assist the institutions in the third market by bringing buyers and sellers together and, in return, receive a fee.

fourth market
a market in which large institutional investors arrange the purchase and sale of securities among themselves without the benefit of broker or dealer

The **fourth market** is even further removed from the world of organized securities trading. Electronic communications networks (ECNs) are computerized trading systems that automatically match buy and sell orders at specified prices. Certain large institutional investors arrange purchases and sales of securities among themselves without the benefit of a broker or dealer. They subscribe to an electronic network in which offers to buy or sell are made known to other subscribers. The offers are made in code, and institutions wishing to accept a buy or sell offer know the identity of the other party only upon acceptance of the offer. A fee is paid to the network provider when the trade is completed. Those who support fourth market trading argue that transfers are often quicker and more economical, but confidentiality is an important feature to many firms.

WHAT MAKES A GOOD MARKET?

NYSE, NASDAQ, third market, fourth market: What are the requirements for a good market? What makes one market better for trading than another for a certain type of transaction?

Competition exists in our product markets. For example, the local Wal-Mart store is a marketplace for buying and selling goods except that Wal-Mart is the lone seller and we, the consumers, are the buyers. Other large stores nearby compete for the consumer dollar, wanting you to enter their store and to "trade" with them.

Competition exists among exchanges, too. NYSE, NASDAQ, and others are encouraging firms to list their shares with them so the exchange benefits from the trading volume. For example, NYSE has been perceived as listing only quality firms that have many shareholders and a history of financial success. NASDAQ has allowed smaller firms and firms without a financial track record to list with them. NASDAQ's emphasis on technology (as trading occurs via market makers and computers rather than in a physical location) has attracted many high-tech firms to list their shares on NASDAQ, such as Microsoft, Intel, Cisco Systems, and Dell Computer.

One exchange will boast of quicker execution of trades to encourage investors to trade securities on their exchange rather than a competitor. For example, NASDAQ has argued its technology will allow faster trade execution than NYSE's DMM system. Over time, NYSE has responded by automating some trades that do not require interaction with a DMM.

A good market will have four characteristics: liquidity, quick and accurate trade execution, reasonable listing requirements, and low costs. Let's discuss each of these in turn:

---

14. Prior to 2007, this organization was known as National Association of Security Dealers (NASD).

PERSONAL FINANCIAL PLANNING
Stock Market Indexes

"What did the market do today?" is an often heard question in financial circles. Although the question sounds ambiguous (which market?), the speakers and their intended listener know which market: the stock market, specifically the performance of the Dow Jones Industrial Average (DJIA). As we mention in the chapter, the DJIA is comprised of only thirty firms, but they are thirty large firms whose market capitalization (that is, the number of shares multiplied by the stock price) is large compared to those of other firms. There are dozens of stock market indexes, and even more examples of indexes abound for the bond markets.

Why are indexes so popular? First, they are a means of representing the movement and returns to the overall market or a segment of the market. The DJIA 30, S&P500, and Wilshire 5000 are measures of stock market performance. The NYSE, AMEX, and NASDAQ indexes measure the performance of the New York, American, and OTC stock markets.

Second, indexes are a useful comparison when you want to benchmark the performance of a portfolio. If your investment advisor recommends a portfolio of stocks that rose 10 percent in value while the S&P500 rose 20 percent, you may feel that his or her recommendations were not good. On the other hand, if his or her selections were all OTC stocks and the NASDAQ index rose only 5 percent, you may judge his or her performance more favorably.

Third, indexes are gaining popularity as investments themselves. Rather than invest to "beat the market," which is difficult to do (as we'll see in Chapter 12 with the discussion of efficient capital markets), more investors are coming to believe the saying, "if you can't beat them, join them." They are choosing to invest in the stocks and bonds that comprise an index in the hope of matching the index's performance over time. Many mutual funds exist so the small investor can do this quickly and easily by purchasing shares of the mutual fund.

A market is liquid if trades are executed quickly at a price close to fair market value. Generally, a market needs to have breadth and depth to be liquid.

A market has depth if it can absorb large buy and sell orders without disrupting prices. This may mean there are investors with deep pockets willing to take the opposite side of a large trade or there are many traders each of whom is willing to help execute the trade. A broad market, or one with breadth, attracts many traders. In general, having many traders makes a market more competitive; a few large traders may be able to set prices in their own favor rather than allowing competitive forces determine price levels. Generally, trading is more liquid if the difference between the bidder's buy and the seller's ask price is small. Otherwise, large price jumps can occur, depending on how anxious a trader is to execute his buy or sell order.

The second characteristic, quick and accurate execution of trades, is reasonably self-explanatory. The quicker the sale or purchase is executed, the quicker the investor can receive confirmation and know the transaction price. Studies have indicated that small stock transactions done electronically average one-tenth of a second to execute whereas larger transactions can take up to 10 seconds.[15] The size of the trade, the liquidity of the stock, and the venue affect the transaction time. Computer trading is quickest, NYSE DMM trading is the slowest, and NASDAQ dealers lie in between. But good recordkeeping is needed, too, to verify the price of the transactions. Portfolio managers (to measure the performance of their stock selections) and individual traders (for tax records) need accurate transactions records.

Thirdly, reasonable listing requirements allow investors to know the quality of the listed firm. The NYSE has the highest standards, in terms of stock ownership, earnings, and cash flow. But many firms that could meet the NYSE standards decide to list their shares elsewhere, believing costs may be cheaper and investor trade execution faster on another exchange. Nonetheless, the average size and profitability is lower for NASDAQ firms than NYSE firms. The "pink sheet" (an OTC market, now computerized, that started trading speculative issues listed on pink sheets of paper)[16] has no listing fees and its quotes are provided only by dealers making a market in the stock. Its securities are fairly speculative.

Finally, a good market will offer reasonable listing fees to issuers (lest they price themselves out of the market for listings) and low costs to investors. Costs to investors include the commissions paid for stock or bond purchases but also "hidden" costs. Hidden costs include the lack of breadth (i.e., few traders) so the buyer must pay the higher ask price of the security (or the seller must accept the lower bid price). Another hidden cost is price pressure, which is another indicator of a

CONCEPT CHECK

What are four characteristics of a good market?

How do market breadth and market depth differ?

---

15. Gregory Crawford, "Inconsistency Haunts Investor Equity Trades, Report Says," *Pensions and Investments*, January 9, 2006, p. 28.

16. "Yellow sheets" refer to OTC bond market quotations for smaller and lower quality bond issues.

market that lacks good liquidity. Price pressure occurs when a large trade moves the market (i.e., it causes the market price to change) before it can be fully executed. Professional traders learn to parcel out large trades into smaller trades and to work with several dealers or market makers to minimize price changes that occur because of the large transaction. But a market that can absorb such trades is a benefit to investors.

A WORD ON COMMISSIONS

INTERNET ACTIVITY

Merrill Lynch (http://www. ml.com) is a full service broker; Charles Schwab (http://www. schwab.com) is a premier discount broker that offers stock trading, some research, mutual funds, annuities, and life insurance. An example of an online broker is E*TRADE (http://www.etrade.com).

CONCEPT CHECK

What factors affect the size of a commission on a trade?

Why has stock trading on the Internet increased so rapidly in recent years?

It costs money to trade securities. About the only market participants that don't pay commissions are the exchange DMMs, supplemental liquidity providers, and registered traders on the NYSE and dealers in OTC stocks.

Stock commissions vary from brokerage firm to brokerage firm. Some brokerage firms, called "full-service" brokerages, assist your trades and have research staffs that analyze firms and make recommendations on which stocks to buy or sell. Their analysts write research reports that are available to the firm's brokerage customers. Examples of full-service brokerages include Merrill Lynch, A.G. Edwards, and Morgan Stanley.

"Discount" brokerages are for investors who want someone to do their stock transactions. Investors who do not desire or need the extra services of a full-service broker use discounters. Stereotypical discount investors make their own investment decisions and wish to trade at the lowest possible costs. Examples of discount brokerages include Brown and Company, Charles Schwab, Muriel Siebert, and Olde Discount. With low overhead costs and offers of basic services, stock trading on some Internet-based brokerages are inexpensive even compared to discount brokers. Falling commissions and ease of access make online trading attractive to those who make their own investment decisions. Trading commissions for some online brokerages are under $7 a trade.

Commissions on security trades depend upon several additional factors. Commissions generally are lower on more liquid securities (more actively traded securities or securities with a popular secondary market). Commissions generally are higher, as a proportion of the market value of the securities purchased, for smaller trades that involve fewer shares or lower-priced shares. Many brokerages charge a minimum commission that may make small trades costly. They charge a transaction fee to cover their costs of processing the trade. Others assess fees if your account is inactive for a year; in other words, even if you don't trade, you still pay the broker some fees. As with so many other things in life, wise investors will shop around for the brokerage firm and broker that best meets their particular needs.

It is possible to buy shares of some companies without going through a stock broker. Some firms sell their shares directly to the public; this is called *direct investing*. Other firms allow shareholders to add to their stock holdings through dividend reinvestment plans; as the name implies, the shareholder's dividends are used to purchase shares (including partial or fractional shares) of the firm.

SECURITY MARKET INDEXES

If one listens to the radio, watches television, or reads the newspaper, the phrases "Dow Jones Industrial Average" or "Standard & Poor's 500 Stock Index" will be encountered daily. The thirty stocks that are part of the Dow Jones Industrial Average (DJIA) are listed in Table 11.4. You are probably familiar with most of their names.

Market indexes are useful for keeping track of trends in an overall market (such as the NYSE index, which tracks all stocks listed in the NYSE), a sector (the S&P400 industrials summarizes the movements in 400 stocks of industrial firms), or specific industries (Dow Jones' various industry indexes, such as those for banks, autos, chemicals, retail, and many others). Market indexes exist for many different countries' securities markets, including a variety of stock and bond market indexes.

There are many ways in which an index can be constructed; the previous paragraph shows that indexes can cover different security market segments. Indexes also can be computed in different ways. For example, the Dow Jones Industrial Average of thirty large "blue-chip" stocks is based upon a sum of their prices; it is an example of a price-weighted index. The S&P500 stock index is computed partly by summing the market values (the stock price times the number of shares outstanding) of the 500 component stocks; it is an example of a value-weighted index. Still other indexes are based upon other computational schemes.

TABLE 11.4

Stocks in the Dow Jones Industrial Average (as of October 2013)

American Express	AT&T	Boeing
Caterpillar	Chevron	Cisco Systems
Coca-Cola	DuPont	ExxonMobil
General Electric	Goldman Sachs	Home Depot
IBM	Intel	Johnson & Johnson
JPMorgan Chase	McDonalds	Merck
Microsoft	3M	Nike
Pfizer	Procter and Gamble	Travelers
UnitedHealth Group	United Technologies	Visa
Verizon	WalMart	Walt Disney

The 500 stocks comprising the S&P500 are not the largest 500 firms or the 500 stocks with the largest market values. A nineteen-member committee of Standard & Poor's Corporation selects the stocks in the index. The committee tries to have each industry represented in the S&P500 index in proportion to its presence among all publicly traded stocks. Most of the changes that occur in the S&P500 index occur because of firms' mergers, acquisitions, or bankruptcies. Because it is an index based upon market values, large market value firms, or "large capitalization" stocks as they are called, are the main influences on the index's movements over time.

Bond indexes exist, too; Barclays (Treasury bonds) and Merrill Lynch (corporates) publish bond indexes that show trends in their respective markets. An "aggregate" bond market index will include different types of bonds. Some of these indexes will favor intermediate-term Treasury securities, longer-term agencies, and corporate bonds.

GLOBAL DISCUSSION

FOREIGN SECURITIES

The growth in the market value of foreign securities has occurred because of general economic expansion, deregulation of exchange rates, and liberalization of regulations of equity markets. The integration of the world's markets is emphasized by the fact that many securities are listed on several markets. The London Stock Exchange, for example, has over 500 foreign listings, of which about 200 are U.S. firms. The major U.S. stock markets, the NYSE and NASDAQ, trade about 600 foreign stocks. Foreign stocks can be traded in the United States if they are registered with the Securities and Exchange Commission (SEC).

INTERNET ACTIVITY

The Bank of New York developed the ADR index (see it on the Internet at http://www.adrbnymellon.com).

Why would foreign companies raise funds in the United States? The reason is similar to the reason U.S. firms will tap overseas markets: to gain access to new funding sources and to finance overseas assets with overseas financing. But another reason that foreign companies want a presence in the U.S. capital markets is their breadth and depth: Companies can find an audience for their shares and raise huge amounts of capital. Some leading world economies have stock markets that are all but ignored by their citizens. Germans prefer the safety of savings accounts and bonds; only 13 percent own stocks. Only 7 percent of Japanese own shares.[17] One reason for this is government pension systems, which diminish the need to invest long-term for one's retirement. Another is a culture that favors conservative investment strategies.

Investors and professional money managers have found it increasingly important to diversify their investments among the world's markets. Such diversification makes possible a broader search for investment values and can reduce the risk in investment portfolios.[18]

American depository receipt (ADR)

receipt that represents foreign shares to U.S. investors

Investment in foreign shares by U.S. investors may be facilitated through the use of **American depository receipts (ADRs)** for short. These ADRs are traded on our exchanges and are as negotiable as other securities. They are created when a broker purchases shares of a foreign company's stock in its local stock market. The shares are delivered to a U.S. bank's local custodian bank in the foreign country. The bank then issues depository receipts. There is not necessarily a one-to-one

17. Sara Calian and Silvia Ascorelli, "Europeans Lose Love for Stocks," *The Wall Street Journal* (May 12, 2004), p. C1; and Craig Karmin, "The Global Shareholder," *The Wall Street Journal* (May 8, 2000), p. R4.

18. The topic of diversification and its effect on the risk of an investment portfolio will be discussed in Chapter 12.

CAREER OPPORTUNITIES IN FINANCE
Field: Securities Markets

Opportunities

Individuals and institutions invest in stocks and bonds to finance assets and to create wealth. Many times, as with large corporations, these investments for any given day may be in the millions of dollars. Most investors, however, have neither the time nor the resources to properly plan these investments. Instead, investors turn to securities specialists to plan and execute investment decisions.

Jobs like these require that individuals have the ability to make sound decisions quickly under heavy pressure. For those who excel though, the opportunities are limitless. Brokerage firms, bank trust departments, and insurance companies typically hire professionals in this field.

Jobs

Account Executive, Securities Analyst

Responsibilities

An *account executive*, or securities broker, sells stocks and bonds to individual and institutional customers as well as manages client funds consistent with client risk-taking objectives. In addition, an account executive must actively pursue new clients and learn about new investment possibilities. Securities firms typically hire account executives to fill entry-level positions. A *securities analyst* includes being a securities analyst or a securities trader for brokerage firms. A securities analyst must evaluate the value of stocks and bonds and present this information to, or act on this information for, investors.

Education

A strong background in finance, economics, and marketing is necessary for these jobs. In addition, these jobs require the ability to communicate and negotiate effectively.

---

global depository receipt (GDR)

listed on the London Stock Exchange; facilitates trading in foreign shares

CONCEPT CHECK

What does an index measure?

What are ADRs?

ETHICAL ISSUES

relationship between shares and depository receipts; one depository receipt may represent five, ten, or more shares of the foreign company's stock. ADRs allow U.S. investors to invest in foreign firms without the problems of settling overseas trades or having to personally exchange currencies. ADRs are traded in dollars, and dividends are paid in dollars as well. A *global depository receipt (GDR)* is similar to an ADR, but it is listed on the London Stock Exchange. U.S. investors can buy GDRs through a broker in the United States.

As securities markets become more global, more foreign firms will seek to have their shares or ADRs listed on a U.S. exchange. There are nearly 2,200 ADRs from ninety countries although significant trading occurs in only a small portion of them.[19] Leading ADRs include telecom firms Nokia (Finland), Ericsson (Sweden), Vodafone (UK) and oil firms British Petroleum (UK) and Royal Dutch Petroleum (Netherlands). Listing an ADR allows U.S. investors to trade a foreign firm's shares more easily. It also gives the foreign firm easier access to a large pool of U.S. investment capital. There is an ADR Index to track price trends.

INSIDE INFORMATION AND OTHER ETHICAL ISSUES

The capital markets are successful in allocating capital because of their integrity. Should investors lose confidence in the fairness of the capital markets, all will lose; investors lose an attractive means for investing funds, and issuers will lose access to low-cost public capital.

Some persons who deal in securities and have access to nonpublic or private information about mergers, new security offerings, or earnings announcements may be tempted to trade to take advantage of this information. Taking advantage of one's privileged access to information can lead to large profits from timely purchases or sales (or short sales) of securities. In the United States, taking advantage of private "inside" information is thought to be unfair to other investors. These factors, combined with the ease with which inside information can be used, explain why insider trading is not allowed under provisions of the Securities Exchange Act of 1934.

The most obvious opportunity for insider trading is that for personnel of a corporation who, by virtue of their duties, have knowledge of developments that are destined to have an impact on the price of the corporation's stock. But "insiders" are not limited to corporate personnel. Investment bankers, by virtue of their relationship with such corporations, may be aware of corporate difficulties, major officer changes, or merger possibilities. They, too, must take great care to avoid using such information illegally. Even blue-collar workers at printing firms that print prospectuses or merger offers have been found guilty of trading on private information based upon what they have read from their presses.

---

19. Craig Karmin, "ADR Issuance Surges as Firms Abroad Tap Market for Capital," *The Wall Street Journal* (December 8, 2000), p. C12.

Because the insider trading law is unclear, it is often difficult to tell when it is illegal to turn a tip into a profit. For example, a stock analyst may discover, through routine interviews with corporate officers, information destined to have an impact on the price of the company's stock. Such information conveyed to the analyst's clients may be, and has been considered to be, insider trading. The almost frantic efforts of large firms to control insider trading is understandable in light of the damage that can occur to their reputations. It is understandable, too, that the SEC has resorted to strong efforts to resolve the question that continues to exist with respect to a meaningful and fair definition of insider information. After all, it is the investing public without access to this information that pays the price for insider information abuses. Regulation FD mandates full disclosure of material nonpublic information, which was sometimes disclosed to a select few, such as security analysts or large institutional investors. Insight into higher or lower earnings, for example, could result in those receiving the information—and their clients—trading securities to make a profit (or avoid a loss) at the expense of others not privileged to have access to the information. Regulation FD mandates that if a company official discloses material nonpublic information to certain individuals, it must announce the information to all via public disclosure.

Another breach of investor confidence can occur via "churning." Churning is when a broker constantly buys and sells securities from a client's portfolio in an effort to generate commissions. Rather than making decisions that are in the client's best interest, frequent commission-generating trades may be made by brokers with selfish motives. There are times when frequent trading may be appropriate, but it should occur only within the clients' investing guidelines and with the client's interests at heart.

Unfortunately, the millions of dollars paid in fees for investment banking fees result in occasional scandal by some who make poor choices. In 2003, several investment banking firms were fined $1.4 billion for ethical lapses. Evidence showed stock analysts, whose stock recommendations should be unbiased, were sometimes rewarded for writing favorable reports to attract investment banking clients. Recall the first-day returns from IPOs in Table 11.3; in another ethical lapse, some banks allocated IPO shares to top officers of their client firms or to firms they wanted to attract as clients. Allocating shares that may enjoy a quick "pop" in price is a means of bribing clients. In addition to paying large fines, firms must separate stock research from investment banking practices and offer clients independent investment research written by analysts from other firms. Because ethics and integrity are at the center of fair and well-functioning securities markets, major professional certifications, such as the Chartered Financial Analyst (CFA®) and Certified Financial Planner(CFP™), have ethics as a central part of their certification programs.

CHANGES IN THE STRUCTURE OF THE STOCK MARKET

In an effort to increase the technological and informational efficiency of the stock market, the SEC has actively promoted major changes in the structure of stock market activities and institutions. Many of the changes proposed have long met with resistance from existing interests, especially the NYSE. However, many of the SEC's recommendations have been adopted and many more will be instituted in due time. The NYSE, which many times resisted change that would de-emphasize its former specialist trading structure, gained new leadership in 2003 and since then has been embracing technology and globalization. As NASDAQ founder Gordon Macklin said in 1987, "How long do you think people are going to stand in a marble hall and trade?"[20]

Indeed, an important change relates to electronic technology. Technology exists to link organized exchanges and OTC markets electronically. The SEC would like to see the stock market take the form of one giant trading floor, all at the command of the broker. The broker would be able to tell which market has the best quote on each stock by punching buttons on the quotation machine. Bid and asked prices on covered stocks would be available in all markets. In a step toward this, NASDAQ offers "dual-listing" to NYSE firms, meaning that NYSE-listed stocks can choose to have their shares listed on NASDAQ. Instituted in 2004, the first firms to take advantage of dual listing were Apache Corp (stock symbol: APA), Cadence Design Systems (CDN), Charles Schwab Corp. (SCH), Countrywide Financial (CFC), Hewlett-Packard (HPQ), and Walgreens (WAG).

---

20. Stephen Miller, "Gordon Macklin, 1928–2007: Ushering in Age of the Electronic Stock Market," *The Wall Street Journal*, February 3, 2007, p. A8.

TABLE 11.5

Current Exchanges and their Predecessors

NYSE EURONEXT	LONDON STOCK EXCHANGE	NASDAQ	CBOE HOLDINGS	DEUTSCHE BORSE	TMX GROUP
Merger of NYSE and Euronext; Euronext was formed from the following exchanges: Lisbon and Oporto LIFFE Amsterdam Brussels Paris; NYSE was formed from the following exchanges: NYSE and Archipelago Holdings	Merger of London Stock Exchange and Borsa Italiana	Merger of NASDAQ Brut INET OMX	Merger of Chicago Mercantile Exchange (CME) Chicago Board of Trade and New York Mercantile Exchange (NYMEX)		

GLOBAL DISCUSSION

Technology can link national markets to one another, worldwide. Long the purview of national market regulators, stock exchanges are reaching across national boundaries to link up and in some cases merge with other exchanges. The NYSE and Euronext, a major European exchange, agreed in 2006 to a merger. In 2007, the NASDAQ owned over 25% of the London Stock Exchange and was seeking its own merger with it. In addition to Euronext, alliances or cross-ownership agreements exist between the NYSE and the National Stock Exchange of India; between the NYSE and the Tokyo Stock Exchange; and the Tokyo Stock Exchange has made alliance agreements with the Singapore Exchange and the Korea Exchange.[21] Table 11.5 shows some of the mergers that have occurred in recent years as exchanges vie for size and technology edges to attract listings and traders.

The goal of global alliances and mergers is to make international investing and the raising of capital easier. One goal of the NYSE–Euronext merger is to cross-list shares on the two exchanges. This will make it easier for U.S. investors to trade securities listed on Euronext and for European investors to trade U.S. stocks. Higher commissions, currency translation, and difficulties in settling trades are large hindrances to investing overseas; efficiencies in having global alliances will make investing in overseas firms easier, quicker, and less expensive.

The European Community (EC) is moving toward greater integration of its financial services, too. Markets in Financial Instruments Directive (MiFID) has the goal of a creating a single market for investment services across the European Union (EU) as well as creating a single set of regulations for financial services firms. MiFID has three main objectives: to create a single EU market for investment services, to coordinate responses to innovations in the securities markets, and to increase protection for investors in a cross-country market.

Electronic trading has been occurring for some time; NASDAQ has an electronic European exchange that it hopes will be the forerunner of an all-European exchange. Another European electronic exchange, Virt-X, is a joint effort of the Swiss exchange and London's Trade-point trading platform.

Which model is better: NYSE's or the electronic trading? For the most part, both systems work to give investors swift trade execution and the best price available. For quicker trades, some will give the advantage to an electronic market. For the best price (lowest price for buyers, highest price for sellers) some argue that NYSE's DMMs or SLPs can intervene to offer better prices to traders. For clearing large trades, the advantage goes to the NYSE; it has more trading volume and offers greater liquidity for handling large transactions.

---

21. Gaston F. Ceron, "NYSE and Tokyo Tie a Knot," *The Wall Street Journal*, February 1, 2007, p. C2.

INSTITUTIONS AND MARKETS

One can easily argue that securities markets exist because of the development of financial institutions and intermediaries over time to collect and allocate capital. In particular, investment banks and brokerage houses help firms and governments raise funds in the public and private markets. They assist investors who want to trade securities and help to provide liquidity to the financial system.

INVESTMENTS

Investors and analysts need to know the different ways to trade (long, short, margin) in securities markets and the risks of each. It is their desire to trade that creates a need for the securities markets and the institutions which facilitate their trading. New information is quickly evaluated by investors as a whole and reflected in changing market prices.

FINANCIAL MANAGEMENT

Firms raise capital in the primary markets. Initial public offerings (IPOs) and secondary offerings are an important undertaking for financial managers who take their firms public; others in private firms will arrange private placements or loans from banks, insurance companies, and other institutions. Securities markets set the interest rates and security prices for the firm; these are a reflection of the quality of the firm, risk, and investors' expectations of future cash flows.

Highly automated securities exchanges now exist in the major money center cities of the world, permitting trading on a global basis. Because of varying time zones, trading is possible twenty-four hours a day. Trading and settlement (issuing securities and collecting funds) go hand-in-hand; currently the United States has a T + 3 settlement standard, meaning all stock trades have to be settled in cash within three business days. With advancing technology, a standard of T + 1, next-day settlement, may become regulatory reality by the middle of the decade.

SUMMARY

The accumulation of funds by business establishments to finance plant, equipment, and working capital is a necessary process of an industrial society. In this chapter, we described the role of the investment banking industry in facilitating this process. The accumulation of funds is supported by the existence of a secondary market for securities. The constant buying and selling of securities not only provides investors with the confidence that their investment is liquid and can be converted easily to cash but also provides information to the firm's managers. Businesses that prosper are rewarded by securities that enjoy price increases. The secondary market is made up principally of the organized securities exchanges and the over-the-counter (OTC) markets. Investing in foreign securities can take place by using ADRs.

Trading on the basis of inside or private information is illegal in U.S. markets although such trading is accepted as the norm in some overseas securities markets. In the United States, ethical norms are such that society frowns upon those who, by virtue of their position or access to information, take advantage of their shareholders for personal gain.

KEY TERMS

aftermarket

American depository receipt (ADR)

ask price

best-effort agreement

bid price

blue-sky laws

broker

buying on margin

commission brokers

dealer

designated market markets (DMMs)

due diligence

Dutch auction

floor brokers

flotation

flotation costs

fourth market

global depository receipt (GDR)

initial margin

initial public offering (IPO)

investment bankers

limit order

maintenance margin

margin

margin call

market maker

market order

market stabilization

odd lot

offer price

pre-emptive rights

primary market

private placement

program trading

prospectus

public offering

registered traders

round lot

secondary market

shelf registration

short sale

spread

stop-loss order

street name

supplemental liquidity providers (SLPs)

syndicate

third market

tombstones

underpricing

underwriters

underwriting agreement

DISCUSSION QUESTIONS

1. Why do corporations employ investment bankers?

2. Identify the primary market functions of investment bankers.

3. Discuss how investment bankers assume risk in the process of marketing securities of corporations. How do investment bankers try to minimize these risks?

4. Briefly describe the process of competitive bidding and discuss its relative advantages and disadvantages.

5. Explain market stabilization.

6. Identify the costs associated with going public.

7. Briefly describe how investment banking is regulated.

8. Describe the inroads into investment banking being made by commercial banks.

9. In 2003, several investment banking firms were fined $1.4 billion for ethics abuses related to the underwriting process. Will this be a deterrent for ethical lapses?

10. What were some of the reasons for the decline in Facebook's stock price after its IPO?

11. What are some of the characteristics of an organized securities exchange?

12. Describe the types of members of the New York Stock Exchange (NYSE).

13. Why is there a difference between bid and ask prices at some point in time for a specific security?

14. Describe the differences among the following three types of orders: market, limit, and stop loss.

15. What is a short sale?

16. Describe buying on margin.

17. What is program trading?

18. Describe several differences between the organized exchanges and the over-the-counter (OTC) market.

19. What factors differentiate a good market from a poor market?

20. A security's liquidity is affected by what influences?

21. Why may a stock trade that takes 1 second to execute be preferable to a trade that takes 9 seconds to execute?

22. How do the third and fourth markets differ from other secondary markets?

23. What are some factors that influence the commission on a stock trade with a broker?

24. Give some examples of market indexes. Why are there so many different indexes?

25. What are American depository receipts (ADRs)?

26. Why is it illegal to trade on insider information?

27. What is Regulation FD, and how does it affect security trading?

28. Visit the Web site of the CFA Institute, http://www.cfainstitute.org. Type the word "ethics" into the site's search function. Discuss, in your own words, the ethics issues that the CFA Institute is analyzing or discussing.

29. Visit the Web site of the CFP Board, http://www.cfp.net. Type the word "ethics" into the site's search function. Describe a few of the pages that appear from the search.

30. What are the advantages of having a specialist-based or DMM (open outcry) trading system? An electronic trading system?

31. Discuss this statement: "Technology and globalization are two current forces impacting stock exchanges."

PROBLEMS

1. You are the president and chief executive officer (CEO) of a family-owned manufacturing firm with assets of $45 million. The company articles of incorporation and state laws place no restrictions on the sale of stock to outsiders. An unexpected opportunity to expand arises that will require an additional investment of $14 million. A commitment must be made quickly if this opportunity is to be taken. Existing stockholders are not in a position to provide the additional investment. You wish to maintain family control of the firm regardless of which form of financing you might undertake. As a first step, you decide to contact an investment banking firm.

a. What considerations might be important in the selection of an investment banking firm?

b. A member of your board has asked if you have considered competitive bids for the distribution of your securities compared with a negotiated contract with a particular firm. What factors are involved in this decision?

c. Assuming that you have decided upon a negotiated contract, what are the first questions that you would ask of the firm chosen to represent you?

d. As the investment banker, what would be your first actions before offering advice?

e. Assuming the investment banking firm is willing to distribute your securities, describe the alternative plans that might be included in a contract with the banking firm.

f. How does the investment banking firm establish a selling strategy?

g. How might the investment banking firm protect itself against a drop in the price of the security during the selling process?

h. What follow-up services will be provided by the banking firm following a successful distribution of the securities?

i.   Three years later, as an individual investor, you decide to add to your own holding of the security but only at a price that you consider appropriate. What form of order might you place with your broker?

2. In late 2009, you purchased the common stock of a company that has reported significant earnings increases in nearly every quarter since your purchase. The price of the stock increased from $12 a share at the time of the purchase to a current level of $45. Notwithstanding the success of the company, competitors are gaining much strength. Further, your analysis indicates that the stock may be over-priced based on your projection of future earnings growth. Your analysis, however, was the same one year ago and the earnings have continued to increase. Actions that you might take range from an outright sale of the stock (and the payment of capital gains tax) to doing nothing and continuing to hold the shares. You reflect on these choices as well as other actions that could be taken. Describe the various actions that you might take and their implications.

3. Which of the following securities is likely to be the most liquid according to these data? Explain.

STOCK	BID	ASK
R	$39.43	$39.55
S	13.67	13.77
T	116.02	116.25

4. You purchased shares of Broussard Company using 50 percent margin; you invested a total of $20,000 (buying 1,000 shares at a price of $20 per share) by using $10,000 of your own funds and borrowing $10,000. Determine your percentage profit or loss under the following situations (ignore borrowing costs, dividends, and taxes). In addition, what would the percentage profit and loss be in these scenarios if margin were not used?

a.   the stock price rises to $23 a share

b.   the stock price rises to $30 a share

c.   the stock price falls to $16 a share

d.   the stock price falls to $10 a share

5. Currently, the price of Mattco stock is $30 a share. You have $30,000 of your own funds to invest. Using the maximum margin allowed, what is your percentage profit or loss under the following situations (ignore dividends and taxes)? What would the percentage profit or loss be in each situation if margin were not used?

a.   you purchase the stock and it rises to $33 a share

b.   you purchase the stock and it rises to $35 a share

c.   you purchase the stock and it falls to $25 a share

d.   you purchase the stock and it falls to $20 a share

6. The Trio Index is comprised of three stocks, Eins, Zwei, and Tri. Their current prices are listed below.

STOCK	PRICE AT TIME (t)
Eins	$10
Zwei	$20
Tri	$40

a.   Between now and the next time period, the stock prices of Eins and Zwei increase 10 percent while Tri increases 20 percent. What is the percentage change in the price-weighted Trio Index?

b.   Suppose instead that the price of Eins increases 20 percent while Zwei and Tri rise 10 percent. What is the percentage change in the price-weighted Trio Index? Why does it differ from the answer to part a?

7. The four stocks below are part of an index. Use the information below:

a.   Compute a price-weighted index by adding their prices at time t and time $t + 1$. What is the percentage change in the index?

b.   Compute a value-weighted index by adding their market values at time t and time $t + 1$. What is the percentage change in the index?

c.   Why is there a difference between your answers to (a) and (b)?

STOCK	# OF SHARES OUTSTANDING	PRICE AT TIME (t)	PRICE AT TIME $(t + 1)$
Eeny	100	10	15
Meeny	50	20	22
Miney	50	30	28
Moe	20	40	42

8. The Quad Index is comprised of four stocks: Uno, Dos, Tres, and Fore.

a.   Given the data below on the number of shares outstanding and their share prices at time (t) and time $(t + 1)$, what is the percentage change in the Quad Index if it is calculated as a price-weighted index? As a value-weighted index?

STOCK	# OF SHARES OUTSTANDING	PRICE AT TIME (t)	PRICE AT TIME $(t + 1)$
Uno	1000	$10	$11
Dos	500	20	21
Tres	250	40	42
Fore	100	50	60

b.   Instead of the prices shown above, suppose we switch the prices for Uno and Fore. That is, Uno's stock price is $50 at time (t) and it rises to $60 by time $(t + 1)$ and Fore's stock price rises from $10 to $11 over the same time frame. What is the percentage change in the Quad Index if it is computed as a price-weighted index? As a value-weighted index?

c.   Explain similarities or differences in your answers to parts (a) and (b).

9. A U.S. firm wants to raise $10 million of capital so it can invest in new technology. How much will it need to raise to net $10 million using the average costs of raising funds in the chapter?

10. A U.S. firm wants to raise $15 million by selling 1 million shares at a net price of $15. We know that some say that firms "leave money on the table" because of the phenomenon of underpricing.

a.   Using the average amount of underpricing in U.S. IPOs, how many fewer shares could it sell to raise these funds if the firm received a net price per share equal to the value of the shares at the end of the first day's trading?

b.   How many less shares could it sell if the IPO was occurring in Germany?

c.   How many less shares could it sell if the IPO was occurring in Korea?

d.   How many less shares could it sell if the IPO was occurring in Canada?

11. Below are the results of a Dutch auction for an IPO of Bagel's Bagels, a trendy bagel and coffee shop chain. Bagel's is offering 50 million shares.

BIDDER	BID PRICE	NUMBER OF SHARES
Matthew	$50.25	15 million
Kevin	49.75	20 million
Amy	49.45	20 million
Megan	49.00	10 million

  a. What will be the clearing price?

  b. How many shares will each bidder receive if Bagel's allocates shares on a pro rata basis to all the successful bidders?

12. Boneyard Biscuits' Dutch auction for an IPO was a great success. The firm offered 100 million shares. Bids appear below.

BIDDER	BID PRICE	NUMBER OF SHARES
Manahan	$25.25	25 million
Campbell	24.95	30 million
Maloney	24.75	25 million
Touma	24.40	10 million
Clark	24.40	30 million
Fry	24.25	15 million

  a. What is the clearing price?

  b. What options do Boneyard and its underwriters have for allocating shares? How many shares will each bidder receive under each option?

13. **EXCEL** Problem: Develop a spreadsheet to do the dollar amount and percentage profit and loss calculations in questions 4 and 5. Use as inputs to the spreadsheet the amount of your funds you are investing, the initial margin percentage, the maintenance margin percentage, and the stock's price. In addition, have the spreadsheet calculate the stock price at which you'll receive a margin call.

14. **EXCEL** Problem: Expand the spreadsheet of problem 13 to consider one extra source of return and one extra cost to using margin. Specifically, modify the spreadsheet to include expected dividends per share and the cost of the margin loan (stated in APR format).

Assume that Broussard Corporation pays a dividend of $0.50 per share, Mattco pays an annual dividend of $0.80 per share, and the margin loan rate is 6 percent.

15. **EXCEL** Problem: Adjust the spreadsheet and its calculations in problem 13 for one more complication, that being to have the length of the holding period (in quarters) be one of the spreadsheet's inputs. Compute the annualized return if the holding period for Mattco stock were (a) three months and (b) six months.

16. **Challenge Problem** Get stock price data from http://finance.yahoo.com/ for ten stocks in the Dow Jones Industrial Average (DJIA) for the prior ten days and use these prices to compute a price-weighted index for each of these ten days. Chart the performance of your index versus the DJIA over this time period. How closely do they track one another? What is the total percentage change in each index? Comment on the differences in performance over this time frame.

LEARNING EXTENSION 11

Introduction to Futures and Options

In addition to stocks and bonds, the financial system has developed other investment vehicles to meet the needs of various market participants. A type of instrument that is gaining widespread use among institutional investors and corporate financial managers is derivative securities. A ***derivative security*** has its value determined by, or derived from, the value of another investment vehicle. They go by a variety of names, such as forwards, futures, options, and swaps. In this learning extension, we will focus on two types of derivatives: futures and options.

derivative security
a security whose value is determined by, or derived from, the value of another investment vehicle

WHY DO DERIVATIVES EXIST?

Most assets that you are probably familiar with, such as stocks, bonds, gold, or real estate, are traded in the cash or ***spot market***. The stock exchanges and the primary and secondary markets we examined earlier in the text are examples of spot markets. Trades occur in these markets, and cash, along with ownership of the asset, is transferred from buyer to seller.

spot market
the cash market for trading securities; where securities are bought and sold

At times, however, it may be advantageous to enter into a transaction with the promise that the exchange of asset and money will take place at a future time. Such an exchange allows a transaction price to be determined today for a trade that will not occur until a mutually agreed upon future date. Such is the case with a futures contract. As an example, in June, wheat farmers may desire to lock in the price at which they can sell their harvest in September. That way, their profits will not be affected by price swings in the wheat spot market between now and harvest.

For others, it may be desirable to enter into an agreement that allows for a future cash transaction but only if contract buyers find it in their best interest to do so. A derivative security called an *option contract* allows purchasers to decide whether or not to execute the trade in the future. For example, real estate developers may purchase an option for $10,000 to buy property at a fixed price of $500,000 sometime in the next year. Should the value of the property rise above $500,000 in the coming year, they will most likely choose to execute the option and purchase the land for $500,000. The wheat farmers may enter into an option contract to sell their harvest at a predetermined price, say, $3.00 a bushel. Should the spot market wheat price at harvest be $2.50/bushel, they will execute their option and receive the predetermined price of $3.00 a bushel. Should the spot wheat price be higher, say $4.00, they will choose to sell their wheat at the higher spot price and let the option contract expire. Similar option contracts exist for financial assets such as individual stocks, stock indexes, interest rates, and currencies.

Thus, derivatives such as futures and options have evolved to fulfill desirable economic purposes. They shift risk from those who don't like risk to those who are willing to bear it. They bring additional information into the market, and their trading mechanisms have evolved so it may be less costly, in terms of commissions and required investment, to invest in derivatives than in the cash market.

hedge
an action which reduces risk; similar to the concept of insurance

The prudent use of derivatives to *hedge*, or reduce risk, is similar to the concept of insurance. For example, auto insurance is used as a hedge against the large dollar expenses that could arise from a car accident. We pay an upfront price or premium to buy a certain level of protection for a limited amount of time. This is comparable to the concept of hedging with derivatives; hedging with derivatives can protect investors from large adverse price fluctuations in the value of an asset.

The growth in the volume of outstanding derivatives increased dramatically. In 1986, one estimate was that $2 trillion in value was traded; this rose to nearly $10 trillion in 1991, over $40 trillion on a worldwide basis by the end of 1995, $370 trillion in 2006, $512 trillion in 2009 and $639 trillion in 2012.[22]

Speculation, or investing in derivatives in the anticipation of a favorable change in the cash market price, is a risky investment strategy. Speculators are not hedging an underlying investment. They hope for a price move that will bring them profits. The complexity of some derivatives has resulted in some investors undertaking risks they were not aware of or so they say. In recent years, firms such as Barings PLC, Gibson Greetings, Metallgesellschaft, Procter and Gamble, several municipalities and colleges, and even well-respected Wall Street firms (Bear Stearns, Lehman Brothers) have suffered large losses and bankruptcy because of inappropriate speculation in the derivatives markets. In the following pages we describe several basic derivative securities.

FUTURES CONTRACTS

futures contract
a contract obligating the owner to purchase or sell the underlying asset at a specified price on a specified day

A *futures contract* obligates the owner to purchase or sell the underlying asset at a specified price (the *exercise price* or *strike price*) on a specified day. Exchange-traded futures contracts are traded on major futures exchanges. Exchange-traded futures contracts are standardized as to terms and conditions, such as quality and quantity of the underlying asset and expiration dates (for example, corn delivered under a futures contract must meet certain moisture content standards, among others). This standardization allows futures to be bought and sold, just as common stocks are bought and sold in secondary markets. Someone purchasing (selling) a futures contract can negate their obligation by selling (purchasing) the identical type of contract. This is called a reversing trade.

exercise price (strike price)
price at which the asset can be traded under a futures or option contract

Today, futures contracts are traded on agricultural goods, precious metals, oil, stock indexes, interest rates, and currencies. Some exchanges on which futures contracts are traded are listed in Table LE11.1.

TABLE LE11.1
Selected U.S. Futures Exchanges

CME Group Inc., a CME/Chicago Board of Trade Company. Formerly two separate entities, the Chicago Board of Trade (CBOT) and the Chicago Mercantile Exchange (CME) merged in 2007. The New York Mercantile Exchange (NYMEX) was merged into the CME Group in late 2009. Items traded on the CME Group include futures contracts for agricultural commodities such as corn, wheat, and soybeans; financial futures contracts, especially those involving Treasury securities, futures contracts on stock indexes, interest rates, and foreign currencies, and metals and energy-related futures contracts including crude oil, gasoline, heating oil, natural gas, electricity, gold, silver, copper, aluminum, and platinum. Website: www.cmegroup.com.

Intercontinental Exchange (ICE) serves the global markets for agricultural, credit, currency, emissions, energy and equity index markets. ICE Futures Europe trades crude and refined oil futures. ICE Futures U.S. and ICE Futures Canada list agricultural, currency and Russell Index markets. Among the commodity futures contracts traded on ICE are contracts for sugar, cotton, and coffee. Website: https://www.theice.com/homepage.jhtml.

22. Fabio Fornari and Serge Jeanneau, "Derivatives Markets," *BIS Quarterly Review* (March 2004), published by the Bank for International Settlements, Basle, Switzerland. Updated data are available at http://www.bis.org including http://www.bis.org/publ/qtrpdf/r_qs0909.pdf and http://www.bis.org/statistics/otcder/dt1920a.pdf. The value mentioned in this statistic is "notational" value, not the actual value of securities traded. Notional value is used to compute the size of the cash flow that is exchanged between market participants. Most futures contracts, for example, require a margin requirement of only 3 to 6 percent of the contract's notional value.

FIGURE LE 11.1
Listing of the S&P500 Futures Contract

MTH/STRIKE	OPEN	SESSION HIGH	LOW	LAST	SETT	PT CHGE	EST VOL	— SETT	PRIOR DAY VOL	— INT
MARXX	1443.00	1443.60	1438.30	1440.30	—	−260	4796	1442.90	40378	591922

See actual listings at: http://www.cmegroup.com/trading/equity-index/us-index/sandp-500.html.

initial margin
deposited funds necessary to purchase a derivatives contract

A risk of entering a contract such as a futures contract is the creditworthiness of the entity on the other side of the transaction. Fortunately, exchange-traded futures have little credit or default risk. Purchasers and sellers of futures are required to deposit funds, or **initial margin,** in a margin account with the exchange's clearing corporation or clearinghouse. The initial margin requirement is usually 3 to 6 percent of the price of the contract. Funds are added to or subtracted from the margin account daily, reflecting that day's price changes in the futures contract. At the end of each trading day, a special exchange committee determines an approximate closing price, called the **settlement price.** Thus, futures are cash-settled every day through this process, known as "marking to the market." As is the case with common stocks, should an investor's margin account become too low, the maintenance margin limit will be reached. Then, investors must place additional funds in the margin account or have their position closed.

settlement price
daily approximate closing price of a futures contract as decided by a special exchange committee

Thus, rather than buying or selling futures from a specific investor, the futures exchange becomes the counterparty to all transactions. Should investors default, the exchange covers any losses rather than a specific investor. But the daily settling of accounts through marking to the market and maintenance margin requirements can prevent investors' losses from growing indefinitely until contract maturity.

Figure LE11.1 presents an example of the futures quotation page from the Chicago Mercantile Exchange (CME or Merc) Web site. Suppose you were considering buying a futures contract on the S&P500 stock market index. Each contract has a value equal to 250 times the value of the S&P500 stock index. The value of the contract traded on the Merc will, over time, closely follow the variations in the actual value of the S&P500 index in the cash or spot market. The March contract opened the day at $1,443.00 per contract (thus having a total contract value of $1,443.00 × $250, or $360,750), and so far during the day's trading had a high of $1,443.60 and a low of $1,438.30. The price of the last recorded transaction was $1,440.30, which is down 260 points (read this as $2.60 in terms of contract price) from the previous day's close.

The settlement price, which is roughly the closing price, is the price at which contracts are marked-to-market; trading is still ongoing for the day when the data were downloaded so no settlement price is given. Trading volume thus far for the day was 4,796 contracts. Data from the previous trading day show a settlement price of $1,442.90, which is $2.60 higher than the current last price. The previous day's trading volume was 40,378 contracts. The open interest, which is the number of contracts currently outstanding, is 591,922.

option
financial contract that gives the owner the option of buying or selling a particular good at a specified price on or before a specified time or expiration date

OPTIONS

An **option** is a financial contract that gives the owner the option or choice of buying or selling a particular good at a specified price (called the *strike price* or *exercise price*) on or before a specified time or expiration date. Most of us are familiar with option arrangements of one sort or another.

In some ways, a sports or theater ticket is an option. We can exercise it by attending the event at the appropriate time and place, or we can choose not to attend and let the ticket expire worthless. As another example of an option, the owner of real estate may be paid a certain amount of money in return for a contract to purchase property within a certain time period at a specified price. If the option holder does not exercise the purchase privilege according to the terms of the contract, the option expires.

call option
a contract for the purchase of securities

put option
contract for the sale of securities within a specific time period and at a specified price

A contract for the purchase of securities is a **call option.** A **put option** is a contract for the sale of securities within a specific time period and at a specified price. Similar to futures trading, exchange-traded options are standardized in terms of expiration dates, exercise prices, and the quantity and quality of the underlying asset upon which the contract is based. Thus, exchange-traded

FIGURE LE 11.2
Stock Option Quotations

Microsoft
Current Stock Price: $25.62

	CALL			PUT		
	LAST	VOL	OPEN INT.	LAST	VOL	OPEN INT.
15 January 20	6.90	336	7451	1.20	100	39387
15 January 30	2.00	17	136164	5.60	10	87389

options are liquid. A secondary market exists for trading in them. While the Chicago Board Options Exchange (CBOE) remains the main market, the New York, American, Pacific, and Philadelphia exchanges deal in option contracts. Today, options are traded on individual stocks, bonds, currencies, metal, and a wide variety of financial indexes. While most exchange-traded options contracts expire in less than a year, the Chicago Board Options Exchange offers long-lived options on select stocks. Long-term Equity Anticipation Securities (LEAPS), have expiration dates up to three years in the future.

Through the organized exchanges, individual investors can sell or create the options. The sellers of option contracts are the **option writer.** The price paid for the option is the **option premium.** It is what call buyers must pay for the right to acquire the asset at a given price at some time in the future and what put buyers must pay for the right to sell the asset at a given price at some time in the future. The sellers or writers of the option receives the premium when they sell the option contract.

option writer
seller of an option contract

option premium
the price paid for the option

Figure LE11.2 presents an example of an option quotation. Suppose you were considering buying a call on Microsoft, and the current price of Microsoft's stock is $25.62. The Web site contains information on a variety of call and put options for Microsoft. We will focus on a LEAPS contract. The notation "15 January 20" refers to the contract's expiration date (January 2015) and strike price ($20). If you had done the last trade on the Microsoft 15 January 20 call, the price would have been $6.90 per option. Because each contract is for 100 calls, the total cost of buying the call option would have been $690.00. During the day, 336 contracts were traded. The number of outstanding 15 January 20 call option contracts is 7,451. The information on the 15 January 20 put option and the 15 January 30 contracts are interpreted similarly.

INTERNET ACTIVITY

The Web sites of futures and options exchanges offer visitors the chance to see time-delayed quotes. See, for example, the CME Group, http://www.cmegroup.com, and the Chicago Board Options Exchange, http://www.cboe.com.

OPTION PAYOFF DIAGRAMS

Futures carry an obligation to execute the contract (unless offset by another contract so the investor's net position is zero). An option contract is just that, meaning it gives the owner the option to purchase (call option) or sell (put option) an asset. Thus, if exercising the option will cause the owner to lose wealth, the option can expire unexercised and have a value of zero. Whereas losses on futures can grow as a result of adverse moves in the value of the underlying asset, the owner of an option contract may be able to limit losses by merely choosing not to exercise the contract.

How valuable is a call option? Suppose Microsoft's January 20 option is about to expire and the price of Microsoft's stock is $25.62. If the call option's price were $3.00, investors could buy the option for $3.00 and immediately choose to exercise it since they could buy the stock by paying only $20 a share. They will sell these shares at Microsoft's market price of $25.62 and receive a profit of $2.62. (They paid a total of $3.00 [option] plus $20 [exercise price] or $23.00; selling the stock for $25.62 results in a $2.62 profit.) This is an example of an *arbitrage* operation in which mispricing between two different markets leads to risk-free opportunities to profit.

Other investors would want to take advantage of this opportunity. The buying pressure in the options market and selling pressure in the stock market by arbitragers would cause the option and/or stock prices to change and eliminate the risk-free profit opportunity. Thus, if the Microsoft January 20 call option were about to expire, its price would have to be $5.62 to eliminate arbitrage opportunities. With a price of $5.62, investors would be indifferent between buying the stock for $25.62 or buying the call for $5.62 and exercising it (total cost, $5.62 + $20 = $25.62).

FIGURE LE11.3
Payoff Diagram for Call and Put Options

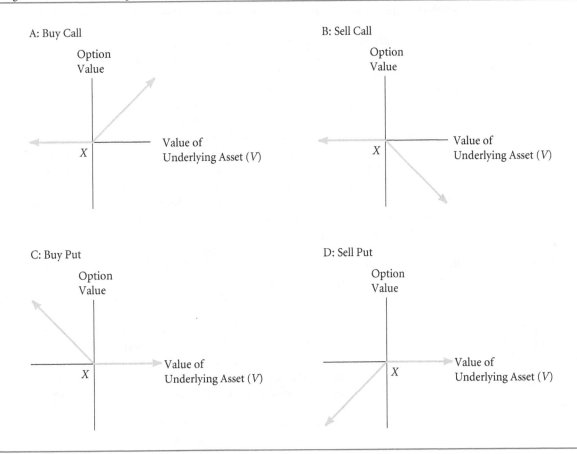

On the other hand, suppose the January 30 call option for Microsoft was about to expire. With the price of Microsoft stock at $25.62, an investor who pays any price for the option is making a mistake; why pay for an option to purchase the stock at $30 per share when the stock can be purchased for $25.62 per share? The value of the January 30 call option, which is about to expire, would be zero.

To summarize, before it expires, the intrinsic value of a call option will be the asset's value minus the exercise price (if the asset's value exceeds the exercise price) or it will be zero (if the asset's value is less than the strike price). If we let V equal the market value of the underlying asset (say, the Microsoft stock price) and X denote the option's exercise price, the value of an option prior to expiration will be the maximum of $V - X$ or 0. This can be written Max $[0, V - X]$. Panel A in Figure LE11.3 illustrates a payoff diagram for a call option.

The payoff diagram for the seller or writer of the call option is shown in panel B of Figure LE11.3; it is the opposite of the payoff to the option buyer. For the option writer, increases in the asset's price above the exercise price are harmful since the call option allows the buyer to purchase the higher-priced asset at the lower exercise price. In the case of the January 20 call option, the writer may be forced to sell Microsoft stock for only $20 a share when its market value is $25.62 per share. As the stock's value climbs, the call writer faces a larger loss.

Payoff diagrams for put option buyers and writers are shown in panels C and D in Figure LE11.3. The put option allows the owner to sell the underlying asset at the exercise price, so the put option becomes more valuable to the buyer as the value of the asset falls below the exercise price.

Let's look at the Microsoft January 30 put option. Arbitrage will ensure this put option's price will be at least $4.38. For example, should the put's price be $0.50, arbitragers will buy the put for $0.50 and buy the stock for $25.62; they will immediately exercise the put, forcing the put writer to purchase their stock at the exercise price of $30. The arbitragers will gain a risk-free profit of

$3.88 on every share (they paid $0.50 [put option] + $25.62 [stock's market value] or $26.12; selling the stock by exercising the put gives them $30, for a profit of $30 − $26.12 = $3.88). Thus, if the put option is about to expire, its price should be $30 − $25.62 or $4.38 to prevent arbitrage.

If the January 30 put option was about to expire and the stock's price is $35, the value of the put option would be worthless. After all, how many people would want to buy a put option that gave them the right to sell Microsoft at $30 a share when they can sell the stock on the NASDAQ, where Microsoft is traded, for the current market price of $35?

This example shows the intrinsic value of the put option at expiration is the maximum of $X − V$ or zero, or Max $[0, X − V]$. As the asset's value falls below the exercise price X, the value of the put option rises in correspondence with the fall of the asset's value, as seen in panel C.

The situation is reversed for the writer or seller of the put option. The payoff diagram for the writer of the put is shown in panel D of Figure LE11.3. As the asset's value falls below the exercise price, the put writer will be forced to purchase the asset for more than its current market value and will suffer a loss. For example, with the January 30 put option, the put writer may have to purchase the stock at the $30 exercise price, thereby paying $4.38 more than the stock's current market price of $25.62.

at-the-money
exercise price equals the market price of the underlying asset

Here's some more option terminology: an option is ***at-the-money*** if its exercise price equals the current market price of the underlying asset. An ***in-the-money*** option has a positive intrinsic value; that is, for a call (put) option, the underlying asset price exceeds (is below) the strike price, X. An ***out-of-the-money*** option has a zero intrinsic value; that is, for a call (put) option, the underlying asset price is below (exceeds) the strike price, X.

in-the-money
the option with a positive intrinsic value

To keep the analysis at a basic level, we have only reviewed the intrinsic value of options. In reality, the option's value will equal its intrinsic value only at expiration. At all other times, the option's premium or price will exceed its intrinsic value. A major reason for this is time. The longer the time to expiration, the greater the chance of the option becoming in-the-money (if it was originally at-the-money or out-of-the-money) or becoming more in-the-money than it originally was. Another important influence on the option premium is the variability in the price of the underlying asset. The greater the asset's variability over time, the greater the chance of the option going in-the-money and increasing in value. Therefore, high volatility in the price of the underlying asset *increases* the option premium for both puts and calls.

out-of-the-money
an option with zero intrinsic value

SUMMARY

From recent headlines to investment seminars, derivatives are an investment vehicle that will become more prevalent. This Learning Extension has reviewed two types of derivatives: futures and options.

A futures contract represents an obligation to buy or sell the underlying asset at a specified price by a certain date. An options contract is similar, except the owner has the option not to exercise the contract.

Futures contracts can be used to "lock in" prices for a transaction that will not occur until later. They can be used to reduce the risk of price fluctuations. For example, the risk of changing prices in a long (you own it) asset position can be countered by a short (sell) position in an appropriate futures contract. The increases in the value of one position will offset the decreases in the value of the other.

Options are useful for hedging positions as well. Some options positions, such as buying a call option, have the added benefit of maintain profit potential should the value of the underlying asset rise while limiting the dollar losses should the underlying asset's value fall.

KEY TERMS

arbitrage

at-the-money

call option

derivative security

exercise price (strike price)

futures contract

hedge

initial margin

in-the-money

option

option premium

option writer

out-of-the-money

put option

settlement price

spot market

DISCUSSION QUESTIONS

1. Briefly describe a derivative security.

2. What is a futures contract?

3. What is an option contract?

4. Indicate the difference between a call option and a put option.

PROBLEMS

1. Determine the intrinsic values of the following call options when the stock is selling at $32 just prior to expiration of the options.

   a. $25 call price

   b. $30 call price

   c. $35 call price

2. Determine the intrinsic values of the following put options when the stock is selling at $63 just prior to expiration of the options.

   a. $55 put price

   b. $65 put price

   c. $75 put price

INSTITUTIONS
AND MARKETS

INVESTMENTS

FINANCIAL
MANAGEMENT

• CHAPTER 12 •

Financial Returns and Risk Concepts

Chapter Learning Objectives . . .

AFTER STUDYING THIS CHAPTER, YOU SHOULD BE ABLE TO DO THE FOLLOWING:

- Know how to compute arithmetic averages, variances, and standard deviations using return data for a single financial asset.
- Understand the sources of risk.
- Know how to compute expected return and expected variance using scenario analysis.
- Know the historical rates of return and risk for different securities.
- Understand the concept of market efficiency and explain the three types of efficient markets.
- Explain how to calculate the expected return on a portfolio of securities.
- Understand how and why the combining of securities into portfolios reduces the overall or portfolio risk.
- Explain the difference between systematic and unsystematic risk.
- Understand the importance of ethics in investment-related positions.

Where We Have Been . . .

We know investors take their savings and direct it in various ways: some to bank accounts and some to stocks, bonds, or other investment vehicles. Investors direct their savings to various instruments by considering a number of factors: How safe is my money? Am I willing to risk a loss in hopes of achieving a large gain? What happens to my investment if security market prices rise or fall?

Where We Are Going . . .

The concepts of risk and return presented in this chapter are important to investors and to the businesses that issue the bonds and stocks that investors purchase. Businesses use a variety of short-term and long-term financing tools; the level of interest rates, expected return, and risk will guide firms as they make financing choices (Chapters 16 and 18) and their investment decisions (Chapter 17).

How Does This Chapter Apply To Me . . .

Perhaps no other chapter can affect your investing future more than this discussion of financial risk and return. When coupled with Chapter 10's discussion of bond and stock valuation, you will have a good working knowledge of investment fundamentals.

Peter Bernstein, a well-known financial consultant and researcher, gives us some insights into the word "risk":

> *The word "risk" derives from the early Italian risicare, which means "to dare." In this sense, risk is a choice rather than a fate. The actions we dare to take, which depend on how free we are to make choices, are what the story of risk is all about.*[1]

A closer look at financial risk will be the main topic of this chapter.

Investors place their funds in stocks, bonds, and other investments to attain their financial goals. But stock and bond market values rise and fall over time, based on what happens to interest rates, economic expectations, and other factors. Since no one can predict the

---

1. Peter Bernstein. *Against the Gods: The Remarkable Story of Risk.* New York, John Wiley & Sons, Inc. 1998

future, the returns earned on investments are, for the most part, unknown. Some may look back and see how different investments performed in the past and predict future returns will be similar. Others do sophisticated economic and financial analyses to estimate future returns.

In this chapter we will first learn how risk is measured relative to the average return for a single investment. We will review historical data showing the risk/return relationship. We will see that higher risk investments must compensate investors over time with higher expected returns. Our emphasis will shift to a discussion of the efficient markets hypothesis and its implications for investors. This leads to a discussion of the use and advantages of portfolio diversification, and we conclude the chapter with a discussion of systematic versus unsystematic risk.

HISTORICAL RETURN AND RISK FOR A SINGLE FINANCIAL ASSET

Figure 12.1 shows monthly prices for the stocks of two firms, Walgreens and Microsoft. Microsoft's and Walgreens' stock prices have moved "sideways" during this time frame, meaning there is some variation over time but no clear uptrend or downtrend. We can compute monthly returns on these stocks, taking their price changes and dividends into consideration. The monthly return is computed as the following:

Dollar return = Stock price at end of month − stock price at beginning of month + dividends

To put things in terms of a percentage return, the month's percentage return is the following:

Percentage return = Dollar return/stock price at the beginning of the month

For example, suppose in one month, Walgreens' stock went from $33.63 per share at the beginning of the month to $34.31 at the end of the month. No dividends were paid that month. The dollar return is the following:

Dollar return = $34.31 − $33.63 = $0.68

The monthly percentage return is $0.68/33.63 = 0.02022 or 2.022 percent.

If a dividend were received, that amount would be added to the dollar return. For example, if a dividend of 4 cents had been received during the month, the dollar return would have been the following:

Dollar return = $34.31 − $33.63 + $0.04 = $0.72

FIGURE 12.1
Microsoft's and Walgreens' Stock Prices, 2007-2012

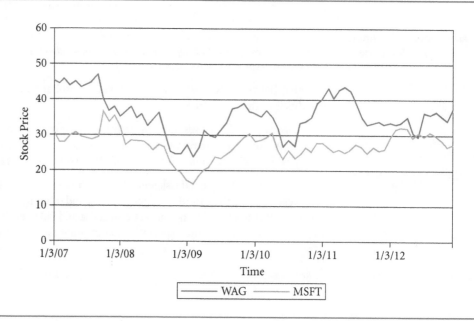

The monthly percentage return is $0.72/33.63 = 0.02141$ or 2.141 percent.

One way to measure the risk of an asset is to examine the variability of its returns. For comparison, an analyst may want to determine the level of return and the variability in returns for these two stocks to see whether investors in the higher-risk stock earned a higher return over time to compensate or reward them for the higher risk.[2]

ARITHMETIC AVERAGE ANNUAL RATES OF RETURN

If historical, or ex post, data on a stock's returns are known, the analyst can compute historical average return and risk measures. If R_t represents the stock's return for period t, the *arithmetic average return*, $\overline{R}$, over n periods is given by the following formula:

$$\overline{R} = \sum_{t=1}^{n} [R_t]/n \qquad (12\text{-}1)$$

The "Σ" symbol means to add or to sum the returns. We compute the arithmetic average return by adding the periodic returns and dividing the sum by n, the number of observations.

Let's assume that Padric held shares of Walgreens stocks over a recent six-year period. Furthermore, Serinca owned shares of Microsoft over the same six-year period. Following is a list of annual rates of returns over the six years for Walgreens and Microsoft stock:

	PERCENTAGE FORM		DECIMAL FORM	
YEAR	MICROSOFT	WALGREENS	MICROSOFT	WALGREENS
2012	8.4%	15.7%	0.084	0.157
2011	−4.6%	16.9%	−0.046	0.169
2010	−6.6%	−19.4%	−0.066	−0.194
2009	59.5%	50.9%	0.595	0.509
2008	−44.1%	−34.1%	−0.441	−0.341
2007	20.6%	−16.3%	0.206	−0.163
SUM	33.2%	13.7%	0.332	0.137
Average	5.5%	2.3%	0.055	0.023

Performing this calculation in Excel is straightforward. Placing the annual returns in columns B and C, we use the SUM function to add the Microsoft returns in cells B2 through B7 by typing =SUM (B2:B7) in cell B8. We divide this sum by 6, the number of observations, to compute the average Microsoft return by typing = B8/6 in cell B9. Similar calculations for the Walgreens data are entered into column C.

	A	B	C	D
1	Year	Microsoft	Walgreens	
2	2012	0.084	0.157	
3	2011	-0.046	0.169	
4	2010	-0.066	-0.194	
5	2009	0.595	0.509	
6	2008	-0.441	-0.341	
7	2007	0.206	-0.163	
8				
9	Sum	=SUM(B2:B7)	=SUM(C2:C7)	
10	Average = Sum/6	=B9/6	=C9/6	
11	Excel's AVERAGE function	=AVERAGE(B2:B7)	=AVERAGE(C2:C7)	
12				
13				
14				

---

2. For simplicity, we will use stocks in our discussion here. The concepts are applicable to any asset.

We can compute the average return by using a special Excel function. If we entered =AVERAGE (B2:B7) in cell B8, we would obtain the same result as above.

Walgreens' stock has an arithmetic average annual rate of return over these six years of 2.3 percent, whereas the average annual return for Microsoft stock over the same six-year period was 5.5 percent. If we are willing to ignore risk as reflected in the variability of returns, an investment in Microsoft stock might be the preferred among the two. However, not all investors have the same tolerance for uncertainty or risk associated with possibly wide swings in Microsoft's returns. Let's see how we might quantify this variability in past returns.

VARIANCE AS A MEASURE OF RISK

deviations
computed as a periodic return minus the average return

The historical risk of a stock can be measured by the variability of its returns in relation to this average. Some quantitative measures of this variability are the variance, standard deviation, and coefficient of variation. All these measures use ***deviations*** of periodic returns from the average return, that is, $R_t - \overline{R}$, where $\overline{R}$ denotes the average arithmetic return over some time frame.

The sum of the deviations, $\Sigma (R_t - \overline{R},)$ is always zero.

variance
derived by summing the squared deviations and dividing by n − 1

The ***variance***, σ^2, from a sample of data, is computed by summing the squared deviations and dividing by n − 1. (You may recall from a prior course in statistics that when a sample is drawn from a population, dividing by n − 1 observations instead of n observations provides a more accurate estimate of the variance and standard deviation characteristics of the population.):

$$\sigma^2 = \sum_{t=1}^{n} (R_t - \overline{R})^2/(n - 1) \tag{12-2}$$

Stated in words, we first find the average annual return, $\overline{R}$, over the time period being analyzed. Second, subtract the average return from the individual annual returns. Third, square each individual difference. Fourth, sum the squared differences and divide this sum by the number of observations minus 1 to get the variance.

We can find the historical variance in returns for Walgreens' and Microsoft's stocks over the past six years as shown in Table 12.1. The results indicate an estimated variance of $979.2\%^2$ for Walgreens and $1171.4\%^2$ for Microsoft. The units, percent squared ($\%^2$), may seem odd, but they are the result of the variance calculation in which the deviations are squared before they are added together and divided by (n − 1).

Use of the SUM function and other Excel operators make these calculations less tedious. Of special note is the Excel function VAR. For example, if Microsoft's returns are in cells B2 through B7, typing =VAR (B2:B7) into another cell computes and displays the variance of Microsoft's returns.

STANDARD DEVIATION AS A MEASURE OF RISK

standard deviation
the square root of the variance

Squaring the deviations can make variance difficult to interpret. What do units like percent squared or dollars squared tell an investor about a stock's risk? Because of this difficulty, analysts often prefer to use the ***standard deviation***, σ, which is the square root of the variance:

$$\sigma = \sqrt{\sigma^2} \tag{12-3}$$

TABLE 12.1

Computing the Variance for the Returns on Microsoft and Walgreens

			MICROSOFT						WALGREENS		
YEAR	RETURN	MINUS	AVERAGE		DEVIATION	DEVIATION SQUARED	YEAR	RETURN	MINUS	AVERAGE		DEVIATION	DEVIATION SQUARED
2012	8.4%	−	5.5%	=	2.9%	8.22	2012	15.7%	−	2.3%	=	13.4%	179.38
2011	−4.6%	−	5.5%	=	−10.1%	101.61	2011	16.9%	−	2.3%	=	14.6%	214.46
2010	−6.6%	−	5.5%	=	−12.2%	147.80	2010	−19.4%	−	2.3%	=	−21.7%	471.04
2009	59.5%	−	5.5%	=	53.9%	2908.99	2009	50.9%	−	2.3%	=	48.6%	2362.38
2008	−44.1%	−	5.5%	=	−49.6%	2463.25	2008	−34.1%	−	2.3%	=	−36.4%	1324.83
2007	20.6%	−	5.5%	=	15.1%	226.99	2007	−16.3%	−	2.3%	=	−18.5%	343.74
Sum =						$5856.86\%^2$	Sum =						$4895.83\%^2$
Variance = Sum/(6 − 1) =						$1171.4\%^2$	Variance = Sum/(6 − 1)				=		$979.2\%^2$
Standard deviation = SQRT (variance) =						34.2%	Standard deviation = SQRT (variance) =						31.3%

The standard deviation formula gives units of measurement that match those of the return data. Taking the square root of the variance of 979.2 for Walgreens stock gives a standard deviation of 31.3 percent. This compares to a standard deviation of 34.2 percent (i.e., the square root of 1171.4) for Microsoft. Thus, Microsoft has a relatively higher average return (5.5 percent versus 2.3 percent) and a higher standard deviation (34.2 percent versus 31.3 percent) when compared to Walgreens for the time period we studied.

The square root can be found using a financial calculator with a square root key as follows:

Financial Calculator Solution:

	Walgreens stock:	Microsoft stock:
Inputs:	979.2	1171.4
Press:	$\sqrt{}$	$\sqrt{}$
Solution:	31.3	34.2

Spreadsheets can be used, too. Since we know the standard deviation is the square root of the variance, Excel's SQRT function can be used by keying in = SQRT(cell containing the variance). To make the calculation simpler, we can use the STDEV function. If Microsoft's returns are in cells B2 through B7, using = STDEV(B2:B7) in another cell computes the standard deviation.

Sometimes calculations using real data may show that one firm had a higher return and a lower standard deviation than another firm. A result like this for two firms, a small sample, is by no means a violation of the second principle of finance that higher returns are expected for taking on more risk. It would indicate only what has happened in the recent past and is based on six years of data. Over time, over many assets, we expect higher risk assets to have higher returns.

Figure 12.2 shows the behavior of stock prices for Walgreens (WAG) and Microsoft (MSFT) for a number of years. Over time, Microsoft's stock has offered more price variability than Walgreens while offering larger percentage gains.

Looking at historical annual returns on these stocks will tell us what their price range has been, namely how low and how high each stock price has been. If we have reason to believe the near future will be similar to the time period we have studied, we can use the standard deviation

FIGURE 12.2

Behavior of Stock Prices for Microsoft (MSFT) and Walgreens (WAG) for over 25 Years

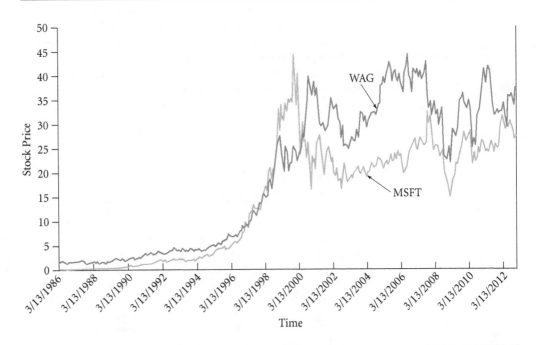

FIGURE 12.3
Normal Distribution

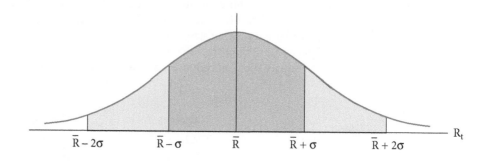

INTERNET ACTIVITY

Stock price data are available at http://finance.yahoo.com. Daily, weekly, and monthly stock prices, adjusted for stock splits, can be downloaded into a spreadsheet. You can use the data to compute returns, average returns over a time period, and risk measures.

to help give an investor an intuitive feel for the possible range of returns that can occur. As shown in Figure 12.3, if the underlying distribution of returns is continuous and approximately normal (meaning bell shaped), then we should expect 68 percent of actual periodic returns to fall within one standard deviation of the mean, that is $\overline{R} \pm 1\sigma$. About 95 percent of observed returns will fall within two standard deviations of the average: $\overline{R} \pm 2\sigma$. Actual returns should fall within three standard deviations of the mean, $\overline{R} \pm 3\sigma$, about 99 percent of the time. Thus, if the mean and standard deviation are known, a rough range for expected returns over time can be estimated.

Applying this to our data for Walgreens and Microsoft, if returns over a long time period were approximately normally distributed and our six years of observations were a reasonable representation of returns over the long run, Table 12.2 should show the range of possible outcomes along with approximate probabilities of occurrence. In words, we can say that 95 percent of the time the annual return on Walgreens' stock will fall between −60.3 percent and +64.9 percent, with an expected average annual return of 2.3 percent. For Microsoft, the annual return will fall within the range of −62.9 percent and +74.0% percent 95 percent of the time, and the expected average monthly return will be 5.5% percent. But with the overall stock market averaging about 10 percent annual return, it is likely that future return distributions for Walgreens and Microsoft will offer investors better returns.

One problem with using the standard deviation as a measure of risk is that we cannot tell which stock is riskier by looking at the standard deviation. For example, suppose stock A has an average annual return of 8 percent and an annual standard deviation of 16 percent while stock B has an average annual return of 12 percent annual standard deviation of 20 percent a year. Stock B has a higher standard deviation, but it also had a higher average annual return of 12 percent versus 8 percent for stock A. Which stock is riskier?

The coefficient of variation allows us to make comparisons because it controls for the size of the average. The ***coefficient of variation*** (CV) is a measure of risk per unit of return. The coefficient of variation is computed in the following way:

coefficient of variation (CV)

a measure of risk per unit of return

$$CV = \sigma/\overline{R} \tag{12-4}$$

TABLE 12.2
Distribution of Returns for WAG and MSFT

STOCK	PERCENT OF RETURNS	ANNUAL RETURN ESTIMATES		
		DOWNSIDE (%)	AVERAGE (%)	UPSIDE (%)
Walgreens	68	−29.0%	2.3%	33.6%
	95	−60.3%	2.3%	64.9%
	99	−91.6%	2.3%	96.2%
Microsoft	68	−28.7%	5.5%	39.8%
	95	−62.9%	5.5%	74.0%
	99	−97.1%	5.5%	108.2%

A higher coefficient of variation (CV) indicates more risk per unit of return. A lower CV indicates less risk per unit of return. Stock A has a CV of 16/8, or 2.0, meaning that it offers 2.0 units of risk for every unit of return. Stock B has a CV of 20/12, or 1.67 units of risk per unit of return. Based upon the CV, stock A is the riskier security based upon its units of risk for every one percentage point of return.

WHERE DOES RISK COME FROM?

Being able to compute risk measures is important for a financial analyst, but perhaps more important is the ability to identify sources of risk and estimate their impact on different investments. For example, companies are affected by many risk sources. Table 12.3 shows a simple income statement for a firm. The income statement, as we will discuss in more detail in Chapter 13 shows the firm's sales revenues and expenses over a time period, such as a month, quarter, or year.

The "top line" of the income statement is the firm's sales. From this, expenses are subtracted. We'll call this difference the firm's operating income. Next, interest expenses on the firm's borrowings are subtracted, leaving pretax income or income before taxes. Subtracting the taxes we owe, we are left with the "bottom line," net income or income after taxes.

Table 12.3 lists sources of risk that affect these components of the income statement. ***Business risk*** leads to variations in a firm's operating income over time. It is caused by changes in quantity sold, changes in the firm's mark-up on its sales (the price − cost margin), and its level of fixed costs.

For example, when the cost of an input increases, such as rising labor costs, oil prices, or raw material costs, competitive pressures may not allow a firm to increase its selling prices to offset the increased expenses. This lowers the price-cost margin and, if all else is constant, will reduce the firm's operating profit. On the other hand, fixed costs can lead to variations in operating profit over time, too. Fixed costs are "fixed" in that they do not change in the face of higher or lower selling prices or quantity sold. When much of a firm's costs are fixed by contract (as in the case of labor union agreements, supply contracts, and lease agreements), a decline in sales revenues is not matched by a decline in expenses. Falling sales combined with stable expenses results in declining operating profits.

Other sources of profit variability include the following:

- ***Exchange Rate Risk***: When a U.S. firm makes an overseas transaction, it may make or receive payment in a foreign currency. If it receives payment in a foreign currency, U.S. dollar sales revenues will fall and rise over time, depending upon if the dollar

CONCEPT CHECK

How is average return computed?

Describe three ways to measure risk.

business risk
variations in operating income over time because of variations in unit sales, price − cost margin, and/or fixed expenses

exchange rate risk
effect on revenues and expenses from variations in the value of the U.S. dollar in terms of other currencies

TABLE 12.3

A Firm's Income Statement Reflects Sources of Risk

COMPONENTS OF A FIRM'S INCOME STATEMENT	POTENTIAL SOURCES OF RISK
Revenue	*Business Risk:* changes in quantity sold; varying price-cost margin
	Exchange Rate Risk: changes in U.S. dollars received from overseas sales
	Purchasing Power Risk: inability to raise prices at the same pace as expenses
Less: Expenses	*Business Risk:* amount of fixed costs
	Exchange Rate Risk: changes in U.S. dollars paid to overseas suppliers
	Purchasing Power Risk: inflation increases costs
Equals: Operating Income	
Less: Interest Expense	*Financial Risk:* amount of fixed financial expenses
	Interest Rate Risk: effect of changing interest rates on variable rate debt
Equals: Income Before Taxes	
Less: Taxes	*Tax Risk:* Changes in tax rates, laws, surcharges either at home or overseas
Equals: Net Income	

purchasing power risk
changes in inflation affect
revenues, expenses, and
profitability

is strengthening (more units of foreign currency are needed to purchase one U.S. dollar) or weakening (fewer units of foreign currency are needed to purchase one U.S. dollar).

Conversely, if the firm needs to pay overseas suppliers in nondollar currency, the firm's dollar-based expenses will fall and rise, depending upon if the dollar strengthens or weakens. To summarize, if all else is held constant, then the following will occur:

	U.S. DOLLAR REVENUES INCREASE FROM OVERSEAS SALES IF:	U.S. DOLLAR REVENUES DECREASE FROM OVERSEAS SALES IF:	U.S. DOLLAR EXPENSES INCREASE TO PAY OVERSEAS SUPPLIERS IF:	U.S. DOLLAR EXPENSES DECREASE TO PAY OVERSEAS SUPPLIERS IF:
U.S. dollar strengthens		X		X
U.S. dollar weakens	X		X	

- **Purchasing Power Risk:** Inflation increases costs and can hurt the firm's profitability if it cannot raise prices to compensate for the increased expenses.

financial risk
variations in income before
taxes over time because fixed
interest expenses do not
change when operating
income rises or falls

- **Financial Risk:** A firm with debt outstanding that requires fixed interest payments faces a situation similar to a firm with fixed operating expenses (see our business risk discussion, above). If sales decline and operating income falls, the fixed interest costs must be paid if the firm is to remain in operation, leading to declines in interest before taxes. On the other hand, rising levels of operating profit do not cause the fixed financial cost to change, so more of the increased operating profit passes through to become an increase in income before taxes.

interest rate risk
variations in interest expense
unrelated to sales or
operating income arising
from changes in the level of
interest rates in the economy

- **Interest Rate Risk:** Some of the firm's debt may have interest rates, which vary according to the level of interest rates in the economy. Such changes in the cost of borrowing are usually unrelated to changes in the firm's sales or operating profits. Thus, variability in interest rates can increase or reduce income before taxes irrespective of sales trends.

tax risk
variations in a firm's tax rate
and tax-related charges over
time due to changing tax
laws and regulations

- **Tax Risk:** Changes in tax rates, laws, and surcharges, at home or overseas, add another layer of risk and potential variability to a firm's income.

ex ante
expected or forecasted

EXPECTED MEASURES OF RETURN AND RISK

The use of historical data to look backward is valuable for examining returns and performance over time, but today's investment and business decisions must be made by looking forward, not backward. Future returns will depend upon our decisions today and upon future events. We need to develop a way to estimate expected, or *ex ante*, measures of return and risk.

SMALL BUSINESS PRACTICE
Should You Start Your Own Business?

Most of us would agree that it is impossible for someone else to answer the question "Should you start your own business?" However, an article by Joshua Hyatt titled "Should You Start a Business?" in *Small Business Success*, a supplement to *Inc.* magazine, provides a list of questions that you should ask yourself. First, "Is my idea good enough?" While it is unnecessary for your idea to be a revolutionary breakthrough, you must believe in it and be willing to commit the time and effort necessary to make it useful and exciting to others.

You should ask, "Do I have the management skills I'll need?" "How important is money to me?" "Can I live with the risk?" People who start companies don't necessarily do so because they thrive on risk. Rather, some entrepreneurs see the starting of a new business as being less risky than the alternative risk of working for a large company. Hyatt attributes the following quote to Paul Hawken of the firm Smith & Hawken: "The best entrepreneurs are risk avoiders. They identify the risk, and then they take actions to minimize the effects of it."

The final question Hyatt suggests you ask is "What do I tell my family?" It is important to talk with family members about the time, money, and energy commitment you will have to make if you decide to start your own business. Hyatt suggests the following: "Have a fallback plan. You can't make the boldest moves with your business if you feel you can't afford to be wrong."

A popular method to forecast future returns is to develop scenarios of future states of nature. A state of nature includes a set of economic trends and business conditions. The investor cannot control or predict what future states of nature will occur. One set of scenarios could be the following:

1. *Boom economy:* The domestic economy will grow at an above average pace; inflation will increase slowly; interest rate trends will be slightly upward. Company sales will be assisted by a healthy export environment.

2. *Normal conditions:* The domestic economy will grow at a pace close to its long-run average. Inflation rates and interest rates will be relatively stable. No major disruptions in our export markets are expected.

3. *Recession:* The domestic economy will grow slowly or maybe contract. Inflation will peak and start to decline; short-term interest rates will fall. Slow export markets will lead to lower levels of foreign sales.

Each of the above three scenarios is a state of nature. The states of nature can be complicated or simple, few or many; as a whole, they should include all reasonable (and maybe a few unreasonable) possible future environments. The above three scenarios assumed inflation, interest rate, and a firm's exports will follow the trends in the overall domestic economy. This, of course, does not have to be the case. A more complex set of states of nature may include separate scenarios for the domestic economy, inflation, interest rates, exports, and any other variables deemed important by the investment analyst.

Once the possible states of nature are projected, the analyst must assign a probability, or a chance of occurrence, to each one. For the above three scenarios, suppose the first scenario of a growing economy has a probability (p_1) of 0.30; the second scenario of normal conditions has a probability (p_2) of 0.40; the third recession scenario has a probability (p_3) of 0.30. In reality, these probabilities are developed from a combination of the analyst's experience or "gut feel," surveying other analysts on their beliefs, economic and industry forecasts, monetary policy, and a review of what has happened in the past under similar conditions. No formula can be used to determine probabilities for each state of nature. The only rules are that each state of nature needs a nonnegative probability assigned to it, and the probabilities of all the states of nature must sum to 1.00.

The analyst must forecast the stock's return for the year under each state of nature. If the above three states of nature are being used, analysts may forecast a 20 percent return under good economic conditions, 10 percent in normal times, and -5 percent in a recession.

The expected return can now be found, using equation 12-5:

$$\text{Expected return } E(R) = \sum_{i=1}^{n} p_i R_i \tag{12-5}$$

p_i = probability of the ith scenario and R_i = the forecasted return in the ith scenario.

The expected return $E(R)$ is a weighted average of the different state of nature returns, where the weights are the probabilities of each state of nature occurring. Using the above probabilities and forecasted returns, the expected return using equation 12-5 is the following:

$$E(R) = (0.3)(20) + (0.4)(10) + (0.3)(-5) = 8.5 \text{ percent}$$

This number, or any other calculated number, represents the average return if the state of nature scenarios could be replicated many times under identical conditions. In any one year, if the states of nature estimates are correct, the outcome will be "boom" (and a return of 20 percent), "normal" (10 percent return), or "recession" (return of -5 percent). If the cycle could be repeated many times, the average return over the cycles would be 8.5 percent. Thus, the expected return does not refer to the expected outcome of a particular situation. It refers only to the long-run average outcome that would occur if the situation could be replicated many times, but this concept does provide analysts with an intuitive measure of central tendency. It also allows us to develop measures of possible return variability or risk.[3]

---

3. The process of computing expected returns from scenarios is difficult to apply practically. Thus, some analysts prefer to estimate expected returns from historical return data and forecasts of future conditions by adding various asset risk premiums, such as a default risk or a liquidity risk premium, to the expected nominal interest rate. For example, an investor may believe a stock investment in AT&T deserves a risk premium of 5 percent over the nominal interest rate. If Treasury bills were currently offering a return of 4 percent, the expected return on an investment in AT&T stock would be 4 percent plus 5 percent, or 9 percent. When using this method, however, it becomes difficult to estimate measures of future risk.

Just as for historical data, measures of dispersion or variance can be computed once the average or expected value is found. The variance, σ^2, is found by using equation 12-6:

$$\sigma^2 = \sum_{i=1}^{n} p_i[R_i - E(R)]^2 \tag{12-6}$$

As with historical or ex post measures, the standard deviation is the square root of the variance. The coefficient of variation is the standard deviation divided by the expected return. As with ex post or historical data, the coefficient of variation is easily interpreted: It represents the risk per unit of expected return.

Let's compute the variance, standard deviation, and coefficient of variation (CV) for the stock return using the three scenarios developed above. The stock return forecast was 20 percent in an economic boom (30 percent probability), 10 percent in a normal economy (40 percent probability), and −5 percent in a recession (30 percent probability). The expected return was computed to be 8.5 percent. Using equation 12-6, the variance of the forecast is the following:

$$\begin{aligned}
\sigma^2 &= (0.3)(20 - 8.5)^2 + (0.4)(10 - 8.5)^2 + (0.3)(-5 - 8.5)^2 \\
&= 39.675 + 0.90 + 54.675 \\
&= 95.25 \text{ percent squared}
\end{aligned}$$

INTERNET ACTIVITY

Do an Internet search of "scenario analysis" to see what examples you can find of this method. To learn more about simulation analysis, visit http://www.oracle.com/crystalball, the Web site of a firm that markets simulation software.

The standard deviation will be the square root of this number, or 9.76 percent. The CV is the standard deviation divided by the expected return, or 9.76/8.5 = 1.15.

Is it practical to develop states of nature, determine their expected probabilities, and estimate expected return and risk? In other words, do investors do these calculations? There is evidence that scenario analysis does have practical implications. First, when the Federal Reserve System (Fed) is expected to decide to act to change short-term interest rates, market watchers and investors anticipate what the Fed may do. Periodicals, such as *The Wall Street Journal* and *USA Today*, survey practitioners on their expectations of Fed action. One news article presented this analysis prior to an expected interest rate cut by the Fed:[4]

SCENARIO	PROBABILITY	LIKELY MARKET RESPONSE[5]
No rate cut	Very unlikely	Stocks and bonds plunge
Quarter-point cut	Possible	Stocks and bonds fall
Half-point cut	Likely	Stocks and bonds could rise, at least initially
Three-quarter-point cut, or more	Unlikely	Stocks and bonds surge

The market evidently anticipated the Fed's actions; that day, the Fed announced it would attempt to reduce short-term rates by one-half point, which was the "likely" scenario. The stock market closed nearly unchanged; the Dow Jones Industrial Average (DJIA) closed down that day 4.36 points (or 0.04 percent of the index's value) while the NASDAQ Composite Index closed up 3.66 points (0.18 percent).[6] As another example, several months later, the market anticipated a quarter-point reduction, from 2.00 percent to 1.75 percent, in the federal funds rate; when the Fed did announce the rate cut to 1.75 percent, the DJIA and Standard & Poor's 500 (S&P 500) indexes moved less than 0.33 percent, reflecting that the market anticipated the move.[7] Other examples of scenario analysis exist in the print media and the blogosphere.[8]

4. E. S. Browning, "Investors Hold Breath, Awaiting Rate Cut," *The Wall Street Journal* (May 15, 2001), p. C1. For a corporate example, see Cari Tuna, "Pendulum is Swinging Back on 'Scenario Planning'," *The Wall Street Journal* (July 6, 2009), p. B6.

5. The likely market responses are based on the market expectations at the time regarding what the Fed might do. The market's responses will not always coincide with those listed here.

6. E. S. Browning, "Fed Delivers Expected Rate Cut, But Investors' Reaction is Muted," *The Wall Street Journal* (May 16, 2001), p. C1.

7. E. S. Browning, "Stocks Fall Back Before Meeting Of Fed on Rates," *The Wall Street Journal* (December 11, 2001), pp. C1, C17; E. S. Browning, "Fed Pessimism and Merck News Abet Late-Day Selloff," *The Wall Street Journal* (December 12, 2001), pp. C1, C19.

8. See, e.g., Russ Koesterich, 3 Potential Scenarios for 2013, Dec 12, 2012, http://isharesblog.com/blog/2012/12/12/3-potential-scenarios-for-2013/, accessed December 20, 2012; Eric Miller, 2013 Global Outlook, Fixed Income Research, Credit Suisse, December 4, 2012, https://doc.research-and-analytics.csfb.com/docView?language=ENG&format=PDF&source_id=em&document_id=1004615281&serialid=10hR0v0HFEeSOAHU05TBjY3yzd2A9HpiLWp7PZf%2BrKk%3D, accessed December 20, 2013. Students can google financial market scenario analysis to find others.

CAREER OPPORTUNITIES IN FINANCE
Personal Financial Planning

Opportunities

Personal financial planning involves preparing for emergencies and protecting against catastrophes, such as premature death and the loss of real assets. Personal financial planning involves planning for the accumulation of wealth during an individual's working career to provide an adequate standard of living after retirement. Job opportunities include the fields of insurance (life, health, and property) and investments (money management, individual bonds and stocks, and mutual funds).

Jobs

Financial Planner
Financial Advisor

Responsibilities

A financial planner helps individuals develop personal financial plans that include establishing current and future financial goals and

assists individuals in setting up steps for carrying out the goals. Financial goals are set for cash reserves, insurance protection, and investing or saving to accumulate wealth over an individual's working lifetime.

A financial advisor focuses on maintaining and increasing the investment wealth of individuals. Investment advice is given in reference to the existing stage in the individual's "life cycle," as well as in terms of the individual's attitude toward investment risk. Advice is given on the target mix among cash reserves, bonds, and stocks. Specific investment recommendations may be provided.

Education

A bachelor's degree usually is a prerequisite. Additional education and training often are needed in the insurance and securities areas. Certification programs must be completed to sell securities. A Certified Financial Planner (CFP) designation also is available.

CONCEPT CHECK

How does computing an expected return differ from finding a historical average return?

Why must the probabilities of the various scenarios sum to 1.0?

The second insight is related to the first, in that although each individual investor may not compute a scenario analysis, the markets as a whole behave as if they do. Expected changes, news, or announcements will generally have little effect on security prices, so if an investor follows the consensus set of beliefs, the investor will find it difficult to earn above-average returns after adjusting for risk differences. To make above-average returns without undue risk, investors must do an analysis and show where the consensus belief is incorrect and invest accordingly. If their analysis is correct, their investments should benefit. Evidence of news "surprises" is many times seen in large stock price reactions following the news event. Following the re-election of President Obama in 2012, the U.S. stock market (as measured by the DJIA) fell 313 points, or 2.4%, the following trading day. Evidently the market was expecting (or hoping) for another result.

The third insight, a more complex form of decision analysis, is called *simulation*. Rather than use a limited number of states of nature with specific values for, say, inflation, economic growth, and so on, simulation allows many different combinations of the important variables that may determine stock returns. After running the analysis several thousand times, the computer can compute the average return from the simulation runs and the standard deviation of the returns. Businesses use this technique for a variety of decisions involving uncertain revenues or expenses.

HISTORICAL RETURNS AND RISK OF DIFFERENT ASSETS

In Chapter 9, we learned that the value of an asset is the present value (PV) of the expected cash flows that arise from owning the asset. To compute a PV, we need to know the size and timing of expected future cash flows from an asset. We must know the appropriate discount rate, or the required rate of return, at which to discount expected cash flows back to the present. Chapter 8 identified three components of the required rate of return: the real risk-free rate of return, inflation expectations, and a risk premium.

The first two components are the same for all investments. Their combined effect is approximated by the yield on a short-term Treasury bill. Expected returns differ as a result of different risk premiums. Thus, finance professionals say that *risk drives expected return* as does our second principle of finance. A low-risk investment will have a lower expected return than a high-risk investment. High-risk investments will have to offer investors higher expected returns to convince (typically) risk-averse people to place their savings at risk. Thus, longer-term Treasury bonds will have to offer investors higher expected returns than Treasury bills. Common stock, by virtue of its equity claim and low priority on company cash flows and assets, will have to offer investors a larger expected return to compensate for its risk.

Evidence that high returns go hand in hand with high risk is seen in Table 12.4, which reports the average annual returns and standard deviations for different types of investments. The return

INTERNET ACTIVITY

Data on asset returns can be found on the Internet, too. For example, visit Prof. Aswath Damodaran's Web site to see annual data on asset returns: http://www.stern.nyu.edu/~adamodar/.

TABLE 12.4

Historical Returns and Standard Deviation of Returns from Different Assets, 1928–2012

ASSET	TREASURY BILLS	TREASURY BONDS	COMMON STOCKS	INFLATION RATE
Average Annual Return	3.70%	5.37%	11.23%	3.15%
Standard Deviation	3.09%	7.74%	20.00%	3.93%

Source: *http://www.stern.nyu.edu/~adamodar/* and author calculations.

distributions for common stocks have a large standard deviation, indicating more risk than the bond investments. However, investors who undertake such risk earn high rewards over the long haul since stock returns reward investors more than conservative bond investments.

The return and risk measures for long-term government bonds show that less risk does result in less return. Treasury bills' average annual return is the lowest in the table, as is the standard deviation of their returns over time.

Although future returns and risk cannot be predicted precisely from past measures, Table 12.4 does present information that investors find useful when considering the relative risks and rewards of different investment strategies. Risk is a real factor for investors to consider. Just because large company stocks have an arithmetic average return of about 11 percent does not mean we should expect the stock market to rise by that amount each year. As the standard deviation of the annual returns indicates, 11 percent is the average return over a long time frame, during which there were substantial positive and negative deviations from the average. The recent behavior of the stock market during 2000–2002 (particularly the technology sector) and during 2007–2009 should remind us that market returns are not always positive. The S&P 500 stock market index lost over 9 percent in value during calendar year 2000, over 12 percent during 2001, and over 22 percent in 2002. The technology sector was hit hard during this time, as bankruptcies and oversupply resulted in some sectors losing 60 percent or more in value in 2000, with losses continuing through 2002. From October 2007 through March 2009, the DJIA lost over 52 percent of its value.

CONCEPT CHECK

Explain what is meant by "risk drives expected return."

How does Table 12.4 illustrate the concept that risk drives expected return?

EFFICIENT CAPITAL MARKETS

Prices on securities change over the course of time. As we learned in Chapter 10, security prices are determined by the pattern of expected cash flows and a discount rate. Therefore, any change in price must reflect a change in expected cash flows, the discount rate, or both. Sometimes identifiable news can cause assets' prices to change. Unexpected good news may cause investors to view an asset as less risky or to expect increases in future cash flows. Either reaction leads to an increase in an asset's price. Unexpected bad news can cause an opposite reaction: the asset may be viewed as more risky or its future cash flows may be expected to fall. Either reaction results in a falling asset price.

A market with systems that allow for quick execution of customers' trades is said to be operationally efficient. If a market adjusts prices quickly after the arrival of important news surprises, it is said to be an *informationally efficient market*, or an **efficient market**. If the market for Microsoft stock is efficient, we should see a quick price change shortly after any announcement of an unexpected event that affects sales, earnings, or new products or after an unexpected announcement by a major competitor. A quick movement in the price of a stock, such as Microsoft, should take no longer than several minutes. After this price adjustment, future price changes should appear to be random. That is, the initial price reaction to the news should, on average, fully reflect the effects of the news.

In an efficient market, only unexpected news or surprises should cause prices to rise or fall. Expected events should have no impact on asset prices since investors' expectations would be reflected in their trading patterns and the asset's price. For example, if investors expected Microsoft to announce that earnings for the past year rose 10 percent, Microsoft's current stock price should reflect that expectation. If Microsoft does announce a 10 percent earnings increase, no significant price change should occur as Microsoft's stock price reflected that information. If, however, Microsoft announced an earnings increase of 20 percent (a good surprise given the market's expectation of a 10 percent increase) or an earnings decline of 5 percent (a bad surprise given the market's expectation), the market would adjust Microsoft's price in reaction to the unexpected news.

efficient market (informationally efficient market)
a market in which prices adjust quickly after the arrival of important news surprises

FIGURE 12.4

Price Reaction in Efficient and Inefficient Markets

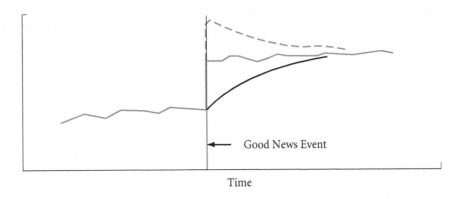

Good News Event

Time

---

* Examples of price reaction in an efficient market(—) and inefficient markets following good news about a company. An inefficient market with an overreaction is indicated by (---); an inefficient market with an underreaction is indicated by (—).

Every time Microsoft's stock price changes in reaction to new information, it should show no continuing tendency to rise or fall after the price adjustment. Figure 12.4 illustrates this. After new information hits the market and the price adjusts, no steady trend in either direction should persist.

Any consistent trend in the same direction as the price change would be evidence of an *inefficient market* that does not quickly and correctly process new information to determine asset prices. Likewise, evidence of price corrections or reversals after the immediate reaction to news implies an inefficient market that overreacts to news.

In an efficient market, it is difficult to consistently find stocks whose prices do not fairly reflect the present values of future expected cash flows. Prices will change when the arrival of new information indicates that an upward or downward revision in this present value is appropriate.

This means that in an efficient market, investors cannot consistently earn above-average profits (after controlling for risk differences among assets) from trades made after new information arrives at the market. The price adjustment occurs so rapidly that buy or sell orders placed after the announcement cannot, in the long run, result in risk-adjusted returns above the market's average return. An order to buy after the arrival of good news may result in large profits, but such a gain will occur only by chance, as will comparable losses. Stock price trends always return to their random ways after initially adjusting to the new information.[9]

random walk
prices appear to fluctuate randomly over time, driven by the random arrival of new information

Efficient markets result from interactions among many market participants, all analyzing available information in pursuit of advantage. Also, the information flows they analyze must be random in timing and content. (In an efficient market, no one can consistently predict tomorrow's news.) The profit motive leads investors to buy low and sell high on the basis of new information and their interpretation of it. Hordes of investors analyzing all available information about the economy and individual firms identify incorrectly priced stocks. Resulting trading pushes those stocks to their correct levels. This causes prices in an efficient market to move in a **random walk**, meaning they appear to fluctuate randomly over time, driven by the random arrival of new information.[10]

strong-form efficient market
a market in which prices reflect all knowledge, including past and current publicly known and private information

Different assumptions about how much information is reflected in prices give rise to different types of market efficiency. A market in which prices reflect all knowledge, including past and current publicly known and private information, is a **strong-form efficient market**. In such an

---

9. Financial periodicals typically feature articles that comment on apparent inefficiencies or to provide evidence in favor of market efficiency. See, for example, Mark Gongloff, "Fed Move: Someone's Sure to Be Surprised," *The Wall Street Journal* (June 24, 2009), page C1and Tony Jackson, "Buffett and other blows to efficient market theory," *Financial Times* (June 29, 2009) page 18.

10. The insightful reader may be wondering how prices can demonstrate a random walk when evidence presented earlier in Chapter 8 shows common stocks increasing in value by almost 12 percent per year on average. Such a return seems to imply an upward trend, not random deviations. Market efficiency does not eliminate long-run upward and downward trends in the economy; it means investors cannot consistently predict which stocks will outperform or underperform the market averages on a risk-adjusted basis.

semistrong-form efficient market
a market in which all public information, past and current, is reflected in asset prices

weak-form efficient market
market in which prices reflect all past information, such as information in last year's annual report, previous earnings announcements, and other past news

chartists (technicians)
people who examine graphs of past price movements, number of shares bought and sold, and other figures to predict future price movements

INTERNET ACTIVITY

Go to http://finance.yahoo.com and see who the day's biggest price gainers and losers in the stock market are. What news may have caused these price changes?

efficient market, even corporate officers and other insiders cannot earn above-average, risk-adjusted profits from buying and selling stock. Even their detailed, exclusive information is reflected in current stock prices according to the strong-form hypothesis. Few markets can pass the test of strong-form efficiency, and insiders can profit from information not known by others. As discussed in the previous chapter, that is a reason why U.S. laws prohibit insider trading, or trading based on important, nonpublic information.

In a **semistrong-form efficient market**, all public information, both past and current, is reflected in asset prices. The U.S. stock market appears to be a fairly good example of a semistrong-form efficient market. News about the economy or individual companies appears to produce quick stock price changes without subsequent trends or price reversals.

A **weak-form efficient market** is a market in which prices reflect all past information, such as information in last year's annual report, previous earnings announcements, and other past news. Some investors, called **chartists** (or **technicians**), examine graphs of past price movements, number of shares bought and sold, and other figures to predict future price movements. A weak-form efficient market implies that such investors are wasting their time; they cannot earn above-average, risk-adjusted profits by projecting past trends in market variables.

Market efficiency has several important practical implications. First, for investors, efficient markets make it difficult to invest to consistently "beat the market" by earning above-average returns after taking risk differences into account. Thus, over time, more individual and institutional investors have chosen to "index," that is, to invest in securities that comprise the market indexes (such as the S&P500 index or Merrill Lynch's corporate bond index) rather than choose specific stocks or bonds. Indexers want to match the market's performance by placing funds in securities in the same proportion as their weight in the chosen index.[11] Over nearly any 10-year to 15-year period, anywhere from two-thirds to three-quarters of professionally managed U.S. diversified stock mutual funds earned lower returns than a broad stock market index. Table 12.5 shows that professional mutual fund managers, except for two years (2005 and 2007), generally earned lower returns than the S&P500 stock market index. This is evidence in favor of the efficient market hypothesis. The bottom row of the table shows that over longer the time frames (3 years and 5 years), the general performance of the equity mutual funds tends to worsen. Over longer time periods, over two-thirds of large-capitalization funds earn returns lower than the S&P500 index.

Second, for corporate financial managers, stock price reactions to a firm's announcements of dividend changes, mergers, and strategies will present a fair view of how the marketplace feels about management's actions. Announcements followed by stock price declines indicate that the market believes the decision will hurt future cash flows or increase the riskiness of the firm. Announcements followed by stock price increases indicate that investors feel future cash flows will rise or risk will fall. By watching the market, managers can see how investors perceive their actions.

Now that we have discussed how difficult it is to earn rates of return higher than risk-adjusted "market" returns, what is should investors do? First, investors can establish the amount of financial

TABLE 12.5

Percentage of Mutual Funds Underperforming the Benchmark Index, various years

	BENCHMARK INDEX	2003	2004	2005	2006	2007	2008	2009	2010	2011	2012	AVERAGE
All Large-Cap Funds	S&P 500	64.6	61.6	44.5	69.1	44.8	54.3	50.8	61.8	81.3	63.3	59.6
	2010-2012		**2008-2012**									
Large-Cap Core Funds	86.5		75.4									

Source: Aye Soe, "S&P Indices Versus Active Funds (SPIVA®) Scorecard," Yearend 2012, S&P Dow Jones Indices LLC.

---

11. In practice, index funds have difficulty exactly matching the performance of the chosen index because of the index funds' need to reinvest dividend or coupon income as well as handle cash coming in from new investors and sell shares from investors who want to take their money out of the index fund.

PERSONAL FINANCIAL PLANNING
Diversification for the Small Investor

Most people do not have the time and expertise needed to manage an asset portfolio. For many, acquiring the investment capital is difficult, too. Fortunately, such "small" investors, as they are called, have a way to obtain professional investment management and portfolio diversification. They can use investment companies.

An investment company is a corporation that invests the pooled funds of savers. Many investment companies purchase the stocks and bonds of corporations. Others specialize in holding short-term commercial paper, bank CDs, and U.S. Treasury bills and are known as money market mutual funds. The funds of many investors are pooled for the primary purpose of obtaining expert management and a wide diversity in security investments. The number and the size of investment companies have increased rapidly in the past decade.

Classification of Investment Companies
Investment companies are of two types: closed-end funds and mutual, or open-ended, funds, the latter of which are much more popular. Both types have the common objective of achieving intelligent diversification, or variety of investments, for the pooled funds of individuals.

Closed-End Funds
Ordinarily, money is initially raised to invest by selling stock or ownership shares in a closed-end fund. Owners of closed-end fund shares may sell their shares just as they would with any corporate security, that is, by selling them to other investors. The shares of closed-end funds are traded either on an organized securities exchange or in the over-the-counter market.

Mutual (Open-Ended) Funds
A mutual fund can invest in equity and debt securities, and it uses dividends and interest from these securities to pay dividends to shareholders. In contrast with closed-end funds, mutual funds continually sell shares to willing investors. Shareholders may sell their shares back to the mutual fund at any time. The purchase and selling price of mutual fund shares is related to the fund's net asset value (NAV). A fund's NAV is the per-share market value of the securities that the fund owns. Some large and well-known mutual fund companies are Fidelity, Vanguard, T. Rowe Price, and Scudder.

Securities and Exchange Commission (SEC) data indicate that more than 8,000 mutual funds hold assets in the form of corporate and government securities in excess of $10 trillion, meaning a popular method of investing indeed.

CONCEPT CHECK
What is an efficient market?

If price trends were predictable, would that be an indication of an efficient or inefficient market? Explain your answer.

How does a semistrong efficient market differ from a weakly efficient market?

portfolio
any combination of financial assets or investments

risk they are willing to accept and then find investments that have demonstrated comparable levels of risk. Second, investors can diversify away that portion of total risk that is said to be "unsystematic," or separate from movements in the economy and the overall market. In the next section, we take a closer look at the trade-off between expected return and risk and the role of systematic and unsystematic risk

PORTFOLIO RETURNS AND RISK

Let's return to our earlier discussion of the stocks of Walgreens and Microsoft. Recall that Padric received a historical arithmetic average annual rate of return of 2.3 percent on Walgreens stock with a standard deviation of 31.3 percent over six years. Serinca's historical average return and risk achieved by investing in Microsoft over the same six-year period were 5.5 percent and 34.2 percent, respectively.

Mary is considering investing in common stocks but is considering purchasing both Microsoft and Walgreens shares. This latter choice would be an example of building or forming a portfolio. A ***portfolio*** is any combination of financial assets or investments.

Mary realizes that future returns and risks for these two stocks may differ from the recent past. She estimates the following for Walgreens and Microsoft:

	WALGREENS	MICROSOFT
Expected Return	7%	12%
Standard Deviation forecast	11%	20%

EXPECTED RETURN ON A PORTFOLIO

The expected rate of return on a portfolio, $E(R_p)$, is simply the weighted average of the expected returns, $E(R_i)$, of the individual assets in the portfolio:

$$E(R_p) = \sum_{i=1}^{n} w_i E(R_i)$$

(12-7)

The value w_i is the weight of the ith asset, or the proportion of the portfolio invested in that asset. The sum of these weights must equal 1.0.

Let's assume Mary is willing to invest 50 percent of her investment funds in Walgreens and 50 percent in Microsoft. We can use equation 12-7 to compute her expected portfolio return, assuming expected annual returns of 7.0 percent for Walgreens and 12.0 percent for Microsoft. Again, assuming these are average expected returns, we have the following:

$$E(R_p) = 0.50(7.0\%) + 0.50(12.0\%) = 3.5\% + 6.0\% = 9.5\%$$

CONCEPT CHECK

What is a portfolio?

How is portfolio return computed?

Now, let's assume that Ramon is willing to accept a little more variability in his portfolio returns relative to Mary as a trade-off for a higher expected return. Consequently, Ramon has decided to invest 25 percent of his investment funds in Walgreens and 75 percent in Microsoft. Using the expected annual returns for each stock, the expected average annual return on his portfolio would be the following:

$$E(R_p) = 0.25(7.0\%) + 0.75(12.0\%) = 1.75\% + 9.0\% = 10.75\%$$

VARIANCE AND STANDARD DEVIATION OF RETURN ON A PORTFOLIO

The total risk of a portfolio can be measured by its variance or the standard deviation of its returns. Extending the concept of portfolio return, one might think that the variance of a portfolio is a weighted average of asset variances. Unfortunately, this first guess is incorrect, and we cannot use an equation like 12-7. To see why, look at the time series of returns illustrated in Figure 12.5.

Consider the relationship between stocks and Treasury bonds. Stock prices are affected primarily by expectations of future economic growth while Treasury bond prices are mainly affected by changes in the level of interest rates. At times, stock and bond returns will move together; at other times they will move in opposite directions.

Figure 12-5a indicates this general condition. It shows the returns of a stock index and a bond index. Bond returns were generally less volatile than stock returns over the 1990–2012 time period.

Suppose, however, investors place funds in stocks and bonds to form a portfolio of 50 percent stocks and 50 percent bonds. The portfolio's combined return in Figure 12-5b shows less risk. Why do the portfolio returns vary so much less?

FIGURE 12.5a
Stock and Treasury Bond Returns 1990-2012

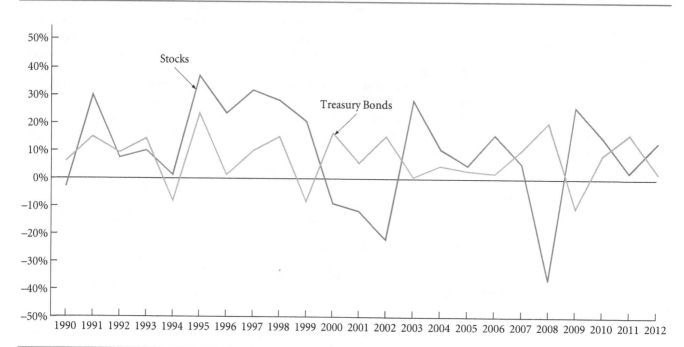

FIGURE 12.5b

Stocks, Treasury Bond Returns, and Returns on a 50/50 Stock/Bond Portfolio, 1990-2012

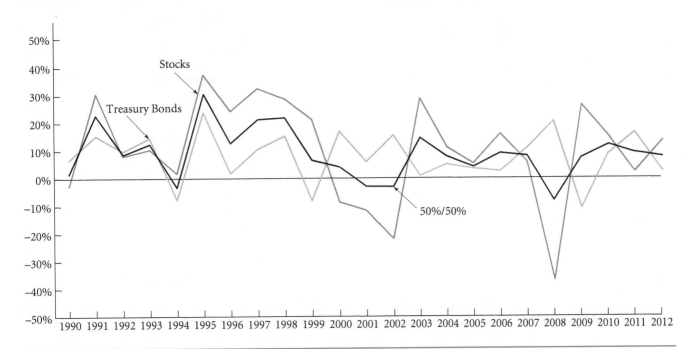

Lower portfolio variability arises from the benefits of diversification. ***Diversification*** occurs when we invest in several different assets rather than just a single one. The benefits of diversification are greatest, as we see in Figure 12.5, when asset returns have ***negative correlations***, that is, they tend to move in opposite directions, such as from late 2000 through 2004 in Figure 12.5a. Two sets of data are said to have a ***positive correlation*** if their returns move together over time, as did the bond and stock returns during the 1992–1999 time frame.

Although the calculation of this measure is beyond the scope of this text,[12] ***correlation*** is a statistical concept that relates movements in one set of returns to movements in another set over time. Part of many investors' strategy is to have investments in their portfolio that are not highly positively correlated with each other. The less positive or the more negative the correlation, the greater the risk reduction benefits from diversifying into different assets. This means that although the individual assets may be risky, combining them in a portfolio may result in levels of portfolio risk below that of any of the constituent assets.

TO DIVERSIFY OR NOT TO DIVERSIFY?

The idea behind diversification is that at times some investments will do well while some perform poorly and vice versa. Since it is difficult to forecast or "time" efficient markets, we should spread our funds across several different investments to prevent us from having a large exposure to any one investment. An example of the benefits of diversification is found in Table 12.6.

Our time frame is twenty-five years; $10,000 invested over this time frame at an average annual rate of 7 percent gives us $54,274.33 in our account. But what might happen if we divide our $10,000 initial investment into five subaccounts, investing $2,000 in each one? Suppose one of the investments turns out to be a total failure and we lose the entire $2,000 invested. The second investment earns no return at all; twenty-five years later we have $2,000 in that account. The third subaccount earns a meager 5 percent annual average return over the twenty-five years. The fourth and fifth subaccounts perform better, one earning 10 percent and the other 12 percent on an average annual basis. Even though some accounts perform poorly, investing $2,000 in each of

diversification
occurs when we invest in several different assets rather than just a single one

negative correlation
when asset returns move in opposite directions

positive correlation
when asset returns move in together over time

correlation
statistical concept that relates movements in one set of returns to movements in another set over time

---

12. The development and calculation of correlations for portfolios can be found in most investments textbooks. See, for example, Frank K. Reilly and Edgar A. Norton, *Investments*, 7th edition (Mason, OH: South-Western College Publishing, 2006), Chapter 8.

TABLE 12.6

Diversification Illustration (Invest $10,000 over 25 years)

	INVESTMENT STRATEGY 1: ALL FUNDS IN ONE ASSET		INVESTMENT STRATEGY 2: INVEST EQUALLY IN FIVE DIFFERENT ASSETS	
Number of assets =		1	Number of assets	5
Initial investment	$10,000		Amount invested per asset=	$2,000
Number of years=		25	Number of years=	25
			5 asset returns (annual)	
Annual asset return =		7%	Asset 1 return	−100%
			Asset 2 return	0%
			Asset 3 return	5%
			Asset 4 return	10%
			Asset 5 return	12%
Total accumulation at end of time frame:			Total accumulation at end of time frame:	
Total funds =		$54,274.33	Asset 1	$0.00
			Asset 2	$2,000.00
			Asset 3	$6,772.71
			Asset 4	$21,669.41
			Asset 5	$34,000.13
			Total funds =	$64,442.25

these five subaccounts will grow to become $64,442.25 over twenty-five years, a gain of more than $10,000 over our single-basket strategy, which earned 7 percent.

Investors should consider investing in a way that cuts across asset classes (such as stocks and bonds), industries, and country borders to benefit from the opportunities in a global investment marketplace. The "U.S. auto industry" used to be known as the Big Three: Ford Motor Company, General Motors and Chrysler. But consider that after the merger between Chrysler and Germany's DaimlerBenz to form DaimlerChrysler, is DaimlerChrysler a German or an American company?[13] Moreover, even though firms such as Ford or Coca-Cola may be headquartered in the United States, much of their product sales and revenue streams are outside the borders of the United States, and they compete globally. Investors need to look for good investments no matter where they may be in the global economy. Some studies have found that a firm's industry sector has more to do with its stock market performance than a "country" effect.[14]

PORTFOLIO RISK AND THE NUMBER OF INVESTMENTS IN THE PORTFOLIO

What happens to portfolio risk as more assets are added to a portfolio? Adding a second asset to a one-asset portfolio may reduce portfolio risk. Will portfolio risk continue to decline if we continue to diversify the portfolio by adding a third, a tenth, or a fiftieth asset to the portfolio?

The answer is no. The greatest reductions in portfolio risk come from combining assets with negative correlations. As each new asset reduces the variability of a portfolio's returns, it becomes more difficult to find additional assets with low correlations to the portfolio because all assets share a common environment. In U.S. markets, most assets' returns react in some way to the ups and downs of the business cycle. Once a portfolio includes a certain number of assets, the pervasive effects of national economic and financial market trends reduce the likelihood that further diversification can offer significant benefits.

We may look beyond our national borders and include non-U.S. assets in the portfolio to gain some additional reduction in portfolio risk since the world's economies and financial markets do not move in lockstep. Even though the global product and financial markets are becoming more integrated, remaining differences suggest a well-diversified global asset portfolio will have a lower total risk than a well-diversified portfolio of U.S. assets. Even with a choice of global assets, however, diversification benefits are limited. The world's economies do not move in lockstep but neither do they have large negative correlations. Eventually, the benefits of further diversification will disappear.

---

13. This question became moot in 2007 when Daimler spun of Chrysler, and it once again became U.S. owned.

14. Craig Karmin, "Investing Overseas Reduces the Riskiness of a Portfolio," *Wall Street Journal* (January 29, 2001), p. R15. Phyllis Feinberg, "Importance of Sectors Grows for International Investors." *Pensions and Investments* (November 27, 2000), p. 56.

FIGURE 12.6
Risk and Portfolio Diversification

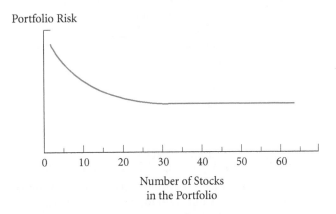

U.S. stock market data confirm this expected pattern.[15] By constructing a number of sample portfolios, with one stock, two stocks, three stocks, and so on, researchers have found that average portfolio risk declines as additional securities are added to the portfolio, as shown in Figure 12.6. After a portfolio includes twenty to thirty stocks, the risk reduction effect of adding more stocks is almost nil. The total risk of a well-diversified portfolio of U.S. stocks appears to be about one-half the risk of the average one-stock portfolio. In other words, constructing a well-diversified portfolio of about twenty stocks can reduce overall portfolio risk by one-half.

Further reductions in portfolio risk are documented when international securities are included in the analysis. It appears that only about fifteen international stocks are needed to exhaust the risk-reducing benefits of diversification. The total risk of a well-diversified international portfolio of stocks is about one-third of the risk of an average one-stock portfolio; that is, up to two-thirds of portfolio risk can be eliminated in a well-diversified international portfolio!

SYSTEMATIC AND UNSYSTEMATIC RISK

Figure 12.6 can be used to show that two types of risk affect individual assets and portfolios of assets: risk that can be diversified away and risk that cannot be diversified away.

Figure 12.7 resembles Figure 12.6 with labels for these types of risks. The risk that is diversified away as assets are added to a portfolio is the firm-specific and industry-specific risk, or the "microeconomic" risk. This is known as ***unsystematic risk***. Table 12.7 lists several sources of risk.

INTERNET ACTIVITY

Mutual fund companies offer investors a means of obtaining professional management in diversified portfolio of stocks and/or bonds for relatively modest investments. Many mutual fund Web sites have investor education links dealing with diversification. See, for example, http://www.vanguard.com and http://www.troweprice.com, as well as other mutual fund firms.

unsystematic risk
risk that can be diversified away as assets are added to a portfolio. Also known as firm-specific risk or industry-specific risk

FIGURE 12.7
Risk and Portfolio Diversification

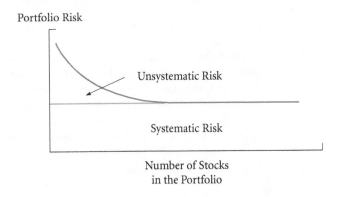

15. J. Evans and S. H. Archer, "Diversification and the Reduction of Dispersion: An Empirical Analysis," *Journal of Finance* (December 1968), pp. 761–67.

TABLE 12.7

Examples of Risk

DIVERSIFIABLE RISK (ALSO KNOWN AS UNSYSTEMATIC RISK OR FIRM-SPECIFIC RISK OR MICRO RISK)	UNDIVERSIFIABLE RISK (ALSO KNOWN AS SYSTEMATIC RISK, MARKET RISK, OR MACRO RISK)
Business Risk	Market Risk
Financial Risk	Interest Rate Risk
Event Risk	Purchasing Power Risk
Tax Risk	Exchange Rate Risk
Liquidity Risk	

systematic risk (market risk)

risk that is inherent in the macro economy and cannot be eliminated through diversification

CONCEPT CHECK

Why is a measure of portfolio risk not a simple average of component asset variances?

How does correlation between assets affect portfolio variance?

What is diversification?

What is the difference between systematic and unsystematic risk?

Information that has negative implications for one firm may contain good news for another firm. For example, news of rising oil prices may be bad news for airlines but good news for oil companies. The announcement of the resignation of a well-respected CEO may be bad for the company but good for competing firms. One firm's announcement of its intentions to build a technologically advanced plant may mean bad news for its competitors. In a well-diversified portfolio of firms from different industries, the effects of good news for one firm may cancel bad news for another firm. The overall impact of such news on the portfolio's returns should approach zero. In this way, diversification can effectively eliminate unsystematic risk. A well-diversified portfolio can reduce the effects on portfolio returns of firm-specific or industry-specific events—such as strikes, technological advances, and entry and exit of competitors—to zero.

Diversification cannot eliminate risk that is inherent in the macro economy. This undiversifiable risk is called **systematic risk**, or **market risk**. General financial market trends affect most companies in similar ways. Macroeconomic events (e.g., changes in GDP, war, major political events, rising optimism or pessimism among investors, tax increases or cuts, or a stronger or weaker dollar) have broad effects on product and financial markets. Even a well-diversified portfolio cannot escape these effects.

Thus, the total risk of an asset has two components: unsystematic or firm-specific risk and systematic or market risk:

Total risk (portfolio variance) = systematic risk + unsystematic risk

In practice and in theory, few investors have only one asset; rather, they own a portfolio of assets.[16] The unsystematic, microeconomic component of an asset's total risk disappears in a well-diversified portfolio. That means the risk that remains, the systematic risk (that is, the sensitivity of the asset's returns to macroeconomic events), is the only risk that should matter to financial markets. When financial markets evaluate the trade-off between risk and expected return, they focus on the trade-off between systematic risk and expected return.

CAPITAL ASSET PRICING MODEL (CAPM)

If markets are efficient, is there still a trade-off between risk and expected return? If so, what will this trade-off look like?

From the previous section, we know systematic or market risk affects all stocks (and more generally, all securities). The U.S. economy's economic trends, changes in interest rates, the U.S. dollar exchange rate, Federal Reserve System (Fed) policy, and so on, are pervasive and affect returns and risk on most securities. All securities are affected by macroeconomic and other national events, so even a well-diversified portfolio will have some exposure to these systematic, or market-wide, sources of risk. Systematic risk cannot be diversified away.

Unsystematic risk is asset-specific or company-specific risk. What is good news for one company (for example, a new product or patent announcement) may be bad news for another competitor.

---

16. Ownership by individual investors of shares of diversified mutual funds helps to achieve overall diversification for an investor.

Or what is good news for one sector of the economy (rising oil prices for oil-producers) is bad news for another (sectors dependent upon oil and gasoline, such as transportation industries). But as more securities are added to a portfolio, the effects of unsystematic risk are diversified away as the positive effects and negative effects on different companies and sectors cancel out leaving only the broad systematic risk exposure.

This has an important implication for the trade-off between expected return and risk. What is "risk"? As we have reviewed, only systematic risk should matter because prudent investors can and should diversify their portfolios to eliminate unsystematic risk. Only systematic risk should remain so only systematic risk will affect an asset's returns over time.

Regardless of their total risk (or standard deviation of returns), assets with higher levels of systematic risk should have higher expected returns; assets with lower levels of systematic risk should have lower levels of expected returns. From this perspective, we see that an asset's total risk is unimportant. What is important is how the asset affects the risk of the overall portfolio.

For example, what is the systematic risk of short-term Treasury bills (T-bills)? Purchasing a T-bill "locks in" a short-term return that is considered risk-free as it is backed by the full faith and credit of the U.S. Government. While an investor owns that security, the return is not affected by economic events. In other words, the systematic risk of a T-bill investment is zero or as close to zero as we can have in this world. If an investor adds T-bills to a portfolio, the effect on the overall portfolio will be to lower its systematic risk. Combining risky assets with a zero-risk asset will lower the overall systematic risk of the portfolio.

As another example, from historical data researchers have found that, by itself, gold is a risky investment. It offers no income stream and its price fluctuates, sometimes with high volatility; in combination with common stocks, an investment in gold can reduce a portfolio's total risk. The reason is that common stocks usually perform poorly when investors fear inflation, whereas gold prices rise when higher inflation is expected. So, including gold in a stock portfolio can have a negative effect on risk; that is, it can make the portfolio less risky. Gold, at times, may have *negative* systematic risk.

market portfolio
a portfolio that contains all risky assets

From the perspective of the financial markets, the **market portfolio**, meaning one that contains all risky assets, is the portfolio that eliminates all unsystematic risk. The only risk contained in the market portfolio is systematic risk. That means that as the value of the market portfolio fluctuates over time, the pure effect of systematic risk is seen.[17]

Since the market portfolio contains all risky assets, some assets that are sensitive to changes in macroeconomic variables, such as interest rates or gross domestic product (GDP), will have higher exposures to systematic risk than the overall market portfolio. Some assets' returns will be less sensitive to these influences and will have less systematic risk. One way we can measure an asset's systematic risk is by comparing its returns to those of the market portfolio. Those assets whose returns rise and fall in line with the overall market will have the same systematic risk exposure as the market portfolio (see Figure 12.8a). Assets whose returns are more volatile (they typically rise higher and fall lower) than those of the market portfolio have systematic risk exposures that exceed those of the market portfolio (Figure 12.8b). Assets whose returns are less volatile (their returns do not rise as high or fall as low as the market portfolio) have less systematic risk exposure than the market portfolio (Figure 12.8c).

From this "portfolio perspective," an asset's risk is measured not by standard deviation but by its systematic risk, namely how it affects the risk of the overall portfolio. Assets with higher systematic risk will tend to increase the systematic risk (and the expected return) of the portfolios in which they appear. Assets with low levels of systematic risk tend to lower the systematic risk (and the expected return) of the portfolios in which they appear.

These insights are the basis for the Capital Asset Pricing Model (CAPM). The CAPM states that the expected return on an asset depends upon its level of systematic risk. The asset's systematic risk is measured relative to that of the market portfolio. In other words, the relative risk of an asset is that asset's contribution to the risk of a well-diversified portfolio.

---

17. It is only in the case of the market portfolio that does the standard deviation (or variance) of returns shows the effect of systematic risk; for all other less-than-perfectly diversified portfolios, the portfolio's variance measures a combination of systematic and unsystematic risk influences.

FIGURE 12.8
Comparing Asset Returns and Market Portfolio Returns Over Time

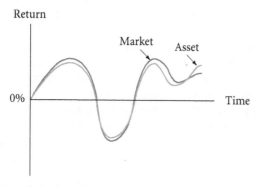

a: Same Systematic Risk as the
   Market Portfolio

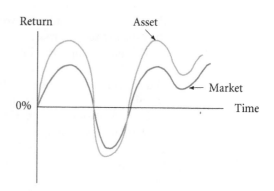

b: Greater Systematic Risk than the
   Market Portfolio

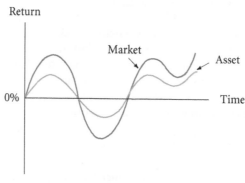

c: Less Systematic Risk than the
   Market Portfolio

CONCEPT CHECK

What is the market portfolio?
What is the relationship between systematic risk and a portfolio's variability relative to the market portfolio?
What is beta?

beta
measure of an asset's systematic risk

Under the CAPM, ***beta*** (β) is the measure of an asset's systematic risk. Beta is a measure of relative risk. Beta measures the volatility or variability of an asset's returns relative to the market portfolio. For example, if an asset's returns are half as volatile as those of the market portfolio, its beta will be 0.5. That means that if the market portfolio changes in value by 10 percent, on average the asset's value changes by 0.5 as much, or 5 percent. If an asset's beta equals 1.4, then the asset's returns are 40 percent more volatile than the market. When the market changes in value by 10 percent, the asset's value changes, on average, by 1.4 times 10 percent, or 14 percent. With this definition of beta, the beta of the market portfolio, β_{MKT}, is 1.0. By definition, the market is exactly as volatile as itself.

Assets that are more volatile than the market, or equivalently, those that have greater systematic risk than the market, have betas greater than 1.0. Whatever the market return, these assets' average returns tend to be larger in absolute value. Assets that are less volatile than the market (that is, those with less systematic risk) have betas less than 1.0. These assets' returns, on average, are less in absolute value than those of the market. Table 12.8 lists the historic betas for some stocks.

In practice, there is no true identifiable "market" portfolio since there are too many assets, including the value of natural resources and human capital (investments in training, educating, and developing) to attempt to measure returns on such a portfolio. What investment professionals use is a proxy, or substitute, for the true market portfolio. A popular measure of the market portfolio is a broad stock market index, such as the Standard & Poor's 500 (S&P500) index or the New York Stock Exchange (NYSE) index. Typically when an asset's beta is estimated, it is measured relative to that of the S&P500 stock market index. How to estimate a stock's beta is the topic of this chapter's Learning Extension.

TABLE 12.8
Examples of Stock Betas

FIRM NAME	TICKER SYMBOL	BETA
Industrial Firms		
AT&T	T	0.39
Caterpillar	CAT	1.79
Coca-Cola	KO	0.38
Disney	DIS	1.09
DuPont	DD	1.48
General Electric	GE	1.40
Ford	F	1.56
McDonald's	MCD	0.34
Transportation Firms		
Alaska Air	ALK	0.81
CSX	CSX	1.31
Delta Airlines	DAL	0.68
FDX	FDX	1.25
J. B. Hunt	JBHT	1.06
Norfolk Southern	NSC	1.13
Utilities		
FirstEnergy	FE	0.29
Ameren	AEE	0.23
American Electric Power	AEP	0.35
Consolidated Edison	ED	0.09
DTE Energy	DTE	0.26
Chesapeake Utilities	CPK	0.27

Source: http://finance.yahoo.com; accessed May 2013

ETHICS AND JOB OPPORTUNITIES IN INVESTMENTS

ETHICAL DISCUSSION

Important components of the financial markets are the laws and regulations governing them. Without regulatory bodies and laws, the financial markets and securities trading would be hampered. Regulations dealing with deposit insurance in banks, the required discussion of risks in a new security prospectus, laws forbidding corporate "insiders" to use their privileged information for private gain, and requirements for fair dealings by brokers and dealers when trading for clients work to increase the public's sense of trust and confidence in the financial markets. Individuals who deal with clients must be registered in the state in which they work and must register with the Securities and Exchange Commission (SEC).

Regulations often arise from past abuses or problems. Much of the long-standing regulations in U.S. markets (the Securities Act of 1933 and the Securities Exchange Act of 1934) resulted from the situation surrounding the stock market crash of 1929. More recently, the Sarbanes-Oxley Act of 2002 arose from corporate accounting scandals. The oversight provided by corporate boards and external auditors failed in some companies, and as a result, false financial statements hid the true condition of those companies. Once uncovered, corporate failure, bankruptcy, job losses, pension losses, and criminal charges involved companies such as Enron, Worldcom, Tyco, Arthur Andersen, and HealthSouth Corporation.

Unfortunately, others entrusted with people's savings have been found less than worthy. Several mutual fund firms and investment banks have been accused of wrongdoing in recent years. Stock analysts who worked at investment banking firms wrote false and optimistic research reports, hoping to attract or to keep clients using the firm's lucrative, high-fee investment banking business. Others allocated shares of "hot" or popular initial public offerings (IPOs) to top executives of firms, which used the firm's investment banking business. Persons and firms involved in such unethical dealings include include Jack Grubman of Salomon Smith Barney and Henry Blodgett of Merrill Lynch. Of recent note is the Ponzi scheme (collecting funds from later investors to pay off earlier investors with what appears to be attractive returns) orchestrated by Bernie Madoff Investment Securities LLC and the firm's owner, Bernie Madoff.

TABLE 12.9

Ethical Standards in Investment Professional Certifications

CHARTERED FINANCIAL ANALYST (CFA®) STANDARDS OF PROFESSIONAL CONDUCT	CERTIFIED FINANCIAL PLANNER (CFP™) CODE OF ETHICS AND PROFESSIONAL RESPONSIBILITY
Standard I: Fundamental Responsibilities	These Principles of the Code express the professional recognition of its responsibilities to the public, to clients, to colleagues, and to employers. They apply to all CFP designees and provide guidance to them in the performance of their professional services.
Standard II: Relationships with and Responsibilities to the Profession	
Standard III: Relationships with and Responsibilities to the Employer	
Standard IV: Relationships with and Responsibilities to Clients and Prospects	Principle 1: Integrity
	Principle 2: Objectivity
Standard V: Relationships with and Responsibilities to the Investing Public	Principle 3: Competence
	Principle 4: Fairness
For additional details, see www.cfainstitute.org.	Principle 5: Confidentiality
	Principle 6: Professionalism
	Principle 7: Diligence
	For additional details, see www.cfp.net

CONCEPT CHECK

What major laws have been created due to ethical lapses in the market?

How do professional designations incorporate ethics awareness?

To maintain the professionalism and ethics of the investments field, professional designations have been developed. Few persons with the Chartered Financial Analyst (CFA®) or Certified Financial Planner (CFP™) designations were involved in these scandals because of the ethics training, which is part of these programs. Persons who receive the designations, by passing exams and having a requisite amount of work experience, show they have a certain level of expertise in their field and agree to abide by a code of ethics and professional standards in their dealings with clients and their employer. An overview of expected behaviors for holders of two investment professional certifications is given in Table 12.9.

Ethics is an important concern in investment-related professions since practitioners advise clients and invest or handle large sums of money. Nearly any career path within the investments field has federal or state regulations on behavior in addition to those required from an earned professional designation. Additional information about investments-related careers can be found on the web pages of financial firms (such as http://www.ml.com, http://www.smithbarney.com, http://www.schwab.com, and https://www.wellsfargo.com/.

APPLYING FINANCE TO...

INSTITUTIONS AND MARKETS	INVESTMENTS	FINANCIAL MANAGEMENT
Banks, brokerages, pension funds, insurance companies, and financial institutions of all types evaluate expected return, risk, and portfolios for their own investments and their clients'. Markets transmit perceived changes in asset risk and expected return through changes in security prices.	The trade-off between risk and expected return is a foundational concept in finance, cutting across markets, investments, and financial management. Knowing how to compute and evaluate return and risk and knowing the important role that correlations play can help investors put together well-diversified portfolios.	Actions by investors affect a firm's stock price and the market interest rates on its bonds. Price changes relative to competing firms and the overall market inform management how investors view their actions.

SUMMARY

Financial risk and return concepts are among the most mathematical and confusing to the first-time finance student, but they are vital to understanding financial markets, institutions, and management. Much of modern investment analysis, portfolio management, and corporate finance is based upon the topics introduced in this chapter.

Historical returns are computed from past income cash flows and price changes. From annualized returns, we can determine the average return on an asset over time as well as measures of risk (variance, standard deviation, and the coefficient of variation). Scenario analysis is a widely used tool for estimating expected return and risk.

When assets are combined into portfolios, diversification effects may mitigate the effects of each individual asset's risk. When some assets' returns are poor, others may perform well. Adding assets to a portfolio may help reduce portfolio risk, but after a certain point, all unsystematic risk has been diversified away and only systematic risk remains.

KEY TERMS

beta
Capital Asset Pricing Model (CAPM)
coefficient of variation (CV)
correlation
deviations
diversification
efficient market

investment
market portfolio
negative correlation
portfolio
positive correlation
random walk
semistrong-form efficient market

standard deviation
strong-form efficient market
systematic risk (market risk)
unsystematic risk
weak-form efficient market

DISCUSSION QUESTIONS

1. Explain how a percentage return is calculated, and describe the calculation of an arithmetic average return.

2. Describe how the variance and standard deviation are calculated, and indicate how they are used as measures of risk.

3. What is the coefficient of variation? How is it used as a measure of risk?

4. Business risk has three possible sources. What are they?

5. What sources of risk does a firm face, and which of those sources are reflected on the firm's income statement?

6. Suppose, in the preceding year, the U.S. dollar strengthens against other currencies. Explain its effect on U.S. dollar revenues and expenses for a global firm headquartered in the U.S.

7. Describe the meaning of a *state of nature*, and explain how this concept is used to provide expected measures of return and risk.

8. Explain the historical relationships between return and risk for common stocks versus corporate bonds.

9. Explain market efficiency. What are the characteristics of an efficient market?

10. What are the differences among the weak, semistrong, and strong forms of the efficient market hypothesis?

11. What type of market efficiency—none, weak, semistrong, or strong—is reflected in each of the following statements?

   a. I know which stocks are going to rise in value by looking at their price changes over the past two weeks.

   b. Returns earned by company officers trading their own firm's stock are no higher than those of other investors.

   c. If a firm announces lower-than-expected earnings, you know the price will fall over a few days.

   d. By the time I heard the news about the dividend increase, the stock had already risen by a substantial amount.

   e. Whatever the stock market does in January, it will continue to move in that direction for the rest of the year.

   f. As soon as the chairman of the Federal Reserve gave his testimony to Congress about future monetary policy, interest rates rose and stock prices dropped.

12. Explain if you agree or disagree with this statement: "After the merger announcement the stock price greatly increased. Then it fell for the next 1–2 days before becoming relatively stable. This is proof against the efficient market hypothesis."

13. How do mutual fund return data present evidence for or against efficient markets? Explain.

14. Define a portfolio, and describe how the expected return on a portfolio is computed.

15. Explain the terms *diversification* and *correlation* in the context of forming portfolios.

16. Explain the fallacy of this statement: "I'd rather put my money into a single high-earning asset than in a portfolio of diversified investments; I'll earn more money with the single asset."

17. Describe what happens to portfolio risk as more assets are added to a portfolio. Are there advantages to international diversification?

18. How does systematic risk differ from unsystematic risk?

19. Classify each of the following as an example of systematic or unsystematic risk.

   a. The labor unions at Caterpillar, Inc. declared a strike yesterday.

   b. Contrary to what polls stated, the President was reelected.

   c. Disagreement about inflation policy leads to a fall in the Euro relative to the dollar.

   d. The computer industry suffers lower profits because of aggressive pricing strategies on new desktop computers.

   e. Every Christmas selling season there is a "hot" toy that many parents try to purchase for their child.

20. What is the Capital Asset Pricing Model? Describe how it relates to expected return and risk.

21. Define the concept of beta, and describe what it measures.

22. What is the market portfolio? Can we invest in such a portfolio?

PROBLEMS

1. From the information below, compute the average annual return, the variance, standard deviation, and coefficient of variation for each asset.

ASSET	ANNUAL RETURNS
A	5%, 10%, 15%, 4%
B	−6%, 20%, 2%, −5%, 10%
C	12%, 15%, 17%
D	10%, −10%, 20%, −15%, 8%, −7%

2. Based upon your answers to question 1, which asset appears riskiest based on standard deviation? Based on coefficient of variation?

3. Recalling the definitions of risk premiums from Chapter 4 and using the Treasury bill return in Table 12.4 as an approximation to the nominal risk-free rate, what is the risk premium from investing in each of the other asset classes listed in Table 12.4?

4. What is the real, or after-inflation, return from each of the asset classes listed in Table 12.4?

5. RCMP, Inc. shares rose 10 percent in value last year while the inflation rate was 3.5 percent. What was the real return on the stock? If an investor sold the stock after one year and paid taxes on the investment at a 15 percent tax rate, what is the real after-tax return on the investment?

6. Find the real return on the following investments:

STOCK	NOMINAL RETURN	INFLATION
A	10%	3%
B	15%	8%
C	−5%	2%

7. Find the real return, nominal after-tax return, and real after-tax return on the following:

STOCK	NOMINAL RETURN	INFLATION	TAX RATE
X	13.5%	5%	15%
Y	8.7%	4.7%	25%
Z	5.2%	2.5%	28%

8. The countries of Stabilato and Variato have the following average returns and standard deviations for their stocks, bonds, and short-term government securities. What range of returns should you expect to earn 95 percent of the time for each asset class if you invested in Stabilato's securities? From investing in Variato's securities?

STABILATO ASSET	AVERAGE RETURN	STANDARD DEVIATION
Stocks	8%	3%
Bonds	5%	2%
Short-term government debt	3%	1%

VARIATO ASSET	AVERAGE RETURN	STANDARD DEVIATION
Stocks	15%	13%
Bonds	10%	8%
Short-term government debt	6%	3%

9. Using the information below, compute the percentage returns for the following securities:

SECURITY	PRICE TODAY	PRICE ONE YEAR AGO	DIVIDENDS RECEIVED	INTEREST RECEIVED
RoadRunner stock	$20.05	$18.67	$0.50	
Wiley Coyote stock	$33.42	$45.79	$1.10	
Acme long-term bonds	$1,015.38	$991.78		$100.00
Acme short-term bonds	$996.63	$989.84		$45.75
Xlingshot stock	$5.43	$3.45	$0.02	

10. Given her evaluation of current economic conditions, Ima Nutt believes there is a 20 percent probability of recession, a 50 percent chance of continued steady growth, and a 30 percent probability of inflationary growth. For each possibility, Ima has developed an interest rate forecast for long-term Treasury bond interest rates:

ECONOMIC FORECAST	INTEREST RATE FORECAST
Recession	6 percent
Constant growth	9 percent
Inflation	14 percent

a. What is the expected interest rate under Ima's forecast?

b. What is the variance and standard deviation of Ima's interest rate forecast?

c. What is the coefficient of variation of Ima's interest rate forecast?

d. If the current long-term Treasury bond interest rate is 8 percent, should Ima consider purchasing a Treasury bond? Why or why not?

11. Ima is considering a purchase of Wallnut Company stock. Using the same scenarios and probabilities as in problem 10, she estimates Wallnut's return is −5 percent in a recession, 20 percent in constant growth, and 10 percent in inflation.

a. What is Ima's expected return forecast for Wallnut stock?

b. What is the standard deviation of the forecast?

c. If Wallnut's current price is $20 per share and Wallnut is expected to pay a dividend of $0.80 per share next year, what price will Ima expect Wallnut to sell for in one year?

12. Ima's sister, Uma, has completed her own analysis of the economy and Wallnut's stock. Uma used recession, constant growth, and inflation scenarios, but with different probabilities and expected stock returns. Uma believes the probability of recession is 60 percent, and that in a recession, Wallnut's stock return will be −20 percent. Uma believes the scenarios of constant growth and inflation are equally likely and that Wallnut's returns will be 15 percent in the constant growth scenario and 10 percent under the inflation scenario.

a. What is Uma's expected return forecast for Wallnut stock?

b. What is the standard deviation of the forecast?

c. If Wallnut's current price is $20.00 per share and is expected to pay a dividend of $0.80 per share next year, what price does Uma expect Wallnut to sell for in one year?

13. Scenario analysis has many practical applications in addition to being used to forecast security returns. In this problem, scenario analysis

is used to forecast an exchange rate. Jim Danday's forecast for the Euro/dollar exchange rate depends upon what the U.S. Federal Reserve and European central bankers do to their country's money supply. Jim is considering the following scenarios and exchange rate forecasts:

CENTRAL BANK BEHAVIOR	PROBABILITY OF BEHAVIOR FORECAST	JIM'S FORECAST EXCHANGE RATE
Euro banks increase MS growth; U.S. does not	.20	1.15 €/$
Euro banks, U.S. maintain constant MS growth	.30	1.0 5 €/$
U.S. increases MS growth; Euro banks do not	.35	0.95 €/$
U.S., Euro banks increase MS growth	.15	0.85 €/$

   a.   What is Jim's expected exchange rate forecast?

   b.   What is the variance of Jim's exchange rate forecast?

   c.   What is the coefficient of variation of Jim's exchange rate forecast?

14. Using the data in Table 12.4, calculate and interpret the coefficient of variation for each asset class.

15. Below is annual stock return data on Hollenbeck Corp. and Luzzi Edit, Inc.

YEAR	HOLLENBECK	LUZZI EDIT
2010	10%	−3%
2011	15%	0%
2012	−10%	15%
2013	5%	10%

   a.   What are the average return, variance, and standard deviation for each stock?

   b.   What is the expected portfolio return on a portfolio composed of

   i) 25% Hollenbeck and 75% Luzzi Edit?

   ii) 50% Hollenbeck and 50% Luzzi Edit?

   iii) 75% Hollenbeck and 25% Luzzi Edit?

   c.   Without doing any calculations, would you expect the correlation between the returns on Hollenbeck Corp. and Luzzi Edit's stock to be positive, negative, or zero? Why?

16. Below is annual stock return data on AAB Company and YYZ, Inc.

YEAR	AAB	YYZ
2009	0%	5%
2010	5%	10%
2011	10%	15%
2012	15%	20%
2013	−10%	−20%

   a.   What is the average return, variance, and standard deviation for each stock?

   b.   If the conditions in the future are expected to be like those in the past few years, what is the expected portfolio return on a portfolio composed of?

   i) 25% AAB and 75% YYZ?

   ii) 50% AAB and 50% YYZ?

   iii) 75% AAB and 25% YYZ?

   c.   Without doing any calculations, would you expect the correlation between the returns on AAB and YYZ's stock to be positive, negative, or zero? Why?

17. Estimate the weights (w_i) for assets in the following portfolios given the following information about the portfolio holdings:

	PORTFOLIO	PRICE	NUMBER OF SECURITIES
A	Stock A	$25	200
	Stock B	$53	100
	Stock C	$119	100
B	Bond A	$975	10
	Bond B	$1,020	20
	Bond C	$888	10
	Bond D	$1,150	10
C	Stock A	$25	1,000
	Stock C	$119	500
	Bond D	$1,150	20
D	Stock B	$53	1,000
	Stock C	$119	100
	Bond A	$975	20
	Bond B	$1,020	10

18. Tim's portfolio contains two stocks, Lightco and Shineco. Last year his portfolio returned 14 percent. Lightco's return was 5 percent and Shineco returned 20 percent. What are the weights of each in Tim's portfolio?

The following year Tim adds a third stock, Brightco, and reallocates his funds among the three stocks. Lightco and Shineco have the same weight in the portfolio, and Brightco's weight is one-half of Lightco. During the year Lightco returns 10 percent, Shineco returns 12 percent, and Brightco loses 5 percent. What was the return on his portfolio?

19. **EXCEL** Spreadsheets are useful for computing statistics: averages, standard deviation, variance, and correlation are included as built-in functions. Below is recent monthly stock return data for ExxonMobil (XOM) and Microsoft (MSFT). Using a spreadsheet and its functions, compute the average, variance, standard deviation, and correlation between the returns for these stocks. What does the correlation between the returns imply for a portfolio containing both stocks?

MONTH	XOM RETURN	MSFT RETURN
November	−4.6%	10.4%
October	0.1%	13.6%
September	−1.9%	−10.3%
August	−3.3%	−13.8%
July	−4.4%	−9.3%
June	−1.6%	5.5%
May	0.7%	2.1%
April	9.4%	23.9%
March	−0.1%	−7.3%
February	−3.2%	−3.4%

20. **EXCEL** If the conditions in the future are expected to be like those in the past, what are the expected portfolio return and standard deviation of a portfolio composed of?

   a.   25% XOM and 75% MSFT?

   b.   50% XOM and 50% MSFT?

   c.   75% XOM and 25% MSFT?

21. **EXCEL** Construct a spreadsheet to replicate the analysis of Table 12.6. That is, assume $10,000 is invested in a single asset that returns 7 percent annually for twenty-five years and $2,000 is placed in five different investments, earning returns of −100 percent, 0 percent, 5 percent, 10 percent, and 12 percent, respectively, over the twenty-year time frame. For each of the questions below, begin with the original scenario presented in Table 12.6.

a. Experiment with the return on the fifth asset. How low can the return go and still have the diversified portfolio earn a higher return than the single-asset portfolio?

b. What happens to the value of the diversified portfolio if the first two investments are a total loss?

c. Suppose the single-asset portfolio earns a return of 8 percent annually. How does the return of the single-asset portfolio compare to that of the five-asset portfolio? How does it compare if the single-asset portfolio earns a 6 percent annual return?

d. Assume that Asset 1 of the diversified portfolio remains a total loss (–100 percent return) and asset two earns no return. Make a table showing how sensitive the portfolio returns are to a 1 percentage point change in the return of each of the other three assets. That is, how is the diversified portfolio's value affected if the return on asset three is 4 percent or 6 percent? If the return on asset four is 9 percent or 11 percent? If the return on asset five is 11 percent? 13 percent? How does the total portfolio value change if each of the three asset's returns are one percentage point lower than in Table 12.6? If they are one percentage point higher?

e. Using the sensitivity analysis of (c) and (d), explain how the two portfolios differ in their sensitivity to different returns on their assets. What are the implications of this for choosing between a single asset portfolio and a diversified portfolio?

LEARNING EXTENSION 12

Estimating Beta

We can estimate beta for a stock or portfolio of stocks relative to the overall stock market using simple linear regression analysis. The reader might recall the following equation from an earlier course in statistics. However, prior work in statistics is unnecessary to grasp the following concepts. In simple equation form, we have the following:

$$R_i = \alpha + \beta R_{MKT} + e_i \qquad \text{(LE12.1)}$$

The value α = the alpha or intercept term, β = the beta or slope coefficient that shows the size of the impact that market returns (R_{MKT}) have on stock returns (R_i), and e_i = an error term reflecting the fact that changes in market returns are not likely to fully explain changes in stock returns. This straight line is shown in Figure LE12.1.

Computer software programs and sophisticated financial calculators can perform the necessary calculations and find the beta coefficient with little effort. Spreadsheet software can perform this analysis, too. In addition, we can estimate beta the "long way" by using simple calculations done by hand or by using a simple calculator. We will demonstrate the long way of estimating beta so the reader can better understand the underlying process.

Let's begin by using the monthly returns over a recent six-month period between the market as measured by the S&P500 and Microsoft. In practice, beta is often computed using sixty months' worth of data, but we will use only six months for the purposes of this illustration:

MONTH	MSFT RETURN	S&P500 RETURN
1	−2.0%	−1.7%
2	4.8%	−1.7%
3	−6.0%	−1.6%
4	−4.1%	1.2%
5	1.0%	1.7%
6	6.5%	5.1%

We want to measure the systematic risk of Microsoft relative to the market. Let's first plot these returns on the graph in Figure LE12.2. The market's returns are plotted along the x (horizontal) axis because we are interested in examining how Microsoft's returns move with or respond to the market's returns. Microsoft's monthly returns are plotted along the y (vertical) axis. There is a positive (upward-sloping) relationship between the returns on the market and Microsoft's returns. We have inserted a line across the scatter plot of annual returns. In addition to having a positive relationship, the steepness of the slope of the line reflects how much Microsoft's returns respond to a change in the market's returns. Thus, the beta coefficient is the slope of this line and indicates the sensitivity of Microsoft's returns to the market's returns.

FIGURE LE12.1

Graph of $R_i = \alpha + \beta R_{MKT} + e_i$

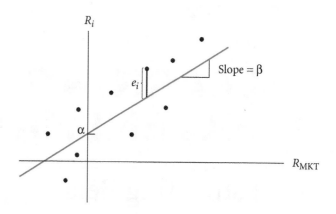

Let's calculate the slope or beta of the relationship between the returns on the market and returns on Microsoft. The calculations used to estimate beta are shown in Table LE12.1. A beta of 0.93 indicates that Microsoft was less risky than the market over this time frame. More specifically, we can say that, based on six months of past data, on average a 1 percent increase (decrease) in the monthly return on the market was accompanied by a 0.93 percentage increase (decrease) in Microsoft's monthly returns. Our estimate was based on only six observations. Normally, betas are estimated using more data points.

SECURITY MARKET LINE

Once an asset's beta is estimated, it can be used to form the basis of return predictions. Another basic aspect of the CAPM is that the expected return/risk trade-off for an asset is given by the security market line (SML):

$$E(R_i) = RFR + \left[E(R_{MKT}) - RFR\right]\beta_i \qquad \text{(LE12-2)}$$

FIGURE LE12.2

Plot of Returns for Microsoft and the S&P 500

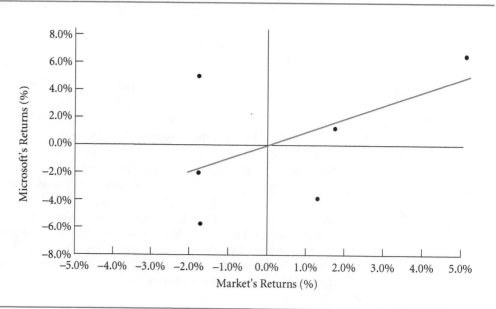

TABLE LE 12.1

How to Calculate a Beta Coefficient or Measure of Systematic Risk

MONTH	RATES OF RETURN S&P 500 X-AXIS	MICROSOFT Y-AXIS	MARKET'S RETURNS SQUARED X²	PRODUCT OF THE RETURNS X × Y
1	−1.70%	−2.00%	2.89%	3.40%
2	−1.70	4.8	2.89	−8.16
3	−1.60	−6.00	2.56	9.6
4	1.2	−4.10	1.44	−4.92
5	1.7	1	2.89	1.7
6	5.1	6.5	26.01	33.15

Sum X = 3.00%   Sum Y= 0.20%   Sum X² = 38.68%   Sum XY = 34.77%

Estimating beta where n = 6 is the number of observations:

$$\beta = \frac{n\Sigma xy - (\Sigma x)(\Sigma y)}{n\Sigma x^2 - (\Sigma x)^2} = \frac{6(34.77) - (3.00)(0.20)}{6(38.68) - (3.0)(3.0)} = \frac{208.02}{223.08} = 0.93$$

$E(R_i)$ = the expected rate of return for asset i

RFR = the risk-free rate, usually measured by the rate of return on Treasury bills

β_i = the measure of systematic risk (beta) for asset i

$E(R_{MKT})$ = the expected return on the market portfolio

The SML is shown in Figure LE12.3. The dependent variable in this relationship is the expected return on the asset and the independent variable is β_i. The asset's risk, as measured by beta, determines the asset's expected return. It is an asset's or portfolio's risk that determines return expectations, not vice versa.

The security market line (SML) shows that the reward for taking on systematic risk is the market risk premium, $E(R_{MKT})$ − RFR, which is the slope of the SML. An asset's risk premium, or extra expected return, equals $[E(R_{MKT}) - RFR]\ \beta_i$.

To illustrate the use of the SML, let's find the expected return on AT&T stock if the market is expected to rise 9 percent. We'll assume the Treasury bill rate is 4.0 percent. We'll need to use equation LE12-2, the Security Market Line, to estimate AT&T's expected return under these conditions. We'll also need to use AT&T's beta listed in Table 12.7. Suppose its beta is 0.65; should the market rise 8 percent, AT&T's expected return is the following:

$$E(R_{AT\&T}) = 4 + \lfloor 9 - 4 \rfloor \times 0.65 = 7.25 \text{ percent}$$

FIGURE LE12.3

Security Market Line

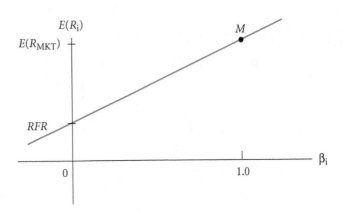

If, for example, the market portfolio were to fall by 15 percent, AT&T's expected return will be the following:

$$E(R_{AT\&T}) = 4 + \left[-15 - 4\right] \times 0.65 = -8.35 \text{ percent}$$

The beta of a portfolio of assets can be estimated at least two ways. First, portfolio returns can be regressed on market returns using equation LE12-1. Second, the beta of a portfolio can be estimated by computing the weighted average of its component's betas:

$$\text{Beta}_p = \sum_{t=1}^{n} w_i \text{beta}_i \qquad \text{(LE12-3)}$$

The value w_i is the weight of the ith asset in the portfolio. Unlike the portfolio variance risk measure, the systematic risk of a portfolio does equal the weighted average of its component's systematic risk.

Beta has several practical uses in finance. It is used to determine investors' required rate of return on an investment. Beta also is used to develop estimates of shareholders' required returns on their investments. As we have seen in here, beta is a valuable measure of the systematic risk of an asset.

QUESTIONS AND PROBLEMS

1. Stock market forecasters are predicting the stock market will rise 5 percent next year. Given the beta of each stock below, what is the expected change in each stock's value?

FIRM	BETA
BCD	1.25
NOP	0.70
WXY	1.10
ZYX	1.00

2. Suppose the estimated security market line is $E(Ri) = 4.0 + 7(\beta_i)$.

   a. What is the current Treasury bill rate?

   b. What is the current market risk premium?

   c. What is the current expected market return?

   d. Explain what beta (β_i) measures.

3. Financial researchers at Smith Sharon, an investment bank, estimate the current security market line as $E(Ri) = 4.5 + 6.8(\beta_i)$.

   a. Explain what happens to expected return as beta increases from 1.0 to 2.0.

   b. Suppose an asset has a beta of -1.0. What is the expected return on this asset? Would anyone want to invest in it? Why or why not?

4 a. What was the risk-free rate in the economy for the year if Stevens Incorporated's stock has a 14 percent return, a beta of 0.85, and the market return is 15 percent?

   b. The stock market of another company had a return of 20 percent. What would you estimate its beta to be?

5. You've collected data on the betas of various mutual funds. Each fund and its beta is listed below:

MUTUAL FUND	BETA
Weak Fund	0.23
Fido Fund	0.77
Vanwatch	1.05
Temper	1.33

   a. Estimate the beta of your fund holdings if you held equal proportions of each of the above funds.

   b. Estimate the beta of your fund holdings if you had 20 percent of your investments in the Weak fund, 40 percent in Fido, 15 percent in Vanwatch, and the remainder in Temper.

6. Using your answers to problems 5a and 5b, estimate your portfolio's expected return if the security market line is estimated as $E(Ri) = 5.2 + 8.4(\beta_i)$.

7. **EXCEL** As mentioned above, spreadsheets can do the work for us of computing beta. Use Excel's "slope" function to estimate the beta of Microsoft using the data in Table LE12.1. Use the "intercept" function to estimate the alpha or intercept term of the regression line.

8. **EXCEL** Below is nine months' return data for Walgreens and the S&P 500.

   a. Estimate the intercept (alpha) and beta for Walgreens stock using spreadsheet functions.

   b. Interpret what the slope estimate means to a stock analyst.

   c. Compute the R-squared of the regression using Excel's RSQ function. What does the R-squared tell us about the relationship between Walgreens' returns and those of the market?

MONTH	WALGREENS RETURN	S&P500 RETURN
1	2.0%	7.5%
2	−5.9%	1.8%
3	0.2%	−8.2%
4	2.0%	−6.4%
5	−2.2%	−1.1%
6	−14.3%	−2.5%
7	−6.0%	0.5%
8	4.9%	7.7%
9	−7.9%	−6.4%

• APPENDIX •

TABLE 1

Future Value of $1 (FVIF)

TABLE 2

Present Value of $1 (PVIF)

TABLE 3

Future Value of a $1 Ordinary Annuity (FVIFA)

TABLE 4

Present Value of a $1 Ordinary Annuity (PVIFA)

TABLE I

Future Value of $1 (FVIF)

YEAR	1%	2%	3%	4%	5%	6%	7%	8%	9%
1	1.010	1.020	1.030	1.040	1.050	1.060	1.070	1.080	1.090
2	1.020	1.040	1.061	1.082	1.102	1.124	1.145	1.166	1.188
3	1.030	1.061	1.093	1.125	1.158	1.191	1.225	1.260	1.295
4	1.041	1.082	1.126	1.170	1.216	1.262	1.311	1.360	1.412
5	1.051	1.104	1.159	1.217	1.276	1.338	1.403	1.469	1.539
6	1.062	1.126	1.194	1.265	1.340	1.419	1.501	1.587	1.677
7	1.072	1.149	1.230	1.316	1.407	1.504	1.606	1.714	1.828
8	1.083	1.172	1.267	1.369	1.477	1.594	1.718	1.851	1.993
9	1.094	1.195	1.305	1.423	1.551	1.689	1.838	1.999	2.172
10	1.105	1.219	1.344	1.480	1.629	1.791	1.967	2.159	2.367
11	1.116	1.243	1.384	1.539	1.710	1.898	2.105	2.332	2.580
12	1.127	1.268	1.426	1.601	1.796	2.012	2.252	2.518	2.813
13	1.138	1.294	1.469	1.665	1.886	2.113	2.410	2.720	3.066
14	1.149	1.319	1.513	1.732	1.980	2.261	2.579	2.937	3.342
15	1.161	1.346	1.558	1.801	2.079	2.397	2.759	3.172	3.642
16	1.173	1.373	1.605	1.873	2.183	2.540	2.952	3.426	3.970
17	1.184	1.400	1.653	1.948	2.292	2.693	3.159	3.700	4.328
18	1.196	1.428	1.702	2.026	2.407	2.854	3.380	3.996	4.717
19	1.208	1.457	1.754	2.107	2.527	3.026	3.617	4.316	5.142
20	1.220	1.486	1.806	2.191	2.653	3.207	3.870	4.661	5.604
25	1.282	1.641	2.094	2.666	3.386	4.292	5.427	6.848	8.623
30	1.348	1.811	2.427	3.243	4.322	5.743	7.612	10.063	13.268

(*Continues*)

Note: The basic equation for finding the future value interest factor (FVIF) is:

$$FVIF_{r,n} = (1 + r)^n$$

where r is the interest rate and n is the number of periods in years.

TABLE I
Future Value of $1 (FVIF) (*Continued*)

10%	12%	14%	15%	16%	18%	20%	25%	30%
1.100	1.120	1.140	1.150	1.160	1.180	1.200	1.250	1.300
1.210	1.254	1.300	1.322	1.346	1.392	1.440	1.563	1.690
1.331	1.405	1.482	1.521	1.561	1.643	1.728	1.953	2.197
1.464	1.574	1.689	1.749	1.811	1.939	2.074	2.441	2.856
1.611	1.762	1.925	2.011	2.100	2.288	2.488	3.052	3.713
1.772	1.974	2.195	2.313	2.436	2.700	2.986	3.815	4.827
1.949	2.211	2.502	2.660	2.826	3.185	3.583	4.768	6.276
2.144	2.476	2.853	3.059	3.278	3.759	4.300	5.960	8.157
2.358	2.773	3.252	3.518	3.803	4.435	5.160	7.451	10.604
2.594	3.106	3.707	4.046	4.411	5.234	6.192	9.313	13.786
2.853	3.479	4.226	4.652	5.117	6.176	7.430	11.642	17.922
3.138	3.896	4.818	5.350	5.936	7.288	8.916	14.552	23.298
3.452	4.363	5.492	6.153	6.886	8.599	10.699	18.190	30.288
3.797	4.887	6.261	7.076	7.988	10.147	12.839	22.737	39.374
4.177	5.474	7.138	8.137	9.266	11.974	15.407	28.422	51.186
4.595	6.130	8.137	9.358	10.748	14.129	18.488	35.527	66.542
5.054	6.866	9.276	10.761	12.468	16.672	22.186	44.409	86.504
5.560	7.690	10.575	12.375	14.463	19.673	26.623	55.511	112.460
6.116	8.613	12.056	14.232	16.777	23.214	31.948	69.389	146.190
6.728	9.646	13.743	16.367	19.461	27.393	38.338	86.736	190.050
10.835	17.000	26.462	32.919	40.874	62.669	95.396	264.700	705.640
17.449	29.960	50.950	66.212	85.850	143.371	237.376	807.790	2,620.000

TABLE 2
Present Value of $1 (PVIF)

YEAR	1%	2%	3%	4%	5%	6%	7%	8%	9%
1	0.990	0.980	0.971	0.962	0.952	0.943	0.935	0.926	0.917
2	0.980	0.961	0.943	0.925	0.907	0.890	0.873	0.857	0.842
3	0.971	0.942	0.915	0.889	0.864	0.840	0.816	0.794	0.772
4	0.961	0.924	0.888	0.855	0.823	0.792	0.763	0.735	0.708
5	0.951	0.906	0.863	0.822	0.784	0.747	0.713	0.681	0.650
6	0.942	0.888	0.837	0.790	0.746	0.705	0.666	0.630	0.596
7	0.933	0.871	0.813	0.760	0.711	0.665	0.623	0.583	0.547
8	0.923	0.853	0.789	0.731	0.677	0.627	0.582	0.540	0.502
9	0.914	0.837	0.766	0.703	0.645	0.592	0.544	0.500	0.460
10	0.905	0.820	0.744	0.676	0.614	0.558	0.508	0.463	0.422
11	0.896	0.804	0.722	0.650	0.585	0.527	0.475	0.429	0.388
12	0.887	0.788	0.701	0.625	0.557	0.497	0.444	0.397	0.356
13	0.879	0.773	0.681	0.601	0.530	0.469	0.415	0.368	0.326
14	0.870	0.758	0.661	0.577	0.505	0.442	0.388	0.340	0.299
15	0.861	0.743	0.642	0.555	0.481	0.417	0.362	0.315	0.275
16	0.853	0.728	0.623	0.534	0.458	0.394	0.339	0.292	0.252
17	0.844	0.714	0.605	0.513	0.436	0.391	0.317	0.270	0.231
18	0.836	0.700	0.587	0.494	0.416	0.350	0.296	0.250	0.212
19	0.828	0.686	0.570	0.475	0.396	0.331	0.276	0.232	0.194
20	0.820	0.673	0.554	0.456	0.377	0.312	0.258	0.215	0.178
25	0.780	0.610	0.478	0.375	0.295	0.233	0.184	0.146	0.116
30	0.742	0.552	0.412	0.308	0.231	0.174	0.131	0.099	0.075

(Continues)

Note: The basic equation for finding the present value interest factor (PVIF) is:

$$PVIF_{r,n} = \frac{1}{(1 + r)^n}$$

where r is the interest or discount rate and n is the number of periods in years.

TABLE 2
Present Value of $1 (PVIF) (*Continued*)

10%	12%	14%	15%	16%	18%	20%	25%	30%
0.909	0.893	0.877	0.870	0.862	0.847	0.833	0.800	0.769
0.826	0.797	0.769	0.756	0.743	0.718	0.694	0.640	0.592
0.751	0.712	0.675	0.658	0.641	0.609	0.579	0.512	0.455
0.683	0.636	0.592	0.572	0.552	0.516	0.482	0.410	0.350
0.621	0.567	0.519	0.497	0.476	0.437	0.402	0.328	0.269
0.564	0.507	0.456	0.432	0.410	0.370	0.335	0.262	0.207
0.513	0.452	0.400	0.376	0.354	0.314	0.279	0.210	0.159
0.467	0.404	0.351	0.327	0.305	0.266	0.233	0.168	0.123
0.424	0.361	0.308	0.284	0.263	0.225	0.194	0.134	0.094
0.386	0.322	0.270	0.247	0.227	0.191	0.162	0.107	0.073
0.350	0.287	0.237	0.215	0.195	0.162	0.135	0.086	0.056
0.319	0.257	0.208	0.187	0.168	0.137	0.112	0.069	0.043
0.290	0.229	0.182	0.163	0.145	0.116	0.093	0.055	0.033
0.263	0.205	0.160	0.141	0.125	0.099	0.078	0.044	0.025
0.239	0.183	0.140	0.123	0.108	0.084	0.065	0.035	0.020
0.218	0.163	0.123	0.107	0.093	0.071	0.054	0.028	0.015
0.198	0.146	0.108	0.093	0.080	0.060	0.045	0.023	0.012
0.180	0.130	0.095	0.081	0.069	0.051	0.038	0.018	0.009
0.164	0.116	0.083	0.070	0.060	0.043	0.031	0.014	0.007
0.149	0.104	0.073	0.061	0.051	0.037	0.026	0.012	0.005
0.092	0.059	0.038	0.030	0.024	0.016	0.010	0.004	0.001
0.057	0.033	0.020	0.015	0.012	0.007	0.004	0.001	0.000

TABLE 3

Future Value of a $1 Ordinary Annuity (FVIFA)

YEAR	1%	2%	3%	4%	5%	6%	7%	8%	9%
1	1.000	1.000	1.000	1.000	1.000	1.000	1.000	1.000	1.000
2	2.010	2.020	2.030	2.040	2.050	2.060	2.070	2.080	2.090
3	3.030	3.060	3.091	3.122	3.152	3.184	3.215	3.246	3.278
4	4.060	4.122	4.184	4.246	4.310	4.375	4.440	4.506	4.573
5	5.101	5.204	5.309	5.416	5.526	5.637	5.751	5.867	5.985
6	6.152	6.308	6.468	6.633	6.802	6.975	7.153	7.336	7.523
7	7.214	7.434	7.662	7.898	8.142	8.394	8.654	8.923	9.200
8	8.286	8.583	8.892	9.214	9.549	9.897	10.260	10.637	11.028
9	9.369	9.755	10.159	10.583	11.027	11.491	11.978	12.488	13.021
10	10.462	10.950	11.464	12.006	12.578	13.181	13.816	14.487	15.193
11	11.567	12.169	12.808	13.486	14.207	14.972	15.784	16.645	17.560
12	12.683	13.412	14.192	15.026	15.917	16.870	17.888	18.977	20.141
13	13.809	14.680	15.618	16.627	17.713	18.882	20.141	21.495	22.953
14	14.947	15.974	17.086	18.292	19.599	21.015	22.550	24.215	26.019
15	16.097	17.293	18.599	20.024	21.579	23.276	25.129	27.152	29.361
16	17.258	18.639	20.157	21.825	23.657	25.673	27.888	30.324	33.003
17	18.430	20.012	21.762	23.698	25.840	28.213	30.840	33.750	36.974
18	19.615	21.412	23.414	25.645	28.132	30.906	33.999	37.450	41.301
19	20.811	22.841	25.117	27.671	30.539	33.760	37.379	41.466	46.018
20	22.019	24.297	26.870	29.778	33.066	36.786	40.995	45.762	51.160
25	28.243	32.030	36.459	41.646	47.727	54.865	63.249	73.106	84.701
30	34.785	40.568	47.575	56.805	66.439	79.058	94.461	113.283	136.308

(*Continues*)

Note: The basic equation for finding the future value interest factor of an ordinary annuity (FVIFA) is:

$$FVIFA_{r,n} = \sum_{t=1}^{n} (1 + r)^{n-t} = \frac{(1 + r)^n - 1}{r}$$

where r is the interest rate and n is the number of periods in years.

Future Value of a $1 Annuity Due (FVIFAD)

The future value interest factor of an annuity due (FVIFAD) may be found by using the following formula to convert FVIFA values found in Table 3:

$$FVIFAD_{r,n} = FVIFA_{r,n}(1 + r)$$

where r is the interest rate and n is the number of periods in years.

TABLE 3

Future Value of a $1 Ordinary Annuity (FVIFA) (*Continued*)

10%	12%	14%	16%	18%	20%	25%	30%
1.000	1.000	1.000	1.000	1.000	1.000	1.000	1.000
2.100	2.120	2.140	2.160	2.180	2.200	2.250	2.300
3.310	3.374	3.440	3.506	3.572	3.640	3.813	3.990
4.641	4.779	4.921	5.066	5.215	5.368	5.766	6.187
6.105	6.353	6.610	6.877	7.154	7.442	8.207	9.043
7.716	8.115	8.536	8.977	9.442	9.930	11.259	12.756
9.487	10.089	10.730	11.414	12.142	12.916	15.073	17.583
11.436	12.300	13.233	14.240	15.327	16.499	19.842	23.858
13.579	14.776	16.085	17.518	19.086	20.799	25.802	32.015
15.937	17.549	19.337	21.321	23.521	25.959	33.253	42.619
18.531	20.655	23.044	25.733	28.755	32.150	42.566	56.405
21.384	24.133	27.271	30.850	34.931	39.580	54.208	74.327
24.523	28.029	32.089	36.786	42.219	48.497	68.760	97.625
27.975	32.393	37.581	43.672	50.818	59.196	86.949	127.910
31.772	37.280	43.842	51.660	60.965	72.035	109.690	167.290
35.950	42.753	50.980	60.925	72.939	87.442	138.110	218.470
40.545	48.884	59.118	71.673	87.068	105.931	173.640	285.010
45.599	55.750	68.394	84.141	103.740	128.117	218.050	371.520
51.159	63.440	78.969	98.603	123.414	154.740	273.560	483.970
57.275	72.052	91.025	115.380	146.628	186.688	342.950	630.170
98.347	133.334	181.871	249.214	342.603	471.981	1,054.800	2,348.800
164.494	241.333	356.787	530.312	790.948	1,181.882	3,227.200	8,730.000

TABLE 4

Present Value of a $1 Ordinary Annuity (PVIFA)

YEAR	1%	2%	3%	4%	5%	6%	7%	8%	9%
1	0.990	0.980	0.971	0.962	0.952	0.943	0.935	0.926	0.917
2	1.970	1.942	1.913	1.886	1.859	1.833	1.808	1.783	1.759
3	2.941	2.884	2.829	2.775	2.723	2.673	2.624	2.577	2.531
4	3.902	3.808	3.717	3.630	3.546	3.465	3.387	3.312	3.240
5	4.853	4.713	4.580	4.452	4.329	4.212	4.100	3.993	3.890
6	5.795	5.601	5.417	5.242	5.076	4.917	4.767	4.623	4.486
7	6.728	6.472	6.230	6.002	5.786	5.582	5.389	5.206	5.033
8	7.652	7.325	7.020	6.733	6.463	6.210	5.971	5.747	5.535
9	8.566	8.162	7.786	7.435	7.108	6.802	6.515	6.247	5.995
10	9.471	8.983	8.530	8.111	7.722	7.360	7.024	6.710	6.418
11	10.368	9.787	9.253	8.760	8.306	7.887	7.499	7.139	6.805
12	11.255	10.575	9.954	9.385	8.863	8.384	7.943	7.536	7.161
13	12.134	11.348	10.635	9.986	9.394	8.853	8.358	7.904	7.487
14	13.004	12.106	11.296	10.563	9.899	9.295	8.745	8.244	7.786
15	13.865	12.849	11.938	11.118	10.380	9.712	9.108	8.559	8.061
16	14.718	13.578	12.561	11.652	10.838	10.106	9.447	8.851	8.313
17	15.562	14.292	13.166	12.166	11.274	10.477	9.763	9.122	8.544
18	16.398	14.992	13.754	12.659	11.690	10.828	10.059	9.372	8.756
19	17.226	15.678	14.324	13.134	12.085	11.158	10.336	9.604	8.950
20	18.046	16.351	14.877	13.590	12.462	11.470	10.594	9.818	9.129
25	22.023	19.523	17.413	15.622	14.094	12.783	11.654	10.675	9.823
30	25.808	22.397	19.600	17.292	15.372	13.765	12.409	11.258	10.274

(*Continues*)

Note: The basic equation for finding the present value interest factor of an ordinary annuity (PVIFA) is:

$$\text{PVIFA}_{r,n} = \sum_{t-1}^{n} \frac{1}{(1+r)^t} = \frac{1 - \dfrac{1}{(1+r)^n}}{r}$$

where r is the interest or discount rate and n is the number of periods in years.

Present Value of a $1 Annuity Due (PVIFAD)

The present value interest factor of an annuity due (PVIFAD) may be found by using the following formula to convert PVIFA values found in Table 4:

$$\text{PVIFAD}_{r,n} = \text{PVIFA}_{r,n}(1+r)$$

where r is the interest or discount rate and n is the number of periods in years.

TABLE 4
Present Value of a $1 Ordinary Annuity (PVIFA) (*Continued*)

10%	12%	14%	16%	18%	20%	25%	30%
0.909	0.893	0.877	0.862	0.847	0.833	0.800	0.769
1.736	1.690	1.647	1.605	1.566	1.528	1.440	1.361
2.487	2.402	2.322	2.246	2.174	2.106	1.952	1.816
3.170	3.037	2.914	2.798	2.690	2.589	2.362	2.166
3.791	3.605	3.433	3.274	3.127	2.991	2.689	2.436
4.355	4.111	3.889	3.685	3.498	3.326	2.951	2.643
4.868	4.564	4.288	4.039	3.812	3.605	3.161	2.802
5.335	4.968	4.639	4.344	4.078	3.837	3.329	2.925
5.759	5.328	4.946	4.607	4.303	4.031	3.463	3.019
6.145	5.650	5.216	4.833	4.494	4.193	3.571	3.092
6.495	5.938	5.453	5.029	4.656	4.327	3.656	3.147
6.814	6.194	5.660	5.197	4.793	4.439	3.725	3.190
7.103	6.424	5.842	5.342	4.910	4.533	3.780	3.223
7.367	6.628	6.002	5.468	5.008	4.611	3.824	3.249
7.606	6.811	6.142	5.575	5.092	4.675	3.859	3.268
7.824	6.974	6.265	5.668	5.162	4.730	3.887	3.283
8.022	7.120	5.373	5.749	4.222	4.775	3.910	3.295
8.201	7.250	6.467	5.818	5.273	4.812	3.928	3.304
8.365	7.366	6.550	5.877	5.316	4.843	3.942	3.311
8.514	7.469	6.623	5.929	5.353	4.870	3.954	3.316
9.077	7.843	6.873	6.097	5.467	4.948	3.985	3.329
9.427	8.055	7.003	6.177	5.517	4.979	3.995	3.332

• GLOSSARY •

A

accommodative function Fed efforts to meet credit needs of individuals and institutions, clearing checks, and supporting depository institutions

adjustable-rate mortgage (ARM) has an interest rate that changes or varies over time with market determined interest rates on a U.S. Treasury bill or other debt security

administrative inflation the tendency of prices, aided by union-corporation contracts, to rise during economic expansion and to resist declines during recessions

advance factoring factor pays the firm for its receivables before the account due date

aftermarket the period after a new issue is initially sold to the public; during this period, members of the syndicate may not sell the securities for less than the offering price

agency costs tangible and intangible expenses borne by shareholders because of the actual or potential self-serving actions of managers

agents the managers hired by the principals to run the firm

American depository receipt (ADR) receipt that represents foreign shares to U.S. investors

amortized loan a loan repaid in equal payments over a specified time period

annual percentage rate (APR) determined by multiplying the interest rate charged per period by the number of periods in a year

annual report contains descriptive information on operating and financial performance during the past year, a discussion of current and future business opportunities, and financial statements that provide a numerical record of financial performance

annuity a series of equal payments (receipts) that occur over a number of time periods

annuity due exists when equal periodic payments start at time period zero or, in other words, the beginning of each time period

arbitrage the simultaneous, or nearly simultaneous, purchasing of commodities, securities, or bills of exchange in one market and selling them in another where the price is higher

ask price requested by the seller

asset management ratios indicate extent to which assets are turned over or used to support sales

assets financial and physical items owned by a business

at-the-money exercise price equals the market price of the underlying asset

automatic stabilizers federal government programs that act on a continuing basis to stabilize disposable income and economic activity in general

automatic transfer service (ATS) accounts used to make direct deposits to, and payments from, checkable deposit accounts

B

balance of payments involves all of a country's international transactions, including foreign investment, private and government grants, military spending overseas, and many other items besides the buying and selling of goods and services

balance of trade the net balance of exports and imports of goods and services

balance sheet statement of a company's financial position as of a particular date, usually at the end of a quarter or year

bank liquidity reflects the ability to meet depositor withdrawals and to pay off other liabilities when they come due

bank reserves reserve balances and vault cash used to meet reserve requirements

bank reserves vault cash and deposits held at Reserve Banks

bank solvency reflects the ability to keep the value of a bank's assets greater than its liabilities

banker's acceptance (1) a promise of future payment issued by a firm and guaranteed by a bank; (2) promise of future payment issued by a firm and guaranteed by a bank

banking system commercial banks, S&Ls, savings banks, and credit unions

bankruptcy costs explicit expenses such as legal and accounting fees and court costs, along with implicit costs such as the use of management time and skills in preventing and escaping bankruptcy

barter exchange of goods or services without using money

base case for project analysis, the firm's after-tax cash flows without the project

bearer bonds have coupons that are "clipped" and presented, like a check, to the bank for payment; the bond issuer does not know who is receiving the interest payments

best-effort agreement agreement which the investment bankers try to sell securities of the issuing corporation; but they assume no risk for the possible failure of the flotation

beta measure of an asset's systematic risk

bid price offered by a potential buyer

bimetallic standard monetary standard based on two metals, usually silver and gold

blanket inventory lien claim against a inventory when individual items are indistinguishable

blue-sky laws protect the investor from fraudulent security offerings

bond markets where debt securities with longer-term maturities are originated and traded

bond ratings assess both the collateral underlying the bonds as well as the ability of the issuer to make timely payments of interest and principal

break-even analysis used to estimate how many units of a product must be sold for the firm to break even or have a zero profit

Bretton Woods system a system in which individual currencies would be tied to gold through the U.S. dollar via fixed or pegged exchange rates

broker one who assists the trading process by buying or selling securities in the market for an investor

brokerage firms assist individuals who want to purchase new or existing securities issues or who want to sell previously purchased securities

budgetary deficit when tax and other general revenues fail to meet expenditures

budgets financial plans indicating expected revenues, spending, and investment needs

business risk (1) variations in operating income over time because of variations in unit sales, price–cost margin, and/or fixed expenses; (2) measured by variability in EBIT over time and is determined by the products the firm sells and the production processes it uses

buying on margin investors borrow money and invest it along with their own funds in securities

bylaws the rules established to govern the corporation and include how the firm will be managed, how the directors will be elected, and the rights of the stockholders

C

call deferment period specified period of time after the bond issue during which the bonds cannot be called

call option a contract for the purchase of securities

call price price paid to the investor for redemption prior to maturity, typically par value plus a call premium of one year's interest

call risk risk of having a bond called away and reinvesting the proceeds at a lower interest rate

callable bonds can be redeemed prior to maturity by the issuing firm

callable preferred stock gives the corporation the right to retire the preferred stock at its option

cannibalization this occurs when a project robs cash flow from the firm's existing lines of business

capacity the ability to pay bills and often involves an examination of liquidity ratios

capital indicates the adequacy of owners' equity relative to existing liabilities as the underlying support for creditworthiness

capital account balance includes foreign government and private investment in the United States netted against U.S. investment in foreign countries

capital budgeting process of identifying, evaluating, and implementing a firm's investment opportunities

capital consumption adjustment (depreciation) the estimate of the "using up" of plant and equipment assets for business purposes

capital formation process of constructing real property, manufacturing producers' durable equipment, and increasing business inventories

capital markets where debt instruments or securities with maturities longer than one year and corporate stocks or equity securities are issued and traded

capital structure firm's mix of debt and equity used to finance a firm's assets

cash budget a tool the treasurer uses to forecast future cash flows and estimate future short-term borrowing needs

cash conversion cycle time between a firm's paying its suppliers for inventory and collecting cash from customers on a sale of the finished product

central bank   federal government agency that facilitates the operation of the financial system and regulates money supply growth

certificates of deposit (CDs)   time deposits with a stated maturity and pay a fixed rate of interest or are sold at a discount

character   ethical quality of the applicant on which one can base a judgment about his or her willingness to pay bills and is best judged by reviewing his past credit history for long overdue or unpaid obligations

charter   provides the corporate name, indicates the intended business activities, provides names and addresses of directors, and indicates how a firm will be capitalized with stock

chartists (technicians)   people who examine graphs of past price movements, number of shares bought and sold, and other figures to predict future price movements

chief financial officer (CFO)   responsible for the controller and the treasury functions of a firm

clean draft   a draft that is not accompanied by any special documents and is generally used when the exporter has confidence in the importer's ability to meet the draft when presented

closed-end mortgage bond   does not permit future bond issues to be secured by any of the assets pledged as security under the closed-end issue

coefficient of variation (CV)   a measure of risk per unit of return

collateral   reflects whether assets are available to provide security for the potential credit

combined leverage   effect on earnings produced by the operating and financial leverage

commercial banks   depository institutions that accept deposits, issue check-writing accounts, and make loans to businesses and individuals

commercial finance company   organization without a bank charter that advances funds to businesses by discounting accouts receivable, making loans secured by chattel mortgages on machinery or liens on inventory, or financing deferred-payment sales of commercial and industrial equipment

commercial letter of credit   a bank's written statement to an individual or firm guaranteeing acceptance and payment of a draft up to a specified sum if the draft is presented according to the terms of the letter

commercial paper   short-term unsecured promissory note issued by a high-credit-quality corporation

common stock   ownership shares in a corporation

common-size financial statements   expresses balance sheet numbers as a percentage of total assets and income statement numbers as a percentage of total revenue to facilitate comparisons between different-sized firms

compensating balance   requirement that 10 to 20 percent of a loan be kept on deposit at the bank

compound interest   involves earning interest on interest in addition to interest on the principal or initial investment

compounding   arithmetic process whereby an initial value increases or grows at a compound interest rate over time to reach a value in the future

conditions   refer to current economic climate and state of the business cycle

constant payout ratio   a strategy in which the firm pays a constant percentage of earnings as dividends; as earnings rise and fall, so does the dollar amount of dividends

Consumer Credit Protection Act   requires the clear explanation of consumer credit costs and garnishment procedures (taking wages or property by legal means) and prohibiting overly high-priced credit transactions

contractual savings   savings accumulated on a regular schedule for a specified length of time by prior agreement

contractual savings organizations   collect premiums on insurance policies and employee/employer contributions from participants and provide retirement benefits and insurance against major financial losses

contribution margin   contribution of each unit sold that goes toward paying fixed costs

controller   manages accounting, cost analysis, and tax planning

conversion ratio   number of shares into which a convertible bond can be converted

conversion value   stock price times the conversion ratio

convertible bond   can be changed or converted, at the investor's option, into a specific number of shares of the issuer's common stock

convertible preferred stock   has a special provision that makes it possible to convert it to common stock of the corporation, generally at the stockholder's option

corporate bond   debt instrument issued by a corporation to raise long-term funds

corporate equity capital   financial capital supplied by the owners of a corporation

corporation   legal entity created under state law in the United States with an unending life and limited financial liability to its owners

correlation   statistical concept that relates movements in one set of returns to movements in another set over time

cost of capital   (1) minimum acceptable rate of return to a firm on a project; (2) the project's required rate of return

cost-push inflation   occurs when prices are raised to cover rising production costs, such as wages

cost-volume-profit analysis   used by managers for financial planning to estimate the firm's operating profits at different levels of unit sales

covenants   impose restrictions or extra duties on the firm

credit bureaus not-for-profit institutions that obtain credit information about business firms and individuals

credit cards provide predetermined credit limits to consumers at the time the cards are issued

credit money money backed by the creditworthiness of the issuer

credit rating indicates the expected likelihood that a borrower will miss interest or principal payments and possibly default on the debt obligation in the form of a loan, mortgage, or bond

credit risk (default risk) the chance of nonpayment or delayed payment of interest or principal

credit score a number that indicates an individual's creditworthiness or likelihood that a debt will be paid according to the terms that were initially agreed to

credit unions cooperative nonprofit organizations that exist primarily to provide member depositors with consumer credit

cross-sectional analysis different firms are compared at the same point in time

crowding out lack of funds for private borrowing caused by the sale of government obligations to cover large federal deficits

cumulative preferred stock requires that before dividends on common stock are paid, preferred dividends must be paid for the current period and for all previous periods in which preferred dividends were missed

currency exchange markets (foreign exchange markets) electronic markets where banks and institutional traders buy and sell currencies on behalf of businesses, other clients, and themselves

currency exchange rate value of one currency relative to another currency

current account balance shows the flow of income into and out of the United States during a specified period

current assets cash and all other assets that are expected to be converted into cash within one year

D

dealer satisfies the investor's trades by buying and selling securities from his or her own inventory

dealer system composed of a closely linked network of dealers and brokers in government securities with an effective marketing network throughout the United States

debenture bonds unsecured obligations that depend on the general credit strength of the corporation for their security

debit cards provide for the immediate direct transfer of deposit amounts

debt management includes determining the types of refunding to carry out, the types of securities to sell, the interest rate patterns to use, and decisions to make on callable issues

debt securities obligations to repay borrowed funds

debt securities markets where money market securities, bonds (corporate, financial institution, and government), and mortgages are originated and traded

default risk risk that a borrower will not pay interest and/or repay the principal on a loan or other debt instrument according to the agreed contractual terms

default risk premium indicates compensation for the possibility that the borrower will not pay interest and/or will not repay principal according to the financial instrument's contractual arrangements

defensive activities Fed activities that contribute to the smooth, everyday functioning of the economy

deficit economic unit spends more money than it brings in and must balance its money receipts with money expenditures by obtaining money from surplus units

deficit financing affects the monetary and banking system when the spending rate is faster than the collection of taxes and other funds

deficit reserves the amount by which required reserves are larger than total reserves of an institution

degree of combined leverage (DCL) percentage change in eps that results from a 1 percent change in sales volume

degree of financial leverage (DFL) measures the sensitivity of eps to changes in EBIT

degree of operating leverage (DOL) measures the sensitivity of operating income to changes in the level of output

demand-pull inflation an excessive demand for goods and services during periods of economic expansion relative to supply

depository institutions accept deposits from individuals and then lend these pooled savings to businesses, governments, and individuals

depreciation devaluing a physical asset over the period of its expected life

depreciation tax shield tax reduction due to depreciation of fixed assets; equals the amount of the depreciation expense multiplied by the firm's tax rate

derivative deposit occurs when reserves created from a primary deposit are made available to borrowers through bank loans

derivative securities markets where financial contracts or instruments that derive their values from underlying debt and equity securities are originated and traded

derivative security financial contract that derives its value from the value of another asset, such as a bond or stock

designated market makers (DMM) assigned dealers who have the responsibility of making a market in an assigned security

development stage requires estimating relevant cash inflows and outflows

deviations computed as a periodic return minus the average return

direct quotation method indicates the value of one unit of a foreign currency in terms of a home country's currency

discount bond bond that is selling below par value

discounted loan   borrower receives the principal less the interest at the time the loan is made; the principal is repaid at maturity

discounting   arithmetic process whereby a future value (FV) decreases at a compound interest rate over time to reach a present value (PV)

dissave   spend accumulated savings rather than further reduce consumption spending

diversification   occurs when we invest in several different assets rather than just a single one

dividend payout ratio   (1) dividends per share divided by earnings per share (EPS); (2) the proportion of each dollar of earnings that is paid to shareholders as a dividend; equals one minus the retention rate

dividend reinvestment plans (DRIPS)   allow shareholders to purchase additional shares automatically with all or part of the investor's dividends

documentary draft   draft that is accompanied by an order bill of lading along with other papers such as insurance receipts, certificates of sanitation, and consular invoices

Dodd-Frank Wall Street Reform and Consumer Protection Act   promotes financial stability of the United States by improving accountability and transparency in the financial system

draft (bill of exchange)   an unconditional written order, signed by the party drawing it, requiring the party to whom it is addressed to pay a certain sum of money to order or to bearer

dual banking system   allows commercial banks to obtain charters from the federal government or a state government

due diligence   detailed study of a corporation

DuPont analysis   technique of breaking return on total assets and return on equity into their component parts

Dutch auction   a bidding process, which allows smaller firms and individual investors to purchase securities

dynamic actions   Fed actions that stimulate or repress the level of prices or economic activity

E

EBIT/eps analysis   allows managers to see how different capital structures affect the earnings and risk levels of their firms

economic risk   risk associated with possible slow or negative economic growth, as well as variability in economic growth

effective annual rate (EAR)   measures the true interest rate when compounding occurs more frequently than once a year

efficient market (informationally efficient market)   a market in which prices adjust quickly after the arrival of important news surprises

electronic data interchange   the use of communications and computer systems to convey ordering, invoice, and payment information between suppliers and customers

enhancement   increase in the cash flows of the firm's other products that occur because of a new project

entrepreneurial finance   study of how growth-driven, performance-focused, early-stage firms raise financial capital and manage their operations and assets

equipment trust certificate   a type of mortgage bond that gives the bondholder a claim to specific "rolling stock" (movable assets), such as railroad cars or airplanes

equity   funds supplied by the owners and represents their residual claim on the firm

equity securities markets   where ownership rights in corporations are initially sold and traded

ethical behavior   how an individual or organization treats others legally, fairly, and honestly

euro   a single currency that has replaced the individual currencies of the eurozone member countries

eurodollar bonds   dollar-denominated bonds sold outside the United States

European Central Bank (ECB)   conducts monetary policy for the twelve European countries that formed the European Monetary Union and adopted the euro as their common currency

European Union (EU)   organization established to promote trade and economic development among European countries

eurozone members   countries that have adopted the euro as their common currency

ex ante   expected or forecasted

excess reserves   the amount by which total reserves exceed required reserves

exchange rate risk   (1) effect on revenues and expenses from variations in the value of the U.S. dollar in terms of other currencies; (2) fluctuating exchange rates lead to varying levels of U.S. dollar-denominated cash flows

exercise price (strike price)   price at which the asset can be traded under a futures or option contract

expectations theory   states that the shape of the yield curve reflects investor expectations about future inflation rates

Export-Import Bank   bank established to help finance and facilitate exports and imports between the United States and other countries

extendable notes   have their coupons reset every two or three years to reflect the current interest rate environment and any changes in the firm's credit quality; the investor can accept the new coupon rate or put the bonds back to the firm

F

factor   a firm that engages in accounts receivable financing by purchasing accounts and assuming all credit risks

Fed discount rate   interest rate that a bank must pay to borrow from its regional Reserve Bank

Fed's Board of Governors seven-member board of the Federal Reserve that sets monetary policy

federal funds short-term loans, usually with maturities of one day to one week made between depository institutions

federal funds rate rate on overnight loans from banks with excess reserves to banks that have deficit reserves

Federal Home Loan Mortgage Corporation (Freddie Mac) formed to aid mortgage markets by purchasing and holding mortgage loans

Federal National Mortgage Association (Fannie Mae) created to support the financial markets by purchasing home mortgages from banks and, thus, freeing the proceeds could be lent to other borrowers

Federal Reserve float temporary increase in bank reserves that results when checks are credited to the reserve account of the depositing bank before they are debited from the account of the banks on which they are drawn

Federal Reserve System (Fed) U.S. central bank that sets monetary policy and regulates banking system

federal statutory debt limits limits on the federal debt set by Congress

fiat money legal tender proclaimed to be money by law

field warehouse a warehouse on the grounds of the borrowing business establishment

finance study of how individuals, institutions, governments, and businesses acquire, spend, and manage money and other financial assets

finance companies provide loans directly to consumers and businesses or aid individuals in obtaining financing

financial assets (1) claims against the income or assets of individuals, businesses, and governments; (2) money, debt instruments, equity securities, and other financial contracts that are backed by real assets and the earning abilities of issuers

financial environment financial system, institutions or intermediaries, financial markets, business firms, individuals, and global interactions that contribute to an efficiently operating economy

financial institutions organizations or intermediaries that help the financial system operate efficiently and transfer funds from savers and investors to individuals, businesses, and governments that seek to spend or invest the funds in physical assets

financial intermediation process by which individual savings are accumulated in depository institutions and, in turn, lent or invested

financial leverage ratios indicate the extent to which borrowed or debt funds are used to finance assets, as well as the ability of a firm to meet its debt payment obligations

financial management involves financial planning, asset management, and fund-raising decisions to enhance the value of businesses

financial markets physical locations or electronic forums that facilitate the flow of funds among investors, businesses, and governments

financial risk variations in income before taxes over time because fixed interest expenses do not change when operating income rises or falls

financial system a complex mix of financial intermediaries, markets, instruments, policy makers, and regulations that interact to expedite the flow of financial capital from savings into investments

first mortgage bonds backed or secured by specifically pledged property of a firm (real estate, buildings, and other assets classified as real property)

fiscal policy involves setting the annual national budget and reflects government influence on economic activity through taxation and expenditure plans

fixed-rate mortgage fixed interest rate with constant monthly payments over the life of the loan, which is typically 15 or 30 years

flexible exchange rates a system in which currency exchange rates are determined by supply and demand

float the delay between when funds are sent by a payer to a payee

flotation initial sale of newly issued debt or equity securities

flotation costs (1) composed of direct costs, the spread, and underpricing; (2) costs of issuing stock; includes accounting, legal, and printing costs of offering shares to the public as well as the commission or fees earned by the investment bankers who market the new securities to investors

follow-up stage determines, through analysis, if a company is meeting expectations

foreign exchange markets electronic markets in which banks and institutional traders buy and sell various currencies on behalf of businesses and other clients

forward exchange rate negotiated exchange rate for the purchase or sale of a currency where delivery will take place at a future date

fourth market a market in which large institutional investors arrange the purchase and sale of securities among themselves without the benefit of broker or dealer

fractional reserve system a system in which banks are required by the Fed to hold reserves equal to a specified percentage of their deposits

full-bodied money coins that contain the same value in metal as their face value

future value value of a savings amount or an investment at a specified time or date in the future

futures contract a contract obligating the owner to purchase or sell the underlying asset at a specified price on a specified day

G

generally accepted accounting principles (GAAP) set of guidelines as to the form and manner in which accounting information should be presented

Glass-Steagall Act of 1933 provided for separation of commercial banking and investment banking activities in the United States

global bonds bonds that are generally denominated in U.S. dollars and marketed globally

global depository receipt (GDR) listed on the London Stock Exchange; facilitates trading in foreign shares

gold standard a standard in which currencies of countries of major countries are convertible into gold at fixed exchange rates

goodwill an intangible asset that represents the excess funds paid when one firm merges with or purchases another over and above the accounting value of the firm's net assets

Gordon model (constant dividend growth model) a means of estimating common stock prices by assuming constant dividend growth over time

government expenditures (GE) expenditures for goods and services plus gross investments by federal, state, and local governments

Government National Mortgage Association (Ginnie Mae) created to issue its own debt securities to obtain funds that are invested in mortgages made to low-income to moderate-income home purchasers

Gramm-Leach-Bliley Act of 1999 repealed the separation of commercial banking and investment banking provided for in the Glass-Steagall Act of 1933

gross domestic product (GDP) the output of goods and services in an economy

gross private domestic investment (GPDI) measures fixed investment in residential and nonresidential structures, producers' durable equipment, and changes in business inventories

H

hedge an action which reduces risk; similar to the concept of insurance

high-yield bonds (junk bonds) with ratings lower than Baa, bonds that have a substantial probability of default

house brokers (commission brokers) act as agents to execute customers' orders for securities purchases and sales

I

identification stage finds potential capital investment opportunities and identifying if a project involves a replacement decision and/or revenue expansion

implementation stage accepted projects are executed in a timely fashion; cash outflows occur as the firm invests in the capital budgeting project

in-the-money an option with a positive intrinsic value

income statement reports the revenues generated and expenses incurred by the firm over an accounting period, such as a quarter or a year

incremental cash flows represent the difference between the firm's after-tax cash flows with the project and the firm's after-tax cash flows without the project

independent brokers handle the commission brokers' overflow

independent projects projects not in direct competition with one another

indirect quotation method indicates the number of units of a foreign currency needed to purchase one unit of the home country's currency

individual net worth sum of an individual's money, real assets, and financial assets or claims against others less the individual's debt obligations

industry comparative analysis compares a firm's ratios against average ratios for other companies in the firm's industry

inflation occurs when a rise or increase in the price of goods or services is not offset by increases in the quality of those goods and services

inflation premium average inflation rate expected over the life of the instrument

initial margin (1) deposited funds necessary to purchase a derivatives contract; (2) initial equity percentage

initial public offering (IPO) initial sale of equity to the public

insurance companies provide financial protection to individuals and businesses for life, property, liability, and health uncertainties

interest rate basic price that equates the demand for and supply of loanable funds in the financial markets

interest rate parity (IRP) states that a country with a relatively higher nominal interest rate will have its currency depreciate relative to a country with a relatively lower nominal interest rate

interest rate risk (1) reflects the possibility of changes or fluctuations in market values of fixed-rate debt instruments as market interest rates change over time; (2) variations in interest expense unrelated to sales or operating income arising from changes in the level of interest rates in the economy

internal growth rate a measure of how quickly a firm can increase its asset base over the next year without raising outside funds

internal rate of return (IRR) method return that causes the net present value to be zero

international banking when banks operate in more than one country

International Monetary Fund (IMF) created to promote world trade through monitoring and maintaining fixed exchange rates and by making loans to countries facing balance of trade and payments problems

international monetary system a system of institutions and mechanisms to foster international trade, manage the flow of financial capital, and determine currency exchange rates

investment bank helps businesses sell their new debt and equity securities to raise financial capital

investment bankers (underwriters) main activity is marketing securities and dealing with the securities markets

investment banking firms sell or market new securities issued by businesses to individual and institutional investors

investment companies sell shares in their firms to individuals and others and invest the pooled proceeds in corporate and government securities

investment grade bonds ratings of Baa or higher that meet financial institution investment standards

investments involve the sale or marketing of securities, the analysis of securities, and the management of investment risk through portfolio diversification

J

junk bonds (high-yield bonds) bonds with ratings that are below investment grade, that is Ba1, BB+, or lower

L

liabilities creditors' claims on a firm, which are the financial obligations of the business

limit order maximum buying price (limit buy) or the minimum selling price (limit sell) specified by the investor

limited branch banking allows additional banking offices within a geographically defined distance of a bank's main office

limited liability company (LLC) an organizational form, similar to a subchapter S corporation, that offers owners limited liability; its income is taxed only once as personal income of the shareholders, and the firm can have an unlimited number of shareholders

limited partners face limited liability to their investments in the firm, meaning their personal assets cannot be attached to settle the firm's debt

limited partnership has at least one general partner who has unlimited liability; the liability of the limited partners is limited to their investment

line of credit loan limit the bank establishes for each of its business customers

liquidity the ease with which an asset can be exchanged for money or other assets

liquidity preference theory holds that investors or debt instrument holders prefer to invest short term so they have greater liquidity and less maturity or interest rate risk

liquidity premium compensation for those financial debt instruments that cannot easily be converted to cash at prices close to their estimated fair market values

liquidity ratios indicate the ability of the firm to meet short-term obligations as they come due

liquidity risk likelihood that a bank will be unable to meet its depositor withdrawal demands and/or other liabilities when they are due

loan amortization schedule a schedule of the breakdown of each payment between interest and principal as well as the remaining balance after each payment

loanable funds theory holds that interest rates are a function of the supply of and demand for loanable funds

lockbox system a system in which payments are sent to a P.O. box and processed by a bank to reduce collection float

M

M1 money supply consists of currency, travelers' checks, demand deposits, and other checkable deposits at depository institutions

M2 money supply M1 plus highly liquid financial assets, including savings accounts, small time deposits, and retail money market mutual funds (MMMFs)

maintenance margin minimum margin to which an investment may fall before a margin call will be placed

margin the ratio of the investor's equity (own money) to the market value of the security

margin call the option of either closing out the position or investing additional cash to increase the position's equity or margin

market order an order for immediate purchase or sale at the best possible price

market portfolio a portfolio that contains all risky assets

market segmentation theory holds that securities of different maturities are not perfect substitutes for one another

market stabilization intervention of the syndicate to buy back securities to prevent a larger price drop

market timing hypothesis firms time the market by issuing stock when their stock prices are high and repurchasing shares when their stock values are low

market value added (MVA) measures the value created by the firm's managers and equals the the market value of the firm's liabilities and equity minus the amount of money investors paid to the firm when these securities were first issued

market value ratios indicate the willingness of investors to value a firm in the marketplace relative to financial statement values

marketable government securities securities that can be purchased and sold through customary market channels

maturity factoring firm selling its receivables is paid on the normal collection date or net due date of the account

maturity risk premium the added return expected by lenders or investors because of interest rate risk on instruments with longer maturities

maturity-matching approach financing strategy that attempts to match the maturities of assets with the maturities of the liabilities with which they are financed

medium of exchange the basic function of money

merchandise trade balance the net difference between a country's import and export of goods

mission statement statement of a firm's main reason for being; sometimes called a vision statement

Mission, Objects, Goals, and Strategies (MOGS) a corporate planning tool that aids in developing project plans that fit well with a firm's plans

modified internal rate of return (MIRR) method a technique that solves some of the problems presented by IRR. MIRR rankings of mutually exclusive projects with comparably sized initial investments will agree with the NPV rankings of those projects

monetary base (MB) banking system reserves plus currency held by the public

monetary policy involves regulating the growth of the money supply and regulating its cost and availability

monetizing the debt the Fed buys government securities, financing some of the deficit and providing additional reserves to the banking system, thus increasing the money supply

money anything generally accepted as a means of paying for goods, services, and paying off debts

money market mutual funds (MMMFs) issue shares to customers and invest the proceeds in highly liquid, short maturity, interest-bearing debt instruments called money market investments

money market securities debt instruments or securities with maturities of one year or less

money markets where debt securities with maturities of one year or less are issued and traded

money multiplier (*m*) number of times the monetary base can be expanded or magnified to produce a given money supply level

mortgage loan backed by real property in the form of buildings and houses

mortgage banking firms help individuals obtain mortgage loans by bringing together borrowers and institutional investors

mortgage markets where loans to purchase real estate (buildings and houses) are originated in primary markets and traded in secondary markets

mortgage-backed security a debt security created by pooling together a group of mortgage loans whose periodic payments belong to the holders of the security

multibank holding companies (MBHCs) permits a firm to own and control two or more banks

municipal bond debt instrument issued by a state or local government

mutual funds open-end investment companies that can issue an unlimited number of their shares to their investors and use the pooled proceeds to purchase corporate and government securities

mutually exclusive projects a project that, when selected, precludes others from being undertaken

N

national debt total debt owed by a government

negative correlation when asset returns move in opposite directions

negotiable certificate of deposit (negotiable CD) short-term debt instrument issued by depository institutions to individual or institutional depositors

net exports (NE) exports of goods and services minus imports

net present value (NPV) present value of a project's cash flows minus its cost

net working capital dollar amount of a firm's current assets minus current liabilities; sometimes used as a measure of liquidity

nominal interest rate interest rate that is observed in the marketplace and that includes a premium for expected inflation

noncumulative preferred stock makes no provision for the accumulation of past missed dividends

nonmarketable government securities securities that cannot be transferred to other persons or institutions and can be redeemed only by being turned in to the U.S. Government

NPV profile the graphical relationship between a project's NPV and cost of capital

O

odd lot sale or purchase of fewer than 100 shares

offer price price at which the security is sold to the investors

one-bank holding companies (OBHCs) permits a firm to own and control one bank

open-end mortgage bond allows the same assets to be used as security in future issues

open-market operations buying and selling of securities in the open market by the Fed through its FOMC to alter bank reserves

operating cycle measures the time between receiving raw materials and collecting cash from receivables

opportunity cost cost of passing up the next best alternative

optimum debt/equity mix proportionate use of debt and equity that minimizes the firm's cost of capital

option financial contract that gives the owner the option of buying or selling a particular good at a specified price on or before a specified time or expiration date

option premium   the price paid for the option

option writer   seller of an option contract

order bill of lading   represents the written acceptance of goods for shipment by a transportation company and the terms under which the goods are to be transported to their destination

ordinary annuity   equal payments (receipts) occur at the end of each time period

out-of-the-money   an option with zero intrinsic value

P

par value   stated stock value in the certificate of incorporation; bearing little relationship to the current price or book value of the stock

par value (face value)   principal amount of a loan or bond that the issuer is obligated to repay at maturity

participating preferred stock   allows preferred shareholders to receive a larger dividend under certain conditions when common shareholder dividends increase

partnership   a form of business organization that exists when two or more persons own a business operated for profit

payback period method   determines the time in years it will take to recover, or pay back, the initial investment in fixed assets

pecking order hypothesis   a theory that states managers prefer to use additions to retained earnings to finance the firm, then debt, and (as a final resort) new equity

pension funds   receive contributions from employees and/or their employers and invest the proceeds on behalf of the employees

personal consumption expenditures (PCE)   expenditures by individuals for durable goods, nondurable goods, and services

personal finance   study of how individuals prepare for financial emergencies, protect against premature death and the loss of property, and accumulate wealth over time

personal saving   savings of individuals equal to personal income less personal current taxes less personal outlays

pledging (pledge)   obtain a short-term loan by using accounts receivable as collateral

poison pills   provisions in a corporate charter that make a corporate takeover more unattractive

political risk   the risk associated with the possibility that a national government might confiscate or expropriate assets held by foreigners

portfolio   any combination of financial assets or investments

positive correlation   when asset returns move in together over time

pre-authorized checks   regular (typically monthly) deductions by a vendor from a customer's checking account

precautionary motives   holding funds to meet unexpected demands

preferred stock   equity security that has preference, or a senior claim, to the firm's earnings and assets over common stock

premium bond   bond that is selling in excess of its par value

present value   amount or value today of a savings or an investment

primary deposit   the deposit of a check drawn on the Fed; it adds new reserves to the bank where deposited and to the banking system

primary markets   where the initial offering or origination of debt and equity securities takes place

primary reserves   vault cash and deposits held at other depository institutions and at Federal Reserve Banks

prime mortgage   a home loan to a borrower with relatively high creditworthiness indicating a relatively high likelihood that mortgage payments will be made when due

prime rate   interest rate charged by banks for short-term unsecured loans to a bank's highest-quality (most creditworthy) business customers

principal-agent problem   a problem in corporate governance in which conflict of interest occurs between the principals and agents

principals   owners of the firm

private placement   sale of securities to a small group of private investors

profitability index (PI) (benefit/cost ratio)   ratio between the present values of the inflows and the outflows

profitability ratios   indicate the firm's ability to generate returns on its sales, assets, and equity

program trading   technique for trading stocks as a group rather than individually; a minimum of 15 different stocks with a minimum value of $1 million are traded

proprietorship (sole proprietorship)   a business venture owned by an individual who personally receives all profits and assumes all responsibility for the debts and losses of the business

prospectus   highly regulated document that details the issuer's operations and finances and must be provided to each buyer of a newly issued security

public offering   sale of securities to the investing public

purchasing power parity (PPP)   states that a country with a relatively higher expected inflation rate will have its currency depreciate relative to a country (or group of countries using a single currency) with a relatively lower inflation rate

purchasing power risk   changes in inflation affect revenues, expenses, and profitability

put option   contract for the sale of securities within a specific time period and at a specified price

putable bonds (retractable bonds)   allow the investor to force the issuer to redeem the bonds prior to maturity

Q

quantitative easing (QE)   a non-traditional monetary policy designed to stimulate economic activity when conventional monetary policy methods are ineffective

R

random walk   prices appear to fluctuate randomly over time, driven by the random arrival of new information

ratio analysis   financial technique that involves dividing various financial statement numbers into one another

real assets   include the direct ownership of land, buildings or homes, equipment, inventories, durable goods, and precious metals

real rate of interest   interest rate on a risk-free debt instrument when no inflation is expected

registered bonds   bonds issued in the United States and for which the issuer knows the names of the bondholders and the interest payments are sent directly to the bondholder

registered traders   individuals who purchase a seat on the exchange to buy and sell stocks for their own account

regulation Z   enacts the Truth in Lending section of the Consumer Credit Protection Act with the intent to make consumers aware of and able to compare costs of alternate forms of credit

reinvestment rate risk (rollover risk)   fluctuating interest rates cause coupon or interest payments to be reinvested at different interest rates over time

remote capture   scanning of paper checks to electronically gather and transmit the payment information

representative full-bodied money   paper money that is backed by an amount of precious metal equal in value to the face amount of the paper money

repurchase agreement   short-term debt security sold by a business firm or financial institution to another business or institution where the seller agrees to repurchase the security at a specified price and date

required reserves   the minimum amount of total reserves that a depository institution must hold

required reserves ratio   the percentage of deposits that must be held as reserves

residual dividend policy   a policy that states that dividends will vary based upon how much excess funds the firm has from year to year

restricted stock   shares of stock, awarded to managers, which vest, or become saleable, after a stated number of years, typically three to five

retention rate   the proportion of each dollar of earnings per share that is retained by the firm

revolving credit agreement (revolver)   a commitment in the form of a standby agreement for a guaranteed line of credit; a legal obligation of the bank to provide up to the agreed-upon borrowing limit during the time the agreement is in effect

risk-adjusted discount rate (RADR)   adjusts the required rate of return at which the analyst discounts a project's cash flows based on the project's risk

risk-free rate of interest   the combination of real rate of interest and the inflation premium, which in the United States is represented by U.S. Treasury debt instruments or securities

round lot   sale or purchase of 100 shares

Rule of 72   a shortcut method used to approximate the time required for an investment to double in value

S

savings   occur when all of an economic unit's income is not consumed and are represented by the accumulation of cash and other financial assets

savings and loan associations (S&Ls)   accept individual savings and lend pooled savings to individuals, primarily in the form of mortgage loans, and to businesses

savings banks   accept the savings of individuals and lend pooled savings to individuals primarily in the form of mortgage loans

savings deficit   occurs when an economic unit's direct investment in real assets exceeds current income

savings surplus   occurs when an economic unit, such as individuals taken as a group, has current income that exceeds its direct investment in real assets

savings-investment process   involves the direct or indirect transfer of individual savings to business firms in exchange for their debt or stock securities

secondary markets   physical locations or electronic forums where debt (bonds and mortgages) and equity securities are traded

secondary reserves   short-term securities held by banks that are quickly converted into cash at little cost to the banks

secured lending (asset-based lending)   collateral or security backing the loan that can be claimed or sold by the lender if the borrower defaults

secured loan   loan backed by collateral

securities firms   accept and invest individual savings and also facilitate the sale and transfer of securities between investors

securitization   Process of pooling and packaging mortgage loans into debt securities

selection stage   applies appropriate capital budgeting techniques to make a final accept or reject decision

semistrong-form efficient market   a market in which all public information, past and current, is reflected in asset prices

settlement price   daily approximate closing price of a futures contract as decided by a special exchange committee

shelf registration allows firms to register security issues (both debt and equity) with the SEC and have them available to sell for two years

short sale sale of securities that the seller does not own

short-term investment policy statement guidelines that detail the type of securities the treasurer can invest in, their safety or default rating, maximum amounts that can be invested in each, and the maximum maturity of the securities purchased

sight draft an instrument requiring immediate payment

simple interest interest earned only on the investment's principal

sinking fund requirement that the issuer retire specified portions of the bond issue over time

sinking fund payments rental or lease payments and periodic bond principal repayments

special dividend an extra dividend declared by the firm over and above its regular dividend payout

Special Drawing Rights (SDRs) reserve assets created by the IMF and consisting of a basket or portfolio of currencies that could be used to make international payments

speculative inflation caused by the expectation that prices will continue to rise, resulting in increased buying to avoid even higher future prices

speculative motives holding marketable securities to take advantage of unusual cash discounts or price bargains on materials if it can pay quickly with cash

spot exchange rate current rate being quoted for delivery of the currency on the spot

spot market the cash market for trading securities; where securities are bought and sold

spread (1) difference between the bid and ask prices; (2) difference between the offer price and the price paid by the investment bank

stand-alone principle analysis focuses on the project's own cash flows, uncontaminated by cash flows from the firm's other activities

standard deviation the square root of the variance

standard of value prices and contracts for deferred payments are expressed in terms of the monetary unit

statement of cash flows provides a summary of the cash inflows (sources) and cash outflows (uses) during a specified accounting period

statewide branch banking allows banks to operate offices throughout a state

static trade-off hypothesis a theory that states firms will balance the advantages of debt with its disadvantages

stock certificate certificate showing an ownership claim of a specific company

stock dividend a dividend in which investors receive shares of stock rather than cash

stock options allow managers to purchase, at a future time, a stated number of the firm's shares at a specific price

stock split a process in which the firms distributes additional shares for every share owned

stop-loss order order to sell stock at the market price when the price of the stock falls to a specified level

store of value money held for some period of time before it is spent

street name an investor's stock certificates are kept electronically at the brokerage firm rather than her taking personal possession of them

SWOT Analysis A review of a firm's internal strengths and weaknesses and its external opportunities and threats

strong-form efficient market a market in which prices reflect all knowledge, including past and current publicly known and private information

subchapter S corporation has fewer than 35 shareholders, none of which is another corporation; its income flows untaxed to the shareholders and is taxed only once, as personal income of the shareholders

subordinate debenture claims of these bonds are subordinate or junior to the claims of the debenture holders

subprime mortgage home loan made to a borrower with a relatively poor credit score indicating a higher likelihood that the borrower will miss mortgage payments when due

sunk cost project-related expense not dependent upon whether or not the project is undertaken

Supplemental Liquidity Providers (SLPs) help add liquidity to the NYSE trading floor, meaning they supplement the work of DMMs by buying and selling shares throughout the day

surplus economic unit generates more money than it spends, and thus, it has excess money to save or invest

sustainable growth rate the estimate of how quickly a firm can grow when it uses internal equity and debt financing to keep its capital structure constant over time

syndicate group of several investment banking firms that participate in the underwriting and distributing a security issue

systematic risk (market risk) risk that is inherent in the macro economy and cannot be eliminated through diversification

T

target dividend payout policy a policy of adjusting the dividend payout dollar amount toward the target dividend payout ratio

tax motives the motive to hold cash outside of the United States due to high U.S. corporate tax rates for bringing cash from overseas profits back into the United States

tax policy sets the level and structure of taxes to affect the economy

tax risk variations in a firm's tax rate and tax-related charges over time due to changing tax laws and regulations

term structure indicates the relationship between interest rates or yields and the maturity of comparable quality debt instruments

third market market for large blocks of listed stocks that operates outside the confines of the organized exchanges

thrift institutions noncommercial bank depository institutions referred to as savings and loan associations, savings banks, and credit unions that accumulate individual savings and lend primarily to other individuals

time draft an instrument requiring payment at a later date

time value of money math of finance whereby a financial return is earned over time by saving or investing money

token coins coins with face values higher than the value of their metal content

tombstones announcements of securities offerings to be placed in newspapers and other publications

trade credit credit extended on purchases to a firm's customers

trade discounts provided to purchasers as an incentive for prompt payment of bills

transactions motive demand for holding cash needed to conduct day-to-day operations

transfer payments government payments for which no current productive services is rendered

traveler's letter of credit issued by a bank in one country and addressed to a list of foreign banks, which have agreed to purchase sight drafts presented to them by persons with appropriate letters of credit

treasurer oversees the traditional functions of financial analysis, including capital budgeting, short-term and long-term financing decisions, and current asset management

Treasury bills federal debt obligations issued with maturities up to one year

Treasury bonds federal obligations issued with original maturities in excess of 10 years, often issued for twenty and sometimes even thirty years

Treasury notes federal obligations usually issued for maturities of one to ten years

trend analysis (time series analysis) used to evaluate a firm's performance over time

trust indenture an extensive document and details the various provisions and covenants of the loan arrangement

trust receipt (1) an instrument through which a bank retains title to goods until they are paid for; (2) lien against specific identifiable items in inventory; whereby the bank retains ownership of the goods until they are sold in the regular course of business

trustee represents the bondholders to ensure the bond issuer respects the indenture's provisions

U

underpricing represents the difference between the aftermarket stock price and the offering price

underwriting agreement contract in which the investment banker agrees to buy securities at a predetermined price and then resell them to investors

undistributed profits (earnings retained in the business) profits remaining after taxes and, in the case of corporations, after the cash dividends are paid to stockholders

unit banking exists when a bank can have only one full-service office

universal bank bank that engages in commercial banking and investment banking

unsecured loan loan that is a general claim against the assets of the borrower

unsystematic risk risk that can be diversified away as assets are added to a portfolio. Also known as firm-specific risk or industry-specific risk

usury the act of lending money at an excessively high interest rate

V

variance derived by summing the squared deviations and dividing by $n - 1$

velocity of money measures the rate of circulation of the money supply

voluntary savings savings in the form of financial assets held or set aside for use in the future

W

warehouse receipt a receipt issued by the warehouse indicating inventory is placed in a bonded warehouse for safekeeping; items are removed as they are paid for

weak-form efficient market market in which prices reflect all past information, such as information in last year's annual report, previous earnings announcements, and other past news

weighted average cost of capital (WACC) represents the minimum required rate of return on a capital-budgeting project; it is found by multiplying the marginal cost of each capital structure component by its appropriate weight and summing the terms

working capital a firm's current assets, which consist of cash, marketable securities, accounts receivable, and inventories

working capital assets needed to carry out the normal operations of the business

World Bank created to help economic growth in developing countries (also called the International Bank for Reconstruction and Development)

Y

Yankee bonds dollar-denominated bonds issued in the United States by a foreign issuer

yield curve graphic presentation of the term structure of interest rates at a given point in time

yield to maturity (YTM) return on a bond investment if it is held to maturity

Z

zero-balance account an account in which just enough funds are transferred into an account to cover that day's checks presented for payment

• INDEX •